HONIARA
VILLAGE-CITY OF
SOLOMON ISLANDS

HONIARA
VILLAGE-CITY OF SOLOMON ISLANDS

CLIVE MOORE

ANU PRESS

PACIFIC SERIES

ANU PRESS

Published by ANU Press
The Australian National University
Canberra ACT 2600, Australia
Email: anupress@anu.edu.au

Available to download for free at press.anu.edu.au

ISBN (print): 9781760465063
ISBN (online): 9781760465070

WorldCat (print): 1306511147
WorldCat (online): 1306509845

DOI: 10.22459/H.2022

This title is published under a Creative Commons Attribution-NonCommercial-NoDerivatives 4.0 International (CC BY-NC-ND 4.0) licence.

The full licence terms are available at
creativecommons.org/licenses/by-nc-nd/4.0/legalcode

Cover design and layout by ANU Press

Cover photograph: Honiara's Solomon Islands National Museum Auditorium on the left and the Anthony Saru building, part of the NPF Plaza complex, on the right. Source: Daniel Evans Collection.

This book is published under the aegis of the Pacific Editorial Board of ANU Press.

This edition © 2022 ANU Press

Contents

List of figures	vii
List of maps	ix
List of plates	xi
List of tables	xxi
Acknowledgements	xxiii
Acronyms and abbreviations	xxv
A note on nomenclature	xxix
Introduction	3
1. *Nahona`ara* before 1942	27
2. *Taem blong faet*: Camp Guadal	63
3. The new capital	115
4. The other Honiara	157
5. Municipal authority and housing	195
6. Building infrastructure	247
7. Building society and the nation	297
8. Stepping-stones to national consciousness	355
9. Since independence	391
10. The village-city	431
Bibliography	487
Index	525

List of figures

Figure 0.1 Honiara's 'worlds' in order of their social, economic, and political importance, 1940s – 2010s. 24

Figure 9.1 The population of Greater Honiara: The Honiara City Council area and the adjacent peri-urban population of Guadalcanal Province, 1959–2019. 392

List of maps

Map 0.1 Solomon Islands. 1

Map 0.2 Guadalcanal Province and Honiara, 2021. 2

Map 0.3 Modern Solomon Islands urban centres. 17

Map 1.1 Languages and dialects of Guadalcanal. 27

Map 1.2 Levers' Tenaru Estate, showing the years various sections were planted and the boundaries with Ilu and Lungga estates. 44

Map 1.3 1920 map showing the Tandai claim and the Occupational Lease claimed by Levers. 51

Map 1.4 Levers' land claim as of 26 May 1920. 52

Map 1.5 1920 map showing the boundaries of Levers' land from the east bank of the Mataniko River to the boundary with William Dumphy's Tenavatu plantation. 57

Map 1.6 The area that became east Honiara, as it was when examined by the Phillips Lands Commission in Claim 17, 12 May 1922. 58

Map 1.7 Map of Guadalcanal, 1930s. 61

Map 2.1 The main Japanese bases in the Bismarck and Solomon archipelagos, between 1942 and 1945. 64

Map 2.2 The north coast of Guadalcanal during World War II, from the Metapona River to Visale. 66

Map 2.3 Iron Bottom Sound between Guadalcanal, Savo, and the Ngela (Florida) islands, showing the sites of some of the Japanese, American, and Australian ships sunk there. 83

Map 2.4 The Carney and Koli airfield complex was the largest of the American airfields on Guadalcanal. 108

Map 3.1 1947 map of Levers' 8,225 hectares of land, stretching from the east bank of the Mataniko River to Tenaru. 126

Map 3.2 The area contested by Baranaba Hoai in 1964 on behalf of the
    Tandai landowners. 127

Map 3.3 The land of Mamara Plantation Limited, 9 March 1948, from the
    coast west of White River, into the headwaters, and east to Vatudaki. 129

Map 4.1 Guadalcanal council wards in the early 1970s, showing details
    of settlements in the north-west, which were the main areas supplying
    Honiara's Central Market. 184

Map 5.1 Honiara Town Council boundary in 1959. 196

Map 5.2 Honiara's town boundary, 1976. 198

Map 5.3 The west of Honiara City Council's land and adjacent
    customary-owned areas of Guadalcanal, 2010s. 199

Map 6.1 Honiara in the 1970s. 247

Map 6.2 Guadalcanal Plains east of the Honiara City Council land in the
    1970s, showing the mixed usage. 249

Map 7.1 The central area of Honiara in 1968, from the Masonic Lodge
    to the tobacco factory. 298

Map 8.1 Honiara in the 1960s, showing the segregated communities. 355

Map 9.1 Honiara town and boundary, 1981. 394

Map 9.2 Honiara (in black) and oil palm plantations (in grey)
    on Guadalcanal Plains, 2009. 408

Map 10.1 Settlements (THA/TOL and squatter) within or on the
    Honiara City Council boundaries, 2019. 433

Map 10.2 A 2015 Honiara citywide structural plan showing the proposed
    bypass road. 436

Map 10.3 A 2015 Honiara city centre structural plan. 436

Map 10.4 Honiara's current and projected urban growth, 2006–25. 480

Map 10.5 Greater Honiara, including the area of the Honiara City
    Council (in green) and Tandai and Malango wards (in red) of
    Guadalcanal Provincial Government. 483

List of plates

Plate 1.1 The area of Guadalcanal that became Honiara. 30

Plate 1.2 A bronze bust of Spanish explorer Álvaro de Mendaña de Neira installed at the Solomon Islands National Museum in 2014. 31

Plate 1.3 Point Cruz in 1944. 41

Plate 1.4 The mouth of the Mataniko River, 1920s. 41

Plate 1.5 Horahi village is in the centre of this 1942 photograph, in a clearing along the beach on the west side of the mouth of the Mataniko River. 53

Plate 1.6 Horahi village in the 1920s. 53

Plate 1.7 The home of the Catholic missionary at Horahi village, 1920s. 54

Plate 1.8 Horahi village in August 1942 overlaid on a modern view of Honiara. 54

Plate 2.1 Coastwatcher Martin Clemens and members of the Solomon Islands Defence Force, August 1942. 68

Plate 2.2 The partly completed Japanese airfield and dispersal area at Lungga, 7 July 1942, which later became Henderson Airfield. 74

Plate 2.3 American troops advancing through the site of the burnt-out Horahi village on the Mataniko River, November 1942. 80

Plate 2.4 American troops at the mouth of the Mataniko River in 1943. 80

Plate 2.5 The Mataniko River footbridge built by the Americans in 1942. 81

Plate 2.6 The Mataniko River vehicle bridge built by the Americans, 1943. 86

Plate 2.7 The 11th Marines firing a 155 mm gun. 87

Plate 2.8 When Solomon Islanders saw the scale of the American landing on Guadalcanal in 1942, it was almost beyond comprehension. 87

Plate 2.9 The American supply base at the mouth of the Lungga River, on the edge of what is now Honiara, 1940s. 88

Plate 2.10 Americans and Solomon Islanders from the Solomon Islands
Defence Force on Kakabona Beach, 25 January 1943. 88

Plate 2.11 Solomon Islands Labour Corps unloading fuel drums at Lungga
Beach, March 1943. 93

Plate 2.12 Solomon Islands Labour Corps unloading cartons of beer
at Camp Guadal, 29 January 1944. 93

Plate 2.13 Solomon Islands Labour Corps unwinding copper wire for the
telephone system, Camp Guadal, June 1943. 97

Plate 2.14 Captain William M. Quiglay, Commander of the Naval Base
at Camp Guadal, 22 August 1942, driving the last spike into the
'Guadalcanal–Bougainville–Tokyo Express' railway, which was built
in three days by the American Seabees. 97

Plate 2.15 Major J.J. Mather paying members of the Solomon Islands
Labour Corps at Camp Guadal, 28 January 1942, while being filmed
for US publicity. 98

Plate 2.16 A US Marine wearing a Japanese sword and water bottle,
and three members of the SIDF, at Camp Guadal on
28 December 1942. 100

Plate 2.17 Three US Marines and a Seabee sharing a drink with members
of the Solomon Islands Labour Corps at Camp Guadalcanal in
August 1943. 100

Plate 2.18 A US Marine and two Solomon Islanders listening to a
gramophone. The man on the right is holding a Japanese bayonet. 101

Plate 2.19 Solomon Islanders taking communion at Camp Guadal,
Easter 1943. 101

Plate 2.20 Guadalcanal women pose with a US Marines recruitment poster
in 1944. Very few of the war photographs depict women. 103

Plate 2.21 Unloading trucks at the lagoon at the mouth of the
Lungga River. 104

Plate 2.22 Fighter I Airfield in the foreground, Henderson Airfield in
the middle, and Fighter II Airfield in the far distance, abutting the
coast, 1943. 107

Plate 2.23 One of the movie theatres at Camp Guadal during
the war years. 110

Plate 2.24 Jacob Vouza and members of the SIDF, 25 January 1944. 112

LIST OF PLATES

Plate 2.25 In 1990, this statue of former policeman, Scout, and war hero Sir Jacob Vouza was added to the war memorial at Rove Police Headquarters. 112

Plate 2.26 The Solomons Scouts and Coastwatchers Memorial in Commonwealth Avenue, Honiara, erected in 2011. 113

Plate 3.1 The Point Cruz area of Camp Guadal in 1944. 115

Plate 3.2 The main coastal highway heading towards Point Cruz, in 1944. The Americans called it the 'Burma Highway'. 121

Plate 3.3 Camp Guadal in about 1945, from Lengakiki Flats to Point Cruz. 122

Plate 3.4 A Queen's Birthday parade in Honiara in the late 1940s. 124

Plate 3.5 The American bridge over the Lungga River on the Honiara side of Henderson Airfield in October 1945. 137

Plate 3.6 Quonset huts of all sizes were everywhere—the most useful remnant of the war years. 138

Plate 3.7 In 1951, the Commonwealth Bank of Australia began operations in Honiara, housed in a Quonset hut. 138

Plate 3.8 The BSIP Trading Corporation Limited was housed in a large Quonset hut in Mendana Avenue, 1960s. 141

Plate 3.9 The staff of the BSIP Trading Corporation Limited, 1960s. 141

Plate 3.10 Alan and Doreen Lindley's house in Mud Alley, 1952. 145

Plate 3.11 Arnold and Mary Cowmeadow's thatched house with woven bamboo walls in the grounds of Government House, 1960s. 146

Plate 3.12 The Mendana Hotel in the late 1950s. 154

Plate 3.13 The Honiara Club, showing murals created by King George VI School art students in 1971. 154

Plate 3.14 The Point Cruz Cinema in Mendana Avenue in the late 1950s. 155

Plate 3.15 West Honiara from the bottom of Lengakiki Ridge, 1956. 155

Plate 4.1 *Walkabout Long Chinatown*, the Viking album featuring the song of the same name by Edwin Sitori, Rone Naqu, and Jason Que. 158

Plate 4.2 Aerial view of Chinatown in the 1950s. 163

Plate 4.3 View down Chinatown's main street in the 1950s. 164

Plate 4.4 View into Chinatown, showing the typical trade stores, in the early 1960s. 164

Plate 4.5 Chinatown in the 1960s. 167

Plate 4.6 The Bailey bridge over the Mataniko River, and part of Chinatown. 167

Plate 4.7 Aerial view of Chinatown, 1968. 170

Plate 4.8 Mataniko River and Chinatown, also showing the beginning of housing on the ridges, 1981. 170

Plate 4.9 Gilbertese migrants in the 1950s. 171

Plate 4.10 Honiara's Central Market was a simple affair when it began in the 1950s. 179

Plate 4.11 Betel nut sellers in Honiara's Central Market, 1970s. 183

Plate 4.12 The *Compass Rose II* carrying thousands of pineapples from Malaita to Honiara's Central Market, 1994. 183

Plate 4.13 Honiara's tobacco factory, 1972. 186

Plate 5.1 Central District Headquarters in Honiara, 1956. 202

Plate 5.2 Flamboyant poinciana trees in Hibiscus Avenue, Honiara, 1968. 202

Plate 5.3 This 1970s photograph shows the typical accommodation for labourers at the back of stores or commercial premises in town between the 1950s and the 1970s. 207

Plate 5.4 This sign was placed on Kukum Beach opposite the Kukum Labour Line by the Honiara Town Council. 209

Plate 5.5 Housing at Mbokonavera in the 1970s, with a bicycle in pride of place. 209

Plate 5.6 The beginnings of Vura housing estate in 1968. 212

Plate 5.7 Ella and John Ru`ugwata Kaliuae in 1988. They were early settlers at Vura. 212

Plate 5.8 Kola`a Ridge squatter settlement on the inland side of the established suburb, 1969. 221

Plate 5.9 The 'Fishery', Honiara's Malaitan Fishing Village, on the beachfront at Kukum, 2008. 226

Plate 5.10 Jack and Margaret Leonga Ramosaea, early settlers at White River, photographed in 1982. 228

Plate 5.11 A Housing Authority home at White River, 2008. 229

Plate 5.12 The typical home of a middle-class White River family, 2008. 229

LIST OF PLATES

Plate 5.13 Kobito 2 in 1968, which was then reminiscent of a Malaitan village.	231
Plate 5.14 The first houses at Kobito 2 were built from local materials. This photograph is from 1968.	232
Plate 5.15 Billy Toa Te`e, originally from Kwara`ae on Malaita, lived at White River, before settling at Kobito 2 in the 1980s. He is seen here with two members of his family in the 1990s.	236
Plate 5.16 Roselyn Aona Toa Te`e, wife of Billy Toa Te`e, 1980s.	236
Plate 5.17 The original 1970s Toa Te`e house at Kobito 2 had ripple-iron walls as well as an unlined roof.	236
Plate 5.18 Urban renewal: The walls of the Toa Te`e home at Kobito 2 were renovated with wood in the 2000s.	236
Plate 5.19 Some of the first minibuses in Mendana Avenue, Honiara, in the 1970s.	241
Plate 6.1 The WPHC High Court building was built in 1964.	248
Plate 6.2 Solomon Islands Museum at the time it was built in 1968.	257
Plate 6.3 In the 1960s, two high-rise residential buildings were constructed in Honiara.	257
Plates 6.4–6.6 Blums' Hometel, built in Hibiscus Avenue in 1964, was the most socially advanced of Honiara's hotels and welcomed everyone.	260
Plate 6.7 Aerial photograph from December 1944 of 'Namba 9', the 9th US Casualty Clearing Station, close to the Mataniko River.	263
Plate 6.8 The tuberculosis ward at Central Hospital, mid-1950s.	265
Plate 6.9 National Referral Hospital, Honiara, 2016.	270
Plate 6.10 BSIP police headquarters at Rove, 1952.	271
Plate 6.11 Queen's Birthday parade, Rove Police Headquarters, 1950s. The building at the rear is the Police Club.	275
Plate 6.12 Honiara Police Station in 1952, constructed from a Quonset hut and scrap US Army materials.	276
Plate 6.13 Honiara's new police station, completed in 1963, was renamed Central Police Station.	276
Plate 6.14 Kukum docks in 1945, built by the Americans. The area is opposite what is now Panatina Plaza.	280
Plate 6.15 In the 1950s, work began on reshaping Point Cruz to create a port.	280

Plate 6.16 RCS *Melanesian* at Honiara wharf in 1958. 281

Plate 6.17 Point Cruz wharves in the 1960s. A Quonset hut from the war years is visible on the shore. 282

Plate 6.18 The interisland shipping wharves in 2017, with the centre of Honiara behind. 283

Plate 6.19 Honiara Airfield in the 1950s, on the site of the Fighter II Airfield at what is now Ranadi. 284

Plate 6.20 The first SIBC Board meeting, 1982. 295

Plate 7.1 The American chapel built for the armed forces and Solomon Islanders, which was dedicated on 12 September 1943. 302

Plate 7.2 St Barnabas' Anglican Cathedral, 2017. It was built between 1968 and 1969. 303

Plate 7.3 Holy Cross Catholic Cathedral (centre), at the foot of the road to Skyline, was built between 1977 and 1978. 304

Plate 7.4 The Ko`o Football Team in 1972, one of the teams playing in the Honiara football competition. 314

Plate 7.5 The front entrance to King George VI School. 318

Plate 7.6 The chapel at King George VI School. 318

Plate 7.7 King George VI School students in about 1968, with school buildings in the background. 319

Plate 7.8 Prize winners at King George VI School in 1970. 320

Plate 7.9 The Teacher and Vocational Training College in the late 1950s. 323

Plate 7.10 Sir Donald Luddington, the final Western Pacific High Commissioner (1973–74) and the first Governor of the BSIP (1974–76), reviewing students at a TS Ranadi Marine Training School graduation ceremony. 326

Plate 7.11 Nurses at Central Hospital in the 1960s. 328

Plate 7.12 A University of the South Pacific graduation ceremony at the Panatina Pavilion in Honiara, 2009. Vice-Chancellor Professor Rajesh Chandra is presenting a student with his degree. 330

Plate 7.13 Gold medal graduates and two of the medal sponsors at the graduation ceremony for the Solomon Islands National University, 2018. 332

Plate 7.14 The senior executive of the Solomon Islands National University at the graduation ceremony, 2018. 332

LIST OF PLATES

Plate 7.15 Honiara Women's Club, 1962. 333

Plate 7.16 Selina Tale (YWCA-SI Kindergarten Supervisor), Christina Maezama (General Secretary, 1980–92), and Vera Sautehi (Extension Officer) outside the YWCA premises at Rove, Honiara, in the early 1980s. 335

Plate 7.17 A YWCA hostel room, probably in the early 1980s. 336

Plate 7.18 The YWCA kindergarten in the early 1960s. 336

Plate 7.19 Lilly Valahoe Ogatini Poznanski was a role model for women in the 1960s and 1970s. 338

Plate 7.20 Women selling barbecued fish at Honiara International Airport—Henderson Field, 2004. 339

Plate 7.21 White River resident Ellen Angofia (centre) selling tie-dyed lap-laps in 1998 at a cultural event. 340

Plate 7.22 A woman selling *bilums* in Honiara, 2010. 340

Plate 7.23 Randall Sukumana preparing for his kindergarten class, at Skyline, 2006. 343

Plate 7.24 Woodford School students, 1976. 343

Plate 7.25 Girl Guides in Honiara, 2006. 344

Plate 7.26 Children at Vura School, 2007. 345

Plate 7.27 Bartholomew Ulufa`alu—trade union leader and, later, politician and prime minister—in the 1980s. 349

Plate 7.28 Joses Taungengo Tuhanuku—trade union leader and, later, politician, cabinet minister, and leader of the opposition—in 1981. 349

Plate 8.1 The High Commissioner's Humber Super Snipe carrying the Duke and Duchess of Kent in 1969, undergoing a traditional challenge from warriors. 357

Plate 8.2 New Government House in 1969. It has since been incorporated into the Heritage Park Hotel. 365

Plate 8.3 The Honiara War Cenotaph was constructed in 1959. 366

Plate 8.4 A government officer's house up on the ridges, 1972. 370

Plate 8.5 The same house as in Plate 8.4, showing its ridge-top position and the view out to sea. 371

Plates 8.6–8.9 Cultural dancers in the 1950s. 375

Plate 8.10 Pelise Moro, leader of the Moro Movement, and some of his followers in Honiara in 1971. 376

Plate 8.11 King George VI School students ready to dance, 1968.   377

Plate 8.12 A Makira canoe crew at Point Cruz in 1969 during the Sea Festival.   378

Plate 8.13 Makira canoes at Point Cruz in 1969 during the Sea Festival.   378

Plate 8.14 Members of the Legislative Council in 1961.   384

Plate 8.15 Chief Minister Peter Kenilorea addressing the motion to adopt the National Constitution, April 1978.   388

Plate 8.16 Prince Richard, Duke of Gloucester, Queen Elizabeth II's representative at the independence ceremony in Honiara, with Prime Minister Peter Kenilorea looking on, 7 July 1978.   388

Plate 9.1 Busy Mendana Avenue in 2014.   391

Plate 9.2 The Honiara waterfront to the east of Point Cruz in 2017, showing international ships at the old main wharf on the right and the smaller interisland shipping wharves to the left.   396

Plate 9.3 Honiara's modern interisland shipping wharves, 2014.   396

Plate 9.4 A prosperous Lengakiki Ridge house, 2014.   398

Plate 9.5 A typical Honiara house combining local and Western materials, 2014.   398

Plate 9.6 Prime Minister Ezekiel Alebua (1986–89), later Premier of Guadalcanal Province (1998–2003), during the Tensions.   412

Plate 9.7 Bartholomew Ulufa'alu, Prime Minister of Solomon Islands (1997–2000), addresses the UN General Assembly in New York on 30 September 1999.   413

Plate 9.8 RAMSI soldiers and RSIPF officers talking to a school group, 2000s.   420

Plate 9.9 RAMSI soldiers outside the Magistrate's Court in Honiara, 2006.   420

Plate 9.10 The entrance of the Pacific Casino Hotel burning during the April 2006 riot.   423

Plate 9.11 Burnt-out buildings in Chinatown after the April 2006 riot.   424

Plate 9.12 The Quan family's QQQ store in Chinatown, 2006, which was not harmed during the riots.   424

Plate 9.13 The RAMSI Memorial in Honiara, opened in June 2017.   427

Plate 9.14 The Solomon Islands National Parliament building, built in 1994, was a gift from the US Government.   428

LIST OF PLATES

Plate 9.15 Prime Minister Sir Allan Kemakeza (2001–06). 429

Plate 9.16 Prime Minister Rick Hounipwela (2017–19). 429

Plate 9.17 Prime Minister Manasseh Sogavare (2000–01, 2006–07, 2014–17, 2019–). 429

Plate 10.1 Hybridity: A rest house at the Honiara Trade Show in 2008—symbolic of the old and the new. 439

Plate 10.2 Hybridity: Neighbouring houses at Fishing Village are often built close together. 440

Plate 10.3 Hendry Billy Toa Te`e's house at Kobito 2, which was built over a few years in the 2010s as money became available. 443

Plate 10.4 Emelda Davis (left), an Australian South Sea Islander, visiting the family of Hendry Billy Toa Te`e at Kobito, 2014. 443

Plate 10.5 'No weapons (sharp or pointed)': The Pipeline Disco, Hibiscus Hotel, Honiara, 1994. 451

Plate 10.6 Youths dressed up for a dance competition entitled 'Battlegrounds', 2016. 451

Plate 10.7 The next generation: Vura Primary School students, 2007. 457

Plate 10.8 Small health clinics run by the Honiara City Council are spread through the suburbs. This one is in White River, 2008. 459

Plate 10.9 The Sunday Fishing Village market on Kukum Highway, 2011. 461

Plate 10.10 Central Market on the waterside, 2017. 461

Plate 10.11 Thousands of people visit Honiara's Central Market every day. 462

Plate 10.12 A market stall at Honiara International Airport—Henderson Field, 2004. 462

Plate 10.13 Chinatown from lower Skyline Ridge, 2011. 465

Plate 10.14 Mendana Avenue, 2008. 465

Plate 10.15 View of the Point Cruz area from Parliament, 2008. 466

Plate 10.16 A women's marching group in Vura, Honiara, 1995. 474

Plate 10.17 Cultures are preserved through cultural groups performing at public events. Here, Malaitan panpipe dancers perform at the Art Gallery in 1995. 474

Plates 10.18–10.20 A Malaitan bride-price ceremony for Clive Maesae and Salome Stella in August 2011. 475

Plate 10.21 Point Cruz Yacht Club, 2008. 481

Plate 10.22 Sabot racing in front of the Point Cruz Yacht Club, looking out to the patrol boat wharf, 2007. 482

Plate 10.23 The front entrance of King Solomon Hotel, 2006. 482

Plate 10.24 Governor-General Sir David Vunagi GCMG KStJ and Lady Mary Vunagi, 2020. 485

Plate 10.25 Isabel Province dancers on Independence Day, 2005, at Lawson Tama. 486

Plate 10.26 Independence Day celebrations at Lawson Tama, Honiara, 2008. 486

List of tables

Table 4.1 Population of Honiara in 1959.	180
Table 4.2 Honiara's gender profile: Melanesian population in 1970.	187
Table 4.3 Age divisions in Honiara's population, 1976 and 1986 (percentage).	187
Table 4.4 Protectorate-born population by island, compared with Honiara's protectorate-born Melanesian population, and the Melanesian male population, 1970.	188
Table 5.1 The number of houses valued up to $6,000 (1975 prices) constructed in Honiara, 1969–1974.	214
Table 5.2 The number of houses valued at more than $6,000 (1975 prices) constructed in Honiara, 1969–1974.	214
Table 5.3 The number of houses constructed in Honiara, 1969–1974.	214
Table 5.4 Housing Authority house models and prices at Mbua Valley, 1975.	216
Table 5.5 Growth of settlements in Honiara, 1970–1979.	220
Table 6.1 Population of Honiara: Ethnic groups, 1959 and 1965.	256
Table 6.2 BSIP Medical Department, 1950, 1956, and 1962.	264
Table 6.3 Solomon Islands airfields and their years of construction.	285
Table 7.1 The numbers of Christian adherents in Solomon Islands and the percentages involved in the main Christian denominations in Honiara, 1970–2009.	305
Table 9.1 Honiara demographic overview, 1959–2009.	393
Table 9.2 Population of wards within Honiara, 1970–2009.	399

Acknowledgements

Many individuals have helped with the preparation of this book, some directly and some never realising that by answering my questions over the past 45 years they were adding to my knowledge of Honiara: David Akin, Rex Akomae, Sam Alasia, Fraser Alekevu, Matthew Allen, Geoffrey Anni, Transform Aqorau, Rex Ringi Angofia, Geoffrey Anii, Graham and Evelyn Baines, Helen Barrett, Patrick and Veronica Barrett, Richard Bedford, Judy Bennett, Simeon Bouro, Terry M. Brown, Murray Chapman, Brian Christie, Robert Cribb, Daniel Evans, Peter Flahavin, Joseph Foukona, Jon Fraenkel, Christal Francis, Ian Frazer, Ian Geering, Eric Grimm, Martin Hadlow, Humpress Harrington, John and Chris Holloway, Johnson Honimae, John Innes, Ishmael Itea and family, Christine Jourdan (whose phrase provides the title for Chapter 7), Tarcisius Tara Kabutaulaka, Brij Lal, Estee Lonamei, John Maetia and Caroline Kaliuae and family, Sir Peter and Lady Margaret Kenilorea and family, Jocelyn Lai (General-Secretary of the Solomon Islands YWCA), Jacqui Leckie, Gordon Nanau, Dr Sir Nathan and Lady Joy Kere, Doreen Kuper, Jacqui Leckie, Andrew Leung, Hadley Leung, Hudson Leung, Alan Lindley, David MacLaren, Mike McCoy, Alan McNeil, Jack Maebuta, Betty and Harry Masae and family, Jeffrey Moore, Rebecca Monson, Martin Otto, Paul Quan, Max Quanchi (who read a draft and helped cull the photographs), Doris Rilifia, Paul Roughan, Tom Russell, David Ruthven, Ellison Sade, Maxwell Saelea, Sir Bruce and Lady Keithie Saunders, Ralph Shlomowitz, John Smith, Ann Stevenson, Ewan Stevenson, Lachlan Strahan, Gideon Sukumana, Philip Tagini, Fred Talo, Karlyn Tekalu, Hendry Billy Toa Te`e, Les Tickle, Sir Paul Tovua, Michael Ben Walahoula (Secretary of the Tandai Tribal Landowners Association), Sir Nathaniel and Lady Alice Waena, Peter Williams, Garth Wong, and Rawcliffe Ziza.

A special thank you is needed for those who provided photographs. Peter Flahavin was always generous with his large collection of photographs of Honiara during 1942–45, and his ability to match them with current sites.

The images from the US National Archives and Records Administration, the British Museum, Wikipedia, and the United Nations are covered by the Creative Commons agreement. Ben Burt facilitated access to the British Museum photographs. The other images are either from my collection or from Transform Aqorau, Patrick and Veronica Barrett, Mary Cowmeadow, Daniel Evans, Wendy Ho, Ian Frazer, Alan Lindley, Lady Keithie Saunders, Garry Scott, Brian Taylor, Les Tickle, John Tod, Greg Tuer, and Robertson Ramsay (Bob) Wright. I acknowledge access to Solomon Islands Government photographs, publications, and media releases, to the archives of the Regional Assistance Mission to Solomon Islands, and to the archives of the General Assembly of the United Nations.

My colleague Chi Kong Lai provided the standard pinyin form of Chinese names. Vincent Verheyen worked on cartography for the book, creating maps and making others more serviceable. I thank him sincerely for the work that he has done to improve the graphic presentation. Dalton Hone, from the National Geographic Information Centre, Ministry of Lands, Housing and Survey, kindly simplified a more complex map of Guadalcanal Province for use in the book. Commissioner of Lands Alan McNeil assisted on various occasions with maps and advice. Regina Souter modified a crucial map on very short notice. Jessica Carmichael created one of the graphs. Stewart Firth and Emily Tinker guided the book through ANU Press. Jan Borrie edited the manuscript.

I have translated some key financial figures into modern-day currency equivalents, using www.measuringworth.com/. These equivalents have many variables and can only be regarded as approximate.

Acronyms and abbreviations

ACOM	Anglican Church of Melanesia
ADB	Asian Development Bank
AMO	assistant medical officer
ANZ	Australia and New Zealand Banking Group
ASA	British Solomon Islands Amateur Sports Association
BM	British Museum
BP	Burns Philp
BSIP	British Solomon Islands Protectorate
BSIP&CWU	British Solomon Islands Ports and Copra Workers' Union
BSIB&GWU	British Solomon Islands Building and General Workers' Union
BSIP AR	*British Solomon Islands Annual and Biannual Reports*
BSIP NS	*British Solomons Islands Protectorate News Sheet*
CDC	Commonwealth Development Corporation
CDF	Constituency Development Fund
FTE	fixed-term estate
GPL	Guadalcanal Plains Limited
HSBC	Hongkong and Shanghai Banking Corporation
IFM	Isatabu Freedom Movement
IS	*The Island Sun*
KGVI	King George VI School
KR	*Kakamora Reporter*

LGBTQ	lesbian, gay, bisexual, transgender and queer
MEF	Malaita Eagle Force
MN	*Melanesian News*
NGO	nongovernmental organisation
NMP	native medical practitioner
PE	perpetual estate
PIM	*Pacific Islands Monthly*
PMB	Pacific Manuscripts Bureau
PNG	Papua New Guinea
PPF	Participating Police Force
RAMSI	Regional Assistance Mission to Solomon Islands
RANVR	Royal Australian Naval Volunteer Reserve
RSIPF	Royal Solomon Islands Police Force
SDA	Seventh-day Adventist
SIBC	Solomon Islands Broadcasting Corporation
SIBS	Solomon Islands Broadcasting Service
SICHE	Solomon Islands College of Higher Education
SIDF	Solomon Islands Defence Force
SIG	Solomon Islands Government
SIGWU	Solomon Islands General Workers' Union
SINA	Solomon Islands National Archives
SINU	Solomon Islands National University
SINUW	Solomon Islands National Union of Workers
SIPF	Solomon Islands Police Force
SIPL	Solomon Islands Plantation Limited
SND	*Solomon News Drum*
SS	*Solomon Star*
SSEC	South Sea Evangelical Church
SSEM	South Sea Evangelical Mission
STT	*Solomons Toktok*
TAA	Trans Australia Airlines
THA	Temporary Housing Area

TOL	Temporary Occupation Licence
TVTC	Teacher and Vocational Training College
UK	United Kingdom
UQ FML	University of Queensland, Fryer Memorial Library
US	United States
USNARA	United States National Archives and Records Administration
USP	University of the South Pacific
WPHC	Western Pacific High Commission
YWCA	Young Women's Christian Association

A note on nomenclature

Several stylistic issues have been difficult to standardise. The first is how to spell Solomon Islands geographic and personal names, which over decades have been written in multiple ways. Glottal stops and extra guiding letters in words—such as 'ng', 'ngg', 'nd', and 'mb'—are single-consonant sounds that show correct pronunciation. Modern linguistic thinking is that in most cases to write 'ng', and so on, is simply to add unnecessary letters. As well, foreigners often have trouble hearing glottal stops, particularly at the beginning of words, and seldom use them in written forms. When words are written incorrectly, the wrong spelling becomes so common it is regarded as normal. I have been guided in my choices by current usage. For example, initially I used Matanikau for the name of the river in the centre of Honiara, which is how it is spelt on most older maps and in earlier texts. Guadalcanal people assure me it should be Mataniko, and I have followed their advice. I have continued to use the 'ng' form for Ngela, and I have left Mbalisuna and Ngalimbiu as the spelling of river names on Guadalcanal, as this is still their usual form. The same applies to Nggosi, the name of the Honiara City Council ward and suburb. Similarly, Lungga River is often written as Lunga, but I have used 'gg' to show the correct longer 'g' sound. Solomon Islanders are aware of the origins of the words and manage to pronounce them correctly, no matter how they are spelt. When names appear on early maps, they have been reproduced using the original spelling. I have left personal names as I found them.

The second issue is capitalisation of titles. The modern publishing style is to keep these to a minimum and only capitalise words when they are directly attached to an individual's name, as in Prime Minister Manasseh Sogavare. Occasionally, I break this rule if the meaning is obscured. The third issue is italics, which I have kept to a minimum: I use them only for book titles and acts of parliament, and for a few keywords, such as *beliga*, *liu*, *kastom*, *kwaso*, *waku*, and *wantok*.

Chinese names present another problem when they are rendered into English in several ways. Sometimes different branches of the same family use different spelling. On the first occasion the name appears, I have added a standard pinyin form (Romanisation of the Chinese characters based on pronunciation) in parentheses directly after, unless it is identical with the modern form. In subsequent references, I have continued to use the original style.

Currency also varies over the years covered in the book. The early pound (£) references are to English pounds sterling. Australian pounds were also used but were of lower value (A£125 to UK£100 in 1965). Pound references are usually to UK currency. Pounds were replaced with Australian dollars in 1966. When values are in US, Australian, or Solomon Islands dollars (the last in use from 1977), I have shown the origin of the currency references by using US$, A$, and SI$, respectively. I have converted most imperial units of measurement to the metric system. One acre is 0.404 hectares, 1 mile is 1.609 kilometres, 1 foot is 30.5 centimetres, and 1 UK gallon is 4.546 litres. Ton has been retained because tonne (0.90718 of a ton) is not an exact equivalent.

Finally, if some references to periodical literature vary slightly from the standard form it is because the copy as published is missing some of the series information. And, in keeping with current usage (since 1975), 'Solomon Islands', not 'the Solomon Islands', is used as the name of the nation. For stylistic reasons, on occasions I use 'Solomons' as a short form for Solomon Islands.

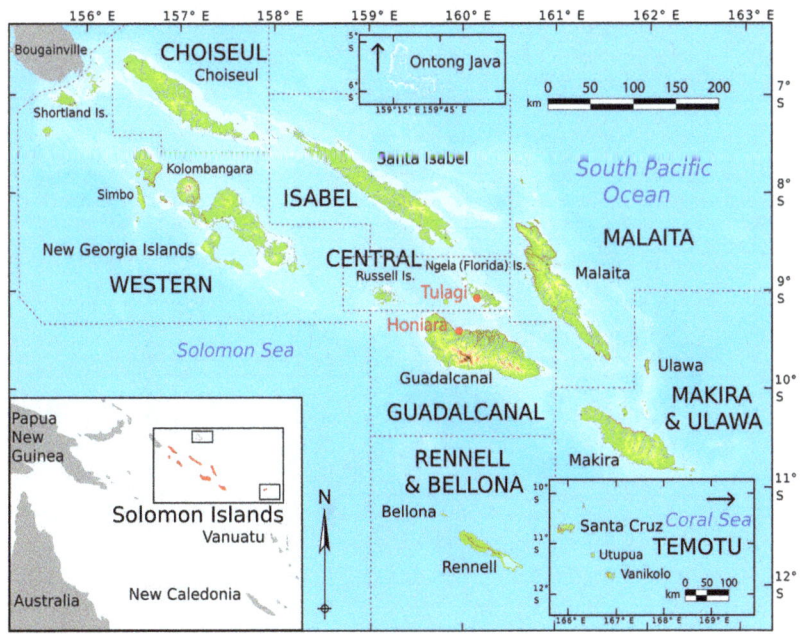

Map 0.1 Solomon Islands.
Source: Cartography by Vincent Verheyen.

HONIARA

Map 0.2 Guadalcanal Province and Honiara, 2021.
Source: National Geographic Information Centre, Ministry of Lands, Housing and Survey, Solomon Islands Government.

Introduction

Honiara

Urbanisation—a 'foreign flower' planted in Oceanic soil—has become an accepted part of all Pacific Island nations.[1] Modern governments and economies function through urban centres and, just as occurs all over the world, the 'bright lights' of towns and cities draw people from villages in the hope of creating better, more interesting progressive lives for themselves and their families. Often, they are disappointed and end up as landless urban poor on low incomes, struggling to exist in a harsh money-driven environment.

The British Solomon Islands Protectorate (BSIP) was declared in 1893. The Tulagi enclave—the capital in the Ngela Group from 1897—was destroyed when World War II reached the islands in 1942.[2] After the war, the new reliance on air transport meant the small Tulagi settlement was no longer suitable to be the centre of government. The capital was shifted to Honiara, where the Americans had built major airfields and a large military base. These created the foundations for the modern city. Like Tulagi, Honiara is geographically central to the nation. The area is midway along the sheltered northern side of the island of Guadalcanal and does not receive the large ocean swells delivered along the southern Weather Coast. The rainfall is also much lower than on the other side of Guadalcanal and in many other areas of the Solomons.

From the 1890s until 1952, the BSIP was a central part but not the hub of the Western Pacific High Commission (WPHC), the bureaucratic mechanism created in 1877 by the British to administer their South Pacific

---

1   Peter Larmour aptly uses 'foreign flowers' in the title of his 2005 edited book on institutional transfers and governance in the Pacific.
2   Moore 2019.

territories. The WPHC administration was transferred from Suva in Fiji to Honiara in January 1953, creating a new importance for the town. This arrangement lasted until 1974–76, when the WPHC was wound down. Solomon Islands was placed under a governor in preparation for independence, which came on 7 July 1978.[3] Then a small city of 20,000 people, Honiara became the capital of both the nation and Guadalcanal Province. I first arrived in Honiara in 1976 during the self-government years, on board *Turkmenia*, a Russian ocean liner that had left Cairns in north Queensland three days earlier. Although I could have taken a plane flight across to the beautiful tropical archipelago, the opportunity for a sea voyage was far more exotic. It was an academic adventure that shaped my entire career. I was 25 years old and beginning research on the participation of Malaitans in the Queensland labour trade in the second half of the nineteenth century, and their migration to the Queensland town of Mackay.[4] I had met Ishmael Itea, an important Malaitan leader from the Fataleka language district, when he was visiting his family, the Fatnownas, in Mackay. His visit was part of the rebirth of the connection between Australian South Sea Islanders and their kin in the islands that began in the 1960s and 1970s, after a lapse of 60 years. Ishmael met the *Turkmenia* and whisked me off to Dodo Creek Agricultural Station on the edge of Guadalcanal Plains, to the home of Mervyn Molia Davis and his wife, Bettrie, who had visited Mackay as part of a Seventh-day Adventist Church group. Along the way, I glimpsed the dusty town and its rural surrounds. A week later, I moved to Vura to the home of John Maetia and Caroline Kaliuae, where I was immersed in a newly developing Housing Authority subdivision—largely a Malaitan community. I knew I was in an unfamiliar cultural milieu one night when a neighbour needed to get a troublesome spirit removed from his house and sent for the *Tasiu*, the Anglican Melanesian Brothers.[5] My first trip to Malaita island a few weeks later was on *Compass Rose II*. I remember the bustling late-night scene as hundreds of Solomon Islanders milled around the wharves seeing off relatives returning home. As with the exorcism by the Melanesian Brothers, that night at the wharves, I realised Solomon Islands was a special place. Although new ships have replaced the old, the scene at the wharves has not changed. Sea transport moving in and out of Honiara is still the nation's lifeblood. Over the intervening years, my arrivals have usually

---

3   The 1972 Select Committee into Constitutional Development recommended that the high commissioner be redesignated as governor.
4   Moore 1981, 1985.
5   Moore 2004b.

been at what is now called Honiara International Airport—Henderson Field,[6] although sea travel is still my favourite means of moving around the islands. For the first time since 1976, in 2017, I arrived at Honiara on a ship, P&O's *Pacific Eden*. We tied up at a much more sophisticated container wharf than the one at which I first stepped ashore.

Honiara has changed over the years as the urban area spread along the coast and inland into the valleys. In the 1950s, Point Cruz—named by Spanish explorer Álvaro de Mendaña de Neira in 1568—began to be expanded into a sizeable port. By the 1970s, a lot of reclamation work had already been completed. In 1976, the main government buildings were clustered on both sides of and inland from Point Cruz. Shops were strung out along Mendana Avenue between Point Cruz and Central Market, which was in the same place as now, but smaller. 'Namba 9'—once the 9th US Casualty Clearing Station, then the Central Hospital, and now the National Referral Hospital—remains close to the Mataniko River. In the 1970s, Chinatown, on the banks of the Mataniko, was the second commercial hub. Riots in 2006 destroyed many of its quaint wooden buildings, although by then the commercial centre of Honiara was at Ranadi, further east.

In 2020, most of the city's houses either balance on the series of undulating ridges or squat on valley floors. In the 1970s, houses along the coast around Rove were the most sought-after residences for government ministers and senior public servants. The middle classes and the rich lived on the ridges, particularly at Lengakiki and Nggosi, or further east at Skyline, Kola`a, and Panatina. Poorer residents lived in the valleys or on the slopes of the ridges. Woodford School, begun in the mid-1950s, was still in the middle of downtown Honiara, opposite the National Museum. The Anthony Saru building and its shopping arcade have replaced it. In the 1970s, large red buses trundled about, along with a few minibuses and cars, and trucks. People often travelled crammed on to the backs of trucks and utilities. They still do when coming from rural areas into town, or travelling for political rallies, or customary ceremonies. There are now large numbers of cars and minibuses, which have made Honiara's

---

6   When the Japanese Government funded an upgrade of Henderson Airport in 2003, they suggested a change of name. A petition against this, and US diplomatic intervention, led to the airfield being renamed Honiara International Airport—Henderson Field.

traffic jams notorious. Since 1994, the National Parliament has sat high on Vavaea Ridge above Point Cruz, creating a central focus. In the 1970s, the High Court building doubled as the parliamentary chamber.

Unlike Port Moresby, Papua New Guinea's capital, positioned on commodious Halifax Harbour, Honiara has no substantial bay. It sits on a curve in the coast with small Point Cruz as the central promontory; the point was originally an island joined to the mainland by a swampy causeway. Unlike Port Vila, Vanuatu's smaller capital on Efate Island, which is set on a safe harbour and is replete with sidewalk cafés showing its French influence, Honiara is often caricatured as a hick town that too hurriedly became a city. It lacks the lush surrounds of Lae or Suva, or the large non–Pacific Islander population of New Caledonia's Nouméa. Yet, for those who live there or who visit regularly, Honiara has a laidback, pleasant nature and is a likeable place—a rumbustious and ever-growing Pacific urban sprawl. On any given day, thousands of residents perambulate constantly along Mendana Avenue, the coastal road that stretches from White River to the Mataniko River. Its name changes to Kukum Highway as the road continues past the National Referral Hospital, the Malaitan Fishing Village, Ranadi industrial estate, Burns Creek settlement, Lungga industrial area, and on to Honiara International Airport—Henderson Field. People walk to Central Market or city offices, or take minibuses to work, school, and shopping, along routes that move travellers about cheaply and efficiently, along the coast and snaking into the hills. The problem is that peak-hour traffic is now so congested that it is often quicker to walk short distances—for instance, from Point Cruz to Central Market—than to take a bus.

Honiara is a homely city made up of long-established middle-class and elite suburbs, as well as large areas of insecure land leases renewed annually, and squatter areas—the last two both best described as urban villages or settlements. Socially, Honiara has much in common with other Pacific cities. Its village-like qualities are hard to come to terms with, but future planners must understand its hybrid links with rural areas if they are to plan wisely and cope with future developments and flashpoints. Sadly, recent town planning documents show few signs of any accommodation of the unusual circumstances of Honiara's development, nor much cognisance of the poor urban planning in the 1960s and 1970s that created the present situation. This point is picked up again in Chapter 10.

A recent Asian Development Bank (ADB) paper described Honiara as a 'village city', which nicely depicts the combination of suburbs and settlements, and provided the title for this book.[7] However, rather than a Pacific village-city, the recent urban plans seem to replicate a modern Australian city, although there are the beginnings of an attempt to come to terms with the dominance of settlements. Despite having its own act of parliament, Honiara City Council is relatively powerless. The mayor and council must always negotiate with national government ministries, and with the administration of Guadalcanal Province. The council and its mayor do not control the city in a way that could be expected of an equivalent large urban area elsewhere.

A city of contrasts

Honiara is a city of contrasts and not everyone is impressed. Many visitors and some residents find Honiara overwhelming and without grace. Eric V. Lawson, a prominent businessman who lived there for 24 years from 1947, uncharitably called Honiara 'just a dump'.[8] Its worst critics emerged before and during the Tension years—the period of violence and civil unrest between 1998 and 2003. Travel writer Paul Theroux visited the city in the early 1990s:

> My first impression was of a place so ramshackle, so poor, so scary, so unexpectedly filthy, that I began to understand the theory behind culture shock—something I had never truly experienced in its paralysing and malignant form. The idea that such a miserable-looking town could be regarded as a capital city seemed laughable.
>
> … The Solomon Islanders in Honiara were among the scariest-looking people I had ever seen in my life—wild hair, huge feet, ripped and ragged clothes, tattoos on their foreheads, ornamental scars all over their faces, wearing broken sunglasses.[9]

Although he softened his attitudes a little once he talked to a few people, such hyperbole is hard to believe from such a seasoned traveller. Perhaps he was trying to be provocative, as he had little good to say about other Pacific cities either.

---

7   ADB 2016; see also 2017. In 1974, Ian Willis published *Lae, Village and City*, the title of which was a similar play on words.
8   *Solomon News Drum* [hereinafter *SND*], 11 July 1975.
9   Theroux 1992: 148, 159.

He was not the only one to deride the city. Will Randall visited during the Tension years, when, admittedly, Honiara was not looking its best. Even so, his unkind description of the city as 'the unsightly boil in the navel of the otherwise dazzling, seductively beautiful Solomon Islands' and as a 'hungover vagrant' gazing 'blearily out across its one main street to the sea'[10] is unfortunate vilification. Charles Montgomery was equally unflattering about Tension-era Honiara, repeating the same style of negative imagery:

> [T]he storm of dust and refuse, the plastic bags that rolled like tumbleweeds across the road, the heaps of garbage that smouldered like castles after a siege. And this, spray-painted across an abandoned building: 'Welcome to Hell'.[11]

After around 60 visits, I must admit to being fond of Honiara. What Theroux, Randall, and Montgomery missed is that Honiara and its surrounds can be very beautiful, and the people are charming, friendly, and gentle, although often shy of foreigners until they get to know them. The city stretches along the coast; the views of neighbouring island groups and the sunsets, with volcanic Savo Island as part of the backdrop, can be astounding. The view into the mountains of Guadalcanal—Mt Popomanaseu, inland from the Weather Coast, reaches 2,335 metres, 107 metres higher than Australia's Mt Kosciuszko—is awe-inspiring. Unlike in Western cities where the inhabitants scuttle past ignoring each other, in Honiara, people do not usually rush about; they amble along—a product of the heat and a desire to put social relationships first. No acquaintance goes ungreeted and everyone is acknowledged. There is an etiquette of respect for personal space that is appealing. Passing directly in front of another person, or between two people who are talking, is considered rude. It is taboo to step over the legs of a sitting girl or woman, although this seldom can occur as they are trained never to allow it to happen. There is no begging in the streets, and in markets there are fixed prices, politeness, and honesty when returning change. When passing, men and youths usually meet your eyes and smile and say hello, using raised eyebrows as part of the greeting, and women and girls will also smile a hello, a little more demurely.

---

10   Randall 2002: 150.
11   Montgomery 2004: 159.

Like any developing-world city, Honiara has its drawbacks. I am not blind to them. The informal settlements overwhelm the formal suburbs, corruption is an ever-increasing problem, and there are too few trees and parks. The pollution of Mataniko and White rivers is a disgrace, and a better rubbish collection service would be a distinct advantage. I have been saddened by the reckless granting of public land to business enterprises; areas once used by the public—for instance, the Town Ground sporting field and the Kukum shore—are now locked away for commercial use. Asian logging businesses have begun to invest in Honiara; the recent Capital Park complex near King George VI School is a good example. But these weaknesses are overridden by the sense among the people of pride in their nation and their capital that makes any shortcomings easy to forgive. And we must not fall into the same trap as many of the planning documents, which seem to presume that Honiara should be a clone of a medium-sized First World city. It never will be. As I argue in this book, it is a village-city in which substantial elements of provincial village life mingle with an emerging 'Solomons' style of urban development. Although I do not underestimate the level of poverty, I can also see the resilience and the beauty.

The final chapter suggests that hybridity is the overriding feature that makes Greater Honiara (the entire city council urban area and its peri-urban surrounds) work as a single unit. Early chapters help build towards this conclusion. Solomon Islands cultural ceremonies and dances continue in Honiara, brought from villages around the nation, some adapted for hotel or cultural show performances. Malaitan bride-price ceremonies take place, in which 50 to 100 strings of shell wealth change hands, accompanied by gifts of cloth and cash. The original canoe transport has turned into travel on open-back trucks, with participants equipped with symbolic decorative paddles. Big-city buildings like Hyundai Mall on the waterfront jostle alongside the modern version of trade stores with unlikely names such as New Generation or Red Carpet. Honiara's markets are a crucial link between villages and the urban centre. Central Market operates seven days a week—a huge undercover area where green and root vegetables, fruit, flowers, chickens, fish, handicrafts, and shell wealth can be purchased. There is a second, smaller council market at Kukum, and a substantial roadside food market flourishes at the Malaitan Fishing Village on Sundays, at which most of the vendors are Seventh-day Adventists, who observe their sabbath on Saturdays. Other local markets operate at White River, Borderline, Mbokona, at the east–west

Kola`a Ridge intersection, and out on the road to the airport, regardless of occasional city council attempts to close some of them. Small makeshift shops sell household items in the settlements and suburbs. Betel nuts, lime, and pepper leaves,[12] and single cigarettes, or cooked chicken or fish, can be purchased from roadside vendors. Potent illegal *kwaso* (homemade alcoholic spirits) and marijuana are readily available in all parts of Honiara, including Central and Kukum markets. Honiara, with its flourishing cash economy, is a complex meeting place for people and products from all over the Solomons.

I feel at home whenever I return, seeking out new buildings and developments, looking at new fashions and interactions. There were low times in the 1990s and 2000s when I was able to judge the weakness of the economy by the size of the potholes in the road from the airport. Viewed from a distance, the drivers appeared drunk as they weaved slowly all over the road, trying to avoid the cavities. Even though repair is now much better on the tar-sealed main roads, this still seems to go in cycles. In late 2013, once more the main roads were falling apart; the repairs were few and inadequate. The contractors had patched the roads for show, not longevity. In mid-2017, when dignitaries arrived from all over the Pacific to mark the end of the Regional Assistance Mission to Solomon Islands (RAMSI),[13] the main roads were full of potholes once more, patched up with gravel, not bitumen. By October that year, the 'drunk drivers' were back, easing cars in and out of potholes. The main Mataniko bridge has been doubled in size, and a Japanese aid project restructured the main road in the Mendana Avenue and Kukum Highway area. Upgrading of the road from Point Cruz to White River has begun. Regardless of the improvements to the coastal road, driving around Kobito, Gilbert Camp, and White River or anywhere in the hills, ridges, and valleys is always a slow experience as cars manoeuvre along decaying roads—a reminder to citizens of Honiara that urban facilities are still limited.

---

12   Chewed together, they have a mildly narcotic effect.
13   Under the auspices of the Pacific Islands Forum, in 2003, RAMSI was begun to bring an end to civil conflict and stabilise the nation. See Chapter 9.

INTRODUCTION

Urbanisation

Solomon Islands, Vanuatu, Fiji, and Papua New Guinea have the most rapidly urbanising populations in the south-west Pacific. As shown in Figure 9.1 and Maps 10.4–10.5, an ever-increasing number of Solomon Islanders—around 25 per cent—now live in what is termed Greater Honiara, beyond the boundaries of the Honiara City Council. The overflow of city boundaries is similar in neighbouring nations. Vanuatu's total population is around 300,000, of whom about 30 per cent live in the Greater Port Vila area. More than 50 per cent of Fiji's total population of 900,000 now lives in urban areas, with 15 to 20 per cent of Greater Suva's 244,000 population living in settlements in the Suva to Nasau corridor. Papua New Guinea now has a population of close to 9 million. Its capital, Port Moresby, is home to 400,000 people, and some estimates suggest that half of them live in informal settlements. Another 600,000 live in other PNG towns and cities.[14]

My training is as a historian, not a geographer or social scientist, which are often the dominant genres of urban academic writing. Cyril Bellshaw's book *The Great Village*, about Hanuabada, Port Moresby, and John Connell and John Lea's *Pacific 2010*, about urban Polynesia, come to mind.[15] In the south-west Pacific, if we exclude settler societies on the fringe in Australia and New Zealand, there are few wide-ranging monograph histories of Pacific towns and cities. There are of course chapters, academic articles, and reports on aspects of Pacific urbanisation, although many of the most recent emerge from allied social science disciplines that study aspects of contemporary development, governance, gender, climate, environment, social change, youth, employment, policing, economics, and politics, not history. Often these publications have little chronological depth, the necessity of which I regard as a hallmark of good urban history. I am interested in the *longue durée*—change over time—and how people use social space and urban settings in their own ways, regardless of attempts by planners to shape and control developments. I also freely borrow techniques from different disciplines to achieve my aims. After all, Solomon Islanders have created their own urban environment, which

---

14 Keen et al. 2017: 31–48. See also Jones 2012; and ADB 2016.
15 Bellshaw 1957; Connell and Lea 1994.

replicates and extends some patterns from rural villages. They use space quite differently from the way the British and post-independence planners envisaged. I have tried to trace the way these changes have occurred.

It is worth a reminder that urban development is alien to Melanesia's pre-contact societies, and that Honiara is a uniquely large urban centre in the nation.[16] Originally, Solomon Islanders lived in small communities—usually hamlets or villages sustained by subsistence agriculture, hunting, and coastal fishing. They came together in large numbers only during warfare and trading, or for feasts and festivities—gatherings of hundreds, not thousands, of people. This all began to change after 1897 when the first substantial urban settlement was begun on Tulagi. Previously there had only been small trading and Christian mission stations.

The urban centres that grew were all government towns, except for Paeu, which was established on Vanikolo Island in the 1920s as a base for a substantial logging company, and Noro near Munda on New Georgia, a fishing port and processing plant begun in the 1990s. Government towns were established on Gizo Island in the New Georgia Group in 1899, at Auki ('Aoke or Rarasu) on Malaita in 1909, Ontong Java Atoll (Luangiua or Lord Howe Atoll) in 1915–16, at Kirakira on Makira (San Cristobal) in 1918, and Lata on Nendö (Santa Cruz) in 1923. There was also a government base at Faisi in the Shortland Islands from 1906, and another began at Aola on Guadalcanal in 1914, neither of which developed into substantial urban areas. By the 1920s, there were eight administrative districts: the Ngela Group; Mala (Malaita); Guadalcanal; Gizo; Shortlands; Isabel and the Russells; Eastern Solomons (Makira and Ulawa); and Santa Cruz. Later, the number of districts was reduced to four: Western (based at Gizo), Eastern (based at Kirakira), Central (based at Tulagi, and then Honiara), and Malaita (based at Auki). Until Honiara was established, the headquarters for Guadalcanal District was at Aola.

Living patterns for some Solomon Islanders began to alter in the late nineteenth century, not only through the government towns but also through large coastal mission villages and plantations. Early in the twentieth century, coconut plantations became new gathering places for labourers, who began and ended their contracts at Tulagi and other government centres.

---

16 Goddard 2019.

INTRODUCTION

Indigenous movements leading to urbanisation

Indigenous social and political movements such as Maasina Rule and the Moro Movement also led to greater concentrations of population in some areas. Maasina Rule (1944–52) began in `Are`are, Malaita, at a time when many Malaitan men were working in the wartime Labour Corps on Guadalcanal and in the Ngela Group. *Maasina* means 'his brother' or 'his sibling', or even 'his friend'. Maasina Rule was a radical reorganisation of Malaitan society with the aim of enabling Malaitans to regain control over their lives after decades of British government. The movement's members were influenced by American servicemen, including African Americans, whose humane treatment of them and political advice encouraged them to take a stand against the old colonial system. The leaders spread a message of the need for Malaitan independence across the island, advocating improvements in agriculture, concentration into larger, cleaner villages, and later, non-cooperation with the BSIP Government and Christian missions. These teachings were coupled at some stages with hopes for liberation by the Americans, and millenarian ideas. This latter aspect of the movement was often exaggerated by contemporary government officials, and later by anthropologists and historians influenced by their accounts. The movement soon spread to all areas of Malaita, and to neighbouring islands, particularly Makira and parts of Guadalcanal. For eight years, the movement dominated the political scene in the central Solomons. It was an indigenous proto-nationalist movement grounded in a desire for self-government and self-determination.

In the late 1940s, Maasina Rule towns were built on Malaita to accommodate several thousand people.[17] Given the preponderance of Malaitan residents in Honiara in the second half of the 1940s and 1950s, should these Maasina Rule towns be considered transitory and ephemeral, or could they have played a part in early Malaitan thinking about Honiara? Many Malaitans never liked the Maasina Rule towns: the imposed social closeness, and having to live with people who were not close kin, far from their gardens and ancestral lands. Solomon Islanders from the provinces often still feel this way about Honiara. Not everyone wants to live there. Some prefer not to visit Honiara at all or, if forced to do so, they escape the hurly-burly as soon as possible. The quiet of rural

---

17   Akin 2013; Bennett 1987: 202–310; Keesing 1978a, 1978b; Laracy 1983.

areas, the support of kin, the ability to live from their own garden produce and fishing, and the comfort of living on ancestral lands will always be important for the majority.

The Moro Movement, the other indigenous movement that influenced Guadalcanal, was begun by Pelise Moro in the late 1950s to gain social, economic, and political improvements on Guadalcanal through cooperative economic enterprises. These changes were combined with a high regard for custom and tradition to synthesise a new social order. It was a 'back to custom' movement and had magical and spiritual elements. Moro was born in the mid-1920s and lived at Makaruka village on Tasimauri (meaning 'live sea'), the name for the Weather Coast of Guadalcanal. The Moro Movement can be partly understood in the context of World War II and the Allied presence on Guadalcanal, the long-term migration of `Are`are Malaitans to Marau Sound at the eastern end of the island, and the government's neglect of the Weather Coast. The Moro Movement called the island 'Isatabu', instead of Guadalcanal (the Spanish-inspired name), and for many decades was a significant regenerative force for traditional life. It was also residually involved in the Tensions that occurred between Malaitans and the people of Guadalcanal in the 1990s and 2000s.

In the same way that the people of the north coast have links to Savo and the Ngela Group, Marau Sound at Guadalcanal's eastern end was settled some 13 generations ago by migrants from the `Are`are language area on the west coast of Malaita. There were already `Are`are links to Marau Sound when the Mendaña expedition visited in 1568, and there was always regular canoe traffic back and forth, and trade and kinship links. This ancient connection seems to have increased in the mid-nineteenth century. The people were divided between those living on the islands around the sound and those on the mainland. During Maasina Rule, the Marau `Are`are felt themselves to be part of the movement. In 1953, preparations began to form the Guadalcanal Council, although in 1954 two of the Marau villages (Hatere and Niu) wanted to join the Malaita Council instead. When this was rejected by the protectorate administration, they, along with the neighbouring Veuru Moli people, asked to be allowed to form their own Marau–Hauba Council, which occurred in 1955. There was considerable tension between the Marau 'saltwater' people, who were determined to expand their interests on Guadalcanal, and the bush people. The Marau Malaitans claimed control of the land from Oniseri to Kakau (Kaukau). Most indigenous Guadalcanal people are inclined to regard the 'Are'are Malaitans as intruders, though they have all been linked for hundreds of years.

Moro suffered a severe illness in 1957 during which he had visions that were incorporated into his social movement. Government records contain the first reports on the Moro Movement in May 1957 and tell of an incident that led to Moro's imprisonment for three months, along with some of his followers. He claimed he was destined to lead the Marau–Hauba peoples and was assisted by two Melanesian Mission–educated men, David Valusa and Joseph Goraiga, who wrote down his version of customs and history. Moro's most important document related to the settlement of Isatabu. He said the core chieftainships of Guadalcanal were in the centre of the island. His own headquarters was at Makaruka in the Veuru Moli area on the Weather Coast.

At the core of the movement was Moro's desire for the economic betterment of his people through social action. His strongly anti-government focus related to land matters and came after the decline of the Marau–Hauba Council. The movement spread along the coast, into the mountains, and to the Guadalcanal Plains on the north coast. It created a structure with district leaders, clerks, and tax collection, much as Maasina Rule had devised. There were also millenarian aspects to the Moro Movement, some of which predicted that the Americans would return, although these ideas were always peripheral. Moro did not promote them.

In 1959, Moro and his followers refused to take part in the government census or cooperate with a government mapping project. By 1960, the movement was renamed the Moro Custom Company. The government dealt carefully with it—first, by trying to increase economic development on the Weather Coast through the establishment of agricultural and health projects. In 1965–66, the Guadalcanal Council aided the construction of an airfield at Avuavu, although this was viewed unfavourably since it served the Catholic Mission, where many people were not movement supporters. Some of Moro's supporters were elected to the Guadalcanal Council, with Moro himself preferring to ignore formal political processes and work separately. By the mid-1960s, the Moro Custom Company had influence over about half of Guadalcanal, mainly in the centre of the island, bounded by the outskirts of Honiara and Rere on the north coast, and Duidui and Balo on the south coast. An estimated 3,000 to 4,000 people were followers, out of Guadalcanal's indigenous population of 20,000 (which included Honiara).

In 1972, more than 1,000 visitors arrived at Makaruka village from all along the Weather Coast and Honiara, including a Canadian television crew and a research team from the University of Hawai`i's East-West Center. Government officials, including District Commissioner James Tedder, also attended. A special feast had been organised to celebrate the first arrival of humans to Isatabu and the creation of the island's strong customs. Moro issued the invitation for people to participate to show that his movement had a rational design and was not a cult. Accompanied by 10 male escorts, Moro was dressed in shell money—an extraordinary display of wealth. All guests were allowed to visit the custom house and the 'house of memory', if they were wearing custom garments: *tapa* breech cloths for men and grass or string skirts for women, with the concession of a *tapa* cloth top for European women. The village normally had only 10 houses; an additional 190 had been constructed for the visitors. Dances were held and displays of fighting were arranged.

At independence in 1978, Moro and his followers were invited to Honiara to join the cultural activities. The movement—strongest in the late 1950s and 1960s—continued to exist into the 1990s. In 1985, it celebrated its 30th anniversary. The Moro Movement had loose connections with the Isatabu Freedom Movement, the militia group that from 1998 to 2003 tried to rid the island of the large Malaitan presence, and to restore control by Isatabu people. Moro died in 2006.[18]

Modern urban settlements

In the early 2020s, there are only five substantial urban areas in a nation of approximately 721,000 people: Greater Honiara, with its population estimated to be 160,000;[19] Gizo, with 7,000 people; Auki, of similar size to Gizo; Noro, with around 4,000 people; and Lata, with 2,300 people. There are now nine provinces, which has meant the creation of new urban centres; Buala in Isabel Province, Taro in Choiseul Province, and Lata in

---

18   Davenport and Çoker 1967; Davenport 1970; O'Connor 1973.
19   Estimates of Honiara's population depend on the boundaries used. The peri-urban population blends into surrounding Guadalcanal Province. As well, the significant daily movement of people from the provinces to Honiara makes estimating the population difficult. This is especially true for movements between Auki and Honiara. Many Malaitans see Honiara (not Auki) as the end of the market route because they are able to get in and out of Honiara on ships daily. Solomon Islands Government [hereinafter SIG] 2009: Basic Tables and Census Description, pp. 5–8. Based on the 2019 national census, the National Statistics Office estimate for the population of the Honiara City Council area is 130,178, with another 30,000 in the peri-urban area. SIG 2020g.

Temotu Province are recent urban developments. Tulagi, the capital of the protectorate until 1942, is now the headquarters of Central Islands Province. The difference between Honiara and the next biggest urban centres is significant.

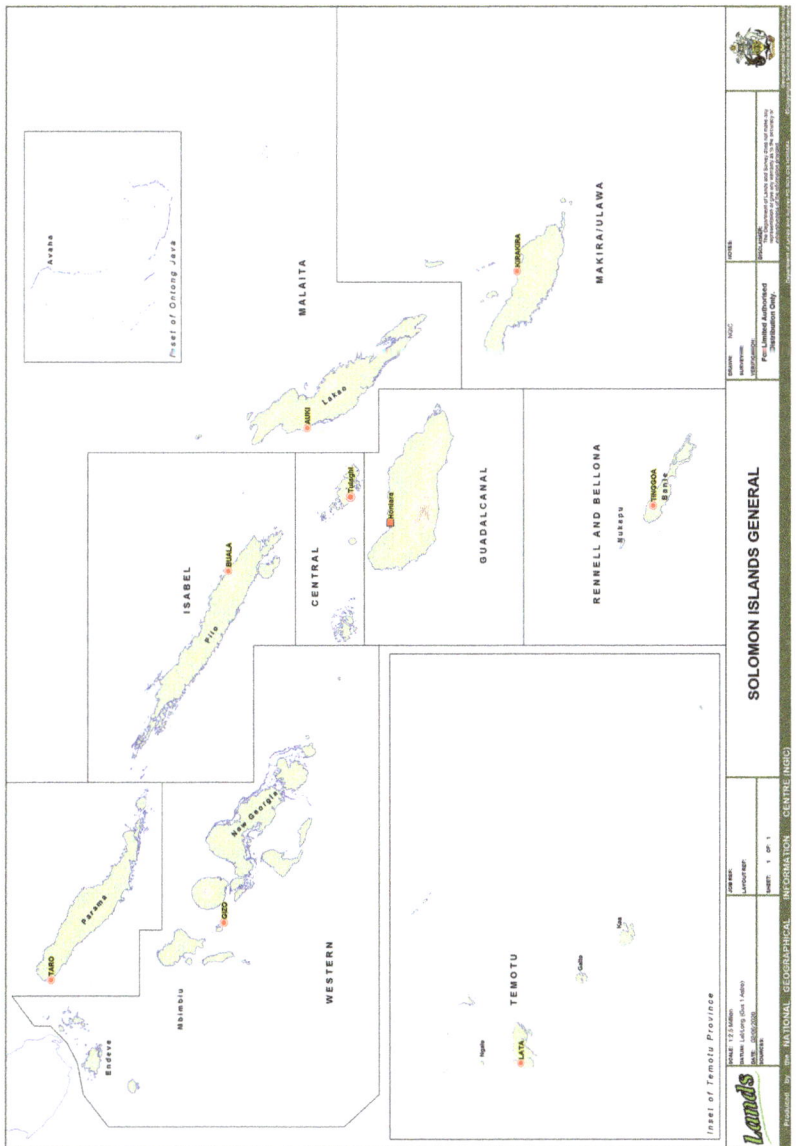

Map 0.3 Modern Solomon Islands urban centres.
Source: SIG (2020h).

The Solomon Islands Government chose a legal status for Honiara similar to the capital territory system used for Port Moresby in Papua New Guinea, and Canberra in Australia. Two acts of parliament are relevant. Under the *Honiara City Act 1999*, the Honiara City Council includes representatives from 12 wards, and the Minister of Home Affairs appoints the three local members of the National Parliament, and the Premier of Guadalcanal Province, as ex officio members, as well as another four members, one of whom must be from Guadalcanal. The *Provincial Government Act 1997*, is also relevant, mainly through Part 2(1), which excludes Honiara, although by tradition the Mayor of Honiara attends premiers' conferences.[20] Honiara is a special district made up almost entirely of perpetual estate (PE) land under the ultimate control of the Commissioner of Lands and is not part of Guadalcanal Province. It is the only urban area in Solomon Islands with its own act of parliament.

Now a sprawling Melanesian city, Honiara's 2020s business, church, and political leaders are very different from the first generation of Solomon Islander residents in the 1940s and 1950s. So far, Honiara does not have the social and criminal problems of Papua New Guinea's larger cities, although the Tension years were testing and, occasionally, serious riots have occurred to mar the urban equilibrium. The most significant riot was in 2006 when Chinatown and several other central areas were destroyed. The causes of the Tension years (1998–2003), discussed in Chapter 9, are unresolved.[21] There are disturbing economic and social trends that indicate that Honiara could well develop into another Port Moresby or Lae, where the rich live behind razor wire and have security guards to stop the unemployed poor preying on them. In Honiara, except for diplomatic and commercial compounds, most residents still manage to live quite comfortably with minimal security. While the *wantok* system (sharing a language and kinship-derived obligations) sustains social and economic equilibrium, and acts as a safety net in an urban society largely bereft of state-sponsored social security, it has its limits. Workers' salaries can never be sufficient to honour customary obligations when relatives come to town, or to sustain family rites of passage that occur in provincial villages.

Honiara will continue to grow and at some stage an accommodation must be reached with the surrounding Guadalcanal landowners to secure an adequate water supply and some agreement as to the eventual maximum

---

20   Refer to SIG 1997, 1999a. I am indebted to Philip Tagini for his assistance.
21   Moore 2004a, 2018; Fraenkel 2004.

population and extent of the city as it extends into the Tandai and Malango wards of Guadalcanal Province. There are obvious solutions for controlling the size, or accommodating the growth, of Honiara. One is to develop provincial towns and rural-based economic projects to make life in the provinces attractive enough to satisfy people in the regions, thus curbing their desire to try their luck in Honiara. The other is to reach an accommodation with the surrounding Guale people on their customary lands. While these solutions are clear, two decades on from the beginning of the Tensions, despite plans, there has been no new large-scale economic development in populous Malaita Province, or anywhere else, that would encourage people to stay home. The government has failed to deal with key issues that provoked the Tensions. Honiara will continue to increase in size.[22]

The village-city

Honiara: Village-City of Solomon Islands outlines life in the area that became Honiara, concentrating on the eight decades between 1942 and 2020. Maps, photographs, tables, and graphs are spread throughout the chapters. Readers can also be viewers, visually appreciating the changes that have occurred. Chapter 1 deals with the north coast of Guadalcanal before Honiara existed, covering the early interaction with Spanish explorers, and the beginning of coconut plantations in the late nineteenth and first half of the twentieth centuries. The nineteenth-century land divisions have in part shaped the modern city. Chapter 2 outlines the Japanese and then Allied invasions between 1942 and 1945. The bulk of the book concentrates on the 1940s to the 1970s and the development of the nation that emerged at independence in 1978. Chapter 3 describes how the Americans' Camp Guadal became Honiara, the British administrative headquarters—first, for the BSIP, and then for the entire WPHC. Chapter 4 covers the same period, focused on the 'other' Honiara—the early parallel community made up of Solomon Islanders, Chinese, Gilbertese, and Fijians.

Chapter 5 examines the development of municipal authority and housing, along with the urban planning necessary to construct the rudimentary town that slowly became a major Pacific city. Chapter 6 examines

---

22   Clifford et al. 1984; Dinnen 2001; Dinnen and Ley 2000.

Honiara in the 1960s as infrastructure was built for the BSIP and WPHC headquarters. Honiara housed the High Court and the Secretariat for the WPHC, Namba 9 (the Central Hospital), the police headquarters at Rove, educational institutions, the National Museum, hotels, shipping and air services, newspapers, and the Solomon Islands Broadcasting Corporation (SIBC). All these were building blocks for creating the modern nation. Chapter 7 discusses further aspects of nation-building, examining religion and sport, and education through to secondary and tertiary levels. The chapter ends with the changing role of women and children in urban society, the beginnings of trade unions and political activism, and the localisation of the public service. Chapter 8 examines the creation of social hierarchies and national politics during the 1960s and 1970s, and the different political iterations that led to the National Parliament. The chapter also examines the public service and the elite who controlled the changing city, ending with independence and Solomon Islander political ascendancy.

The final two chapters are broad essays on the development of Honiara over the 40 years since independence. Two major arguments are pursued throughout. The first is that a hybrid society exists that has drawn its characteristics from several sources, both indigenous and international, as Solomon Islands has joined the community of nations. Second, as summarised in Figure 0.1, an overarching argument from Chapter 3 through to Chapter 10 is that over decades there have been four and sometimes five changing and intersecting Honiara 'worlds' (or spheres) operating at any one time, each with different social, economic, and political significance. Although there were few Solomon Islanders living in Honiara until the early 1950s, even at this stage, the beginning of Malaitan dominance was clear. Four or five Honiara 'worlds' were in operation by the 1960s and 1970s: one British, one Solomon Islander, one Chinese, and one made up of Gilbertese migrants and other Pacific Islanders who were in Honiara for employment or education. A Malaitan 'world' grew strong, both in numbers and in social significance, far more so than for other Solomon Islanders in the capital. While the Chinese extended their economic power, at the same time, Malaitans overwhelmed Honiara numerically and in many social ways. In my suggested divisions in Figure 0.1, the Gilbertese are not listed separately after the 1970s and 1980s, because they have become citizens of Solomon Islands.

Likewise, Fijians and Indo-Fijians were only significant in early decades, usually arriving as tradesmen, and the presence of other Pacific Islanders undertaking education was transitory—a product of the 1960s and 1970s.

Chapters 9 and 10 carry the book's argument from independence until 2020. In the 1980s and 1990s, Honiara's Asian population broadened to include old and new Chinese families (the *waku*) and other Asian groups. They took over most of the modern economy of the independent nation in a manner that had never been possible for the Chinese in Tulagi before World War II. Indigenous national consciousness also developed, partly planned by the British through the creation of local and national political and educational institutions, but inevitably also home grown, taking on unique Solomon Islander characteristics. During these recent decades, there have been significant issues as the nation both lost and found its way politically and economically. Along the road there were mismanagement and corruption, and the Tension years, when the nation came to the brink of anarchy and was described by some as a 'failing state'. The arrival of RAMSI (2003–17) was a Pacific Islands Forum initiative, attempting to rebuild major governance structures. The book ends in 2020, with Solomon Islands once more a totally independent Pacific nation. Honiara is woven into these recent events.

Writing about the Solomons

Although my career as a historian has also covered diverse topics in the history of Australia and Papua New Guinea, I have an abiding fascination with the peoples of the Solomon Islands archipelago and the modern Solomon Islands nation. In some ways, I have been in training to write about Honiara for 45 years, and my work on Malaitan history has enabled me to deal with one of the key aspects of Honiara: the substantial number of residents of Malaitan descent. Understanding their background and place in Honiara is an important part of the book. As well, Honiara is intimately involved in the history of the nation and cannot be written about in isolation. Often, I have had to set explanations into a wider context to make sense of developments in Honiara. I have not dealt in detail with the history of the BSIP before World War II, as that was covered in my book *Tulagi*, the companion volume to *Honiara*, and in my *Making Mala*. The history of the capital city is also a history of the modern nation; Honiara is the urban hub that makes it all function. My path to the book began in the first half of the 1970s when I first interacted with Australians of Solomon Islander descent while collecting oral history, and particularly after 1976 when I first visited Honiara and Malaita. The route is now paved with several earlier books and publications that are precursors to, or augment, the present volume.

Malaita has long been the most populous island in Solomon Islands and Malaitans became the major labour force travelling in circular labour migrations outside and inside what in the 1890s became the BSIP. From the 1870s, Solomon Islanders were involved in the labour trade to Queensland, Fiji, Samoa, and New Caledonia and, from the 1900s, within the protectorate. Malaitans have always been the dominant ethnic group in Honiara. I argue that we cannot account for Malaitan dominance unless we also understand the history of the archipelago and particularly of Malaita and labour movements. Just as my apprenticeship to write a history of Honiara has been long, so is my background in examining the role of Malaitans in developing the nation. In a broad sense, this is the fourth book I have written that is fully or partially centred on Malaitans. The first two were *Kanaka: A History of Melanesian Mackay* and *Happy Isles in Crisis: The Historical Causes for a Failing State in Solomon Islands, 1998–2004*, both of which link to arguments presented in my later *Making Mala: Malaita in Solomon Islands, 1870s–1930s*.[23] Over the same years, I have constantly broadened my knowledge of Solomon Islands. My *Tulagi: Pacific Outpost of British Empire*, while about the first capital of the protectorate, also widened my understanding of the place of Malaita in the establishment of government processes. These books are supported by my online *Solomon Islands Historical Encyclopaedia 1893–1978*, which contains aspects of them all and serves as an extension of the present book.[24] In the course of this journey, I have both broadened and narrowed my understanding of the history of the nation. My 2004 history of the background and course of the Tension years, much of which was played out in Honiara, forced me to present all sides of the argument as I strove not to be branded as a Malaitan partisan. During 2005–08, I edited *Tell It As It Is*, the autobiography of Sir Peter Kenilorea, who lived much of his life in Honiara. His book was published as part of the 40th anniversary celebrations for the nation of which he was the first prime minister.[25] This provided me with new perspectives on decision-making processes and a close acquaintance with the Malaitan who is regarded by many

---

23 Moore 1985, 2004a, 2017a, 2019.
24 Kenilorea 2008; Moore 2013c: entry for Kenilorea, 2017a, 2019.
25 Kenilorea 2008.

as the most important leader the nation has produced. I also edited the proceedings of a 2013 RAMSI seminar[26] and chaired the final RAMSI symposium in June 2017. Both occasions provided me with a wider perspective on Solomon Islanders in the mid-2010s.

Two other books have particularly influenced my thinking. Judith Bennett's *Wealth of the Solomons: A History of a Pacific Archipelago, 1800–1978* is an exceptional history of the colonial years; my copy never leaves my desk and is regularly consulted. David Akin's *Colonialism, Maasina Rule, and the Origins of Malaitan Kastom* is equally useful.[27] In his exhaustive, forensic look at Maasina Rule (1944–52), Akin examined the way Malaitans constructed a proto-nationalist movement that repositioned Solomon Islanders vis-a-vis the British administration. Although *Making Mala* is a useful precursor to understanding this political movement, anything I could write on Maasina Rule would be superfluous to Akin's book on these crucial years, the final stages of the creation of one Malaitan people from a dozen language and cultural regions. As this political development coincides with the beginning of Honiara, it is essential to understanding Malaitans and the influence of Maasina Rule in early Honiara.[28]

Honiara's 'worlds'

To conclude this introduction, I have attempted to summarise Honiara's history in one figure, which illustrates historical events over almost 80 years. Hopefully, it will make readers think about historical and cultural processes and developments, and ponder the future. *Honiara: Village-City of Solomon Islands* amplifies the abbreviations depicted.

As the book proceeds, I often refer to this figure and explain the changes illustrated. Viewed over several decades, the division into 'worlds' or spheres operates as a summary and argument, helping guide the reader through the changes that have occurred. Nevertheless, it is important not to be confined by the simplification offered in the figure. There were always intersections and a melding of these 'worlds' caused by religion, education, travel, finances, and so on, which no one figure can express. Each 'world' had a distinct social identity, largely self-contained, but also permeable.

---

26 Moore 2014.
27 Bennett 1987; Akin 2013.
28 Akin 2013: 187–91.

HONIARA

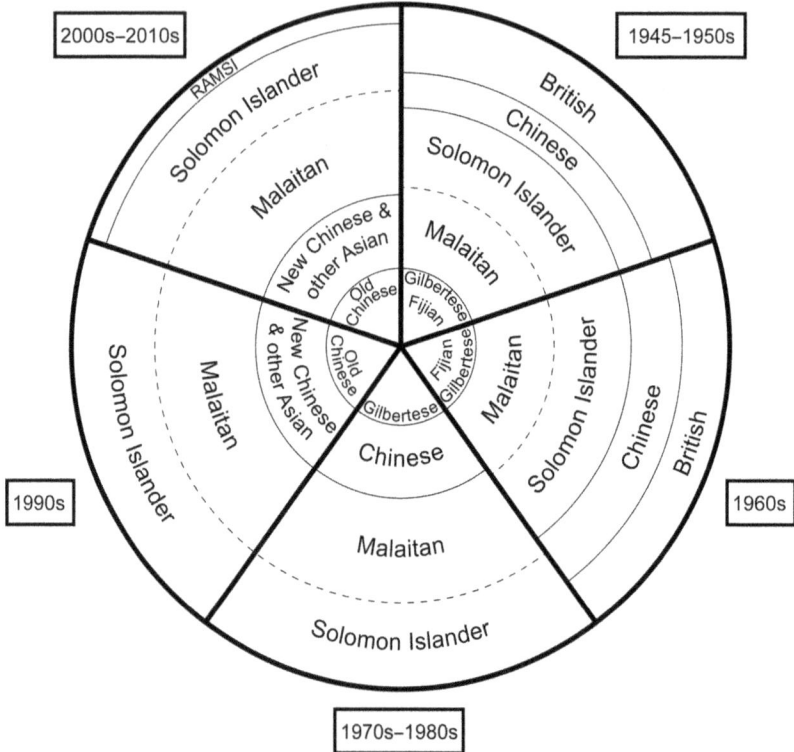

Figure 0.1 Honiara's 'worlds' in order of their social, economic, and political importance, 1940s – 2010s.
Source: Figure by Vincent Verheyen.

I suggest that a rudimentary Malaitan world separate from, and dominant over, all other Solomon Islander urban communities has existed in Honiara since the 1940s and emerged very clearly well before independence in 1978. Honiara's Malaitan world has since grown ever stronger numerically and culturally. I am not advocating Malaitan dominance, superiority, or separation, but as a historian, I cannot ignore what has occurred. It is a unique situation, not matched in the history of neighbouring nations such as Papua New Guinea and Vanuatu. Yet, I expect this influence will wane and not remain such a strong difference.

The only way forward is for all Solomon Islanders to be equal, and for future development to assist all areas of the nation—the smaller provinces just as much as the larger, more populous ones. The processes of modernisation will ensure that over the next few generations there will be further intermarriages that will eventually create one nation. Islands of origin will become less significant. This is already beginning to be evident in modern Honiara, although even when urban Solomon Islanders become disconnected from their village origins, they still maintain a strong sense of connection to their island of origin. At present, it is inescapable that Malaitans are the major ethnic group in the nation, in their numbers in Malaita Province (173,347 in 2019), in other provinces, and in Honiara. Within the context of Honiara, it is necessary to try to understand the historical circumstances that have led to the large number of residents of Malaitan descent, and to come to terms with other development issues such as those that have left the Guale as an urban minority in a Honiara steadily encroaching on their customary lands.

Solomon Islands has a centralised system of government with weak provincial governments,[29] alongside strong regional cultures. Creating a federal system has been discussed for many years, with no significant progress. Regardless of this seemingly failed dialogue, the citizens of Solomon Islands will become more united, although for the moment home provinces and islands of origin remain significant. The Malaitan dominance in Honiara is a local historical peculiarity that will decline over the next century as intermarriages, nationalism, and modern education become more significant than regionalism. Christine Jourdan described this as 'cultural creolisation'.[30]

If I may be allowed to do what historians usually avoid—to forecast the future—over the next 50 years, I would expect to see the emergence of a more united people with class and income variations becoming more significant than tribal, language, or regional ancestry. This will particularly occur in urban areas.[31] There are of course moderating factors: customary ownership of most non-urban land in Solomon Islands is a basic right enshrined in the constitution; and circular migration from rural to urban areas, and vice versa, will continue, always renewing traditional cultural patterns. At the same time, sacred sites have been abandoned and offerings are no longer made to ancestors, except among a small number of people, mainly in the Kwaio area on Malaita. The people's relationship with their land has altered, and in urban areas landownership and occupancy have

---

29   Provincial governments were largely formed out of the protectorate's administrative districts of the 1960s and 1970s. The terminology came into use after independence in 1978. On Guadalcanal, this meant the government of the entire island, excluding the area of Honiara, with a provincial headquarters based in Honiara.
30   Jourdan 1995b.
31   Gibson 2019.

been individualised. There are also signs that some urbanites are losing fluency in their parents' indigenous languages and are using Solomon Islands Pijin and English as their primary languages. While rural customary influences will remain important, urban areas are growing fast and the residents are adopting new versions of custom and culture, mixed with influences from the 'foreign flowers' of Christianity and government requirements, alongside often insecure land tenure. As Jaap Timmer suggests: 'The cultural openness of Melanesian societies has enabled the creation of new forms of organisation and identity in the contemporary era.'[32] In the long run, the most enduring urban characteristic will probably be not Malaitan dominance or cultural retention, but the dominance of the immigrant East Asian business community with its strong economic influence in the nation.

***

Finally, every historian has moments of self-doubt, and we are only as good as our sources allow. I am conscious that I will always be an outsider, no matter how well-informed. And even though I have cumulatively spent a few years of my life in Honiara, I have never lived there permanently. This has advantages and disadvantages. My view is clearer from not being involved in day-to-day events, although I can never hope to have the detailed knowledge of changes and geography available to a permanent, long-term resident. To my friends whom I have pestered with questions about obscure details, now you know why. I apologise for any shortcomings. I hope Solomon Islanders will gain some appreciation of their past from my endeavours. No doubt, they will agree and disagree with some of my interpretations. It is my hope that the current generation will be inspired by what I have retrieved and go on to write their own histories of Honiara and the other urban centres in Solomon Islands.

Clive Moore
The University of Queensland
February 2022

---

32   Timmer 2019: 133.

1
Nahona`ara before 1942

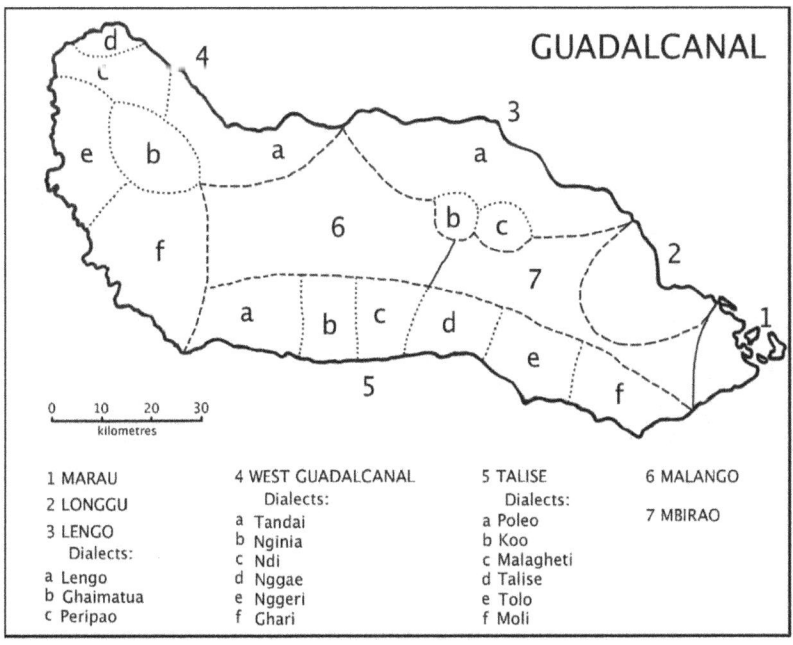

Map 1.1 Languages and dialects of Guadalcanal.
Source: Adapted from Tryon and Hackman (1983: Map 3). Cartography by Vincent Verheyen.

HONIARA

Guadalcanal and *Nahona`ara*

The history of Honiara can never be separated from that of Guadalcanal, the second-largest island (after Bougainville) in the Solomon archipelago. The chapter begins with a discussion of the short Spanish interlude in 1568. This well-documented view of Guadalcanal from centuries ago allows us to draw some conclusions about population levels, the nature of the people on Guadalcanal's north coast, and their responses to the incursion. During the sixteenth century, coastal settlements around what is now Honiara were much larger and more numerous. The second section of the chapter examines the plantation developments of the nineteenth and early twentieth centuries, when the number of Guale (the people of Guadalcanal) was considerably lower.

The Spanish explorers named several of the main Solomon Islands, including Guadalcanal, which they called after a municipality in the province of Sevilla in Andalusia, Spain. The name comes from the Arabic term *Wād al-Khānāt*, which translates as 'Valley of Stalls'—an indication of the refreshment stalls constructed there centuries earlier during the time of Muslim rule. *Wād al-Khānāt* became Guadalcanal (also Guadalcanar in early sources). Although smaller islands usually have one indigenous name, this is not always so with the larger Melanesian islands, where multiple languages, geographic regions, and tribes predominate. Malaita, Guadalcanal's neighbour, was usually called Mala, Choiseul was known as Lauru, and Makira (San Cristobal) was known as Hanuato`o. Bougainville and Guadalcanal seem not to have been known by single names.[1] Guadalcanal—160 kilometres long and 45 kilometres wide—was perhaps too big and too regional in its groupings to have one name, although the south coast is always known as Tasimauri (Weather Coast).

In 1888, Charles Woodford, a naturalist who became deputy commissioner (1896) and the first resident commissioner (1897–1915),[2] was told by Legacy, a man from neighbouring Savo Island, that Guadalcanal was called Launa by its inhabitants, and that his people called it Kulengela.[3] He may have been referring only to the north-west coast. Ian Hogbin, who conducted anthropological research on Guadalcanal's north-east

---

1   Oliver 1991; Regan and Griffin 2005.
2   Lawrence 2014; Moore 2019.
3   Pacific Manuscripts Bureau [hereinafter PMB] 1290, Woodford Papers, Reel 5, Bundle 29, C.M. Woodford Diary, 16 August 1888 to 3 January 1889, entry for 1 October.

coast in 1933, used the name Guadalcanal,[4] and BSIP reports make no mention of one indigenous name. Former district officer (and later district commissioner) James Tedder told me that during his years in the Solomons (1952–74), many of them based on Guadalcanal, he knew of no single name for the island.[5] Tarcisius Tara Kabutaulaka, a Tasimauri man, in his 2002 biography of his grandfather Dominiko Alebua, and other writing, uses Guadalcanal and Tasimauri.[6] All the central Solomon Islands are close together and there is evidence of migration to and from neighbouring islands.

As mentioned in the Introduction, more than 400 years ago, `Are`are people from west Malaita established a colony at Marau on the south coast. There was also migration from the Ngela Group to the Guadalcanal coast around Tasimboko, and Savo is close to the Visale area.[7] During the time of the Moro Movement, and later the Tensions, many Guadalcanal people used 'Isatabu' as an all-encompassing name for their island. Guale is now used, both for the name of the island and for its people, which appears to be of modern origin.

Archaeological evidence suggests that human occupation of Guadalcanal can be dated back 6,000 years. With confirmed dates going back 28,000 years in the north of the archipelago, it is possible that earlier dates will be established.[8] Evidence of deliberate clearing of vegetation by regular burning on the extensive plains east of Honiara, and of past irrigation of root crops on inland slopes, suggests early higher population levels along the coast. Linguists Darrell Tryon and Brian Hackman identified seven languages and 15 dialects on Guadalcanal. There are four main tribes, each with distinct totems, and land inheritance is usually matrilineal. The other important division is between interdependent but distinct inland (bush) and coastal (saltwater) communities.[9] Tandai on the north coast (Map 1.1: 4a) is the language area that includes Honiara, bordered to the east and south into the central mountains by the Malango, the Lengo along the coast to the east, and the coastal Ndi and inland Nginia groups to the west.

---

4   Hogbin 1964; Beckett 1986; Beckett and Gray 2007.
5   Conversations with James Tedder during the 2000s; Oliver 1991.
6   Kabutaulaka 2002a, 2019.
7   SIG 2001: 5.
8   Roe 1993: 2, 182.
9   Tryon and Hackman 1983: Map 3, p. 24; Roe 1993: 19; Kabutaulaka 2002a: 25.

Plate 1.1 The area of Guadalcanal that became Honiara.
This August 1942 photograph shows Horahi village to the west of the mouth of the Mataniko River.
Source: USNARA.

The Tandai use '*Nahona`ara*' as the name for the coastal land west of what is now known as Point Cruz—the area around old Government House, which is now the Heritage Park Hotel. It means 'facing the `*ara*', the place where the south-east trade winds meet the land.[10] It is unclear who suggested the town be called Honiara. The name was in use by mid-1945, replacing the more prosaic Camp Guadal—the American name for their military base. Presumably, the local Guale used the name, which Europeans liked and applied to the whole urban space. Greater Honiara, on a curved section of Guadalcanal's coast, now spills out from Point Cruz in both directions, stretching from Kakabona (or Kakambona) to Alligator Creek (also called Ilu River), with new settlements steadily moving inland.

---

10   Manakako and Mangalle 2018. Some sources suggest it is a Ghari word. This was the Guadalcanal language often used by the Catholic mission as their Guadalcanal *lingua franca*. The word is also used in the Tandai language.

1. NAHONA`ARA BEFORE 1942

The Spanish, 1568

In 2014, a bronze memorial bust of Spanish explorer Álvaro de Mendaña de Neira was unveiled in the grounds of the Solomon Islands National Museum in Honiara. Four-and-a-half centuries earlier, Mendaña and his crew were the first outsiders known to have reached the Solomon archipelago since Austronesian migrations from further north a few thousand years earlier—the origin of most of the modern Pacific languages and cultures. The Spanish accounts are useful as they allow us to assess the size of the population in the sixteenth century and, to some extent, patterns of behaviour.

Plate 1.2 A bronze bust of Spanish explorer Álvaro de Mendaña de Neira installed at the Solomon Islands National Museum in 2014.
Source: Christopher Chevalier Collection.

The Spanish were impressed by the potential of the north coast of Guadalcanal. Looking for the sources of King Solomon's gold (part of the justification for the expedition), they found limited amounts of alluvial gold, but largely this desire went unfulfilled.[11] What they located was the well-watered coastal plain that broadens east of modern Honiara into the best agricultural land in the Solomon archipelago. As they gazed at Point Cruz and its surrounds, the Spanish noted extensive short coastal ridges, most less than 60 to 80 metres high, with a few extending to 1 kilometre in length. The valleys they saw were 15 to 120 metres wide at their bases, with soil at the bottom but barren on the slopes and tops. They also found major coastal rivers with swampy, mangrove-clad mouths. Some of the valleys around the Mataniko River, Rove Creek, and Tau`utu (White) River, and the Mbumburu, Lengakiki, Vavaea, and Mbokonavera ridges were deep and heavily forested. Even allowing for some exaggeration—aimed at convincing the Spanish Government that they had not wasted their money on the expedition—the records indicate a substantial population on the north coast settled in large villages, with agriculture based on yam and taro cultivation, and the use of irrigation.

Honiara in 2020 is still centred on Point Cruz. On 12 May 1568, Mendaña's ships anchored near a small island they named Puerto de la Cruz ('Port of the Cross'). Gomez Catoira, the chief purser, recorded that they were watched by a crowd of 1,000 Guale when they disembarked at the beach. By the size of the crowd, curious Guale may have come from a wide area to meet them. The friars travelling with the expedition brought a large wooden cross ashore, celebrated mass, and carried the Christian symbol to the top of a nearby hill—still within sight of the ships—placing its base in the ground. Claims that this is the site of the present-day Catholic cathedral are unlikely to be true as it is too far away to fit the description. Vavaea Ridge where the National Parliament sits is a more likely site. Catoira wrote:

> [W]hilst this was happening [erecting the cross] several natives came to us, and the General showed them much friendship, embracing them and making them signs of peace, and giving them to understand that we would do them no harm.[12]

---

11 Hansell and Wall 1974: 106.
12 Amherst and Thomson 1901: 303.

As the Spaniards returned to their ships, there were loud shouts and threats from 300 men who had been hiding in a nearby valley. The Spanish fired arquebuses (long-barrelled guns on stands) and killed two of the attackers before retreating. The villagers took away the cross, although the following day they returned it. Next, there were altercations over coconuts, which the Spanish had taken without providing any compensation.

Over the next few days, two parties set out to search for gold. One substantial group went inland, and Mendaña set off in another direction with a second party, coming across many villages with substantial taro, yam, and pana (another tuber) gardens:

> And after they had gone a quarter of a league [1.3 kilometres] into the interior, entering a palm-grove they went up a hill, whence they saw a ravine, and on the sides of it they saw some villages, very bright and pleasant to look at, encompassed by groves of palm-trees and plantains and other trees, and many fields near the villages planted with their food, which is *pana* and *ñame* [yams and taro].
>
> … On our return we saw many villages upon the hills and many plantations (*chacaras*) of food on the slopes, arranged very well so that they could irrigate them, which they did. It was well laid out; and by each cleft there was a stream of water. The place whence the water came is full of trees. And soon we returned to the ship under the cool shade of the trees, without inconvenience from the sun.[13]

A few days later, Mendaña and 27 of his crew set off again:

> We went into the interior of the land, and after we passed through a little thicket in the plain, we were up to the hill-tops, having some difficulty in getting up on account of the thick grass, which remains throughout the year. We saw so many villages on the hill-tops that it was marvellous, for more than thirty villages, of ten and twenty houses and more, could be counted within a league and a half of road. And all of the slope round the hills was full of huts, clearings and plantations, kept in very good order, and the villages were surrounded by very tall palm-trees; and it is certain that one of these clearings would grow food enough to sustain all that we saw, as far as we could judge.

---

13 ibid., 305–6.

> ... In some parts of it there were hills, but of no great altitude, the rest being savannah. We saw much smoke in the plains, which was not surprising as the land is so densely populated. We saw some rivers, which traversed the plain and went down to the sea. We entered a small village of about seven or eight houses, but did not find anyone, and near it was another one, smaller, where there were no Indians. We sat down to rest in the village, and we took some *pana*, which we roasted, and we did the people no harm. We returned by another road which seemed to lead straight on; and entered another village, where there were seventy houses, placed in regular order, with a street between them, made of baskets of earth, piled against the houses.[14]

The only creeks and rivers close to Point Cruz are the Mataniko, Tanakua (Cruz Creek), Vutudaki (Rove, or Le Sage Creek), and Tau`utu (White River). Perhaps the irrigation was near the Mataniko or White rivers, given that a considerable water flow would have been needed, although the description seems to indicate areas west of White River.

The other party proceeded for 12 or 14 kilometres east, which would have taken them past the Lungga River and on to Guadalcanal Plains. The party was continually attacked by locals with arrows and stones. While not mounting a full-scale battle, the Tandai, Malango, and Lengo groups seem to have tried to discourage the invaders. The Spanish came across several villages where they helped themselves to root crops and some poultry, which would not have endeared them to the Guale.[15]

The Spaniards were short of food and affected by fever, probably malaria. Always wary of attack, their accounts carry constant references to fear of cannibalism, although without proof. Once more, they set off exploring, going further than before. They came to a village on the coast, searching it for food, and finding none. Nearby on the beach, 1,000 Guale are reported to have gathered. Again, the size of the crowd may indicate that they had come together from the surrounding areas and assembled to meet the Spaniards, or that the numbers were exaggerated. The Spaniards' supplies were dangerously low, and the villagers refused to barter for food, which led the interlopers to seize garden produce they found buried at one village. They were attacked by people from what may have been a village at the mouth of the Lungga, during which members of the crew were

---

14   ibid., 308–9.
15   ibid., 313–15.

killed. A nearby village was burnt in retaliation and food seized. A few days later, the Spaniards came across Tayla village, where the headman was named Tuadubi. At Tayla, they recorded more than 150 huts and a fighting force of 700 men. They claimed to have counted 200 houses in another village. On several occasions, they slept in villages overnight and seemed in some places to have established amicable relations.[16]

Violence increased on both sides, with another nine Spaniards killed and severely mutilated. Retaliatory punitive expeditions were organised; many villages were burnt and more than 20 Guale killed. Two men are mentioned: Lunga from a village at a river mouth (possibly the Lungga), and Nano, said to have been an enemy of Lunga. Skirmishes occurred constantly over weeks. Later, when a canoe brought a pig as compensation, its occupants were killed and quartered and laid out at the spot where the Spanish had been massacred. The Spanish burnt houses and pillaged as much garden produce as they could carry away. Realising that relations were at a low ebb, on 13 June, the Spanish ships departed.[17]

We cannot be certain of the size of the population of Guadalcanal in the sixteenth century. Given that the Spanish stayed around the Tandai area for a month, this may have attracted people from surrounding areas, skewing the estimates. Because the Spanish recorded that there were many villages in the Honiara area, the general impression is of a substantial population on the north coast. On occasions, the Spanish, having travelled along the coast as far as Marau Sound, claimed to have seen 1,000 or 2,000 Guale at one time. As Amherst and Thomson summarise in their 1901 edition of the diaries from the expedition:

> The whole country was under cultivation; irrigated taro plantations covered every hillside; and in the broad plains to the westward, intersected by rivers, he saw smoke rising in every direction. After reading Catoira's enumeration of the villages through which he passed, one is less inclined to doubt the number of the fighting men who are described as assailing the Spaniards later.[18]

Even allowing for exaggeration, the coast was heavily populated, the people lived in large villages with plentiful gardens, and practised irrigated agriculture.

---

16   ibid., 316–21.
17   ibid., xxxiii–xxxviii, 325–81.
18   ibid., xxxv.

The Spanish claimed to have seen irrigated yams growing west of Point Cruz, possibly in Poha or Vura valley. This site can no longer be located, although there is evidence of irrigation and ponding around Visale, much further west.[19] Severe depopulation seems to have occurred during the mid to late nineteenth century due to raids emanating from Savo, Russell Islands, and New Georgia, which, as on nearby Isabel Island, forced the survivors on Guadalcanal to move inland, away from the coast. These raids were part of much wider aggression emanating largely from New Georgia over a few hundred years, which was probably exacerbated in the nineteenth century by the introduction of European weaponry by whalers and traders.[20] For instance, Legacy from Savo Island, who knew the Tandai area in his youth in the 1850s, told Woodford that there had once been a much larger local population on the coast around Point Cruz, which had been dispersed by raiders from Savo and the Russell Islands during headhunting raids and the search for slaves—all part of the larger aggressive movement south from New Georgia.[21] Resettlement along the coast only occurred once the protectorate began and headhunting was subdued in the 1900s. From the 1870s, diseases introduced by the labour trade to Queensland and Fiji may also have caused further depopulation, possibly by half.[22] Although not mentioned by Woodford in his 1888 description, Magagili village was on the east bank of the mouth of the Mataniko River, Kakabona village was several kilometres to the west of Point Cruz, and Lungga village was a similar distance away between Tenaru River and Koli Point to the east. In the 1930s, anthropologist Eugen Paravicini found few villages along the north coast. Only Kakabona was of any size—a village of about 80 houses.[23] The other villages present in the sixteenth century had disappeared.

Plantations on Guadalcanal

We know very little about the years between the Spanish sojourn and the British arrival in the second half of the nineteenth century. Clearly there had been a significant decline in the population level, which is

---

19 Roe 1993: 159–75, 182–86.
20 ibid., 23.
21 PMB 1290, Woodford Papers, Reel 5, Bundle 29, C.M. Woodford Diary, 24 October 1888.
22 My calculations for Malaita suggest the population there could have been reduced by 40 to 50 per cent between the 1870s and 1930s. Moore 2017a: 429–34. For Makira, see also Scott 2007: 84–87.
23 Roe 1993: 23–24.

unlikely to have been solely caused by raiders from New Georgia and other islands to the north. We need to consider the numbers of Guale who worked outside the Solomons between 1870 and 1886: about 5,266 indenture contracts in Queensland and 892 in Fiji, plus a few labourers in Samoa and New Caledonia. If we apply general Queensland statistics, 96 per cent of workers were male and the mortality rate would have been about 25 per cent. More than 6,000 left Guadalcanal and around 4,600 returned—probably about one-fifth of the population.[24] The labourers were exposed to a measles epidemic in 1875, which, although early in the Solomons labour trade, may have caused deaths on Guadalcanal. Overall, labour recruiting must have caused significant population declines and may have altered the size of Guadalcanal descent groups, and land control on the north coast. The protectorate's colonisation process may also have caused changes to local cultures, altering languages, cosmologies, and values.

Land in Melanesia is an integral part of communities and societies. The relationship is symbiotic. On Guadalcanal, as elsewhere, all land has 'owners' (or perhaps, better, 'custodians'), as do the surrounding sea and reefs, and there are a variety of political and territorial safeguards. Some land was in permanent use, while other areas were used seasonally or according to needs. Shifting agriculture clearly requires local movement and villages were also re-sited for a variety of reasons. As Guadalcanal academic Gordon Nanau reminds us, land is life, providing food and subsistence. It is also a spiritual place where the ancestors and spirits live alongside the present generation.

There is no standard way to describe descent group divisions on Guadalcanal and, compared with neighbouring Malaita, there has been little written about Guadalcanal by anthropologists. Basing his comments on the Lengo language area, Nanau identifies two key social entities: the *kema* (tribe) takes care of the integrity of its land and its members; the *mamata* (clan) is a political entity that safeguards the interests and welfare of clan members. Being born into a family gives an individual the right to use and live on the group's land. These rights shape behaviour and the attitudes of individuals and families, both to their local areas and to the lands of other *kema* and *mamata*. Permission must be obtained when harvesting produce from old garden or village sites. *Kukuni* (respect) must

---

24   Price with Baker 1976: 114; Siegel 1985: 49; Moore 1985: 235–73.

be given to the rights of all residents, and *kikinima* (reverence) is expected from all actions carried out on the land. Movement relates to *kema* and *mamata* and there is etiquette involved in establishing altars and sacrifices to *tidio* (spirits/gods). In Nanau's words, it 'signifies the human bond between people and relationships sealed through land':

> Within a piece of land owned by a *mamata*, there are multifaceted rights from members of the same *mamata* as well as those of non-*mamata* members. The *vunivae* and *ghatumba* rights are two extremely important rights that cannot be interfered with. Even the landowning *mamata* and *kema* cannot do as they please in a family or person's *vunivae* and *ghatumba*. Permission has to be sought from the *ghatumba* or *vunivae* holders. From this vantage point, it can be confidently asserted the landownership is not exclusive but reflects the subsistence and social cohesion amongst members of a particular society.[25]

Another Guale academic, Tarcisius Tara Kabutaulaka, prefers not to use the terms 'clan' or 'tribe', which he suggests can be ambiguous in their meaning, instead substituting the Solomons Pijin term *laen*, derived from the English words 'line' and 'lineage', and referring to a group of people who claim the same lineage or ancestry.[26] Information about land is not freely given and is often contested. The number of *laen* identified varies, depending on where on Guadalcanal the information is gathered. The relationship between a group and its territory is flexible and fluid, changing over time. In short, what Europeans attempted to do—purchase permanent land rights from a few compliant individuals—was not accepted by the Guale, who had no similar concept of land alienation.

Ownership of customary land in Melanesia is always fraught. Claimants within one descent group or tribe do not always agree, and neighbouring groups often disagree over boundaries. It would also be wrong to present the nineteenth-century Tandai as a totally united group. Joseph Foukona and Matthew Allen list numerous examples of disagreements since 2000 among the Tandai over the finer points of landownership.[27] Nevertheless, there is no doubt that modern Honiara is within land acknowledged by surrounding Guale groups and the government to have been under Tandai control. Another complication is that the Guadalcanal Provincial

---

25   Nanau 2014: 174.
26   Kabutaulaka 2019: 119–20.
27   Foukona and Allen 2017: 103.

1. NAHONA`ARA BEFORE 1942

Government has made recent claims on behalf of the Tandai and has included them in much wider negotiations with the national government, which include surrounding areas of alienated land.

The Tandai, particularly those originally living around the Mataniko River, have never agreed with the legitimacy of the Kukum–Lungga–Tenaru land transfer in the 1880s. Nor did those in the area to the west that became Mamara plantation support the acquisition of their land or its later inclusion in urban lands. Although the Tandai acknowledge negotiating the 1886 land purchases, they have always sought to preserve their ownership of a triangular piece of land beginning along the coast from Tanakake to Point Cruz, and from there inland along the boundary line with what is marked on Map 1.3 as Svensen and Rabut's Mamara plantation for approximately 12.8 kilometres.[28] As well, there was seldom any concept of permanent alienation of land in Melanesian society. The Europeans who negotiated to obtain the land had a quite different concept of land rights and ownership from that understood by the Tandai.

The first plantation in the Honiara area was begun at Kukum (Kokomu) in 1886. The Kukum–Lungga–Tenaru land deal (or rather its boundaries) was disputed all through the early twentieth century. Suala, chief of the Gombata *laen* from Magagili village, was a child at the time of the 1886 land agreement. In 1917, he told the Guadalcanal district officer that Thomas Garvin Kelly, John Williams, and Thomas Woodhouse had only purchased the land 3.2 kilometres east of Tanakake, which he said belonged to the Simbo people. He also complained to the BSIP administration about the behaviour of Levers Pacific Plantations Limited (Pacific Islands Company) employees who cut down all the vegetation surrounding the village and attempted to drive his people away from their coastal homes.[29] In turn, Levers claimed freehold ownership over the coastal area and inland from Point Cruz to just east of Tenaru River. Levers also held a certificate of occupation over the headwaters of the Mataniko and Tenaru rivers, and down to the coast, but excluding Lungga village.[30]

---

28   This boundary marking appears to be incorrect.
29   The relevant Solomon Islands National Archives [hereinafter SINA] BSIP file is 18/I/2.
30   SINA BSIP 18/I/2, J.S. Symington to Resident Commissioner, 26 May 1920, and accompanying maps. The area in dispute was registered in the Red Book, No. 229, Folio 121, 122. See also SINA BSIP 18/I/21c, hand-drawn map by F.L. Langdale, authorised by S.G.C. Knibbs, Crown Surveyor, 16 June 1917.

When Woodford visited north Guadalcanal as a naturalist in 1888, he said the area that is now Honiara was known locally as Tandai, meaning the landowning and language group in the area. He also called it 'Kokoma', by which he meant the geographic area, and he recorded the name of the nearby river, now called the Mataniko, as 'Nanago', which may be a mishearing or variation of the same name. On 21 October 1888, Woodford recorded the following description in his diary:

> At daylight we came back towards the island at Port la Cruz. We anchored before breakfast off the mouth of the river about ½ a mile SE of the island. We saw three natives fishing and they told us it was called the Nanago R. This, after inspecting the island and the remainder of the coast to the west, I have come to the conclusion is the Rio Gallego [named by the Spanish]. The name by which the island is known among the natives is Kokoma (the island). We took the boat and went ashore and I took photos of the mouth of the river & of the island as seen from it. Just behind the fringe of trees on the coast some low grassy hills rise for about 100 to 120 ft [30–37 metres] upon one of which doubtless the cross was planted ...
>
> The island is of coral formation and covered with low trees & scrub. It is connected with the mainland by a reef-flat almost dry at low water and on the eastern edge of it there is at present a sand spit joining the island & mainland along which some stunted bushes grow. This is probably of recent accumulation but there could not have been [space] even at the time of the Spaniards [for] passage for a boat between the island and the mainland except at high water. To the westward of the anchorage there are some sunken coral patches shewn by coloured water. We landed for an hour & I took some photos. There are no natives now living on the coast, a few scattered huts are some distance back in the bush and the natives visit the coast to fish as those had whom we met this morning ... As to Port la Cruz I cannot call it a good harbour, & the bottom is uneven, we had 7 fathoms [13 metres] just ahead of us and 15 [27 metres] just astern. While there are coral patches a short distance away to the westward. Still it was better than an anchorage on an open coast.[31]

---

31   PMB 1290, Woodford Papers, Reel 5, Bundle 29, C.M. Woodford Diary, 21 October 1888.

Plate 1.3 Point Cruz in 1944.
The sandspit joining the original island to the mainland had grown since the 1568 visit by Mendaña, and the 1888 visit by Charles Woodford.
Source: USNARA.

Plate 1.4 The mouth of the Mataniko River, 1920s.
Source: Raucaz (1928: 150).

Woodford first visited Solomon Islands in 1886. He was aware that Europeans seeking to purchase land had a different perspective from Solomon Islanders agreeing to part with their land. When he took up his BSIP appointment in 1896, Woodford issued the Solomon Islands (Land) Regulation, which declared all previous land 'contracts' to be provisional until investigated by protectorate officers, although in fact this rarely occurred. The regulation stipulated the necessary improvements for land acquired as trading stations, or for agricultural purposes, and provided for negotiation of leases with Solomon Islanders. Woodford believed the protectorate government had the right to control land and to declare land to be 'vacant', although the Colonial Office felt Woodford's regulation was invalid. It was superseded by an 1899 ruling that it was legal to declare land to be Crown land if the inhabitants were 'practically savages without any proper conceptions of ownership of land'. The solution was to issue certificates of occupation on land 'neither owned, cultivated nor occupied by any native or non-native person'.[32] A subsequent law, the Waste Land Regulations, 1900–04, enabled the WPHC to declare land to be waste and vacant. Woodford created the position of government surveyor in 1911, which was the forerunner of what became the Department of Lands and Survey. In the late nineteenth century, the depopulated Tandai, Malango, and Lengo coast appeared to be more 'waste and vacant' than it would have a few centuries earlier.

Some of the alienated land in the BSIP became freehold, with other areas held under certificates of occupation. Levers—English soap manufacturers who became the largest landholders in the protectorate—used these legal mechanisms to acquire land east of the Mataniko River, and to secure their extensive landholdings elsewhere along the north coast of Guadalcanal, and on other islands.[33] Through their Pacific Islands Company, Levers purchased freehold land directly from the customary landholders, amassing 80,937 hectares in the protectorate under certificates of occupation. In the 1900s, the company began negotiating purchases of freehold land directly from the indigenous owners (11,683 hectares) and from existing traders and planters (20,638 hectares). By 1907, the company controlled 121,405 hectares in the protectorate. As well, Levers was happy to keep

---

32 Heath 1981: 64.
33 The original company was Levers Pacific Plantations Limited (1902, registered in the United Kingdom), the Solomon Islands activities of which were transferred to Levers Pacific Plantations Pty Ltd (1928, registered in Australia). The usual short form is Levers, or Lever Brothers.

using certificates of occupation, negotiating with the Colonial Office to extend them from 99 to 999-year leases. These were the years when Levers acquired their land in and around what became Honiara.[34]

In 1906, Woodford requested but was refused permission to pass regulations enabling his government to purchase land directly, to resell at reasonable prices. He continued to negotiate with the WPHC and, in 1911, it was agreed there would be no more private land purchases after 1 January 1912. A new Solomon Islands land regulation issued in March 1914 enabled leases of 10 to 99 years, with a forfeiture clause if there was no development of the land. The 1914 regulation included a provision for standard leases such as for building, cultivation, and grazing, which replaced the 1900–04 regulations. This ended the 'millennium' leases, although occasionally after 1914 leases in perpetuity were still granted.[35] Compulsory registration of land title deeds was introduced in 1918—still with no provision for investigation of their validity.[36] With minor amendments, the 1914 regulation remained in force until 1959, when it was repealed and replaced.[37]

Kukum–Lungga–Tenaru, Tenavatu (Ilu), and Mamara plantations

To the 1880s European eye, north Guadalcanal had a low population, and the land was suitable for coconut plantations. Europeans began coastal plantations on Guadalcanal, negotiating land purchases, which they registered with the WPHC in Suva, Fiji. Three European agricultural landholdings developed on Tandai land within what has become Honiara, with most of the growth taking place between 1900 and about 1916. The land under coconut palms increased rapidly after 1906 and many estates had reached their maximum capacity by 1917. In the 1920s, serious losses because of premature nut fall caused by *Amblypelta cocophaga* (coconut bug) significantly reduced production.

---

34 Hookey 1969.
35 *British Solomon Islands Annual and Biannual reports* [hereinafter *BSIP AR*] 1971: 23.
36 PMB 1371, Nigel Oram Collection, Memorandum from Commissioner of Lands and Surveys, H5/20, 18 October 1969.
37 BSIP 1959.

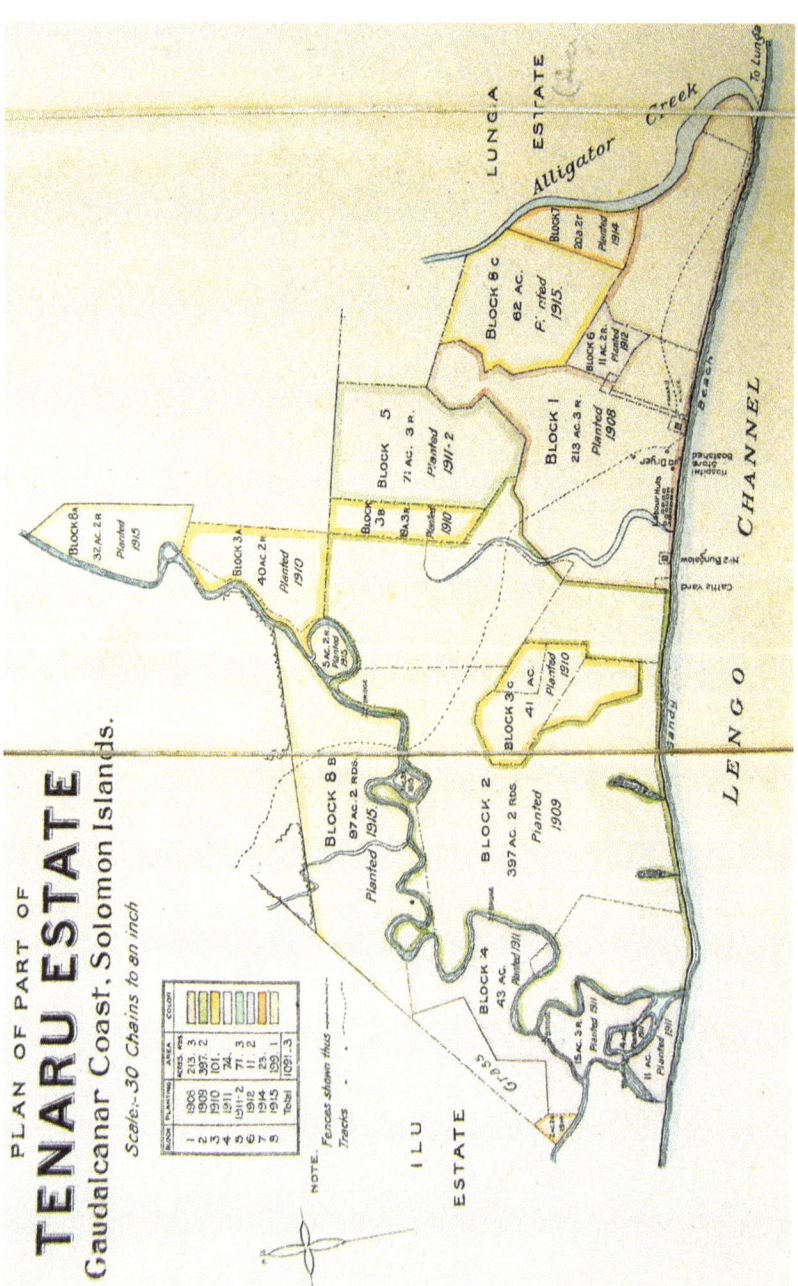

Map 1.2 Levers' Tenaru Estate, showing the years various sections were planted and the boundaries with Ilu and Lungga estates.
Source: Peter Flahavin Collection.

The core area of modern Honiara became a combination of freehold and certificates of occupation over plantation land, separated until January 1947 by an area of indigenous ownership (Mataniko to Rove), as well as disputed indigenous ownership east of the Mataniko (Maps 3.1, 3.2). The 450-square-kilometre Guadalcanal Plains are unique in the Pacific Islands because of the large, level areas with evenly distributed good-quality alluvial soil, and an ample river system. Areas of the plains more distant from the coast remained undeveloped, covered with natural grassland or forest, but the coastal land was soon covered with coconut palms.

Kukum–Lungga–Tenaru estates

The central area of Greater Honiara, from Point Cruz to Tenaru, and known at various times as Kukum, Lungga, and Tenaru estates or plantations, was purchased on 7 November 1886 for £60 of trade goods. The deal was done by Robert Bain and Harry Stevens on behalf of partners Kelly, Williams, and Woodhouse, New South Wales–based traders with commercial interests in the Shortland and New Georgia islands, and Ontong Java Atoll. The land was purchased from Woothia (or Uvothea) of Lungga, Allea of Manago (or Nanago), his son Manungo (or Maneuqu), with Mosey (or Mosee) from Tasimboko as a witness. The agreement described the land area in this way:

> All that Peice [sic] of land on the north coast of Guadalcanal one of the Solomon Islands called Moreo and Nanago extending from a remarkable grass patch in Langa [Lengo] bay Westwardly to a point in Le Cruz bay called Bah from Bah Point S.S.W. to the main range from thence eastwardly to meet a line S.W. from the grass patch to Langa bay.[38]

The area extended into Tandai, Malango, and Lengo lands. As this area is disputed in court cases, it is worth noting that in 2017 Michael Ben Walahoula, secretary of the Tandai Tribal Landowners Association, told me that Moreo and Nanago are the names of two warriors from the time, Mare (Moreo) and Maneugu (Nanago), not of pieces of land. There is no Tandai land that matches the description. This may be a basic flaw in the original alienation of the land. Yet, in 1888, Charles Woodford also used Nanago as a geographic description.

---

38 SINA BSIP 18/I/2, WPHC Land Notice No. 229, copy of original dated 18 December 1886. Joseph Foukona provided me with a copy of the original agreement, which I have used here. The spelling and capitalisation vary slightly from the SINA version.

The next owners were Carl Oscar Svensen and his partners, and then Levers. Svensen's name first appears in Solomon Islands history in 1888 when he passed through as a seaman, before returning in 1890 in partnership with Alex Monrad, based at Marau Sound. Monrad became ill and sold out to Svensen, who was joined by his brother Theodore, and the Nerdrum brothers, forming the Norwegian Solomon Islands Trading and Plantation Company Limited. In Norway, Theodore Svensen, who owned a small fleet of sailing ships, was forced out of business by the changeover to steam ships. He was in his element with the company's sailing ships in the Solomons. Oscar Svensen and his partners prospered, purchasing Tavanipupu Island in Marau Sound, which they used as their main base. Then, as the focus of the protectorate moved to Tulagi, in 1903, they purchased Gavutu Island (opposite Tulagi) from Lars Neilsen. Oscar Svensen became the most entrepreneurial trader in the protectorate. For a few years early in the twentieth century, he owned most of the plantation land within modern Honiara. Svensen ingratiated himself with Woodford, and always assisted the administration, and the missionaries, although he and his partners used their Norwegian citizenship to circumvent British authority, particularly when selling guns and ammunition. Another reason given for their success was that they are said to have treated Solomon Islanders better than did most of the other traders and planters.[39] Svensen and his partners' most lucrative early investments were in pearling, using beds in Maramasike Passage (Malaita), Manning Straits (between Isabel and Choiseul), and Mboli Passage (Ngela). Pearl shell (*Pinctada maxima*) was worth £150 to £180 a ton on the London market. Pearls were a bonus and large, fine specimens were worth £200 to £400 each—a small fortune.[40] They also purchased land for plantations around Marau Sound and at Aola, which was augmented a few years later by their Honiara lands.

Early land transfers are not always easy to track. In the late 1890s, Oscar Svensen met Alex J. Rabut (or Rabuth) in Santa Cruz, where he was the unhappy partner of A.E.C. Forrest. Rabut was persuaded to take over management of Svensen's Aola plantation, which he had purchased from the bankrupt Kelly, Williams, and Woodhouse partnership in 1898.[41] Over the next two years, Rabut proved his worth by planting more than

---

39 Bennett 1981: 170–73, 180, fn. 24.
40 Mullins (2019: 78) provides an excellent account of the values of pearls, pearl shell, and other marine products around northern Australia.
41 Golden 1993: 118.

66 hectares of coconut palms. At the same time, Svensen purchased the Kukum–Lungga–Tenaru land. Between 1903 and 1905, Svensen, with Rabut as his partner, sold the land to Levers, which then held a certificate of occupation for 99 years over 7,284-hectare 'Tinaru Estate'. In 1903, at the age of 42, Svensen claimed to have been earning £2,000 to £6,000 (approximately A$276,300 to A$828,900) annually since 1899, and to be collecting half of the local produce sold in the archipelago.[42]

Svensen had watched Levers' Pacific Islands Company select large amounts of land for plantations in the western Solomons. Knowing that Woodford supported commercial plantation development, Svensen decided to purchase as much coastal land as he could. He spent very little (£1,000 in cash and goods) to purchase 10,400 hectares throughout the protectorate. To keep his costs down, he made provisional purchases, only offering part-payment.[43] This becomes important when we try to work out the complexity of the Mamara plantation purchase.

Svensen offered to sell some of his holdings to Burns, Philp & Company—a prominent Australian shipping, retail, and plantation operation in the Pacific until the 1970s—for £10,000, which the company declined. Then, between 1903 and 1905, he sold most of his property to Levers for £40,000 (approximately A$5.6 million in 2020). Initially, he committed to stay on as manager, although he soon resigned and concentrated on his remaining Guadalcanal plantations. As well, he negotiated a deal with Burns Philp to arrange the repatriation of around 4,000 Solomon Islanders from Australia who had been deported under the 1901 legislation to create the White Australia Policy. By 1908, he had made £9,000 (the equivalent of more than A$1 million in 2020) from this venture.[44]

Aside from adjustments to their title after the 1920s Lands Commission, and the hiatus during World War II, when the area became a Japanese base, a battlefield, and then an American base, Levers maintained ownership until 12 February 1947, when it sold the Protectorate Government 2,274 hectares of land stretching from the Mataniko River east to Kukum–Lungga–Tenaru.

---

42   SINA BSIP C18/I/7, Civil Case No. 3 of 1964, Provisional decision of the Registrar of Titles on the claim raised by Baranamba Hoai; Certificate of Occupation for 99 years granted to Pacific Islands Company Ltd in 1903. If it is correct that Rabut died in 1902, presumably his estate had not been finalised. (Joseph Foukona provided a copy of this case.)
43   Bennett 1981: 179–80.
44   ibid., 181, 183.

Tenavatu (Ilu) plantation

The other plantation that was part of the Greater Honiara area, but beyond the town council and then city council boundaries, was Tenavatu (Ilu) plantation, east of Kukum–Lungga–Tenaru plantations (Map 1.2). Maps from the 1920s show Tenavatu as beginning at Red Beach and similar in size to Mamara plantation between Rove and White River, which were both much smaller than the Kukum–Lungga–Tenaru estates. The plantation's western boundary seems to have begun within Tandai territory, which ended at Alligator Creek, a short distance east of the end of the modern runway of Honiara International Airport—Henderson Field. The lease over Tenavatu was taken up by another Svensen employee, William Dumphy, about the same time as Mamara was established in the 1900s. Dumphy arrived in the Solomons in about 1900 as one of the crew of a pearling lugger owned by Svensen. It seems likely that Svensen was involved in financing both Dumphy and Joseph T. d'Oliveyra at Mamara. Just as with Rabut, they did the work and Svensen provided the money.

Bill Dumphy also had land at Tauvutu Island and Aola. He sold Tauvutu in 1917 and moved to Aola. In about 1921, he suffered an attack of the bends while diving and left for medical treatment in Australia, never to return. Historian Graeme Golden recorded Tenavatu as covering 6,812 hectares (which is much larger than it appears on maps).[45] Levers purchased Tenavatu soon after this, although it may be that Svensen was in control of Tenavatu all along. Evidence from a 1964 court case suggests Svensen sold the Tenavatu land to Levers in 1927.[46] To further complicate matters, the names and boundaries of the various plantations altered over time. Kukum became part of Lungga, and Lungga and Tenaru were amalgamated in 1935, including Tenavatu, which was renamed Ilu. Levers Solomon Limited, now Russell Islands Plantation Estate Limited, still holds part of this land as fixed-term estate (FTE, effectively long leases).[47]

---

45   Golden 1993: 146.
46   SINA BSIP C18/I/7, Civil Case No. 3 of 1964.
47   Foukona and Allen 2017: 103–4.

Mamara plantation

The other area within the Honiara land alienations was Mamara plantation. The coastal area to the west, between Rove and White River, was called Tau`utu (and, variously, Tautu, Tuutu, Ta-Ut, or Ta-wtu). It became the 366-hectare Mamara plantation, consisting of two contiguous blocks of land, which explains why there are discrepancies in some accounts and maps. To further complicate matters, it is not on the Mamara River, which is further west.

An investigation by the Honiara City Council in 2011 suggested the Mamara land transactions first took place in 1911. I believe the research is mistaken and has missed earlier documentation. Joseph T. d'Oliveyra purchased a smallholding first, which was called Mamara plantation. Svensen joined d'Oliveyra on the contiguous block, which was known as Tau`utu. In 1943, Svensen's son said the original owners were Melbourne Solomon Islands Proprietary Limited.[48] D'Oliveyra, who had spent several months studying rubber production in Malaya, experimented with cotton and rubber production at Mamara, although copra remained the mainstay. Evidently all went well, as by 1910 they had erected a cotton ginnery and a sawmill to service their Guadalcanal plantations.[49]

Some sources suggest the Mamara–Tau`utu partnership became one between Svensen and Rabut, with d'Oliveyra no longer involved. If Rabut died in 1902 (as sources suggest), any Mamara partnership involving him is unlikely. Golden gives 1907 as the starting date for Mamara plantation, although he provides no reference. A prospectus for Mamara Plantation Limited was promulgated in 1911, with Svensen as the major shareholder and managing director.[50] What the City Council investigation failed to consider is Svensen's habit of only paying part of the purchase price until he was certain the plantation would be a commercial success.

By the mid-1900s, Svensen was a wealthy man—a multimillionaire in modern terms. The order of the north-west Guadalcanal land purchases was that, in 1907, Svensen negotiated for land on north Guadalcanal near Poha River on the west side of Kakabona, and the next year began the

---

48 *Pacific Islands Monthly* [hereinafter *PIM*], February 1964, 80; SIG 2012a.
49 Bennett 1981: 185; Svensen 1943. I have not been able to find any registration details for this company.
50 Golden 1993: 121; Bennett 1981: 185. The prospectus has no date. Bennett identified it as 1909, although when Svensen died in 1964, his son had a copy dated 1911. *PIM*, February 1964, 77–80.

partnership with d'Oliveyra at Mamara–Tau`utu. Then, in 1910, Svensen and d'Oliveyra made a joint purchase for £5,000 of Domma plantation to the west, which was begun by William Pope in 1907. Svensen sold Domma in 1912 but retained a major portion of the shares and became director of the new company, Domma Plantation Limited.[51]

In 1911, the western part of Mamara plantation consisted of 233 hectares—an area beginning at Chachapa Kondomamba (west of the White River area, near the present-day Tandai parish church), running east to Vatuboia on the coast, and then inland for 1.6 kilometres. This was acquired from two men, Voka and Tevu, for £55 on 24 January 1911. The 133-hectare eastern part of Mamara plantation, from Vatuboia east to Vatudaki, also running inland for 1.6 kilometres, was acquired from one individual, Nana, on 18 July 1911 for £30 (Map 3.3).[52] From 1912, Mamara Plantations Limited had capital of £120,000, with Svensen as managing director and owner of one-quarter of the shares.[53] This may explain why Svensen was paying landowners in 1911, as he had altered his title from leasehold to freehold and was making a final payment.

Svensen seems to have believed that Mamara covered the land as far east as the Mataniko River, or at least he tried to intimidate the people living on that land into believing he had legal control. Sualu, chief of the Ramtata (Gombata) descent group, living at Horahi village, reported to the 1920s Lands Commission that Svensen had cleared people off the land and they had moved to Kakabona.[54] There is an indication in 1919 correspondence by Commissioner of Lands Stanley Knibbs that part of the problem was the vagueness of the original boundaries:

> [S]ubsequent conveyances to Svensen and Levers show that the [Kukum] boundary extends as far west as Pt. Cruz, and runs S.S.W. inland to the 'Main range'. There has been continuous trouble with the natives living near Kookoom [Kukum], and they all consider that they have been swindled.[55]

---

51 Bennett 1981: 186.
52 SIG 2012a: 18.
53 Bennett 1981: 185; Golden 1993: 121, 133, 142, 143, 146, 314, 330.
54 SINA BSIP 18/I/2, Claim No. 17, Lands Commission; see also Golden 1993: 133.
55 SINA BSIP 18/I/2, Knibbs to Resident Commissioner, 15 September 1919.

1. NAHONA`ARA BEFORE 1942

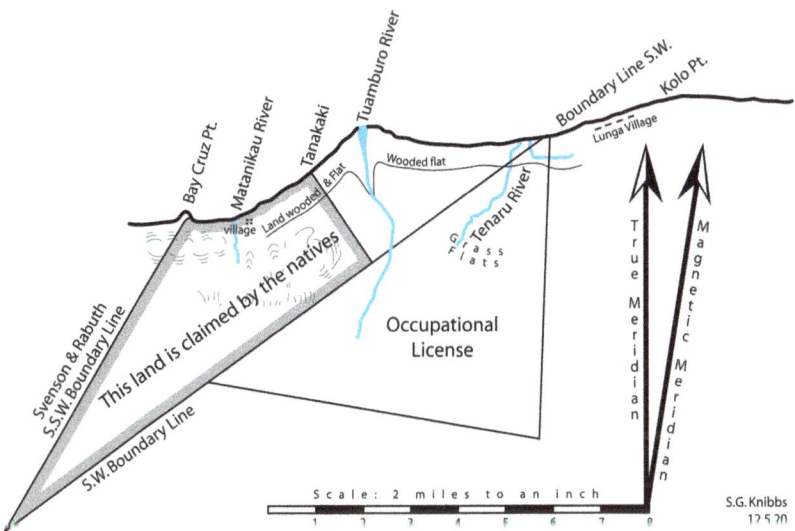

Map 1.3 1920 map showing the Tandai claim and the Occupational Lease claimed by Levers.

Svensen and Rabut's Mamara plantation (between Tau`utu [White] and Kohove rivers) is shown on the western boundary of the Tandai land claim, and includes Point Cruz. BSIP officials interpreted the Tandai claim as relating only to Malagili village at the mouth of the Mataniko River. All spelling and wording are as they appear on the original map.
Source: SINA BSIP 18/I/2, J.S. Symington to Resident Commissioner, 26 May 1920. Cartography by Vincent Verheyen.

There is conflicting evidence over the eastern boundary of Mamara plantation. Map 1.3, drawn by Knibbs in 1920, shows Svensen and Rabut as owning land right up to Point Cruz, when Rabut was long dead. Map 1.5, also drawn by Knibbs in 1920, shows Mamara or Tawtu (Tau`utu) as beginning at Rove. Maps 1.5–1.6 (1920, 1922), both by Knibbs, show the area west of Point Cruz as 'native land', which suggests Mamara stopped at Rove. Perhaps Knibbs was careless with the 1920 sketch (Map 1.3). On Map 3.1 (from 1947), Mamara plantation is marked as consisting of 325 hectares and appears to be between White River and Kakabona, but it excludes the area from Rove to White River. Because Mamara plantation was not investigated by the 1920s Lands Commission, there was never a definitive survey of its boundaries.

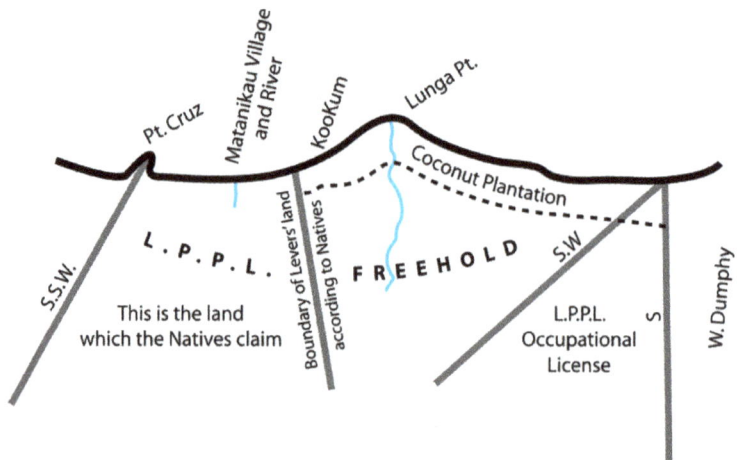

Map 1.4 Levers' land claim as of 26 May 1920.
The map shows the area from Point Cruz to Koli Point, which they claimed they held under a combination of freehold and a certificate of occupation. William Dumphy's Tenavatu plantation is further east. All spelling and wording are as they appear on the original map.
Source: SINA BSIP 18/I/2, J.S. Symington to Resident Commissioner, 26 May 1920. Cartography by Vincent Verheyen.

The Tandai and their land

The land deals that created Honiara were made between the 1880s and 1960s—all beyond the modern statute of limitations, which only allows legal challenges within 12 years. Any further negotiation can only be at a political level. The Tandai land and sea-holding descent group, on whose land Honiara was built, divide their area into five sections: Lakuli, Haubata, Kakau, Simbo, and Kidipale. Generations ago, people originating from Tinana Vera migrated down to coastal Tandai. Kukum, Lungga, Tenaru, and Tenavatu are part of Tandai lands. They share the eastern plains area with the Lengo to the east, the Honiata at upper Betikama, the Kosumba in the west, and the Biti in the south. The Tandai lands over which most argument has occurred are Lungga, Tenaru, and Tenavatu, extending from Saravitu (the mouth of the Lungga River) to Betinavua east along the coast on the Tandai's eastern boundary. They list their main village sites as Mae, Matabilo, Takusa, Vatuliva, Vatubebea, Veraliva, Taonavua, Tana`aru, Haviha, Kindy, and Haikoku.[56] Tandai lands continue west past

---

56 Tandai House of Chiefs and Tandai Landowners Association n.d. [2010s].

1. NAHONA`ARA BEFORE 1942

the Mataniko River to include other suburban land and peri-urban land to the western boundary of Honiara City Council land, and beyond to Kakabona and Ruaniu. They also hold rights over the sea around their land.

Plate 1.5 Horahi village is in the centre of this 1942 photograph, in a clearing along the beach on the west side of the mouth of the Mataniko River.
Source: USNARA.

Plate 1.6 Horahi village in the 1920s.
Source: Raucaz (1928: 135).

Plate 1.7 The home of the Catholic missionary at Horahi village, 1920s.
Source: Raucaz (1928: 187).

Plate 1.8 Horahi village in August 1942 overlaid on a modern view of Honiara.

The village was on the site of the present octagonal United Church building and the old Solomon Islands Electricity Authority headquarters, now owned by Fair Trade Co. The building on the coastal side is the Sea King restaurant. The area is on Mendana Avenue just east of Central Market.

Sources: USNARA; Google Earth (www.google.com/earth/; 2010); with insertion and markings courtesy of Peter Flahavin, 1 June 2015.

1. NAHONA`ARA BEFORE 1942

There was no government presence on Guadalcanal until 1914, when Aola station was opened 40 kilometres further around the north coast, far from Tandai land. Svensen and Levers were able to be ruthless in their attempts to gain control of the entire coastal area around what is now Honiara. As reported by Suala and corroborated by eyewitnesses, in the mid-1900s, Rivers, a Levers' employee, arrived with two boats carrying labourers. They burnt down 15 Malagili village houses, destroyed their gardens, shot 12 pigs, and smashed canoes. At this stage, the Mataniko village was on the east bank of the river, near the mouth. For the next two years, the Mataniko area people fled inland up the river, and then returned to their coastal village site, still on the east bank. Suala said he was from the Rabata (Ravutu) descent group but did not know who had been involved in the 1886 negotiations. In about 1913, Nangana of Wouuna, accompanied by Jilivi (Tsilvi) and Lia, head of the village, went to Tulagi to report their dissatisfaction to Resident Commissioner Woodford. In a 1917 statement, Nangana claimed Woodford had told them they could stay in their coastal village. Nangana acknowledged Suala as the senior male.[57] In 1919, acting District Officer C.G. Norris had no doubt that Levers had behaved 'outrageously' at Mataniko and Visale in the past, and the company was continuing to behave badly. He described Levers as a 'menace':

> Since then [1917] Lever's Pacific Plantations Limited have felled some hundred acres of land on all sides of their village—land of which they had been monstrously deprived—and now they appear to think denied British Justice, they are forced to abandon the splendid houses built after 1917 because Lever's Pacific Plantations Limited prevent them growing food for subsistence.[58]

In 1916–17, the Mataniko people rebuilt their village at the original coastal site, against ill will from Levers, who still claimed ownership.[59] According to Norris:

---

57 The eyewitnesses to the Rivers incident were Oliboa, Pura, Managu, Miru, Vurulu, Vogi, Honania, Pino, and Garibala. SINA BSIP 18/I/2, statements by Suala of Mataniko (Malagili village) and Nangana of Wouuna to acting District Officer C.G. Norris, 7 March 1917.
58 SINA BSIP 18/I/2, acting District Officer C.G. Norris, Aola, to acting Resident Commissioner F.J. Barnett, 18 August 1917.
59 ibid., 10 March 1917.

55

> These natives who have rebuilt their Village consisting of more than thirty houses inform me that Lever's representative is now continually harassing them—by felling trees, ordering them to leave, preventing them from using the coconuts of which they have been deprived, spoiling their gardens and generally using threats—to such an extent that they have decided to again forsake their Village and for a second time retreat inland to exile.[60]

Woodford seems to have investigated the purchases in 1902, and again in about 1913.[61] In September 1919, Norris listed the principal complainants as the Tandai occupants of the areas named Rere, Bulibui, and Kookoom (Kukum), along with Runbatu (Ravatu), Kakau, Tenaba (Tevavatu), and Lavaro (Lavuro)—all of whom he understood to have an interest in the land.[62] Acting Resident Commissioner Jack C. Barley decided matters should be dealt with by the Lands Commission (1919–24), which was appointed to investigate previous land alienation in the protectorate. In mid-1920, there were 74 villagers living at the mouth of the Mataniko. The new Resident Commissioner, Charles Workman, suspended Levers' claims until after the Lands Commission hearings.[63] Suala reiterated to Commissioner of Lands G.C. Alexander and his deputy Stanley Knibbs that Woodhouse had purchased only the land east of Tanakake, which did not include any Gombata land to the west. Knibbs thought the Gombata people would only be willing to part with the areas west of Tanakake, which Levers had already cleared.[64]

At Alexander's suggestion, in June, Guadalcanal's district officer Ralph Hill met with Levers' staff and the Gombatas' representatives. J.S. Symington, Levers' manager at their Gavutu headquarters, suggested that Malagili village should be moved from the east to the west bank of the Mataniko, and that Levers be granted control of the land east of the river for a payment of £25 and the cost of surveying the boundaries.

---

60   SINA BSIP 18/I/2, District Officer C.G. Norris to Barnett, 18 August 1919; acting Resident Commissioner Barley to acting District Officer, 20 April 1917; Resident Commissioner C.R.M. Workman to Lands Commissioner Alexander, 3 May 1920. See also Moore 2013c: entry on Phillips Lands Commission.
61   J.S. Symington, Manager, Levers Pacific Plantations Ltd, Gavutu, 26 May 1920, in SIG 2012a: 33, Honiara City Council. No correspondence was found to substantiate this.
62   SINA BSIP 18/I/2, District Officer C.G. Norris, Aola, Guadalcanal to Resident Commissioner, 4 September 1919. The new spelling in parentheses was provided by Michael Ben Walahoula, September 2017.
63   SINA BSIP 18/I/2, 19/II/5, District Officer R. Broadhurst Hill to Resident Commissioner, 10 June 1920; Resident Commissioner Charles Workman to Lands Commissioner, 3 May 1920.
64   SINA BSIP 18/I/2, Knibbs to District Officer, Aloa, Guadalcanal, 12 May 1920.

1. NAHONA'ARA BEFORE 1942

Although they had requested payment of £50, the Malagili villagers were said to have agreed to transfer a narrow strip of coastal land east of the Mataniko (about 81 hectares) to Levers. The company voluntarily gave up all claims to the land west of the Mataniko, requiring only a right-of-way from the river to Point Cruz, which it used as an anchorage. Levers purchased the right-of-way for the government and, acting on the advice of Commissioner of Lands Alexander, paid the full £50 requested.[65]

In London in 1924, the Secretary of State for the Colonies confirmed the recommendations of the Lands Commission, which were gazetted on 23 May. Levers gave up its old title and received conveyance of a piece of land that included the modern Honiara land east of the Mataniko River—the land contested by the Tandai landowners. Levers had improved its situation and achieved freehold of the entire area.

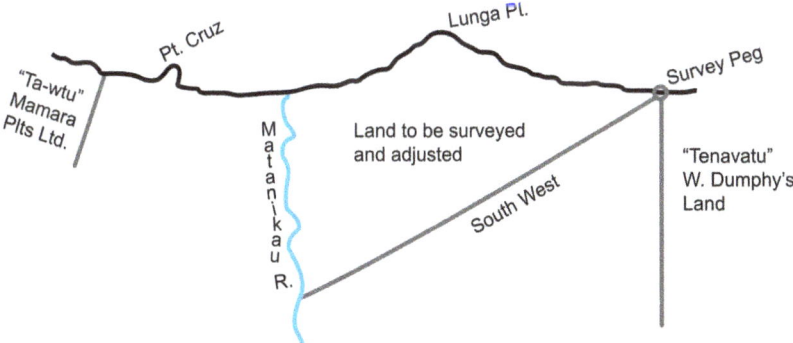

Map 1.5 1920 map showing the boundaries of Levers' land from the east bank of the Mataniko River to the boundary with William Dumphy's Tenavatu plantation.

These boundaries were negotiated on or before 18 June 1920 as a result of investigations by the Phillips Lands Commission. Part of the solution was that the Tandai's Malagili village be moved from the east to the west bank of the Mataniko River. It was renamed Horahi. Mamara plantation is shown west of Rove, but with no exact western boundary. The site of the survey peg between Lungga and Tenavatu is not on the border between the Tandai and Lengo language/cultural areas, which would have created further problems. All spelling and wording are as they appear on the original map.

Source: SINA BSIP 18/I/2, S.G.C. Knibbs to Resident Commissioner, 18 June 1920. Cartography by Vincent Verheyen.

---

65 SINA BSIP 18/I/2: Lands Commissioner Alexander to Resident Commissioner, 12 April 1920; District Officer R. Broadhurst Hill Aola, Guadalcanal, to Resident Commissioner, 10 June 1920 (2 letters); Alexander to Resident Commissioner, 9 August 1920.

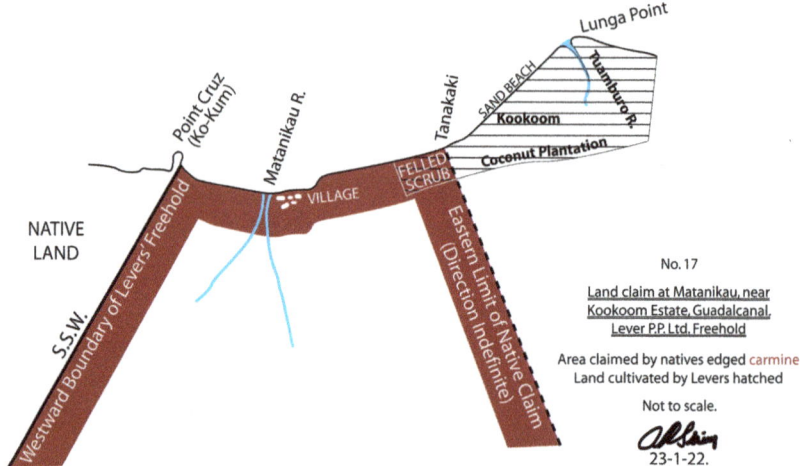

Map 1.6 The area that became east Honiara, as it was when examined by the Phillips Lands Commission in Claim 17, 12 May 1922.

The map shows the Kookoom (Kukum) coastal plantation developed by Levers, and the claim by Tandai villagers over part of the same area. The land west of Point Cruz is shown as still in indigenous hands and not part of Mamara plantation. Malagili village was then on the east bank of the Mataniko River. As part of the negotiations, the village was shifted to the west bank and renamed Horahi. All spelling and wording are as they appear on the original map.

Source: SINA BSIP 18/I/2 and 18/11/5, Claim 17, Lands Commission; Plans A and B, S.G.C. Knibbs to District Officer, Aola, Guadalcanal, 12 May 1922. Cartography by Vincent Verheyen.

Malagili village (renamed Horahi) shifted to the west bank of the river. There are photographs from the 1920s of the river, the village, and its Catholic mission house.[66] Marist Catholic Father D.J. Moore arrived on Guadalcanal in 1931 and knew the area well. In reminiscences written in 1968, Moore said:

> Prior to 1942, Honiara did not exist, not a trace of it, not even the name. The site of the present town was occupied partly by the village of Mataniko which consisted of a group of leaf houses, located in the vicinity of the present clerk's quarters near the Government Stores. The people who formerly lived there now dwell along the banks of the Mataniko River upstream. The remainder of the present site of Honiara was occupied by gardens, coconuts and scrub.[67]

---

66   Raucaz 1928.
67   *British Solomons Islands Protectorate News Sheet* [hereinafter *BSIP NS*], 14 February 1968.

1. NAHONA'ARA BEFORE 1942

Between the 1880s and 1930s, much of Guadalcanal's coastal land was divided into coconut plantations. This occurred in and around what is now Honiara, except for the area between Point Cruz and Rove, which remained under customary ownership until 1947. Before World War II, the coastal region that became Honiara was part of the Vulolo administrative subdistrict—a huge expanse of the island, covering the central mountains through to Talise on the Weather Coast. The 1931 census estimated the entire Guadalcanal population as 14,264, which had increased to 15,620 in 1941. Vulolo was assessed as having a population of 1,273 in 1929, 1,211 in 1931, 1,299 in 1936, and 1,392 in 1941, but only 602 in 1946—the majority presumably living along the coast.[68] These population numbers are far smaller than those reported by the Spanish in 1568.

More than 130 years after the first alienation of Tandai land from customary ownership, and 75 years since the protectorate's capital moved to Guadalcanal, the loss of control for paltry compensation remains a major point of contention with the Guale. The Tandai House of Chiefs and the Tandai Tribal Landowners Association have long protested the poor compensation and lack of consultation they received during the process of hosting a major urban development on their land. The same is true for the Malango and Lengo language, cultural, and landowning groups on neighbouring Guadalcanal Plains. This dissatisfaction helped fuel the beginning of the Tensions in the 1990s (Chapter 9).[69] Statements are still being made that the alienated Honiara land and its sea frontage belong to the original customary owners. Although the government and the Honiara City Council have held consultations with the Tandai people, the government always retreats to the legality of the original alienation of the land.

***

Cities are an ever-evolving form of settlement, and their growth seldom directly benefits the original inhabitants. This has been the case with Honiara. The land alienation occurred during the colonial era when fairness was far from the minds of the original plantation owners and the government. The planters paid the Tandai a total of £195 in cash and goods for the coastal land from Tenaru to White River (excluding the

---

68 SINA BSIP F14/22, District Census, 1941; F14/9 Annual Report, Guadalcanal District, 1936; SINA BSIP F14/19, Annual Report, 1944. These figures are from research by Richard Bedford, provided to Ralph Shlomowitz, and passed to me in 1996.
69 Moore 2004a; Fraenkel 2004.

Mataniko to Rove section). Factoring in inflation, this was a bargain—about SI$50,000 in 2020 currency. During 1947–48, the BSIP Government secured permanent alienation of the Honiara land by paying £6,971 to the traditional owners and two plantation owners. This is the equivalent of about SI$1.5 million in 2020. The area had been devastated by war and housed a temporary American military town. The plantations were wrecked, and the local Tandai were in no position to bargain. Most of the compensation went to the plantation owners, not the Tandai, and the remaining section of their land (Mataniko to Rove) was compulsorily resumed. Honiara City Council controls 3,424 hectares of land and sea (Map 9.1). The land (2,273 hectares) is now valued at hundreds of millions of dollars. Adding in Greater Honiara (the peri-urban spread beyond the declared area of the city) would increase the value substantially.

Modern Honiara contains a mixture of landownership types, and any government would blanch at a challenge to the right of the capital city to exist. The modern legal system upholds agreements made as far back as the 1880s, although these laws and agreements have no relationship to the traditional land system of Guadalcanal, and to the *chupu* concept (outlined in Chapter 5), which binds individuals and communities when compensation takes place. At the heart of the modern legal system is also a presumption that the original agreements were made with the correct custodians, which may not be accurate. The surviving evidence is fragmentary, and insufficient to be totally sure. In the case of the land surrounding the Mataniko in central Honiara, the original compensation seems to have been based on who lived in the village at the mouth of the river at the time of the deal, not on who were the rightful custodians of Tandai land. Part of the compensation was for agreeing to move the site of the village, not for the sale of the land.

An ever-increasing extra problem is that Honiara's legal boundaries are too small to accommodate its current population, which spills over on to Tandai and Malango lands inland and along the coast (Maps 10.1 and 10.4). Even if other urban areas in Solomon Islands expand and absorb migrant populations, and a new urban centre develops within Guadalcanal Province, Honiara will continue to expand, encroaching further on to customary lands. A satisfactory mechanism needs to be worked out that will enable the growth of Honiara, while also placating the Guale. This chapter has provided empirical background information but leaves it to Solomon Islanders to make ethical and political judgements about their past, and the best way forward.

The land around what became Honiara was not unique. What made it different was the Japanese decision to build an airfield there in 1942, and the American counter-invasion that created Camp Guadal, and eventually Honiara.

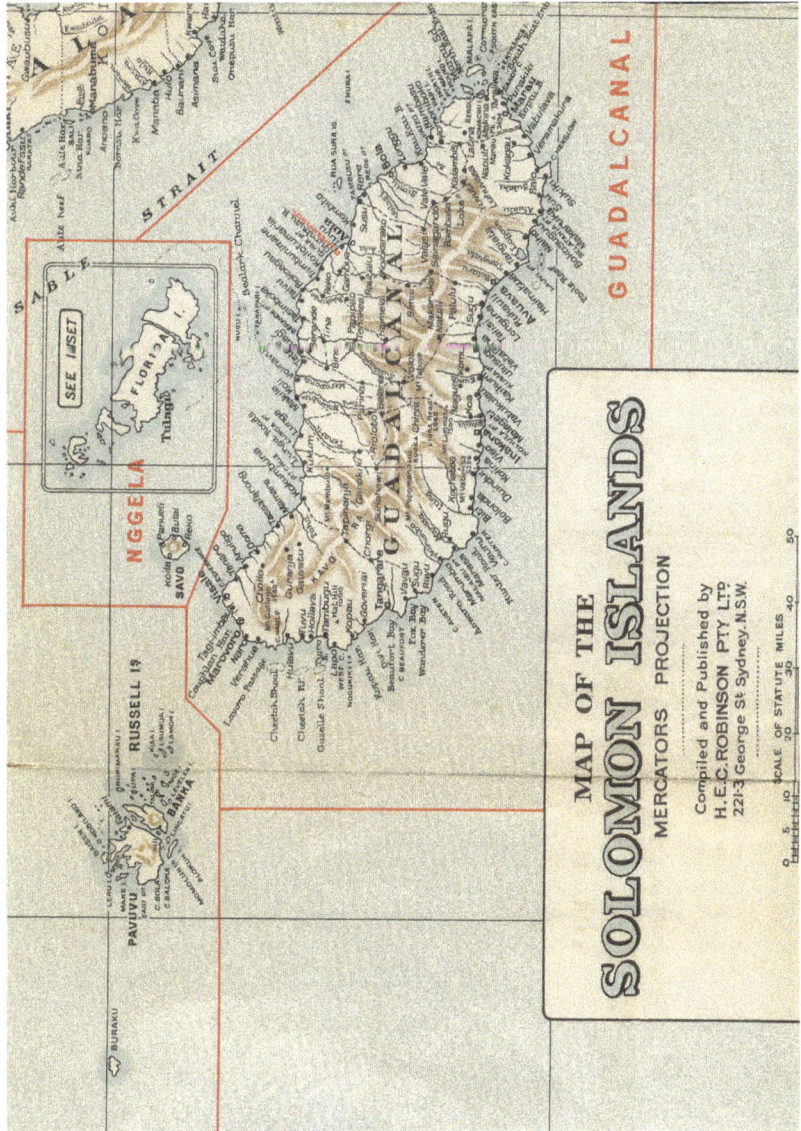

Map 1.7 Map of Guadalcanal, 1930s.
Many of the coastal sites are villages, plantations, and missions.
Source: Robinson (c. 1940).

2
Taem blong faet: Camp Guadal

The Pacific War

After China lost the First Sino-Japanese War (1894–95), between 1895 and 1945, Taiwan became Japan's first overseas territory, with Korea added in 1910. When World War I broke out, Australia captured German New Guinea and Japan captured German Micronesia. After the war, Japan was awarded Micronesia and Australia received control of north-east New Guinea, both of which were League of Nations Class C Mandated Territories. Japan began to expand militarily, conquering Manchuria in 1931, the next year developing military defences in Chuuk (Truk) in the Caroline Islands, and in 1933 walking out of the League of Nations after censure. Chuuk had the best anchorage in Micronesia and Dublon Island in Chuuk Lagoon became Japan's Pearl Harbor for its fleet—a strategic base from which to cast covetous eyes on South-East Asia. In 1937, Japan invaded coastal China, initiating war in the Pacific region.

When World War II began, Japan was an ally of the Axis powers Germany and Italy. With the capture of South-East Asia in mind, on 7 December 1941, Japan made a pre-emptive strike on Pearl Harbor, the American military base in Hawai`i, bringing the United States into the war. The action destroyed the US Pacific Fleet and the largest US military base beyond the American mainland.

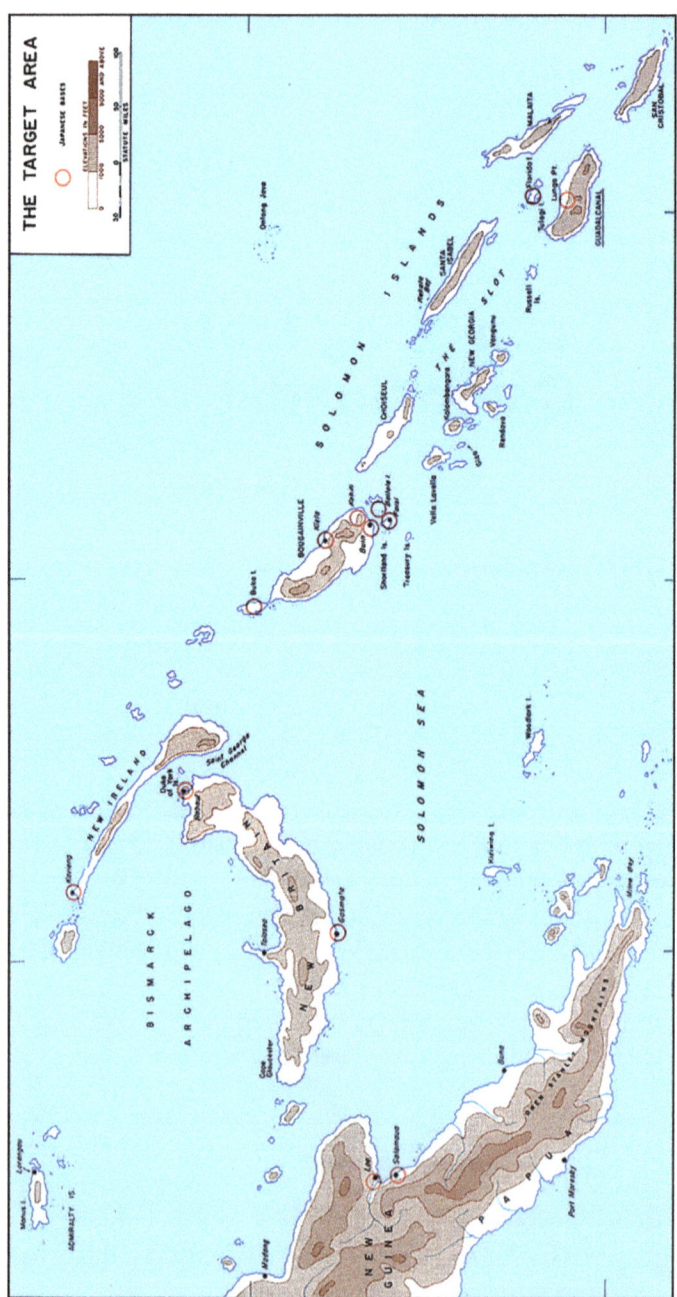

Map 2.1 The main Japanese bases in the Bismarck and Solomon archipelagos, between 1942 and 1945.

Source: Public domain file provided by the US Government. By derivative version Angelus, in the public domain (commons.wikimedia.org/w/index.php?curid=15311575).

Between May 1942 and early 1943, the Japanese and the Americans (and their allies) fought one of the deciding battles of World War II in the Pacific, to gain control of Guadalcanal and its airfield, along with Tulagi and Gavutu harbours. Guadalcanal and Milne Bay, on the south-east New Guinea mainland, were the southern limits of the Japanese advance. The Battle for Guadalcanal was crucial in deciding the result of the war in the Pacific. It was about control of an airfield established on Levers' Lungga coconut plantation. In the Pacific, it was primarily a sea war, and whoever controlled the ocean was able to assure supply to their land bases. The Americans learnt that to control the ocean they had also to control the air above. This was a new kind of warfare and explains the importance of what became Henderson Airfield. Whoever held the airfield could launch attacks on enemy ships and aircraft hundreds of kilometres away.[1]

Along with the Battles of Buna-Gona and Milne Bay in Australian Papua, which ended six months of Japanese occupation of sections of south-east New Guinea, the victory on Guadalcanal was the first milestone in the American advance north towards Tokyo. The Japanese were no longer on the offensive and thereafter had to adopt a defensive strategy right through to their surrender in August 1945. The difference was that in the central Solomon Islands, the Japanese Navy suffered crushing and irreplaceable losses in a series of sea battles. This helped make the Battle for Guadalcanal an important Allied victory.

The Australian evacuation of Rabaul on New Britain, the largest town in the islands off eastern New Guinea, began on 11 December 1941. The Japanese first bombed Rabaul on 4 January 1942 and, by 23 January, the town had fallen.[2] They wanted to control Rabaul because it had the best harbour in the islands off New Guinea, had enough flat land for airfields, and was only 1,029 kilometres from Chuuk, their largest base in the central Pacific. At the same time, although the British attempted to defend the Malay Peninsula from the Japanese advance, Singapore fell on 15 February—the largest surrender of British-led military personnel in history. The war then moved south.

---

1   The distance depends on the type of aircraft, the number of engines, the weight of the bomb load and the fuel, how difficult the target might be to find, climatic conditions along the way, and the type of target. For instance, ships at sea are much more difficult targets than a land base like an airfield. A 370-kilometre range would be correct for single-engine planes flying out of Henderson Airfield hunting ships early in the war. Later in the war, when US planes had multiple engines, the distance could be stretched to 550 kilometres. My thanks to war historian Peter Williams for his valuable advice on these figures, and generally with this chapter.
2   Aplin 1980; Stone 1995.

HONIARA

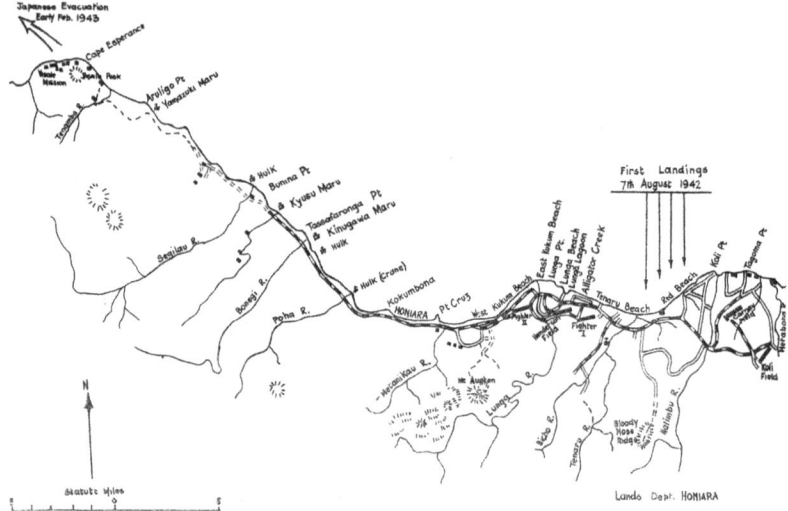

Map 2.2 The north coast of Guadalcanal during World War II, from the Metapona River to Visale.
The map shows the first American landing at Red Beach and the progression of American fighting in 1942 and 1943, the sites of Japanese wreckage left along the coast, and the final Japanese evacuation at Cape Esperance. The position of present-day Honiara is indicated.
Source: Based on the map in BSIP (1960). Cartography by Vincent Verheyen.

With Chuuk and Rabaul under their control, next, the Japanese constructed an airfield on Buka Island, which was contiguous with north Bougainville. The Guadalcanal Plains were a suitable site for extending their air network. The Japanese strategy was to create a semicircle of smaller airbases south of Rabaul to prevent their New Britain base being bombed. The Allied fight to remove the Japanese from New Guinea and Solomon Islands was under the control of General Douglas MacArthur, Supreme Commander of the Southwest Pacific Area, who was based in Brisbane. MacArthur's strategy was to isolate Rabaul, not to directly attack the garrison, which remained under Japanese control until late in the war. The Japanese planned to take control of Port Moresby (which failed) and Milne Bay (from where they retreated). Holding Guadalcanal was also part of the Japanese plan. With Buka and Bougainville secured between 9 March and 5 April 1942, it was a short hop to the Shortland Islands in the far north of the BSIP, which fell to the Japanese on 30 March. The Japanese constructed further airfields on Bougainville at Bonis Peninsula, Kahill, and Keita. As we shall see later in the chapter, construction of another airfield, at Buin in south Bougainville, aided their attack on the Allies on Guadalcanal. The British evacuation of the Tulagi enclave—Tulagi, Makambo, Gavutu-Tanambogo, and Bungana islands, and Taroaniara on Ngela Sule—and the Anglican base at Siota in Mboli Passage, began in late 1941, and the process continued during the early months of 1942 as Japanese planes began to bomb and strafe the islands. After heavy air raids on 1 and 2 May, Tulagi fell and, by 4 May, was totally under Japanese control.[3] While this occurred, attacks were monitored and reported on by an Allied network of Coastwatchers and indigenous Scouts.

The Americans, forced on to the defensive, were determined to keep open the lines of communication with Australia. It was imperative that Allied shipping be able to travel freely between America and Australia, which required a string of Allied bases across the southern Pacific. The Americans already held Hawai`i and American Samoa. An airfield was hastily constructed on New Caledonia, along with other bases in the New Hebrides Condominium. When Admiral Chester W. Nimitz, Commander of the US Pacific Fleet, ordered a counteroffensive, Guadalcanal became crucial to these plans.

The Japanese called Guadalcanal *Ga Tō* or *Gadarukanaru*, and their codename for their airfield was 'RXI'. The Americans used 'Cactus' as their codename for Guadalcanal and 'Operation Watchtower' as the codename for the plan to retake Guadalcanal and Tulagi. The 'Cactus Air Force' was later the nickname of the American planes based at the captured and renamed Henderson Airfield. 'Tokyo Express' was the American nickname for the Japanese supply ships and aircraft attacking Guadalcanal. 'Camp Guadal' was the American name for the military camp that became Honiara. Solomon Islanders called the war *taem blong faet*: the time of the fighting.

Coastwatchers and Scouts

Once war began in Europe, and the Japanese advance continued through Asia, the British began to prepare the BSIP for invasion. The policy was fivefold: create a small defence force; evacuate the expatriate population; destroy anything that could be useful to the Japanese; maintain a skeleton administrative staff at Auki on Malaita, and then in the hills inland; and create a unique small organisation called the Coastwatchers.

---

3   Moore 2019: 373–413.

Plate 2.1 Coastwatcher Martin Clemens and members of the Solomon Islands Defence Force, August 1942.
Standing, left to right: Daniel Pule, Martin Clemens, and Andrew Langabaea.
Seated, left to right: Olorere, Gumu, Chaparuka, and Chaku.
Source: USNARA.

The Coastwatchers (the Coast Watch Organisation) were Allied military intelligence operatives on Pacific Islands. The organisation consisted of military officers, planters, government officers, and missionaries. In the BSIP, recruitment of Coastwatchers began in October 1939, although the final round of recruitments was not until 1941. The members were Australians, British, New Zealanders, and Solomon Islanders who went into hiding once the Japanese invasion began. Along with the Solomon Islander Scouts, the Coastwatchers were part of a secret communication system to monitor enemy shipping and planes for the Allies. They also rescued Allied personnel if they became stranded after plane and ship disasters. There were around 100 European Coastwatchers in the South Pacific. Many were stationed in eastern New Guinea, along with 23 Coastwatcher bases in the Solomon archipelago, including two on Bougainville.⁴ It is difficult to count the number of individual Coastwatchers; some were official Coastwatchers with military rank, while others were civilians. Their activities were crucial to alert the Allied forces of approaching Japanese air and sea movements. The coded Coastwatcher call sign was 'Ferdinand', after the 1936 children's story about a fictional bull that preferred to smell flowers than fight in the ring. This drove home the point that Coastwatchers and Scouts were there to observe, not to take defensive or offensive action.

These teams performed magnificently throughout the war and were a constant thorn in the side of the Japanese. Coastwatchers on Bougainville, along with their colleagues in the protectorate, supplied information on Japanese planes flying the 1,040 kilometres south from Rabaul to attack Tulagi and Guadalcanal. The distinction between Coastwatchers and Scouts is artificial, based on military rank and colonial authority. For instance, Sergeant Major Jacob Vuza, the chief of Martin Clemens's Scouts on Guadalcanal, proved to be tough and efficient. The Scouts were the majority, and some of the Coastwatchers were mixed-race Solomon Islanders. The European Coastwatchers could never have survived without their Scouts.

The Coastwatchers and Scouts sometimes had to reposition their bases to avoid capture. This was never easy as their tele-radios were heavy and required a team of carriers to move them. The Bougainville Coastwatchers, W.J. (Jack) Read in the north and Paul Mason in the south, were crucial. A glance at a map shows why. Planes flying from Kavieng in New Ireland to Lungga on Guadalcanal passed over Read's base at Porapora in the central mountains. Read's reports were 30 minutes ahead of those from Mason at Buin, and an hour or more ahead of the bases further south. Planes flying from Rabaul to Lungga passed directly over Mason at Buin. The Japanese bombers and Zeros from Kavieng could be counted with certainty at Porapora while their formations were still at low altitude and Read could also see flights coming from Rabaul.⁵ The Coastwatchers provided notice of imminent attack for the troops on the ground and for ships, and enabled fighter aircraft to be scrambled to intercept the Japanese planes. Forty-five minutes was all that was needed to get American fighters into the air and in position at 7,600 to 9,100 metres,

---

4   Lord 1977; Horton 1970; Clemens 2004; Feldt 1946; Feuer 1992; Lee 2019; Trench 1956a, 1956b, 1956c.
5   Lee 2019: 217.

enabling them to attack the lower-flying Japanese bombers from above. Without the Coastwatchers, hundreds of US aircraft on Guadalcanal would have been destroyed on the ground. The Bougainville reports, along with others from Coastwatchers further south, saved innumerable Allied lives.

There were several BSIP-based Coastwatchers north of Guadalcanal. Henry Josselyn, a government officer, and John Keenan were based on Vella Lavella and Rendova islands. D.C. (Dick) Horton, another district officer, spent time on Rendova with Josselyn.[6] Donald G. Kennedy, who had been the Ngela and Isabel district officer, established a base at Mahaga on Isabel from which to observe Thousand Ships Bay and New Georgia Sound. He also set up a secondary base on Rennell Island, and later moved from Isabel to Seghe on New Georgia.[7] Bill Bennett, a mixed-race Solomon Islander, served on New Georgia as Kennedy's second-in-command. Hugh Wheatley, also a mixed-race Solomon Islander, trained as a Native Medical Practitioner (NMP), was based at Isabel, and then sent to the Shortlands, where he was captured and killed.[8] Harry Wickham, another mixed-race Solomon Islander, trader, and plantation manager at Marovo Lagoon, was a successful Coastwatcher on New Georgia.[9] Alexander (Nick) Waddell and Carden Seton were on Choiseul, the latter owning a plantation there. Waddell was a government officer. Geoffrey Kuper (another mixed-race Solomon Islander NMP) was on Isabel at Tataba, and Mogao near Suavana. Royal Australian Air Force Flying Officer J.A. Corrigan, Albert M. (Andy) Andresen (Royal Australian Naval Volunteer Reserve), and planter Frederick Ashton ('Snowy') Rhoades, also served at Mogao during 1943.[10] Michael Forster, the district officer at Kirakira on Makira, remained at his post all through the war and was part of the network, even though there were no Japanese on the island. He had little to report. Ruby Olive Boye, married to Samuel S. Boye, manager of the Vanikoro Kauri Timber Company on Vanikolo, was the only female Coastwatcher. She was the link with Port Vila early on when the radio at the temporary BSIP headquarters on Malaita was out of action. Those north of Guadalcanal were able to give warning of the arrival of new waves of Japanese torpedo and dive-bombers.

---

6   Clemens 2004: 42.
7   Butcher 2012: 5, 59.
8   Clemens 2004: 42.
9   Kwai 2017: 18.
10 White 1988: 150.

Initially, there were three Coastwatcher bases on Guadalcanal. Martin Clemens operated one at Aola, where he was still trying to perform district officer duties. Lieutenant Don Macfarlan, a naval liaison officer, was first based on Tulagi, and then operated from a base inland from Berande plantation near Tasimboko, Guadalcanal. Veteran BSIP entrepreneur Kenneth Hay worked with Macfarlan. When the Japanese took Tulagi, Macfarlan shifted his base to Gold Ridge, high in the mountains, looking down on the north coast. Hay followed, transporting his supplies cross-country using a truck and carriers. Hay had been given the keys to the warehouse of Burns Philp (BP) on Makambo Island opposite Tulagi. Over several months, he had shifted large amounts of supplies to Guadalcanal, including alcohol. At Gold Ridge, Macfarlan first met Andresen, a miner turned Coastwatcher who had lived in the Solomons for 25 years. The north-west base in the mountains behind Visale was operated by 'Snowy' Rhoades from Lavoro (Lavuro) plantation further around the coast. He later moved to an upstream area beside Hylavo River. Lief Schroeder, an elderly trader, was first based on Savo, using a patched-up old tele-radio. He joined Rhoades soon after the Japanese arrived. The pair remained at the western end of the island until September 1942, close to the Japanese.

Even though they had greater range than the US aircraft, the Japanese planes were fully stretched over the distance from Rabaul and could remain for only a few minutes over their target areas. Fully laden Mitsubishi G4M 'Betty' bombers had a range of about 2,300 kilometres. Rabaul to Guadalcanal and return was 2,084 kilometres and they needed spare fuel as a safety margin in case they had to manoeuvre around bad weather or Allied aircraft or ships. The margin was even lower for planes returning to Kavieng. The best and most direct route was straight down the Solomon archipelago and through The Slot (Map 2.1), even with the disadvantage of being spotted by Coastwatchers.[11] As soon as a Japanese airfield was established at Buin in southern Bougainville (in October 1942), Zero fighters stationed there had short-range access to Guadalcanal.[12] The bombers out of Rabaul or Kavieng

---

11   The Slot is the passage of water between the double line of islands in the north of the protectorate. The Japanese twin-engine Mitsubishi G4M 'Betty' bombers had a greater range than the early US aircraft, plus the target was an easy-to-find large island. The Japanese fighters, bombers, and reconnaissance planes all had a much longer range than the US aircraft—double in most cases. Information from Peter Williams.
12   Before October 1942 and the opening of Buin Airfield, only half the Japanese fighters had sufficient range to make return flights between Rabaul and Guadalcanal, which limited their ability to strike Guadalcanal. Once Buin was in use, they could base their short-range fighters there to supplement the fighters coming from Rabaul. Information from Peter Williams.

tended to pick up their Zero fighter escorts over Buka, 320 kilometres closer to Guadalcanal, and then flew down Bougainville, heading south. The Coastwatchers reported on their tele-radios as the formations of 40 to 60 planes passed over their hidden observation posts. Initially, they reported to Vanikolo, Port Moresby, and Townsville. Once the Americans were in control of Henderson Airfield, messages were passed to Lieutenant Commander Hugh Mackenzie, a deputy supervising intelligence officer in the Royal Australian Navy, who was based there. The Japanese bombers passed over Bougainville mid-morning, attacking Tulagi and Guadalcanal just before midday. Once they were ensconced on Guadalcanal, the Americans could counterattack. Then, in the early afternoon, the Coastwatchers saw the often-depleted fleets of Japanese planes struggle home. Planes unable to reach Rabaul landed at Buin or Buka or crash-landed. Each evening, Mackenzie provided a score on the attacks. Sometimes the Japanese bombers lost all their Zero fighter escorts. After late August, there were also night-time Japanese flights over Guadalcanal, which were intended more to demoralise and stop the Americans sleeping than to inflict damage. The Americans nicknamed their night visitors 'Washing Machine Charlie' and 'Louie the Louse'. Some of these were long-distance flights from Rabaul, although cruisers also carried seaplanes and, by August, there was a Japanese seaplane base in the Shortland Islands.[13]

One final point needs to be made. The real skill in maintaining the Coastwatcher bases came from the Scouts, who knew how to operate successfully in jungle terrain. Even though the 'official' Coastwatchers—the Europeans and a few mixed-race Solomon Islanders—had better knowledge of radio technology and an overall understanding of the war, they were totally dependent on their Scouts. After the war, various Coastwatchers wrote quite romanticised accounts of their success, seldom naming or fully acknowledging their Scouts. To Solomon Islanders, jungle was advantageous territory in which they excelled. At conferences in the 1980s, Solomon Islands war heroes like Sir Jacob Vouza and Bill Bennett were quite ambivalent in their attitudes to the authoritarian European Coastwatchers who often used harsh discipline.[14]

---

13 Feuer 1992: 66, 67, 69, 94.
14 Laracy and White 1988; White et al. 1988a.

The Japanese on Guadalcanal

An astounding 30,000 Japanese died in the effort to hold on to Guadalcanal. The Americans were more numerous, better supplied, and had a much lower death rate. The Japanese Navy had superior weapons to the Americans, their aircraft had a better range, and their army had some excellent large guns. They had also perfected night land travel and warfare. In the fight for Guadalcanal, the Japanese controlled the land and sea at night and the Americans controlled the land during the day. The Japanese forces were tenacious and imbued with a moral code (*bushido*: 'the way of the warrior') that meant they never gave up and were willing to die for their emperor. The battles raged back and forth, and it was quite possible the Japanese could have won the long Battle for Guadalcanal. There were five crucial differences between the Allies and the Japanese that enabled American success in the Pacific. The first was the work of the Coastwatchers and Scouts. The second was the use of Atabrine (Mepacrine) to suppress malaria; the Japanese only had access to Quinate (based on quinine), which was less effective. The third were the shorter American supply lines from Australia; Brisbane is 2,131 kilometres from Honiara and 2,092 kilometres from Port Moresby. There were also American airfields around Townsville and on the Atherton Tableland. The Americans rested their Solomons-based troops in New Zealand (and their New Guinea-based troops in Queensland) before sending them back into battle. The Japanese supply line was overstretched as they did not have total control of South-East Asia. Japan was 4,600 kilometres away, and they could not rest their troops adequately. The fourth difference was that the American economy was bigger and better resourced, enabling seemingly unending war supplies. The fifth was the imperative American strategy to keep control of southern supply routes and never allow Australia to be cut off from the Allies.

During their first three weeks in control, the Japanese confined their occupation of the central Solomons to Tulagi; then, on 27 May, they made their initial inspection of the area around Tenaru and Lungga on Guadalcanal. Over the next two weeks, they became a constant presence along the coast, looting plantations and butchering cattle to take back to Tulagi. The choice of Lungga as the site of the airfield is credited to Captain Shigetoshi Miyazaki, commander of the seaplanes from the Yokohama Air Group based at Tulagi. He was responsible for the establishment of Honiara, as the Japanese and Allied military camps were based around the airfield. On 8 June, the Japanese began to erect tents at Lungga. Their occupation of the coast of Guadalcanal began in earnest on 19 June when a destroyer arrived and began landing supplies and men. Admiral Shigeyoshi Inoue, commander of the Japanese 4th Fleet and advocate of naval aviation, toured the area. After building a camp and a small wharf at Kukum, they began to clear large areas of coconut palms and long grass. At Gold Ridge, the Coastwatchers and the gold prospectors watched, puzzled. On 6 July, a 12-ship convoy arrived and disgorged heavy equipment: 100 trucks, generators, an ice-plant, tractors, road rollers, rails, small locomotives, and hopper wagons.[15]

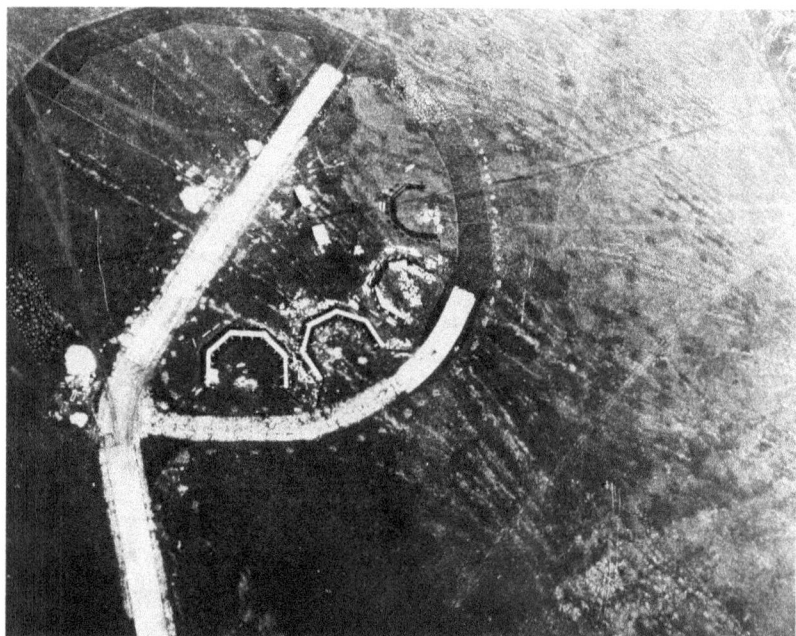

Plate 2.2 The partly completed Japanese airfield and dispersal area at Lungga, 7 July 1942, which later became Henderson Airfield.
The U-shaped revetments in the centre are for protection against strafing attacks.
Source: USNARA.

The Japanese plan was now clear to the Coastwatchers: they were building an airfield from which to attack Allied shipping in the Pacific and as a base for activities in nearby Australian Papua, as well as a platform from which to attack Allied bases on Espiritu Santo in the New Hebrides and

---

15   Innes 2017: 96; Frank 1990: 31.

further south. The South Pacific bases were vital to maintaining Australia's communications with the United States, and ultimately the security of northern Australia.[16] A Japanese photograph from 7 July indicates the area of coconut palms on Levers' Lungga plantation to be cleared for the airfield.[17] From that day, American priorities in the South Pacific changed. Task One, as it was called, had been to regain control of Tulagi and the adjacent seaplane base at Gavutu-Tanambogo. The events of early 7 July meant Task One was reoriented to stopping the Japanese from building their airfield on Guadalcanal. Tulagi and the seaplane base became lesser concerns.

The Japanese landed 492 troops and 2,269 Korean labourers: the 84th Guard Unit under Lieutenant Akira Tanabe, formerly part of the Kure 3rd Special Landing Force; and the 11th and 13th Construction Units led by Lieutenant Commander Norinaga Okamura and Captain Kanae Monzen.[18] The number of Japanese on Guadalcanal was unclear to the Allies. On Malaita, Resident Commissioner William Marchant received reports via Coastwatcher Clemens that there were 700 Japanese based at Kukum, others at Visale, and another 500 on the Weather Coast, spread between Lambi and Marau Sound. The report noted large quantities of stores in dumps spread from Lungga to Tenaru and that coconut palms had been cleared. Local labour was conscripted to assist with the construction. Machine guns and heavy guns were being installed along the shore.[19] Later, the initial estimates of Japanese numbers were revised down. The Allies thought there was a large force of Japanese on Guadalcanal, when in fact the military numbers in the Honiara area were low, bolstered by the Korean labourers working on the airfield. Monzen, in charge of the Lungga construction operation, had good reason to be pleased when, by 6 August, the airfield was almost complete. Okamura had overall control and, with Monzen, was proudly expecting two staff officers from Rabaul the next day to discuss deploying planes to Guadalcanal. The Japanese and Koreans were celebrating that night and were not expecting the US landing early the next morning at Red Beach (then codenamed Beach Red), about 5 kilometres from the airfield.

---

16   SINA BSIP 5/IV/1, William S. Marchant 1942–43, Diary for 2 January 1942 to 6 May 1943, transcribed by J. French, Aide-de-Camp to the High Commissioner, 29 December 1962, Diary entry for 20 June 1942.
17   Innes 2017: 97–98.
18   Smith 2000: 34.
19   SINA BSIP 5/IV/1, Marchant 1942–43, 16 July 1942.

HONIARA

Watching from Gold Ridge

The Coastwatchers were not the only expatriates to remain in the protectorate during the war, although they stayed the course, while others left later in the war. Marist Catholics remained at Visale, Tangarare, Avuavu, and Marau Sound, and Reverend Leslie Stibbard and Frederick Rowley remained at the Anglican school at Maravovo. Four missionaries were killed. Mistakenly, they believed the Japanese would respect their neutral religious status.[20] One planter who stayed was the elderly Clarry Hart, who had served as a nongovernment member of the BSIP Advisory Council. Determinedly, he remained on his Kakau Bay plantation (between Rere and Marau Sound) in the early years of the war, and then helped with the Solomon Islands Labour Corps.[21]

The Coastwatchers at Gold Ridge (Map 0.2) in the mountains inland from Honiara were military officers, although there were civilians with them at the facilities of the Guadalcanal Sluicing and Dredging Company. Gold prospector Fred Campbell (police commandant and district officer in the 1910s, and then a plantation owner on Makira) was nearby with his two sons, Jack and Pat, as were Bert Freshwater, A. Wilmot, and Andy Andresen.[22] The prospectors continued to search for gold, maintaining an uneasy relationship with the official Coastwatchers, who were not supposed to be responsible for civilians. The numbers were swelled by Macfarlan's Scouts, Hay's servants, and 30 labourers employed by the Campbells. The Gold Ridge community was known to the Japanese, who sent patrols, forcing the Coastwatchers and prospectors to evacuate further inland. They continued to use Gold Ridge as the best site from which to watch the Japanese building the airfield.[23]

Coastal Guale fled into the mountains away from the fighting, and some helped the Coastwatchers or joined the Solomon Islands Labour Corps. Others did not. The Coastwatchers could not blindly rely on the Guale. Some of the villagers at Tasimboko and Visale (east and west of the airfield) were pro-Japanese.

---

20 *PIM*, November 1942, 19.
21 Golden 1993: 117–18, 181–82.
22 ibid., 183–85, 309.
23 Lord 1977: 29–35.

The Americans on Guadalcanal

By late July 1942, the Americans had decided to make their first land offensive in World War II: an attack on the Japanese in the Tulagi enclave and on Guadalcanal. The BSIP came within the region under the control of General MacArthur, although he delegated his authority over the protectorate to Admiral Nimitz, who was in command of forces in the Central and South Pacific. The manoeuvre required a large American military force and the only unit immediately available was the 1st Marine Division. Some of the marines were still at sea in a move from North Carolina to Wellington, New Zealand, and the 7th Marines had been detached to garrison Samoa—another strategic area between Australia and the United States. In compensation, Major General Alexander A. Vandegrift had been given temporary control over the 2nd Marine Division, the crack 1st Raider Battalion, and the 3rd Defense Battalion. The United States also faced a lack of shipping, although on 22 July, Vandegrift was able to muster 80 ships and almost 12,000 troops for a rehearsal in Fijian waters for the amphibious invasion.[24]

The Japanese drive to capture Port Moresby, across New Guinea and by sea, was first thwarted by the Battle of the Coral Sea (7–8 May 1942) and weakened again at the Battle of Midway (3–6 June 1942), which halted the main Japanese offensive and reversed the strategic situation in the Pacific. The Battle of Midway was relevant because the Japanese Navy lost four aircraft carriers there (half their carrier fleet), which, had they been available, might have made the Americans reconsider the risk involved in capturing Guadalcanal. Without their losses at Midway, the Japanese could have prevailed over the Americans on Guadalcanal.

Gaining complete control of Guadalcanal took five months and cost 7,400 American lives. A fleet of American and Australian naval ships carrying Vandegrift's marines, commanded by Rear Admiral Kelly Turner, set sail from Fiji. Miraculously, the fleet, including the Australian heavy cruisers *Australia* and HMAS *Canberra*, and the light cruiser HMAS *Hobart*, escaped detection. The ships were aided by heavy cloud and rain, cloaking their approach. The fleet's path north was designed to look like a convoy heading for Australia, until it reached just south of Rennell Island, where they turned their bows towards Guadalcanal. Once the fleet

---

24 Smith 2000: 1–4; Table 1, p. 15.

reached Cape Esperance at the north-western tip of Guadalcanal, it split into two, with one section sailing around Savo to Tulagi, and the other moving along northern Guadalcanal. Three days of attacks commenced at dawn on 7 August. They bombarded the Japanese garrison on Tulagi, and the 1st Marine Division went ashore, securing Tulagi the next day. The Japanese seaplane base at Gavutu-Tanambogo fell to the Americans just before midnight on the same day. Early on 7 August, the marines landed on Guadalcanal east of Lungga Point, at Red Beach between Alligator and Tenavatu creeks.

It is difficult to imagine how the young marines felt while waiting on ships and in barges off Guadalcanal; many were only 18 to 20 years old, and they knew the death rates were expected to be high. The troops landed, supported by firepower from three cruisers and four destroyers, and subsequently by bombardment from the 75 mm howitzers of the 11th Marines. Dive-bombers swept in from the fleet's aircraft carriers—USS *Saratoga*, USS *Enterprise*, and USS *Wasp*—which had taken up a covering position to the south. The marines followed up later in the day with an attack using 105 mm howitzers as they landed. By 8 pm, 10,800 troops had gone ashore without opposition and, on the afternoon of the second day, they had taken control of the Japanese airfield. Over one month, from 7 July to 7 August, Guadalcanal's population doubled, increasing by two-thirds of its 1941 indigenous levels on just one day, 7 August.[25] The watchers up at Gold Ridge had an extraordinary view of the proceedings.

The Japanese were caught unprepared and ignominiously retreated. As soon as Vice-Admiral Gunichi Mikawa, who was in charge of the 8th Japanese Fleet at Rabaul, heard of the major Allied attack, he ordered a counterattack. On the same day, he dispatched all his submarines and warships (five heavy and two light cruisers, and a destroyer) plus 27 high-level two-engine, and 17 Zero fighters. Mikawa suspended much of the fighting on New Guinea to concentrate on the Solomons. Coastwatchers Mason and Read on Bougainville watched the planes pass over and sent messages on their tele-radios. The resulting naval and air battles were crucial in turning back the Japanese southern advance into the Pacific, through New Guinea and to Australia. Early on the morning of 9 August, Mikawa's fleet steamed down The Slot to Tulagi and Guadalcanal, inflicting heavy damage in the Battle of Savo Island. The cruisers USS *Astoria*,

---

25 *BSIP NS*, 22 May 1967.

USS *Vincennes*, USS *Quincy*, and HMAS *Canberra* were sunk, and the USS *Chicago* was badly damaged. Luckily, the marines' transports were not attacked, although Admiral Turner's American fleet retreated, failing to land many of the marines' essential supplies. Strangely, Allied communications did not warn all the fleet of the approaching Japanese ships and their planes.[26]

The almost completed 1,151-metre runway was under Allied control by 4 pm on 7 August. Two days later, the US 1st Marine Engineer Battalion took over work on the airstrip, using Japanese equipment, because their own had not yet been landed. There was little initial opposition from the Japanese and Koreans, who had retreated to the surrounding hills, into the upper reaches of the Mataniko River, and west of Point Cruz. The Japanese had constructed fortifications and foxholes (small pits used as defensive positions) on the ridges overlooking the airfield, which they used to attack the American efforts.

Charles Widdy, pre-war manager of Levers in the Solomons, arrived with the ships as one the Americans' local guides. He contacted the Coastwatchers at Gold Ridge. Martin Clemens, the only British official on Guadalcanal, marched his men down to meet Widdy, Lieutenant Commander Hugh Mackenzie, and finally Major General Vandegrift. Two government officers, Henry Josselyn and Dick Horton, had also arrived back with the fleet as honorary lieutenants, guides, and liaison officers for the marines.[27] The retreat of the American fleet left the marines short of equipment and with only 14 days of food supplies. They did not have radio communications for the first three days, until a captured powerful Japanese shortwave radio was made operational.[28]

The first US plane to land at what became Henderson Airfield was a Catalina piloted by Lieutenant W.S. Sampson on 12 August; just to have the honour, he lied that his seaplane was damaged and could not land on water.[29] On 17 August, Vandegrift was able to announce that the airstrip was open to fighters and bombers. Three days later, 20 F4F Grumman 'Wildcat' fighters and 12 dive-bombers from USS *Long Island* landed. On 22 and 27 August, 14 P-400 fighter aircraft from the US Air Force 67th Squadron arrived as reinforcements. The planes pounded the

---

26 Horton 1970: 83; Smith 2000: 17.
27 Lord 1979: 35–55, 37–39.
28 Horton 1970: 83; Smith 2000: 17.
29 Innes 2017: 100–3.

Japanese all along the north coast of Guadalcanal. The Americans landed mountains of supplies and built defences along the shore from the mouth of the Alligator Creek to Kukum. Heavy fighting took place all along the north Guadalcanal coast.

Plate 2.3 American troops advancing through the site of the burnt-out Horahi village on the Mataniko River, November 1942.
Source: USNARA.

Plate 2.4 American troops at the mouth of the Mataniko River in 1943.
The remains of Japanese tanks destroyed in October 1942 are visible along the beach and sandbar.
Source: USNARA.

Plate 2.5 The Mataniko River footbridge built by the Americans in 1942.
Source: USNARA.

The Allied fight against the Japanese

The American and Japanese troops were mainly young and faced not only fighting and fear of the unknown, but also the trials of life on a mountainous and swampy tropical island. They suffered from war injuries, malaria, dengue fever, dysentery, gastroenteritis, infected cuts that festered into major sores and ulcers, foot (or jungle) rot from wearing constantly wet boots, heat stroke, exhaustion, malnutrition, and psychological trauma. The Japanese were more exposed to malaria than the Americans, which may have affected their ability to retake the airfield.[30] As mentioned above, the availability of Atabrine to the Americans as a malaria suppressant was a distinct advantage. The long battle to control Guadalcanal and Tulagi cannot be told fully here. Many books have been written that do it justice. The gaps in the literature lie in the limited amount of writing in English detailing the Japanese side of the story, and Solomon Islander involvement.[31]

---

30   Mason 2004: 83–86.
31   See Kwai 2017: 8–11. Frank (1990) contains information based on Japanese sources.

Both the Japanese and the Allies brought in reinforcements and supplies by sea. Between August and November, the Japanese attempted to recapture Henderson Airfield, receiving constant reinforcements and supplies dropped along the Guadalcanal coast on both sides of present-day Honiara. These attempts led to naval battles in Iron Bottom Sound as the Japanese fleet covered the arrival of transport ships carrying troops and supplies. All moves to recapture the airfield failed. In phase two, between December 1942 and early February 1943, the Japanese realised they could not recapture the airfield, so they decided to withdraw, slowly and quietly. By January, the Americans had forced the Japanese west towards Cape Esperance, unaware of the Japanese evacuation plan, which led to their complete withdrawal by the evening of 8 February.

Some of the best surviving 1940s aerial views of what is now Honiara were taken in mid-August 1942 at 3,261 metres by the daily B-17 Flying Fortress reconnaissance missions. Point Cruz and the Mataniko River feature in many of them. The site of Horahi village can be seen in a clearing near the coast just west of the mouth of the river. It was burnt down soon after by American marines pursuing Japanese troops. The coast and the river were fringed with low undergrowth, and most of the stony hills behind were clear of vegetation, other than kunai or blady grass (*Imperata cylindrical*).

The air attacks were monotonous and ferocious. The naval battles were horrific. Over several months, the surrounds of the Mataniko River were a 'no-man's land' between the Japanese and the American forces. Tulagi and Gavutu eventually became an Allied base for PT boats and seaplanes, and a safe harbour for Allied ships. Later in the war, there were 6,500 US troops stationed in the Ngela Group, and many more on Guadalcanal.[32] Iron Bottom Sound was the name given to the waters between Guadalcanal, Savo, and Ngela islands, its deep bottom strewn with ships and planes, plus the many wrecks along the coasts (Map 2.3). Around 70 ships were sunk (60 of them in Iron Bottom Sound) and 1,000 aircraft were lost. The Japanese were victorious in the short Battle of Savo Island on 8–9 August, during which the Allies lost four heavy cruisers and a destroyer, and another heavy cruiser and two destroyers were damaged—one of the worst defeats ever suffered by the US Navy in wartime. More than 1,000 American sailors died. Two Japanese heavy cruisers were also badly damaged. This was followed by further major sea battles: the Battle of the Eastern Solomons

---

32   Cline and Michel 2002: 225; Horton 1970: 86.

(24–25 August), the Battle of Cape Esperance (11–12 October), the Battle of Santa Cruz (25–27 October), the Naval Battle of Guadalcanal (12–15 November), the Battle of Tassafaronga (30 November), and the Battle of Rennell Island (29–30 January 1943). The Naval Battle of Guadalcanal (really two battles fought at night with a night in between) was even more severe than the Battle of Savo Island, with 1,700 American sailors killed and 10 ships lost or badly damaged.[33]

Map 2.3 Iron Bottom Sound between Guadalcanal, Savo, and the Ngela (Florida) islands, showing the sites of some of the Japanese, American, and Australian ships sunk there.
Source: Creative Commons by User: W. Wolny, Upload from German Wikipedia by user:Vvulto, CC BY-SA 3.0 (en.wikipedia.org/wiki/Ironbottom_Sound#/media/File:Wrecks_in_the_Ironbottom_Sound.jpg).

Although there was no adjacent sheltered harbour, large American ships with front-opening cargo doors unloaded directly on to the beaches, and there was room to build new airfields. The Japanese fought to regain control of Guadalcanal and its airfield. Right from 7 August, the Americans had to face Japanese raiders in Mitsubishi G4M 'Betty' medium bombers and Aichi 'Val' dive-bombers, escorted by Zero fighters flying out of Rabaul and Buka. The Japanese long-range Zeros were faster and more manoeuvrable

---

33 Ballard 1993; Hornfischer 2011: 435–36. Innes (2017: 8–15) provides a neat summary of these battles. I have also used Frank (1990), and information from Peter Williams in my calculations.

than the equivalent American planes. Because the marines had only short-range radar, they had no way of knowing when the Japanese planes were coming, except through the Coastwatchers. Short of supplies, initially, the marines could only create a defensive perimeter, which enabled the Japanese to regroup to the west. The Americans fortified Lungga Point Beach but could do little else.

The Goettge Patrol incident illustrates how little the Americans knew about the *bushido* culture of the Japanese military and the tenacity of their forces. Captain Kanae Monzem had ordered his 13th Construction Unit to withdraw to the ridges west of the Mataniko. They had little food and relied on raiding sweet potato gardens and collecting coconuts. The Americans seemed to have believed—foolishly—that the Japanese might surrender. With this in mind, Vandegrift authorised Lieutenant Colonel Frank Goettge from the 1st Marine Division to mount a 25-man patrol into Japanese-held territory. They landed between Point Cruz and Horahi village (on the west side of the mouth of the Mataniko, now the site of the United Church) on the night of 12 August, only to be repulsed by a Japanese force on Vavaea Ridge. The Japanese picked off the marines one by one, until by dawn the next day only four were still alive. Three were shot dead while running to hide in the jungle; one survived by swimming back to Lungga Point—a remarkable feat. Horahi village was destroyed on 19 August when American marines began a second assault, during which 65 Japanese were killed. The Goettge Patrol is well recorded—even lauded—in the American histories of Guadalcanal, even though it was a disastrous underestimation of the Japanese. The Mataniko River area remained the scene of major fighting between September and December.[34]

The Japanese also misinterpreted the Americans. Tokyo headquarters underestimated the size of the Allied force and its intentions, believing the Americans were not capable of mounting a full-scale counteroffensive so quickly. Captain Monzen established his defences along the Mataniko, while another group, of 113 men, led by Lieutenant Tatsunosuke Takahashi, was landed from the destroyer *Oite* and dug in at Tassafaronga Point to the west, establishing a front along the Bonegie River. Tokyo sent Colonel Kiyoano Ichiki's elite detachment to the Solomons.[35] On 16 August, the First Echelon (917 men in the 28th Infantry Regiment) and the Yokosuka 5th Special Naval Landing Force were on their way

---

34   Smith 2000: 36–42.
35   ibid., 29–36.

to Guadalcanal in a convoy controlled by Rear Admiral Raizo Tanaka. Ichiki had been an instructor at the Imperial Army's Infantry School and was an expert infantry tactician. His troops went ashore at Taivu Point on 19 August, then headed for Tetere. Intelligence sources alerted the American troops that Ichiki was on his way.[36]

Clemens' Scouts provided information on Japanese numbers and positions. Japanese ships shelled Lungga Point, then resupplied Kadomae's troops stationed at Kakabona, which became the major Japanese supply and headquarters area, until it was captured by the Americans in January 1943. What occurred became known as the Battle of Tenaru River—misnamed, as the body of water was Ilu River (Alligator Creek) near Henderson Airfield. Ichiki decided to approach along the beach on the night of 20 August, then planned for his men to fan out and seize the airfield, while also creating a base on the Lungga River. He was contemptuous of the US Marines, expecting an easy victory. By the morning, many of his men were dead, their bodies embedded in the sand at the mouth of Alligator Creek. During the day, the marines used M3A1 Stuart light 'Honey' tanks, against which the Ichiki detachment's grenades and mortars were no match. About 4.30 pm, Ichiki and his senior officers, having sustained huge losses, buried the regimental colours, and committed suicide. The survivors—128 men, including those left on guard at the landing base—retreated to Taivu Point. Ichiki's Second Echelon (about 1,100 men) was held back until later in August.[37]

This was the battle in which Jacob Vouza was captured. An ex-Armed Constabulary Sergeant Major, and then a Scout, he was recognised by one of the officers (Ishimoto, who had lived on Tulagi before the war) and tortured for information about the US troops. Vouza was tied, clubbed, and bayoneted, then taken with his captors when they attacked the marines at Lungga River. He managed to escape and reported to the Americans what he knew of the Japanese strength and positions. Although he was near death, he eventually recovered. His bravery was lauded by the Americans and the British and is still remembered by Solomon Islanders.[38] General Vandegrift awarded him the Silver Star Medal and made him a Sergeant Major of the US Marine Corps—the first of his many honours, which included the British George Medal for gallantry, and a knighthood.[39]

---

36   ibid., 221; Frank 1990: 143–48.
37   Frank 1990: 154–58.
38   Moore 2013c: entry on Vouza.
39   Frank 1990: 153–54; Kwai 2017: 25.

More US supplies arrived on 21 August, and the American marine garrison at Lungga Point was reinforced with 1,100 troops from Tulagi, lifting their number to 12,000. The Japanese underestimated American numbers at between 7,000 and 8,000.[40] The Americans had to contend with constant bombardment of the airstrip from Japanese artillery in the surrounding hills. Nevertheless, the Seabees (the 6th Naval Construction Battalion) worked on the airfield, lengthening the runway to 1,158 metres, and widening it to 46 metres. The Seabees also began work on Fighter I Airfield nearby. In its first years, it was muddy and not favoured by pilots. Once improved, the airfield remained in use until 1945.[41] An American carrier force arrived, which led to the Battle of the Eastern Solomons, the first aircraft carrier–based battle of the campaign since the Battle of the Coral Sea, which was augmented by an air attack from Henderson. Tanaka's force was defeated and the convoy of transports bringing troops to Guadalcanal was delayed.[42]

Plate 2.6 The Mataniko River vehicle bridge built by the Americans, 1943.
Source: USNARA.

---

40 Frank 1990: 145.
41 Jersey 2008: 219.
42 Smith 2000: 77–82.

2. TAEM BLONG FAET

Plate 2.7 The 11th Marines firing a 155 mm gun.
Source: USNARA.

Plate 2.8 When Solomon Islanders saw the scale of the American landing on Guadalcanal in 1942, it was almost beyond comprehension.
Source: USNARA.

Plate 2.9 The American supply base at the mouth of the Lungga River, on the edge of what is now Honiara, 1940s.
Source: Lieutenant Robert Porter, Signal Corps photograph, in Peter Flahavin Collection.

Plate 2.10 Americans and Solomon Islanders from the Solomon Islands Defence Force on Kakabona Beach, 25 January 1943.
Source: USNARA.

The final days of August were full of warfare. The Japanese sent Major General Kiyotake Kawaguchi and his elite detachment of 4,700 men to Guadalcanal. They landed at Taivu Point between 28 and 30 August. The Japanese 11th Air Fleet renewed its assault on Henderson Airfield and, at the same time, Vandegrift redoubled his efforts to destroy Japanese forces between the Mataniko and Kakabona rivers. In turn, in early September, the Japanese sent barges of troops south from the Shortlands to build up their base at Taivu Point.[43] The newly christened Kumar (Bear) Battalion advanced on Henderson Airfield and the Lungga base, moving first to Koli Point, within sight of Lungga Point, ready to attack on 12 September, from inland but supported from the air and sea.[44]

The Americans, aware of the enemy build-up, landed to the east at Tasimboko to force the Japanese back, using Colonel Merritt A. ('Red Mike') Edson's 1st Raider Battalion. Kawaguchi marched 3,000 men through the thick jungle, using compasses to navigate, heading for the ridges behind Henderson Airfield. Troops on both sides suffered from great physical and mental strain. The Americans spent 11 and 12 September digging in, creating foxholes. The Japanese slowly advanced.

The Battle of Edson's (or Bloody) Ridge (Map 2.2) was the largest clash so far between the Japanese and the Americans on Guadalcanal. As usual, just before lunch, on 12 September, 'Betty' bombers arrived over Lungga Point, causing damage. Next, Kawaguchi's troops emerged from the jungle on the southern side of the airfield, beginning their attack, which continued until 14 September. The Japanese failed to retake the airfield. Had they been able to hold on, they could have turned their firepower on to the airfield, closing the American air base. They lost 800 men, and the Americans lost 104, with 278 wounded. War historian Michael Smith's assessment is that the Japanese could have won the battle and had sufficient reserve troops to hold the airfield. The Americans were lucky. They had superior firepower, although they did not have the troop numbers to match the Japanese. Kawaguchi's men literally limped off, carrying their wounded, into the Mataniko Valley to recuperate. Starving and dejected, they then moved west to Kakabona, which they reached on 19 September.[45]

---

43 ibid., 82–109.
44 ibid., 110–18.
45 ibid., 161–91.

At this stage, the US Marines received 4,262 reinforcements, which enabled them to hold their positions.[46] On 16 September, the 3rd Battalion 2nd Marine Regiment arrived on Guadalcanal from Tulagi, and two days later the 1st Marine Division was joined by the 3rd Infantry Battalion 7th Marine Regiment. In October, the 164th Infantry Regiment of the Army's American Division landed on Guadalcanal—the first major army unit to join the marines. Some of the marine units departed. This increase in troop numbers enabled the Americans to complete their defensive perimeter and to mount decisive attacks. There was constant heavy fighting along the beaches and in the foothills, and Japanese aircraft and ships prevented the Americans from landing cargo. The Americans' supplies of aviation fuel were running critically low.

The Japanese were shattered by their September failure at Bloody Ridge. Although they outnumbered the Americans two to one, they had been defeated. Next, the Japanese landed 4,000 men and a company of tanks (a dozen) at Tassafaronga on the north-west coast, intending to force their way across the sandbar at the mouth of the Mataniko and east to Henderson. Although an advance headquarters was established at Kakabona on 6 October, access by the main group of reinforcements waiting in the Shortland Islands was slowed by an American blockade. Lieutenant General Masao Muruyama, commander of the 2nd Division, replaced Major General Kawaguchi. In the early morning of 14 October, two Japanese battleships shelled Henderson Airfield, closing the runway, which enabled the Japanese to land reinforcements. The Americans managed to make the airfield operational again by the next day. On 23 October, the Japanese infantry attacked again, under cover of heavy artillery fire, with troops and tanks crossing the sandbars at the mouth of the Mataniko. The next day, the Japanese circled east from inland, crossed the Lungga River, and moved towards the airfield. This second Battle of the Mataniko ended on 27 October. The Japanese outperformed the Americans, who were defeated. Both sides were battered, with men dead, wounded, and traumatised.

Another naval battle occurred on 26 and 27 October, close to the Santa Cruz Islands. American and Japanese fleets launched air strikes against each other. The Japanese fleet was bigger, with two large and two light aircraft carriers. The American fleet included two large aircraft carriers,

---

46   Mason 2004: 33.

the USS *Hornet* and USS *Enterprise*. American losses were substantial. Although the lengthy land battle continued, by 29 October, the dishevelled Japanese 17th Army retreated west to Kakabona and the Shoji Butai (the 230th Infantry Regiment) withdrew east to Koli Point. The Americans had won the battle and were able to hold their ground, with Japanese losses estimated at 2,000 men.[47] In early November, the Americans attacked the Japanese again, pushing them west from Kakabona to Poha River. More Japanese landed at Metapono River (west of Koli Point; Map 2.2) in early November. They were attacked by the US Raider Battalion, with the battle fought through to the end of the month.[48] The area between the Mataniko River and White River was a devastated battlefield. Wrecked Japanese tanks were scattered about the mouth of the Mataniko, which the Americans called 'the river of death'.

Up to November, the Japanese had landed around 36,000 troops on Guadalcanal, against 44,000 American troops. The figures are a little misleading as the Americans were also operating from Tulagi and moving troops back and forth. During November, the Americans' eastern perimeter was extended as far as Koli Point, and their western flank edged slowly beyond the Mataniko. The Japanese used Cape Esperance (Visale) as their resupply base, dropping off cargo and fresh troops at night, and evacuating their wounded. Further Japanese reinforcements were on their way in mid-November: 11 transport and cargo ships escorted by 12 destroyers. Sighted by American aircraft when they were about 240 kilometres north of Guadalcanal, they were bombed throughout the day. Nine transport ships were hit and seven sunk at sea. Only four reached the Guadalcanal coast, under cover of darkness. The American aircraft continued to attack and, by morning, the four remaining transports were all burning on the coast. The Americans estimated that of the 10,000 Japanese troop reinforcements, only 4,000 survived to land. Maps 2.2 and 2.3 show the sites of the wrecks. The Battle of Tassafaronga was fought on 30 November. An American cruiser and destroyer taskforce encountered eight Japanese destroyers midway between Savo Island and Tassafaronga on Guadalcanal. All four American heavy cruisers were critically damaged, and one sank, although a light cruiser and six destroyers escaped damage. The Japanese lost one destroyer. It was a major American defeat.

---

47   Jersey 2008: 248–93.
48   Merillat 2010: 217–27.

The Japanese arrivals on Guadalcanal in November were the last major attempt at reinforcements. From then on, the Japanese continued to fight the Americans in a hard land war, which they slowly lost. The defeat in November left them quieter and on the back foot. Both sides were suffering from lack of supplies, and exhaustion. Their clothes were in tatters, boots were constantly wet, and socks rotted. Accounts written after the events are often too sanitised. Herbert Merillat, who was directly involved, more accurately describes the 'stench of bodies rotting quickly in the sun on a tropical battlefield', the loneliness, and the fear of 'battle-hardened veterans barely out of their teens'.[49]

This is when phase two of the Guadalcanal campaign began. The Japanese had difficulties maintaining their supply chain out of Rabaul, which left them short of ammunition, food, and medical equipment. They realised they could not regain control of the airfield and chose a defensive strategy to hold on to the area to the west and south (inland). The American supply lines were also under strain. The Japanese infantry was now dug in high on Mt Austen and its ridges and gullies (Map 2.2)—a combination of rocky ground and jungle. They had constructed interlocking well-armed 'pillbox' defences. During December, when Mt Austen was under siege, there were major changes to the American forces. The 1st Marine Division was replaced with the 2nd Marine Division, together with two army units, the 35th Infantry Regiment of the 25th Division, and the 27th Infantry Regiment. Supplies improved and the Solomon Islands Labour Corps was formed to handle the unloading, movement, and storage. At the same time, the Japanese numbers were dwindling. On 18 December, the Americans began to attack the Japanese positions around Mt Austen, locating the most heavily fortified position on 24 December, just west of the summit, which was captured on 3 January 1943. Then they drove the Japanese up the coast, finally capturing Kakabona and reaching Poha River two days later, on 25 January. What they did not know was that on 12 December the Japanese began to consider leaving Guadalcanal and, on 26 December, the Tokyo headquarters took the decision to evacuate.[50]

---

49   ibid., 236, 237.
50   Information provided by Peter Williams.

Plate 2.11 Solomon Islands Labour Corps unloading fuel drums at Lungga Beach, March 1943.
Source: USNARA.

Plate 2.12 Solomon Islands Labour Corps unloading cartons of beer at Camp Guadal, 29 January 1944.
Source: USNARA.

The Americans were uncertain of the Japanese plans and suspected they might land more reinforcements for another attempt on Henderson Airfield. In January, they began to pursue the Japanese to their base at Cape Esperance in the north-west, and around to Beaufort Bay. They also dropped pamphlets advising surrender. The Japanese maintained their weakening hold on Mt Austen, until ordered to withdraw on 14 January 1943. A small rump remained, intending to never surrender. In late January, fighting occurred at the Bonegie and Mamara rivers as the Japanese moved west. The Americans, aware that a Japanese armada was gathering at Rabaul, suspected another attack was brewing, not realising it was for a withdrawal from Guadalcanal.[51] The Naval Battle of Rennell Island occurred on 29 and 30 January. An American cruiser and destroyer taskforce with two escort aircraft carriers was covering troop movements to Guadalcanal. The Japanese planes attacked, crippling an American cruiser, which was sunk by torpedoes while under tow, and two destroyers were damaged.

Fighting on Guadalcanal continued through late January and early February, masking the withdrawal of the remaining 10,660 Japanese on Guadalcanal, who quietly slipped away, and were all gone by 8 February, retreating to New Georgia, Buin in southern Bougainville, and Rabaul.[52] Although there were still naval and air battles in the Solomons, the land battle for control of Guadalcanal—the turning point of the war in the Pacific—was over. Occasional Japanese air raids on Guadalcanal continued until the middle of 1943.

Solomon Islanders during the war

Annie Kwai's book on Solomon Islanders during the war gives a detailed picture of their involvement, mostly as Scouts and labourers. Her conclusion is:

> Islanders were not bystanders in the war but active participants. They were recruited as guides for military patrols, they infiltrated, observed and reported on the Japanese, they rescued personnel; they were the primary (and often the only) communication link between coastwatchers, they provided the manpower that kept the

---

51   Jersey 2008: 350–83.
52   ibid., 384–401.

logistic side of the campaign moving and they actively engaged in combat in several different units and modes of fighting. These varied contributions significantly aided the Allied victory in the Pacific. Local recollections make it clear that the dangers endured by Solomon Islanders were no less than those faced by foreign troops. Islanders displayed great courage, and many showed great strength and skill in difficult circumstances. Despite the hardships and losses endured, Solomon Islanders overwhelmingly remained true to the Allied cause until the end of the war in 1945.[53]

The intense fighting on and around Guadalcanal involved 100,000 foreign soldiers, sailors, and airmen, and continued for six months on the sea, in the air, and on the land. The Guale could only watch—some of their men conscripted on both sides. Villagers moved inland, trying to stay away from the fighting. By avoiding the Japanese, they seem largely to have escaped the atrocities that occurred in other parts of island Melanesia and on New Guinea, including the sexual exploitation of women and the spread of venereal diseases. The total indigenous population of the BSIP during the war years was around 100,000, about 15,620 of them on Guadalcanal.[54]

Solomon Islanders served as casual labourers for the Japanese and the Allies, as part of the small British Defence Force and the larger Labour Corps, and as South Pacific Scouts attached to a Fijian guerilla company.[55] As soon as they established a footing on Guadalcanal, the Americans began to employ Solomon Islander males to help unload supplies at Lungga. Around 400, mainly from Guadalcanal, were involved early on, under the supervision of district officer turned Coastwatcher Martin Clemens. The Solomon Islands Labour Corps was established by proclamation of the military governor (the rebadged resident commissioner's position) on 30 November 1942. Within two months, there were 1,450 members—1,100 at Lungga and 350 at Tulagi. Recruitment accelerated during December 1942 and January 1943, mainly from Guadalcanal and Malaita. As the war moved north, recruitment extended to the Russell Islands and Isabel. By mid-1944, there were 3,700 members. While most worked unloading supplies at the wharves, a few drove trucks, graders, and bulldozers.[56]

---

53 Kwai 2017: 49.
54 BSIP 1970: Table IC, p. 4.
55 Kwai 2017: 33–35.
56 White et al. 1988b: 128–29; Gegeo 1991; Lawson n.d. [c. 2000s]: 10.

The Solomon Islands Defence Force (SIDF) consisted of 800 men, initially drawn from members or ex-members of the Armed Constabulary. Divided into small groups, they were assigned to American, New Zealand, and Fijian units. They acquitted themselves well and were responsible for killing 350 Japanese and taking 43 as prisoners, for a loss of seven SIDF men within the Solomons. Some of them travelled with American detachments; two, Selo and Leon, are buried at Bitapaka war cemetery outside Kokopo on New Britain.

Annie Kwai has raised questions about the motivations of the loyalty of Solomon Islanders during the war:

> Indigenous wartime involvement was inspired by various factors, some pushing through perceived duty or responsibility and some pulling through attraction. There was a sense of familiarity and obligation toward the longstanding British colonial administration, so despite Japanese propaganda casting themselves as anti-colonial liberators, when Japanese troops invaded the Solomons they were immediately regarded as outsiders and 'enemies'. But the war was also a very new and exciting event that fuelled the curiosity of local men and prompted them to take part. The easy abundance of food in labour camps at Lunga and elsewhere was another draw, and the attraction of paid wages lured men from their villages. There was also a sense of prestige attained from joining ranks with the Allied soldiers and sailors as fellow warriors.
>
> But there were more coercive factors that drove local participation that shouldn't be ignored. Some Coastwatchers imposed harsh punishments upon mere suspicion of any sympathy for or collaboration with Japanese troops ... Punishments imposed by some Coastwatchers included severe beatings [that were] unrealistic for the 'crime' committed. This was done with the intention to instil fear in the minds of locals, in order to deter contact of any sort with Japanese troops.[57]

While this harshness is true, the rules of war applied, and most Coastwatchers were military officers, regardless of their pre-war occupations.

---

57 Putz 2018.

2. TAEM BLONG FAET

Plate 2.13 Solomon Islands Labour Corps unwinding copper wire for the telephone system, Camp Guadal, June 1943.
Source: USNARA.

Plate 2.14 Captain William M. Quiglay, Commander of the Naval Base at Camp Guadal, 22 August 1942, driving the last spike into the 'Guadalcanal–Bougainville–Tokyo Express' railway, which was built in three days by the American Seabees.
He is watched by men from the SIDF. The man on the far right is wearing his sergeant's stripes on a band on his left arm.
Source: USNARA.

Plate 2.15 Major J.J. Mather paying members of the Solomon Islands Labour Corps at Camp Guadal, 28 January 1942, while being filmed for US publicity.
Source: USNARA.

The number of Guale and other Solomon Islanders who died from war causes is unknown but may have been a few thousand. Along the north coast of Guadalcanal, gardens, villages, and ancestral sacred sites were destroyed. Those living near fighting zones were forced to flee inland to areas where they had kinship links, where they often had to subsist on wild foods, just as they would during a natural disaster. The fighting on Guadalcanal ended after six months and, once away from the north coast, the Guale were relatively safe.

There is another aspect of the war that Solomon Islanders may never have realised. Although much has been made of Solomon Islanders' relationships with the American troops, particularly African Americans, and the spirit of camaraderie that developed (which had never occurred with the British), their living quarters were kept segregated from the Americans. Solomon Islanders were seen as malaria-carriers who could increase infection rates among the troops, which coincided with British desires to keep Solomon Islanders 'in their place'. Given that African Americans were also segregated from white troops, and that the British wanted to maintain pre-war authority structures, there were probably multiple reasons for the separation. The result was that, in 1944, Labour Corps camps were moved further away from American camps.[58] The British had great misgivings over the generosity of the Americans—in friendship, working conditions, higher wages, and the way in which soldiers gave out gratuities in cash and kind.

The Labour Corps was created to provide a manual labour force to assist the Allies. It was housed in military-like camps and subject to discipline. Despite lack of safety and deaths suffered during Japanese bombing, most members stayed and were responsible for unloading at the wharves and beaches and transhipping to warehouses. They benefited from American generosity, were amazed by the huge stockpiles of supplies available, and by the friendliness they encountered. They worked and ate, drank soft drink and beer, and smoked tailor-made cigarettes alongside Americans, and talked to them as they had never been able to do with the pre-war British 'masters'. The African-American troops were part of segregated construction battalions, although to Solomon Islanders they appeared to be the equals of the white troops. The Americans played their 1940s music to the Solomon Islanders in the Labour Corps, introducing them to country and western, bluegrass, Tin Pan Alley songs, and tunes from musicals. They also taught them how to jive. The war also introduced the ukulele and the guitar, which eventually led to the string band popular music scene from the 1950s.[59] It was a subversive experience that led to post-war changes and had an influence on the formation of Maasina Rule, the post-war proto-nationalist movement described in the Introduction to this book.[60]

The Solomon Islanders called Americans 'Joe', with the name entering Pijin English in the phrase '*iumi Joe, ia*', which roughly translates as 'we can do this' or 'we can do anything'.[61] It was a favourite phrase of Solomon Mamaloni, the country's first chief minister and second prime minister.

---

58   Mason 2004: 86–89.
59   Webb 2005: 289–90.
60   Akin 2013.
61   Information provided by Christopher Chevalier.

Plate 2.16 A US Marine wearing a Japanese sword and water bottle, and three members of the SIDF, at Camp Guadal on 28 December 1942.
Source: USNARA.

Plate 2.17 Three US Marines and a Seabee sharing a drink with members of the Solomon Islands Labour Corps at Camp Guadalcanal in August 1943.
Source: USNARA.

Plate 2.18 A US Marine and two Solomon Islanders listening to a gramophone. The man on the right is holding a Japanese bayonet.
Source: USNARA.

Plate 2.19 Solomon Islanders taking communion at Camp Guadal, Easter 1943.
Source: USNARA.

The Americans used herbicides to clear large areas of vegetation on the coast that then remained useless until the chemicals lost potency.[62] After the war, there was no financial compensation, although there were benefits. Some of the European residents collected scrap metal for resale, and the local people were also able to help themselves to leftover materials: metal pipes, Marston matting,[63] buildings, roofing iron, tools, other equipment, and food. Such largesse had never been available in pre-war days, and to this extent they did receive compensation indirectly from the Americans, but not from the British. In 1976, I spent three months living in Ambe village in east Fataleka on Malaita with Ishmael Itea and his family in their large house. The roof was galvanised ripple-iron that Itea, a member of the wartime Labour Corps, had salvaged from Honiara and brought back to Malaita. It easily survived the next 30 years.

Judith Bennett provided a thoughtful description of the effect of the war on northern Guadalcanal:

> The war was like an extended cyclone. It came like a fury, causing upheaval. Then the armies departed and only the rusting, abandoned wrecks and Marston matting reminded people of the tumult of battle and the busy routines of the airfields and camps. The forests were stripped in a few places, but natural regeneration soon closed the gaps and covered most of the eroded paths of tractors and trucks. It was only where the forest was not able or not permitted to re-assert itself that cleared areas remain. On Guadalcanal, between the Mataniko river and Kukum and south to Mt Austen, post-war urbanization has meant that the forest is gone.[64]

There is now little sign that Honiara was once a battlefield. Modern travellers land at Honiara International Airport—Henderson Field without realising that a Japanese officer chose the site. They travel along Kukum Highway to the Mataniko River and Point Cruz, little knowing that thousands of men died there. Modern residents of Naha 3 have no idea that after the Battle for Henderson Field in October 1942, Second Lieutenant Mitchell Paige made a desperate stand on the ridges of their suburb against the Japanese after they had killed all other marines in his machine-gun section. His own gun was destroyed, after which he moved

---
62 Mason 2004: 56–59.
63 These strong steel mats measured about 1.8 metres by 0.91 metres, with holes in them. There were flanges on one side and slots on the other to clip into. They were mainly used to surface airfields.
64 Bennett 1987: 127–28.

from gun to gun in a withering solo attack until reinforcements arrived. Next, he led a bayonet charge that drove the Japanese back and stopped them breaking through the American lines. He received a Medal of Honor. And locals and visitors who spend their Sundays swimming at Bonegie, and stop on the way home to buy grilled chicken on the roadside at Kakabona, do not understand that these areas were all battlefields.

Plate 2.20 Guadalcanal women pose with a US Marines recruitment poster in 1944. Very few of the war photographs depict women.
Source: SINM, Bob Archibald Collection.

Camp Guadal

Retaking Tulagi, and Guadalcanal with its airfield, was crucial to the South Pacific theatre of operations under Vice-Admiral Robert L. Ghormley, and ultimately Admiral Nimitz and General MacArthur. The Japanese had intended to make Guadalcanal a major training and equipment base for their operations as far north as Iwo Jima (between Japan and the Mariana Islands) and Okinawa (Japan's southernmost prefecture). The airfield on Guadalcanal was a crucial part of the Japanese strategy.

Rather than try to capture northern Australia, the Japanese attempted to cut the supply line, which would also have weakened the Allied war effort under General MacArthur in the south-west Pacific theatre of operations, which was centred on Australia and New Guinea. In the same way, the five airfields the Americans constructed on Guadalcanal were integral to their strategy. Camp Guadal became a huge air force and army base. Late in the war, some of the airfields could take the four-engine Boeing B-17 bombers. Where earlier the Japanese had the advantage of being able to send bombers south from Rabaul, the Americans could also send their big bombers, each loaded with 1,000 kilograms of bombs, to islands as far north as New Britain.

Plate 2.21 Unloading trucks at the lagoon at the mouth of the Lungga River.
Source: USNARA.

After the Japanese withdrew from Guadalcanal, between mid and late 1943, the Allies managed to retake Isabel and most of Western District (Rendova, New Georgia, Vella Lavella, and Mono), although other large Japanese bases remained in the Shortland Islands and on Bougainville and Buka.⁶⁵ Guadalcanal became a staging base for further operations in the central and northern Solomons, with successive landings made northwards towards the Japanese base at Rabaul. Once the Japanese were removed from around Henderson Airfield, the Americans set up their main base at Lungga, with the huge 1st Marine Division spread over the former Levers plantations.

The Americans rebuilt and extended the original Japanese airfield and, by the end of the war, had built another four substantial airfields and two crash strips east of present-day Honiara. There were also three railway lines: the original temporary narrow-gauge line taken over from the Japanese and used by the Americans to excavate tunnels; the main railway, the 'Guadalcanal–Bougainville–Tokyo Express', connecting Kukum docks to the warehouses; and a short marine railway at Kukum docks. From January 1943, Camp Guadal began to change from a fighting zone to the second-largest base in the South Pacific, through which everything needed to retake Bougainville passed. Roads and railways were extended, and bridges were built over rivers. There were several hospitals, a telephone system, and a local radio station. Three hundred and twenty kilometres of sealed roads were built, with the beachfront arterial road nicknamed the 'Burma Highway'.⁶⁶ Thousands of buildings were erected—none intended to last more than a few years, although a few have survived, such was the quality of the materials and the skill in construction. There were water treatment plants, bakeries, laundries, movie theatres, a newspaper (the *Island Times*), as well as iceworks to keep food supplies chilled, Coca-Cola cold, and ice-cream frozen. There were huge gardens around Camp Guadal to provide fruit and vegetables for the troops. By August 1944, the gardens were producing 600 tons of vegetables a month. Two years later, there were 333 hectares of American food gardens in Solomon Islands. After the Americans departed, these returned to the wild, although they still provided some food. Large amounts of local timber were cut and used. There were six logging operations on the Guadalcanal Plains. Judith Bennett records that almost 255,000 cubic metres of timber was harvested on Guadalcanal during the war years, most of it passing through sawmills at Tenaru and Ilu. Some of the bridges on the Guadalcanal Plains were constructed from large kauri logs imported from New Zealand.⁶⁷

---

65   *BSIP AR* 1951–52: 45–46.
66   *PIM*, September 1943, 6.
67   Mason 2004: 45, 54–56; Bowman 1946: 421–23, 427; Hadlow 2004; Bennett 2000: 122–24.

Solomon Islanders and other personnel constructed a beautiful chapel from local materials, next to a large cemetery, east of the mouth of the Lungga River.[68]

Map 2.2 includes the positions of the five airfields. In November 1942, the expanded Japanese airfield was named Henderson Airfield after US Marine Air Corps Major Lofton R. Henderson, who the previous June had crash-dived his plane on to a Japanese warship in the Battle of Midway—a strategic move that opened the way for the campaign to retake Guadalcanal. The beaches around the mouth of the Lungga River were used as the main area to land supplies, with huge front-opening ships disgorging directly on to the beach. Now, Henderson is the only airfield, although older residents will tell you about Fighter II Airfield at Kukum on the eastern side of Honiara, which is now the site of the golf club and Ranadi industrial estate. The other three have been forgotten. Henderson Airfield was the middle airfield. Fighter I Airfield was further inland, also known as the 'Cow Pasture' from its early swampy days. There was a crash strip inland from Fighter I Airfield, to which damaged aircraft were diverted on their return from missions. Further east along the coast between the Metapona and Naumbu rivers there were another two airfields and a second crash strip, called Koli (after the point) and Carney airfields,[69] built to take long-distance bombers. These two airfields were also known as Bomber II Field (Maps 2.2 and 2.4).[70] They hosted several US Army Air Forces command organisations and fighter squadrons, along with US Navy PBY-4 Catalina squadrons.[71] Henderson and Fighter II were solidly decked with crushed coral, as well as Marston matting, which was also used to cover the other three.

---

68 The building team was supervised by BSIP personnel, assisted by officers and men of the US military, primarily the 1st Platoon 45th QM (GR) Company, 46th Naval Construction Battalion, Mica Engineer Depot, 472nd Engineer Heavy Maintenance Company, and the 362 Engineer Regiment. The chapel was constructed in two months from local materials and dedicated on 12 September 1943, presented to the Americans by Jason, a leader in the Labour Corps. The surrounding cemetery was begun on 12 August 1942. By the time it was decommissioned, it held 3,407 bodies: 3,340 Americans, nine Allied servicemen, and 58 Japanese. After World War II, the American bodies were disinterred and taken back to the United States for burial or cremation. The Anglican and Catholic cathedrals were destroyed during the war, which for some years left the chapel as the largest church in the islands. The chapel was on the west side of what is now Lungga Beach Road. This is partly based on information provided by Martin Hadlow, 22 March 2019.
69 Captain J.V. Carney of the US Navy Civil Engineer Corps was Commanding Officer of Naval Construction Battalion 14 (Seabees). He was killed on 16 December 1942 while flying aboard a Douglas SBD Dauntless dive-bomber.
70 Tedder 2008: 188. Information from Alan Lindley, Adelaide, 30 June 2011.
71 Tedder 2008: 188.

Plate 2.22 Fighter I Airfield in the foreground, Henderson Airfield in the middle, and Fighter II Airfield in the far distance, abutting the coast, 1943.
Guadalcanal, with its five major airfields, became one of the largest clusters of air power in the Pacific.
Source: USNARA.

While the fighting was still at a peak, in late August 1942, Martin Clemens was instructed by Resident Commissioner Marchant to resume his duties as district officer for Guadalcanal. On 3 September, Marchant was flown to Tulagi and Lungga to consult with the American commanders, with the aim of re-establishing civilian government. Marchant returned to Lungga on 12 September, ready to travel to Suva for a 25 September conference with High Commissioner Sir Philip Mitchell on the future of the BSIP administration.[72]

---

72   SINA BSIP F1/1, Military Administration HC Sir Philip F. Mitchell to Secretary of State, and Ambassador to Washington, Sir John Dill, 25 September 1942; Secretary of State to WPHC HC Mitchell, 3 October 1942; Courts (Constitution and Powers) Proclamation 1942.

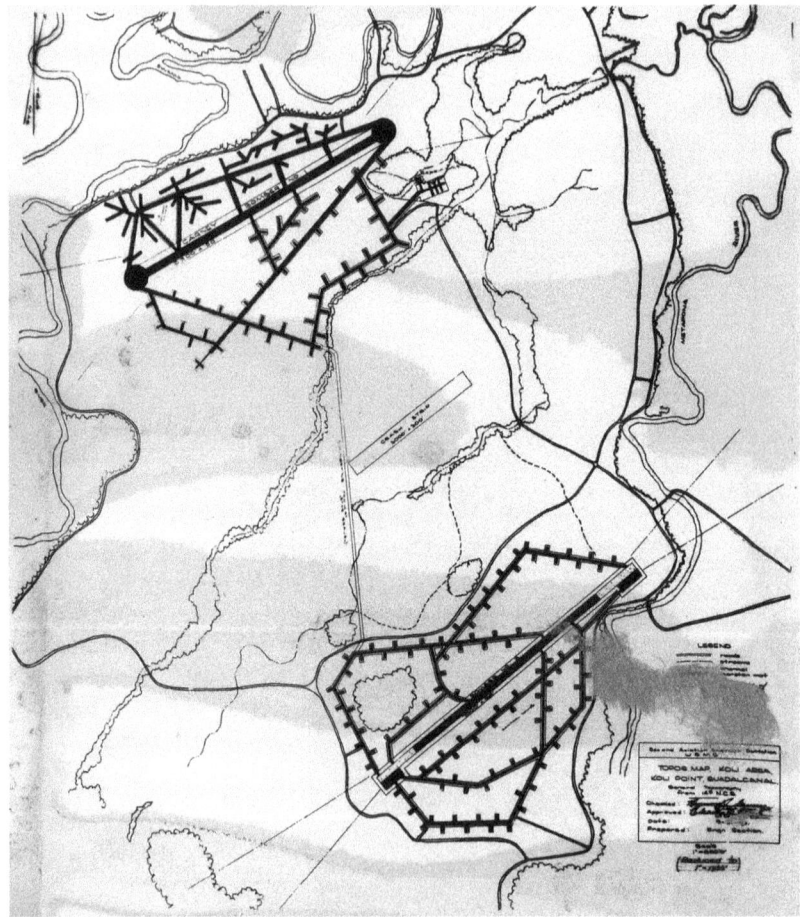

Map 2.4 The Carney and Koli airfield complex was the largest of the American airfields on Guadalcanal.
The two airfields and a crash strip were built inland from Koli Point.
Source: USNARA.

Mitchell refused a recommendation from the Secretary of State for the Colonies that Marchant be made a temporary WPHC special commissioner. Instead, from 5 October, he was given increased legal powers and the higher title of military governor, with the rank of lieutenant colonel. Marchant travelled from Suva to Nouméa and Brisbane, then on to Sydney, where he consulted with Frederick ('Pop') Johnson and Eustace Sandars at the temporary BSIP office. By 3 November, Marchant was back on Guadalcanal, arranging for administration to begin again on Tulagi. A series of new regulations was passed to cope with the different circumstances of the war years.[73] Marchant returned to Lungga on 2 December, this time accompanied by Mitchell, enabling accommodations to be worked out between the Allied forces and the BSIP Government.[74] The Solomon Islands Labour Corps was formed—its officers all pre-war residents, although it was financed and maintained by the Americans.[75] In late 1942, Alexander ('Spearline') Wilson, Charles Bengough, Michael Forster and Dr Nathaniel Critchlow were made WPHC special commissioners to strengthen British authority. Mitchell returned in January 1943, mainly to discuss the Labour Corps, which was subdivided to include a Service Battalion.[76] Marchant, who was often in poor health because of injuries sustained in World War I, had worked hard during the war and endured privations on Malaita. Ill and totally exhausted, he spent several days in Tulagi hospital at the end of March and early April. He left for Suva at the end of April, ordered out on medical grounds. He was replaced with Owen Cyril Noel, previously a district commissioner in Uganda, who arrived on 16 October 1943 and served until 1950. David C.C. Trench acted in the position in the intervening months, and later whenever Noel was absent.[77]

The area from Point Cruz to Kukum Beach became Camp Guadal, a supply and transit base for the Americans. A road extended on both sides, 32 kilometres to the east and 10 kilometres to the west—the first extensive road system in Solomon Islands. The British decision not to rebuild on Tulagi was made late in 1945, and the temporary BSIP headquarters at Camp Guadal began to expand. Honiara had begun.

---

73 SINA BSIP F1/1, HC Mitchell to BSIP RC W.S. Marchant, minute 5 October 1942; BSIP 5/IV/1, Marchant 1942–43, 3, 25 September to 4 November 1942.
74 Clemens 2004: 204, 221.
75 List of members of the Solomon Islands Labour Corps in Laracy and White 1988: 117–37. See also White et al. 1988a.
76 SINA BSIP 1 F43/60, Frederick J. Bentley, acting DO, Malaita District, 4 August 1946, to Secretary to the Government.
77 BSIP 5/IV/1, Marchant 1942–43, 2 February, 27–31 March to 7 April 1943; SINA BSIP F1/1, HC Mitchell to RC W.S. Marchant, telegram, 14 December 1942; University of Queensland, Fryer Memorial Library [hereinafter UQ FML, Wilson Papers], Alexander H. and Jessie Wilson, 1930s–1950s, Papers and photographs of Alexander and Jessie Wilson, including material from their daughter Andrea Gordon Bannatyne, Marchant to A.H. Wilson, 28 April 1943.

Plate 2.23 One of the movie theatres at Camp Guadal during the war years.
Source: USNARA.

Memorials to the dead

Sometimes when I travel around Honiara, I wonder whether the ghosts of the war dead are still there. Tens of thousands of Japanese died on Guadalcanal, and the US Marine Corps air arm shot down 427 Japanese planes, the crews of which were not counted in the numbers of dead on Guadalcanal. The usual figures given are that the Japanese landed 40,000 men on Guadalcanal, 24,000 of whom died, with thousands more dead in sea battles.[78] The true number of Japanese deaths may be many thousands higher. The American statistics are easier to calculate, but even they vary depending on the origin and author. Historian Stanley Jersey suggested that America landed 65,000 Marine Corps, army, navy, and air force personnel on Guadalcanal, and that 6,088 died in combat, around 3,000 were wounded, and many others died from malaria and other tropical diseases.[79] Some were captured and never heard of again. Richard Frank's 1990 book on Guadalcanal is considered the most accurate. Frank says 26,000 Japanese died on land, 3,000 at sea, and 1,200 in the air. Few of the Japanese dead were taken home, although since the war there have been many Japanese expeditions to retrieve skeletons and cremate the remains. There are still 7,000 to 10,000 Japanese dead unaccounted for

---

78   Information from Peter Flahavin, 1 June 2015. See also Innes 2017: 57.
79   Jersey 2008: 402–3.

on Guadalcanal. By Frank's estimates, the Americans lost 2,000 dead on land, 5,000 at sea, and 400 in the air. The total number of wounded and sick would have been many thousands.[80] The number of indigenous inhabitants of Guadalcanal who died during the fighting in 1942 is unclear. The 1941 population estimate of 15,620 had fallen to 13,787 in 1944.[81]

In 1978 in the Mendana Hotel garden bar, I met an American dressed in expensive white clothes, his long sleeves held together with gold-coin cufflinks. He asked me to take his photograph with the same camera he had used as a soldier on Guadalcanal in 1942. He told me he was a Hollywood animal trainer, which I doubted, until he showed me a photo of himself with his arms around a lion and a tiger. He had come a long way since the war, but like all the soldiers had never forgotten the comrades he left behind. Many books have been written. Movies have been made, such as *The Thin Red Line* (1998), a semifictional account of part of the Battle for Guadalcanal. Tourists come to visit the war sites and the memorials.

There are five Honiara war memorials, and a memorial grove of trees at Honiara International Airport—Henderson Field, plus plaques at the airport and at Tenaru, and other small memorial sites. The oldest memorial is the small cenotaph next to Central Police Station, built in 1959 and used for general commemorations. This site now also houses a Japanese memorial originally erected at Bloody Ridge in 1993 for the members of the Japanese 124th Infantry Regiment who fought there. Difficult to access, it was moved to the cenotaph grounds in the 2010s. In June 2017, a RAMSI memorial was added to the cenotaph site to mark the Pacific Islands Forum initiative (2003–17). The second-oldest memorial site, for the Japanese, was constructed at Mt Austen (the Allies' Hill 35) in 1984. The third oldest was built by the Americans at Skyline Ridge, which was dedicated in 1992. Both the American and the Japanese memorials are stark white compounds that look moodily over the battlefields. Allied soldiers, sailors, and airmen from Australia, New Zealand, Fiji, and Tonga, and Solomon Islands labourers, members of the SIDF, and Scouts are commemorated through a monument at Rove, where a 1990 statue of Sir Jacob Vuza looks down vigilantly. On 7 August 2017, the 75th anniversary of the American landing on Guadalcanal was marked by ceremonies and the declaration of Bloody Ridge as a national park.

---

80   Frank 1990: 613–14.
81   BSIP 1970: Table IC, p. 4.

Plate 2.24 Jacob Vouza and members of the SIDF, 25 January 1944.
The presentation plaque reads: 'To the United States Navy with appreciation from the people of the British Solomon Islands, Guadalcanal, 1943.'
Source: SINM, Bob Archibald Album.

Plate 2.25 In 1990, this statue of former policeman, Scout, and war hero Sir Jacob Vouza was added to the war memorial at Rove Police Headquarters.
Photograph from 2016.
Source: Daniel Evans Collection.

In the 2010s, war commemorations in Solomon Islands shifted focus to include remembrance of local participation. Another memorial, 'Pride of Our Nation', specifically for the Coastwatchers and Scouts, was erected at Point Cruz in 2011, in Commonwealth Street adjacent to the local shipping wharves. The sculpture was the work of local artist Frank Haikiu and the memorial was built locally. Since 2020, the magnificent towering Solomon Islands flagpole erected at the end of the street close to the Ports Authority has augmented the memorial and created a special enclave. Solomon Islanders arriving or leaving for the provinces on interisland ships can read about and recognise with pride the efforts of their *wantoks* from *taem blong faet*. There is a sense of local ownership of 'Pride of Our Nation' that is missing from the other memorials. As Annie Kwai suggests:

> Monument building is part of this awareness, and is a significant symbol of unity within a broader contemporary Solomon Islands society. This sense of unity was initiated by our ancestors during the difficult times of the war and grew throughout the journey to political independence. It is one of the pillars of our patriotism to our country. Islanders' war memorials, in this regard, are symbolic of a unified sense of nationhood, and gratitude to those who laid the foundations for Solomon Islands sovereignty.[82]

Theses memorials are sad markers of the enormous waste of human life that created what is now Honiara.

Plate 2.26 The Solomons Scouts and Coastwatchers Memorial in Commonwealth Avenue, Honiara, erected in 2011.
Source: Clive Moore Collection.

---

82 Putz 2018.

3
The new capital

Plate 3.1 The Point Cruz area of Camp Guadal in 1944.
Source: BM, Alexander Wilson Collection.

While some of the pre-war foreign residents of the BSIP re-established themselves after the war and prospered, most of the early planters, traders, missionaries, and government officers never returned. Some had been killed during the war, in the protectorate or in military service elsewhere, or had reached retirement age. Piecemeal between 1944 and 1946, Honiara became the capital of the protectorate. It then slowly changed from being a cast-off American military base to a thriving new town, which has become a major Pacific city.

HONIARA

The American legacy

Between late 1942 and 1945, Camp Guadal developed into the second-largest American military base in the south-west Pacific, exceeded in size only by the US base at Nouméa on New Caledonia. Once the Japanese withdrew from Guadalcanal in February 1943, the island became a major transit and supply base, sustaining operations elsewhere to drive the Japanese back north. The huge logistical operation was centred on Lungga. It spread along the Guadalcanal coast, east on to the plains, and west to Point Cruz and beyond to Rove.

Planning for the rehabilitation and post-war development of the BSIP began on 18 May 1944 at a conference held at Tenaru, attended by High Commissioner Mitchell, the new BSIP Military Governor Owen Noel, and eight administrative officials. Turning Camp Guadal into Honiara was a tempting proposition. The Tulagi enclave was wrecked and returning the BSIP headquarters to the island would have meant total rebuilding. As well, Tulagi was small with no space for expansion. If an airfield was to be constructed there, it would have to be on Ngela Sule Island across the passage—not ideal for a major airfield for a capital. The advantages of Tulagi—except for its safe harbour and excellent wartime wharves—had passed. However, the move from Tulagi to Honiara was vociferously opposed by many pre-war residents, particularly Anglican Bishop Walter Baddeley, aided by the *Pacific Islands Monthly*'s editor R.W. Robson.[1] Eventually, even the doubters had to accept the inevitable. The British military administration ended on 31 March 1946. Until then, the wartime protectorate staff wore khaki uniforms. For some time afterwards, they did the same, minus badges of rank, as few had any civilian clothes.[2]

The Americans were vacating their Guadalcanal military base: a complex of roads, the wharves at Kukum, and a smaller wharf at Point Cruz, hundreds of Quonset huts (huge, curved-roof, galvanised ripple-iron buildings with low eaves and concrete floors),[3] water and power supplies, five major airfields, and several hospitals. It was a readymade town. Lennox Barrow was a district officer in the BSIP between 1942 and 1947 and was stationed in Honiara in September 1944 and for a few other periods over the next few years. He could see the potential:

---

1   *PIM*, February 1946, 22.
2   UQ FML, Wilson Papers, A.H. Wilson to J.A. Wilson, 6 February 1946.
3   The World War I version was called a Nissen hut—the name sometimes carried over to World War II. They were metal prefabricated huts that varied in size, with larger versions produced late in the war.

3. THE NEW CAPITAL

It was not a pleasant place to live. It was dusty and ugly and seemed to be perpetually on the verge of a nervous breakdown, but at the same time you always felt that it might be the beginnings of something. You might scoff at the beautiful town plan of the Honiara of tomorrow which hung in the Resident Commissioner's office, but at times you could not help picturing that ridge behind dotted with neat cheerful little bungalows, that derelict expanse of dusty ground as public gardens with a fountain and a bandstand and a children's playground, that broken down camp around the corner as the commercial quarter with fine shops with plate glass windows, and that bit of reef at the end of Point Cruz as a pier at which your ship could tie up.[4]

The British Government gave little thought to rebuilding its Solomons protectorate, or constructing a new capital, and was churlish in dealing with the Americans, who offered to sell Camp Guadal for US$10.4 million.[5] The WPHC could have purchased any of the American infrastructure at bargain prices. Britain wanted the main hospital, but aside from that, it was only willing to accept American infrastructure if it was free.[6] The British 'line' was that it did not need charity and would not accept any 'lend-lease' arrangements. Commercial companies were less choosy: it is said that when Burns Philp took over the US cigarette supply at Tulagi, the profit repaid all its losses there from the war. In Honiara, the few early British residents were delighted when they were allowed to remove as much as they could carry from the PX (Post Exchange) stores on one vehicle each, piled high. No one worried too much about where leftover goods and buildings ended up, and both expatriates and Solomon Islanders helped themselves. Solomon Islanders fenced homes and pig yards with Marston matting, and used plywood and galvanised ripple-iron for house construction. Food, building materials, weapons, boats, jeeps, motors, and refrigerators found their way to plantations, Honiara houses, and villages on Guadalcanal and other islands.[7]

---

4   PMB 517, G. Lennox Barrow, 1942–47, *An Account of Life in the British Solomon Islands Protectorate Where the Author was a District Officer, 1942–1947*, 8.
5   Bathgate 1977: 5.
6   WPHC 7/II, File F.58/28/1, Military buildings in Honiara, Minute to Resident Commissioner from Secretary, WPHC, 26 July 1945; File F.58/28/13, United States Surplus Heavy Military Equipment other than buildings in BSIP. Reference courtesy of Martin Hadlow; see also Hadlow 2016: 215–16.
7   Lindley 2011a.

Although the Japanese and Americans had clear-felled vegetation, used herbicide on gardens, and destroyed coconut plantations, neither nation felt any obligation to repair the damage it had caused. The Americans had sent mountains of supplies to the Pacific—more than 60 million tons. When the war ended, the United States had huge amounts of surplus supplies still at home, on top of the supplies overseas valued at US$12 billion. For instance, all the materials for the planned invasion of Japan were still stored on Guadalcanal Plains.[8] By 1944, some buildings on Guadalcanal had been disassembled and shipped closer to the current war front. As well, small amounts of the supplies were shipped back to America.[9] The usual policy was to try to sell or, failing that, destroy most of the property, bulldozing equipment into holes in the ground, or dumping it at sea. The Royal New Zealand Air Force (RNZAF), based in the Ngela Group and on Guadalcanal, did the same on a lesser scale. From a government point of view, selling meant they could recoup at least a small part of the costs of the war. Some of the American surplus on Guadalcanal eventually was sold to the British for use in Malaya, Hong Kong, and China, while other materials were donated to the United Nations. Both Australia and New Zealand blocked imports of war surplus materials from New Guinea and Solomon Islands, to stop competition with their reviving domestic production.[10]

The decision to rename Camp Guadal Honiara was made by May 1945. The *Pacific Islands Monthly* used the name that month, although the magazine was uncertain whether it was to be 'Honiara' or 'Harira'.[11] On 22 October 1945, at the first meeting of the BSIP Advisory Council at the end of the war, two sites were considered for the capital. Halavo Bay, the RNZAF No. 6 Flying Boat Squadron base opposite Tulagi on Ngela Sule Island, was a serious contender, although America's Camp Guadal won the day.[12] From December 1945, civilians were allowed to return to the protectorate without a special permit, although shipping services were limited and did not fully resume until 1946.[13]

---

8   Mason 2004: 137, 139.
9   ibid., 140.
10 ibid., 145–49.
11 *PIM*, May 1945, 5.
12 *PIM*, December 1945, 15.
13 *PIM*, January 1946, 7.

3. THE NEW CAPITAL

By early 1946, the Americans had only a token garrison at Honiara, which made disposal operations quite difficult. While the BSIP administration was settling into leaf-thatch houses and flimsy temporary buildings walled with tar paper, just west of Point Cruz, the Americans were busy dismantling or burning substantial buildings, destroying plant and machinery, and folding up tent suburbs. Some things could not be removed. The roads (valued at US$4.6 million) and port facilities (valued at US$1.3 million) were left intact.[14] One account suggests there were more than 102,000 tons of army materials left behind on Guadalcanal: 27,000 tons to be shipped out, 28,000 tons still required by the residual armed forces on the island, 34,000 tons available for sale, and 13,000 tons for which there were no plans for disposal.[15] The Americans did not have it all their own way. In February 1948, the high commissioner asked them to remove Quonset huts from Guadalcanal and the Russell Islands, where they were interfering with efforts to replant coconut plantations. Ten years after the war ended, the BSIP Government was still doing deals, allowing salvage only if surrounding areas were cleaned up as well. W.R. Carpenters & Company was interested in purchasing Quonset huts and, in 1947, offered US$70,000 for 507 steel buildings on Guadalcanal. The Americans had no idea how many huts they had and, when a count was made, there were only 337. Eventually, the BSIP Government assumed control, salvaging and selling off Quonset huts.[16]

No direct compensation was ever paid to companies, villages, or individuals for wartime damages. The Japanese economy was broken, its government unable to pay, although a token amount gained from selling Japanese assets in Asia went into the British Colonial Development and Welfare Fund, which helped finance the creation of the post-war Trade Scheme to re-establish commerce in the BSIP.[17] The Americans estimated that 116,573 trees (mainly coconut palms) were destroyed on Guadalcanal during the war by both Japanese and Allied forces, through bombing, fighting, clearing land for construction, and the making of roads.[18] There was a rumour in 1944 (which was denied) that Levers was to receive US$25 from the Americans for each coconut palm destroyed within its

---

14 Mason 2004: 164.
15 ibid., 167.
16 ibid., 168–69, 173–79.
17 Allan 1990: 113.
18 Information from Martin Hadlow, Brisbane, 22 March 2019, based on USNARA and US Army sources.

Guadalcanal plantations.[19] As soon as the war was over, residents who had lost assets began applying for compensation. After a drawn-out assessment of the huge damages, in 1949, the BSIP Government decided against offering any support. It has been suggested that Britain was unwilling to spend money on rehabilitation while there was the possibility that Solomon Islands could be transferred to the United Nations as a Trust Territory, or to Australia as a territory. Britain could barely repair its damages at home and left far-flung colonies and protectorates to recover by themselves.[20] The small planters were ruined and the big companies like Levers, Carpenters, and Burns Philp wrote off their pre-war assets and never returned to their previous retail and merchant businesses. Although Burns Philp continued to run shipping services, it never reinvested in copra plantations.[21] Levers and Fairymead[22] restored only their best plantations, mainly in the Russells. In 1948, a nine-year deal was signed with the British Ministry of Food to take the entire BSIP copra crop at a low price, with the first exports in 1949, of only 494 tons.[23] The Chinese merchants also suffered large losses, some of them returning to rebuild their business ventures in Honiara's new Chinatown. The only compensation Solomon Islanders received was indirect, through purloining surplus American equipment.

Turning Camp Guadal into 1940s Honiara

Set on a mountainous tropical island just 8 degrees from the Equator, Honiara lies in a partial rain shadow. Compared with the old capital and most areas on neighbouring islands, the climate is drier and the humidity relatively low. Honiara receives about 2 metres of rain a year—the highest falls between December and April—with a temperature range (22°–31°C) that is more diurnal than seasonal. From June to October, the *Ara*, the south-east trade winds, blow from the north-east, providing pleasant sea breezes, although from January to March, the *Komburu*, the reverse north-

---

19   *PIM*, June 1944, 7.
20   *PIM*, October 1946, 12, May 1951, 10.
21   Waters 2016; *PIM*, March 1951, 25. In Papua New Guinea, the Australian Government set up the War Damage Compensation Scheme that reimbursed people for losses. Downs 1980: 40.
22   Fairymead Sugar Company Limited belonged to the Young family, who founded the South Sea Evangelical Mission and Church. Initially, their commercial arm was Malayta Company, which was sold in 1936 to the Fairymead company, their Bundaberg sugar plantation company. They never grew sugar cane in the Solomons.
23   *PIM*, April 1951, 91; Bennett 1987: 303–4.

3. THE NEW CAPITAL

westerly winds, can be warmer. Honiara can be hot and dusty, although it is also capable of being wet and muddy, and periodically cyclones cause floods and damage.

The topography and physical characteristics have largely determined the shape of the city's urban development. Early Honiara had no sheltered anchorage equivalent to that at Tulagi. The city grew in a long thin coastal strip spread over 15 kilometres between White River and Burns Creek (part of the mouth of the Lungga River), extending further inland in the east than the west. Greater Honiara has now extended well past the airport in the east, and past White River in the west, adding another 5 to 10 kilometres to the coastal front. The coastal strip is backed by a series of low coralline limestone ridges, the bases of which vary in width from 4 to less than 1 kilometres. Some of the ridge tops are barely wide enough to allow space for one house and a road. The subsoil contains coral debris. Guadalcanal is subject to minor earth tremors and occasional large earthquakes. The tidal range is about 1.25 metres. Although Honiara is on the north coast and does not face into the western Pacific, which limits its exposure to cross-ocean tsunamis, Savo Island, a dormant volcano, is within sight. Tsunamis and cyclones are always a possibility.

Plate 3.2 The main coastal highway heading towards Point Cruz, in 1944. The Americans called it the 'Burma Highway'.
Source: USNARA.

Plate 3.3 Camp Guadal in about 1945, from Lengakiki Flats to Point Cruz.
The officers' hospital that became the Government Residency is close to the beach in the middle of the photograph.
Source: BM, Alexander Wilson Collection.

Point Cruz is small and provided little protection until the port area was expanded by reclaiming and extending swampy land. It took until the late 1950s and early 1960s to begin to accomplish this, and it is an ongoing project. In the meantime, Tulagi continued to serve as the major port for the protectorate. East of Point Cruz, the Mataniko River is tidal upstream for 1.5 kilometres, flowing down its narrow valley, fed by several tributaries that pass between the many steep-sided ridges, which were once thickly forested.[24] Map 5.1 illustrates the centrality of the Mataniko Valley and its coastal floodplain. Further east around Kukum, the coastal plain widens. West of Point Cruz, White River provides a steep but plentiful water supply. Vegetation is sparse on the ridges and is mainly grass. As the town developed, high-quality houses were built on the tops of the ridges or along the beach, and middle-income and lower-standard housing developed in the valleys and on slopes. The ridges and valleys are

---

24 Heavy rain in April 2014 caused bad floods in Honiara, which were exacerbated by deforestation upstream that had altered the way the river drained at the coast.

suitable for residential zones, and the coastal strip has been used mainly for administrative, commercial, and industrial development, and for playing fields, which double as ceremonial sites.

Some areas of Honiara still bear American names. Stateside is the area around the Ministry of Works workshop on the western side of the bridges over the Mataniko in Mendana Avenue, opposite the roundabout at the city council building. Namba 9 is the colloquial name of the post-war Central Hospital, now the National Referral Hospital. Originally the 9th Casualty Clearing Station for the US forces, it consisted of 18 Quonset huts, some of which were still in use in the 1960s. The modern street plan of coastal Honiara still shows evidence of the design of the original American camp, which provided the airfield and the basic road structure. The east of the town is backed by a neglected national park created in 1954, then truncated in 1973, after it had largely been stripped of timber and turned into gardens for urban Honiarans. The unregulated urban sprawl spread on to unoccupied town council land and surrounding Guadalcanal customary land. How this occurred and the consequences of the development of the city of Honiara are a major subject of the remainder of this book.

Honiara grew slowly during its first five years. There was space for an extensive urban settlement and the area was close to the huge plains nearby to the east, which were suitable for agricultural development. There was also hope of future goldmining at Gold Ridge in the mountains nearby, although E.G. (Ted) Theodore, an Australian politician and mining magnate with investments in Fijian mining, withdrew his interest in 1946. In 1955, Placer Development Limited considered taking up a mining lease, but decided the reward was not sufficient, leaving the field to small-scale miners until the 1990s.[25]

A huge number of buildings left over from the war were converted for multiple uses. Aerial photographs of Honiara in 1945 show the extent of Camp Guadal. It would be another 40 years before the same density of buildings along the coast was re-created. No one thought about asking permission from the Tandai landowners, nor offering further compensation. Most of the land had already been alienated for more than half a century. The Tandai people moved inland and along the coast

---

25   UQ FML, Wilson Papers, 1945; Emberson-Bain 1994: 35, 76, 83, 86, 138, 149; *PIM*, November 1955, 18, March 1956, 25.

to the west on to customary land beyond the reach of the new urban settlement. For further financial compensation, the traditional owners were 'persuaded' to part permanently with their remaining coastal land between the Mataniko River and Rove Creek. No one thought to ask Solomon Islanders whether they would like a new capital perched on a narrow coastal strip backed by dry ridges—all very sunny, exposed, treeless, and infertile—with no harbour.

Plate 3.4 A Queen's Birthday parade in Honiara in the late 1940s.
The Armed Constabulary is under review. The Europeans are probably the acting Resident Commissioner J.D.A. Germond (in white) and Superintendent of Police Frank Moore (in black trousers). They are followed by a civilian and an aide-de-camp. The site could be Stateside, opposite the present-day Guadalcanal City Council building on the west bank of the Mataniko River.
Source: Alan Lindley Collection, in Clive Moore Collection.

Acquiring the land for Honiara

From the Mataniko, west to Rove

The first move by the British administration was to secure the land that is included within the boundaries of present-day Honiara, which was acquired in four main stages. The first three pieces cost £6,971, about $1.5 million in modern Solomon Islands currency.[26]

---

26   I would like to acknowledge the assistance of Michael Ben Walahoula, Secretary of the Tandai Tribal Landowners Association, during September and October 2017 in correcting the spelling of names and refining my interpretation.

The first acquisition was the land from the west side of the Mataniko River, down as far as Rove. On Map 3.1 (from 1947), the western side of Honiara—the land between Mamara plantation and the west bank of the Mataniko River—is clearly marked 'native land', and not part of any plantation. The Tandai land west of Point Cruz begins at Nahona`ara, then includes Raqachaphau (the Solomon Islands Broadcasting Corporation area), Matavale (the Coral Sea Casino area), Parikukutu (St John's area, and Iron Bottom Sound Hotel on the coast), and Rove Creek. Through a 21 January 1947 civil case in the High Commissioner's Court for the Western Pacific, the government forced the landowners to relinquish this land, which was compulsorily acquired and incorporated into Honiara.[27] The landowners were compensated with £4,495—a generous amount compared with what was paid to Levers for the Mataniko to Kukum land, or the money paid for Mamara plantation.

From the Mataniko, east to Kukum

In 1947, Levers held 7,988 hectares between the Mataniko River and Tenaru (as well as more land further east on the plains). The second acquisition for Honiara was 2,274 hectares, the western end of which began on the east bank of the Mataniko River, including Kukum but stopping short of the Honiara Airfield (Fighter II) and Burns Creek. This land was acquired from Levers in February 1947 for £2,174. The Tandai continued to dispute Levers' ownership and in 1964 took a case to court over the land, which they lost (Map 3.2).[28] The area had been devastated by the war and then overtaken by the Americans' construction of Camp Guadal. Levers must have been relieved to receive even this much money. Map 3.1 shows Levers' east Honiara land in 1947 as far out as Tenaru. Map 3.2 shows the parcel of land still under dispute in 1964.

---

27 The defendants were Tsilivi, Kosi, and Lovanea on behalf of the landowners. Interestingly, Baranaba Hoai, the main Tandai chief, was not included. He had been jailed for spurious reasons relating to *vele* (destructive magic) visited on his daughter. This may have been deliberate manipulation and intimidation by the British, which is how the modern Tandai people interpret his imprisonment.
28 WPHC 16/II/165/2/11, Great Britain, High Commission for Western Pacific Islands, Western Pacific Archives, 1875–1976; Indenture of Sale for Kukum–Lungga–Tenaru Plantation, 12 February 1947; Application to Purchase Land in BSIP 1954–59. Copy provided by Joseph Foukona.

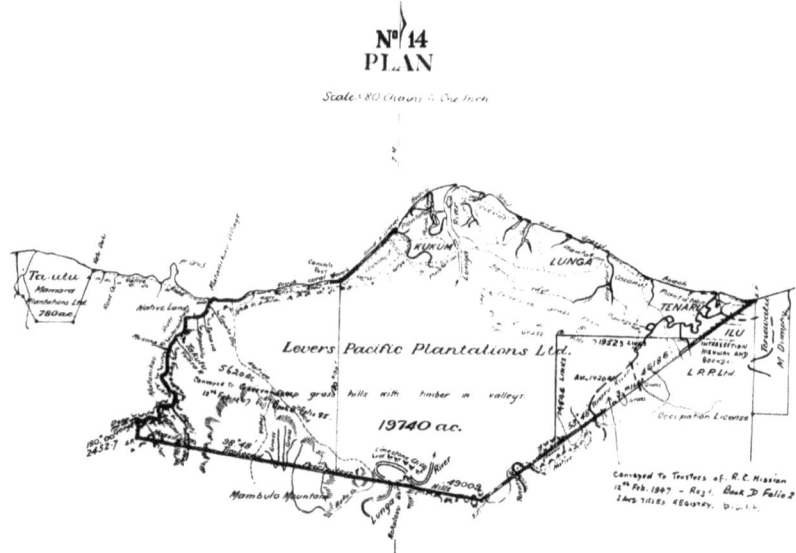

Map 3.1 1947 map of Levers' 8,225 hectares of land, stretching from the east bank of the Mataniko River to Tenaru.

Mamara plantation is also shown, between White and Kohove rivers. The area from the Mataniko to White River is shown as 'native land'. All this area is now included in Greater Honiara.

Source: PMB 1121, Levers Pacific Plantations Pty Ltd/Levers Solomons Ltd, Papers relating to Levers Pacific Plantations Pty Ltd and related companies. Copy provided by Joseph Foukona.

Over several decades, the unfortunate Tandai villagers living around the Mataniko were squeezed out of what became Honiara. Earlier planters and then Levers had turned their land into coconut plantations. Malagili village at the mouth of the Mataniko was threatened and moved, then Horahi village, which replaced it, was destroyed in 1942. The war raged around the Tandai, forcing the villagers to flee inland. The exact area of the 1947 Rove land acquisition is not stated in 2012 Honiara City Council documentation from the BSIP archives. Based on a map comparison with the Tau`utu (Mamara) block, it would appear to have been about 430 hectares. The site of Horahi village at the mouth of the Mataniko was never returned, although the Tandai landowners were allowed to keep small areas for customary use, such as Komulevuha, a canoe reserve on the beach on the west side of Mataniko River—now the Lord Howe (Ontong Java or Luangiua) settlement—and a right-of-way (width unspecified) along the west bank of the Mataniko River to a spring below the site of the present-day US War Memorial, within what is now the Koa Hill settlement (Map 10.1: #25).[29]

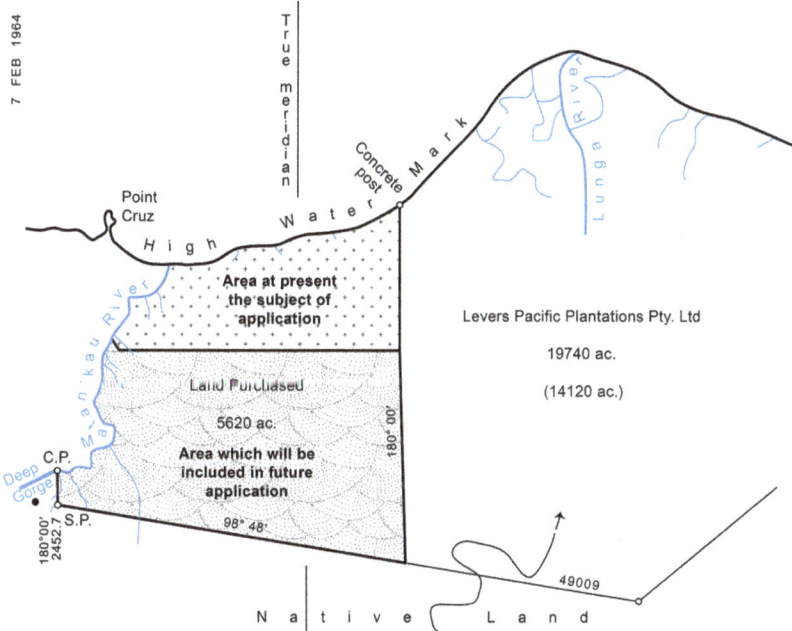

Map 3.2 The area contested by Baranaba Hoai in 1964 on behalf of the Tandai landowners.
Marked from the east side of the mouth of the Mataniko River (approximately 833 hectares centred on the old village site), part of 2,341 hectares extends along the east bank of the river, which Levers and the Tandai both claimed. All spelling and wording are as they appear on the original map.
Source: Case 3 of 1964, High Court of the Western Pacific. Copy provided by Joseph Foukona. Cartography by Vincent Verheyen.

The Americans had built on the Horahi village site on the west side of the Mataniko. In 1947, the BSIP Government negotiated to acquire the land. Agreement was reached that the village be shifted to its present site inland on the banks of the Mataniko River beyond the present-day southern Honiara City boundary.[30] Other Horahi villagers moved to Kakabona and Vatamunu. Unlike other Melanesian urban areas—Port Moresby in Papua

---

29 R.L. Clark, Surveyor, BSIP document in *A Report on the Claim by Landowners that West of Honiara Starting from Rove to the Western Town Boundary Has Not Been Properly Acquired*, in SIG 2012a; Oram 1980: 140.
30 SINA BSIP, Civil Case No. 3 of 1964, High Court of the Western Pacific.

New Guinea, for instance, where the Motu-Koita people still possess considerable areas of land within the city boundary—the customary owners of Honiara were stripped of their land and relocated away from the coast or pushed away to the east and west.[31]

The Tandai people continued to protest the unfair terms of the land acquisition. In 1964, on behalf of himself and the Kakau and Haubata descent groups, Baranaba Hoai claimed ownership of 2,341 hectares— the western third of Levers' land (Map 3.2).[32] As had also occurred in the 1910s and 1920s (Maps 1.3–1.6), they challenged Levers' right to freehold ownership of the land from the east bank of the Mataniko River and along the coast as far as Tanakake. They alleged that £50 had been paid only as compensation for their moving from Malagili to Horahi village, not for the land. The inland section of their claim also extended into the Queen Elizabeth National Park surrounding east Honiara.

Chief Justice G.G. Briggs sat in judgement, basing his decision on the history of land alienation back to 1886. He noted that there were three indigenous groups involved: Simbo, Kakau, and Haubata (Habata). The High Court found in favour of Levers, ruling that the 1923–24 arrangements were still valid, denying any further rights to compensation. The Phillips Lands Commission had been validated by legislation passed in 1924, which made the decisions final. The Chief Justice found no new reliable evidence had been produced to support the 1964 claim.[33]

Rove to White River: Tau`utu

The third acquisition was 320 hectares of land known as Tau`utu (Ta-Utu; Map 3.3), which ran from Rove to the current western boundary of Honiara at White (Tau`utu) River. Purchased from Mamara Plantation Limited, this consisted of two parcels of land that had been sold to Oscar Svensen and Joseph T. d'Oliveyra in July 1911, although their occupation preceded this date (see Chapter 1). Just as it had with the Kukum–Lungga–Tenaru land, the war years turned Mamara plantation into a battle zone. Nothing much survived other than damaged vegetation. The Tau`utu land was sold to the government on 9 March 1948 for £302.

---

31   Golden 1993: 121, 146, 202–3; SINA BSIP, 18/II/5, 18/I/2.
32   SINA BSIP, Civil Case No. 3 of 1964. See also Bellam 1970: 72; *BSIP NS*, 29 February 1964, 4–5.
33   SINA BSIP, Civil Case No. 3 of 1964; Ruthven 1979b: 245; *BSIP NS*, 15 March 1964.

Like Levers, the company must have been happy to receive any payment for the devastated land. Svensen's other plantations were sold to R.C. Symes Proprietary Limited in 1950.

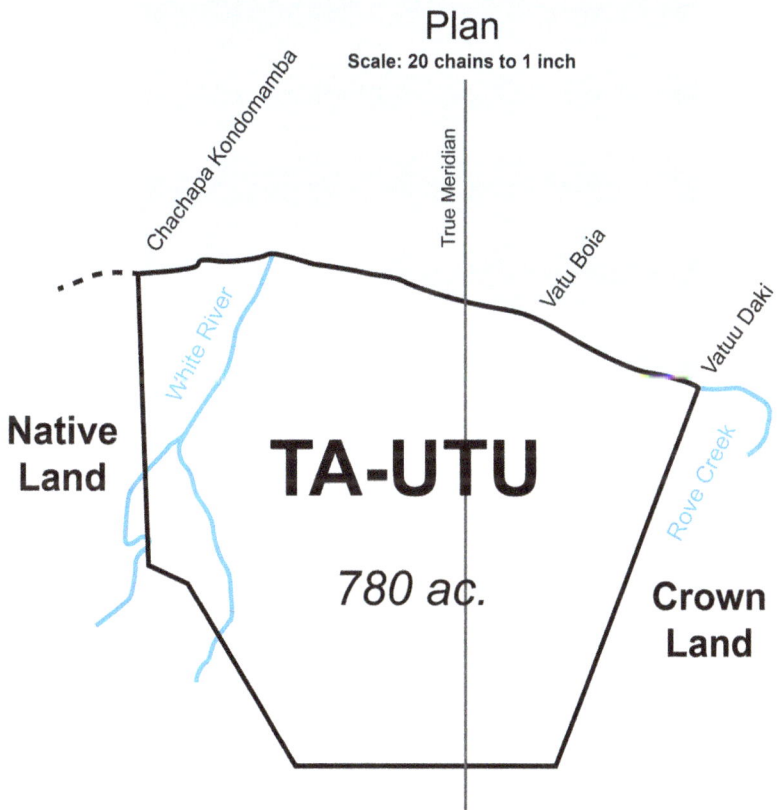

Map 3.3 The land of Mamara Plantation Limited, 9 March 1948, from the coast west of White River, into the headwaters, and east to Vatudaki.
All spelling is as on the original.
Source: SIG (2012a: 25). Cartography by Vincent Verheyen.

Queen Elizabeth National Park

The fourth acquisition came several years later. In 1954, to mark the coronation of the new monarch and to provide nature reserves and recreational areas in the protectorate, the National Park Regulation was passed.[34] Although no details of any parks were included, this enabled

---

34   BSIP 1954.

the formation of Queen Elizabeth National Park on 6,070 hectares of Tandai land at the back of east Honiara, beginning in the headwaters of the Mataniko River, out to Mt Austen, and along the back of Kola`a Ridge. James Tedder, District Commissioner for Central District, was responsible for the negotiations. Tandai memory is that he discussed temporary acquisition but never permanent alienation. They had no understanding of the concept of a national park; it was alien in a nation consisting overwhelmingly of customary land. The ordinance stated that fauna could not be hunted within the park, but made no mention of flora, and there were no rangers or any management plan. It was a very European concept that did not translate well into Solomon Islands ideas of land use, and the Tandai people still dispute the government's right to the land. Insult turned to injury when the national park was taken over by Honiara's growing population, cleared of timber, and used for gardening. In 1973, the national park was reduced to 1,093 hectares and the remainder was added to the Mataniko, Kola`a, Vura, and Panatina wards of Honiara City Council's land (compare Maps 5.1 and 5.2), enabling urban expansion around Kobito and Gilbert Camp.[35] Little is known about this significant land acquisition and whether there was any compensation in 1954, or consultation in 1973.[36]

The old national park is virtually defunct. In 2017, plans were announced for a 1,392-hectare community-sanctioned Barana Nature and Heritage Park with an environmental and resilience centre. The park, expanded to 5,000 hectares of forest area, was formally launched on 27 June 2019. It is in the vicinity of the Queen Elizabeth National Park, on Tandai land in the upper catchment of the Mataniko River. The project is supported by the Tandai and the national government, with assistance from a nature conservation group funded by the German Government.[37]

***

---

35   Tedder 2008: 177; Allan 1989: 55–56; *BSIP NS*, 7 May 1973.
36   Under the subsequent subsidiary legislation, Queen Elizabeth Park was proclaimed as No. 1 of 1973 and gazetted under legal notice 29/1973. It was referred to as Lot 3 of LP83/1, being reduced in size to 1,093 hectares. The *BSIP NS* (7 May 1973) says the national park was reduced to 809 hectares with 5,260 hectares added to the Honiara Town Council boundaries. I have taken the gazetted notice to be correct. Under the Act, there was provision to pay compensation, although it was not mandatory. My thanks to Michael Ben Walahoula, Secretary, Tandai Tribal Landowners Association, Honiara, September 2017, and Jeffrey Moore, former BSIP Commissioner of Lands, Brisbane, 9–12 May 2020.
37   SIG 2019a.

3. THE NEW CAPITAL

Having legally secured the land from White River to Kukum by 1948, then added the land inland to Mt Austen in 1954 (the national park), and extended the area along the coast east as far as Burns Creek in 1964,[38] the government had control of almost all the area included within the boundaries of the modern Honiara City Council. Despite their early lack of interest, the British did purchase some of the American wartime equipment through the Foreign Liquidation Commission, including the waterpipe supply, generators, electric light and refrigeration plants, and bulldozers.

What eventually became the Government Secretariat (now the site of the cenotaph and Central Police Station in Mendana Avenue) began operating in plywood and tar-paper huts. Quonset huts of all sizes were scattered about in plentiful supply, as was Marston matting. A few of the Quonset huts remain—reminders of Honiara's wartime beginnings. Thousands of Marston mats were used to create firm surfaces for planes to land on; they were also used on roads in boggy areas. The Americans decided there was too much work involved in removing the many hectares of Marston matting covering the airfields. Two businesses in particular, R.C. Symes and Ken Hay's K.H. Dalrymple Hay Proprietary Limited, made substantial fortunes from onselling this scrap steel, as well as salvaging copper, brass, and lead.[39] There was also money to be made in selling the many wrecks along the coast for scrap metal—some to Japanese companies between 1958 and 1960.

Coronation Gardens (the present National Museum enclave) was named on 4 July 1953, a few days after the coronation of Queen Elizabeth II. It had been an American vegetable garden on the banks of the small Cruz Creek, which still flows down its now polluted path between the National Museum and Central Police Station. There were other vegetable gardens near the end of Henderson Airfield and another area at Ilu.[40] A small American force remained near Henderson Airfield until October 1949, surrounded by empty army huts, defunct open-air picture theatres, and basketball courts from the war years. The remaining Americans were charged with selling off as much wartime equipment as they could, and continued to provide antimalaria spraying of mosquitoes around Honiara.

---

38   *BSIP NS*, 29 February 1964, 6.
39   Ken Hay's full name was Kenneth H. Dalrymple-Hay. *PIM*, May 1953, 18; Lawson n.d. [c. 2000s]: 17–18.
40   Tedder 1966: 36; *BSIP NS*, 31 March 1969.

They left in early 1950.[41] Rusted landing barges dotted the shoreline, ammunition dumps in big underground 'igloos' were built into the foothills, and unexploded mortar bombs were a constant problem. The first automobiles were left-hand-drive American jeeps and trucks—to such an extent that it was 1947 before there were enough British right-hand-drive cars to make the change to driving on the left of the roads. During and after the war, land inland from Hell's Point was used as a storage area for unexploded ordnance, which was placed there by the Americans and later by Australian bomb-disposal units. Solomon Islanders entered this 'off-limits' area to collect brass shells casings and to remove the explosive materials to use to dynamite fish—a dangerous pastime.[42]

Honiara in the 1940s was in transition from an American military base to a British colonial town. The last word on this early period goes to two famous individuals, James A. Michener and Sir Fred Osifelo. Osifelo, from Baegu, Malaita, joined the public service in Honiara at age 17 in 1945 as an orderly—an office messenger.[43] Writing in the 1980s, he remembered his uniform as 'a dark grey sulu with a red sash and a black canvas belt with a silver buckle':

> Honiara in April 1945 was very small. Its eastern boundary was the present road which goes down to the Yacht Club, between Solomon Motors and Quan Hong's Store on Mendana Avenue. Its western boundary was between the Prime Minister's Office and Government House's western boundary. The Secretariat Office at that time was situated in the area now known as Mendana Garden where the Cenotaph now stands. It was T-shaped, its eastern wing occupied wholly by the Treasury. The western wing consisted of the Labour Office and Medical Office. The northern wing consisted of the Resident Commissioner's Office and office of the Secretary to the Government, Chief Clerk, typist and general office occupied by Walter Togonu and Walter Kanaf, two local clerks from Reef Islands.[44]

He remembered some of the difficulties he had with communicating in Solomons Pijin, with some very funny results until he became fluent. Housed at Mataniko No. 3 'Labour Line' (workers' barracks) at Vara Creek (Map 8.1), he remembered his weekly rations from the Government Trade

---

41 *BSIP NS*, 31 January 1969; *BSIP AR* 1949–50.
42 Lindley 2013: attachment to Map 4.
43 Moore 2013c: entry on Osifelo.
44 Osifelo 1985: 26.

Scheme store as 7 pounds (3 kilograms) of rice, 1 pound (500 grams) of sugar, three tins of Ox & Palm corned beef, a quarter-pound (100 grams) of tea, 21 hard navy biscuits, three sticks of tobacco, and 3 inches (7.6 centimetres) of washing soap.[45]

American novelist James A. Michener returned to Guadalcanal in 1948, retracing his wartime steps. He could see the future possibilities for Honiara:

> Leave Henderson Field and go west along Highway 50 past Fighter One [he means Fighter II], past Kukum Docks, across the Matanikau, and on to Point Cruz, where the ammunition dump was [he means Hell's Point]. At the base of Point Cruz, which forms the meagre semblance of a harbour, Honiara has been built. The word means 'where the wind blows', which, as the planter observed 'is so perfect a name for a capital that any comment from me would be superfluous.'
>
> Honiara will be a better town than Tulagi ever was. King-size Quonsets have been moved in for barracks, and grass shacks have been tucked away under broad trees to serve temporarily as government offices. Behind the town is a high ridge where lovely homes are being built in breezes that keep them permanently cool and mosquito-proof.[46]

UXBs: Cleaning up munitions dumps and unexploded bombs

The site of Honiara had been a huge battleground for the Japanese and Allied forces. Unexploded bombs (UXBs) and lesser munitions were everywhere. The Americans used land on the east bank of Alligator Creek between Henderson and Fighter I airfields to store unwanted munitions (as it was opposite Hell's Point on the coast, the area was also known by this name). When Michener visited Honiara after the war, road graders were still uncovering unexploded shells in the main street, many of which he said were quietly covered over again. He claimed to have asked an official what would happen if one detonated and was told, with typically understated British humour, 'There'd be a tremendous bang, I should think'.[47]

---

45 ibid., 25–28.
46 Michener 1951: 131.
47 ibid., 133.

A huge uncontrolled explosion at Hell's Point in November 1943 proved the potential for extreme damage. Once the fighting ended, the Japanese were gone and the Allied forces in the Solomons—the United States, Britain, and New Zealand—felt no particular need to clean up war debris, let alone unexploded munitions. Dealing with Quonset huts and rusting hulks, tanks, and jeeps was a minor issue by comparison. There were four main aspects to the problem: unexploded bombs and shells; small arms such as hand grenades, and bullets; munitions stockpiles; and the deterioration of all of them in the tropical climate. The bulk of the American forces left so quickly there was little time to dispose of ordnance. The situation was not helped when local villagers and plantation staff used fires to clear large areas of land. The BSIP officials did not have the skills to remove the UXBs. If munitions were found, all they could do was close an area and make a report.

In 1948, the Australian Army's Bomb Disposal Section was called in and was still at work in the early 1950s collecting and disposing of unexploded shells.[48] It was daunting work and early reports show the task to have been almost unending. On one day in 1948, the team disposed of more than 200 hand grenades, 100 mortar rounds, a dozen 4-inch shells, 234 small-calibre shells, and rifle ammunition.[49] In April 1949, the 2nd Australian Bomb Disposal Section arrived for the long haul. The humid conditions over several years had made everything more precarious. In the 1940s and 1950s, Hell's Point was a dangerous place. Some of the bombs were still fused and live. There were also chemical weapons—prepared for use in Japan, then 'shelved' and stored on Guadalcanal. The Hell's Point munitions dump was close to Kukum Airfield, a mission, and schools, and far too close to Honiara.

Large uncontrolled explosions occurred in February 1950, which led to the evacuation of eastern parts of Honiara and St Joseph's Catholic Mission at Tenaru. Another bomb emergency occurred in June the next year. The precautionary arrangements were typical of the colonial segregation of the time: European women and children were told to shelter at Rove Police Depot (in comfort and far away), 'natives' were told to shelter in Cruz Creek (next to the present museum, and at a midrange distance), and the Chinese were instructed to shelter down on the banks of the Mataniko River (next to Chinatown, closest to Hell's Point). Each area was reasonably safe, but the races were not to mix. Smaller deadly

---

48 Lindley 2014: 17.
49 Mason 2004: 188.

accidents occurred regularly, and several bomb-disposal labourers were killed or maimed. The 1950–51 incidents reminded everyone just how dangerous Hell's Point was. If the whole dump had exploded, it certainly could have affected the nearby mission and airfields. The team of workers had stacked 75,000 shells there, with no end in sight. As well, after the horrific deaths, labourers were, understandably, reticent to work at Hell's Point.[50] Clearing Hell's Point was beyond the ability of the government, and there were many more areas in the protectorate to clear, including Visale, Koli Point, Tulagi, Munda, and the Shortland Islands.

In the early 1950s, Hell's Point still contained 3,000 to 4,000 tons of ammunition.[51] There was debate over the best way to proceed. One suggestion was to fence off Hell's Point and erect a blast wall to create an exclusion zone to contain any explosions; another was to continue the existing policy of exploding ordnance or dumping it at sea. The costs were prohibitive either way, and the trucks and vessels used were old and unreliable. Attention was focused on Hell's Point in late 1952 when the newly arrived high commissioner toured the site. The plan became to aim each week to move 100 tons of ammunition down to the beach, to be dumped at sea. In the end, the main stock was cleared, and the area was closed off through a proclamation issued on 22 October 1953, with a 1.8-kilometre danger zone declared around the dump.

Bombs continued to be found around Honiara and in other areas of the protectorate. In the first few years of the British Solomon Islands Training College at Kukum, more than 400 shells were destroyed after being uncovered in the grounds. The largest bomb found after the war was exploded in 1968: a 227-kilogram device detonated at Henderson Airfield, which was thought to have been dropped by the Japanese.[52] Later the same year, a man was killed when a bomb exploded in a fire at Kukum and, in 1970, several 75 mm shells, two mortar bombs, and three hand grenades were found in a valley at Kola`a Ridge.[53] In the mid-1970s, the Australian Government trained a Solomon Islands Police Force bomb-disposal squad. Australian ordnance disposal experts are still involved in training Solomon Islanders to continue the task, and Hell's Point remains fenced off. The United States has seldom participated in the clean-up operations. In 1991, a squad arrived in Honiara after President George H.W. Bush promised to destroy all American chemical weapons.

---

50 ibid., 182–97.
51 ibid., 208.
52 *BSIP NS*, 14 February 1968.
53 ibid., 15 May 1968, 15 September 1970.

With much fanfare, they took away one hundred 155 mm artillery shells, each filled with 5.5 kilograms of mustard gas. The Japanese have totally ignored the issue.[54]

There can be no doubt that many pieces of ordnance are still buried around Honiara and, after 75 years, they must be in poor condition. In February 2018, a 135 mm shell was located near White River market—probably fired from a ship during the war. The Police Explosive Ordnance Disposal Unit transported the shell to Hell's Point for destruction. Then, in September 2020, two expatriate ordnance disposal experts were killed when a bomb exploded in their apartment at Tasahe Ridge in west Honiara. Other munitions were found to be stored close by, raising many questions. In May 2021, a US 105 mm bomb exploded at Lengakiki after being inadvertently uncovered while a group was preparing a site for a stone oven, killing one man, and injuring three others.[55] The Japanese and US governments must take responsibility for removing their decaying ordnance from around Honiara and other sites.

Creating urban and communication services

Honiara began, slowly, to develop a full range of urban services. Once Burns, Philp & Company resumed regular shipping services in 1948; the *Morinda*, *Muliama*, or *Malaita* turned up every few weeks from Sydney and, beginning the next year, Bank Line ships arrived four times a year to export the protectorate's copra to Britain. Air transport was easy to establish as Honiara was unusually well served by airfields. Kukum (Fighter II) Airfield became Honiara's main civilian airfield between 1945 and 1957, although its position was too confined to meet international civil aviation standards. However, problems with access across the Lungga River between Henderson Airfield and Honiara kept the use of that airfield patchy until it was reopened permanently on 5 December 1960. Until the late 1960s, Kukum Airfield was brought back into service whenever the Lungga River was impassable, or while Henderson Airfield was being expanded. Honiara Golf Club was established alongside Kukum Airfield in 1957, with the original airport building converted into the club's recreation building.[56]

---

54 Mason 2004: 182–223.
55 Sei 2018; Wickham and Eremae 2020; Mamu 2021.
56 *PIM*, November 1955, 23; Tedder 2008: 188; Information from Alan Lindley, Adelaide, 30 June 2011.

Plate 3.5 The American bridge over the Lungga River on the Honiara side of Henderson Airfield in October 1945.
The area was surrounded by American military facilities. In 1948, the Seventh-day Adventists used these huts and facilities to begin their Betikama Primary School.
Source: USNARA.

In 1946, Qantas Empire Airways investigated extending its Territory of Papua and New Guinea 'Bird of Paradise' service to Solomon Islands via New Britain and Bougainville.[57] This route opened two years later, subcontracted to Trans Australia Airlines (TAA). Flights began in Sydney, then flew via Brisbane and Port Moresby, Lae, Rabaul, Bougainville, Barakoma (on Vella Lavella), Levers' private airstrip at Yandina in the Russell Islands, and on to Honiara. TAA used DC-4s from Sydney to Port Moresby and DC-3s onwards to Honiara. In June the next year, Qantas also subcontracted to Trans Oceanic Airways to begin regular monthly Catalina seaplane charter services out of Sydney to New Caledonia, the New Hebrides, and Tulagi.[58] Alan Lindley, who arrived in Honiara in 1952, remembered one bizarre detail: there was no radio communication at Kukum or Henderson airfields before 1958. To create a radio link, the local radio station used its frequency to play *Slowcoach* by Pee Wee King and his Golden West Cowboys on its transmitter to enable the planes to home in on the radio signal using their automatic direction finder.[59]

---

57   *PIM*, December 1946, 7.
58   ibid., December 1947, 26, June 1948, 16, May 1952, inside front cover; *BSIP AR* 1949–50: 5, 1953–54: 41; Tedder 2008: 15.
59   Information from Alan Lindley, Adelaide, 30 June 2011 and 26 October 2015. My investigations suggest the use of the song is possible, not for the music but for the regular radiowave pattern.

Plate 3.6 Quonset huts of all sizes were everywhere—the most useful remnant of the war years.
This one was still in use at Solomon Islands National University in 2017.
Source: Martin Hadlow Collection.

Plate 3.7 In 1951, the Commonwealth Bank of Australia began operations in Honiara, housed in a Quonset hut.
The new bank was built alongside in the early 1960s.
Source: Brenda Cantwell Collection, in Clive Moore Collection.

In 1945, once the decision was made to shift the capital to Honiara, a town plan was prepared, and £250,000 requested from the Western Pacific High Commissioner—only one-fifth of which was allocated.[60] It took until well after 1953—the year the WPHC headquarters shifted from Suva to Honiara—for extra attention to be given to shaping the development of Honiara. More housing was needed for the increased number of public servants, and temporary government buildings had to be improved or replaced. The Americans left behind a rudimentary but extensive road system, although there were no permanent bridges over the rivers. In late 1947, five Bailey bridges were imported at a cost of £24,000 to replace dilapidated timber bridges on Guadalcanal. The first Bailey bridge erected was over the Mataniko River at Chinatown, which was completed in June 1950, replacing an American pontoon bridge.[61] The Chinatown Bailey bridge lasted until floods in 2014, after which the original structure was replaced—with a new Bailey bridge.

In 1948–49, Honiara's population consisted of about 80 Europeans (including 23 women and 18 children), 100 Chinese, living mainly in Chinatown, the workers in Fijian Quarter, Solomon Island labourers, and Maasina Rule prisoners. The initial labour supply for building Honiara came from rotated batches of 60 Fijian and Indo-Fijian workers from Suva, who were housed in the area still known as Fijian Quarter near Chinatown. There were also Solomon Islanders originally from the Labour Corps and the Defence Corps who remained after these units were disbanded. Although the exact number is unknown, there were thousands of Maasina Rule prisoners in Honiara between 1946 and 1952. At any one time, the number swung between 100 and 1,000. Some of the trials were held in Honiara; the town was used for the transit of prisoners being moved to Western District and, when the jails on Malaita overflowed, prisoners were sent to Honiara. These prisoners included the head chiefs and their co-defendants. They were kept isolated in a low-security lock-up, which enabled other Malaitans in Honiara to talk to them through the fence.[62] Until 1948, Maasina Rule caused a severe labour shortage in Honiara because the movement's policy was to not allow its supporters to work as labourers. The labour supply improved in 1949 and, by 1950, was adequate.

---

60   *BSIP NS*, 31 May 1969.
61   A Bailey bridge is a portable, prefabricated truss bridge developed by the British during World War II. They have the advantage of not requiring heavy equipment in construction. *PIM*, February 1948, 24; *BSIP AR* 1953–54: 8.
62   According to Jonathan Fifi`i, they were held somewhere near the present-day National Archives. Akin 2013: 283, 427 fn.64; Information from David Akin, 12 September 2017.

Central Honiara was fully surveyed in 1949, 24 new houses had been built for European residents, and a 'Labour Line' had been constructed at Kukum, which was extended further in the early 1960s. As the supply of sago palm leaves for the thatching of roofs and walls was insufficient, the government often had to fall back on timber and iron for house-building and relied extensively on second-hand American buildings and materials. By 1954, Honiara had a population of 1,400, about 150 of whom were of European origin.[63]

After the war, due to a shortage of wholesale and retail shops, the BSIP Government began the British Solomon Islands Trade Scheme, which was based at a wharf and Quonset hut on the site of Point Cruz Yacht Club. The Quonset hut was later moved to Mendana Avenue beside the cinema. Known as the Government Trade Scheme, it was envisaged as a temporary replacement for the large retail businesses, and organised the sale of copra. With plantations ruined, no compensation provided, and little chance of quick regeneration, Burns Philp and Carpenters had no reason to re-establish their retail and merchant businesses. Although Burns Philp eventually resumed its shipping service between Australia and the Solomons, it never returned to its pre-war dominance. Air transport took away its old mail-run subsidies, copra was marketed directly to the Ministry of Food in Britain, and there were other shipping competitors. Directly after the war, the Government Trade Scheme was managed by Bob Firth, and then by Jack Lotze (the pre-war manager of Carpenters on Tulagi). He was replaced in 1947 with Eric. V. Lawson, who had been merchandise manager for Carpenters in Suva.[64] A second branch, with its own wharf, was opened in Gizo, in two Quonset huts also used for storing copra. In the 1950s, the Government Trade Scheme was broken up. Its wharves were taken over by the Ports Authority, which was formed in 1956. Copra buying passed to the Copra Board, and European and Chinese companies began to arrange their own overseas buying of merchandise. The Trade Scheme became BSIP Trading Corporation Limited on 29 September 1955,[65] before a new regulation in July 1960 allowed the corporation to be sold to private industry.

---

63   *BSIP AR* 1949–50: 26, 1972: 2; Tudor 1953b: 75.
64   Eric V. Lawson became a prominent businessman. After running the Government Trade Scheme in Honiara, he became manager of the Fairymead Sugar Company (which owned coconut plantations) and secretary-manager of the Copra Board. Lawson was a member of the Legislative Council from 1959 to 1966. In 1971, he sold his business to C. Sullivan (Export) Pty Ltd. 'Honiara just a dump says "EV"', *SND*, 11 July 1975.
65   *PIM*, November 1955, 93.

Plate 3.8 The BSIP Trading Corporation Limited was housed in a large Quonset hut in Mendana Avenue, 1960s.
Source: Brenda Cantwell Collection, in Clive Moore Collection.

Plate 3.9 The staff of the BSIP Trading Corporation Limited, 1960s.
Source: Brenda Cantwell Collection, in Clive Moore Collection.

The government could not persuade any of the large pre-war companies to take over its Trade Scheme. Then, in March 1962, the corporation, excluding the plantations it had acquired, was sold to a partnership between Mitsui & Company and D.J. Gubbay & Company (New Hebrides) Proprietary Limited—the latter also operating the South Pacific Fishing Company, based on Santo, New Hebrides. The corporation finally closed its doors on 29 June 1962, though its assets were not fully liquidated until 1966. The new company maintained the existing Honiara and Gizo branches and opened another in Auki on Malaita. It sold basic items such as tinned foods, rice, and clothing, collected and stored copra for shipping, and acted as an agent for a long list of international companies.[66] The Gubbay store gradually became less dominant as other commercial companies cut into their market during the 1960s.

The pre-war system of transferring money via bank agencies at the Trade Scheme and the post office continued. Although there was estimated to be A£227,020 in circulation, there were no banks in the protectorate directly after the war. Commercial normality returned in 1951 when Australia's Commonwealth Bank opened a Honiara branch and soon after established agencies in Auki, Gizo, Kirakira, Lata, and Yandina.[67] The bank introduced chequebooks, which ended the practice of expatriates operating accounts at shops, the one club, and the one hotel.

The cost of living for expatriates was high and supplies were limited.[68] Shortages often occurred in the interim between the arrival of Burns Philps' ships. The cost of meat was exorbitant, although attempts at breeding local cattle were proceeding at nearby Ilu experimental farm, and efforts were made to market fish cheaply. An Agriculture Department farm opened at Kukum in 1950, experimenting with alternative crops to coconuts: rice, maize, root crops, sunflowers, sorghum, sesame, soybeans, and groundnuts.[69]

---

66 Bennett 1987: 303–4; *PIM*, April 1953, 12. D.J. Gubbay & Company were agents for many companies. *BSIP NS*, 31 July 1960, December 1961, 31 March 1962, 15 April 1962, 30 May 1964; Close 2011: 112, 152, 169, 171, 173, 179.
67 *BSIP NS*, 31 January 1969, 7 May 1966, 31 March 1969; *PIM*, July 1951, 35; *BSIP AR* 1951–52: 15; Bennett 1987: 257.
68 Tudor (1953b: 70) provides domestic commodity prices.
69 *BSIP AR* 1949–50: 22.

Several prominent pre-war businessmen and public servants re-established themselves in 1940s Honiara. The only early social centre (for Europeans) was the Guadalcanal Club on the west Honiara beachfront, which was built by the government to replace the Tulagi Club from before the war. The first leaf-clad structure burnt down in May 1949; it was partially rebuilt before a cyclone blew it down. The third structure was about 500 metres from the first, made from two Quonset huts firmly anchored with concrete-filled iron pillars, with a hardwood floor and wide verandahs.[70] In its absence, the Trade Scheme built a small, primitive hotel, the Woodford, using wartime and new materials, on the site of the current Kitano Mendana Hotel. This was purchased in 1949 by Ken Hay, a pre-war plantation manager and former Coastwatcher. Until the Guadalcanal Club was rebuilt in 1951, Hay's hotel held the only liquor licence in Honiara. It accommodated air crews, travelling salesmen, planters, and traders. Directly after the war, Hay had been acting general manager for Levers' Yandina plantation; he then set up on his own as a scrap metal dealer, recycling wartime materials. Next, Hay purchased the Trade Scheme's Honiara butchery, and leased Levers' Three Sisters plantation in the small island group of that name near Makira, as well as Tetere plantation on Guadalcanal, and Tetepare plantation on a small island of that name in the New Georgia Group. His K.H. Dalrymple Hay Proprietary Limited and, later, Guadalcanal Plains Limited (GPL) developed extensive agricultural interests on Guadalcanal Plains, including the purchase of Ilu farm to supply the hotel.[71]

The Hotel Woodford was extended in 1950 to include a small residential wing, mainly for permanent guests. Journalist Judy Tudor, a seasoned Pacific traveller, was not impressed. When she stayed there in mid-1953, Honiara was in the middle of a heatwave and Tudor said the rooms were the hottest she had ever used.[72] The original buildings were located where the front driveway entrance to the Kitano Mendana's foyer is now. The accommodation was opposite to the west. Honiara's main fresh meat supply was controlled by J.A. ('Johno') Johnstone (the pre-war Hollis Brothers' New South Wales Fresh Food and Ice Company manager at Tulagi). He had been a major in the BSIP Labour Corps and in the new capital he ran the Government Trade Scheme butchery, which operated from an ex–

---

70   *PIM*, February 1951, 76.
71   ibid., June 1949, 64, October 1951, 89, June 1957, 79, 139, October 1966, 139, January 1969, 123; Kendrick 1968; Information from Alan Lindley, Adelaide, 30 June 2011; Moore 2013c: entries for Ilu Experimental Farm, Hay, and Mendana Hotel.
72   Tudor 1953b: 70.

US Marines walk-in refrigerator in the grounds of the Hotel Woodford. Meat and butter were rationed and distributed by Johnstone. By 1953, Johnstone—who had led a colourful career, including participation in the 1927 government attack on the Kwaio on Malaita—had been awarded an MBE and with Jacob Vuza was off to the coronation of Queen Elizabeth II as the two official BSIP representatives.[73] Hay's Mendana Enterprises Limited took over the butchery. The hotel's dining and lounge area was in a '*haus win*' (a thatched open structure) on the beach approximately where the front garden lounge is now situated. The hotel's name changed to Mendana in 1958.

The other source of fresh meat was a farm near the Mataniko River bridge run by Geoffrey Kuper, the son of German-born planter Heinrich Kuper and his wife, Augusta Kafagamurironga, from Santa Ana. Trained in Fiji before the war as an NMP, Geoff Kuper bridled under British racism against mixed-race families. A Coastwatcher during the war, he began the farm soon after.[74] Access to fresh food improved in about 1954 when Central Prison developed a large farm run by the prisoners, near the beach at Nggosi, which also supplied key government institutions and often government officers as well.

Government departments were slowly re-established in Honiara. The Lands and Survey Department was one of the first to be restaffed, under Spearline Wilson, its pre-war head. The land records, which had been evacuated to Sydney during the war, were all returned. Initially, the secretariat at Point Cruz housed the Resident Commissioner's Office, the Departments of Lands, Labour, Health, Police, Justice, and the Treasury. The Public Works Department, the Government Stores, and the Armed Constabulary operated from Stateside, next to the Mataniko River. The Marine Department continued to operate from Tulagi and, in 1950, preparations began to build a slipway there to service the 14 ships in the government fleet. The largest, *Kurimaru*, was about 200 tons.[75] Despite setbacks—such as cyclones in February 1951 and January 1952 that buffeted Honiara and demolished the Kukum wharves (reminding everyone of the exposed nature of the new town)—development progressed.[76]

---

73 *PIM*, May 1953, 16. Interestingly, Johnstone is mentioned but not Vuza, the decorated war hero who was clearly in Johnstone's charge. By 1953, they had known each other for more than 30 years. See also Keesing and Corris 1980; Moore 2017: 227–43.
74 Lindley 2014: 5; Moore 2013c: entries for Heinrich Kuper, and Augusta Kuper.
75 *BSIP NS*, 31 January 1969; *BSIP AR* 1949–50: 34–35.
76 *PIM*, March 1952, 122.

Accommodation and amenities

Expatriate accommodation in the late 1940s and early 1950s was mainly in former American military buildings. When Spearline Wilson returned to Honiara in 1945, he was allocated living space in the secretariat compound, where an ex-Tulagi Chinese cook catered for the 24 occupants. Then Wilson moved to a building that he used as both his home and the department's offices. His former Tulagi house servants Bennie Verali and Eric joined him. Wilson managed to scrounge a decent bed from the hospital, which enabled him to give up his camp stretcher. The government controlled all food supplies and initially did not distribute to individuals, only to the headquarters mess. Accommodation was scarce: Wilson had Anglican Bishop Walter Baddeley and Reverend John Goldie from the Methodist mission as his house guests during November 1945.[77]

Plate 3.10 Alan and Doreen Lindley's house in Mud Alley, 1952.
Source: Alan Lindley Collection, in Clive Moore Collection.

---

77 UQ FML, Wilson Papers, A.H. Wilson to M. Wilson, 9 October 1945, and A.H. Wilson to A. Wilson, 10 November 1945.

Plate 3.11 Arnold and Mary Cowmeadow's thatched house with woven bamboo walls in the grounds of Government House, 1960s.
Source: Mary Cowmeadow photograph, in Clive Moore Collection.

Soon after, one-bedroom 'dongas' were built for the single and married but childless government employees. They were situated in a coconut palm grove east of the secretariat and close to the Government Residency known as 'Shickers Alley' (slang for being drunk). Each had one small bedroom, a lounge/dining room, kitchen, and bathroom. The floors were concrete, the roofs consisted of sago palm thatch, and the walls were made from woven bamboo strips.[78] By about 1953, there were three main types of housing for expatriates: the one-bedroom thatched cottages along the shore; converted Quonset huts with new linings and fittings, usually with two bedrooms; and new bungalows up on the ridges, which were usually 'L'-shaped and clad in fibro sheeting, with push-out shutters and wide eaves. There were also a few unique creations that dated from the American years, with new interiors. In the early 1950s, Alan and Doreen Lindley lived on the corner of Mud Alley and Mendana Avenue in one of these, opposite the entrance to the Government Residency. Lindley described his house as 'a very ordinary, roughly built, one-bedroom house with attached kitchen and storeroom'.[79] The building was on short stumps with a galvanised ripple-iron roof over the bedroom, a thatched roof over the living room and kitchen, and a front door with no lock. It was typical

---

78 Lawson n.d. [c. 2000s]: 7–8; Email from Mary Cowmeadow, 14 April 2018.
79 Lindley 2014: 5.

of houses in Honiara in these years. When Lindley returned to Honiara in 1960 as officer-in-charge of Central Police District, his accommodation for the first few weeks was worse—in Fijian Quarter. There, he was given a long room with a bed in one corner, a toilet, a shower, and wash basin in another, plus a small benchtop electric stove on one side. Next, he was given a house in Shickers Alley, although he considered this also below the standard of his Mud Alley home.[80]

Another early official, Dr J.D. Macgregor, was appointed to Central Hospital in 1957. His house was on the site of what is now the Anglican Cathedral, and had belonged to Romulus Dethridge, whom Macgregor described as a 'crocodile hunter and entrepreneur'. The house next belonged to Ken Hay, who sold it to the government. It was built in 'local style with a thatched roof, plaited and patterned pandanus leaf walls, and shutters to lower when the weather was stormy'.[81] The house was surrounded by fruit trees and had two large ngali nut trees in the garden.

Electricity and water supplies were developed piecemeal as needs increased.[82] The original power supply for the town was provided by a mixture of Japanese and American generators, three working at any one time, with two more as back-up. In early 1949, after new generators were purchased, electricity became available 24 hours a day. Even though the system was only 110 volts, this was enough to allow permanent refrigeration to be used. In October 1951, the ageing powerplant was about to expire and residents were given a choice: they could use either electric lighting or their refrigerator, not both. Sales of candles and hurricane lanterns skyrocketed. Two new engines and generators arrived late in the year and a completely new power station was erected. The entire town as far as Kukum was placed on the 240-volt system. Meters were installed in nongovernment higher-quality residences and commercial premises in 1963, with 200 meters in use at the end of 1964.[83] Honiara's power consumption more than doubled in the second half of the 1960s and continued to grow—by 9 per cent in 1970 alone. This necessitated developing Lungga power station, which was opened on 6 November 1971, adding 4 megawatts to the Honiara power grid. Establishing a water supply was (and still is) a

---

80 ibid., 10.
81 Macgregor 2000.
82 *BSIP NS*, 31 January 1969.
83 *PIM*, November 1952, 66; *BSIP AR* 1963–64: 60.

problem in Honiara. Boreholes at Kukum and springs at Lengakiki were used, with the water fed into small dams and distributed by gravity.[84] The higher areas were supplied by pumping stations.

A small telephone system was included with the American facilities handed over to the British. It was a manual exchange: users had to crank handles on their phone-sets to generate power before making a call. A new automatic 100-line telephone exchange was installed in 1954, with lines extending east to Kukum Airfield and west to Rove. In the same year, small local exchanges were installed at Gizo and Auki; calls could only be made between the three exchanges from the post offices. In 1963, a radio-telephone circuit was opened to Suva with a connection to New Zealand. Three years later, it was possible to call Gizo and Auki from Honiara homes. Until 1968, all local calls were free.[85]

Anglican priest Con L. Montford, who had been in the protectorate since the 1920s, was transferred to Honiara with his new wife in December 1955. They sailed from Sydney on BP's *Muliama*:

> At Honiara eight or nine days later we were not very impressed. All we could see from the ship was a small scattered place sprawling over several steep ridges. On landing it was not much better. There was no wharf, only a jetty for launches and small craft. First came the customs sheds, then the businesses consisting of two stores, a butcher's shop, two garages, a picture theatre, and further back all the government administration buildings. Everything was housed in old military huts adapted for the purpose for which they were being used.
>
> … Later on we were to discover China Town, a collection of some thirty or forty stores and shops, all of them made of old military huts of varying sizes. A little further on was the government Hospital with all its wards and administration buildings made from converted military huts.[86]

After its transfer from Suva to Honiara, the WPHC Secretariat occupied ramshackle wartime structures. Colin (later Sir Colin) Allan arrived as a district officer in 1946. He became a senior public servant and governor (1976–78):

---

84   *BSIP AR* 1951–52: 35–36; 1971: 4.
85   See Moore 2013c: entry for Telephone Service; Lindley 2014: 10.
86   Montford 1994: 80.

> Constructed of poor-quality sago-palm leaf, wire-netting, tarred paper, rusty corrugated iron and riddled with termites, the buildings were unbelievably hot and unpleasant. In the hurricane season rain drove through by the bucket despite the rickety shutters. Only a few offices had ceiling or desk fans. Furniture had come from Suva, some of it dating back to the beginning of the century. File trays were of rusty metal or wood. Many of the typewriters would today fetch impressive sums at Christies [sic]. Tables were stabilised by ancient out-of-date legal volumes or government-issue loo paper … Distinguished visitors from Whitehall, were frankly appalled and some doubted the wisdom of even supporting such a Mickey Mouse outfit with cold hard development aid. Visitors from Fiji seemed to regard us with contempt. Those from Papua New Guinea took comfort—at least we were no better off.[87]

Allan noted one advantage: Solomon Islanders were not intimidated by the dilapidated secretariat buildings.

The population rose quickly; Honiara doubled its size during the 1950s. In 1959, the town was home to 3,534 of the total BSIP population of 124,000. By the early 1960s, Honiara had improved enormously, compared with 10 years earlier. Sir John Gutch was high commissioner between 1955 and 1961. He described the rapid expansion of Honiara, with new government bungalows built along the coast and on the hills behind. Mendana Avenue was still not sealed, except for a small section opposite the stores and the cinema in the centre of the town. As Sir John remembered:

> Road improvements were under way in both directions from Honiara and bridges were under construction. Along the coast west of Honiara the shore was littered with the wrecks of Japanese cargo vessels which had been run ashore under naval bombardment. One of the first problems with which I had to deal was an application by Japanese interests to remove these wrecks and export the salvaged material to Japan for new ship construction. It was suggested in some quarters that Solomon Islanders might object actively to the presence of Japanese from whom they had suffered during the war. The application was granted and there were no untoward results.[88]

---

87 Allan 1990: 112.
88 Gutch 1987: 114.

Gutch also described the leisure activities available to the 1950s expatriate residents, and the dangers:

> We used to picnic at various spots along the coast, but unfortunately sharks were prevalent and crocodiles were also a danger in the rivers and were reputed to travel by sea from one river mouth to another. We did, however, bathe at one or two sheltered spots amongst the reefs and also in the rivers, particularly in a pool to the east of Honiara where one could swing out on a rope from a convenient tree and drop into the cool water.[89]

Despite Honiara Town Council's valiant attempts at beautification, European residents who had lived in pre-war Tulagi were slow to call Honiara home, and in early years never called it 'the Capital', out of nostalgia for Tulagi, preferring 'protectorate headquarters'. Ever so slowly, urban services developed enough to make Honiara into a comfortable public service posting. Honiara's first coffee shop was begun in 1966 by Augustine Quan Hong (Guan Houyuan), a member of the Honiara Town Council and President of the British Solomon Islands Chinese Association.[90] The first barber and women's hairdressing shop was opened in 1967 by Kwok Hing Chung (Guo Xingzhong), who had trained at the Hong Kong School of Arts, Beauty and Fashion, and also ran an optical service.[91] Girl Guides, Brownies, Scouts, and Cubs troops and packs began, and children made their own fun in the local creeks, rivers, and at the beaches.

Trips to the cinemas at Point Cruz and Kukum opened a world outside the Solomons.[92] Reverend Montford, a member of the BSIP Censorship Board, remembered Point Cruz's cinema well. It was built in 1953 from Quonset huts and operated until the 1980s. It was also used for theatrical performances and as a live music venue:

> One of the delights for those who could afford it was the picture theatre which was a great thrill and ran to full houses. The walls were partly open and it never became unbearably hot. A back seat cost five shillings but the front seats only one shilling, so that the Melanesians very sensibly elected to sit in the front. Love scenes

---

89 ibid., 120.
90 *BSIP NS*, 7 October 1966, 19 December 1966, 31 April 1969.
91 ibid., 7 September 1967.
92 ibid., 6 October 1967, 15 August 1970.

were not at all popular, fighting scenes were fully appreciated, but we the censors did not allow too much of that and we absolutely censored any brutality. The favourite picture was 'Quo Vadis' and had to be brought back time and again.[93]

During the 1960s, George Yee Fai owned the cinema. The films did not always run smoothly, as one resident complained in 1969:

[T]he audience has had to contend with a sound system which cannot be interpreted. Generally it is the case of the volume being turned to a pitch which renders the sound just as indecipherable as when it is scarcely audible … The showing of 'The Sound of Music' recently is a case in point. Any musical depends to a major extent on the quality of the sound track. This may not be the case with 'westerns' to which a less critical audience is attracted.[94]

By 1966, Honiara had 55 registered shops and stores, nine tailors, and three bakers. A substantial Chinatown had developed on the eastern bank of the Mataniko River, containing a non-residential hotel (just a rough bar) and 39 of the registered businesses in Honiara, drawing most of the Solomon Islander customers.[95] The government administrative centre was concentrated around Point Cruz. Buildings varied from modified Quonset huts to modern airconditioned banks and a supermarket. Four businesses were registered at White River, two at Kukum, and three on Kola`a Ridge.

Urban associations began to form, more hotels were built, and main roads were given names. A Jaycees branch, a Masonic Lodge (see Map 7.1), a Chamber of Commerce, and a St Andrew's Society were established.[96] A multiracial Solomon Islands Club, later called the Honiara Club, was begun in July 1964 on the coastal side of Mendana Avenue, in a Quonset hut next to the Central District office and the first courthouse. Officially opened on 2 March 1965 by Chief Secretary Michael Gass, the club was granted a piece of land overlooking the Mataniko River for a permanent

---

93 Montford 1994: 44–45.
94 *BSIP NS*, 30 September 1969.
95 ibid., 7 April 1966.
96 ibid., 19 December 1966, 31 January 1969; *SND*, 3 June 1977. A Rotary club was formed in Honiara in 1987.

building.[97] In the club's first year, membership grew from 17 to 80. Work began on the new structure in 1969.[98] It was decorated with traditional motifs painted by King George VI School students, directed by their art teacher, Les Tickle.

The Guadalcanal Club was the early centre of expatriate entertainment. It revived one of the competitions from the Tulagi Club: the Five Events Cup (swimming, tennis, cricket, golf, and snooker), which was held annually. As on Tulagi, this was always followed by a dinner and a beer-guzzling finale.[99] The club was expanded in the 1960s, using Honiara's classic building material, Quonset huts, with an extra touch as they were lifted into place using derricks taken off Japanese wrecks.[100] During the 1950s and 1960s, square dancing was in vogue, short plays and sketches were presented, and betting occurred on Saturday-night crab races. Europeans also flocked to the comfortable golf club, with its local-style sago-leaf thatch clubhouse. In 1959, plans were unveiled to extend the course to nine holes. Expatriates also congregated at the Mendana Hotel and the Point Cruz Yacht Club (from 1968)—neighbouring sites west of Point Cruz along the beach.

There were also cultural pursuits that did not include drinking alcohol. The more literate appreciated the opening of Honiara's Public Library in mid-1968 with space for 12,000 books—a target almost achieved in 1970 when there were 10,000 volumes, and 782 expatriate and 403 indigenous borrowers.[101] Musical expatriate residents joined or listened to the 'Honiara Hotspots', also called the 'Honiara Deadbeats'—

---

97 It is interesting to see who members of the early executive were: Dr Gideon Zoleveke (a Choiseul-born medical practitioner and radio broadcaster, later knighted) was elected president, Albert Kuper (brother of Geoff, mentioned above) was vice-president, Bartholomew Buchanan (a senior public servant) was secretary, and Solomon Dakai (in charge of the x-ray department at Central Hospital, president of the Red Cross, and a famous singer) was treasurer. The trustees were Fred Osifelo (a Malaitan quickly making his way up in the public service), and Ron Lawson (a Honiara businessman and vice-president of the Honiara Town Council). By 1966, the Solomon Islander members of its committee were Zoleveke, Osifelo, Michael Musuota, Luke Dangopiru, Michael Rapasia (Member for Guadalcanal), Silas Sitai (a senior public servant from Santa Ana), Peter Naturanga, Joseph Molia (from north Malaita), Olle Torling (an ex-government cocoa officer who owned Tambea Resort), and Gerald Malkmus.
98 *BSIP NS*, 15 August 1964, 15 March 1965, August 1965, 11 August 1966, 21 August 1967, 31 July 1969, 31 October 1972.
99 Lawson n.d. [c. 2000s]: 20; Moore 2019: 208.
100 Jock Stevenson, the senior architect of the Public Works Department, supervised the task. Information from Ann Stevenson, 28 July 2019.
101 *BSIP NS*, 13 December 1967, 31 August 1968, 30 November 1968, 28 February 1970.

the 'hottest jazz band in two million square miles of the Pacific'.[102] Locals also performed in local repertory shows organised by the Honiara Hams. Others joined the British Solomon Islands Society for the Advancement of Science and Industry, formed in 1951, the Solomon Islands Museum Association, formed in 1972, or the chess club, and the film society. Scottish country dancing was taught by Jock Stevenson for the St Andrew's Society, slightly incongruously at the Yacht Club, where he was commodore. Some of the best dancers were Solomon Islanders. The society celebrated St Andrew's night in November and Burns Night in January—both formal occasions held at the Honiara Hotel, with haggis, and a Solomon Islander bagpiper borrowed from the police band. Each New Year's Eve, a party was held at the Guadalcanal Club with the New Year's Honours announced at midnight. The main public celebration each year was the Queen's Birthday in June, when a ceremony was held, and decorations and awards were presented, followed by a garden party and ball at Government House.[103]

By the late 1960s, Honiara was a fully functioning small British Pacific settlement. The post-war public servants and colonists usually had quite different ideas and motivations from their pre-war equivalents. Most of the public servants belonged to a new generation of technocrats who were less colonial in their thinking and willing to embrace British Prime Minister Harold Macmillan's 1960 'wind of change' speech, which signalled a new British attitude to its dependencies. Although there were a few 'old Africa hands' seeing out their contracts and trying to hold back the tide, most of the expatriates were amenable to implementing change.

---

102 ibid., June 1966.
103 Gutch 1987: 115–16; Russell 2003: 117; *BSIP NS*, June 1966, 31 January 1968, 16 October 1972.

Plate 3.12 The Mendana Hotel in the late 1950s.
Source: BM, Patrick Barrett Collection.

Plate 3.13 The Honiara Club, showing murals created by King George VI School art students in 1971.
Source: Les Tickle Collection.

Plate 3.14 The Point Cruz Cinema in Mendana Avenue in the late 1950s.
The cinema was constructed from Quonset huts with open sides to enhance air flow.
Source: BM, Patrick Barrett Collection.

Plate 3.15 West Honiara from the bottom of Lengakiki Ridge, 1956.
Source: Peter Flahavin Collection, US CIA Photograph 221961 supplied to *New Commonwealth*, 14 May 1956.

4

The other Honiara

Wokabaoti long Saenataone	**Walkabout in Chinatown**
Wokabaoti long Saenataone,	Walkabout in Chinatown,
Mekamu kosi angga long kona,	Make a course for the corner,
Suti apu sekem hedi,	Shoot, shake head,
Kikim baket enikaeni,	Kick bucket, any kind
Iasi iu laf hafu sens wata nating.	Yes, you laugh, mad, water on the brain.
Tingting baek long iu,	Think back to you,
Lusim hom long taem,	A long time since leaving home,
Tu yia ova mi no lukim iu,	More than two years haven't seen you,
Tasawai mi no laekim iu,	Which is why I don't like you,
Man i karangge hed i luism mani.	Man stupid, stupid head to lose money.
Namata mi dae long Honiara,	Doesn't matter if I die in Honiara,
Samting mi lus long taem long iu,	What's lost, is lost a long time with you,
Bat sapos iu ting long me,	But if you think of me,
Iu kan weit fo tu yia moa,	You can wait for two year more,
Letem kam laet sikin lelebet.	Let my skin get a little lighter here.

Source: Frazer (1985: 185).

Plate 4.1 *Walkabout Long Chinatown*, the Viking album featuring the song of the same name by Edwin Sitori, Rone Naqu, and Jason Que.
The recording was made during the first half of the 1950s by Solomon Dakei and his Solomon Singers.
Source: Brian Taylor Collection.

Honiara's worlds

Wokabaoti long Saenataone, the best-known song from Solomon Islands, was co-written in the first half of the 1950s by Edwin Sitori from Malaita, Rone Naqu from Kolombangara, and Jason Que from Vella Lavella. The song was made famous by Solomon Dakei and his Solomon Singers. It has now also been absorbed into the popular culture of Papua New Guinea, Vanuatu, and Fiji. Sung in Solomons Pijin English and originally played in country-music style, it nostalgically describes aimlessly walking about in Honiara's Chinatown, and the trials of living in the foreign urban setting, separated from home and loved ones. Sitori, from the Onepusu area of west 'Are'are on Malaita, was fascinated by modern music and had taught himself to play the guitar. Like so many of his contemporaries, he arrived in Honiara to seek his fortune, eventually finding a maintenance job with the government. *Wokabaoti long Saenataone* struck a chord of recognition with many rural Pacific peoples faced with the alienation of life in town. The song was recorded by the Solomon Islands Broadcasting Service, issued as a Viking Records 45 rpm record, and popularised outside the Solomons by Fijian musician Sakiusa Bulocokocoko, who produced a more up-tempo version.

Two Malaitan musicians from the 1960s and 1970s, Fred Maedola and Jim Baku, also recorded with Viking. Music was one aspect of change in Honiara after World War II when the US troops introduced modern American music and new musical instruments. Until then, Solomon Islanders' access to world music had been limited to Christian hymns. Some of the missions saw songs like *Wokabaoti long Saenataone*, Sitori's *Honiara Girl*, or Baku's *Lucky Girl* as the work of the devil, leading inexorably to promiscuity and decline. While these were hardly provocative songs by modern standards, the reactions point to other aspects of Solomons culture in decades past: the hold of Christianity and *kastom* taboos still observed among some Solomon Islanders (particularly Malaitans) that meant public displays of sexuality could lead to demands for compensation.[1]

This book argues that there were (and still are) several parallel Honiaras: the official Honiara largely governed by administration and commerce, which began as a British 'world' but is now controlled by Solomon Islanders; an Asian Honiara, the members of which have social, economic, and political influence well beyond their numbers; and an indigenous hybrid Honiara, which combines elements of all the 'worlds', including the rural village 'world' that is still the major driving force of the nation. These divisions began in the colonial years and each has altered in importance as the decades progressed (Figure 0.1).

In the 1959 census, the national population was estimated to be 124,000, with Honiara home to 2,664 males and 827 females. Six years later, the population had almost doubled.[2] Honiara in the 1940s, 1950s, and early

---

1 Hægland 2010: 32–37.
2 BSIP 1961. See also Tables 4.1 and 6.1, this volume.

1960s was primarily an administrative centre dominated by expatriate officials. The 'other' Honiara was made up of several parallel communities, with Chinese and Solomon Islanders—Melanesian and Polynesians—and other Pacific Islanders living alongside in a symbiotic relationship that depended on the cash economy but remained segregated from the European community. The Solomon Islander labour force—which was most of the population—lived mainly in the squalid Labour Line at Kukum. Chinese were added to the pattern from 1948, establishing Chinatown on the east bank of the Mataniko. And there were other groups, particularly the immigrant Gilbertese, Fijians of indigenous and Indian descent, and a small Nauruan community.[3] In Tulagi, Solomon Islanders always outnumbered the Europeans, Chinese, and other Pacific groups. It did not take long for this also to occur in Honiara. This chapter examines the early years of these parallel but interwoven communities.

James Tedder and M.P.E. Bellam both conducted research in Honiara in the 1960s. Bellam, a geographer, created a schematic plan for Honiara in the mid-1960s (Map 8.1), which showed how the small town was divided up. In early Honiara, physical segregation was based on a combination of income, occupation, and race. Honiara in the 1950s and 1960s had two distinct areas, divided by the Mataniko River and Chinatown. Tedder, a senior government officer, lived in Honiara in the late 1950s and more substantially in the 1960s and 1970s. His description of Honiara, written in 1966, is accurate:

> Partly due to the town plan and partly to conditions which can be placed upon leases of crown land, housing development had been carried out in an orderly pattern which has, however, resulted in rather strict stratification by income. Thus, most of the higher-grade Government houses and more expensive commercial houses are situated in one of four areas—Lengakiki, Kola, or Vavaya ridges, and along the coast west of Rove. For the most part, these houses are occupied by Europeans. The middle-grade houses on the flats north of Lengakiki and Vavaya ridges in the Matanikau Valley, and on the lower slopes of Kola Ridge are generally occupied by Solomon Islanders and Fijians, though on the Lengakiki Flats most of the houses and apartments are occupied by Europeans.

---

3   Tahal and Oxenham 1981. In the mid-1970s, one Nauruan family at White River owned the largest car in Honiara, a red American convertible. One of the sights of Honiara was watching the car being driven slowly about town with the occupants waving, almost regally. The family owned the Kukum movie theatre. 'Who brought the Nauruans in?', *Kakamora Reporter* [hereinafter *KR*], July 1975, 9–10.

> The lower-grade houses and barracks occupied by the semi-skilled artisans, junior clerks, and labourers are situated around the eastern end of Vavaya ridge and the Kukum housing estate and are occupied by Solomon Islanders.[4]

Housing for Solomon Islanders was established inland from Central Market and Fijian Quarter, spreading to Mbokonavera and Kukum. Chinatown, which was home to most of the Chinese and some of their employees, was a neutral zone accessed by all. Accommodation for single and married labourers was developed in the Labour Line housing spreading inland from Kukum Beach. Young Solomon Islanders, mainly males, making their way up through the public service and church hierarchies, lived nearby in the Single Officers' Quarter. The new indigenous middle class—public servants and church workers—lived on the lower slopes of the ridges behind Central Market and on Kola`a Ridge. Most expatriates had little need to visit east Honiara, except to pass through on the way to the airfields at Kukum or Henderson, once it was reconditioned. Likewise, most Solomon Islanders lived in barracks, shopped in Chinatown, and had little need to proceed west of the Mataniko, except for trips to Central Market, the beachside churches, and the Point Cruz wharves. A few worked as domestic servants or in the government offices at Point Cruz.[5] The closest Tandai villages were Kakabona to the west and higher up the Mataniko behind Honiara. White River, Kukum, and Vaivila (the Malaitan fishing community on the coast at Kukum) developed as village-style modern residential areas within Honiara's boundaries. Initially, indigenous house construction used local or leftover American building materials.

While the protectorate's expatriate officers thought of Honiara as their town, in many ways, it was a Solomon Islander creation, and the way it became incorporated into Guadalcanal was certainly very 'Solomons'. The argument put forward here and in later chapters is that over decades Honiara has become a hybrid society that has many village-like characteristics. The etiquette of exchange is a feature of Solomon Islands cultures. Circulation, not one-way migration, is basic to movement in the islands. This is best illustrated in the discussion below of Central Market. But first, the origins of Chinatown.

4 Tedder 1966: 38.
5 ibid., 36–41, 43.

HONIARA

Chinatown and Chinese business interests

Permanent Chinese residents arrived in Solomon Islands in the 1910s, creating Chinatown on Tulagi. From the 1920s and until 1942, they developed numerous trading companies, which operated a fleet of small interisland boats from rickety wharves off Chinatown, and began trade stores in the western Solomons, on Isabel, Malaita, and a few other islands. There was never a comfortable relationship between European and Chinese commerce. Several attempts were made to limit the number of Chinese allowed to enter the protectorate and their right to become traders. Neither was there a close relationship with Solomon Islanders, as the Chinese were exploitative in business dealings. About half the Chinese left during the war years, with small communities remaining on Makira, Malaita, and Isabel.[6] During the war Kwan How Yuan (Guan Houyuan)[7] and a few other Chinese accepted an offer from Military Governor Trench to move to Camp Guadal. They ran laundry and other services, and some joined with Kwan How Yuan to sell artefacts. Kwan worked as a middleman between the Americans keen to take home grass skirts, weapons, and carvings, and local villagers and members of the BSIP Defence Force and Labour Corps who made the items in their spare time. They also had artefacts and shells sent to them from their home islands. Sir Fred Osifelo remembered his mid-teenage years on Malaita, when he gathered shells off reefs and made walking sticks, grass skirts, and combs for his relatives in the Labour Corps to sell to the Americans on Guadalcanal. The Chinese 'marooned' on Makira during the war also manufactured their own versions of artefacts. The Americans bought them all.[8]

Several Quan/Kwan brothers and cousins migrated to BSIP before the war. Augustine Quan Hong (Guan Kang) arrived in the Solomons in 1920s, then lost everything during the war. His brother Kwan How Yuan (or H.Y.) had arrived at Gizo in 1933 when he was 18 years old, establishing a store there. After his stint selling artefacts at Camp Guadal during the war, he returned to Hong Kong in 1947, where he established businesses that restored some of his finances. Persuaded to return to BSIP in 1952, he had plans to develop extensive business interests, first restoring his Gizo store and, with his brother Kwan Toor, purchasing a new ship to resume their

---

6   Laracy 1974; Moore 2008a; 2019: 113–21, 213–27, 389–90.
7   There are complex issues with Chinese nomenclature, as several English-language versions are used in the sources, and different branches of the same family choose to spell the same names differently. I have followed the advice of my colleague Chi Kong Lai and placed a standard pinyin form in parentheses after the version found in the source unless they are identical to modern forms.
8   Osifelo 1985: 23.

interisland trading. On the way to BSIP, he left his children in Sydney for education; the eldest, James, was already studying there. Fairly quickly the brothers extended to Honiara. Other Chinese merchants joined them—often from Hong Kong after the communist takeover on the mainland in 1949. In the 1950s, Honiara's Chinatown was a separate shopping centre catering almost exclusively for Solomon Islanders.[9]

The Chinese built what are still called 'trade stores'. In the beginning, they used scrap materials left by the Americans, then they began to construct typical Chinese stores. Some of the early buildings still exist, having survived the 2006 riots that destroyed much of old Chinatown. The small wooden shops with galvanised ripple-iron roofs were painted in bright colours. They had front verandahs with crossed railings, leading into cool, dark commercial spaces full of tinned goods, rice, and cheap household items. The traders and their families lived at the rear. There were usually small alters set high on an interior wall, where ancestors were venerated with prayers, offerings of fruit and other foods, and burning incense. The shops were similar to those that had existed in Tulagi and in other places like Gizo and Auki before the war. The Chinese operated with three prices for any item: the lowest for other Chinese, a middle price for Europeans, and the highest for Solomon Islanders.

Plate 4.2 Aerial view of Chinatown in the 1950s.
Source: BM, Patrick Barrett Collection.

---

9   O'Brien 1995: 227; *Solomon Star* [hereinafter *SS*], 8 February 2016; Emails from Joyce Tshe (née Kwan), 21 and 28 March 2022.

HONIARA

Plate 4.3 View down Chinatown's main street in the 1950s.
Source: BM, Patrick Barrett Collection.

Plate 4.4 View into Chinatown, showing the typical trade stores, in the early 1960s.
Source: BM, Bob Wright Collection, in John Tod Collection.

In Solomons Pijin English, the Chinese are now known as *waku*. The origin of the word is from the Cantonese *wah kiu*, which translates literally as 'residing outside', although it is better translated as 'expatriate' or 'overseas' Chinese. In Mandarin, the phrase is *wai ju*. Originally used self-descriptively by Chinese immigrants, the word has been adopted by Solomon Islanders.[10] The Chinese and Chinatown have been central to Honiara since the late 1940s, although the use of *waku* as a Pijin name for them is relatively new. The standard descriptor until the 1960s was 'Chinaman'.

The Chinese community in its separate Chinatown was integral to the new Honiara. The Chinese prospered in the pre-independence years— still outsiders in a social sense, and mainly isolated from the European elite, but far more important to the economy than they had been back in Tulagi days. Because the large pre-war merchant houses (Burns Philp, Levers, and Carpenters) never returned to dominance in the post-war retail trade, the Chinese merchants were able to achieve a substantial monopoly. They also began to diversify their interests into business areas once the preserve of the large merchant companies, such as coastal trading, and in the case of James Wang, plantations. The Chinese community had its own elite and they socialised quite separately from Solomon Islanders and Europeans, although there were always crossovers and friendships.

Beginning in the late 1940s, they began to adopt Christianity and established a Chinese-language school. Seldom invited to European 'society' functions, they controlled much of the retail trade in the country and became dominant in Honiara and in the main provincial towns. One of the first signs of this change was the establishment of Honiara's Chung Wah School (Chinese School), which was organised and financed by Chinese residents. The school was officially opened by acting Resident Commissioner J.D.A. Germond on 15 October 1949. In the mornings, teaching was in English by the wife of the secretary to the government, and in the afternoons in Cantonese by a teacher from China. The first professional teacher was Fung Shiu Kat (Feng Shaoji) from Hong Kong, who arrived in July 1952 through arrangements between the Anglican

---

10   I am indebted to Garth Wong, Chi Kong Lai, Tarcisius Tara Kabutaulaka, and David Akin for their help with the meaning of the word.

Melanesian Mission and the Bishop of Hong Kong.[11] The school went from strength to strength and remains one of the major schools in Honiara, although it is no longer exclusively for Chinese children.

In the early 1950s, there were around 300 Chinese living in the protectorate who were involved in technical and commercial services, based mainly in Chinatown, running small trade stores, and travelling in their own ships throughout the protectorate to purchase copra, bêche-de-mer, and trochus shells. They were also skilled artisans and craftsmen, filling many trades positions for the government and private enterprises.[12] A few Chinese also lived at the Kukum (now Ranadi) industrial area and above their shops in the Point Cruz commercial area.

The Chinese were fluent in Pijin, but seldom in English. One who was fluent in English was Chan Chee (Chen Zhi), general manager of Kwan How Yuan Proprietary Limited, the largest Chinese company in the protectorate. He was also president of the Chinese community group in Honiara during the 1950s and until he returned to Hong Kong in 1962. Chan Chee was succeeded by Lai Yuen Wo (Li Yuanhuo). The better-educated Chinese also had friends in the European community. As owners of trade stores and as employers, they had an ambivalent relationship with Solomon Islanders, although there were some early intermarriages that created substantial links. In the 1950s and 1960s, many Chinese residents applied for British citizenship. This was easier to gain if they were Christian, and many became Roman Catholics, encouraged by Fathers van Mechlin and Leemans. In October 1961, 43 Chinese from Chinatown were christened, watched by another 60 Chinese Catholics in the congregation. The British Solomon Islands Chinese Association was formed in November 1965,[13] with advisors from the wider community. The overlap with the executive of the multiracial Honiara Club gives some idea of who were the major racial integration advocates of the 1960s.[14]

---

11 *PIM*, November 1949, 16.
12 Information from Paul Quan, Sydney, September 2017.
13 Peter Lai was president, James Wang was chairman, C.K. Ching (Qing) was vice-chairman, Henry Quan (Guan) and K.H. Ip (Ye) were secretaries, and Chow Leong (Zhou Liang) was treasurer. Stephen Yee (Yi), Leong Fat (Liangfa), and Paul Sze-tu (Situ) were responsible for social and educational activities.
14 These were Michael Rapasia, Mariano Kelesi (Legislative Council Member for North Malaita), Father Wall (Anglican priest and Legislative Council Nominated Member), Silas Sitai, and Dr Gideon Zoloveke.

Plate 4.5 Chinatown in the 1960s.
Source: BM, Bob Wright Collection, in John Tod Collection.

Plate 4.6 The Bailey bridge over the Mataniko River, and part of Chinatown.
Source: BM, Bob Wright Collection, in John Tod Collection.

At the time of the 1959 census, there were 366 Chinese in Solomon Islands, all but three of them in Honiara, and another 100 or so in the 'mixed' category, some of whom were of part-Chinese descent. There were 624 Chinese in Honiara in 1968, and 577 in 1970. By the early 1970s, the Chinese were considering their futures, and many were leaving to join relatives in Australia, Canada, and the United States. About 200 departed and a further 60 were preparing to leave before self-government in 1976. In mid-1975, there were said to be 30 shops for sale in Chinatown, Kukum, and Point Cruz. The main motivations of those who left were to obtain a better education for their children and to secure the future of their families. Un Tak Fook (Yu Defu), the main commercial photographer in Honiara, was one of those preparing to leave in 1975.[15] The children of the first generation were blocked from taking expatriate-salaried government jobs. Although many were Australian educated, they were domiciled in Solomon Islands and not eligible for the overseas salary supplement. In 1976, 452 remained. Numbers had declined again, to 342, by the time of the 1986 census.

Honiara's Chinatown of the 1950s, 1960s, and 1970s was the classic two-sided street of trade stores. A few Chinese businesses had become major commercial operations. The largest was Kwan How Yuan Pty Ltd, importers and exporters, plantation and ship owners, and general merchants, famous for their Joy Biscuit factory opened in the late 1950s in the Kukum area that became Panatina. The factory made 'hard navy biscuits' for local consumption, which are still a favourite Solomons breakfast item. The company also manufactured soft drinks. There were increasing numbers of Chinese importers and exporters, plantation owners, shipowners, and general merchants.[16] Some of the younger Chinese left their family trade stores and branched out into other commercial ventures. They supplied logging camps, marketed trochus shell and bêche-de-mer, and began specialist shops in the central business district along Mendana Avenue. There were always tensions because Solomon Islanders resented the Chinese stranglehold on retail and wholesale business, but they worked hard and served the nation and themselves well. The families who remained prospered, becoming leading hoteliers, parliamentarians, and owners of a wide range of businesses.

---

15 *SND*, 25 July 1975; Email from Joyce Tshe (née Kwan), 30 November 2016.
16 *BSIP NS*, 7 June 1967.

4. THE OTHER HONIARA

Some of the Chinese men married Solomon Islands women, which has stood them in good stead in periods of conflict in Honiara when local connections were crucial. The Chan, Leong (Liang), Leung (Liang), and Wang families have entered the mainstream as hoteliers. The Chans entered politics. Sir Tommy Chan was in parliament and was the head of a political party, while his son Laurie served as Minister for Foreign Affairs and Trade. The Leong family set up the Pacific Casino Hotel. The Leung family started with their father's electrical shop in the 1960s, moved into commodity trading, then took over The Bookshop in Mendana Avenue, which in the 1990s effectively became Honiara's first department store. Next, they moved on to run restaurants and bars at the Pacific Casino Hotel, and now operate Iron Bottom Sound (IBS) Hotel. The Quans, early settlers in Tulagi, are in business in Honiara; their QQQ store in Chinatown is famous. A few other early Asian settlers also prospered, such as Japanese businessman Yukio Sato, who established himself in Western District in the 1950s, before shifting his business interests to Honiara. He went into national politics for one term.

Honiara's Asian community is now much more complex, including Japanese, Taiwanese, Koreans, Filipinos, Malaysians, and Bangladeshis. There are clearly two Chinese groups in Solomon Islands, classified by the length of time they have resided there: old *waku* and new *waku*. The new *waku* are Chinese (and other Asian) residents who have arrived in recent decades, from South-East Asia (particularly Malaysia, the Philippines, and Vietnam), Taiwan, and mainland China (Figure 0.1). One tendency is a move into the small businesses usually reserved for Solomon Islanders, forcing some local canteens out of business. The same applies to bus and taxi ownership. Although there is also long-term smouldering resentment of the old *waku*, these more established Chinese families 'belong' in the Solomons. They understand and respond quite differently to local cultural issues. The difference was made clear in 2006 when large amounts of new *waku* property were damaged in riots, while the businesses of some of the old *waku*—notably, the Quan and Chan families—escaped unscathed.[17]

---

17   Moore 2008a.

Plate 4.7 Aerial view of Chinatown, 1968.
Source: Les Tickle Collection.

Plate 4.8 Mataniko River and Chinatown, also showing the beginning of housing on the ridges, 1981.
Source: Wendy Ho photograph, in Clive Moore Collection.

The Gilbertese Migration

Solomon Islands is unusual among Pacific nations for having three substantial Pacific ethnic communities: Melanesians, Polynesians, and Micronesians,[18] the latter group recent migrants from what is now Kiribati. The Gilbertese resettlement scheme began in the 1950s to provide new homes for the people from the Phoenix (Rawaki) Group: eight atolls including Orona (Hull), Birnie (Manra, or Sydney), and Nikumaroro (Gardner) islands. The Phoenix Group, west of the Line Islands and east of the Gilbert Islands, was uninhabited until the 1930s and was then settled due to overcrowding in the southern Gilbert atolls. Poor soils and low rainfall caused famines and resettlement was suggested for humanitarian reasons. The scheme was only possible because the Crown Colony of Gilbert and Ellice Islands and the BSIP were both administered by Britain's WPHC, based in Honiara.[19] By the time independence arrived in 1978, there were 2,753 Gilbertese living in Solomon Islands, with a few Ellice Islanders included in the migration.

Plate 4.9 Gilbertese migrants in the 1950s.
Source: BM, Patrick Barrett Collection.

---

18   Continuing to use this racial classification terminology rightly has its detractors (due to its racist connotations and the fact that the migration of Pacific peoples is extremely complex). Nevertheless, it is still widely used, not least by Pacific Islanders themselves.
19   A group from Banaba Island, which was devastated by phosphate mining, was moved to Rabi Island in Fiji. Kituai 1982; Teaiwa 2000, 2015.

A pilot party of 10 Gilbertese arrived in 1954, visiting Gizo and surrounding islands. They were followed by 30 adult men at the end of 1955, who were accompanied by assistant administrative officer Te Karibanang—the intention being to build up to a balanced community of 120 by 1957.[20] The next group to arrive were 500 from Manra and the southern Gilberts during 1955–57. The first settlement was at Titiana, in the south of Gizo Island, with later settlers placed on small islands close to Gizo. By 1962, there were 600 living at Titiana.[21] A few more families joined the transplanted Gilbertese communities during the second half of the 1950s. Further settlements were begun in the Shortland Islands in 1962–63 for about 120 people who had arranged their own journeys. In 1963, an advance party of 70 cleared land on Wagina Island off southern Choiseul, which became home to 1,200 people from Orona and Nikumaroro islands. The Wagina settlers were government-sponsored, completing the evacuation of the Phoenix Group. A fourth group arrived in the 1960s: 350 came as public servants and students, while some others joined the migration to look for work. Most of these settled near Honiara, some at Red Beach, and others at White River. Two brothers helped with the 1950s transition: Takarebu Tarakabu was an ordained United Church minister, and his brother Tim was soon also ordained. They attended an orientation course at Goldie College and then took up duties at Wagina and Titiana.[22]

The migrants all signed agreements that they would decide within five years whether they intended to remain in the BSIP. The UK Government provided funds to purchase land, mainly that which had been already alienated as coconut plantations. The first and third groups were offered government freehold land if they promised to give up all land rights in the Phoenix Group. The second and fourth groups were not promised any land, although settlers in the second group were able to purchase government perpetual estate (PE, closely resembling freehold) land.[23] They could also apply to join resettlement schemes within the BSIP or apply for land in fixed-term estates (FTEs) in urban areas. In 1971, some of the settlers purchased 8 hectares of an old plantation on the Guadalcanal Plains as freehold land, and another group moved nearby to Komuvada

---

20 *PIM*, July 1955, 87, November 1955, 110.
21 Pitakaka 1979.
22 Bobai 1979: 131–32.
23 A PE is the most common form of landholding in Honiara and, unlike FTE, it is not time bound. It can only be owned by citizens. Evans 2012: 1.

under a land resettlement scheme (Map 6.2). The Wagina Island land in Western District proved to be poor quality, forcing many to look for work elsewhere, with some moving to Honiara.[24]

Questions were asked in the Legislative Council in 1963, expressing fears that the migration could lead to a situation like that in Fiji with its Indian immigrants. In 1971, the Governing Council effectively stopped all further migration by restricting the automatic right of entry of children of existing settlers. The path of the Gilbertese migrants was not smooth. Five years later, the government recommended that if they chose to become citizens, the Gilbertese could keep their existing PE land, but any further land acquisitions should only be leases. Under the terms of early 1970s land ordinances, Gilbertese settlers were defined as Solomon Islanders, which meant they could also acquire customary land with the approval of local councils. The year before independence, the Land and Titles Ordinance was amended, no longer recognising Gilbertese residents as Solomon Islanders, removing their right to purchase PE and customary land from indigenous citizens. The same legislation turned PE land held by non–Solomon Islanders into 75-year FTEs. At home, the Gilbertese had access to individual ownership of land and expected the same conditions in Solomon Islands. Later that year at independence talks in London, a compromise agreement was reached allowing Gilbertese residents automatically to become citizens on application. Although they were allowed to keep their PE land, their access to leased land was limited.[25]

They re-created their original lifestyles, building *maneaba* (large meeting houses) and churches, and maintaining distinct cultural ways, which were particularly obvious in singing, dancing, and martial arts. Coming from atolls, they were unaccustomed to forested land and found it difficult to adapt their maritime skills to Solomons-style agriculture. This was aggravated by the poor quality of land they had been allocated. The Catholic Diocese in Gizo established close relations with the new community, augmenting the United Church connection.[26]

---

24 ibid., 134; Pitakaka and Bobai 1979.
25 Bobai 1979: 134–41; see also McIntyre 2014: 182–95.
26 *BSIP NS*, 12 July 1955, 31 August 1957, 31 May 1963, 31 July 1963, 31 August 1963, 15 November 1963; *BSIP AR* 1969: Part 2, pp. 182–83; Gina 2003: 59–63; Knudson 1965, 1977; Laxton 1951; Cochrane 1970; Bedford 1967.

The 2009 National Population Census recorded 6,446 Micronesians, almost all of whom would have been of Gilbertese descent. For several decades, they have held significant positions in the public service, and Gilbertese dancing has become a tourist mainstay in Honiara and Gizo hotels. The Gilbertese have also intermarried successfully with indigenous Solomon Islanders. The census does not differentiate the offspring of these marriages, and the total population of Gilbertese descent would be much higher than the statistics indicate—equal to the number of indigenous Polynesians in Solomon Islands. The Gilbertese settlers have become citizens, are well integrated into the nation, and a constant presence in Honiara, Gizo, Munda, and on the small islands where they were resettled.[27]

Fijians

The link between Fiji and Solomon Islands was always strong as the BSIP and Fiji were part of the WPHC and, aside from Australia, Fiji provided the main overseas communication channels, whether shipping, telecommunications, or international flights. Two different groups came to Honiara: indigenous Fijians and Indo-Fijians (the descendants of the Girmitiyas, who were indentured labourers from India). Fijian tradesmen on contracts were employed from the 1940s and 1950s when skilled labour was scarce in Honiara, and others worked as clerks in the public service. Fijian Quarter near Chinatown is the original site of their barracks and houses. The Indo-Fijian workers were usually plumbers, mechanics, carpenters, or joiners, most of whom worked for the government, along with a smaller number working for private businesses. For example, of 18 mostly single Indo-Fijian men who arrived during the 1950s and 1960s, seven stayed in Honiara and five married local women. The two groups mixed in Fijian Quarter, on special occasions combining Fijian *Tabua* (whale's tooth) presentations, feasts, and Indian *Taralala* dances.[28] The most senior were in the police force or were assistant medical officers (AMOs) trained at the Fiji School of Medicine. The most significant were probably Ratu Dr Tom Dovi, an AMO and brother of Ratu Sir Lala Sukuna, Fiji's leading early twentieth-century statesman, and Timoci

---

27 They are often still known as Gilbertese, which is not a slight on their Solomon Islands citizenship but differentiates them from the i-Kiribati who are citizens of Kiribati.
28 Tudor 1953a: 119.

Bavadra, who was later briefly Prime Minister of Fiji and who also worked in the Solomons as an AMO (1966–69).[29] A few, such as James Prasad Tahal, went into business and one became general manager of the Tulagi shipyard, until it was bought out by the National Fisheries Development Company in 1978.[30] The families of those who stayed are so blended into the Solomon Islands population as to be inconspicuous.

Solomon Islanders, markets, and exchanges

The chapter now turns to discussion of the presence of Solomon Islanders in modern Honiara—the subject of much of the remainder of the book. The British, busy re-establishing their pre-war regime, were slow to realise that the war had changed everything. Solomon Islanders, particularly in the north and central islands, had experienced invasion, war on land, sea, and air, and had seen almost unbelievable numbers of foreigners and their supplies arrive. Perhaps more than anything else, they had witnessed their colonial 'masters' run away in fear. As well, thousands of men had joined the Defence Force, the Labour Corps, or worked as Scouts with the Coastwatchers. They had learnt about new ways of life, interacting with the American troops, particularly African Americans, who encouraged them to think differently. They had also passed through the years of Maasina Rule (1944–52), the proto-nationalist movement that began on Malaita and spread to neighbouring islands, making demands of the British and cleverly using passive resistance as a tactic. They also experienced the Moro Movement, a social and political force on Guadalcanal over decades. Solomon Islanders had had to deal with war, and protectorate and indigenous-derived forces of progress and national and regional unification. They would never be the same again.

Honiara was also a new phenomenon—much bigger than Tulagi. The problem for Solomon Islanders in its early years was not so much the social segregation or the shortages of various foods, but a lack of money to buy anything at all. An article in the *BSIP News Sheet* looking back on 1949 from 1969 noted:

---

29 Moore 2013c: entry for Bavadra.
30 Tahal and Oxenham 1981.

A little went a long way in those days, with unskilled labourers getting $4 [£2] a month plus $6 [£3] worth of rations. Even so, employers were alarmed at the spiralling cost of living, which in 1949 was two and a half times as high as in 1939.[31]

Other problems emerged as the new urban centre began to expand. Disease epidemics were difficult to control. In late 1949 and early 1950, the Medical Department battled a whooping cough epidemic. Several hundred deaths occurred in the BSIP, and Honiara was a major centre for the disease.[32]

Access to food also became a major issue. Solomon Islanders have always traded commodities at regular markets, and Honiara needed a local food supply. The two needs came together in the establishment of Honiara's Central Market. Murray Bathgate's excellent 1970s studies of the Honiara market supply and the role of the Ndi-Nggae (Map 1.1) people from north-west Guadalcanal show that selling market produce in Honiara was initially an extension of long-established social mechanisms. Items freely given to kin in a village environment were usually sold to outsiders and, while the buyer set the price within a village, it was the seller who established the value outside the village. Cash became a major commodity from the 1940s and 1950s, and the main medium of exchange in Honiara, but never the sole means. Traditional shell valuables and pigs were also traded, and what developed was an amalgam of old and modern trading systems. Inland and coastal peoples on Guadalcanal have always required products from each other. Gifts generated obligations and values were not fixed, varying between individuals and groups. Even though exchanges in Honiara were no longer strictly traditional, elements of *sinei* (exchange with no fixed-equivalent values), *tsabiri* (a form of fixed-equivalence trading expedition), and *voli* (nonceremonial exchange between Ndi-Nggae individuals) remained.[33] Bathgate continues:

> Even though *sinei* exchanges declined following the early change in settlement pattern, and there is no longer *tsabiri* of a traditional type with Malaitans, the people of Santa Ysabel, Savo and the Florida [Ngela] Islands in pigs, valuables and canoes, and the Ndi-Nggai [Nggae] today [in the 1960s], nevertheless they view marketing in Honiara as a *tsabiri*, the purchases made by townsmen as a *voli*, making it quite clear that traditional precedents and associated

---

31 *BSIP NS*, 31 January 1969.
32 *BSIP AR* 1949–50: 24.
33 Bathgate 1973, 1977, 1978a, 1978b, 1985.

exchange concepts have been translated into modern day market place trade. In fact it can be said that in selling food to Malaitans and other Solomon Islanders in Honiara, the Ndi-Nggai are not only carrying out an activity consistent with traditional practice but they are also catering for many of the people with whom, before the place of exchange was centralised to the urban centre, they had trade relationships in the past. It can also be said that where once the Ndi-Nggai acquired shell valuables, canoes and sundry items from Solomon Islanders, they now acquire money in their *tsabiri* which allows them to buy goods in Honiara.[34]

Central Market

Honiara's early expatriate residents always complained about the lack of fresh fruit and vegetables, having to rely on cold room supplies brought by ship from Australia, which usually arrived wilted and unedifying. While they were able to obtain basic supplies from the Government Trade Scheme of anything that was frozen, tinned, bottled, or bagged, they also craved fresh foods. Spearline Wilson, an 'old hand' from Tulagi, was based in Honiara during 1945–46 as Commissioner of Lands, and for a short time was acting government secretary.[35] He knew his way around:

> I get a couple of frozen chickens a week from an unknown (to anybody else) source, and today I expect to acquire about 10 lbs [4.5 kg] of boned roast sirloin. Sunday I had crayfish, Monday a pigeon (shot with my new gun) and Bennie and the orderly produce a fish occasionally. My only expense at home is about 6d per day for bread, which I have to buy at 1/- a loaf from the Chinabloke.[36]

He spent part of his spare time pigeon and pig-shooting, which endeared him to the Solomon Islanders to whom he gave most of his trophies. A few of the 1940s residents grew their own fruit and vegetable gardens. Wilson was growing tomatoes, cabbages, watermelons, rockmelons, and cucumbers. He lived on a coral-topped area with not much soil and went to the trouble of having soil brought in from Tulagi for a flower garden, with asters and zinnias in pride of place.[37]

---

34 Bathgate 1977: 23–24.
35 UQ FML, Wilson Papers, A.H. Wilson to J.A. Wilson, 13 December 1946.
36 ibid., 6 April 1946.
37 ibid., 17 and 30 December 1945, 14 and 15 March 1946.

Honiara has poor soils in many areas, which discouraged gardening, and the residents longed for garden produce to be brought in from surrounding areas. What they needed was a regular marketplace. After the war, the Agriculture Department distributed yam and pana seeds to surrounding villagers to replenish agriculture disrupted by the war, although sweet potatoes were still available. From 1946, once the government's experimental farms at Ilu and Kukum were established, seeds for other vegetables—corn, shallots, watermelon, pumpkin, tomatoes, and beans—were distributed. The next year, the government suggested that surrounding villages might supply root crops for consumption in Honiara and other urban centres, and that they could pay their taxes in this way. This never happened. The first Solomon Islanders to sell produce in Honiara were door-to-door hawkers who first arrived in about 1947 from north coast villages on Guadalcanal, mainly Ndi-Nggae people from near Visale, and others from nearby Kakabona and Mataniko villages. They established contacts with labourers employed in the town and began selling root crops. Once they understood urban market requirements, the villagers added bananas, citrus fruit, varieties of Chinese cabbage, and watercress to their cultivation.[38] Until then, Honiara residents had relied entirely on imported food, and vegetables and fruit supplied from the prison gardens and Kukum and Ilu farms.

A year later, plans were made to build a marketplace and the hawkers were encouraged to become vendors. By 1949, Ho Man (also Ho Min or Ho Nan), an ex-Tulagi Chinese businessman, had established a market garden and Honiara's first restaurant (on the site of today's King Solomon Hotel).[39] Mission farms were operating at Tenaru and Lungga, swelling supplies. The government built a market house as accommodation for visiting vendors, which Ho Man managed to take over for his own business purposes. In early 1950, people from the Ngela Group began to sell produce in Honiara in the same way they had on Tulagi. The government assisted them with transport. The next step came in May when Central Market began on the beach east of Point Cruz. On its first day, the produce sold out in one hour. Two more market days were held later in the month, although transport issues overwhelmed the Ngela villagers. Once more, Honiara was left dependent on local supplies. The district officer then began marketing produce twice weekly out of his own office, mainly to expatriates. Clearly, there had to

---

38 Bathgate 1978b: 11–12.
39 Lawson n.d. [c. 2000s]: 9. By 1952, Ho Man had established another small restaurant, behind the Kukum Married Quarters. Information from Alan Lindley, Adelaide, 2 November 2014.

be a better method than 'feast or famine' to provide food supplies for the growing town. This led the district commissioner to revive the idea of a permanent Central Market supplied from villages to the east and west, and from the south coast. To accomplish this, the government needed to overcome transport problems.[40]

The first permanent Central Market facilities were constructed in 1952 next to the office of the district commissioner. There was a fenced area, several leaf-thatch houses with tables, and produce spread out on leaves on the ground. Marketing occurred on Wednesdays for a few hours in the morning, under police supervision to stop disputes over prices. The police also discouraged hawkers from operating anywhere in Honiara, diverting them to the market. Government produce was sold at fixed prices, which set the standards to which villagers eventually had to conform. The Ndi-Nggae, Mataniko, and Kakabona villagers gradually increased their production. Vura and Tabuku villagers began to participate and, in 1953, once the road was extended up into the Poha Valley, Tapinanja villagers also joined them regularly (Map 4.1). Transport was by road and by canoe. Supplies of produce from the south coast were slower to develop as the government had difficulties providing a reliable transport service.

Plate 4.10 Honiara's Central Market was a simple affair when it began in the 1950s.
Source: Mary Cowmeadow photograph, in Clive Moore Collection.

---

40   Bathgate 1978b: 7–9.

A small market also operated three days a week at the prison gardens.[41] Bathgate reported that, by 1956, Central Market was operating twice a week, on Wednesdays and Saturdays, and the variety and quantity of produce available had improved. Although in 1955 the government sold its 65-hectare Ilu farm to Romulus Dethridge,[42] the government farm at Kukum, which was used to train agricultural extension officers, continued to supply produce. The government also distributed vegetable seeds to surrounding villages to stimulate production. The main customers continued to be European and Chinese.

Table 4.1 Population of Honiara in 1959.

Racial origin	Male	Female	Total
Melanesian	2,154	464	**2,618**
European	201	162	**363**
Chinese	139	127	**266**
Polynesian	137	48	**185**
Fijian	13	11	**24**
Gilbertese	8	6	**14**
Other	12	9	**21**
Total	**2,664**	**827**	**3,491**

Sources: BSIP (1961: 51, 57, 60); Tedder (1966: 37).

Accommodation for Solomon Islanders initially was in leaf-thatch houses, which slowly were replaced with the cement-walled and floored, rather soulless Kukum Labour Line houses, and the Single Officers' Quarter. Over the years, the gender proportions became more equal, although male dominance remained strong during the first few decades. The young single male workers were not major market customers; they were supplied with rations—mainly rice, hard navy biscuits, and tinned meat— although they also purchased small amounts of fruit and vegetables. The government was aware that this limited diet was not satisfactory. During the 1950s, the senior medical officer insisted that the hospital's patients be provided with increased amounts of root and green vegetables, and fruit. This reduced rice to 15 per cent of hospital diets and raised

---

41 Initially, these gardens seem to have been on the site of the present-day National Archives and the National Museum, but by 1953 they were flourishing near the new Rove police headquarters. Tudor 1953b: 69.
42 Hilder 1957.

the root crop proportion to 80 per cent. Fairly quickly, the Mataniko villagers, and those from Tamatangga, Kakabona, Tapinanja, and west Tasimboko, began to sell produce to the hospital. The oversupply was sold in the Honiara market, as was Kukum farm produce. While increasing the availability of fresh produce had a health basis, the government also realised that food imports were costing them £50,000 a year. There was an immediate saving from encouraging local produce and all government departments were advised to purchase local food. For instance, in 1957, the Police and Prisons Department increased the root crop content of staff diets to 50 per cent, and prisoner diets to 85 per cent.[43]

By the end of the 1950s, the amount of market produce reaching Honiara had increased, mainly coming from around Guadalcanal, with Ngela villagers making occasional contributions, and Malaitans also entering the fray. There was never enough produce and, in the 1950s, the settlers at Fishing Village regularly hired trucks from the town council to visit surrounding Guale villages to purchase root crops. During 1957 and 1958, the people around Auki began sending market ships loaded with betel nuts, fish, pigs, and root crops. Between 1956 and 1960, *Bina*, a government ship, brought produce each month from Guadalcanal's south coast and, by 1958, a local boat out of Tasimboko, east of Honiara, brought regular produce to market and to supply the hospital. Ken Hay, whose GPL company had purchased Ilu farm, was producing exotic vegetables for European and Chinese tastes. The Police and Prisons Department was also supplied from a village to the east of Honiara.

Murray Bathgate divided suppliers into three groups (Map 4.1). In the first were people from Mataniko, Kakabona, Chiri, Tapinanja, and Veramboli. This part of the supply chain was interfered with by expatriates with cars, who began intercepting the vendors when they overnighted at Kakabona before market day. This left Honiara's Solomon Islanders with reduced supplies in the market; they complained to the district commissioner. The second group was from Vura, Taboko, Vatusii, Vilu, and Takemboru. In the second half of the 1950s, as more people in these villages purchased vehicles, their participation increased, although Vura people were the main enthusiasts. Nearby villagers also walked to Honiara or cadged lifts with government and mission vehicles. Outsiders—namely, a Malaitan

---

43   Bathgate 1978b: 9–12.

and a mixed-race woman—also established commercial gardens in this area, supplying the Police and Prisons Department and Central Market. The third group was from further away in west Guadalcanal, between Takemboru and Lambi Bay. With no direct road access, they preferred to produce export crops and dive for trochus shell to earn cash income.[44] For them, copra production was still greater than production of market vegetables.

The old labour recruiting system (a hangover from the days of indenture contracts) ceased in 1960. Labourers no longer received rations and were paid marginally higher wages to compensate. They had to obtain their own food, which stimulated the sale of produce in Honiara's market.[45] By 1970, Honiara had a population of more than 11,000 people. The cash-crop production escalated during the 1960s and 1970s, providing a substantial urban market for agricultural produce. The road infrastructure improved, allowing reasonably easy access to Honiara's market from as far west as Visale. Government agricultural extension work also expanded. Demonstration farms were established at Komimbo (near Visale) and at Vatakola (near Kakabona), allowing people to be educated about new crops, hygienic packaging, and transport. The Agriculture Department established vegetable marketing cooperatives—the first at Mataniko in 1961 and the second at Vatakola in 1965. A market was built at Vatakola, operating on Saturdays, but like the earlier ambush of supplies at Kakabona, Chinese businessmen arrived at 5 am and bought up all the produce to onsell in Honiara.[46] Central Market and other smaller markets operated on the 'shilling economy': items for sale were sorted into piles valued at 1 shilling; pennies and sixpence coins were not used. It was a picturesque scene, as the rural women sold their produce, while their menfolk watched and chatted. All the Guale men and women smoked pipes, often keeping a plug of stick tobacco threaded through a hole in their earlobe. Everyone chewed betel nuts.

---

44 ibid., 13–14.
45 Bellam 1970: 75.
46 Bathgate 1978b: 15–16.

Plate 4.11 Betel nut sellers in Honiara's Central Market, 1970s.
Source: Ian Frazer Collection.

Plate 4.12 The *Compass Rose II* carrying thousands of pineapples from Malaita to Honiara's Central Market, 1994.
Source: Clive Moore Collection.

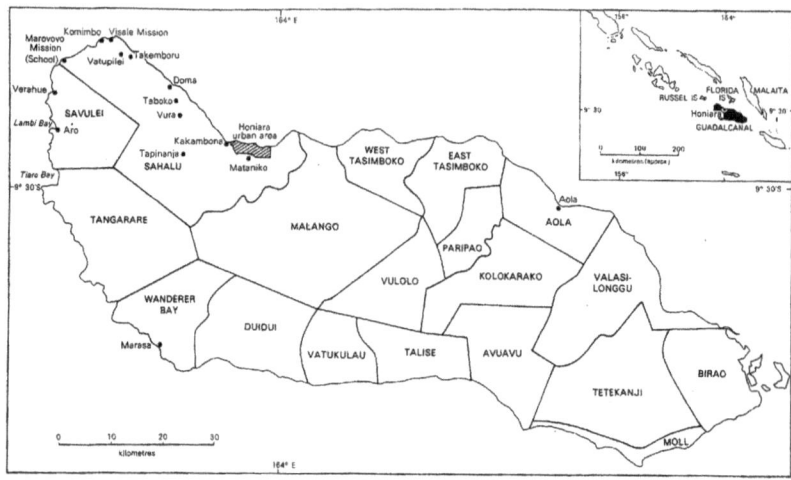

Map 4.1 Guadalcanal council wards in the early 1970s, showing details of settlements in the north-west, which were the main areas supplying Honiara's Central Market.
Note: Bathgate used Kakambona as the spelling on this map; elsewhere in the book, it is Kakabona.
Source: Bathgate (1978b: 64).

Migration to Honiara

The 1959 census (Table 4.1) spelled out clearly what had worried authorities since Honiara was established. Although the proportion of males and females was well balanced in the overall BSIP population, in Honiara, 82 per cent of the indigenous population was male and most were young adults from Malaita. One of what I have called Honiara's 'worlds' (Figure 0.1) had emerged: Malaitans dominated overall and were the main labour force in Honiara. However, all islands were represented in the new urban centre. For instance, Choiseulese, who were smaller in number, came to Honiara to find work and pursue lifestyles and education impossible on their own island, as did other groups from the central Solomons. The same applied to migrants from the Outer Islands. Quite large numbers from the Reef Islands, and Polynesians from Tikopia, Anuta, Sikaiana, and Ontong Java Atoll migrated to Honiara. Eventually, these communities outnumbered the populations on their home islands. The Guale were always there, too, as it was their island and they had easy access to Honiara.[47]

---

47   Donner 2002; Feinberg 1996, 2002; Kengava 1979.

Ian Frazer's early 1970s study of the To`ambaita from north Malaita exemplifies the movement that took place from the 1950s, usually with no intention of a permanent shift of residence. Honiara provided alternative employment to plantation work. The main drive was to find employment in the new town and to better their economic and social circumstances. Young men regarded the migration as an adventure, much as their grandfathers had in working as indentured labourers in Queensland and Fiji, with the intention of eventually returning home to marry.[48] Working in Honiara and on the Guadalcanal Plains had become the new Malaitan 'rite of passage'. The W.D. & H.O. Wills Company tobacco factory (Map 7.1), with its Dickensian working conditions, was an urban replacement for plantation work. Older married men with families also participated, taking the chance to earn wages, which, although low, were more than anything they could earn in their villages or anywhere on Malaita. If they failed to find work, their *wantoks* supported them and, if necessary, paid to send them home again. And there was also extra excitement available, as Frazer described:

> Honiara has all the attractions associated with a fast growing town, such as picture shows, recreational and sporting clubs, drinking facilities, and trading stores with a wide range of consumer goods available at prices more favourable than in rural areas.[49]

After a while, as still occurs, the momentum was increased by migration to join *wantoks*' existing families, or individuals who had succeeded in Honiara. Much of the unskilled labour force was transitory, wages were low, and there was insufficient accommodation available for families. In 1958, 40 per cent of Honiara's labourers worked there for three months or less, 20 per cent for three to seven months, and 15 per cent for six to 12 months, before returning to their villages.[50] By 1960, building contractors, other employers, and the Public Works Department were able to engage all necessary labour in Honiara. Only the Ports Authority still recruited stevedores from elsewhere for Honiara-based activities.[51] The first meeting of the Legislative Council in 1961 discussed the problems created by Solomon Islanders visiting Honiara without sufficient means of support, thus causing financial hardship for permanent residents. The government was requested to report on possible remedies.[52]

---

48 Moore 1985, 2017.
49 Frazer 1973: 115.
50 Tedder 1966: 37.
51 *BSIP AR* 1959–60: 8.
52 *BSIP Legislative Council Debates*, 2 May 1962, 48.

Plate 4.13 Honiara's tobacco factory, 1972 (see position on Map 7.1).
Solomon Islanders first smoked tobacco in the nineteenth century, bartered from whalers and traders, and obtained when working on plantations overseas and in the protectorate. Initially smoked in clay pipes, the tobacco was also rolled in strips of newspaper or pages from school exercise books. W.D. & H.O. Wills Company built Solomon Islands Tobacco Company at Ranadi in 1967. Production of twist tobacco began that July, with 5 tons of cut and twist tobacco manufactured each month — enough to supply the Solomon Islands and New Hebrides markets. In 1968, its first full year of operations, the company produced 66.74 tons of twist tobacco worth $249,208. The leaf came from the United States and Africa.
Source: Ian Frazer Collection.

Demographic trends in the 1970s and 1980s

Census statistics for the BSIP are poorly enumerated before 1970. The first BSIP-wide census was in 1931. Another planned for 1949 was only complete for Western and parts of Eastern and Central districts. This was in the middle of the Maasina Rule years and the government received no cooperation from Malaitans and some other island groups. There was another partial census in 1959—deliberately so this time—as the government seems to have been unable to finance a full national census. A complete census did not occur until 1970, which was repeated in 1986, 1999 (another year with difficulties that made those results unreliable),

2009, and 2019.⁵³ The 1959 census (Table 4.1) tells us little about Honiara, beyond basic numbers. Over decades, indigenous male/female ratios became more equal, with the predominance of indigenous males dropping from 81.7 per cent in 1959 to 58 per cent in 1976, and 53 per cent in 2009. The number of households has more than tripled since 1978 and household sizes are bigger. In the 1960s, 1970s, and 1980s, the population was overwhelmingly young, with 39 per cent aged under 14 years. Honiara was predominantly a very young male Malaitan town.⁵⁴

Table 4.2 Honiara's gender profile: Melanesian population in 1970.

Age	Female	Male	Total
0 to 4	546	624	**1,170**
5 to 9	373	429	**802**
10 to 14	340	437	**777**
15 to 19	400	1189	**1,619**
20 to 24	400	1070	**1,470**
25 to 29	254	773	**1,027**
30 to 34	157	497	**654**
35 to 39	111	265	**376**
40 to 44	65	160	**225**
45 to 49	62	130	**192**
50 to 54	33	96	**129**
55 to 59	19	47	**66**
60 to 64	12	38	**50**
65+	13	46	**59**

Source: BSIP (1970).

Table 4.3 Age divisions in Honiara's population, 1976 and 1986 (percentage).

Year	1–14 years	15–29 years	30–40 years	45–59 years	Over 60 years
1976	39.20	35.7	17	5.80	2.1
1986	39.23	35.7	14	5.12	2.1

Source: SIG (1988a: 5, 15).

---

53   The latest national census occurred in November 2019. The full statistical analysis had not been released when this book was finalised in late 2020. SIG 2020g.
54   BSIP 1961; SIG 1988a: 5, 15, Table 2, p. 57.

Table 4.4 Protectorate-born population by island, compared with Honiara's protectorate-born Melanesian population, and the Melanesian male population, 1970.

Islands/Sub-Districts, Urban Area, Districts	Total Population by Island/Sub-Districts, Urban Area, Districts	Melanesian Population of Honiara	Solomon Islander Males in Honiara Over 15 Years
Guadalcanal	23,996	2,039	540
Honiara	11,191	(see total)	(see total)
Ngela	5,351	346	236
Rennell & Bellona	1,504	0	1
Russell	2,715	19	5
Santa Isabel	8,653	536	318
Savo	1,352	48	34
Central District	**54,762**	**2,988**	**1,134**
Anuta	157	n.a.	n.a.
Makira	10,921	241	151
Reef	4,053	228	176
Santa Cruz	3,433	51	35
Tikopia	1,040	n.a.	n.a.
Ulawa	1,469	64	38
Utupoa	232	n.a.	n.a
Vanikoro	163	n.a.	n.a.
Other	0	4	8
Eastern District	**21,468**	**588**	**408**
Malaita	50,659	4,183	2,291
Pelau, Luaniua & Sikaiana	1,063	n.a.	9
Other	0	0	9
Malaita District	**51,722**	**4,183**	**2,309**
Choiseul	8,017	165	109
Marovo	4,538	87	44
Roviana	8,499	311	174
Shortland	1,950	42	32
Vella Lavella	9,227	173	92
Western District	**32,231**	**778**	**451**
TOTAL	**160,183**	**8,537**	**4,302**

Source: BSIP (1970: 23, 32). These statistics come from two different sources in the census report. Except for the total population by island, they can only be taken as an overall approximation. I have excluded the Polynesian islands from the Honiara Melanesian population statistics, while leaving in islands that are Melanesian with Polynesian influences.

4. THE OTHER HONIARA

Kastom and *wantokism*

As well as maintaining traditional gardening practices, Solomon Islanders in Honiara adapted other customary ways of behaving to survive in the urban environment. Two terms are relevant, *kastom* and *wantok*. *Kastom* (shared traditions and customary ways of behaving) was applied and adapted constantly. In Solomon Islands, *kastom* is not a hegemonic ideology. Anthropologist David Akin suggests this is because some of the leading Christian churches, particularly in the past, opposed the retention of what they saw as 'customary ways', and because the most *kastom*-conscious large island is Malaita, where *kastom* emerged after the war as an anti-government ideology.[55] *Kastom* is a fluid concept that is used selectively as part of Solomon Islanders' ability to cope with modernisation and change.[56] *Kastom* affects the way a physical dwelling is used. If sexual separation is practised—which is still typical in many villages—then customary special divisions will be observed, even in a small urban house full of visiting family members. In a one-bedroom house, a couple and their children retreat to the bedroom as a family unit, leaving the rest of the house to the visitors, who occupy the living and outdoor kitchen areas. Or the house could be divided into male and female domains. No-one is ever turned away because of lack of space.[57]

Wantokism is derived from *wantok* ('one talk'), meaning from the same language group, and implies giving preference to kin in the expectation of reciprocal obligations being fulfilled. Once *wantoks* are outside their village situation (where everyone usually speaks one language), the same-language social category applies, particularly in urban, school, or plantation/work situations. As political scientist Tarcisius Tara Kabutaulaka has noted, increasingly, *wantokism* has become a term used 'to identify people from the same region or island to distinguish them from outsiders, even if they speak a different language'.[58] In its broadest form, it identifies all Solomon Islanders (when they are overseas) as one people, or all Melanesians as one people. In the Solomons, the added complication is that there are also substantial Polynesian and Micronesian communities, which practise their own type of *wantokism*, broadening the base of the concept.[59]

---

55   Akin 2005: 98.
56   Keesing 1982, 1993; Keesing and Tonkinson 1982; Babadzan 2004; Gooberman-Hill 1999: 29–31.
57   Jourdan 1985: 55–96.
58   Kabutaulaka 1998: 24; Nanau 2011.
59   Nanau 2011.

Wantokism operates like a social security system, providing food, shelter, and care to the wider group. They do so not just out of obligation. It comes from a belief about what is necessary to support societal stability. In Honiara, this means supplying hospitality to visiting kin and relatives. At moments of crisis and rites of passage, they send remittances to immediate and extended family members. Remittances are used to pay school fees or church requirements, and to help with supplying food and clothing, as well as playing a part in ceremonial activities on their home islands. In optimum circumstances, Solomon Islanders will return to their villages, even if only briefly when they are working, to take part in weddings or funerals. There is no strong concept of a nuclear family, and equal place goes to extended families. First, second, or third cousins are regarded as brothers and sisters, and aunts and uncles are treated as parents. Adoption of children between families is part of normal life. If unable to attend a social activity in their home village, Solomon Islanders will send money or bags of rice, provide fares for relatives to attend, and eventually return themselves, with compensatory goods, cash, and sometimes customary wealth items. Being a Solomon Islander carries deep and meaningful obligations, freely given, and love for their families. For those who have migrated to another area there is the added need to maintain their rights at home. They are quite aware that long absences and lack of participation in communal responsibilities make them lesser members of their descent groups, which in the long term will dilute their access to land and ceremonial rights. When the main wages activity revolved around plantation work, there was little chance of returning home to fulfil one's obligations, except at the end of contracts. In urban situations, it became usual for Solomon Islanders to try to keep, but also to restructure, their kin obligations.

In an urban setting, *wantokism* develops both horizontally and vertically. In the 'valley' communities in Honiara, *wantokism* has been remade through weekend neighbourhood gatherings for gardening, sporting or church events, birthdays, and other social events. Some of these ties emerge from equivalent personal circumstances. For instance, in the 1960s and 1970s, senior public servants worked alongside junior labourers in their gardens in Honiara's valleys on land either leased from the Guale or in Queen Elizabeth National Park. The common factors were their agricultural backgrounds, the paucity of root and green vegetables in the market, which created the need to supplement wages to supply food for extended families, and gardening as a form of exercise. The same applied to fishing after work or on weekends, and to hunting. As Honiara grew, there was less spare space in the valleys; animals such as possums and birds became rarer, hunted to extinction. Great strain was caused from feeding the extended family members who flowed in and out of Honiara while they were job-hunting, shopping, seeking medical care, on church group trips, or selling copra and trochus shells, or artefacts for the tourist market. Nothing has changed. They still often stay for extended periods, overcrowding houses and straining finances.

Initially, Solomon Islanders from outside Guadalcanal saw Honiara as a place to earn quick money and return home. Home remained their island of origin, to which most families returned on annual holidays and to fulfil social obligations. As the Tandai population had long been displaced from the Honiara area, and was not large, Honiara was never the equivalent of Papua New Guinea's Rabaul, Lae, and Port Moresby, where nearby villagers supplied much of the manual and clerical labour. Children, even if born in Honiara, still identified with their parents' islands of origin. Over decades, there has been a shift as many Honiara-born residents have now lost touch with their ancestral roots and seldom return to their parents' villages. This is discussed in the final chapter.

***

Honiara was a readymade town based on American wartime facilities. It was excised from what became the Guadalcanal Sahalu Council Ward, neighboured by the Malango and West Tasimboko wards (Map 4.1). The British were slow to invest in the development of new infrastructure. Ten years after the end of the war, the Solomons plantation economy had been re-established and confidence was beginning to be restored. Honiara's early development depended on obtaining funds from the British Government through the WPHC, although eventually independent commercial development spread, first to Chinatown and then around Point Cruz, and at Ranadi. Honiara quickly became much more of a focal point for Solomon Islanders than Tulagi ever had been. This process was never an alienation from village roots; it was a circulation and extension, based on cultural concepts that continued to operate in the districts and, later, the provinces.

HONIARA

By the time independence arrived in 1978, Honiara was a thriving and expanding urban area, an entity that functioned separately from the rest of the island. The Guale were becoming aware that urban growth and the presence of the 'foreigners'—Europeans, Chinese, Gilbertese, other Pacific Islanders, and other Solomon Islanders, particularly Malaitans—living there had made their island different. There was a sense of pride that Guadalcanal had become the centre of the new nation, accompanied by a growing sense of unease as Guale realised they were not reaping many of the benefits.

The argument put forward in the Introduction and summarised in its Figure 0.1 is that several intersecting 'worlds' existed in Honiara, the importance and composition of which altered over time. From the late 1940s and 1950s, Solomon Islanders began to live in Honiara on a temporary basis, as an extension of a pattern of circular mobility that dated back to the nineteenth-century labour trade, and to plantations and Christian missions in the protectorate in the twentieth century. Just as they had overseas on Queensland and Fijian plantations, and on BSIP plantations, Malaitans predominated in Honiara's labour force. Solomon Islanders from all over the protectorate and nation lived in Honiara, but, other than Malaitans, never in such large numbers that any other island group became dominant.

There are pan-Malaitan characteristics that bind them together as *wantoks* in a whole-island sense and, just as earlier labour movements and Maasina Rule united them, so, too, have their Honiara experiences. Nevertheless, it is wrong to depict Malaitans as one united group. They come from a dozen language and cultural regions on the island. Malaitans moved to Honiara roughly in the same proportions as their numbers in various language areas at home. The Kwara`ae were always the main group and those from the north were also numerous. The move to Honiara made intermarriages easier, both with other Malaitans and with other Solomon Islanders. They also made marriage links into the European, Chinese, and other Pacific Islander communities.

There came a stage—probably beginning as early as the late 1950s, and certainly in the 1960s and 1970s—when there was a significant enough Malaitan urban community to claim that they inhabited their own Honiara 'world', measured not in terms of economic or political control, but through indigenous social dominance. If we use the 1970 census as our guide (Table 4.4), Honiara had a population of 11,191 people, or close to 7 per cent of the national population of 160,183.[60] Malaitans made up 37.4 per cent of Honiara's total population. The next largest island group was from Guadalcanal: 2,039 or 18.2 per cent. The 2,291 Malaitan males made up 54.7 per cent of Honiara's Melanesian male population over 15 years of age.[61]

60 BSIP 1970: Table IID, p. 20.
61 ibid., 32, 33.

5
Municipal authority and housing

The modern boundary of Honiara City Council includes 2,273 hectares of land and another 1,151 hectares of water off the coast (Map 9.1).[1] Most often the land, not the water, is the centre of the story. Then, in 2017, the Tandai won a court case over ownership of the sea surrounding Honiara—a reminder that, in the Pacific Islands, customary land includes areas of sea, in the same way as modern nations claim ownership of the surrounding ocean. Honiara land is vested in the government as Perpetual Estate (PE) and is regulated by the *Land and Titles (Amendment) Act 2014*.[2] In 2006, there were said to have been 6,078 PEs within Honiara.[3] The Commissioner of Lands is trustee for the government over PE titles. The commissioner (now governed by a Land Board) has the power to create fixed-term estates (FTEs), Temporary Occupation Licences (TOLs), and Temporary Housing Areas (THAs), to transfer them or enable subleases, and has also to deal with squatters occupying land to which they have no legal claim. Strategic planning for land use comes under the Honiara Local Planning Scheme and the Ministry of Lands, Housing and Survey. There is also a very small amount of Tandai customary land, and one right-of-way, within the boundary.

---

1 BSIP 1970: 24; Foukona and Allen 2017: 92.
2 SIG 2014c.
3 Evans 2012: 1.

HONIARA

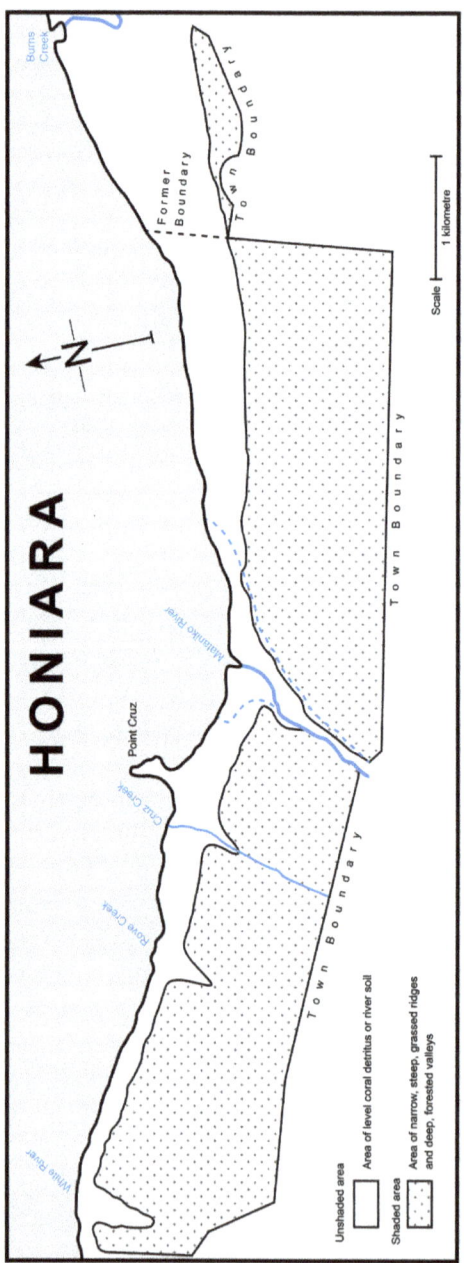

Map 5.1 Honiara Town Council boundary in 1959.

Note the extension to the east to incorporate the land for educational institutions. Kukum Airfield and Ranadi industrial estate had not yet been included. The dotted lines around the Mataniko River indicate its floodplain.

Source: Based on a map in Tedder (1966). Cartography by Vincent Verheyen.

Map 5.1 illustrates the land area of Honiara in 1959, with the narrow coastal plain backed by steep grassed ridges and deep forested valleys. The early town area stretched for 10 kilometres along the coast, with a national park added in 1954, abutting the south-east of the urban area. Honiara was surrounded by large tracts of alienated land to the east and customary-owned land to the west and inland. The boundaries of the Honiara City Council area have been extended over time and are of complex origin. As explained in Chapter 3, in 1947–48, the BSIP Government acquired nearly all the land within the boundaries of the new town. Customary and plantation lands from the west bank of the Mataniko River to White River were resumed, as was Levers' Kukum plantation to the east. In 1954, the government negotiated to obtain a large parcel of Tandai land inland from east Honiara, extending to Mt Austen, which became the 6,070-hectare Queen Elizabeth National Park. A small area of customary land was exempted from the resumptions—although this is now under the control of squatters—at the mouth of the Mataniko and in the settlement at the base of Koa Hill. Two other anomalies occurred: at Mbumburu in the 1970s, when a two-storey block of units was built partly over the boundary, and a water tank that was built wholly over the boundary.[4]

Map 5.3 is a 2010s map of west Honiara, which blends into traditional Tandai land centred on Kakabona. Map 6.2 depicts the Guadalcanal Plains as they were divided in the 1970s, showing the complex land-use patterns that had evolved on what were once coconut plantations and then a battlefield. The boundary to the east, which was initially quite limited, was extended in the second half of the 1950s to include the new educational institutions at Kukum and Panatina, but not yet including what is now Ranadi industrial estate.[5] After Kukum Airfield closed, the land around it was included in Honiara's urban area, which enabled the expansion of Ranadi industrial estate. Further areas to the east of the original Honiara City boundary were acquired from Levers in 1965 and 1970, although there were few people living there. Several small areas of freehold land close to the eastern boundary, belonging to Levers and Christian missions, were converted into FTEs.[6] Clearly, it was easier to expand east than west. When the southern city boundary absorbed a large part of the failed national park in 1973, the Mataniko, Vura, and Panatina wards were expanded (Map 5.2).[7]

---

4   Information from Jeffrey Moore, 5 May 2020.
5   It was originally called the Kukum industrial estate.
6   Oram 1980: 137–38. See Section 3 of the Town Planning Ordinance (6/1954 as amended) under L.N. 13/1969.
7   BSIP 1970: 24; Foukona and Allen 2017: 92.

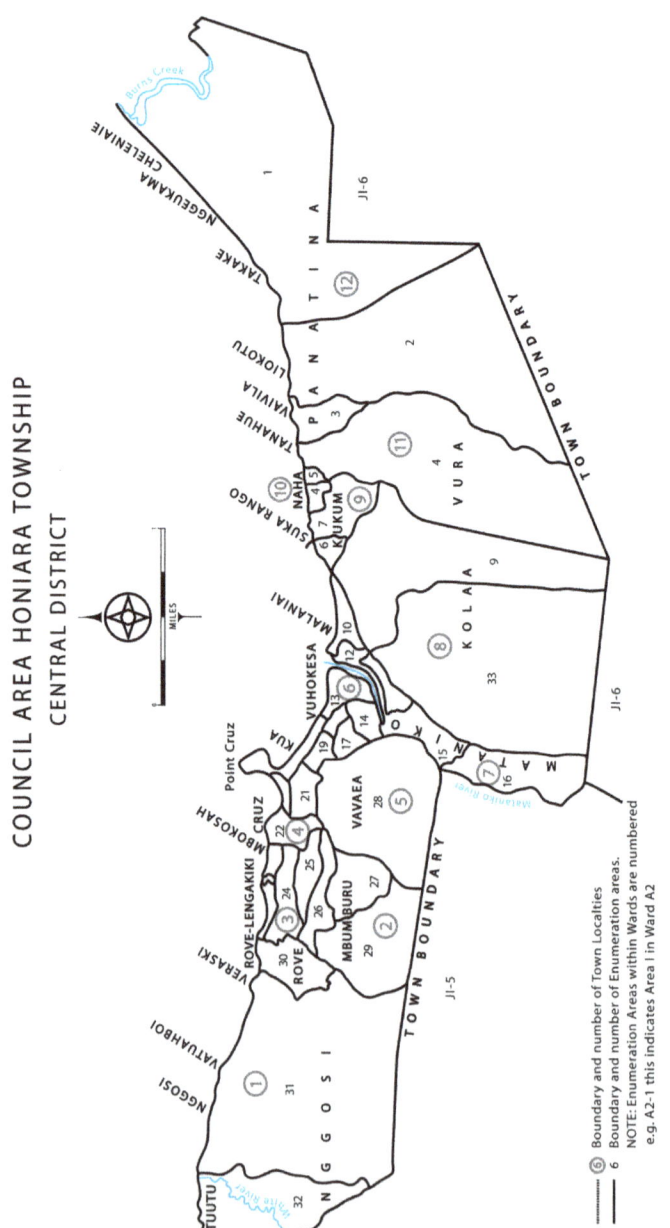

Map 5.2 Honiara's town boundary, 1976.

Note the changes to the Kola`a, Vura, and Panatina boundaries to include areas of Queen Elizabeth National Park resumed in 1973, and the resumption of Kukum Airfield in 1957, which enabled the creation of Ranadi industrial estate and the golf course.

Source: Based on Floyd (1976: 25). Cartography by Vincent Verheyen.

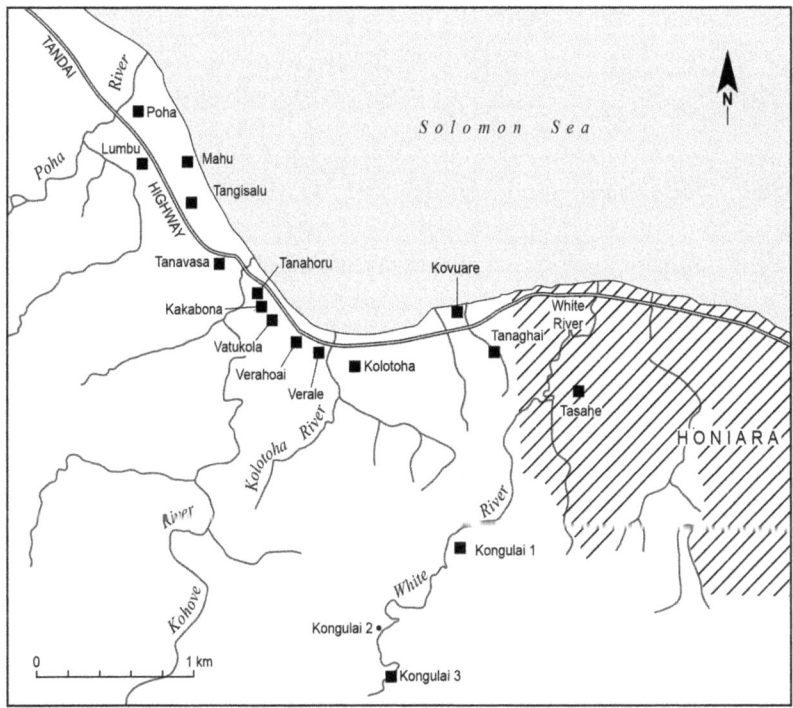

Map 5.3 The west of Honiara City Council's land and adjacent customary-owned areas of Guadalcanal, 2010s.
Source: Monson (2015: 438).

All of this was accompanied by an initial attempt to regularise the settlement patterns of Solomon Islanders arriving in Honiara. Village-style settlements were created in the early 1950s at Malaitan Fishing Village at Kukum and at White River, and about the same time squatters began to move on to vacant land elsewhere. As often happened in Honiara, modern authorities had to accommodate residential patterns based on customary land use, rather than migrants fitting with the municipal regulations governing settlement. Compromises were reached. The largest group of inward migrants came from Malaita, followed by those from Western, Guadalcanal, and Central provinces.[8] The valleys behind Honiara soon began to fill with village-style houses.

---

8   SIG 1988a: 5, 15; 1988b.

As mentioned in Chapter 3, the first Honiara town plan was prepared in 1945. Separation of Honiara's affairs from those of the BSIP Government began in the late 1940s when a six-man Town Board was established. A Town Planning Ordinance was passed in 1954 to provide a framework under which an area of land could be declared a town. Honiara Town Council was constituted under the 1957 Town Councils Ordinance by a warrant issued by High Commissioner Gutch on 1 March 1958. The 1957 ordinance was reconstituted under the 1963 Local Government Ordinance, which was further amended in 1969. There were 12 council members, one for each ward, all appointed by the high commissioner, with one member each supplied from the Departments of the District Commissioner Central, Public Works, Lands and Survey, and Medical Services.[9]

There were no town planners employed in the BSIP until just before independence.[10] Since the 1940s, Honiara's suburban area has extended further along the coast to the east and inland along valleys, ridges, and hills. The number of people recorded as living in Honiara can be deceptive, as the statistics only count those living within the official boundary. Official statistics suggest that, in 1954, there were 1,400 residents in Honiara, 3,548 in 1959, 6,684 in 1965, 11,191 in 1970, 13,300 in mid-1971, and 17,000 by 1974. Even though these statistics are conservative, this is an increase of 10 to 15 per cent a year. Unfortunately, the number of new jobs available only covered about 5 per cent of the annual population increase. The official population almost doubled in the six years between 1959 and 1965 and more than trebled between 1959 and 1970. There was also the beginning of a peri-urban population that was part of Honiara but living beyond the city boundaries (Figure 9.1).

While detailed planning was lacking, the ridges and valleys were reserved for residential zones, and the coastal plain was set aside for government departments, commerce, industry, educational institutions, and sports and community facilities. Forty-five per cent of the early population was employed by the government. The Honiara Town Council had specific responsibilities and duties to pass by-laws (which still required higher approval) and had only limited powers to raise revenue, instead relying

---

9   District Commissioner Central, D.G. Cudmore, was the first chairman of the council. The first indigenous members were Alphonse Daga from Western District, Jesimiel Afia from Malaita, and J. Tamana. *BSIP NS*, 31 May 1969.
10   Floyd 1974; Heath 1975, 1978.

mainly on an annual subvention from the BSIP Government. The District Commissioner Central, based in Honiara, served as the executive officer of the council, with similar duties to those of a council clerk in the districts. Although early planning was very ad hoc, in 1958, there was a report into urban housing for Solomon Islanders. In 1960, Honiara was divided into zones with appropriate building standards gazetted: commercial and industrial areas had to be built in concrete, usually in the form of concrete blocks. Chinatown was largely exempt from these requirements because many of its buildings preceded the regulation, which left its quaint wooden trade stores intact. The Town Planning Board was set up in 1961 and a more substantial town plan was completed the next year. By designating areas as low and high-density residential zones, the new plan created spatial separation of Solomon Islanders and expatriates, with a blurred line at Chinatown and the Mataniko River (Map 8.1). This separation established a model quite different from urban areas elsewhere—for example, in many South-East Asian cities, which have mixed occupancy. This ensured that central parts of Honiara were very European in character.[11]

The issue of squatters occupying town council land began to be discussed during the 1960s. The council chairman warned that 'iron shanties' or 'slum dwellings' constructed without permits could be ordered to be demolished, except at White River and Malaitan Fishing Village at Kukum, where by-laws were relaxed.[12] The council encouraged the digging of individual and communal pit-latrines, and attempts were made to stop pigs and dogs roaming around. There was an existing but limited coastal piped-water system left by the Americans, although most government and expatriate private houses usually also had water tanks. Other residents used natural springs and boreholes, hand-carrying water to their homes. Residents living near the upper Mataniko and White rivers were the only ones with an excellent free-flowing freshwater stream and late in the afternoons people there went upstream to bathe. Sadly, both are now too polluted for this use.

---

11   Bellam 1970: 78.
12   PMB 1371, Nigel Oram 1962–93, Papers on Town Planning in Bougainville and Honiara, and Provincial Government in Papua New Guinea: Town Planning Ordinance, No. 6, 1954; Honiara Town Building By-Laws, *BSIP Gazette*, Notice No. 152, January 1960; BSIP 1962; BSIP SINA, Chairman, Honiara Town Council Circular No. 4/67, File LAN 2/1/5, 1 September 1967.

Plate 5.1 Central District Headquarters in Honiara, 1956.
The building was on the beach on the Point Cruz side of the present Central Market.
Source: Alan Lindley Collection, in Clive Moore Collection.

Plate 5.2 Flamboyant poinciana trees in Hibiscus Avenue, Honiara, 1968.
The Honiara Town Council planted many flowering trees to beautify the town. They are immediately obvious in photographs from the early years and Solomon Islanders remember being able to walk along Mendana and Hibiscus avenues shaded by the fringe of red-flowered poincianas. Sadly, most of them have now been cut down.
Source: Les Tickle Collection.

A new Town Council Ordinance was introduced in 1968, allowing for future elections, along with a core of appointed members. This came under the Honiara Town Council (Constitution of Wards) Order in 1969, which created the 12 wards. Plans for the Honiara recognisable in the 2020s first developed during the 1970s, with commercial, residential, and industrial zones. Soon after independence, conflicts began to arise between council plans and those of government departments and agencies, which often ignored the council and sometimes tried to make decisions that were contrary to existing town planning.

Council elections were held in 1969.[13] The council's budget was $121,000, of which only $11,000 came from a service tax. The main expenditure was on capital works. The council took over responsibility for the provision of junior primary education in Honiara—initially only at the main primary school. Then, several new primary schools were built to cater for the new housing estates.[14] The Kukum shoreline was cleared and made into a park for public use, and the Rove Botanic Gardens were established in 1971, along with an orchid house.[15] By 1974, the council's revenue was $339,000, and was mainly used for public health and education, the construction of a new Central Market building, and an abattoir.[16] The town council became a municipal authority in 1980. *The Honiara City Act 1999* created a city council of 20 members.[17]

Expanding Honiara and anticipating other urban developments in the protectorate provided a planning dilemma. The government buildings were clustered west of Point Cruz and the central business district was close by on Mendana Avenue. There was recognition that the port facilities at Point Cruz had to be enlarged, and that there needed to be a new bridge

---

13   The new council members were: Nggosi (Lilian Poznanski), Mburumburu (Dr R.B. Thompson), Rove–Lengakiki (Ron Lawson), Cruz (Rose Dettke), Vavaea (Peter Smith), Vuhokesa (Peter Salaka), Matanikau (D. Chinn), Kola`a (John Lee), Kukum (Stephen Sipolo), Naha (Gordon Billy Gatu), Vura (C.H. Cheng), and Panatina (J. Kari). The high commissioner appointed Mr Sheehan, a surveyor from the Lands Department, Chief Health Inspector Mr Dunn, and acting Deputy Director of Public Works Mr MacNaughton. *BSIP NS*, 31 March 1958, 31 March 1969, 30 September 1969.
14   These were at White River and Tuvaruhu (1969), Mbokonavera (1970), and Vura (1971). Three more were planned for Rove, Koloale (between Chinatown and west Kola`a Ridge), and a site near the training college at Kukum (now Panatina). *BSIP NS*, 31 March 1958, 31 October 1971; *BSIP AR* 1958–59: 63–64.
15   It appears the Botanic Gardens may meet the same fate as the Queen Elizabeth National Park. In 2019, there were squatters living within its upper boundary. SIBC, 3 July 2019.
16   *BSIP AR* 1974: 146.
17   As noted in the Introduction, 12 members are elected to represent the wards and the Minister for Home Affairs appoints the three parliamentarians with Honiara constituencies, the Premier of Guadalcanal Province, and four other members (one of whom must be from Guadalcanal).

over the Mataniko River in line with Mendana Avenue. Central Market was established midway between Point Cruz and Chinatown. Community facilities were also slated to be built close to the west bank of the Mataniko River, although this was flood-prone land. Another failing in the rather haphazard growth of downtown Honiara was the overemphasis on, and consequent increasing congestion around, Mendana and Hibiscus avenues. Two more troublesome features of modern Honiara have never been resolved. First, the convenience of having the fuel storage facilities close to the port is overwhelmed by the potential for explosions in the centre of the city. Second, the National Referral Hospital is on the coast, too close to the mouth of the Mataniko River and the adjacent beach, and exposed to possible tsunamis. Discussions on moving the hospital and the fuel tanks have continued over decades.

Ranadi industrial estate

The town plan included Ranadi industrial estate, midway between Point Cruz and Henderson Airfield, which was originally known as Kukum industrial area and was developed for use by light manufacturing and to support the agricultural industries on Guadalcanal Plains. In the mid-1960s, a small industrial area already existed at Ranadi, housing the Joy biscuit factory, a tin-container factory, a joinery, and a bakery, but the area was inadequate for expansion.[18] The growth that occurred was further east along Kukum Highway. Once the airfield was relocated to Henderson, there was enough spare land to use as a golf course, and to expand the commercial and industrial areas.

Honiara's educational institutions are described in Chapter 7. All were positioned along the coast at what was once all called Kukum and is now Kukum, Ranadi and Panatina. Nearby Kukum Beach had been developed, but only to a limited extent as it always took the brunt of heavy cyclonic seas. Burns Creek, on the western side of the streams and channels at the mouth of the Lungga River, closed off the urban area. In the 1970s, a small ferrocement shipbuilding enterprise operated at Kukum Beach, as did the town council abattoir, and a commercial soap factory.[19]

18 Tedder 1966: 39.
19 Floyd 1975: 31–44.

In 1975, the area was zoned for light industrial use, with plans for further medium-scale industry. The western portion of the site (next to T.S. Ranadi Marine Training School) was allocated for the Queen's Warehouse (the Government Store), with land for other governmental instrumentalities close by. Slowly, over decades, Ranadi became the major light industrial and warehouse area for Honiara. The only real failure is that plans to shift the oil storage tanks from central Honiara to Ranadi never eventuated.[20] The industrial area now extends east as far as the Lungga River.

Housing in Honiara

Honiara of the 1950s was centred on Point Cruz and Rove, along with a thinly settled seafront. A decade later, Lengakiki and Mbumburu ridges were beginning to become middle-class housing areas, as were Vavaea and Mbokonavera ridges between Point Cruz and the Mataniko River. Chinatown and the hospital were across the river, and the Labour Line was further east at Kukum. The official early 1950s version of Honiara's emerging lifestyle sounded enticing:

> Here every effort is made to provide as attractive an environment for them as circumstances permit. In 1949 a Central Committee for Native Recreation was established which deals with all matters of outdoor recreation. The seven sports clubs have now increased to eight and hold league matches and knock-out competitions in football and cricket … The Native Welfare Centre in Honiara, which was opened in December, 1950, contains a canteen, wireless and facilities for indoor games. All sections of the community have used its stages once a week with films provided by the Central Office of Information, London.[21]

Reality was never as glossy. The predominant leisure occupations for Solomon Islanders were gardening, fishing, and hunting, attending church on the sabbath, sport, and family responsibilities. Recreation centred on playing soccer, both in organised leagues and in impromptu games when teams of 30 to 40 took to the fields for up to three hours. Those with spare money took themselves off to the cinemas to watch mainly Hollywood 'Westerns' or attended informal parties and dances. Males still predominated, as wives and families were usually left at home in their

---

20 Heath 1978: 2–15.
21 *BSIP AR* 1953–54: 32.

villages—separations that lasted many years. Even in Honiara, men left their wives at home with the children when they went out socialising. The 1961–62 *BSIP Annual Report* recorded that there were 2,500 men employed in Honiara, of whom less than 300 lived with their families.[22] Reverend Montford, the Anglican priest resident in Honiara in the 1950s and 1960s, was realistic in his description. Rather than a need for welfare centres, the basic problem was accommodation:

> The Melanesian population was crowded into a variety of buildings. Small houses were being built for families but there were more families than houses. Most of the population consisted of single men, or men who had had to leave their families in their home villages. Wherever there was a roof there were people crowded in. It was not good but that was all there was. It took time to assemble the material for new houses and people kept coming. Somehow the people kept cheerful in spite of the living conditions. They seemed to be able to manage on so little. They slept on the ground or floor if there was one. Very often they cooked on an open fire under sheets of iron. Their food was rice, or root crops if they could procure them, with a tin or two of meat shared among a number of people. For ablutions there were a few streams or, luxury of luxuries, a shower where they never seemed to turn off the tap. Their lavatory was the open beach. Yet they turned up on Sundays looking spick and span in white shorts and shirts. As more and more houses were built more and more people crowded into them.[23]

Government records show worries about early squatter settlements, overcrowding of housing, and disharmony in families when low wages were too often used for the purchase of alcohol. Domestic violence became common. In 1958, a special committee reported on the problems of housing for Solomon Islanders, concluding that the accommodation provided for employees was below acceptable standards. The committee recommended improving house designs and setting aside special areas where village-style structures could be built. The report also recommended encouraging longer periods of employment to try to create a settled family-oriented population.

---

22   *BSIP AR* 1961–62: 52–53; Bedford 1967; Knudson 1965.
23   Montford 1994: 83.

Plate 5.3 This 1970s photograph shows the typical accommodation for labourers at the back of stores or commercial premises in town between the 1950s and the 1970s.
Source: Ian Frazer Collection.

The committee discussed establishing a housing authority, although the concept was initially shelved due to lack of finances. Three areas were created specifically for Solomon Islanders: Fishing Village at Kukum, where a Lau Malaitan community developed on the shore; at White River on the edge of west Honiara, an area of mixed ethnicity where private houses could be built in village style; and Kukum Labour Line, which was a planned community including space for housing for 700 government and private employees in both single and married barracks quarters. Kukum had a playing field, market, cinema, school, community centre, Christian churches, and shops. Government and city council labourers were housed at Kukum, with low-level housing estates developed in surrounding areas further inland. Some sites of around 1,000 square metres (one-quarter acre) were made available at low rentals. Building materials were in short supply and, by the mid-1960s, fewer than 20 houses had been constructed on the Kukum blocks. The government also built single men's quarters and a few basic houses suitable for junior married clerks and married artisans. The latter comprised two small bedrooms, a living and verandah area, and an external ablutions block. They cost about $2,000 to construct and were rented at a rate related to salary. The building cost was too high and the government began to consider how to build more cheaply using prefabrication methods.[24]

Wages for Solomon Islanders varied depending on skill. The highest wages in 1954 went to assistant medical officers (AMOs), at £240 to £500 per annum, along with cost-of-living allowances in some cases. Middle-range employees such as clerks, artisans, agricultural field assistants, medical dressers, sanitary inspectors, and wireless operators received £72 to £240 per annum. Lower-range workers received wages of between £60 and £144 per year, supplemented by rations. Domestic servants were paid £24 to £36 per year, with unskilled workers receiving £24 to £30 per year, plus rations, free accommodation, clothing, and medical care.[25] A decade later, in February 1966, the Australian currency in use changed from pounds to dollars. In that year, government labourers received an average of A$249 per annum, domestic servants received A$240, government-classified workers received A$374, mechanics and clerical workers received A$360, while senior public servants earned up to A$1,000 a year.[26] Lower-income workers could barely scrape an existence in Honiara, and their accommodation was of poor standard.[27]

---

24 Tedder 1966: 38; Bellam 1970: 88.
25 *BSIP AR* 1953–54: 11.
26 Bellam 1970: 82.
27 Bellam 1964.

Plate 5.4 This sign was placed on Kukum Beach opposite the Kukum Labour Line by the Honiara Town Council.

It says it is forbidden to defecate on the beach. It was quite usual for coastal communities to use the shallow water at beaches as a public toilet.

Source: Alan Lindley Collection, in Clive Moore Collection.

Plate 5.5 Housing at Mbokonavera in the 1970s, with a bicycle in pride of place.

Source: Ian Frazer Collection.

In 1974, Honiara's town planning was described as an 'ordered drift': 'ordered' because the government owned the land, and 'drift' because there was no clear idea of how expansion should occur.[28] After the initial 1945 town plan, building by-laws were prepared and, in 1960, a town map at a scale of 1:2,000 was produced.[29] A new town plan was issued in 1962, then revised in 1966, and in 1971. These early plans detailed a port and an administrative hub, including the secretariat building, High and Supreme courts, plans for a Legislative Council chamber, post office, natural resources and social services departments, a central sports arena and playing fields, and fuel storage depots. Little attempt was made to deal with expanding suburban development. In 1972, Mr Berry, a water engineer with the Public Works Department, prepared a report recommending a series of high-density housing estates, based on the logistics of providing water services, which, because of the lack of a competent town plan, became de facto the basis for future planning.

Housing estates

Quite large numbers of government-owned houses were built in Honiara during the 1950s and 1960s for the mainly expatriate public servants. Government housing styles were classified using Roman numerals, from III to X. The top of the range X houses were commodious but never grand. As localisation occurred in the late 1960s and 1970s, Solomon Islanders began to occupy these houses, paying rents that averaged about 20 per cent of their salaries. They were also given priority to purchase the houses as the government divested itself of residential property. Although the provision of housing was a contractual requirement for expatriate public servants, this was not the case for most local employees, and maintaining housing was an expensive business, which the government could ill afford.

During the late 1960s and 1970s, Honiara's urban sprawl moved away from the coast and into the rolling valleys, with the expansion achieved mainly through developing government-financed housing estates.[30] In 1967, the government constructed the first 112 houses at Vara Creek, inland on the Mataniko River, then 60 at Rove, the latter mainly for police families

---

28 Floyd 1975: 14.
29 *BSIP AR* 1959–60: 43.
30 Bellam 1964; 1968: 3–4.

(Map 8.1). A hostel for single young women was planned.[31] The next area developed was the three-stage Vura housing estate (Map 6.1), with a plan to construct 300 family homes, a primary school, and a retail area. The Housing Authority, a statutory body under the Ministry of Public Works and Utilities, began operations in 1970, responsible for the allocation of residential land to Solomon Islanders and providing them with home loans. The government provided land to the Housing Authority under a 99-year lease, which was in turn leased to individuals for houses. Land could also be purchased privately, and some companies built houses for their employees. These houses were half the price of those built in the 1960s. They were very basic, lined up in rows, and looked unappealing until vegetation grew around them. The Commissioner of Lands made the land available (at no cost) to the Housing Authority, attempting to guard against speculative purchases. The land was released as FTEs, and there were no survey fees or charges for the initial installation of sewerage, electricity, and other services. Between 1970 and 1973, the Housing Authority spent A$1,010,600 to build 290 houses in estates, with another 110 houses built before 1976.[32]

Plots of land cost A$100, with tenure for 50 years. The smallest houses—with two bedrooms, a verandah, kitchen, septic toilet, and shower—cost just over A$1,500, which could be borrowed from the Honiara Town Council. Whatever one's salary, it was a slow process to pay off a house. Payments made to the Housing Authority varied with salary levels, and for those on lower salaries, payments were capped at a level below repayment costs.[33] Some of the purchase prices for the lower-quality houses were below building cost, although middle-range and elite housing was sold at cost price. While the Housing Authority was able to increase Honiara's housing stock during the 1970s, overall, it was not an economic operation and was faltering around the time of independence in 1978. The Housing Authority picked up again and continued into the 1980s.

---

31   *BSIP NS*, 7 June 1967.
32   Floyd 1975: 46; 1976: 10–11.
33   Tedder 1966: 37–38; *BSIP NS*, 15 March 1970.

Plate 5.6 The beginnings of Vura housing estate in 1968.
Source: Brian Taylor Collection.

Plate 5.7 Ella and John Ru`ugwata Kaliuae in 1988. They were early settlers at Vura.
Source: Clive Moore Collection.

New housing estates opened at Kola'a Ridge, Mbua Valley (between Kukum and Kola'a Ridge), Mbokonavera, Tuvaruhu, Tehamurina (near Lengakiki), Vara Creek, and Vura 1, 2, and 3 (Maps 6.1 and 8.1). Research by Nigel Oram, an expert on Port Moresby's urbanisation, showed that, by 1977, about 520 houses had been built or were under construction— around one-fifth of all conventional (non-traditional) housing in Honiara. Anyone purchasing through the council or the Housing Authority had to provide a 5 per cent deposit, on 15-year terms for older buyers and 20-year terms for younger buyers. House prices began to rise dramatically in the late 1970s: what was known as a '485' style of house, which cost $2,900 in 1975, was selling for $5,500 in 1977. The government provided a grant of $300 to public servants wishing to purchase houses, although there was no clause in the agreements to ensure the money was invested in a house. The Housing Authority, which received interest-free and 'soft' loans, managed to build many houses, even though it seems to have been disorganised when it came to the finer points of payments received. The wealthier members of the urban population benefited most.[34]

The future of suburban accommodation in Honiara was tied to housing estates, although Solomon Islanders had to be encouraged to live there. Plus, there was a need for private housing, beyond Housing Authority and government housing. Estimates suggest there were about 2,000 houses in Honiara by 1969, most owned by the government and some dating back to the days of the American base. Twenty-four of these structures were barrack blocks, most of which were at Kukum. Initially, the government built all levels of housing, although once the Housing Authority began, the government removed itself from the lower end of the construction market. By the end of 1974, the Housing Authority estimated that 450 houses had been or were in the process of being purchased by Solomon Islanders, while there were another 380 houses constructed in the urban Temporary Occupation Licence (TOL) settlements (see below), which were being brought within the control of the town council. Housing construction kept pace with population growth during the 1970s, although the real growth was largely unsupervised in the settlements.[35]

---

34 *BSIP AR* 1971: 4, 1974: 81–82; *SND*, 4 April 1975.
35 Floyd 1976: 35.

Table 5.1 The number of houses valued up to $6,000 (1975 prices) constructed in Honiara, 1969–1974.

Year	1969	1970	1971	1972	1973	1974	Total
Housing Authority	0	0	50	100	100	114	**364**
Government	71	106	49	10	23	9	**268**
Private (incudes village development)	57	25	27	55	65	41	**270**
Subtotal	**128**	**131**	**126**	**165**	**188**	**164**	**902**

Source: Floyd (1976: 34).

Table 5.2 The number of houses valued at more than $6,000 (1975 prices) constructed in Honiara, 1969–1974.

Year	1969	1970	1971	1972	1973	1974	Total
Housing Authority	0	0	0	0	0	0	**0**
Government	26	8	7	22	16	0	**79**
Private	23	12	16	27	19	10	**107**
Subtotal	**49**	**20**	**23**	**49**	**35**	**10**	**186**

Source: Floyd (1976: 34).

Table 5.3 The number of houses constructed in Honiara, 1969–1974.

Year	1969	1970	1971	1972	1973	1974	Total
Housing Authority	0	0	50	100	100	114	**364**
Government	97	114	56	32	39	9	**347**
Private	80	37	43	82	84	51	**377**
Total	**177**	**151**	**149**	**214**	**223**	**174**	**1,088**

Source: Floyd (1976: 34).

The 1959 Land and Titles Ordinance developed out of Colin Allan's extensive 1957 report on customary land.[36] Not fully operational until 1963, it was amended during 1963–65, then replaced in 1968 with a new ordinance. There were three types of land in the protectorate: customary land, unregistered alienated land, and registered land. Only the government could convert land held under customary tenure to statutory tenure. There was also provision for compulsory acquisition. As mentioned in Chapter 4, in relation to the Gilbertese community, in August 1977, the Legislative Assembly amended the Land and Titles Ordinance so that

---

36 BSIP 1957.

all PE land held by non–Solomon Islanders became FTEs held by the government and allocated on long-term leases.[37] FTEs could be issued for up to 75 years, although in Honiara they were originally allocated for 50 years or lesser periods, subject to a fixed payment and annual rent. The land could be disposed of during the lifetime of the holder of the FTE or at their death. Residential FTE land usually consisted of around 2,000 square metres (about half an acre), costing $1,500, and with an annual rental value of $50 to $100. Industrial sites cost about 50 per cent more, with a similar annual rent.[38] In the early decades, FTE land was beyond the finances of almost all Solomon Islanders.

Berry's 1972 report recommended housing developments for new areas: SDA Valley (south-west of Vura), Rove South, Symes Valley (between Vura and Panatina), Kuromulevuhu (on the west bank of Mataniko River), Mbokona (behind the old power station), Mbumburu (west of Mbokonavera, near Lengakiki), Kombuvatu (south of Kula'a Ridge), and at White River (on the western edge of Honiara) (Map 6.1). The density of housing developments varied, with an average of eight houses per hectare. These were generous proportions, allowing for the expansion of the house, gardening land, and space for children to play. Initially, Solomon Islands public servants were not keen on moving out of centrally located, heavily subsidised government housing into their own houses on the edge of town. This was accomplished during the mid-1970s by increasing the rents paid for government houses, which made the move more financially attractive. Under the sixth development plan in 1977, the strategy was to transfer the houses in the government housing pool to the Housing Authority, although valuations were slow and difficult to obtain.[39]

Another housing problem was that there were very few privately owned houses in Honiara suitable for letting to short-contract technical assistance staff from aid agencies. The government attempted to obtain overseas aid to build suitable houses, to be constructed by the Housing Authority, with the idea that in the long term these houses would be purchased by senior Solomon Islanders.[40]

---

37 Heath 1978: 11.
38 PMB 1371, Nigel Oram Collection, Commissioner and Lands and Surveys, Memorandum H5/20, 18 October 1969.
39 Floyd 1976: 44–45.
40 ibid.

Honiarans remember the houses by their model numbers. Taking low-covenant housing at Mbua Valley estate as an example, in 1975, there were 89 houses of various models. They were constructed on short steel-pipe stilt foundations, with wooden frames and floors, Masonite interior walls, fibro outer walls, insulated ceilings, and galvanised ripple-iron roofs. They cost between A$1,337 and A$4,800. Deposits were between A$50 and A$500.

Table 5.4 Housing Authority house models and prices at Mbua Valley, 1975.

Model no.	Cost (A$)	Deposit (A$)	Size (sq m)
240	1,337	50	6.1 x 3.6
384	1,598	100	7.3 x 4.8
485	2,600	200	8.2 x 5.4
700	3,434	300	9.1 x 5.4
800	4,800	500	12.1 x 6.1

Source: Floyd (1975: 53–55).

The '240' was a one-bedroom house with a separate concrete service capsule outside, containing the toilet, shower, and washtub. The '384' was similar, but bigger and the ablutions block could be built inside. Type '485' had two bedrooms, a living room, kitchen space, and indoor ablution facilities. The '700' was similar to the '485', but larger, with two extra bedrooms. The '800' was clearly the deluxe model, with four bedrooms, a living room with dining space, a separate kitchen with a stove, indoor ablution facilities (including a washbasin), ceilings, flyscreens, and built-in shelves. While the lower-range houses provided only basic accommodation, their residents built extensions roofed with sago palm fronds, and outdoor kitchens, seating, and sleeping areas—usually low wooden platforms designed to catch the breeze. A combination of urban and village styles ensued, which were suitable for cheap urban development.

Model '240' was designed to be within the reach of middle-level public servants, while the '700' was for top-level public servants, as was the '800'. There were no Model '1,000' houses at Mbua (Map 6.1), but where they were built, they required two high incomes to meet the repayments.[41] The original selling price did not include the site development costs, which largely explains the demise of the Housing Authority, as it could ill afford

---

41 Floyd 1975: 53–55.

to absorb the costs.[42] Even so, the owners also needed to purchase furniture and appliances, and to attend to maintenance, which, with electricity and water, the repayments, and feeding and clothing large extended families, meant that incomes were stretched to the limit. Repayment defaults were common. These were the living conditions available for public servants, unless they were lucky enough to have access through localisation to one of the older houses built for expatriate public servants.

The demand for housing eased in the late 1970s. There were few new jobs in Honiara, although labour was being drawn to commercial activities on Guadalcanal Plains at the Commonwealth Development Corporation (CDC) oil palm project, the Brewer Solomon Associates rice scheme, Foxwood Timbers, and Levers' activities (Chapter 6). Inflation pushed house prices beyond average income levels, while the plan to introduce economic rents for government houses was slow to be implemented. Other Honiara valley areas were opened—such as Mbokona and Kaibia (Map 10.1: #23, #44)—and there was infilling: building new houses in already established areas on Housing Authority estates. Plans for a 400-house SDA Valley estate were shelved for a few years. A middle-class housing estate eventuated at Panatina Ridge—a suitable supplement to this educational, commercial, and industrial area.

Home gardens did not flourish on the estates as the soils were poor and the settlers required large areas for root-crop gardens, which they obtained by colonising the surrounding national park and through customary arrangements with Tandai landowners. The planners had designed conventional suburbs that did not consider Solomon Islands shifting cultivation practices or the poor soils.

The settlements: Early THA/TOL and squatter areas

The housing estates and the more formal urban areas are overwhelmingly made up of FTE leases, although there are always small squatter areas within these, or close by, even in areas as solidly middle class as Kola`a Ridge. Temporary Housing Area (THA) schemes under TOLs are arguably now as important and permanent as FTE areas, even though this was not part of the original urban concept.

---

42   Floyd 1976: 38.

The Allies' Camp Guadal was largely a tent city, along with Quonset huts, and a few substantial buildings. Photos of downtown Point Cruz in 1945 show rows of tents, which were dismantled when the Americans withdrew. When Solomon Islanders first arrived in Honiara in the late 1940s, they required accommodation and, after work, they needed to supplement their meagre incomes by continuing food-gathering and cultivation practices learnt in their home villages. What became increasingly obvious was that 90 per cent of Honiara's residents could not afford even the cheapest houses provided by the authorities, and they needed to supplement their wages with extensive subsistence gardens to feed their families, and to sell excess food in the market. The result was the growth of the first settlements in what are now THA/TOL and squatter areas on the fringes of central Honiara.[43] Individuals from these settlements established gardens on Honiara Town Council or BSIP Government land, or Tandai customary land, and they fished, hunted, and foraged. From about 1950, men who were living in the Kukum Labour Line accommodation began to make gardens further inland, which the government encouraged.[44] To protect their crops, they arranged for *wantoks* to build small huts as guard houses. This led to the establishment of several of the earliest settlements in the valleys leading away from the coast.

The accommodation provided by employers was usually substandard. To compensate, Honiara's residents began to build houses using bush materials, or a combination of bush and scavenged materials. On their customary lands at home, they were free to begin new hamlets or villages, and to build houses for themselves using local materials. They applied the same principles to vacant land around Honiara. A good example was men occupying the single men's quarters at Kukum who brought their families to join them. Honiara was populated by Solomon Islanders who had migrated from their home villages and were trying to make their way in the urban settlement. They earned low wages and could not afford to rent houses, even when they were available. If they moved, it was to nearby squatter settlements where sanitation was poor and there was no reticulated water. As they did in their home islands, people depended on rivers and streams, and tapped into small springs, although overall Honiara had a poor supply of natural groundwater, and lower rainfall than surrounding areas.

---

43   PMB 1371, Nigel Oram Collection, J.B. Twomey, Advisor, Natural Resources Committee, BSIP Secretariat, Public Notice No. 40/73, 11 April 1973; Floyd 1974: 11.
44   *PIM*, April 1953, 129.

The THA/TOL concept, introduced in 1960, was intended to provide short-term permits to erect one house, and the initial idea did not include transfer, lease, or renting to another person. THAs were intended to regularise the use of government land within Honiara through formalising temporary occupancy. Settlers could obtain a licence for $5 to occupy land for 12 months. The blocks were not surveyed, no facilities were provided (such as roads, water, electricity, garbage disposal, or human waste removal), and the placement of houses was haphazard. As long as a house was built on the land, the licence could be renewed each year until some future date when the BSIP Government or the Honiara Town Council had an alternative purpose for the land.

Honiara's residents needed somewhere to live beyond the Labour Line and shanties behind their employers' properties. They also needed to supplement their small incomes. District Commissioner Tedder described the situation in 1966:

> All types of fishing are practiced on weekends. Fish is a useful dietary supplement, and the surplus fish is sold for cash. Hunting and foraging parties are held during most weekends along the river valleys within easy reach of Honiara.[45]

The most senior civil servant and the most junior labourer could be found during weekends working in adjacent gardens in the valleys. There was no declared official policy until 1964, when Honiara Town Council tried to place limits on shifting cultivation to prevent soil erosion. Gardening permits were introduced, allocating 1,300 square metres for each member of a household, but banning the burning or cutting of larger trees, and encouraging composting. These permits increased in number from 250 in 1964, to 719 by June 1971.[46] Residents of the settlements suffered from poor health. A report from Kobito in 1976 showed elevated levels of sickness among children. The principal diseases were those of the skin, diarrhoea, and hookworm—all indications of poor sanitation.[47]

---

45   Tedder 1966: 40.
46   Bathgate 1978b: 3, fn. 2.
47   Oram 1980: 146.

In 1974, an investigation was under way in 12 urban squatter settlements—an attempt to regularise titles, construct roads, and provide water and refuse services. The Housing Authority and the council wanted to provide basic services and even sketched the minimum type of structure they would like to see built. This was hardly a unique idea as the sketch was typical of many basic Solomon Islands village structures then and now, with public and private areas, and a detached kitchen with a fireplace, all made from local materials.[48]

In the mid-1970s, the government and the council were very aware of the growing number of urban and peri-urban village settlements constructed from local or mixed materials. Nigel Oram described the way these settlements grew between 1970 and 1979, noting that the statistics he collected were probably too low. The settlers were almost all Malaitan, except for settlers from Ontong Java Atoll and Rennell Island on Tandai customary land at the mouth of the Mataniko River opposite the hospital. The oldest of these settlements are at Malaitan Fishing Village and White River, which was the first attempt by the BSIP Government to come to terms with the needs of Solomon Islanders in Honiara. As Figure 0.1 in the Introduction indicates, the Malaitan community was beginning to dominate.

Table 5.5 Growth of settlements in Honiara, 1970–1979.

Year	Houses	Settlements	Population
1970	148	7	?
1972[a]	196	9	?
1973	346	15	1,168
1976[b]	428	?	2,407
1979[c]	337	17	2,330
1979[d]	147	6	961

[a] Survey dated 3 July 1973.
[b] November 1976 Housing Survey.
[c] Inside the town boundary, 1979 Honiara Census, pp. 22, 46.
[d] Outside the town boundary, 1979 Honiara Census, pp. 22, 46.
Source: Oram (1980: 139).

---

48   PMB 1371, Nigel Oram Collection, Sketch of a Honiara-style village house, 1970s.

5. MUNICIPAL AUTHORITY AND HOUSING

Plate 5.8 Kola`a Ridge squatter settlement on the inland side of the established suburb, 1969.
Source: Brian Taylor Collection.

Squatting on empty land became a considerable problem as more people migrated to Honiara, attracted by hoped-for employment opportunities. In September 1967, Jim Tedder, as Chairman of the Honiara Town Council, issued a stern warning against squatters building houses without permission:

> Frequently, though the actual building under construction is not in sight, people can be observed carrying old Masonite, corrugated iron, sewn sago-palm leaf, bush timber, etc, into the wooded valleys in the town—which always means that a structure is being built there … The Council hopes to expand the areas in which proper village-type houses can be built. But it is essential both now and in the future to prevent the erection of unlawful shanties.[49]

Ten years later, a report to the government extoled the THA/TOL system:

> Migrants from rural areas and other islands who are still living according to traditional patterns can obtain a temporary occupation license permitting them to construct a house, usually

---

49 PMB 1371, Nigel Oram Collection, Circular No. 4/67, File LAN/2/1/5, James Tedder, Chairman, Honiara Town Council, 1 September 1967.

of traditional materials. In providing temporary housing areas, wherein basic housing can be constructed, subject to simple control, the Government avoided the development of squatter areas. There are just a few isolated squatters.[50]

In 1976, the Honiara City Council recognised about 16 'villages' in Honiara, containing 500 houses and a population of around 2,000, all on land designated as THAs under TOL.

Wishful thinking in the 1970s was not mirrored by what happened over the next 40 years.[51]

Migration from rural areas to Honiara increased rapidly and there was nowhere to live except in the squatter or THA/TOL settlements. Traditional arrangements were mixed with urban concepts. Map 10.1 from 2019 shows 92 contemporary THA/TOL/squatter settlements, and there are also many squatter areas not shown on the map as they are outside the council boundaries. In some cases, when the initial settlement began, the squatters compensated the Tandai for the land. In east Honiara, this was before the land was incorporated into the 1953 national park, or later into the Honiara City Council area. This suggests that under customary law they may have had usufructuary rights. Most of the residents in any THA/TOL or squatter area are from one language area, one island, or one Christian denomination. Some families have lived on these temporary sites for half a century and have built substantial homes. As well, there are nearby leaf houses, which are cheap to rent and provide a low-cost urban base.

Although most residents continue to identify with their home island, they now see Honiara as their permanent place of residence.[52] The interpretation explored in this book is that these THA/TOL and squatter settlements are an extension of customary village patterns transferred to the urban setting. Rather than the people accommodating municipal regulations, the Honiara City Council and the government have had to accommodate the needs and traditional land-use and housing patterns of the people. In 2020, close to half of Greater Honiara's residents lived in settlements—either on THA/TOL land or as squatters—areas

---

50   ADB 1977: 5.
51   ibid., 25.
52   Keen et al. 2017: 79.

with no permanent security of land tenure. The majority are from Malaita. They are an urban reality and will play a powerful role in shaping future economic and social developments.

Unfortunately, the THA/TOL system has broken down and the authorities have lost control. The initial concept included no urban services, which gave way to minimal services: roads, electricity from the grid that can be connected, and a communal water supply that can also be connected to houses—both for a fee. Many TOL residents cannot afford grid electricity, although small solar systems are now often used. The standard of housing now varies from dwellings that would not be out of place in rural villages to four-bedroom houses that could just as easily have been built in FTE suburbs. The bulk of the residents have failed to pay their annual licence fees. Squatters have shifted on to government land within the city boundary and on to surrounding alienated and Tandai land. The system continued to grow (and deteriorate) as the number of squatters and THA/TOL residents increased. In the 1960s and 1970s, the small TOL fee provided a minimal form of legal security—a licence to squat— and guided people to settle in concentrated areas, creating urban villages or settlements. Twenty years later, the THA/TOL system was providing land for at least 23 per cent of Honiara's population. Some of these areas were authorised by the government or council, while others regularised what were family initiatives to begin new settlements.

The council has had to amend its by-laws to accommodate these urban villages, building roads and paths, supervising health services, the spacing of houses, and implementing rubbish removal services.[53] The council and government are now in the early stages of providing more permanent legitimacy to THA/TOL tenure, if occupants pay their annual land rents and organise a conversion of title. In recent years, bowing to the way in which the THA/TOL areas developed over several decades, and for a survey and title transfer fee of around SI$10,000, the land can now be registered as FTE, providing more permanent tenure. There also needs to be an education campaign to explain the responsibilities inherent in urban residence, which includes paying fees to live on the land. While the government and the Honiara City Council gradually provided services, most THA/TOL residents have failed to pay their annual TOL fees, with many of them 20 to 25 years in arrears. A 2006 survey found that of 3,000

---

53 WPHC 1958, *Housing Committee Report*, 28/I CF 252/4/6, vol. 1.

TOLs, only 10 were up to date with their annual licence fees. By 2013, there had been a slight improvement, with 168 up-to-date TOL parcels of land—still a long way to go. In the mid to late 2010s, there were 38 THA/TOL settlements within or on the city boundary (Map 10.1).[54] The fee has increased over the decades and is now SI$1,000 for a three-year TOL. Most THA/TOL residents will never afford to convert their land to FTE title.[55]

There is another category of people with no formal urban status: families who occupy land as squatters, either under customary arrangements with the surrounding Tandai or Malango landowners or on land that was alienated but unused. The Honiara City Council attempted to differentiate between THA/TOL settlements and squatter areas (where no TOLs exist), although THA/TOL settlements also fall into administratively unclear land categories, particularly so if the payment of TOL fees is not up to date.[56] Over the decades, what began as squatter settlements often progressed to become THA/TOL areas—a regularising of an indigenous *fait accompli*. The difference between squatters and THA/TOL residents who fail to pay their annual TOL fee (the majority) is small, although lapsed THA/TOL residents can pay their arrears and have their licences reinstated. The Honiara City Council's maps make the attitudes of urban planners clear, with headings that depict 'Temporary Housing Areas' as squatter areas. This is because, as a 2014 report says:

> The vast majority of the remainder [other than the 168 up to date with payments] are still occupying that land that their expired TOL was issued for. The use of the term 'temporary' is a misnomer, as occupation of land in Honiara's squatter settlements is rarely ever of a temporary nature.[57]

The next section examines the best-known settlement areas: Fishing Village, White River, Kobito, Gilbert Camp, Koa Hill, and Burns Creek.

---

54 ibid., 92.
55 Foukona and Allen 2017: 91–92; Tozaka and Nage 1981; SIG 2014a: 16.
56 Oram 1980: 147.
57 SIG 2014a: 16.

Fishing Village

Ellison Sade and Harry Maesae have recounted to me the early history of Fishing Village on the shore at Kukum. Gilbert Talo was one of the founders of Fishing Village, which was Honiara's first and most visible urban village settlement. The area is also known as 'Fisherie' or Vaivila Fishing Village (Maps 6.12, and 10.1: #24). It was first settled in the mid-1950s by people from Funafou Islet in Lau Lagoon on Malaita's north-east coast. Talo, from Lau Lagoon, was working at the mental hospital at Kilu`ufi on Malaita when the facility was shifted to Honiara in 1955. He led a group of four medical workers who moved with their families to work at the new mental hospital (Map 6.1), which was on the site of the modern Woodford International School. The colonial government found it difficult to obtain enough protein for hospital patients, and even root vegetables were in scarce supply. One easy protein source was fish and, although the nearby sea abounded with marine life, there was no organised commercial fishing. The doctors at the hospital asked Talo to help establish a regular supply of fish. Talo wrote to his younger brother Loea Mamata, who was a student at Batuna Seventh-day Adventist (SDA) school in Marovo Lagoon, in the western Solomons, asking him to come to Honiara to begin a commercial fishing venture. Mamata agreed and travelled to Funafou to recruit the first large group of Lau fishermen to live in Honiara.[58]

Over the decades, the size of Fishing Village increased, and eventually an eastern extension of the 'Fisherie' stretched along the coast to Vagamatotora, opposite the present-day main campus of Solomon Islands National University. Vaivila and Vagamatotora are rocky infertile areas on the shore, hemmed in by reefs. This rugged area of coast was no less hospitable than the artificial islands on which most of its inhabitants had lived on Malaita, and the position offered advantages. Many of the first inhabitants were employed at the nearby hospitals or as domestic servants at the Agricultural College across the road. They made extra money through participating in fishing cooperatives and selling their catch at Honiara's Central Market. In the 1960s, one BSIP Government policy was to develop the local fishing industry. Three 'F'-class fishing boats were provided, two to Lau cooperatives operating from Mamanawata (Lokea) at the mouth of the Mataniko and from the Fishing Village, the division marked by religion.

---

58 The first Fishing Village settlers were Loea Mamate (their leader), Toata Talo, Tom Abanaai, Lomo Rofeta, Kabolo Adaisi, Adaisi Abakai, Sarui, Tagele, Satini Dara, Magi Misimisi, Maelasi Molia, and Gilbert Talo. Information from Ellison Sade, 26 November 2017.

HONIARA

The Loya Brothers (SDA) formed the Kukum Private Fishery in 1960, and the other group, Ganomela, was Catholic. The Honiara Co-operative Fish Marketing Association was formed in 1965, with cold-room facilities constructed the next year.[59] Fishing Village residents lived in clan groups. They built leaf-thatch houses in traditional Lau style on the shore, but they were squatters with no land licence or tenure. The administration did not confirm their village as permanent until the residents marched to confront them. In 1972, 28 Fishing Village households were granted 57 THA/TOL licences, establishing the family and clan patterns that continue. All their THA/TOL areas have now been converted to FTEs.[60]

Plate 5.9 The 'Fishery', Honiara's Malaitan Fishing Village, on the beachfront at Kukum, 2008.
This was one of the first areas allocated for 'village-style' living in the 1950s. The old Malaria Centre (left) and Woodford International School (right) are on the other side of the main coastal road.
Source: Clive Moore Collection.

---

59 Fishermen from Langalanga Lagoon, Malaita, also established themselves in Honiara in 1967, further expanding the Malaitan fishing community. WPHC 29/11, 312/2/3, Great Britain, High Commission for the Western Pacific Islands, General Correspondence Files, 300–499 series, relating to the WPHC and BSIP: 1967–71 (1962–72).
60 Information from Harry and Betty Masae, Fishing Village, Honiara, 19 October 2007, 29 November 2016; *BSIP NS*, 15 February 1970; Oram 1980: 139.

White River

The government had begun to realise that not all settlement in Honiara would be through high-covenant housing, purpose-built estates, and labour barracks. Solomon Islanders took the initiative to negotiate for land in ways that were familiar to them. White River on the west side of Honiara (Maps 5.3, and 10.1: #77) was different from Fishing Village. It was a government-planned area—the first acknowledgement that there needed to be settlements where planning regulations were relaxed. It seems likely that the earliest people to live at White River were Malaitans. Two brothers from east Fataleka, Malaita, Rau and Jack Ramosaea, were among the first settlers. Their families claim they arrived in the late 1940s, which if true probably means they were initially squatters. They were certainly living there in the early 1950s. Jack Ramosaea's children say their father named the river for the white stones on its bed, although James Tedder said it was named after a Lieutenant White of the US Armed Forces.[61] Originally, the river was called Tau`utu. The Ramosaeas chose a downstream location with plentiful water nearby.

In the 1960s and 1970s, there were government attempts to guide development of the settlement, which was a different start to that at Fishing Village, Kobito, Gilbert Camp, or much later at Burns Creek. The area was acknowledged as a 'village area' although in practice it became a THA/TOL settlement. Roads and drainage were laid out and, in the 1970s, an extra 60 plots of land were released, doubling the settlement's size. White River officially became an 'estate'. Small stores and a primary school were established and, by the 1970s, there were some substantial houses at the coastal end of White River. It became a racially mixed community. Its Malaitan, Santa Cruz, Polynesian, and Gilbertese residents were among the first Solomon Islanders to identify Honiara as their permanent home. Settlement also spread inland to Kongulai (Map 5.3) on the ridges at the top of the river.

---

61 After a search through books on Guadalcanal during the war years, I can find no record of a Lieutenant White.

Plate 5.10 Jack and Margaret Leonga Ramosaea, early settlers at White River, photographed in 1982.
Source: Clive Moore Collection.

5. MUNICIPAL AUTHORITY AND HOUSING

Plate 5.11 A Housing Authority home at White River, 2008.
Source: Clive Moore Collection.

Plate 5.12 The typical home of a middle-class White River family, 2008.
Source: Clive Moore Collection.

White River is on the border between Tandai and Honiara land. During the Tension years (Chapter 9), many residents fled. The young men of the area joined a community watch group that became the Iron Eagles, within the Malaita Eagle Force. They guarded the empty houses of those who had evacuated to their home islands and safeguarded the remaining White River community. Like other Honiara settlements, since the 2000s, White River has witnessed an influx of settlers, although because of the extent of its existing settlement, there was less space for newcomers. The area is different to the other settlements as it has a multiethnic heritage and is a mixture of THA/TOL and FTE land. What was once considered an area of Honiara too isolated to settle is now within easy access of the city centre.[62]

Kobito, Gilbert Camp, and Koa Hill

Many Solomon Islander residents continued to cultivate gardens on the town's fringes for family food and cash crops. In the 1980s, more than half of Honiara's women had root-crop gardens, and about one-quarter had leaf-vegetable gardens—all away from their homes.[63] In the early 2020s, THA/TOL settlement and squatter area residents were still walking long distances to their sweet potato and tapioca gardens on customary land rented from the Tandai. When heavy rains destroy these and other gardens on Guadalcanal, as occurred after floods in April 2014, supplies to Honiara's markets are low, prices are high, and residents suffer.

One of Honiara's planning failures was the 6,070-hectare Queen Elizabeth National Park, created in 1954 to celebrate the accession to the throne of the new monarch. The park was placed under the charge of the local district commissioner. It is doubtful whether the traditional landowners ever recognised government control of the park, nor did they understand the later incorporation of most of it (5,261 hectares) within the Honiara City Council boundary. They continued to make customary transactions to allow urban settlers to use the land. By the time money was eventually allocated for rangers, in 1973, squatters and 'weekend farmers' had cleared much of the rainforest from the slopes of Mt Austen. The government acknowledged that the concept had failed.

---

62   I am indebted to Daniel Evans for allowing me access to a draft section of his doctoral thesis, which has expanded my knowledge of White River settlement.
63   Jourdan 2010: 270; SIG 1988b: 23, 27.

Kobito (Map 10.1: Kombito, #39–41) had pockets of good soil and the residents also had gardens further out, which were rented from the Tandai landowners. Michael Kwa`ioloa, a senior resident of Kobito originally from the Kwara`ae language area on Malaita, commented on the origins of the gardens on Mt Austen:

> Tapioca is the main food which we plant in the outlying settlements, and sweet potato. We live on tapioca because we can replant it in the same place and it will grow over and over again for many years, if we can't extend our gardens because the land belongs to others. Our way is that if it is regrown forest, no-one can work it and if you do they will chase you out, because the area belongs to the man who worked it when it was virgin forest. So on land we were the first to settle we make tapioca gardens, harvest them, and repeat this again and again. When it will no longer grow well, we leave it for the forest to regrow and no-one will come to work it, because it is ours. In this way we worked the whole area of Mount Austen before the ethnic tension. People from Matariu, `A`ekafo, Namoliki, Fulisango and Kombito settled everywhere, all of them from home on Malaita.[64]

Plate 5.13 Kobito 2 in 1968, which was then reminiscent of a Malaitan village.
Source: Les Tickle Collection.

---

64 Kwa`ioloa and Burt 2012: 68.

Plate 5.14 The first houses at Kobito 2 were built from local materials. This photograph is from 1968.
Source: Les Tickle Collection.

Kobito is now a sprawling permanent settlement divided into several sections. Most of the early settlers around Kobito and Gilbert Camp came from the Kwara`ae, Fataleka, and Baegu language areas in north and central Malaita. The first settlers in the 1950s approached the Tandai landowners for permission to settle on the outskirts of Honiara. Even though most (although not all) of this land was within the town council boundaries or inside the national park, Solomon Islanders used traditional methods to acquire rights to use the land. Kwa`ioloa described what happened when the Malaitan settlers approached the Tandai. While they may initially have been squatters (under the definitions used by the municipal authorities), they employed customary processes to settle on Tandai land. Kwa`ioloa recorded other settlement patterns, using a style reminiscent of recited Malaitan genealogies, and explained the Tandai's reason for encouraging settlement on their land. Many of the sites mentioned below can be located on Map 10.1:

Their names were Baranaba, Ben Baenosi and Manimosa, Domeniko and Kosi, from Gaobata and Kaokao in the Tandai Shahalu clan lands. Their aim in giving out those areas was to safeguard their customary land against further expansion of the town boundary by the government, with the Malaitans there to witness that they were the land-owners. However, as I told Orodani, when more of our relatives flooded into Honiara for employment, instead of consulting the land-owners they called at the Lands Department office for permission to occupy these outlying settlements. Without consulting the land-owners either, the Lands Department automatically issued temporary occupation licences with a yearly rent of five shillings, which rose to ten shillings, then two dollars, rising to thirty dollars by 1994, and now to one hundred dollars.[65]

Kwa`ioloa said his brother John Maesatana was the first to settle at Kobito. Solodia (meaning 'soldier' or 'policeman') and Maniuri from Fataleka, and Laua`a from Baegu, also settled at Kobito 1. Laua`a's descendants are Dongafaka and his son Konongūi. Kaobata established his family at Kobito 2, where Michael Kwa`ioloa and his family are his descendants. Tua settled at Mamulele (Namulele), where his grandson Jimmy Ga`ea still lived in the 2010s. Salebanga settled at Dukwasi, where Benjamin Ramo is his descendant. Dioko began Ferakuisia and was represented in the 2010s by Michael Ngidui. Kamusu settled at Adaliaua, along with Jack, Deobasi, and `Au from `Ataa, who arrived a little later. Suxon Talo and Ini are their descendants. Tega and Amagele settled the Matariu land, where Tega's son Fito`oa and Amagele's grandson Cedric Kemanu lived in the 2010s. Ngwaa and Lafunua settled at Taba`a above Rove Market in west Honiara.[66] Some of these settlements were on leased government land, but even so, the new occupants conducted traditional exchanges with the Tandai landowners to make certain their welcome was long term. Originally, their homes were made from 'bush' materials, then, slowly over years, they used more permanent materials, and the land was incorporated into the THA/TOL system.

---

65   ibid., 198.
66   From the memories of Michael Kwa`ioloa, and the Toa Te`e, Itea, Masae, and Kaliuae families. See also ibid., 64, 199.

Lau Valley (Map 10.1: #36) was begun by a leader from Lau Lagoon, represented by Inito`o in the 2010s. Maelaua was the first to settle at Kaibia, which was named after a tapioca (*kaibia*) garden there. `Ofi`olo was begun by Robert, a man from the South Malaita section of `Are`are. Gua from east Fataleka was the first settler at Abira`ado`e, which he named after his home area.[67] As Michael Kwa`ioloa notes, these settlements were arranged through traditional procedures:

> We must also realise that when our 'fathers' sought permission to settle this land they offered gifts of shell-money and pigs to the land-holders, who had to offer sacrifices to their ancestral ghosts to declare everything before anyone settled or cleared an area of land. Otherwise the ghosts would not know those persons and would cause sickness or even death to those settling the land. They also offered the land-holders food such as sugar, tinned meat, biscuits, rice or whatever, and even handed them tools such as machetes, axes, saws, hammers and nails. They provided the land-holders with everything, because they were friends, demonstrating the rights of Solomon Islanders to freedom of movement to settle anywhere as long as we seek permission from the rightful land-holders, avoiding fighting, killing and parting people from their property.[68]

The ethnic origins of settlements are usually clear from their names, which come from particular islands and languages. Settlement names such as Adaliua, Aekafo, Feraladoa, Fulisango, Koa Hill, Lau Valley, and Tolo all have Malaitan origins. Malaitan residents are also clustered in other settlements such as Borderline, Burns Creek, Gilbert Camp, Green Valley, Kaibia, Kobito 1, 2, and 3, Mamulele, Adaliua, New Mala, and Sun Valley.[69] Alongside this formal permission there was a blend of occupation types on Tandai and THA/TOL land, which now cover large areas of the city. Several of the outer settlement areas grew in these years, particularly those in east Honiara dominated by Malaitans. The pattern of settlement relates to language and extended kin relationships back on Malaita.

Anthropologist Rodolfo Maggio's research suggests that between 1949 and 1952, Moses and Benjamin Ko`oru`u were the first to settle at Gilbert Camp (Map 10.1: #18). Benjamin made an arrangement with Baranaba O`ai from the Tandai Kakau descent group: he worked at Ilu

---

67   Kwa`ioloa and Burt 2012: 199.
68   ibid., 201.
69   Foukona and Allen 2017: 91.

farm and, in return for access to produce, his family was allowed to live at Gilbert Camp. As this was before the national park was proclaimed in 1954, it was a normal customary arrangement preceding later government declarations. The Malaitans say the current Tandai landowners of Gilbert Camp land regard the arrangement as a Guadalcanal *chupu*, a traditional arrangement involving the exchange of food and valuables for land.[70] However, traditional arrangements seldom operate in perpetuity and need to be regularly maintained, which has not always occurred, and which became part of Guale disquiet during the Tension years.

A similar pattern developed on Koa Hill (Map 10.1: #25), between the Mataniko River and Skyline Ridge.[71] There are two entry points to Koa Hill: down from Skyline Road and across the Mataniko, using a bamboo raft. The river end of this area is one of the two remaining Tandai customary areas within Honiara. A man from Koa in west Kwara'ae asked permission from Baranaba to settle there. Others followed in the 1970s and 1980s, and gradually there was more of a mix of housing materials, using bush materials and modern milled wood and galvanised ripple-iron sheeting. Talo settled at Namoliki, while 'Aitorea, Adam from Kwaio, and Dick Maetoe settled at Kena Hill. Kalaka established Kalaka, and Kofiloko was founded by Paul Ata, Kasile, and Ben Beuka—all from east Kwaio.

Not all Tandai landowners would support Kwa'ioloa's analysis of Malaitans' customary negotiations. The Tandai complain that many Malaitans did not continue to pay compensation or rent for their houses and garden land. Guale customs relating to land and residence differ from those on Malaita. Although unhappy with the Malaitans, the Guale did not feel able to terminate the arrangements. They say they approached the Guadalcanal Council for assistance but were told it was their own responsibility. When the matter was raised in the Legislative Assembly, Malaitan members are said to have blocked any discussion.[72] These issues simmered for decades and eventually boiled over during the Tensions.

---

70 Maggio 2016; see also 2014.
71 Ariki 2020: 72–94.
72 Oram 1980: 140–41.

Plate 5.15 Billy Toa Te`e, originally from Kwara`ae on Malaita, lived at White River, before settling at Kobito 2 in the 1980s. He is seen here with two members of his family in the 1990s.
Source: Clive Moore Collection.

Plate 5.16 Roselyn Aona Toa Te`e, wife of Billy Toa Te`e, 1980s.
Source: Clive Moore Collection.

Plate 5.17 The original 1970s Toa Te`e house at Kobito 2 had ripple-iron walls as well as an unlined roof.
Source: Clive Moore Collection.

Plate 5.18 Urban renewal: The walls of the Toa Te`e home at Kobito 2 were renovated with wood in the 2000s.
Source: Clive Moore Collection.

Burns Creek

The Burns Creek coastal settlement abuts the easternmost Honiara City Council land. The name Burns Creek was originally applied to a sluggish stream feeding into the mouth of the Lungga River, and then to a rubbish dump, an area used for agriculture and education, and a squatter settlement. Levers—under a new company entity, Russell Islands Plantation Estate Limited—originally controlled the land. It is low-lying and Japanese and American photographs from mid-1942 indicate that the area was never planted with coconut palms.[73] It was known as Burns Creek as far back as 1945 and wartime photographs show a scattering of American buildings there. The SDA mission took over the American facilities at nearby Betikama to begin a primary school in 1948. Negotiations began in the 1960s to start a secondary school at Betikama and the mission arranged to shift its existing primary school to the Burns Creek area on the opposite side of the highway.

The city rubbish dump was also known as Burns Creek, even though it was on the fringe of Ranadi outside the area of Burns Creek settlement (Map 10.1: #7). During the 1970s, cattle holding grounds were established there, with plans for an abattoir under the Livestock Development Authority, which collapsed in the 1990s (Map 6.2). From the 1980s until 2019, about 12 hectares of the area, where it bordered the highway, became the Taiwan Technical Mission's experimental rice farm, which is often still referred to as the 'KGVI farm', which presumably indicates its original use when KGVI transferred from Malaita to Honiara in the 1960s. A decade later, part of the Burns Creek land was sold to private interests and part reverted to the government, when the Commissioner of Lands is said to have allowed squatters to settle there.

Daniel Evans' informants suggest the current squatter settlement at Burns Creek began in 1992, facilitated by John Seti Iromea from Baegu, Malaita. He was on the Honiara City Council and seems to have invited settlers, mainly migrants from north-east Malaita. He is said to have 'sold' land to the squatters, trading on his authority as a councillor. Another prominent early settlement leader was Peter Usi, who also invited people to settle. Burns Creek was sparsely populated during the 1990s, then came into its own in the early 2000s, housing many of those who returned after

---

73 I am indebted to Peter Flahavin for providing relevant photographs.

having fled Honiara and Guadalcanal Plains during the first years of the Tensions. The settlement expanded rapidly during the 2000s and 2010s. Finally, in 2010, a portion of the area was obtained by the National Sports Council on a 50-year lease to construct a sports stadium. Part of this land was already included in the squatter settlement. In 2013, the National Sports Council issued squatters with letters demanding they quit the land, which they ignored. Burns Creek is the best example of an area recently 'colonised' by migrants in need of homes. In essence, what occurred there is the same as in other settlements like Kobito and Gilbert Camp in the 1960s, 1970s, and 1980s: newcomers in search of a place to live squatted on land that was empty. It became theirs through long-term occupancy.[74]

Figure 0.1 in the Introduction shows the transition to a separate dominant Malaitan community, much of it in east Honiara in the settlements described above.

Creating modern social patterns

Chapter 10 concentrates on hybridity and aspects of village life that maintain and sustain modern Honiara. These urban social patterns developed over several decades. This short concluding section attempts to begin to explore some aspects that have fed into the making of modern Honiara.

First, there is the overwhelming Malaitan presence in Honiara. The Malaitan THA/TOL and customary/squatter communities, along with the other more well-to-do Malaitans living on FTE land, created a Malaitan urban 'world' of such size that it operates as a separate entity, as well as being part of the wider Solomon Islands section of the urban population. The majority is from central and north Malaita, particularly from Kwara'ae, or from Lau and Langalanga lagoons, Fataleka, and Baegu. Yet, Malaitans are not a united group and they have also intermarried with Solomon Islanders from other provinces (including Guadalcanal), adding to the complexity. In *Making Mala: Malaita in Solomon Islands, 1870s–1930s* (Moore 2017a), I discussed the way in which, decades earlier, Malaitans overcame their differences to unite during Maasina

---

74 I am indebted to Daniel Evans and Martin Hadlow for assisting in the quest for the origin of the Burns Creek name. We were not successful in establishing who Burns was.

Rule (1944–52). David Akin extends this analysis into the Maasina Rule years.[75] Their urban lives, particularly in Honiara, were built on these earlier experiences.

Second, modern Honiara combines elements similar in urban settings around the world, along with aspects specific to Solomon Islands. Over decades, there were changing consumption patterns and expectations. In the 1960s and 1970s, all urban working-class and middle-income earners had rising expectations as they became used to town life. Whereas a bicycle was a paramount urban status symbol in the early 1950s and 1960s, at the end of the decade, bicycles had been replaced with autobikes, small motorcycles, or motor scooters. Young Peter Kenilorea, a KGVI secondary schoolteacher, provides a good example of the changing consumption patterns of elite indigenous workers. In 1969, he became the proud owner of a Honda 150cc motorcycle, then a few years later he graduated to a small British car. In 1976, he became the country's second chief minister and, in 1978, the first prime minister, with a car and a driver.[76] His final car in the 2010s was an ageing Land Cruiser, which was a remnant of his time as Speaker of Parliament. His accommodation also changed. Sir Peter moved from government accommodation at the new KGVI to the 'Red House' (the prime minister's residence), and then to his own comfortable home on Kola`a Ridge.

Third, as in any city, Honiara developed communal urban facilities. The Christian denominations led the way in providing facilities such as multipurpose halls adjoining churches. The United Church and the South Sea Evangelical Church established their main churches on the beach near Central Market. The Catholic and Anglican cathedrals were constructed further east. Other churches are spread through the suburbs and settlements. The first community centre was built in 1971, between Chinatown and Lawson Tama sports ground, close to the new urban sprawl, providing multipurpose space for indoor sports and meetings.[77] There are shopping centres, community facilities, food markets, sporting associations and facilities, spaces for public events, and a growing sense of belonging to a complex urban community.

---

75   Akin 2013.
76   Kenilorea 2008: 132.
77   *BSIP AR* 1971: 5; *BSIP NS*, 7 May 1973; Oram 1980: 143.

Fourth, alongside these trappings of a modern city, the Tandai landowners feel that their ownership of the land on which Honiara is built has never been extinguished. The government's arrangements to resume the land were made legally in 1947–48 and 1954. Back then, it was easy for the government to set a low price. Between the 1950s and 1990s, the Tandai were also compensated in cash and traditional wealth items by other Solomon Islanders who had come to live in Honiara. I am aware of Tandai land at Kongulai (Map 5.3), on the ridges behind White River settlement, which was purchased (using cash and *chupu* concepts) by Malaitans in the 1990s, in a style of acquisition like that for the land around Gilbert Camp decades earlier. Evidence was presented to the Truth and Reconciliation Commission (2008–12) on these land transactions, some of which were paid for through cash compensation, but in other areas, the land reverted to the Guale with no recompense.[78] Other Solomon Islanders are quite aware of the ambivalent attitudes of the people of Guadalcanal to the existence of Honiara.

A related land issue is the nature and size of the squatter and THA/TOL settlements. While the city council and the national government have legal claim over the FTE, THA/TOL, and other 'vacant' lands within the city's boundaries, and lament that most TOL fees are in arrears, they seem to have no ability to regularise or close squatter settlements. Evicting about half the occupants of Greater Honiara from their homes is not an option. Planners are treading carefully in this area, aware of the issues, but unsure how to deal with them.

Fifth, Solomon Islanders have made Honiara their own, creating a hybrid indigenous culture. In the early decades, many Solomon Islanders did not feel comfortable in downtown Point Cruz, and various of Honiara's early facilities, such as the clubs and hotels, were dominated by, and almost exclusively for, expatriates. The core of indigenous Honiara was formed by the Central Market, Chinatown, Kukum, the hospital, and the churches—all located close to the Mataniko River. Central Market was always a meeting place for everyone: expatriates shopped there once or twice a week; Solomon Islanders without refrigeration to preserve food visited the market every day.

---

78   SIG 2014b.

The dynamics of Central Market are useful for explaining Honiara's hybridity. By the 1960s and 1970s, the market ran six days a week and supplies were coming in from all over Guadalcanal and other islands. When in season, Malaitan pineapples flooded the market, and root vegetables arrived by the shipload from other provinces. Villagers from all around Guadalcanal, Savo, and Ngela were constant visitors, bringing produce. The market has always been a place where Solomon Islanders can laze about and socialise, chew betel nuts with *wantoks*, pass on messages, and look for relatives just arrived on ships. Murray Bathgate noted in the 1970s that 'the market compound was divided into discrete social territories',[79] which were never marked but always adhered to. Customary exchange cycles interacted with the modern economy. It was a microcosm of the Solomons world in which foreigners were tolerated but never quite felt comfortable.

Plate 5.19 Some of the first minibuses in Mendana Avenue, Honiara, in the 1970s.
This scene is of the centre of the Point Cruz shopping centre in Mendana Avenue, opposite the gas company, Acor Bookshop, and Solomon Airlines. There were trees in the main street, which, sadly, have now disappeared in the name of progress.
Source: Ian Frazer Collection.

---

79   Bathgate 1977: 18; *SND*, 14 March 1975.

The same patterns apply to established *wantok* communities. There are large parts of Honiara that most foreigners never visit: the settlements—the THA/TOL and squatter areas. Solomon Islanders live comfortably there, combining the need to earn money to support urban life with the need to fulfil family and customary obligations. One of the most interesting things about Honiara is the way it brought about an amalgamation and intertwining of different systems of *kastom* from various islands and broadened the *wantok* system beyond its origins in separate local languages. Another interesting aspect is the way Solomon Islanders' concepts of public space have been transferred from villages and language groups to the urban setting. One theme in this and other chapters is the idea of parallel Honiara 'worlds'. Although some urban compounds and private houses are fenced off and access is clearly restricted, most of Honiara is one large public arena.[80]

North Malaitans introduced a word into Solomons Pijin: *liu*, meaning to 'hang around', stroll, or loiter casually. Young single men have always been the main performers of this social art, although the practice can apply to families and women as well. They, too, enjoy the freedom of wandering about Honiara's public places. *Liu* allows new contacts to be made and old relationships to be supported. *Lilui la* became a lifestyle for many Malaitans and other urban Solomon Islanders. The term *masta liu*, coined in the 1970s, is still well-known, and means to have no work and depend on *wantoks* for sustenance. In 1975, in his final year as a student at Betikama SDA High School, Ellison Sade wrote the following lyrics for a song about *masta liu*. Like the lyrics for *Wokabaoti long Saenataone* (*Walkabout in Chinatown*), *Masta Liu* struck a chord with the people of Honiara:

> Master Liu
> I'm Master Liu
> And it's not something new
> If I come your way
> At any time of the day
> I'll walk the streets
> Till the soles of my feet
> Know every grain of sand
> In all of this land
> [Chorus]

---

80 Frazer 1985: 191.

> Hey Master Liu, please show us the way
> To travel along the Kukum High Way
> It was long, long ago since we have come
> So take us home
> Master Liu, Master Liu[81]

The *master liu* concept entered Solomon Islands culture. On the district stations in the 1950s, the unemployed were given free passage home by the district commissioners or district officers. This did not occur in Honiara, although in the 1960s there were some 'district houses' built for *lius* (the plural form) next to the district commissioner's office.[82] *Lius* have always been a large portion of the Honiara population, staying with their extended families in overcrowded housing. Ian Frazer interpreted 'to *liu*' as strategic behaviour, a way of learning, and of supporting social cohesion. He also described comparative terms and behaviours among the Guale, and from other areas of the nation. This peripatetic but acceptable lifestyle can extend over years, and include movements and circulations between islands, all encompassed in an extension of local area activities rooted in culture.[83] What foreigners often see as rootless wandering and parasitic dependence on *wantoks* are part of the creation of a sustaining modern national consciousness, a dynamic and creative process that blends with traditional cultural norms. It also easily tips over into criminal activity.

***

Planners never envisaged the Greater Honiara of 2020, with its population of 160,000 in a nation of 721,000 people. Future forecasts are difficult, although the Ministry for Lands, Housing and Survey estimates that Greater Honiara's population could reach 350,000 by 2050.[84] Honiara has always had a high rate of inward migration, with the population increasing sevenfold between independence in 1978 and the 2010s. There have been two falls in population numbers. The first was during the Tension years (1998–2003), when 25,000 to 35,000 residents left Guadalcanal Plains and Honiara, although many returned after 2003, once RAMSI arrived (Chapter 9). The second was in 2020 during the COVID-19 pandemic, when many people returned to their home villages.

---

81 My thanks to Ellison Sade for allowing the reproduction of his lyrics.
82 In 1967, there were several hundred people without employment, which was of concern to local and central government authorities. *BSIP NS*, 7 May 1967.
83 Frazer 1985: 185–205; Gegeo 2015.
84 Keen et al. 2017: 19.

Solomon Islands Government processes are often frustrating to outsiders. Citizens seem to behave in ways that appear to be not in the national interest. There are deeply felt beliefs about preserving the rights of customary landholders, which hold up development opportunities. Government decisions almost always err on the side of humanitarianism, recognising that there are social pressures at work as village societies transition into the modern world, which do not always fit into bureaucratic rules. As well, the government seldom uses force on its people; almost never in land matters. While this may seem inefficient, negotiation and respect are the key mechanisms that preserve the fabric of society and cultural values. I have heard senior Solomon Islanders complain about squatters in shanties wedged into urban crevices on Kola`a Ridge, next to their prestigious urban allotments. Yet, they also prefer to let the squatters stay there and would be horrified if the government used strong-arm tactics to remove them. I suspect that, deep down, they realise that they, too, are only one or two generations away from villages where land is held under customary ownership. All the Solomon Islands elite have relatives living in Honiara's settlements or in provincial villages, to whom they are obligated. The elite remember their own less-affluent days, and Christianity also plays its part in shaping a modern belief system that is forgiving of difference.

In the standoff at Burns Creek over land reserved for sporting facilities, the squatters seem to have won, as it is unlikely the government will evict them. There are other recent similar examples. In 2017, news broke of squatters from Temotu Province fighting back against Hatanga Limited at Tinge Ridge in west Honiara. They retaliated against the company, which had FTE ownership and the legal right to clear them off the land. The company, chaired by Jay Bartlett, who is also a member of the Solomon Islands Chamber of Commerce and Industry board, had owned the land for 20 years, with the long-term plan to subdivide it into a residential estate. The company claimed to have entered negotiations with the illegal settlers. Appeals were made to the owners and the squatter/settlers to remain calm and deal with the dispute in a peaceful manner. In another 2017 case, at Ranadi, two different Chinese companies were said to have been sold the same piece of land (which belongs to the South Sea Evangelical Church and had a tenant, a local company, Timol Enterprises

Limited).[85] Ministry of Lands officers seem to have connived for personal gain. The bubbling tensions are obvious. Disputes between settlers on the land and the legal owners will continue as Honiara grows.[86]

The Honiara City Council has never really been autonomous, always hamstrung by the BSIP Government and the post-independence national government and its instrumentalities such as the Housing Authority, the Ports Authority, and the Ministry of Infrastructure Development, which maintains Honiara's road system.[87] While Honiara is only a small region excised from Guadalcanal Province, the city belongs to the nation, not to the province. The 1998–2003 Tension period and continuing disturbances such as those between Hatanga Limited and the Temotu squatters show the complexities of life in Honiara. Deep social issues relating to land and society are never far below the surface.

---

85 Tatua 2014.
86 Koli 2017; Bartlett 2017.
87 Osifelo 2018.

6

Building infrastructure

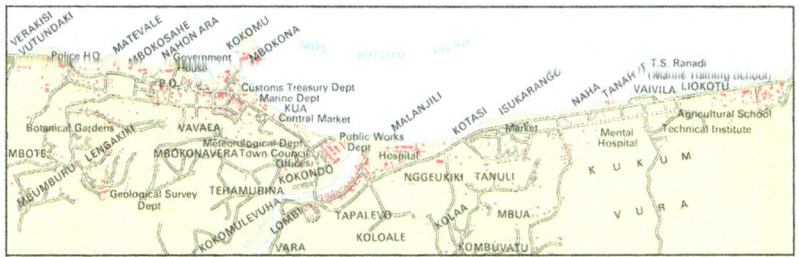

Map 6.1 Honiara in the 1970s.
This map uses local names while also showing the developed areas.
Note: Mbokona is wrongly positioned; it should be inland, not on Point Cruz.
Source: Clive Moore Collection.

In European tradition, cathedrals, exhibitions, art galleries, sporting facilities, large hospitals, excellent schools, and tertiary institutions are markers of the difference between a town and a city. In Honiara, the foundation stone for the Anglican St Barnabas' Cathedral was laid in 1961, with the completed building consecrated in 1969. The Catholic Holy Cross Cathedral was completed during 1977–78. Both cathedrals replaced earlier temporary structures.[1] The other Christian denominations also built central churches, although none is as imposing as the Anglican and Catholic structures. Judged by its cathedrals, Honiara in the 1960s and 1970s qualified as a city. In reality, it was still a small tropical British colonial town replete with racial attitudes that segregated indigenous and non-indigenous inhabitants.

---

1   *BSIP NS*, 7 July 1967, 31 July 1957, 31 June 1960, 28 February 1961, 30 November 1969; *BSIP AR* 1968: 82, 1969: 80–81; *SND*, 18 March 1977.

HONIARA

Plate 6.1 The WPHC High Court building was built in 1964.
It was also used as the BSIP court building and for meetings of the BSIP Legislative Council and the National Parliament, until the new parliamentary building was constructed in 1994. This photograph is from 1971.
Source: Brian Taylor Collection.

This chapter discusses some of the major infrastructure developments that shaped Honiara and Guadalcanal in the 1960s and 1970s—the urban development that changed the town into a city. The British envisaged a new capital that would also be the headquarters of the WPHC, with adjoining agricultural development. The areas discussed here are medical services, the police, shipping, air services, and the media. Each of these institutional themes concentrates on Honiara but reaches out to networks created throughout the archipelago. Together, they helped create a national consciousness, and a sense of belonging to one political entity and society, rather than to individual islands. Developing these institutions was part of the process of building a nation. An associated development was commercial agriculture on the Guadalcanal Plains. The British also had longer-term hopes for mining development, which eventually came to pass (briefly) when Gold Ridge mine opened in the late 1990s. Inadvertently, these three developments—Honiara, agriculture on the plains, and Gold Ridge—fuelled Guale discontent as they saw their land eroded from their control, and large-scale migration, all with too little compensation.

Guadalcanal Plains, 1960s – 1970s

After World War II, one of the government's goals was to encourage commercial agricultural development on the Guadalcanal Plains. They were part of the parcel of land that made Honiara a suitable base for the protectorate's headquarters. The initial development began at the edge of east Honiara, and the port was the conduit for labour. In the early 1940s, when Levers abandoned Ilu plantation east of its Kukum–Lungga–Teneru land, it reverted to the government. During the American years, Ilu became a military farm to produce vegetables for Camp Guadal. After the war, the government put the land to use as an experimental farm. It also purchased the remainder of Levers' land out to Lungga River and some further out on Guadalcanal Plains.

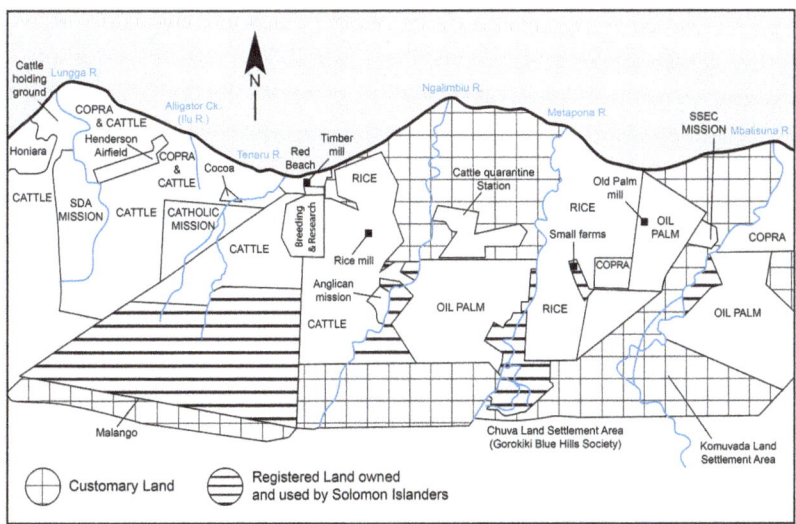

Map 6.2 Guadalcanal Plains east of the Honiara City Council land in the 1970s, showing the mixed usage.
The eastern boundary of Tandai land is at Betanivua, between the Tenaru and Ngalimbiu rivers. The land further east belongs to the Malango and the Lengo.
Source: Based on Ruthven (1979a: 59). Cartography by Vincent Verheyen.

Honiara lies on the edge of the Guadalcanal Plains, which have witnessed intensive agricultural development and contestations over land use and land rights since the 1880s and 1890s. During the 1900s and 1910s, Levers developed coconut palm estates on the plains, having bought up earlier plantations. Levers always concentrated on copra production, although it also experimented with other tropical crops such as cacao and palm oil.² In 1916, Levers introduced a 40–50-hectare trial of oil palms on part of its Ilu plantation.³ The war years turned the coast into a battlefield, destroying most of the coconut palms and plantation buildings. During 1944–45, the Americans trialled dry rice cultivation at Ilu, with 200 hectares planted by late 1945. Although the yields were disappointing, in 1946, a further 25 hectares of dry rice were planted, only to be attacked by insects when harvesting machinery was late arriving. By 1948, the government had given up; then, in the 1960s, it attempted a trial of wet rice production.[4]

In the 1950s and 1960s, the British Colonial Development and Aid Fund investigated the commercial possibilities of crops other than coconut palms. In 1963, the Commonwealth Development Corporation (CDC) leased 10 hectares of land at Ilu to trial oil palms, and wet and dry rice. It was part of development planning to restore and diversify commercial agriculture, creating a sounder economy for the protectorate. This was followed in 1965 by the announcement of a new company, Guadalcanal Plains Limited (GPL), under the direction of Honiara businessman Ken Hay, with nominal capital of £750,000 and plans to develop the plains for rice, soybean, sorghum, and beef cattle. When questioned in the Legislative Council about the alienation of the plains from their customary owners, Director of Agriculture F.N. Spooner said the government had reserved 2,600 hectares on the eastern side of the Mbalisuna River for a Solomon Islander settlement scheme. There were also significant amounts of customary land interspersed with the commercial development (Map 6.2).

In late 1965, GPL received a 33-year lease over 1,666 hectares at Tetere and prepared 291 hectares for dry rice, soybeans, and sorghum, and introduced Hereford cattle. The amount of dry rice planted by GPL increased from 30 hectares in 1965, to 154 hectares in 1967, and 833 hectares in 1968.[5]

---

2   Raw cacao is made by cold-pressing unroasted cacao beans. The process keeps the living enzymes in the cacao and removes the fat (cacao butter). Cocoa powder is raw cacao that has been roasted at high temperatures. Palm oil is an edible vegetable oil derived from the reddish pulp of the fruit of oil palms. Along with coconut oil, palm oil is one of the few highly saturated vegetable oils that is semisolid at room temperature, which makes it a cheap substitute for butter. Oil palm processing involves picking the fruit bunches, sterilising and threshing the bunches to free the palm fruit, mashing the fruit, and pressing the crude palm oil, which is then further treated to purify and dry for storage and export.
3   SINA BSIP 18/I/2, Knibbs, Deputy Lands Commissioner to RC Workman, 17 June 1920.
4   Hansell and Wall 1974: 34.
5   *BSIP NS*, 7 May 1967, 20 October 1967.

Hay's other assets included the Mendana Hotel, a store, butchery, and what became Tetere rice plantation. The first dry rice crop produced 200 tons, which was sold in Honiara in mid-1966, with investigations under way to develop an irrigated rice scheme.[6] Dry rice farming was rotated with soybean production; the beans were exported.[7] In 1966, the government invited applications for the lease of another 1,916 hectares on the plains, with three-year leases paid at A$1.10 per hectare per year, with an option to extend for another 35 years. GPL took this up. Rice exports firmed up in 1969 when 200 tons of brown rice were exported to Fiji.[8]

The rice project was enlarged and wet rice became the main crop, with 1,800 kilograms of paddy rice expected in 1971, with plans to expand the irrigated area to 2,000 hectares.[9] GPL produced sweet potatoes for the local market, raised cattle, and operated Ilu farm. Two thousand laying chickens produced 1,000 eggs each day, with a potential daily market for 1,500 eggs.

In September 1973, GPL was taken over by the Mindoro International Corporation, a company based in Millersville near Philadelphia, in the United States. This company hired Hawaiian Agronomics Company International, a subsidiary of C. Brewer & Company, to operate GPL's rice and other agricultural operations, and, in May 1974, announced expansion plans worth A$2.3 million. This would have increased rice production fivefold, trebled the cattle herd, increased pig and poultry production, and begun to produce farmed seafood. Overstretched, in October 1974, GPL went into receivership. In February 1975, GPL was taken over by the Brewer Group, in a new company known as Brewers Solomons' Associate Limited.[10] Some years earlier, the Hotel Mendana had been split off as a separate company.

The BSIP had more success with the CDC. In 1970, the government had reached agreement with the CDC to establish a 3,333-hectare oil palm project between the Ngalimbiu and Barande rivers on Guadalcanal Plains. Planting began the next year, with 680 hectares of palms under cultivation

---

6 ibid., 27 July 1966.
7 There were several Australia-based directors: W.F. Moses and F.B. Moses, E. Sly (from a NSW grazing family), David Thompson (a partner in stockbroking firm Ors, Minnett and Thompson of Sydney), and Mr Pennyfather (a Hereford cattle breeder from Victoria).
8 *BSIP NS*, 15 February 1969; Hansell and Wall 1974: 34–35.
9 *BSIP NS*, 30 June 1971.
10 *SND*, 25 October 1974, 28 February 1975.

by the end of 1972, and the factory expected to begin operations five years later.[11] The company, known as Solomon Islands Plantation Limited (SIPL), was a partnership between the CDC (68 per cent), the BSIP Government (30 per cent), and local landowners (2 per cent). The land, formerly alienated as coconut plantations, had become government-owned and was converted to 75-year leases, with PE rights reverting to the landowners. The initial cost, to be provided by the CDC, was expected to be $6 million, with around 800 employees in the early stages. The decision to proceed was based on the CDC's trial plantings begun in 1965. SIPL began operations in 1973, built a mill, and by 1976 was exporting palm oil. The original concept, which never eventuated, envisaged smallholder outgrowers. SIPL chose to run an estate-based operation. Nevertheless, the venture was successful: palm oil products made up an average of 11.3 per cent of national exports between 1976 and 1998, and between 1988 and 1998, were Solomon Islands' most important agricultural export.[12]

The other major business on the plains was Foxwood Timber Limited, a Queensland-based company that in 1973 bought out the British Solomons Timber Company. It had extensive logging operations inland and around Red Beach, where it had a sawmill.[13]

Just as land issues in Honiara sowed the seeds for future discontent, so, too, did the division and commercialisation of the Guadalcanal Plains, which attracted large numbers of labourers from other islands. By the late 1990s, 6,300 hectares of the plains were under oil palms, and the company employed 1,800 people—the largest numbers from Malaita Province (65 per cent) and Temotu Province (16 per cent). With their families, this added 8,000 to 10,000 people to the population of the plains—a level that remained until mid-1999. Although companies provided barracks-style accommodation, once the labourers settled permanently with their families, they wanted their own land for houses and gardens. The labourers became friendly with the local landholding groups; sometimes they, or their family members, ceased employment with the companies and worked for the landowners. They negotiated rights to start small villages and gardens, providing compensation for land use in a complex web of intermarriages, customary exchanges, cash, and goods. These agreements

---

11   Hansell and Wall 1974: 34.
12   *BSIP NS*, 15 June 1965, 31 October 1965, 7 May 1966, 7 October 1966, 15 October 1970; Kendrick 1968; Fraenkel et al. 2010: 66–67.
13   Bennett 2000: 178, 312.

were seldom written down and were extended when new members of the immigrant families arrived. The Guale landowners became worried and tried to remove some of the squatters, and the Guadalcanal Provincial Government suggested that in future formal applications must be made, in consultation with the landowners, before permission could be granted to settlers. Twenty years later, in the late 1990s, the issue had escalated and militant Guale caused forced the evacuation of tens of thousands of non-Guale Solomon Islanders from Honiara and Guadalcanal Plains.

Honiara in the 1950s and 1960s

There can be little doubt the British neglected the development of Solomon Islands during the second half of the 1940s and into the 1950s. The protectorate's economy was based on coconuts, and the 900 islands in a far-flung corner of the Pacific were of little concern to Whitehall. The war had done so much damage it was difficult to rehabilitate the protectorate. As there were no radical pressures for change, such as it faced in several African and Asian colonies, Britain was able to hold back on establishing an agenda for economic and political development.

In 1951, the decision was made to separate the position of Western Pacific High Commissioner from that of Governor of Fiji, and to transfer the WPHC headquarters to Honiara. The stated reason was to place more emphasis on the development of the BSIP, but the war had caused the British to rethink their rather unwieldly 1877 WPHC, which was always a sideshow to the administration of the Crown Colony of Fiji. The delay was because of uncertainty about whether the BSIP would remain British, as the Australian Government had discussed with Britain and France the possibility of taking over the BSIP and the New Hebrides.[14] Robert (later Sir Robert) C.S. Stanley was appointed the new high commissioner, separate from the position of Governor of the Crown Colony of Fiji. Arrangements to move the WPHC headquarters continued throughout the year. Stanley made his first visit to Honiara in September and transferred there permanently on 22 December. On 1 January 1953, the new resident high commissioner took over the administration of the protectorate from acting Resident Commissioner Peter Hughes, combining his BSIP duties

---

14   *PIM*, May 1951, 5, 10.

with those of the WPHC.[15] The High Commission Secretariat plus its records were transferred to Honiara, and the High Commission's chief secretary and financial secretary held conjoint appointments as officers of the BSIP administration. An officer of the colonial legal service was appointed as BSIP Attorney-General and concurrent legal adviser to the High Commission, replacing the Attorney-General of Fiji. The office of the resident commissioner lapsed, and the BSIP Secretariat was merged with that of the High Commission. The Inspector-General of the Health Service in Fiji continued as adviser to the high commissioner on medical matters. Stanley departed on 7 July 1955 on pre-retirement leave, succeeded by John (later Sir John) Gutch, who began his duties on 26 September 1955.[16]

Until then, the development of the BSIP had been tied to the level of its internal revenue, which in 1952 was only £483,445. Once the High Commission shifted its headquarters to Honiara, the town served not only as the capital of Solomon Islands, but also as the WPHC headquarters, which included the administration of the Crown Colony of Gilbert and Ellice Islands, the British half of the New Hebrides Condominium, and several smaller territories.[17] Regular development plans began to be created in the 1960s and proceeded until after independence. Between 1955 and 1967, total revenue increased eightfold. In 1967, $4.5 million of the BSIP's $7.7 million expenditure related to the WPHC headquarters' move to Honiara.[18]

Slowly, urban and rural transport infrastructure developed. By the mid-1960s, it was possible to drive the 40 kilometres from Honiara to Maravovo Anglican School in the north-west of the island. To the east, the Tenaru River was bridged in the early 1960s, although the Ngalimbiu, Mbalisuna,

---

15 *PIM*, January 1953, 19.
16 *BSIP AR* 1955–56: 59–60.
17 Cook Islands and Niue were removed from the WPHC in 1901 when they were transferred to New Zealand. Tokelau was transferred to New Zealand in 1926 and removed from the WPHC in 1948. By 1952, the remaining WPHC territories were Canton and Enderbury Islands (a US and British Condominium), the Kingdom of Tonga (a protected state), Fiji, Gilbert and Ellice Islands Colony, the BSIP, and New Hebrides (the British side). Pitcairn Island was removed from the WPHC in 1952; it became a separate territory administered by the Governor of Fiji. In 1971, the British High Commissioner in Wellington became the non-resident Governor of Pitcairn. Tonga and Fiji became independent nations in 1970, the Crown Colony of Gilbert and Ellice Islands was split in two in 1975 in preparation for independence as two separate nations: Tuvalu in 1978 and Kiribati in 1979. Canton and Enderbury Islands were included in Kiribati in 1979. The BSIP became independent in 1978, followed by the New Hebrides (Vanuatu) in 1980.
18 Australian dollars were used from February 1966.

and Metapona rivers (Map 6.2) continued to be forded until later in the decade. The rehabilitation of Henderson Airfield, plus the beginnings of the new wharf complex, were all completed during these years.

The US Army Quonset huts that had been a feature of Honiara were disappearing. Several new public buildings were constructed, such as the airconditioned High Court, the secretariat building, the post office, the National Museum, King George VI School, and the public library. Educational institutions were expanded, and roads and bridges on Guadalcanal were improved. When Jock Stevenson joined the Public Works Department as senior architect in 1963, he had the dream job of designing and supervising the construction of new buildings, many of which remain in use today. He also completed the first sketch plans for the new Government House on the beach at Nahona`ara. Stevenson went into private practice in 1968, adding to his list the University of the South Pacific Extension Centre, Kukum cinema, Forum Fisheries, industrial buildings such as the abattoir, the tobacco company, the Joy biscuit factory, the octagonal-shaped Tourist Authority, the Solair office, and The Bookshop, CDC housing, and various church buildings. He also designed other buildings throughout the nation until he retired in the 1990s. The Stevenson stamp remains on the architecture of Honiara.

The urban labour force grew, as did the overall population. The combined WPHC–BSIP administration also enabled more Solomon Islanders to become public servants. There were 320 indigenous civil servant positions in 1958, which had increased to 580 in 1966.[19] Honiara's gender divisions changed considerably. Between 1959 and 1965, the number of males in Honiara had increased from 2,297 to 3,980—up 40 per cent. The number of women almost tripled, from only 520 in 1959, to 1,426 in 1965, creating a more balanced community. The size of the European population grew from 363 in 1959 to 624 in 1965, and the number of Chinese residents increased from 266 to 414. Nevertheless, as before, Solomon Islanders were the majority population. These increases meant that housing and services had to expand fast, and one further result was the increase in the number of indigenous women who had moved to Honiara. Males still predominated and about 90 per cent lived singly, although a large minority were married and had left their wives and families on their home island. Slowly, the arrival of women changed the nature of Honiara society.[20]

---

19 Bellam 1970: 72–75.
20 *BSIP AR* 1965: 5; 1969: 90; 1971: 7.

Table 6.1 Population of Honiara: Ethnic groups, 1959 and 1965.

Ethnic group	1959	1965
Solomon Islander	2,817	5,469
European	363	624
Chinese	266	414
Other[a]	102	145
Total	3,548	6,652
Further divisions of ethnic groups		
Melanesian	2,618	4,535
Polynesian	185	238
Micronesian (Gilbertese)	14	166
Not stated	0	532

[a] Fijians, Indo-Fijians, and mixed-race
Sources: *BSIP* (1961); Bellam (1964, 1968, 1970).

M.E.P. Bellam conducted a survey in 1962 that revealed that most adult Solomon Islander males in Honiara intended to return to their home village. Only around one-fifth of those interviewed expressed a wish to spend all their working life in Honiara:

> This seems to apply to men who may spend all of their working lives in wage employment as well as to migrant labourers whose sojourn in town on any one visit may be restricted to three or six months. To date virtually all civil servants have returned to the village on retirement from government service.[21]

Bellam discerned the development of embryonic class-like relationships, mainly among skilled workers. He concluded that a small number of workers was beginning to see advantages in permanent urban residence, particularly because of the educational assistance this could provide for their children.[22] Many of Honiara's earliest indigenous public servants were from Western District—the area of greatest early economic development and modern education. Most other Solomon Islanders in Honiara were labourers or semiskilled workers on short-term wage-earning ventures. They lived among kin or *wantoks*, often in barracks, and much of their earnings were remitted home.

---

21   Bellam 1968: 11.
22   ibid., 11–12.

Plate 6.2 Solomon Islands Museum at the time it was built in 1968.

The museum's collection was begun in 1951 and was displayed at various sites before the present museum enclave was established at Coronation Gardens in central Honiara. The original structure remains the central exhibition space, augmented by newer exhibition areas, offices, a library, storage areas, an artefact shop, and an auditorium constructed from traditional materials.

Source: *BSIP AR* (1969: 89).

Plate 6.3 In the 1960s, two high-rise residential buildings were constructed in Honiara.

Source: *BSIP AR* (1963–64: 52).

Three substantial hotels began operations in Honiara. The Mendana Hotel had a monopoly over 'high-level' accommodation until the mid-1960s. Jack Close, who arrived in 1962 to run the British Solomon Islands Trading Corporation Limited for its new owners, Mitsui & Company and D.J. Gubbay & Company, described the Mendana:

> The accommodation at the hotel was a series of rooms in a long single-story [sic] wooden building with a veranda running along the front. The rooms were Spartan but adequately furnished. Mosquito mesh covered the windows and the screen door, but all the rooms and the shower-blocks were hot and generally airless.[23]

The father of the present owner of the Honiara Hotel (Sir Tommy Chan) began the 13-room hotel on the edge of Chinatown in 1968. The Mendana Hotel doubled its capacity in the same year.[24] Another hotel, Kwong Chow (Kuang Zhou) in Chinatown, built by R.C. Symes for Chinese interests, was a basic drinking place with no accommodation. A few years earlier, in 1964, Americans Alvin J. and Gertrude Blum began their Hometel (a word play on 'homely hotel') in Hibiscus Avenue, with rooms, a café, and dining room.[25] Their philosophy combined religious beliefs and capitalism.

The Blums were two of Honiara's characters in the 1950s and 1960s. Alvin was born in New Jersey in the United States in 1912. He spent 10 years in the southern US as a commercial traveller. When World War II began, he joined the American Army Corps. Blum served four years in the Pacific, including on Guadalcanal, in a non-combat medical position, rising to the rank of sergeant. After the war, he married Gertrude Gewartz from New York. They moved to Little Rock, Arkansas, where their daughter Keithie was born in 1947.[26] Lady Keithie Saunders' history of her parents, *Of Wars and Worship*, tells the story of this remarkable American couple who were of the Bahá`í Faith, which they introduced to Solomon Islands. The family moved to New Zealand, then in 1953 toured Ceylon (Sri Lanka), India, Pakistan, and Israel, where they pursued their interest in religions, chiefly the Bahá`í Faith. They arrived in Solomon Islands in March 1954, and Alvin Blum spent his first three months as acting manager of the

---

23 Close 2011: 169.
24 *BSIP NS*, 31 August 1968.
25 ibid., 21 September 1967, 30 September 1968, 30 September 1970, 23 June 1976; Saunders 2013: 269–72.
26 'Festivities honor community service', Bahá`í World News Service, 1 March 2004, available from: news.bahai.org/story/291/.

Mendana Hotel. An inveterate entrepreneur, he set up a taxi service, and began a general store and bakery in Honiara. The couple traded as A.J. and G. Blum and Company. Other ventures followed: a dry-cleaning business, a peanut oil mill, production of iceblocks and soft drinks, a fish and chip shop, and in 1959, a general store, bakery, and cinema in Auki, Malaita. Not all these ventures succeeded, but the Blum's Hometel endured. Built like a motel and based on temperance principles, it was on the site of what is now King Solomon Hotel. Individual bathrooms were added in 1966 and the accommodation wing was extended to 15 rooms in 1968. These rooms are now the shopping arcade of the King Solomon Hotel. As recounted in *Of Wars and Worship*, the Blums began their Hometel largely as a reaction against Ken Hay, who would not allow Solomon Islanders into his Mendana Hotel, except in the '*boi* bar'. Blum's Hometel was a comfortable, alcohol-free environment with a friendly atmosphere where all races were welcome.

The main concern of the Blums was always the Bahá`í Faith, in which they were pioneers and international figures. Alvin was an active member of the town council from its inception in 1958 until August 1967. He was also a leading member of the Chamber of Commerce, serving as its president for several years in the 1960s. The Blums were overseas for part of late 1967, when they visited Bahá`í centres around the Pacific. In their absence, their businesses were run by Owen Battrick, another Bahá`í follower. Alvin died in 1968, survived by his wife and daughter, Keithie, who had married Bruce (later Sir Bruce) Saunders. She returned to Honiara to take over her parents' businesses and, with her husband, expanded into tourism, artefacts, real estate and property management, insurance, and international trade. Alvin and Gertrude Blum received a Knight of Baha`u`llah Award. Gertrude helped establish the National Council of Women and the Red Cross Society, and was awarded an MBE in 1989 for her community services and her dedication to the Bahá`í Faith. In 1970, Gertrude left Honiara for two or three years to spread the Bahá`í Faith in New Zealand. The Blums' Hometel was sold in 1976 to Hibiscus Hotels Limited. Gertrude remained in Honiara until her death in June 1993.[27] The Blum company still operates, with Sir Bruce running the business, as well as BJS Agencies Limited, while Lady Keithie is the US Consular Agent for Solomon Islands.

---

27 Saunders 2013; *BSIP NS*, 7 April 1966, 21 September 1967, 15 April 1968, 30 September 1968, 30 September 1970, 30 June 1976; Letter from Alan Lindley, Adelaide, 30 June 2011.

Plates 6.4–6.6 Blums' Hometel, built in Hibiscus Avenue in 1964, was the most socially advanced of Honiara's hotels and welcomed everyone.

The food in the café was excellent and affordable. The Hometel guestrooms are now part of the shopping arcade of King Solomon Hotel. In keeping with the Blums' Baháʼí Faith, their Hometel did not serve alcohol.

Source: Lady Keithie Saunders Collection.

6. BUILDING INFRASTRUCTURE

New Honiara

Honiara changed rapidly during the 1960s. In March 1966, the Honiara Town Council named some of the important roads and facilities in Honiara, although street signposts and maps have never been a strong point. One of the city's continuing peculiarities is the lack of readily available maps. A quiet secret of RAMSI's 2003–17 success was a book of large maps made from aerial photographs, which the personnel used to navigate Honiara. Although digital maps of Honiara can be viewed online, revealing its pattern of nameless streets, there is still no paper-based street directory.

The coastal road west from the Mataniko River to Rove Creek is Mendana Avenue, which then changes name at Rove to become Tandai Highway as far as Poha River. Prince Philip Highway, now usually known as Kukum Highway, runs east from Mendana Avenue along the coast. Both highways were named in 1966. Skyline Road was named, as was Commonwealth Street from Mendana Avenue to the Point Cruz docks. Mud Alley already had its name, based on the 'quality' of its road in the 1940s and 1950s. Footpaths were constructed along main roads and beautification projects were undertaken.[28] Poincianas and other flamboyant shade trees were planted along the roads, adding character, which, sadly, has been depleted in recent years.

The remnants of the American wartime camp gradually disappeared, replaced with new buildings and facilities. Several problems were difficult to solve. Removing munitions has already been mentioned. Another problem—still Honiara's biggest weakness—was the water supply. As mentioned in Chapter 2, Honiara's original water supply was provided by a combination of rainwater tanks, boreholes at Kukum, and springs at Lengakiki. Electric pumps were submerged in two boreholes and supplemented by six permanent springs whose water was caught in a small dam.[29] After 1965, the upstream section of the Mataniko River was also used as a source, with water stored in a series of large tanks in different locations. Water pressure has always been poor in hilly areas like Skyline, Kola`a Ridge, and the other ridges as new houses were built. For 75 years, Honiara's residents have complained about rationed and inadequate water

---

28 *BSIP NS*, 20 October 1967.
29 *BSIP NS*, 31 January 1969; *BSIP AR* 1949–50: 32–33.

supplies, with little solution in sight and larger problems looming as Honiara continues to grow. Recently, a Japanese aid project has expanded the network of boreholes. Another possibility is to build a treatment plant upstream on the Lungga River and pipe in water.[30] Residents on the ridges are used to water coming and going in the pipes and sometimes must wait hours for it to return. I lived on Skyline Ridge in the mid-2000s in a household where rain was welcomed and captured in drums and buckets to supplement the often-empty reticulated system. The supply of electricity was similarly erratic. The problems continue. Honiara has water rationing, as well as poor water quality. Residents are advised to boil drinking water. As Matthew Wale, leader of the parliamentary opposition, remarked in 2019, 'it is totally unacceptable that the capital city of a country should go without water for an extended period'.[31]

Honiara's public and commercial facilities became permanent and more substantial during the 1960s. Honiara Town Council's new fish market opened in May 1966, with a freezer, cold store, and ice-making facilities, leased to the Honiara Co-operative Fish Marketing Association Limited. Guadalcanal Bus Service began in 1968, travelling from King George VI School to White River, operated by partners Monty Ho (He), William Chan (Chen), James Kwan (Guan), and Nga Kwak Kwan (Yan Weiqun), with Chan as general manager. A second bus was added in 1969 and a third in 1970.[32] The big red buses trundled back and forth until the introduction of minibuses made them obsolete. A permanent wharf was constructed next to the fish market in 1969, which allowed small ships and fibreglass canoes to bring produce directly to the market.[33] Supplementing the existing Commonwealth Bank, the Australia and New Zealand Banking Group (ANZ) opened a branch in Honiara in mid-1966, and the Hongkong and Shanghai Banking Corporation (HSBC) did likewise in December 1973.[34] In 1969, Honiara held its first National Agricultural and Produce Show—the forerunner for many similar events. Substantial churches and cathedrals were also built and remain the major focal points of life for many Solomon Islanders.

---

30 Sei 2019a.
31 Salani 2019. See also Bau 2019a.
32 *BSIP NS*, 31 August 1968, 15 May 1969, 31 December 1969. The company was purchased by Mark Lewis in 1975. *SND*, 6 February 1975.
33 *BSIP NS*, 15 April 1969.
34 ibid., 7 May 1966; Moore 2013c: entry for Banking.

Namba 9: Central Hospital

Plate 6.7 Aerial photograph from December 1944 of 'Namba 9', the 9th US Casualty Clearing Station, close to the Mataniko River.
This became Honiara's Central Hospital, initially consisting of Quonset huts.
Source: USNARA, Air Force aerial photograph, 11 December 1944.

One of the most important facilities in Honiara is Namba 9, once the 9th US Casualty Clearing Station, which became Central Hospital and is now known as the National Referral Hospital. During the war, the Americans developed extensive medical facilities for their troops and, to a limited extent, Solomon Islanders also benefited. When Honiara began, the buildings of the most conveniently placed wartime hospital became the main hospital for the protectorate. They were Quonset huts with wooden internal walls and plywood floors—all of which were intended to be temporary. The operating theatre had wire-netting walls (spectators had to be removed during operations), the roof leaked, and there was no plumbing.[35] Medical services were disorganised in the early post-war years, with a restructuring partly achieved by 1948. Various extensions and rebuilding schemes were made possible by grants under Britain's Colonial Development and Welfare Fund. In the early years, the European section was painted inside, while the Solomon Islander section still had plain tar-paper walls.[36]

Table 6.2 BSIP Medical Department, 1950, 1956, and 1962.

Position	No. of staff		
	1950	1956	1962
Senior medical officer/director	1	1	1
Medical officers	4	4	5
Assistant medical officers	11	11	16
Pharmacist	1	1	1
Dressers, medical assistants, and nurses	71	83	90
Trainee medical assistants	0	0	28
Matron	0	1	1
Sister-tutor	0	0	1
Nursing sisters	4	3	5
Nurses	0	5	18
Trainee nurses	0	n.a.	19
Local council nurses	0	n.a.	22

n.a. Not available
Sources: *BSIP AR* (1949–50: 24; 1955–56: 37; 1961–62: 49).

In the early 1950s, the BSIP Medical Department was quite limited. Central Hospital was equipped with 120 beds and able to provide surgical, x-ray, and laboratory services. The wartime buildings were dilapidated and being consumed by termites. In March 1950, a new European ward was constructed with accommodation for six patients. In 1950, Central Hospital received 1,376 inpatients, 8,259 outpatients, and conducted 2,871 laboratory tests, and 750 x-ray examinations. Planning to rebuild the entire hospital commenced in 1951, with construction between 1954 and 1958. The first new wards to open were for outpatients, dental surgery, and tuberculosis patients, along with a dispensary.[37]

---

35 *PIM*, September 1952, 59.
36 ibid., March 1953, 19.
37 *BSIP AR* 1953–54: 31; *BSIP NS*, 1 July 1955, 12 July 1955; Information from Alan Lindley, Adelaide, 30 June 2011.

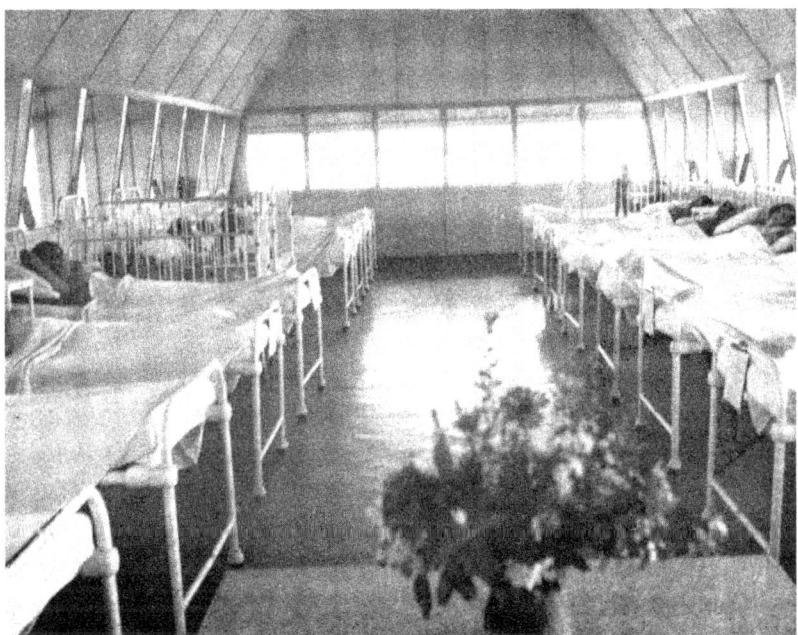

Plate 6.8 The tuberculosis ward at Central Hospital, mid-1950s.
Source: *BSIP AR* (1955–56: 36).

Dr J.D. Macgregor became the senior medical officer in 1957, remaining until 1974. Until Macgregor arrived, there had been no expansion in the senior staffing since the late 1940s, although there was some growth in the number of indigenous dressers, medical assistants, and nurses (Table 6.2). As Macgregor recounts, it was an exciting time to practise medicine in the Pacific:

> For example, penicillin was becoming available in place of the old arsenical preparations to treat Yaws. It was far more effective and infinitely less toxic. Streptomycin and other drugs were revolutionising the treatment of Tuberculosis. Even Leprosy was responding to treatment with the new drug Dapsone. Blood transfusions could be contemplated in remote places like the Solomons; anaesthesia was much safer despite the fact that we had no anaesthetic gases in the islands; new insecticides, especially DDT [dichlorodiphenyltrichloroethane], held out promise for the eventual control on Malaria; and a vaccine was at last available against Poliomyelitis.[38]

38 Macgregor 2000.

When he began work, Mcgregor found himself the only fully trained doctor at the hospital, as the other two expatriate doctors were about to depart. Macgregor was aided by several very competent AMOs—two of whom, Enele Karuru and Sefanaia Tabua, were on secondment from Fiji—a very experienced matron (Christine Woods), several expatriate nursing sisters, a pharmacist (Ben Crone), and an excellent executive officer (Reg Pullen). There was no blood bank, but the local branch of the British Red Cross Society (formed in 1951) kept a register of potential donors. Transfusions were organised by Solomon Dakei, the chief laboratory technician, who also doubled as the radiographer (his other claim to fame was as the mainstay of Honiara's best string band in the 1960s and 1970s). Until anaesthetic gases were available, surgical procedures were performed using local, regional, and spinal injections. The major causes of death were malaria, yaws, tuberculosis, and Hansen's disease (leprosy). Other prominent conditions were related to poor hygiene and sanitation, including fungal skin conditions and intestinal worm infections. The effects of early 1950s poliomyelitis epidemics were also very evident.[39]

Malaria has long been the scourge of the Solomon archipelago. Malaria is transmitted by the nocturnal bite of the female Anopheles mosquito, which transmits a protozoan parasite from an infected human to someone uninfected. Until Atabrine was developed in the 1930s, the only effective treatment was Quinate, a drug with quinine as its active ingredient. Atabrine was a better drug, although it still only supressed and did not cure malaria and had the disadvantage of turning one's skin yellow. It remained in use until superseded by Chloroquine, which was also invented in the 1930s but not in common use until the 1960s and 1970s.[40] While seldom fatal in adults, malaria reduces the general efficiency of a person by about 20 per cent. Residents learned to live with malaria and to take prophylactics, although most Solomon Islanders waited until the fevers struck, then used a high suppressive dose, if they had access to a clinic or hospital. Removing mosquito breeding grounds in stagnant water and DDT spraying were used to reduce the risk. This all changed in the 1990s when research by Sir Dr Nathan Kere showed that bed nets treated with insecticide were better preventative measures, along with community education. Although not eradicated, malaria is no longer a major health issue.

---

39   *PIM*, February 1948, 15; June 1951, 49; July 1951, 79.
40   Mason 2004: 66–101.

6. BUILDING INFRASTRUCTURE

Central Hospital catered for Honiara and was the referral hospital for the protectorate. In addition, there were government hospitals in each of the other district headquarters: Gizo (Western), Auki (Malaita), and Kirakira (Eastern); and two rural hospitals, at Malu'u (Malaita) and Tataba (Isabel). Some district councils employed dressers (medical assistants) and provided funds for buildings and equipment for dispensaries.[41] The Christian missions also maintained hospitals: at Fauaabu (Anglican Diocese of Melanesia) and Atoifi (SDA Mission) on Malaita, and at Kukudu (SDA Mission) and Bilua (Methodist Mission) in Western District. These hospitals and their rural clinics were all feeders for the Central Hospital. Fauaabu was also the Anglican training school for nurses.

Eventually, there were also 62 rural health centres and 22 rural maternity and child welfare centres, each staffed by nurses, and all connected to Central Hospital. Dressers were in charge of the rural health centres and locally registered nurses or midwives ran the maternity and child welfare centres. There was also a government leprosarium at Tetere, 32 kilometres from Honiara, and small mission-run leprosaria in Western and Malaita districts. Metropolitan-trained doctors were in charge at Fauaabu Hospital, and at Munda Hospital on New Georgia. Most of the many mission stations throughout the protectorate also provided medical care, which varied from basic first aid to simple hospitals run by foreign nursing sisters.[42] In June 1966, a new hospital was opened at Buala on Isabel, and work had begun on another at Auki.[43]

During its first year based in Honiara, the WPHC put aside £106,000 to reconstruct the main hospital and build a small mental hospital at Kukum, which was completed between 1954 and 1956.[44] In the 1960s, the expansion in the government medical staff was at the level of medical assistants and nurses, many of whom were working in the districts. By 1967, the principal government medical institutions were still Central Hospital in Honiara (148 beds), and district hospitals at Kilu'ufi at Auki (100 beds), Kirakira (56 beds), and Gizo (46 beds). Rural hospitals operated at Malu'u (36 beds, plus a hostel for transient patients) and Buala (36 beds). Kilu'ufi Hospital at Auki was opened in October 1967. The government leprosarium at Tetere was staffed by three nursing sisters

---

41 *BSIP AR* 1953–54: 28.
42 *BSIP AR* 1959–60: 41; 1963–64: 51.
43 *BSIP NS*, No. 11 [n.d.] June 1966, 27 July 1966.
44 *BSIP AR* 1955–56: 6.

from the Catholic Marist Order, who were joined in 1967 by a fourth sister qualified as a physiotherapist. The New Zealand Leper Trust Board assisted in establishing a physiotherapy department at Tetere.[45]

The first specialist surgeon in Honiara was Dr Tony Cross, who was appointed in the 1960s. One of his specialities was assisting people who had been crippled in the 1950s poliomyelitis epidemics. He conducted hundreds of operations to restore some degree of mobility. A team of eye specialists visited each year in the 1970s for around three weeks, headed by Dr J.E.K. (Dick) Galbraith from Melbourne, attending to cases in Honiara, Gizo, Auki, Atoifi, and Kirakira.

Central Hospital was expanded in 1970 with a 12-bed ward for people with mobility problems, mainly those suffering the effects of poliomyelitis. In 1974, a hostel run by the Society for Crippled People opened at the hospital, funded by the Ryder Cheshire Foundation and local donations. It accommodated 10 male and eight female patients undergoing rehabilitation. In 1974, government hospitals contained just 500 beds, supplemented by another 275 beds in mission-run hospitals; 775 beds for a population estimated to be 178,940 was disastrously below the world average.[46] The Nurses and Dressers Training Centre also began at Central Hospital.[47] Providing medical care was crucial, but so, too, was the training of local nurses, which created one of the few working environments for Solomon Islander women (the other was the teaching profession). Training for nursing and teaching is discussed later in the chapter.

One difference in 1970s medical treatment was the new emphasis on community health through malaria eradication—usually via DDT spraying and the use of chemically impregnated bed nets—and attempts to lessen the occurrence of tuberculosis, Hansen's disease, gastroenteritis, and measles. Health inspectors received training overseas. Some of their tasks were to ensure standards in meat production at the abattoir, and to mitigate air and water pollution. One thing remained the same: without the medical services of the Anglican Diocese of Melanesia, the United Church, and the SDA Church, patients in the districts would

---

45   *BSIP AR* 1967: 55.
46   In 1975, the world average number of hospital beds per 1,000 population was 2.4; the Solomon Islands statistic for 1974 was 0.0043 per 1,000 population. 'Hospital beds (per 1,000 people)', *World Bank Data* [online], available from: data.worldbank.org/indicator/SH.MED.BEDS.ZS.
47   *BSIP AR* 1974: 80.

have been far worse off. Although the government was developing services in the districts, overwhelmingly, they concentrated on building up Central Hospital.[48]

The National Referral Hospital

Namba 9, as it is still affectionally known, is the nation's tertiary care hospital, taking referrals from the 12 smaller provincial hospitals, and dealing directly with the population of Guadalcanal and Honiara. In 2020, there were 50 doctors, 304 beds, 12 clinical departments, 12 inpatient wards, and 10 outpatient clinics. The available treatments include emergency care, injury and trauma care, advanced obstetrics care, as well as paediatric, surgical, and general medical care. The National Referral Hospital also treats increasing numbers of diabetes, cardiopulmonary, and cancer patients, and is a training centre for medical, nursing, and other allied health professions. The hospital staff interact with 110,000 patients a year, providing direct care for 4,500 to 5,000 patients a month. There are 11,000 admissions each year. The hospital has three functioning operating theatres (two of them major), although in 2016, two of these were closed temporarily for safety reasons. Diagnostic equipment remains limited.

Additional buildings were added to Namba 9 in the 1970s and 1980s. The current main building was constructed by the Republic of China (Taiwan) in 1993. The biggest future issue is the need to relocate the hospital away from the beach and the mouth of the Mataniko River, as the ground is only 1.5 metres above high tide. Wastewater is discharged out to sea, but during high tides, this backs up. In a cyclonic area, subject to earthquakes, and with a volcanic island within sight, the possibility of tsunamis is high. The current site is not safe for a medical facility integral to the wellbeing of the nation. Construction of a larger, modern hospital on a new site is crucial.[49] An offer in 2016 from the Republic of China to provide a new National Referral Hospital was rejected because the plan was to rebuild on the existing coastal highway and there was no gynaecological ward included, even though Solomon Islands has the highest level of prenatal and neonatal deaths in the Pacific. Plans for relocation are still under discussion.

---

48   ibid., 75–80.
49   SIG 2014d; Sasako 2016; Sei 2017.

HONIARA

Plate 6.9 National Referral Hospital, Honiara, 2016.
This is the nation's major hospital. On the site of the former Central Hospital, it was rebuilt by the Republic of China (Taiwan) in 1993.
Source: Daniel Evans Collection.

The Royal Solomon Islands Police Force

The modern police force was created after World War II, rebuilt from the pre-war Armed Constabulary, which began in 1897 as a small paramilitary force. Its original headquarters was at Tulagi, with regional forces in each district. Primarily, the police were used for 'pacification' and to assert British law; then, from the 1920s, they accompanied tax-collecting expeditions. During the war, the police were absorbed into the Defence Force. On its re-establishment after the war, the force consisted of a commandant and a sub-inspector, and 150 sub-officers and constables. Urban areas depended on regular policing, which was slowly expanded in Honiara after the war. After spending 1944–45 with his 'Honiara Guard' crowded in with other BSIP departments at Stateside close to the Mataniko River, and supervising three prisons (in Honiara, at Ilu farm, and at Rove), the acting commandant, Inspector Frank Moore, wrote to the government secretary suggesting a move for the headquarters detachment and all prisons to 'Rove Camp', a site large enough to cope with any expansion. The area adjoined the western portion of what had been the US engineering depot and 690th Heavy Equipment Company base. The move was agreed to on 24 December 1945. The constables built the new buildings using thatch and scrap wartime materials. The new prison consisted of one barrack block containing lock-up cells built from salvaged lumber and wartime prefabricated huts. A grassed parade ground doubled as a sports ground, with a pavilion. The creek provided cooking and washing water. Drinking water was carted in—some of it from the wells at the nearby Heavy Equipment Company site.[50]

Plate 6.10 BSIP police headquarters at Rove, 1952.
A Japanese field gun is in front of the main office block (at left). The buildings beside the white entrance gate are the guard house and the armoury.
Source: Alan Lindley Collection, in Clive Moore Collection.

Moore, an Australian, only lasted one more year, then reverted to his substantive rank of inspector. He left soon after, but his 1945–49 task had not been easy. The Armed Constabulary was shambolic, and the task of reform seemed impossible without recruitment of new expatriate police officers. Few police records survived the war, the police were untrained, and there were sometimes as many as 1,000 prisoners in Honiara because of Maasina Rule arrests. In 1949, Moore was replaced

---

50   Holloway 1973.

with Superintendent Hugo Colchester-Wemyss, who had been with the Palestine police (1933–38), the Barbados police (1938–41), and in Jamaica (1941–49). Looking forward to retirement, not to building a new, efficient police force, he left the Solomons in 1955.[51] In his early years, Colchester-Wemyss had only two senior officers, both of whom were sub-inspectors: Ronald Yates, who had been a post-war Palestine police building inspector and was in charge of the prison; and Dick Richardson, of African-American and Solomon Islander descent, who had previously been a sergeant major. All three were stationed at the Rove headquarters in the early 1950s. There were 210 sub-officers and constables in the force. The police headquarters, depot, and training school were gradually expanded and, by 1953, were fully operational, with offices, teaching facilities, a clubhouse, and canteen (which was reported to be superior to the facilities at the Guadalcanal Club), lawns, paths, and gardens. Detachments were also stationed at the various district administration centres. In addition to Honiara (later Central) Police Station, there were stations at Auki and Malu`u in Malaita District, and at Kirakira in Eastern District. Police detachments were also stationed at Gizo, and at Tataba on Isabel Island.[52]

New expatriate police officers did not arrive until the early 1950s. The delay was probably because Britain concentrated on Palestine and Kenya and other colonial flashpoints considered more important than a far-away Pacific protectorate. Eventually, 10 new expatriate officers were appointed during the 1950s, which enabled the establishment of the modern Solomon Islands Police Force (SIPF). The first of these officers, Inspector John Buckingham, a former London Metropolitan Police officer close to retirement, arrived in February 1952. He was based at Honiara Police Station, which also served all of Central District. The second to arrive was Alan Lindley, a sub-inspector, at the end of March 1952. Two more sub-inspectors arrived in June, Edward Bradley and James Semple. They were followed by John Holland early in 1953. Lindley was from Nottingham and had completed his National Service in the Royal Berkshire Regiment, serving in Eritrea, and then as a constable with the Coventry Police in England. The war had removed many middle-aged officers, enabling these young British men to advance rapidly in the colonial service. Most were aged in their twenties (Lindley was 22 years old when he arrived) and barely prepared for working in the protectorate. Semple came from the Nottingham Police and had also been in Palestine in the post-war years.

---

51   Hilder 1955; BSIP 1949.
52   Golden 1993: 290; *BSIP AR* 1949–50: 30; BSIP 1949.

Buckingham was moved from Honiara Police Station to Auki in about May 1952, as commanding officer on Malaita during the later years of Maasina Rule. Semple was posted to Malu`u in north Malaita. Soon after he arrived, Bradley, also from Coventry, was put in charge of the training school and central prison. Lindley was transferred to Honiara Police Station, replacing Buckingham. He remembered his annual salary as Fijian £550 (about £500 Sterling), plus a 10 per cent rent allowance. There was no uniform allowance, which made for difficulties as dress uniforms, which included a sword and long boots, were expensive. The jobs were far from the standard police duties in the United Kingdom. The superintendent (chief) of the SIPF was also superintendent of prisons, although most prison duties fell to their deputy, who carried the extra title of Inspector of Prisons. Lindley added prison officer and executioner to his duties.[53] He was also responsible for Honiara's fire services, which included the airfield. Later he was appointed an immigration officer, as well as being firearms control officer, and in charge of all traffic matters.[54]

The prison was near the police station and inmates were taught wood and cane work, making furniture for the hospital and government offices.[55] The 'Haus Hang' was behind the prison; condemned prisoners had to walk around the wall to get to the place of execution. When Lindley arrived, there was a flogging stool at the central prison, shaped like a lectern, about 1 metre high in the front and 1.2 metres high at the back, with a piece of wood on which the offender could lean. The Honiara device had never been used, and the ordinance that allowed flogging was repealed in 1951.[56]

A new Queen's regulation issued on 14 November 1954 renamed the Armed Constabulary as the Royal Solomon Islands Police Force (RSIPF). At the end of that year, the approved establishment was eight commissioned officers, and 200 sub-officers and constables. Not all the posts were filled and there were only six or seven commissioned officers. The police headquarters, depot, and training school remained at Rove, with police detachments located at various district administration centres. European commissioned officers were in charge of stations at Honiara, Auki, and Gizo. Police officers were also stationed at Malu`u, Yandina in the Russell

---

53   The death penalty was not used after 1959 and was formally abolished in 1966.
54   Lindley 2013: 3.
55   Tudor 1953b: 74.
56   A 1934 regulation introduced flogging in certain circumstances. This was not repealed until 1951. Lindley 2015: 19; 2011a: 2.

Islands, and Gizo and Korovo in Western District, the last station opened in 1954. Increasing emphasis was placed on literacy for new recruits; they had to be at least 1.6 metres tall and unmarried. Government reports suggest that in 1954 a start had been made to establish a criminal records office at Honiara. This may have been 'window-dressing' as Lindley had no memory of it and said the criminal investigation division was not established until many years later.

Most of the pomp and ceremony in Honiara were provided by the police. Their strict dress codes mixed British colonial 'military' uniforms with Pacific-style adaptations. The uniforms were made by a tailor at the Rove headquarters. The early police uniform for constables was a khaki *sulu* made from drill material and a black belt, with no shirt or shoes. Before shirts were common apparel, to which rank stripes could be attached, cummerbunds were worn. These were red for constables, light blue for corporals, black for lance corporals, white for sergeants, white with a wide 'Sam Browne' belt[57] for sergeant majors, and red and white for a senior sergeant or station sergeant.[58] In 1952, Station Sergeant Waneba at Central Police Station in Honiara had a shirt with his rank on the sleeve, which was unusual. In the late 1950s, the *sulus* were tailored, with cloth straps and buckles. When Honiara was chilly at night, duty police wore full European clothing. Hair was worn long and bushy, with one strange habit: on ceremonial or special occasions, the men darkened their hair by using a mixture of ash from burnt sago palm leaves and coconut oil, to achieve uniformity of hair colour.[59]

On occasions like the Queen's Birthday parade, Solomon Islander police wore starched white jackets with tailored blue *sulus* and red sashes, along with black leather sandals made in Fiji. Expatriate officers wore khaki British colonial police uniforms with a 'Sam Browne' black leather sash-belt and, on formal occasions such as parades, buff-coloured trousers. On special occasions, they wore khaki trousers and long-sleeved shirts. In 1954, this dress uniform changed to dark blue. On formal occasions, such as the Queen's Birthday, officers wore white linen jackets with a belt passing from the left shoulder and under the right arm, which held a leather 'message box' (left over from battlefield uniforms). Tight-fitting

---

57   A wide belt, usually leather, supported by a narrower strap passing diagonally over the right shoulder to the left hip.
58   Parakoro 1971: 9.
59   ibid.

woollen trousers with buff-coloured stripes were worn with half-length wellington boots with patent leather tops that reached up to the knees. White pith helmets with a pointed silver top, a dark-blue puggaree, and a strap under the chin, along with a ceremonial sword, completed the outfit. Pith helmets were used until 1968, after which they were replaced with caps. The ceremonial swords were modelled on straight infantry weapons; they were pointed, but always blunt. Another eccentricity of early police formal uniforms was that superintendents wore spurs (there were no horses).[60]

The new Central Police Station (the present one) opened in April 1963, with accommodation built behind it in 1966, consisting of a block of rooms for single men and eight married quarters. The Rove headquarters was rebuilt in late 1963, and the first training course passing-out parade occurred there on 3 June 1964. The examinations were of similar standard to those used in the United Kingdom, and Constable Baekalia earned the top score. By 1966, the SIPF comprised 10 gazetted officers and 275 non-commissioned officers and other ranks.[61]

Plate 6.11 Queen's Birthday parade, Rove Police Headquarters, 1950s. The building at the rear is the Police Club.
Source: Brian Taylor Collection.

---

60   Information from Alan Lindley, Adelaide, 30 June 2011.
61   *BSIP AR* 1966: 54.

Plate 6.12 Honiara Police Station in 1952, constructed from a Quonset hut and scrap US Army materials.
Source: Alan Lindley Collection, in Clive Moore Collection.

Plate 6.13 Honiara's new police station, completed in 1963, was renamed Central Police Station.
The Central Bank building is on the right. This photograph is from 2011.
Source: Clive Moore Collection.

Routine police work began to change in the 1960s once alcohol was legally available, and in the same decade the first stirrings of protest began, related to racial discrimination, trade unionism, and labour politics. Honiara became more volatile in the late 1960s and early 1970s when trade union activism began. There were also new social and religious movements such as the Moro Movement on Guadalcanal and the Christian Fellowship Church in the western Solomons. This led to the formation of a field force and a riot unit under Superintendent Ray Viggor, who had previously had a posting in Africa. Honiara's first riot occurred in April 1965, when the police used teargas (actually CN or CS gas—a far worse form) to quell a crowd of Malaitans who were marching past the Treasury building to Central Police Station, demanding the release of a man arrested at the Kukum Labour Line. This incident is further examined in Chapter 7, in the section on the development of trade unions and labour activism.

As independence approached in the mid-1970s, there were 13 gazetted police officers, 16 inspectors, and 328 non-commissioned officers, along with 17 clerical staff. There were 14 police stations and posts within the four police districts, which coincided with the BSIP administrative districts. The headquarters remained at Rove, along with the training school and the mobile unit. All police stations were linked by a radio network: Honiara, Gizo, Kirakira, Auki, and Korovou had 100-watt base sets, while Munda, Ringi Cove, Yandina, Buala, Tulagi, Malu'u, Santa Cruz, and Mohawk Bay used 15-watt Racal base sets. The police training school also taught constables from the Crown Colony of Gilbert and Ellice Islands.[62]

By 1968, three of the four police districts were commanded by Solomon Islanders. The first two senior Solomon Islander police officers were W.B. (Ben) Kiriau and Simon Siapu. Kiriau, a Malaitan, joined the force in 1950. By 1952, he was a corporal, and was promoted to sub-inspector in 1957, and to superintendent in 1968. David Morgan took over as chief of police in 1963, with Superintendent Alan Lindley as deputy chief (later senior superintendent). After Morgan and Lindley left the force at the end of 1969, Kiriau, who had trained in 1951 at Hendon Police College in the United Kingdom, was offered but declined the deputy's position. Siapu had a similar record of service and was the first Solomon Islander to be promoted to superintendent. Kiriau was given command of Malaita in 1968.[63]

---

62   *BSIP AR* 1974: 88–89.
63   *BSIP NS*, 31 January 1968.

John Holloway, appointed as officer-in-charge of the Special Branch in 1964, had previously worked in Northern Rhodesia. He was appointed the first police commissioner in 1975, with Ben Kiriau as his deputy. Holloway held the position until 1982, when he was replaced with the first indigenous police commissioner, Fredrick Soaki from Tikopia, who held the position until 1995. Knighted for his services to the nation, Sir Fredrick was assassinated at Auki on 1 February 2003 during the Tensions.

During the self-government years, the SIPF comprised Rodger Edwards as commissioner, Kiriau as deputy commissioner, H. Brown as senior superintendent, Fred Soaki and B.S. Ward as assistant superintendents, several inspectors, 70 sergeants, 272 constables, and 16 administrative staff. 'Royal' was added to the title of the police force in 1978. The title can only be granted after a visit by the monarch, which occurred in 1974. The actual gift of the title was made by the Duke of Gloucester as Queen Elizabeth II's personal representative at independence on 7 July 1978.[64]

Another feature of the Royal Solomon Islands Police Force (RSIPF) is the police band, formed in 1950, which always faced great difficulties. None of its members could read music, they lacked confidence, and their instruments were in poor repair. In 1962, new instruments arrived from New Zealand and the band was rejuvenated by new bandmaster John Kabwere, a Gilbertese who had trained with the Fiji police band. It has remained the major band used on all formal occasions in Honiara, particularly for the Queen's Birthday and Independence Day parades.[65]

Shipping services

Contrary to the pattern in many countries of government divestment of essential services, the Solomon Islands Government continues to control water, electricity, ports, broadcasting, postal services, a printery, Solomon Airlines, and the Investment Corporation. These are all based in Honiara. From the end of the war until the late 1950s, almost all contact with the outside world was by ship, and the ocean was also the essential path for communication within the protectorate. The main pre-war BSIP ports were at Tulagi, Yandina, Gizo, Tulagi, and Vanikolo. The smaller harbours

---

64 Information from Maxwell Saelea, Honiara, 15 July 2015.
65 *BSIP NS*, 31 October 1962.

at Auki, Gizo, and Kirakira could only be used by vessels of light draft. Viru and Allardyce harbours, Nila, and Ringi Cove were also used, and there were several sheltered lagoon anchorages formed by barrier reefs off New Georgia, Isabel, and Malaita, which allowed safe navigation, provided the skipper had local knowledge. Gizo wharf was controlled by the British Solomon Islands Trading Corporation, although the harbour was shallow. The wharves at Yandina were in deep water, as was the Vanikolo wharf operated by the Kauri Timber Company. Both were too far from Honiara to be useful substitutes. The wartime Tulagi wharves remained in use until the 1970s, by which time Honiara's port facilities had improved.[66] Control and operation of the official ports were vested in the BSIP Ports Authority, which was an independent statutory body based in Honiara.

Honiara has no natural sheltered port other than Point Cruz, which has been constantly expanded and modified since the 1950s. It is barely recognisable as the small island joined to the mainland by a narrow neck of reef and sand observed by Mendaña and his crew in 1568. During the American occupation in the 1940s, the main wharf was at Kukum, with a smaller temporary jetty at Point Cruz. The Kukum wharves had three sections, two at right angles to the shore and one parallel, forming three sides of a rectangle. The most easterly section fell into disrepair and was demolished; the other sections were destroyed by cyclones, in February 1951 and January 1952.[67] Inland from the Kukum wharves were copra and cargo sheds, the customs house, and the headquarters of R.C. Symes, the largest private company after the war. Brothers Bob, Jim, and Matt Symes made their money on the New Guinea goldfields and at Tulagi, before the war, then returned and set up business in Honiara. In the early years, when the Meteorological Office issued storm or cyclone warnings, ships anchored at Point Cruz would make a dash for the safety of Tulagi Harbour, 32 kilometres away.[68] With the wharf gone, ships arriving from overseas had to use lighters, or tranship at Tulagi on to smaller vessels. The first stage of new port facilities for Honiara was approved in September 1955.[69]

---

66 In the 1940s, the Tulagi wharves were difficult to use as, when they departed, the Americans had dumped trucks and other vehicles off the end, blocking the anchorage.
67 *PIM*, March 1951, 17; March 1952, 122.
68 *BSIP AR* 1957–58: 47.
69 *BSIP NS*, 1 September 1955, 12 September 1955, July 1960, 15 February 1963, 31 March 1964, 14 February 1965, 21 February 1966.

Plate 6.14 Kukum docks in 1945, built by the Americans. The area is opposite what is now Panatina Plaza.
Source: USNARA.

Plate 6.15 In the 1950s, work began on reshaping Point Cruz to create a port.
Source: BM, Patrick Barrett Collection.

6. BUILDING INFRASTRUCTURE

Plate 6.16 RCS *Melanesian* at Honiara wharf in 1958.
The ship was built in Kowloon in 1956 for the BSIP Government. Thirty-six metres long with a 7.9-metre beam, the ship had a maximum speed of 9.5 knots. It left Sulufou in Lau Lagoon, Malaita, on 9 July 1958, heading for Sikaiana, with 64 people onboard. The *Melanesian* disappeared, and only limited amounts of wreckage and one partial body were found, along the east Malaita coast. No clear explanation was ever established for the tragedy. The most likely reason was faulty manufacture of the hull, which may have split in two when hit by rogue waves, causing the ship to sink immediately with total loss of life.
Source: Alan Lindley Collection.

During the 1950s, Burns Philp's *Muliama* arrived at Honiara every four weeks and its *Malaita* every six weeks. They were the main means of travelling to and from Australia. A major study was conducted during 1954 into how to develop Honiara as a port. The first stage of the new port facilities was approved the following year, the *Ports Act* was passed in 1956, and the Ports Authority was gazetted in 1957. The next year, a new 128-metre concrete wharf was constructed with a 3-metre depth, augmented by a 9-metre-deep stub jetty for larger overseas ships. Cargo handling sheds were added in 1959.[70] Plans to build a deep-water wharf began in mid-1960, including surveys to extend the existing wharf and install heavy mooring buoys to accommodate overseas vessels, which still had to use lighters to unload. In 1963, funding was approved to construct a deep-water berth, financed by the Ports Authority through a bank loan. Tenders were considered during early 1964. Brisbane-based Hornibrook Constructions won the contract and began work early the following year.

---

70   *BSIP Gazette*, No. 213, November 1957; *BSIP AR* 1957–58: 47.

The berth, 71 metres long with a minimum depth of 8.5 metres, was used for the first time on 15 February 1966. Soon after, around 70 overseas ships were visiting Honiara every year.[71] This also enabled cruise ships to visit, the first of which was probably TSMV *Oriental Queen* in 1965; in 1967, P&O's SS *Orcades* began regular visits for a few years, which provided an occasional market for artefacts.[72]

By 1974, the deep-water berth had been expanded to take vessels up to 213 metres long and there were also three small jetties for local ships. Two jetties had a capacity to take vessels up to 35.5 metres and the other was owned by Shell Oil Company, which supplied overseas shipping with fuel via a submarine pipeline that ran out to a moored buoy.[73] In 1977, the Asian Development Bank provided funds to improve the port. Over subsequent decades, Point Cruz has been extended with landfill, creating the present facilities for the major container ship traffic.

Plate 6.17 Point Cruz wharves in the 1960s. A Quonset hut from the war years is visible on the shore.
Source: BM, Bob Wright Collection, in John Tod Collection.

---

71   *BSIP NS*, 1 September 1955, 12 September 1955, 15 July 1960, 15 February 1963, 31 March 1964, 14 February 1965, 21 February 1966; *PIM*, June 1965, 115.
72   The *Oriental Queen* information is from Ian Geering, 30 May 2020.
73   *BSIP NS*, 16 December 1977.

6. BUILDING INFRASTRUCTURE

Plate 6.18 The interisland shipping wharves in 2017, with the centre of Honiara behind.
The Bank of the South Pacific is on the corner of Commonwealth Avenue at bottom right, the Anthony Saru building and NPF Plaza (opened in 1986) are at top right, with part of the accommodation block of King Solomon Hotel showing above it. The lower, grey-coloured structure in the centre is the City Centre building, and the NPF building is on the left.
Source: Clive Moore Collection.

The modern Solomon Islands Ports Authority operates two international ports, Honiara and Noro, which is the fishing and cannery base near Munda in Western Province. Development over the past 60 years has transformed Point Cruz into a container terminal for overseas ships, with a new large wharf that can also accommodate visiting cruise ships. On the eastern side of the port, the original wharf remains, along with local shipping wharves. The patrol boat base is on the western side.[74] Further extensive improvements of the Point Cruz facilities occurred during the late 2010s and, despite a tumultuous few years under chief executive officer Colin Yo, who was dismissed in 2016, the port functions well.[75]

---

74 Keen et al. 2017: 110. The combined annual income from each cruise ship is now around S$270,000 (comprising port fees, markets, hotels, and tours), with the revenue increasing each year until the COVID-19 pandemic began in 2020.
75 *Pacific Islands Report*, [Honolulu], 1 February 2017.

Air services

While sea transport will always be the main way to move around Solomon Islands, a quicker transport method was established: by air. The first seaplane landed at the Shortlands, Gizo, and Tulagi in 1926. It took the war to provide the beginnings of the airfield infrastructure still in use today.

In 1954, there were only three airfields functioning in the protectorate: Kukum (Fighter II), Yandina, and Barakoma on Vella Lavella. Air traffic linking Honiara to the districts developed gradually as wartime airfields were reconditioned or new airfields were constructed between the 1950s and the 1970s (Table 6.3). These made access to Honiara easier. Henderson Airfield was reconditioned during 1957 to a standard suitable for Douglas DC-3s, and officially opened as the main airfield on 19 May 1958. The first overseas flight, a new Qantas service via Lae in Papua New Guinea, arrived on 9 June 1958. Air navigation aids, including a beacon, were installed in May 1960 in preparation for an extension of air services. Henderson Airfield was extended again in 1966, from 1,654 to 1,828 metres, and tar-sealed to enable Douglas DC-6 piston-powered aircraft to land. Two years later, it was extended further and a 182-metre overrun was added, with another upgrade in 1970.[76]

Plate 6.19 Honiara Airfield in the 1950s, on the site of the Fighter II Airfield at what is now Ranadi.
Source: SINA, ACOM, Fauaabu Melanesian Mission Box.

---

76 *BSIP NS*, 31 October 1957, 30 April 1958, 29 February 1960, 31 December 1960, 30 April 1961, 30 May 1961, 21 March 1966, 7 May 1966, 15 March 1969.

Table 6.3 Solomon Islands airfields and their years of construction.

Airfield	Year	District/province
Kukum	1943	Central
Yandina	1945	Central
Barakoma (Vella Lavella, Methodist)	1945, 1955	Western
Munda	1955	Western
Henderson	1942, 1957	Central
Gwaunaru'u	1963	Malaita
Seghe	1963	Western
Barakoma	1963	Western
Mono	1963, 1966	Western
Kirakira	1964	Makira-Ulawa
Avuavu (Guadalcanal, local council)	1965	Central
Marau (Guadalcanal)	mid-1960s	Central
Nusa Tupe (Gizo)	1969	Western
Parasi	1969	Malaita
Hatangua (Rennell)	1970	Rennell–Bellona
Graciosa Bay (Santa Cruz)	1970	Temotu
Lomlon (Reef)	1970	Temotu
Taro	1971	Western/Choiseul
Fera	1971	Isabel
Sterling (Treasury)	1971	Western
Ghongau (Bellona)	1971	Rennell–Bellona
Atoifi (SDA)	n.a.	Malaita
Afutara (SDA)	n.a.	Malaita
Kwailabasi (SDA)	n.a.	Malaita
Kakuda (SDA)	n.a.	Western
Batuna (SDA)	n.a.	Western
Viru Harbour (SDA)	n.a.	Western
Ramata (SDA)	n.a.	Western
Vella Lavella (SDA)	n.a.	Western

n.a. Not available
Source: Compiled by Clive Moore.

Beginning in April 1961, TAA introduced a prop-jet Fokker Friendship service between Lae and Honiara, which soon after included Buka in its run. Fiji Airways also began regular flights, in mid-1961. In October, Captains M. Lewis and P. Bennett arrived in Honiara to investigate beginning an internal air service. The next year, Captain Laurie Crowley began charter flights to Honiara out of Papua New Guinea, using a Piper Aztec plane. Late in 1963, Crowley purchased a Series 6 de Havilland Dove aircraft to operate as Crowley Airways, and within the protectorate as Megapode Airways. There was a sharp increase in air traffic between 1965 (2,911 flights) and 1966 (6,130 flights) due in large measure to the activities of planes conducting an aerial geophysical survey of the country.[77] Each week in 1966, Henderson Airfield serviced 125 to 250 passengers travelling on Fiji Airways, TAA, and Megapode Airways. Early in 1969, Fiji Airways and Solair both applied for licences to operate in the BSIP, much to the annoyance and resistance of TAA, which had extended its international service to Munda and Yandina. Fiji Airways proposed to operate from Fiji to Port Moresby via Honiara, and Solair wanted to operate from Honiara to Kieta via Munda and Gizo (once Nusa Tupe Airfield was completed in 1969).

Crowley Airways was purchased by Macair Holdings of Papua New Guinea in 1968 and incorporated into Megapode Airways. By March the next year, four regular air services a week were operating to Munda.[78] The company became Solomon Islands Airways in 1975, trading as Solair but owned by Macair Holdings. Macair was purchased in the same year by Talair (Tourist Airlines of Niugini), a company owned by Dennis Buchanan, which gave Talair control of Solair. At the same time, the Solomon Islands Government bought 49 per cent of the Solair shares, with a right to purchase the remaining shares within the next five years. This full government takeover was negotiated between 1984 and 1987. The current name, Solomon Airlines, was adopted when the airline became fully state-owned.

One issue was the need for an alternative airfield to land international flights if Henderson was closed. In 1963, Auki's Gwaunaru'u airfield was lengthened by 152 metres as an alternative, although as planes became

---

77   *BSIP AR* 1966: 63; *BSIP NS*, 7 May 1966.
78   *BSIP NS*, 31 October 1961, 31 August 1962, 31 January 1962, 31 July 1962, 15 September 1963, 30 November 1963, 31 July 1964, 14 November 1964, 14 February 1965, 15 June 1965, 15 November 1965, 21 February 1966, 7 March 1966, 7 April 1966, 7 May 1966, 11 August 1966, 15 May 1968, 31 January 1969, 15 February 1969, 15 April 1969.

larger, Gwaunaru'u was no longer suitable.⁷⁹ Munda, once a large wartime Japanese airfield, was upgraded in 2017 with New Zealand Government aid funds to become the alternative international airfield. This also enabled international flights to land in Western Province, thus boosting its tourist industry.

By the early 1970s, Solomon Airlines was the sole commercial domestic provider of air services, operating Beechcraft Baron and Britten-Norman Islander aircraft. Honiara was the centre of operations, reaching out to 18 protectorate destinations. TAA (on behalf of Qantas) and Air Pacific (formerly Fiji Airways) provided overseas services. There were links to the New Hebrides and Fiji three times a week, to Port Moresby once a week, and to Kieta and Rabaul via Munda twice a week. In 1973, the Air Transport Licensing Authority allowed the SDA Mission to operate non-scheduled air services on routes linking airstrips they had developed, and to other licensed or government airstrips. Over many years, the SDAs developed their aviation services. They used SDA-owned airfields (Atoifi, Afutara, and Kwailabasi on Malaita, as well as Batuna and Kakuda in Western Province) and 'affiliated' airfields managed by community groups on customary land adjacent to SDA villages (at Viru Harbour, Ramata, Vella Lavella, and on Choiseul).⁸⁰ The next year, the Mission Aviation Fellowship was given permission to operate a Cessna seaplane for public non-scheduled transport on six-month permits to United Church and South Sea Evangelical Church (SSEC) bases.

Air Pacific inaugurated its first direct flight from Honiara to Brisbane in 1973. Four years later, the first Boeing 727 jet landed at Henderson Airfield. Henderson's passenger terminal and facilities were upgraded for independence in 1978, with several more upgrades since. The old international terminal is now the domestic terminal. Also in the 1970s, the Australian Bureau of Meteorology, on behalf of the South Pacific Air Transport Council, began operating several meteorological reporting stations and a meteorological office in Honiara. In 1980, the council's assets were distributed and its member nations took over individual control.⁸¹

---

79 ibid., 15 September 1963.
80 My thanks to David MacLaren, Humpress Harrington, and Fraser Alekevu for this information, 12 August 2017.
81 *BSIP NS*, 22 June 1973; *SND*, 13 January 1978, 17 February 1978; *BSIP AR* 1971: 89, 1974: 100.

This web of international and domestic flights serves the nation well and contributes to national infrastructure. Twenty-three domestic airfields can now be reached out of Honiara. The international carriers and their routes have altered over decades. Current links include Australia, Fiji, Vanuatu, Papua New Guinea, Nauru, and Kiribati. The national airline remains 100 per cent owned by the Solomon Islands Government through the Solomon Islands Investment Corporation and Solomon Islands Holdings. Air transport has enabled quick communication between islands and further developed the feeling of being linked into one nation. Another way this has been achieved is through the introduction of modern media.

Media and communication

A mix of media provide flows of information to the citizens of the nation. These have helped unify the population and foster nationalism. Recently, the arrival of modern media (Facebook and other digital and online services) that is available on mobile devices and computers has changed the scene.[82] While the usefulness of print media relates mainly to literacy, this is not true for radio or mobile phones—the communication mediums with the best outreach. The future expansion of the new digital communications is an unknown quantity, although the new undersea fibreoptic cable will cause great advances. The Solomons Government negotiated first with China and then with Australia for a cable to improve its antiquated telecommunication services. As part of a policy to limit Chinese expansion into the Pacific, Australia provided A$137 million for a new cable linking Australia, Papua New Guinea, and Solomon Islands. Agreements were signed in early 2018 and the cable was installed in late 2019.[83]

The first periodicals and newspapers specifically related to Solomon Islands were produced by the various Christian missions, which circulated along with weekly newspapers and periodicals from overseas. News specific to the protectorate was not produced until 1955, when the Government Information Service began the *BSIP News Sheet*, initially every two months, then upgraded to monthly in 1957, and to fortnightly in 1962. The *News Sheet* dealt with BSIP news and was distributed to missions,

---

82 Hobbis 2017a, 2017b, 2017c.
83 Sas 2019.

all schools, local councils, government headmen, health clinics, cooperative societies, government departments, on request to private citizens within the BSIP, news services, and Solomon Islands students overseas. With no local press, the *News Sheet* was intended to express government aims and policies and provide general public relations, as well as limited overseas news for Solomon Islanders. It contained centre spreads on a wide variety of subjects, such as therapy for polio victims or the tourism potential of Solomon Islands. The text, produced by mimeograph machine, was kept as simple as possible and the *News Sheet* was illustrated with photographs. The *News Sheet*'s letters to the editor became an early outlet for Solomon Islanders wishing to communicate widely with their own people.

The number of copies produced increased rapidly, to 1,000 in 1966 and 3,500 in 1969.[84] In 1972, the *News Sheet* and the Information Service were included in the Department of Information, Broadcasting, Museum and Library Services. Advertising in the *News Sheet* began in 1974. Circulation in that year was around 4,000 copies, 400 of which were sent overseas, mainly to students, while 1,930 went to schools, and around 400 began to be sold via distribution points throughout Solomon Islands.[85]

The Anglican Diocese of Melanesia press (now the Provincial Press) became a commercial printery in 1973 with an offset press and the ability to print to tabloid newspaper size. Two years later, this enabled the *News Sheet* to be turned into a weekly newspaper renamed the *Solomon News Drum*, a successful trial edition having been published in October 1974, with the final *News Sheets* published in December. In mid-1982, the *Solomon News Drum* was taken over by five Solomon Islanders (the government sold it to them for one dollar) and renamed the *Solomon Star*. It has been run as a private newspaper ever since.

Another early newspaper was the cyclostyled *Kakamora Reporter* (1970–75), also published in Honiara, which came out monthly or bimonthly. It was produced by a group of volunteers and contained the views of 'educated' Solomon Islanders, generally presenting 'radical' nationalist opinions in a satirical and often quite scathing style. The *Melanesian Nius* (also called *Kiokio Nius*) came next, published from January to March 1977. Edited by George Atkin, it closed due to financial difficulties. Atkin then edited *Solomons Toktok* from August 1977 to December 1978. The newspaper

---

84 *BSIP AR* 1966: 68; 1969: 79.
85 *BSIP AR* 1974: 111.

began with a print run of 800 copies and, by December, had increased its run to 1,500 copies a week.[86] District commissioners also issued monthly newsletters in simple English to communicate issues of local interest within their districts. In 1977, the Nationalist (later Nationalist Democratic) Party started a 10-page news sheet called *Nadepa* to publicise its views, and the proceedings of the Legislative Assembly. Honiara was at the centre of this new media industry, working alongside the Solomon Islands Broadcasting Corporation. Creating a nation is a political process. By encouraging local newspapers and its government radio station, the BSIP also fostered independent debate about issues that concerned all Solomon Islanders, and provided education on international issues.

Solomon Islanders remain inveterate readers of newspapers. The *Solomon Star*, the *Island Sun*, and *Sunday Isles* are sold on the streets of Honiara. The *Solomon Times* has an online format. There is an ever-increasing number of magazines, for business, for women, for youths, and so on, which come and go.

Solomon Islands Broadcasting Corporation

The other improvement in communications was through radio, which continues to be the main medium of communication at the village level. There are many synergies here with other Pacific nations where there is no mainline power system in rural areas.[87] During the war, American military radio operated a 'Mosquito Network' from Camp Gudal.[88] The first attempt at regular local broadcasting after the war was in 1947. Station VQJ2 transmitted each Sunday at 10 am for 30 minutes from a leaf-thatch hut on the beach in Honiara. It used a rebuilt American war-surplus transmitter operated by Wireless Officer Ron F. Calvert. Known as 'The Shoestring Network', the station began its short weekly radio service primarily for planters, missionaries, and colonial officials, keeping them in touch with world news, copra prices, and shipping schedules. In 1948, a grant of British aid money enabled the purchase of broadcasting equipment, the installation of which was delayed until

---

86   *Solomons Toktok* [hereinafter *STT*], 13 December 1978.
87   Bolton (1999) shows a similar pattern of usage and importance in Vanuatu.
88   Martin Hadlow's (2016) research suggests that public broadcasting in Solomon Islands began in 1923, when the Methodist Mission in the western Solomons broadcast a concert.

1949 when a new communications building was erected on Vavaea Ridge. From 1949, Calvert was helped by Bill Bennett, an assistant Coastwatcher during the war and later the Honiara postmaster. In 1970, Bennett became the head of the broadcasting section, retiring five years later after 25 years in broadcasting.[89]

Gradually during the 1950s and 1960s, Solomon Islanders gained access to radio, enjoying the advantages provided by a diversity of music, personal 'service messages', education, and general information. Just as televisions were initially expensive for modern users, radios were similarly prohibitively expensive for most villagers. The government distributed 200 'saucepan' wireless receivers in 1951 to extend the listening audience to Solomon Islanders in villages near Honiara.[90] Another 600 radios were donated by the Foundation for the People of the South Pacific in 1969.[91]

A 400-watt war-surplus transmitter was obtained and converted in 1951. Solomon Islands Broadcasting Service (SIBS, now Solomon Islands Broadcasting Corporation, or SIBC) began operations on 23 September 1952 with a medium-wave transmission on 400-watt Station VQO each night between 6 pm and 7 pm on a frequency of 1030 kilohertz (kHz). Reception was usually good for about 160 kilometres. The first broadcast lasted two hours and included a message from the high commissioner, a history of the station, musical numbers by Fred Kona's string band, and music from the stage show *South Pacific*. On Wednesday evenings, there was a 90-minute program primarily for Solomon Islanders.[92]

The first British Broadcasting Corporation (BBC) transcriptions were received in 1954 and, in the same year, indigenous music, recorded by G.F. Milner of the London School of Oriental and African Studies in 1950, began to be broadcast. SIBS also purchased a high-quality tape machine to record more indigenous music. At Gizo in 1953–54, the Sunday news broadcast was treated as an expatriate social event when, in turn, the district commissioner, district officer, doctor, and police commander hosted a brunch of curry, beer, brandy, and gin and tonic.[93]

---

89 Tedder 1973; Moore 2013c: entry for Solomon Islands Broadcasting Corporation; Hadlow 2015.
90 'Saucepan' radios were invented in the 1930s as the 'poor man's radio', literally using half a saucepan, an antenna, a coil, and a tuning capacitor. Smyth 1984; Hadlow 2004; *BSIP NS*, 31 January 1969; *BSIP AR* 1949–50; *SND*, 4 April 1975.
91 *BSIP NS*, 15 February 1969.
92 *PIM*, November 1952, 57; *BSIP AR* 1953–54: 43.
93 Information from Alan Lindley, Adelaide, 30 June 2011, who was stationed in Gizo during the 1950s.

In October 1955, an experimental shortwave service was added, Station VQ02, which broadcast on Sunday mornings. In many ways, radio broadcasts emanating from the SIBC created a new social communication network for Solomon Islanders and expatriates alike.

Solomon Dakei, Fred Osifelo, and Silas Sitai[94] were members of the SIBS board, which first met on 12 November 1958. New studios were opened in Honiara in January the next year, with medium and shortwave transmitters, replacing the first studios on Vavaea Ridge. This provided more audience space for programs such as Belshazaar (Bill) Gina's children's program. A permanent Broadcasting Advisory Committee was established the next year to give guidance on policy. It was reconstituted in 1970 and advised the Governing Council on broadcasting strategies. The SIBS became an associate member of the Asian Broadcasting Union, which had members throughout Asia and the Pacific, and arranged program exchanges, staff training, and technical liaison. Until the end of 1964, the SIBS operated under the Colonial Development and Welfare Scheme, after which the BSIP Government met recurrent expenditure.[95]

Short commercial advertisements began to be broadcast in 1961 and, in 1965, service messages were initiated to disseminate essential information to individuals or families on behalf of government departments, private individuals, or groups. Service messages were the quickest way to pass information to people living in rural areas and to the nation as a whole. Between 1968 and 1970, 1,400 of these messages were broadcast annually[96] and, by 1973, the rate was 2,000 per year. Service messages became integral to the nation's communication system; they reached people with no other means of speedily receiving messages. Deaths, marriages, money transfers, family matters, shipping arrival times, and staff and private transport movements became everyday knowledge throughout the islands. In villages, even if not used at any other time, radios were always turned on for the service messages, and the news in Solomons Pijin. The personal nature of service messages helped create the modern nation. They enabled everyone in the protectorate to feel part of one extended family, since all listeners knew quite intimate details

---

94   Moore 2013c: entries for Dakei, Osifelo, and Sitai.
95   *BSIP AR* 1963–64: 73.
96   *BSIP AR* 1970: 85.

about families and individuals throughout the archipelago. Radio service messages still exist, broadcast twice a day, although in reduced numbers, and now mainly replaced with mobile phones and text messaging.

Evening radio programs were extended and, in November 1965, the first live broadcast occurred when a Honiara versus Auki rugby match was transmitted from Auki. The SIBC also began to record local popular music, such as Peter Lui's band, for broadcast in the BSIP and Papua New Guinea. A 1967 survey of 314 Honiara listeners reported that about half listened to the radio every day. Their favourite programs were those in Solomons Pijin: the local news, shipping movements, and the world news summary, as well as Dr Gideon Zoleveke's[97] 'Good Health' talks. The largest numbers of listeners tuned in between 6 am and 7 am, and 6 pm and 8 pm.[98]

From the 1960s, radio listening became part of village and urban life in Solomon Islands. Good reception was available in most areas early in the morning and in the evenings, and there were even listeners in the New Hebrides, Papua New Guinea, and the Gilbert and Ellice Islands. By 1968, 2,200 radios had been imported to be given away to village and urban communities.[99] Broadcasting increased from 1,400 total hours in 1966 to 3,400 hours during 1968. A grant in 1969 from the British Government enabled installation of two new transmitters near Henderson International Airport, and expansion of other facilities.

The broadcast buildings at Rove were expanded and weekly broadcast time increased from 24 hours in 1965 to more than 80 hours in the 1970s. Overseas news was provided each day by two relays of the BBC World Service and three of Australian Broadcasting Corporation (ABC) bulletins, and there was also a daily news summary in Solomons Pijin. Regular programs covered a range of subjects, including school and adult education, and special broadcasts concerning women, youth, and farming. Excerpts from Governing Council proceedings were broadcast, beginning the tradition of parliamentary broadcasts. About this time, the SIBS also began publishing its own magazine, *Preview*, which was issued six times each year and contained information and publicity about programs, editorial opinions, and advertising. Each print run was about 2,000 copies.[100]

---

97 Moore 2013c: entry for Zoleveke. See also Zoleveke 1980.
98 Moore 2013c: entry for Solomon Islands Broadcasting Corporation.
99 *BSIP AR* 1968: 1.
100 *BSIP AR* 1970: 85.

Two years later, the government's broadcasting and information departments were joined with the library and museum into one department. The SIBS provided 57 hours of its own programming, together with 14 hours of school broadcasts over 10 weeks in each school term. A new format was introduced during 1973, with 10 hours a week of local and relayed news, including one hour of Solomons Pijin news, 7.5 hours of locally produced features, two hours of religious broadcasts, 19 hours of music requests, and 18 hours of music and plays. This increased the time allotted to requested music (both traditional and modern local music) by 14 hours, which was the most popular programming. Strategic placement of the request programs attracted larger audiences to adult education programs in public health, agricultural extension, and political education. Broadcasting the proceedings of parliament, as with the service messages, helped to create a united Solomons listening community. Each year during the early 1970s, advertising netted the SIBS around $18,000. There was no licence fee required and by then there were an estimated 7,800 radio sets in the Solomons, reaching a listening audience of 8,000 in rural areas and 12,000 in urban areas, from a 1974 population of around 178,940.[101]

When Bill Bennett retired, he was replaced with R.J. (Dick) Hoskins, who resigned in October 1977, claiming the government was interfering through the chief minister's office.[102] Initially broadcasts came in batches, with some gaps in between; all-day programming (6 am – 10.30 pm) began in 1975, and in that year Chief Minister Solomon Mamaloni laid the groundwork for what would become the Solomon Islands Broadcasting Corporation (SIBC), a statutory body. This occurred on 1 January 1977 under legislation introduced by Chief Minister Peter Kenilorea. Both chief ministers, Mamaloni (1974–76) and Kenilorea (1976–78), realised the importance of providing the nation with an independent, high-quality radio service. Kenilorea obtained further funding from the Australian Government, enabling construction of the present Rove studio complex, which opened in 1982.[103] Solomon Islanders became 'hooked' on radio. In every Honiara settlement and suburb, and every village in the nation, radios received service messages and local and international news, Solomons music was played, and a potent communication network was at work. The SIBC remains the dominant radio network, although there are now also four independent FM services.

---

101 *BSIP AR* 1974: 108–9.
102 *STT*, 5 October 1977, 23 November 1977.
103 Information from Sir Peter Kenilorea, Honiara, June 2007.

Plate 6.20 The first SIBC Board meeting, 1982.
Left to right: A.B. Wickham (general manager and secretary to the board), F. Wa'ahero, E. Gagahe, M. Abana, Bill Bennett MBE MM (chairman), G.B. Gatu MP, W. Teilo, and J. Fifi'i MBE. Absent: M. Sibisopere (deputy chairman).
Source: Martin Hadlow Collection.

Another aspect of Solomons radio was the ease with which radio signals from the east coast of Australia and elsewhere in the Pacific were picked up in the evenings. Alan Lindley reported being able to listen to Hawaiian radio on Malaita in the 1950s. I know from personal experience in the 1970s that in east Malaita and Honiara, I was able to tune into 4AY (Ayr) and 4TO (Townsville) in north Queensland, and that shortwave receivers could reach the BBC, Radio Australia, Radio New Zealand, Radio Moscow, and the American overseas service. The SIBC also carried some international religious programs such as Garner Ted Armstrong's *World Tomorrow* (an American syndicated religious program), which may have affected some local religious developments.[104] While of diverse quality, radio reception was crucial to the education of Solomon Islanders in the late protectorate years. At a stage when many countries had moved on to television, Solomon Islands discovered radio.

---

104 Timmer 2015.

Solomon Islands now has two SIBC stations broadcasting from Honiara, one from Gizo (Western Province), and one from Lata (Temotu Province), plus FM stations in Honiara. Where once the *News Sheet* arrived in the mail, now Solomon Islanders overseas can listen to their local radio stations streamed live anywhere in the world.

Television was introduced much later than radio. The wealthy have satellite dishes and can tap into numerous overseas channels. Television is received in Solomon Islands from overseas services and relayed locally. There is a limited local television service, One News, which began in 2008, producing 15 minutes of local news and content, broadcast over the top of the Australian Network. By 2016, the SIBC was investigating beginning its own television station, then late in December 2017, the corporation announced that the government had not paid its financial subvention for more than a year, which meant the SIBC was behind in paying its bills. Broadcasting was reduced to shortwave, with limited hours, and staff lay-offs were contemplated. In early January 2018, the government found SI$1.2 million, but still owed the SIBC SI$150,000. Services have been restored and a limited SIBC television news service began in May 2019 in collaboration with Telekom. However, the financial difficulties show how less essential 'essential' services become when the money runs out.[105]

***

Honiara, once the centre of a substantial and crucial American wartime garrison, inherited some of those wartime facilities. New government buildings were erected in the late 1950s and 1960s—some of which are still in use—and the town altered from its origin as a second-hand former American base into a small, quaint British colonial city. Honiara lacked much of the grace of Suva, but bubbled along and grew fast, with hospitals, airlines, radio, newspapers, an international port, hotels, and clubs. Many of these infrastructure developments assisted the growth of nationalism and they all impacted largely on Honiara. Partly provoked by changes in the physical infrastructure came related social and political changes, which are the subject of the next chapter.

---

105 Dorney 2012; Runa 2017; 'Govt settles $200,000 of arrears to SIBC', *SIBC*, 4 January 2018.

7
Building society and the nation

Greater Honiara is a Pacific creation where concepts of village land and society rub uncomfortably against town planning regulations and an overlay of modern urban social hierarchy. There is something very 'Solomons' about the way urban village settlements mingle with and are equal in number to the population in formal suburban areas. One of the major ways the transference of Solomons' village values to the urban setting has occurred is through Christian denominations, which permeate every part of the city and its surrounds, and through employment and trade unions, participation in sports, and education. These are the themes discussed in this chapter. In 1962, there was a ceremony marking the 20th anniversary of the US Marine Corps landing in August 1942. Honiara had come a long way in two decades and progressed much further in the next two. Women, children, and youths have now become the majority of Honiara's residents and are woven into its support services and the general operation of the urban area. This chapter concentrates on Honiara's middle years and the institutions that developed, helping to push Honiara and the protectorate along the road that led to the modern nation.

HONIARA

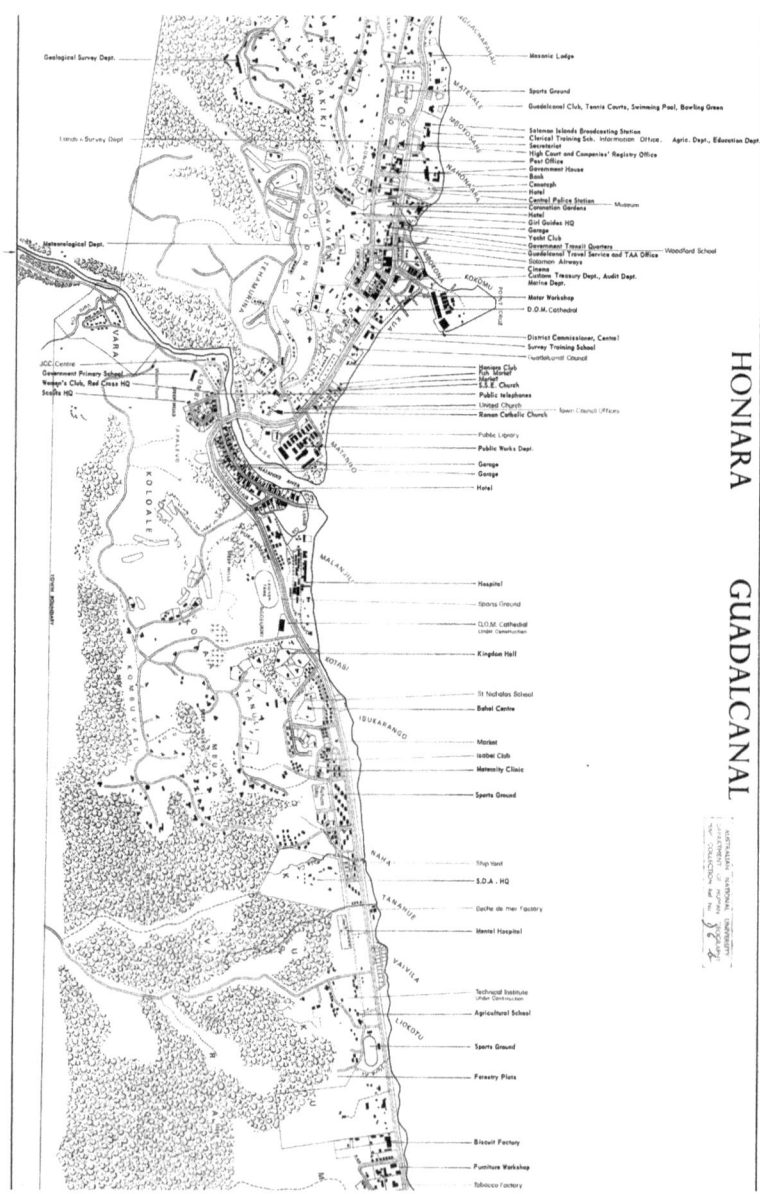

Map 7.1 The central area of Honiara in 1968, from the Masonic Lodge to the tobacco factory.

Source: 'Solomon Islands, Guadalcanal, Honiara, Sheet 967b, 1968, 1:10,000', ANU Open Research Library, available from: openresearch-repository.anu.edu.au/handle/1885/145247.

Religion: Christianity, Bahá`í Faith, and Islam

Religion has always been important to Solomon Islanders, both the many variations of spiritual and ancestral beliefs in pre-colonial times and their adoption and adaptation of Christianity, including a strong degree of syncretism. Just as *wantokism* and *kastom* are linked into everyday life, so, too, are religion and the myriad ethical and philosophical systems that accompany spiritual beliefs. Melanesian culture is never static. As Jaap Timmer suggests, it pursues experimentation and cultural openness. Christianity has created forms of connection that 'cross ethnic boundaries and tend to unite people in a Christian public sphere'. Timmer continues:

> People say that they have found their origins and foundational truth of their customary ways as versions of Judaic and Mosaic rules. This realisation motivates many to institute Christian forms of governance, to forge links with like-minded Christians and to instigate political leaders to build covenants with God. Such elements become the foundation of an imagined nation that encompasses a worldwide community of believers.[1]

This chapter provides a brief outline of the history of modern religious beliefs in Honiara. The complexity is great and explains much about the successful cultural hybridity that is obvious in urban life. The major influence from world religions has been through Christianity. From 1945, Honiara became the headquarters for all the major denominations, other than the Christian Fellowship Church, which began in the Western District in 1960 and still has its core congregation there.[2] The outliers are the Bahá`í Faith and, more recently, Islam, and even Scientology.

Catholicism arrived first. Marist Catholics were given the eastern Pacific to evangelise in 1836, with subdivisions created in the 1840s. Between 1844 and 1889, the Catholic Church established the Vicariate Apostolic of Melanesia, spread from Timor to Solomon Islands. Discounting the Catholic Spanish explorers of the sixteenth century (mentioned in Chapter 1), the Catholics began proselyting in the Solomon archipelago in 1845, and then withdrew until 1898 when a new push began.

---

1 Timmer 2019: 137.
2 Harwood 1971; Tuza 1975; Hviding 2005; Ishimori 2007.

Northern Melanesia was allocated to the Missionnaires du Sacré-Coeur–Issoudun (Missionaries of the Sacred Heart of Jesus), although their numbers were too small to extend to the Solomons. The Society of the Divine Word was established on the north coast of New Guinea in 1896, and two prefectures apostolic were erected in the Solomons, both under the Marists. During the early protectorate years, the Marists operated in both the German and the British Solomons. Ecclesiastical boundaries were not brought into line when political territorial changes occurred in 1899, although in 1904 the names of the prefectures were altered to North Solomons and South Solomons. On Guadalcanal, the Marists established a base at Visale in west Guadalcanal in 1904, followed by subsidiary bases at Rua Sura, Avuavu, and Tangare. Isabel was added to the southern prefecture in 1912—the justification for which was the fact it was the 'martyr' island, where Catholic Bishop Jean-Baptiste Epalle was killed in 1845. They made no progress on Isabel.[3]

The Church of England (Anglicans) came next. Outreach into the Solomons began in 1852 when their Diocese of Melanesia started to recruit students for their schools in New Zealand and, after 1867, at Norfolk Island. They enticed mainly young men away for about seven years, with a trip home in the middle, before returning them to begin mission schools in the islands. The Anglican mission presence became permanent from 1861, and more substantial by the 1870s. Some islands, such as Isabel, and the Ngela and Santa Cruz groups, remain predominantly Anglican. The Anglicans proselytised around Guadalcanal to obtain students for their mission on Norfolk Island, then established themselves minimally at Maravovo in west Guadalcanal in the 1900s. They were outpaced by the Marist Catholics and the South Sea Evangelical Mission (SSEM).

Men and women who had participated in the overseas labour trade became Christians and brought their new beliefs back to their islands; other missionary groups followed them during the early twentieth century. The Queensland Kanaka Mission arrived in the islands informally in 1894 and formally from 1904. It became the South Sea Evangelical Mission in 1907.[4] The Methodist Mission began its outreach in 1902, based in Roviana Lagoon, New Georgia. The Seventh-day Adventists, who arrived in 1914, were initially also based in the western Solomons. Several other of the current religious groups arrived after World War II. The Assemblies

---

3   Laracy 1976: 38–45.
4   Moore 2013a; 2013c: entry for South Sea Evangelical Mission.

of God began in the Solomons in 1971, and the Jehovah's Witnesses in 1977.[5] The Bahá'í Faith arrived with the Blum family in 1954. Sunni Islam began in the 1990s and has grown quickly, particularly on Malaita and to some extent among Malaitans in Honiara, although recent reports suggest a decline.

There were Catholic, Anglican, SSEM, and SDA missions on Guadalcanal, and a Catholic mission church in Horahi village at the mouth of the Mataniko River in the 1920s. The first substantial Christian church in modern Honiara has long been forgotten: the large, thatched chapel near Lungga Beach built by Solomon Islanders for the Americans during the war. It was surrounded by American graves, until the bodies were exhumed after the war and taken back to the United States for reburial. As the number of Solomon Islanders in Honiara increased, so did observation of the sabbath and other aspects of Christianity. Once Honiara was established, the Anglican Diocese of Melanesia headquarters was relocated to Guadalcanal from Taroaniara in the Ngela Group, to where they had moved from Siota in the early 1940s.[6] Honiara's All Saints' Pro-Cathedral (a parish church utilised as a cathedral) was constructed from two large Quonset huts in the late 1940s. That served well enough until St Barnabas' Cathedral on Kukum Highway, positioned at the turn-off to Kola'a Ridge, was built during 1968 and 1969.

After the war, Catholic Bishop Jean M. Aubin settled at Kakabona, west of Honiara. Initially, a leaf-thatch chapel in Honiara was used early each morning as a Catholic church, mainly for wharf labourers from Langalanga Lagoon, Malaita, and then during the day as an office. Their printing press was moved from Visale to Kakabona, and the bishop built his headquarters at Tanagai. St John's School was begun at Rove, and Villa Maria Training College was built at Visale on the foundations of the old church, taking its first students in 1959. Holy Cross Pro-Cathedral was built at the foot of Vatuliva Hill, at the turn-off to Skyline Ridge. Like the Anglicans' temporary cathedral, it was initially a large Quonset hut.

---

5   Tippett 1967.
6   St Luke's Cathedral at Siota in the Ngela Group was destroyed during World War II. As the move to Taroaniara across Tulagi Harbour on Ngela Sule had already been made, there was never an attempt to re-establish Siota, except as a school. After the war, the Anglican headquarters shifted to Honiara.

Plate 7.1 The American chapel built for the armed forces and Solomon Islanders, which was dedicated on 12 September 1943.

The chapel was constructed by Solomon Islanders under the direction of BSIP personnel Lieutenants Harkins and Borgon. They were assisted by officers and men of the US military, primarily the 1st Platoon 45th QM (GR) Company, 46th Naval Construction Battalion, Mica Engineer Depot, 472nd Engineer Heavy Maintenance Company, and the 362nd Engineer Regiment. It was surrounded by a cemetery for Allied and some Japanese dead.

Source: The photograph was taken by Bob Porter, a Signal Corps photographer who was later General Douglas MacArthur's personal photographer in Japan. It is in the Peter Flahavin Collection.

Two vicariates were established in the BSIP in 1959. In the north, one was based at Gizo, covering the protectorate as far south as Isabel, although the only Catholics were on Choiseul and the Shortlands. This was staffed by the Order of Preachers (Dominicans). The islands south of Isabel, including Guadalcanal, became the second vicariate and a Marist preserve.[7] The Catholics decided to relocate their secondary school from St Paul's Aruligo to St Joseph's Tenaru on the outskirts of east Honiara. Year 1 students were the first to move, in 1972. The policy was to transfer

---

7   Laracy 1976: 160–61.

all junior primary schools from mission station grounds to villages, and the staff of all junior primary as well as several senior primary schools was localised—a process that continued in the priesthood and administration, including at the cathedral in Honiara. The Catholics introduced Dominican Sisters in 1956, including the first Solomon Islander Sisters in the late 1960s. An Order of Solomon Islands Sisters, the Daughters of Mary Immaculate, also developed. In the 1970s, a new cathedral was constructed on the site of the pro-cathedral.

Plate 7.2 St Barnabas' Anglican Cathedral, 2017. It was built between 1968 and 1969.
Source: Clive Moore Collection.

The third-biggest Christian denomination is the SSEM and its church, the SSEC, which grew out of it in 1964 and was registered in 1968. The SSEC had its origins in the Plymouth Brethren beliefs of the Young family of Fairymead sugarcane plantation in Bundaberg, Queensland, in the 1880s.[8] Until the early 1950s, there was no general church organisation; then the board of directors began to discuss how to link together the 300 village churches. Each local church group appointed officers to share pastoral and business responsibilities, and clusters of churches were brought together in district associations, each with a president, vice-

---

8   Moore 2013c: entries for Queensland Kanaka Mission, and South Sea Evangelical Mission/Church; 2017a: 231–300.

president, and secretary. There was also a general president of all the associations (recently given the title of bishop). The SSEM/SSEC drew funding from independent Protestant evangelical churches in Australia and New Zealand, and from tithing within local congregations. As with all the Christian denominations, the SSEC became increasingly localised during the 1970s. The central Honiara SSEC building was established next to the main Methodist/United Church building, on the beachfront near Central Market.

Plate 7.3 Holy Cross Catholic Cathedral (centre), at the foot of the road to Skyline, was built between 1977 and 1978.
The main United Church is on the right of the photo, on the beach. This photograph is from 2017.
Source: Clive Moore Collection.

Honiara's SDA congregation is a similar size to that of the SSEC. An SDA primary school was begun in 1948 at Betikama near Henderson Airfield. The site also housed a secondary school from 1970. The primary school was moved to the nearby Burns Creek area across the highway.[9] A new administrative headquarters was constructed for the SDA Western Pacific Union Mission on the Betikama campus in the early 1970s, and the union staff transferred there from Rabaul in 1973. The main city SDA church is situated where Vura Road meets Kukum Highway.

---

9   Information from Ellison Sade, Honiara, 26 November 2016.

As Honiara grew, even though their strength was in Western District, the Methodist mission had to cater for ever-increasing numbers of followers in the capital and, on 12 November 1960, Reverend George Carter opened the new central Methodist church in Honiara, which was expanded in 1968.[10] The Methodists were incorporated into a regional United Church in 1967 with Lesley (later Sir Lesley) Boseto as the first Solomon Islander bishop.

Jehovah's Witnesses had a more difficult introduction than any other denomination. The BSIP Government and the influential established Christian denominations opposed the church because of its non-trinitarian beliefs. Jehovah's Witnesses had some connections with the BSIP as far back as 1948, although their magazines, *The Watchtower* and *Awake!*, were banned until 1974. The church was not registered as a charitable trust until 1977, which enabled its first missionaries to arrive.[11]

Throughout Solomon Islands, all the Christian denominations concentrated on the provision of welfare, schools, health clinics, and hospitals. They were far more important than the government in providing social welfare in the districts, and although there were many church schools in Honiara, only in the capital did the government rival and exceed them in providing education and health services.

Table 7.1 The numbers of Christian adherents in Solomon Islands and the percentages involved in the main Christian denominations in Honiara, 1970–2009.

Religion	1970	1976	1999	2009	2009 Honiara, main denominations
Anglican Church of Melanesia	54,004 (33.5%)	67,370 (34.2%)	134,288 (32.8%)	164,639 (31.9%)	30%
Catholic Church	30,117 (18.7%)	36,870 (18.7%)	77,728 (19%)	100,999 (19.5%)	15%
South Sea Evangelical Church	27,772 (17.2%)	33,306 (16.9%)	69,651 (17.02%)	88,395 (17.1%)	23%
Seventh-day Adventist	14,939 (9.3%)	19,113 (9.7%)	45,846 (11.21%)	60,506 (11.7%)	16%
United Church	18,075 (11.2%)	22,209 (11.3%)	42,236 (10.32%)	51,919 (10%)	6%

---

10   *BSIP NS*, 30 November 1960.
11   Ernst 2006: 188.

Religion	1970	1976	1999	2009	2009 Honiara, main denominations
Christian Fellowship Church	3,878 (2.4%)	4,822 (2.4%)	9,693 (2.3%)	13,153 (2.5%)	n.a.
Jehovah's Witness	2,496 (1.8%)	3,530 (1.8%)	7,485 (1.8%)	9,444 (1.8%)	n.a.
Christian Outreach	0	0	3,841 (0.9%)	5,303 (1.02%)	n.a.
Bahá'í	0	873 (0.4%)	2,300 (0.56%)	2,427 (0.47%)	n.a.
Customary beliefs	0	7,130 (3.6%)	2,633 (0.64%)	4,191 (0.8%)	n.a.
No religion or faith, or not stated	1,280 (0.8%)	1,600 (0.6%)	2,203 (0.54%)	818 (0.15%)	n.a.
Other	n.a	n.a	11,138 (2.7%)	14,076 (2.7%)	n.a.
Total population	**152,561**	**196,823**	**409,042**	**515,870**	

n.a. Not available
Sources: SIG (1988b: 15; 2009: Vol. 1, 4.2, pp. 81–82; 2011b).

The various denominations behaved quite differently in their attitudes to the localisation of their clergy and teachers. The Anglicans installed their first indigenous deacons and priests in the late nineteenth century, and developed an indigenous order, the Melanesian Brotherhood (Ira Retatasiu), in 1925, as well as another, smaller order, the Community of the Cross, in 1927, which included Solomon Islander Sisters from 1932. This order was disbanded in 1950 (the few remaining Sisters transferred to the Catholic Church). It was replaced in 1970 with the Community of the Sisters of the Church. The SSEM always encouraged localisation because it never had a clergy in the same style as the Catholics and Anglicans. The message of the early Methodist mission was spread by Pacific Islanders from other countries and increasingly by local pastors. The first ordained Solomon Islander Methodist ministers were Bill Gina in 1938, Jobi Rotoava and Leslie Boseto in the 1960s, and Esau Tuza in the 1970s. The Catholics were more rigid and relied mainly on French Marist priests and Sisters, while also developing local orders for Sisters. The first Solomon Islander to be ordained by the Catholic Church was Michael Aike in 1965, followed by Donasiana Hitee and Timothy Bobongi in 1967, and Lawrence Isa in 1968.

Since the 1970s, there has been a significant growth in Pentecostal and charismatic Christian groups. While it is difficult to generalise, these denominations promote a personalised relationship with God, and members of their congregations experience the gifts of the Holy Spirit. They 'speak in tongues' (glossolalia), interpret prophecies, and heal the sick. These churches are more likely to be found in the suburbs and settlements of the urban centres, with some outreach to rural areas in the provinces. The Calvary Temple in Honiara in 1974 was the first church established by the Assemblies of God in Solomon Islands. It was the headquarters, until the pastor of the Christian Life Centre was elected General Secretary of the Assembly of God in Solomon Islands.

Two more religious groups arrived to stay: the Bahá'í Faith, in the 1950s; and, since the 1990s, Islam, which has made limited inroads, mainly on Malaita and in Honiara, with several thousand converts. The Bahá'í Faith was introduced to Solomon Islands in 1954 by Americans Alvin and Gertrude Blum. Their business background was outlined in Chapter 6. Bahá'í believe there is only one God, who was revealed to humanity through a series of divine messengers, each of whom was the founder of a great religion. The founder, Bahá'u'lláh, who was born in Tehran, Persia (Iran), in 1817 and died in Palestine in 1892, is believed to have been the latest of these divine messengers. Solomon Islanders were attracted to the Blums because they treated them as equals without prejudice or discrimination. They shared the Bahá'í message with whomever was interested, and soon significant numbers of people declared their belief in Bahá'u'lláh's revelations. By 1956, the first local assembly of Honiara was elected, and the message of the faith began to spread to most major islands. In 1971, the National Spiritual Assembly of Solomon Islands (the administrative body) was elected from the community of more than 25 local assemblies. The assembly was incorporated under the *Charitable Trust Act*, Bahá'í marriages were recognised, and land was registered for a future house of worship. Currently, the faith claims more than 4,000 Bahá'í throughout all provinces of Solomon Islands, although the 2009 national census only recorded 2,427 (Table 9.1).[12]

The first Muslims in Solomon Islands may have been several students from Iran and Pakistan who attended the Auki Boat-Building School in 1963. A few well-educated Solomon Islanders were drawn to Islam during

---

12   I am indebted to Sir Bruce and Lady Keithie Saunders for this summary, October 2017.

the 1980s and 1990s, with the real progress made during the Tension years (Chapter 9). The first converts met Muslims while studying at universities overseas, particularly on the main Suva campus of the University of the South Pacific in Fiji, and talked with the few Muslim expatriates in Honiara. A (Sunni) Muslim League was formed and, in the late 1980s and the 1990s, an Ahmadiyya (a moderate branch of Shia Islam) missionary began to visit. The converts were attracted to what anthropologist Debra McDougall described as Islam's 'elegant monotheism' and unified focus. Often, they drew similarities with *kastom* and indigenous Solomons religions, with their gender separation, taboos, and ideas about retribution rather than forgiveness.

The late 1990s and 2000s were a time of much soul-searching for Solomon Islanders. Some blame for the Tensions was laid on the laxity that Christianity allows, compared with *kastom* beliefs. There was a feeling, particularly among some Malaitans, that Christianity had diminished the importance of ancestral religious beliefs and weakened the social fabric. Islam's rules are much stricter and, in some ways, more comfortable for those seeking absolute moral and philosophical guidance. Sunni Islam made inroads on Malaita, particularly among less formally educated men. Several thousand converted, although often it was only the men, with their wives and children remaining Christian. Many did not follow the strictures of Islam and continued to eat pork and drink alcohol, which made their conversion seem opportunistic. There was the attraction of trying something new, and conversions occurred in Honiara where there were concentrations of Malaitans. A small mosque was built at Gilbert Camp, there is a Sunni centre at Mbokonavera, and an Ahmadiyya Centre on west Kola`a Ridge. Christian leaders in Solomon Islands seem to resent the incursion of Islam and to fear the growth of the religion. They forget that some denominations (the Jehovah's Witnesses and Pentecostal groups, and splinter groups from the larger denominations, such as the Remnant Church)[13] were also opposed by mainstream Christianity when they first began, but grew strong in the archipelago.[14]

---

13   Maeliau 1976, 2003; Maetoloa 1985; Burt 1983.
14   This section on Islam is based on McDougall (2009) and my own experience on Malaita and in Honiara.

Such a short discussion is perhaps misleading. Religion is central to life at spiritual, social, and behavioural levels. Through both regular observance and actions, the residents of Honiara exude Christianity and, to a lesser extent, the Bahá`í Faith, and now Islam. There is also a degree of syncretism in teachings and behaviour in all faiths.

Sporting facilities

Honiara inherited sporting facilities from the American's Camp Guadal. There were plenty of basketball courts and even the BSIP Secretariat buildings had their own tar-surfaced tennis courts and a sports field.[15] Solomon Islanders and expatriates put these to good use. Weekends were dominated by religion and sport, which became a central part of the lives of Solomon Islanders. Attending educational institutions went hand in hand with organised sports, and students or ex-students were some of the main participants. One early town council plan aimed to allocate 2.4 hectares of sporting facilities for every 1,000 residents—an idea that soon lapsed. The first of the modern playing fields was at Rove, and the next at the British Solomon Islands Teachers' Training College.[16] The Honiara Football League began in 1957, using the police facilities at Rove. A more permanent public sports ground was needed and, in August 1961, businessman Eric V. Lawson convened a meeting to consider future sporting facilities in the protectorate. This led to the inauguration of the British Solomon Islands Amateur Sports Association (usually called ASA), with a six-man committee. Lawson became president and Val J. Andersen (a senior public servant) was vice-president. Town Ground at the foot of Lengakiki Ridge was the first public sports field in the 1960s, with a cricket pitch built there.

Honiara's main sports grounds and playing fields became known as *tama*.[17] Honiara educational institutions, such as the Teachers' Training College, Honiara Technical Institute, and King George VI School, also built sporting ovals. Two major public sporting areas developed: Town Ground and Lawson Tama. Other sports fields now exist in the inland suburbs

---

15 Lawson n.d. [c. 2000s]: 6.
16 Expatriate cricket matches were organised at the Rove police ground in 1951. *PIM*, March 1951, 72.
17 All attempts to find the origin of *tama* have failed. *Tama* is a word in some Guadalcanal languages for 'father'. One possibility is that the term was applied to Eric Lawson as the 'father' of public sports facilities in the protectorate.

and settlements, such as the oval at Kobito. Unfortunately, in the 2000s, Town Ground was leased for a Chinese shopping complex development, which stalled for years, leaving construction half-completed due to arguments over building specifications. For a long time, the playing field was unusable. Now operational once more, it is also used for ceremonies. The other major area allocated for public sporting facilities was near the hospital and Chinatown. Originally called the Town Sports Ground, as Honiara grew, this sports field became more central, and suggestions were made to rename it. Calling the area Hospital Tama was not appealing. Instead, the decision was made to use the name of the man who had done the most to create the facility, Eric Lawson. For decades, Lawson Tama has been the site for major sports games and public ceremonies and will remain so at least until better facilities are built for the 2023 Pacific Games. The sheltered stadium seating and the sloping hill behind provide excellent viewing platforms for all events. The basic preparation of Lawson Tama was completed in early 1964, jointly managed by the town council and the ASA. A subcommittee consisting of Lawson, Reverend Charles Fox, and Reverend Bill Gina was appointed to oversee the use of funds allocated for improvements. A pavilion and various sporting facilities were planned, and other improvements were made during 1965.

Solomon Islanders engaged in sports before the days of the British, although these activities were not designated solely as recreational and usually related to everyday occurrences. Training for warfare began when boys practised spear-throwing and the use of bows and arrows and other weapons, or practised hand-to-hand combat. Wrestling is said to have been popular in pre-British times on the Melanesian islands; it continued on the Polynesian Outliers, and *tika*, a team spear-throwing competition, continued on Tikopia and Anuta. Women also played games related to their traditional activities.[18] Most famously, the Australian 'crawl' swimming stroke had its origins in Roviana Lagoon in the western Solomons, given world prominence by two Roviana brothers, Alick and Harry Wickham.[19]

Solomon Islanders first participated in Western sports through the auspices of the Anglican Melanesian Mission, which organised cricket teams to play in various places. They also began to participate in modern sporting events while on plantations in Queensland and Fiji in the nineteenth century, and early in the twentieth century on plantations, missions,

---

18 Treadaway 2007: 86–88; *BSIP AR* 1969: 86.
19 Osmond 2006.

and government stations within the protectorate. There are accounts of cricket games played among coconut palms on plantations, and there were Solomon Islander cricket teams on Tulagi before the war. British traditions meant that soccer, rugby football, and cricket predominated. The first local Honiara soccer team was the Melanesian Team in 1946, with Albert Kuper as manager. Their first meeting was held at Namba 9, the Central Hospital. The team's colour was yellow, which was achieved by dyeing the players' singlets in a bucket of Atabrine (antimalarial) tablets from the hospital dispensary.[20]

The equipment for many of these sports was expensive and, initially, there were more expatriates than Solomon Islanders involved. Gradually, Solomon Islanders, particularly those who had been exposed to organised sports at schools in the protectorate and overseas, began to participate. Sport became a central part of the lives of Solomon Islanders and large crowds came to watch cricket and football matches on Sunday afternoons. In 1951, the first Solomon Islands soccer team travelled to New Zealand on the Anglican Diocese of Melanesia's *Southern Cross*. They played barefooted against New Zealand teams. In the 1950s, the Anglican Church had a soccer team, as did the Public Works Department; others were formed soon after.[21] The ASA raised funds to send representatives to the first South Pacific Games in Suva in 1963, as well as establishing a playing field at Kukum, and creating better sporting grounds in the districts.

Eight Solomon Islanders travelled to Australia in late 1963 to undertake a two-month refereeing course run by the Queensland Soccer Referees Association. The Honiara Rugby Union Football Club was formed in April 1964, followed by the Bicycle Club in July the same year, with the aim of affiliating with the Amateur Cyclists' Union. During 1962, the South Pacific Commission founded the South Pacific Games (now the Pacific Games). Solomon Islands teams have taken part in all South Pacific Games. Initially, the games were held at three-year intervals, which was subsequently expanded to four years. Most BSIP participants came from Honiara, and each time there was great excitement as training and selection trials progressed.

---

20 'Albert Kuper to editor', *KR*, September 1970.
21 Montford 1994: 95.

During 1971, an interisland rugby series for the Andersen Shield was successfully completed and soccer teams competed for the Rothmans Cup. Amateur boxing was introduced in 1969. Three years later, a team of boxers was sent to the New Hebrides, and a Bougainville rugby team made a five-match tour of the Solomons.[22] The ASA affiliated several national sporting bodies: the Amateur Athletics Association, the Basketball Association, the Amateur Boxing Association, the Cricket Association, the Netball Association, the Amateur Football Association (also affiliated to the English Football Association), and the Rugby Football Association. In addition, local groups for the following sports were affiliated into the ASA: golf, hockey, judo, table tennis, skindiving, underwater spearfishing, and volleyball. Netball leagues were organised in Honiara for girls and women, and the game was also played in some larger villages, where it was organised by Women's Clubs. Hard-court tennis was played in Honiara and all regional centres, and yachting and sabot racing were popular in Honiara under the auspices of the Point Cruz Yacht Club, which began in 1968.[23] The Honiara Golf Club was established in 1957, at the eastern end of town on land once part of Kukum Airfield. Competitive swimming was another early sport. In the 1970s, there were three large swimming pools in Honiara: at the Police Club, the Guadalcanal Club, and a short-lived pool built at the Community Centre in 1973.[24]

League cricket began in the 1960s, although there were few regular cricket teams during the years before and immediately after independence. A six-team league existed in 1968. King George VI School had a team of teachers and students, and the Australian banks (ANZ and Westpac) had a team called the Bank Boys. There was also the High Commissioner's XI, and teams called the Packers' Mob, Finance, Tenavatu, and Teneru School. Two of the earliest Solomon Islander champions were John Wilikai and Billy Boso. One of the best remembered cricket teams was the multiracial Barbarians, captained by Solomon ('Solo') Mamaloni during the 1970s and 1980s. It had several well-known members: Henry Isa, Dominic Otuana, Robert Waigagu, Francis Talasasa Aqorau, and, Ashley, Adrian, and Martin Wickham; and many expatriates over the years, including David Roe, Christopher Chevalier, Barry Hayes, Nick Constantine,

---

22 *BSIP AR* 1971: 103.
23 *BSIP AR* 1969: 85.
24 *BSIP NS*, 31 August 1961, 31 October 1961, 31 July 1962, 15 October 1962, 15 May 1963, 16 August 1963, 15 November 1963, 30 November 1963, 30 April 1964, 31 July 1964, 31 August 1964, 7 April 1966, 21 May 1966, 7 November 1966, 19 December 1966; *BSIP AR* 1970: 94, 1974: 121.

Bart Kirby, and Tony Hughes. The Barbarians played at various places around Honiara, but usually at Town Ground. Early on, 'Solo' was the proud owner of a small motor scooter and was always willing to pick up participants, if they were happy to sit on the luggage rack and look after the betel nuts and stubbies, which were essential parts of his cricket equipment. He was just as shrewd a cricket captain and administrator of league cricket as he was a politician, although he always fielded in the deep and did not try too hard to run after balls. When 'Solo' became prime minister, his cricket team's transport became easier and the cricket supplies increased. A memento has survived in the form of an advertisement from 1982 when the Prime Minister's Barbarians played the 'Diplomatic Devil-Devils'; and at one stage they played as the Governor-General's XI, at the request of Sir Baddeley Devesi.[25]

If there is a failing in sports planning, it is the lack of a large national stadium in Honiara, and making do with Lawson Tama, Town Ground, and a variety of other smaller sites. There were plans after independence to build a stadium opposite the golf course, on land already in use as part of the playing fields for King George VI School. This area is also close to other educational institutions (described below) that are now part of the Solomon Islands National University.[26] Land for a sports stadium was reserved near Burns Creek, which by the 2000s and 2010s had become a large squatter settlement. These were major chances missed, which should have provided unified sporting facilities for Honiara. The 2023 Pacific Games are to be held in Honiara and the lack of a stadium is embarrassing. In 2019, the Indonesian Government agreed to build a stadium. Planning began for a three-court stadium at the KGVI–Panatina Sports Complex, to be completed by 2021. Then, late the same year, the Solomon Islands Government changed diplomatic horses from the Republic of China (Taiwan) to the People's Republic of China. With this move came the promise of a new stadium. Hopefully, these government manoeuvres will lead to the creation of more unified sporting facilities, which have been part of planning since the 1970s.[27]

---

25 My thanks to David Roe and Christopher Chevalier for recounting their years as members of the Barbarians, and to Christopher Chevalier for the following references: Lewis 2017: Cricket chapter; 'Cricket season begins', *SND*, May 1975; 'Parkers tame Barbarians', *STT*, 12 November 1979; 'Cricket league still first round', *STT*, 9 September 1982.
26 Heath 1978: 41–42.
27 Aruafu 2016; '2023 Pacific Games stadium in doubt', *The Island Sun* [hereinafter *IS*], 3 November 2017, 24; SIBC, 18 December 2019, 5 March 2020. Late in 2019, as part of the diplomatic move from Taiwan to the People's Republic of China, mainland Chinese funding was also discussed.

Plate 7.4 The Ko'o Football Team in 1972, one of the teams playing in the Honiara football competition.

The team's name comes from the To'ambaita language in north Malaitan, in which it means 'grandparent'/'grandchild'. It is also used to address a friend (not necessarily a relative) and is the common name by which the To'ambaita were known in Honiara. The captain (standing in the centre back row) was Jim Iro, who worked as foreman at the tobacco factory. One of the team members (front row, far right) was Lawrence Foana'ota, who became director of the Solomon Islands National Museum.

Source: Ian Frazer Collection.

Education

Once its central place in the country's transport infrastructure was established, Honiara was able to host the key educational institutions of the nation. After the WPHC headquarters was moved to Honiara in the early 1950s, the BSIP also became a hub for education and other facilities for neighbouring areas of the Pacific. A small Education Department was established in Honiara in 1946 (with three staff), which functioned under considerable difficulties. The missions still conducted all education in the protectorate, except for a part-time school in Honiara for European children, and the Chung Wah School for Chinese children. Honiara's Woodford School for European children began in the mid-1950s, housed in the British Red Cross Society's building, with the students enrolled in the New Zealand Correspondence School. As student numbers were increasing, from July 1954, the government decided to convert an existing building into a school and to follow a normal curriculum conducted by a trained teacher.[28]

The post-war BSIP Government's initiatives flowed from the appointment of C.A. Coleman-Porter as Director of Education. A November 1947 conference for all educators outlined a new policy to create state institutions to provide skills for the BSIP and other WPHC territories in teaching, nursing, agriculture, commerce, carpentry, and engineering. The only concession to the Christian missions was a strange plan to allow colleges within the institutions to be organised according to religious denominations. This development was delayed after Coleman-Porter resigned in 1948—once he realised he did not have the support of the government or the missions. A new conference was held in Honiara in March 1949, organised by Howard Hayden, Education Adviser to the WPHC, the result of which was no more conciliatory to the Christian missions. New BSIP education regulations circulated in 1953 stipulated the creation of multi-course colleges to produce practitioners in all the skills needed to develop the protectorate.[29] This was the foundation of what eventually became the Teacher and Vocational Training College, the British Solomon Islands Teachers' Training College, the Agricultural Staff Training Institute, Central Hospital's Dressers School, the Nurses' Training Centre (both later combined as the Hospital Training School), Auki Boat-Building School, and the T.S. Ranadi Marine Training School. All these institutions brought a new generation of young Solomon Islanders to Honiara, along with a mix of fellow students from the Crown Colony of Gilbert and Ellice Islands, the New Hebrides Condominium (Vanuatu), and other Pacific colonial territories in Micronesia.

The first change was the Auki Experimental Primary School, which was the forerunner of plans for wider government participation in the education system. Funds were also approved in 1951 for an elementary school in Honiara. Its first principal was Reverend Bill Gina, who was sent to Fiji in 1952 to complete teacher training. He remained principal of the Honiara Government Primary School until he retired in 1965 and was responsible for educating the first generation of Solomon Islands children

---

28   *BSIP AR* 1953–54: 26.
29   Laracy 1976: 151–52.

in the town. By the late 1950s, there were five government schools in the protectorate providing education up to Standard IV, and the Government Primary School providing education for the primary range up to Year 7.[30]

King George VI School and secondary education

Until 1965, King George VI School was based at Aligego, just outside Auki, on Malaita. It began as the Auki Experimental Primary School in 1947 and floundered along until an adequate headmaster was appointed in 1952. The school became the first government senior primary school. After the death of the British king in February 1952, on 25 September of that year, the school was renamed the King George VI School (KGVI).

By the end of 1954, KGVI provided education up to a higher primary standard for 92 boys. The construction of the school buildings was completed in 1955. The curriculum included English, which was the only instructional or wider language of communication used at the school, as well as arts and crafts, hygiene, arithmetic, agriculture, and social studies. Sport flourished—mainly soccer, cricket, and athletics. The school farm, staffed by the students, provided 90 per cent of the root vegetables they consumed.[31]

From 1945, BSIP Government planning had been to move towards mass primary and eventually more limited secondary education within the BSIP. This coincided with one of the demands of the Maasina Rule movement—that a government secondary school be established on Malaita—and led to secondary education beginning at KGVI in January 1958. KGVI became a secondary school in 1962. About half its secondary students came from Malaita, and half from other areas of the protectorate, the New Hebrides, and the Gilbert and Ellice Islands, where government schools only went to Year 8. By 1960, there were three secondary classes and two senior primary classes. In 1962, the school had 62 students. Under headmaster Hugh Hall (1960–67), the secondary education section of KGVI adopted the Cambridge syllabus. Candidates began to sit for their Cambridge School Certificate (O Levels) in 1960, with the

---

30 *BSIP AR* 1953–54: 5; 1957–58: 33.
31 Palmer and Medobu 2003; Geoffrey Anii, interview with Clive Moore, Honiara, 23 February 2007; *BSIP NS*, 21 August 1967, 6 October 1967; *BSIP AR* 1951–52: 4, 1953–54: 26.

first passes in 1962.³² Most of these early students went on to further education and found their way into the BSIP public service. Thirty boys obtained their O Levels between 1962 and 1966. The school introduced a system of prefects and dormitories named after European explorers (such as Mendaña and Lieutenant John Shortland).

KGVI had also begun to take a few girls as day students and, in 1963, it began to accept larger numbers of girls. KGVI was moved to Honiara at the end of 1965 to cater for the growing capital city. The first buildings on the Honiara site were constructed in 1963 near the British Solomons Teachers' Training College at Panatina. The foundation stone was laid on 8 February 1964, and the new school was officially opened in January 1966.³³

KGVI supplemented the Christian school system and was crucial to producing the new educated elite in Solomon Islands. The Honiara-based KGVI was initially large enough to cope with 210 students, with plans to expand to three hundred. As it had been on Malaita, it was also a boarding school. When it opened in Honiara, there were 159 students, five of whom were female day students. The school became fully coeducational in 1967, with a student body of 223, including 34 girls, with the intention of expanding the female student intake to 80. This move was bitterly opposed by some conservative members of the Legislative Council, who called it a disregard for established customs—although, as it was pointed out, the Methodists had operated coeducational boarding schools in the protectorate since 1902. In 1969, KGVI provided a four-year course of education up to Cambridge School Certificate level. That year, there were 281 students (212 boys and 69 girls) with 98 new students, including 25 girls. There were 18 teachers, and extra buildings were under construction. The next year, the school had 305 students (228 boys and 77 girls) and one new teacher.³⁴

---

32   *BSIP NS*, 7 January 1967, 21 August 1967. In 1963, James Roni was the first to obtain a First-Class Division—equivalent to matriculation—after which he was sent to Gatton Agricultural College in Queensland. Two others who sat for their O Levels that year were William Fa'arondo and Bobby Oifena Kwanairara, who received school certificates with six subjects each. Kwanairara was appointed an Assistant Administrative Officer Cadet, working in Central District, and Fa'arondo worked at the Lands Department before attending a draughtsman's topographical course at the School of Military Survey in Melbourne.
33   The old Aligego site became a senior primary school for children on Malaita and BSIP's first Local Government Training School, which opened in 1967 under Michael Forster, the newly arrived Local Government Training Officer, who had served previously in the BSIP (1939–50) as a district officer and Coastwatcher. The initial courses were for executive officers, council clerks, subdistrict clerks, and court clerks. *BSIP NS*, 21 February 1967, 6 October 1967, No. 24, December 1967.
34   *BSIP NS*, 13 December 1967; *BSIP AR* 1969: 47, 1970: 51. Also see Moore 2013c: entry for King George VI School.

Plate 7.5 The front entrance to King George VI School.

The sculpture is a collective work by students Henry Sitai, George Kuper, Rollance Hilly, Lawrence Foana'ota, James Kamasai, Isaac Molia, Mark Bisili, and others.

Source: Les Tickle Collection.

Plate 7.6 The chapel at King George VI School.

Source: Les Tickle Collection.

Plate 7.7 King George VI School students in about 1968, with school buildings in the background.
Source: Les Tickle Collection.

The KGVI's intake was from government and church senior primary schools, with a 'credit level' necessary to be eligible to enter secondary school. In the 1960s, the major churches established equivalent secondary schools in Honiara. Four Christian secondary schools in the protectorate took students through to Year 8: All Hallows at Pawa (boys), St Joseph's Tenaru (boys), Goldie College on New Georgia (coeducational), and St Mary's Pamua (girls). By 1969, there were six church secondary schools: St Paul's Aruligo (Catholic), Su`u on Malaita (SSEM), Goldie College (United Church), Betikama in Honiara (SDA), All Hallows Pamua, and St Mary's Pawa (Anglican). At the end of that year, the last two combined into a new school: Selwyn College, 29 kilometres west of Honiara. Betikama Adventist School introduced Year 8 in 1968 as part of its plans to extend to Year 9 in 1969 and Year 10 in 1970. The Catholics' St Joseph's School at Tenaru was also expanded at this time. These schools fed students through to the post-secondary government and church educational institutions in Solomon Islands and overseas. The alternatives to attending secondary school were to enrol in the training college for vocational courses and primary school teachers, or to enter the workforce.

Plate 7.8 Prize winners at King George VI School in 1970.
Source: Les Tickle Collection.

KGVI was responsible for other less obvious changes that are now incorporated into the modern culture of Solomon Islands. Art students developed new motifs based on traditional designs, learning how to incorporate them in murals and into the fabric of modern buildings. KGVI students designed and painted murals on the walls of the Honiara Club, which were also incorporated into the new 2 cent, 10 cent, and 1 dollar coins. Les Tickle, teacher in charge of the art department (1968–72), painted a mural for the entrance to the Legislative Council's committee rooms, with the design later incorporated into the banknotes used from 1977 until 2013. Even the designs on the decorated 'planters' (plant pots) now used in the centre of Mendana Avenue owe their origin to the early KGVI art students.[35]

KGVI remains an important national secondary school, although it has now been overtaken in academic performance by St Nicholas College, Florence Young School, Bishop Epalle School, and Honiara High School.

British Solomon Islands Teachers' and Vocational Training College

The second plank in modern secular education in the Solomons was the creation of the British Solomon Islands Teachers' and Vocational Training College (TVTC). This was later split into the British Solomon Islands Teachers' Training College and the Honiara Technical Institute.

Plans were drawn up in 1954 and a site selected for a college to train artisans, electrical and clerical workers, and teachers. The government's aim was to strengthen the training programs already existing through the various Christian denominations and government departments. In 1955, the BSIP Government received a £56,000 grant to establish the TVTC. In June, High Commissioner Stanley laid the foundation stone of the first building on the Kukum campus, on the site of wartime battles and an American storage area. The first staff houses were built in 1956 and the initial intake of students also occurred that year. Completion of the main block was delayed until 1957, owing to the slow delivery of steel from the United Kingdom.[36] The college was fully operational by 1959, when 20 students began the teacher training courses to teach in junior primary schools (Years 1–4). Two-year courses for teachers, clerical workers, and

---

35 Email from Les Tickle, 22 December 2018; Tickle 1970.
36 *PIM*, March 1956, 71; March 1957, 27.

carpenters were planned, to be followed by others in metal work, electrical, and radio operation, as the college expanded. There were some unusual early dangers for students, such as the hundreds of unexploded wartime shells discovered on the college grounds during these early years.[37]

The first 18 primary Year 3 teachers graduated from a two-year course at the end of 1960, as did the first 14 manual arts (mainly carpentry) students. In conjunction with the South Pacific Commission, there were two schemes for full-time technical education introduced for Solomon Islands students and others from Pacific territories, in printing and boatbuilding. The Literature Production Training Centre began a one-year course in offset printing in 1960, for 12 students from six Pacific territories. The second group of carpenters graduated in 1962.[38] A boatbuilding course began in 1960, based in Auki, Malaita.[39]

By 1961, the government was investigating ways to increase the TVTC's intake for the full two-year teacher training courses and, under the Australian Commonwealth Education Scheme, short courses were provided to improve the methods of unqualified teachers. Late in 1964, plans were formulated for construction of a 'polytechnic', to provide facilities for a limited range of technical training, to coordinate the common features of various training programs, and to provide adult education classes.[40] Residential accommodation was expanded from 48 to 96 places in 1964, using a grant from the Nuffield Foundation. The first women attended the college in 1964; they graduated five years later and, in 1970, the female intake increased from 20 to 30.[41]

---

37   *BSIP NS*, 8 July 1966, 21 September 1966, 19 December 1966.
38   *BSIP AR* 1959–60: 4; *BSIP NS*, 31 October 1960, 30 November 1962.
39   The Boat-Building School was established in Auki and was funded by the Pacific Commission and the World Health Organization, with male students enrolled in a two-year course. The second intake was in 1963, with students from the BSIP, Papua and New Guinea, the New Hebrides, Niue, the US Trust Territory in Micronesia, Iran, Pakistan, Indonesia, and the Philippines. The first three fishing boats were built in 1961, and seven 7.6-metre launches were built at the school between 1960 and 1964. Work also began on the *Walande*, a 15.8-metre touring vessel for the Marine Department, which was completed in February 1965. The third boatbuilding course began in May 1966, with BSIP students and others from the Crown Colony of Gilbert and Ellice Islands, the New Hebrides, and Niue. By 1968, they were building four 7.9-metre vessels for the protectorate fleet. *BSIP AR* 1959–60: 38, 1963–64: 46; *BSIP NS*, 31 August 1961, 31 October 1962, 15 March 1962, 30 April 1963, 16 August 1963, 15 May 1964, 28 February 1965, 7 February 1966, 21 May 1966, 31 March 1968.
40   BSIP 1960–69: G.F. Bovey, *BSIP Legislative Council Debates*, 6 June 1961, 68; *BSIP AR* 1963–64: 16.
41   Veronica Kafa and Sally Hakatuna were enrolled in 1964, and four more women followed in 1965. Afia-Maetala and Pollard 2009: 16–19.

Plate 7.9 The Teacher and Vocational Training College in the late 1950s.
Source: *BSIP AR* (1957–58: 36).

British Solomon Islands Teachers' Training College

The technical courses were split off into the Honiara Technical Institute and the college continued to provide two-year courses for teacher training. Selection was by competitive examination and 36 new students joined the college in January 1967, including five women. By the end of that year, there were 94 teacher trainees, a dozen of them women. In 1970, the college increased its female intake from 12 to 30, and the BSIP scholarship board agreed that teachers were eligible to apply for scholarships under the Commonwealth bursary scheme.[42] Thirty-four Year 3 teachers successfully completed their second year of training in 1970, and another 49 were selected to begin the course. Untrained teachers went through a crash course and were awarded certificates. By 1974, there had been a change in the length of the pre-service Year 3 course, from two to three years. Curriculum development was improved and, in anticipation of a substantial increase in the future output from the Year 3 course, 70 students began in 1975. Additional students trained

---

42   *BSIP NS*, 14 February 1964.

in vocational subjects with an emphasis on home craft, rural science, art and craft, and woodwork. In-service courses also operated in the school holidays, bringing in teachers from around the protectorate.[43]

The training college provided a major new pathway for young Solomon Islands women to obtain a higher education and to enter the workforce. Along with nursing, teaching enabled women to be independent and to participate in building the modern nation. Along with other government training institutions in Honiara, it was the precursor of the Solomon Islands College of Higher Education (SICHE), which began in 1984, and the Solomon Islands National University (SINU), which began in 2013.

Honiara Technical Institute

A 1966 report recommended that a technical college be established in Honiara, separate from but complementing what would become the British Solomon Islands Teachers' Training College. The separate technical college would provide basic and advanced pre-vocational courses on a full and part-time basis. Entry was to be from Year 7 into three-year courses, beginning in 1970. Initially, government departments had their own small training schools.[44] The Agricultural Staff Training Institute (ASTI) had begun at Kukum in 1959. Its first students, from Solomon Islands and the Crown Colony of Gilbert and Ellice Islands, graduated at the end of 1962. The report suggested combining the ASTI and the small Survey and Draughting Institute with a new Honiara Technical Institute, all based in the ASTI grounds. Supervised by its principal George Hardcastle, work began on the new buildings in May 1968. The Honiara Technical Institute opened in 1969 with five schools: Marine, Agriculture, Commerce, Survey and Draughting, and Trades. The institute drew students from neighbouring Pacific territories. By 1970, there were 200 students enrolled, from Solomon Islands, Tonga, New Hebrides (11 per cent of the enrolment), and Saipan in the Northern Mariana Islands. At the end of the institute's first two years, 422 students had attended some type of full-time training. The institute added clerical training to its syllabus and, in 1969, the first seven women sat the elementary typewriting examination from Pitman's College in England.[45]

---

43 *BSIP AR* 1970: 52; 1974: 69.
44 *BSIP NS*, 12 July 1955, 16 August 1963, 8 July 1966, 21 September 1966, 19 December 1966.
45 Afia-Maetala and Pollard 2009: 19. They were Maxine Bretchefield, Elizabeth Maelaua, Urmila Singh, Selina Har, Daisy Sikori, Jocelyn Mamupio, and Maetofea Waleilia.

As localisation increased in the public service and private industry expanded, there was a need for trained workers. Basic electrical training and building courses, a full-time course in clerical work, and a short course for coxswains (ships' navigators) were introduced. In 1974, the enrolment was 587 full-time students, attending courses of six months to one year in technical and commercial subjects. The remainder attended short courses in management, auto electrics, outboard motor servicing, and coxswains' training. Evening classes were held in typing, shorthand, and Pijin English for expatriates, with a total enrolment of 409 during the year. There were also part-time courses in bookkeeping, correspondence and report writing, and refrigeration.[46]

TS Ranadi Marine Training School

The TS (Training Ship) Ranadi Marine Training School was named after MV *Ranadi*, a steam yacht that was the main government vessel during the 1920s, and eventually became the resident commissioner's yacht.[47] Through its Marine Department, the BSIP Government in 1960 began making plans to establish a Maritime (later Marine) Training School in Honiara to train crews for government vessels. The first course began in April 1961, temporarily using facilities at Tulagi, pending completion of permanent buildings on the shore at Tanakake in November. Its first training officer was Captain James C. Anderson, later vice-principal of the Honiara Technical Institute.[48] The school was expanded during 1962 to include a dormitory for 30 male students. The first Solomon Islanders received Outer Islands Masters tickets in 1963. In 1968, there were 50 students, 20 of them receiving advanced instruction as marine mechanics.[49] The Marine Training School became part of the Honiara Technical Institute and later a section of the School of Marine and Fisheries Studies of SICHE, before incorporation into SINU. The Marine Training School provided the name for the Ranadi Industrial Estate.[50]

---

46   *BSIP NS*, 31 May 1968, 31 January 1970; *BSIP AR* 1969: 4, 1971: 60, 1974: 71.
47   MacQuarrie 1946: 25–26.
48   *BSIP NS*, February 1969.
49   *BSIP NS*, 31 July 1960, 2 November 1961, 1 November 1962, 31 June 1965, 31 January 1968.
50   Floyd 1978.

Plate 7.10 Sir Donald Luddington, the final Western Pacific High Commissioner (1973–74) and the first Governor of the BSIP (1974–76), reviewing students at a TS Ranadi Marine Training School graduation ceremony.
Source: John Holloway Collection, in Clive Moore Collection.

Nurses' and dressers' training schools

The other aspect of education that was eventually to become part of SICHE, and now SINU, was nurse training, which was dominated by women. The early nurses in the protectorate were Europeans working for the various Christian missions or for the government. The first government nurse, Edith Elizabeth Elliot, arrived at Tulagi Hospital in 1914. Many Solomon Islands women, particularly church Sisters, received informal training as nurses. In 1922, the BSIP Government began training male 'native dressers' (medical orderlies) at Tulagi Hospital and, in 1929, the first Solomon Islander attended the Fiji Medical School, graduating in 1931 as a Native Medical Practitioner (NMP). In 1956, the title changed to Assistant Medical Officer (AMO). From the late 1920s, the government began to extend medical services and established small hospitals at district stations, which were staffed by local dressers. In 1941, the first six young Melanesian women began training as nurses at the Melanesian Mission

(Anglican) Hospital of the Epiphany at Fauaabu, Malaita. After World War II, a nurses' school was established at Fauaabu, with between 20 and 30 nurses enrolled each year in four-year courses.

Central Hospital in Honiara trained dressers, with the course increased from 18 months to three years in 1953. The only entry specification was that trainees had to be able to read and write. By the end of 1954, four dressers had graduated as medical assistants.[51] The Nurses' Training Centre was opened at Central Hospital by High Commissioner Gutch on 13 December 1956; it was intended to supplement the output of nurses from the training centre at Fauaabu. The Central Hospital system was renamed the Hospital Training School, providing three-year courses for nurses. Male graduates were called medical assistants (what had been the male dresser or orderly positions) (Table 6.2).

The protectorate's Nurses and Midwives Ordinance was passed in 1958. Amended in 1961, this allowed the temporary registration of qualified nurses and midwives, until a formal meeting of the Nurses and Midwives Board could be arranged. The change enabled nurses arriving from overseas to begin work immediately.[52] The Central Hospital School of Nursing continued to train local nurses, with the program funded by the United Nations Children's Fund (UNICEF) and the World Health Organization. In 1970, six women and nine men (one from the New Hebrides) passed the BSIP Nurses and Midwives Board final examination. A new nurses' hostel was completed with accommodation for 32 and a flat for the 'house mother'. In 1974, there were 57 students in local training, with three student nurses, and three registered nurses training overseas.[53]

The School of Nursing at SINU was established in 2011, beginning with a Bachelor of Nursing, with a postgraduate diploma course added in 2017. Two years later, the annual intake was 75, which was large enough to replace the number of nurses lost to retirement or who left the Solomons to work overseas, mainly in Vanuatu.[54]

---

51   *BSIP AR* 1953–54: 29.
52   *BSIP AR* 1961–62: 50; *BSIP NS*, 31 December 1956, 31 January 1961; Fox 1958: 248–54; BSIP 1960–69: *BSIP Legislative Council Debates*, 31 May 1961. Nurse training continued at the Anglican Fauaabu Hospital and the Methodist hospital at Munda. Fauaabu nurses were considered the same standard as those trained by the BSIP Government. The SSEC also ran a training course for midwives at Nafinua.
53   *BSIP AR* 1970: 62; 1974: 80.
54   Faculty of Nursing, Medicine & Health Science, SINU website, available from: www.sinu.edu.sb/fnmhs/; Bau 2019b.

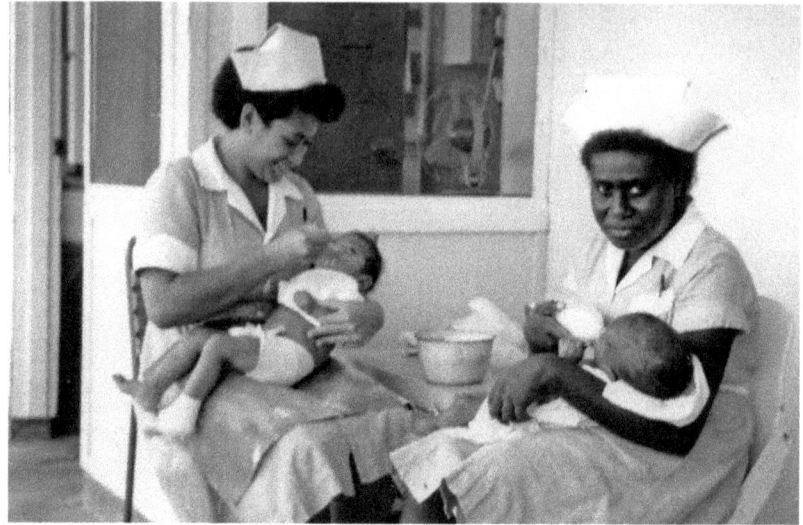

Plate 7.11 Nurses at Central Hospital in the 1960s.
Source: Alan Lindley Collection, in Clive Moore Collection.

Tertiary study

From the 1950s, there was a realisation that Solomon Islanders needed to be trained in specialist post-secondary education and that Honiara could become a regional training hub for Pacific students. The various training institutions attracted their share of students from other Pacific territories, and a few from Asia. These students helped alter the nature of Honiara, making it more cosmopolitan, as well as training Solomon Islanders in a variety of occupations. Overall, the training also improved the ability of all students to be articulate citizens of modern Pacific nations.

In the years before independence, there was only one university presence in Honiara, a campus of the University of the South Pacific (USP, centred in Suva, Fiji).[55] When the USP opened in 1968, there were eight Solomon Islanders among its first students.[56] The USP Extension Centre in Honiara opened in November 1971, using three temporary buildings. In 1967, it moved to its permanent premises, backing on to the ridges between Chinatown and Lawson Tama. A feature of the building are four

---

55   University of the South Pacific Solomon Islands Centre 1983; 2018: 47, 65–67, 98, 128.
56   In 1971, Sister Mary Emmanuela and Walter Ramo were the first Solomon Islands students to receive the Diploma of Education. Francis Billy Hilly, prime minister in 1993–94, was the first graduate, with a BA in 1973. University of the South Pacific Solomon Islands Centre 1983: 1.

carved posts at the entrance, depicting traditional life and legends from all areas of the nation, and woven matting on the foyer walls. These are in keeping with the overall USP philosophy of cultural preservation and social involvement.[57]

Under a system known as 'Extension Studies', initially, the centre taught introductory and foundation courses and, from 1977, one course within a BA degree. Correspondence materials were used, which were bolstered from August 1974 with innovative voice tutorials using a satellite communication system linked to teachers in Fiji. Tutors also visited from the main campus and travelled to the districts. Extension studies enabled students to begin their tertiary studies while in Honiara or in remote areas of the nation, using paper-based resources backed by attendance at intensive residential schools for short periods in Honiara. The best students went on to study at the Laucala campus in Suva. There were other continuing education courses offered at the Honiara campus—for instance, in-service training for primary schoolteachers, adult education informal discussion groups on economic development, and courses in music, creative writing, dance and drama, *tapa*-making, small business planning, and learning Solomons Pijin (for foreigners). In 1983, there were 106 Solomon Islander full-time undergraduate students studying at the USP in Suva, with 3,957 enrolments in individual extension studies courses. Many Solomon Islanders received their first chance for higher education through the USP centre, which has continued to expand. Discussions began in 2012 to construct a fourth major campus of the university, on land at Domma, west of Honiara, which had been earmarked for a new urban centre. Plans changed and the new campus, financed by the Asian Development Bank, will now be located on land at KGVI. In 2016, USP had the equivalent of 1,701 full-time students in Honiara. Solomon Islands students were the second-largest group on the Laucala campus in Fiji and, overall, Solomon Islanders made up the full-time equivalent of 2,945 students in the USP system, which now has campuses in all its member nations.[58] The USP centre has been instrumental in training vast numbers of Solomon Islanders, and preserving local culture.

---

57   These were carved by Jonathan Taingo and his son Faletau Aeui Taingo from Munda in Western District, Gabriel Fousitau from Malaita District, Frank Haikiu from Bellona, which was then in Central District, and Francis Sufake from Santa Ana in Eastern District. Leckie 2018: 66.
58   *BSIP AR* 1974: 112; *SND*, 16 July 1976, 27 May 1977. These figures are cumulative by course enrolment and do not indicate individual students. My thanks to Jacqui Leckie for providing the recent statistics.

Plate 7.12 A University of the South Pacific graduation ceremony at the Panatina Pavilion in Honiara, 2009. Vice-Chancellor Professor Rajesh Chandra is presenting a student with his degree.
Source: Clive Moore Collection.

The Solomon Islands College of Higher Education (SICHE) was formed in 1984 under an Act of parliament that amalgamated all post-secondary government educational institutions in Honiara. The initial SICHE schools were Education, Finance and Administration, Marine and Fisheries Studies, Nursing and Health Studies, Industrial Development, and Natural Resources. In 2008, the Act was amended to include the School of Tourism and Hospitality, and any other schools as needed.

Sir Nathaniel Waena, a former government minister and governor-general, became chairman of the SICHE board in 2011, and was charged with guiding the transition to university status. Two years later, SINU took over from SICHE and became the Pacific Islands' newest university, with Dr Glynn Galo as the first vice-chancellor. There are now six faculties: Business and Tourism; Agriculture, Fisheries and Forestry; Nursing, Medicine and Health Services; Science and Technology; Education and Humanities; and Distance and Flexible Learning. The second vice-chancellor, Fiji-born Professor Ganesh Chand, who was appointed in 2019, fell out with the staff and government in 2020. Dr Jack Maebuta is now acting vice-chancellor.

SINU is designed to encompass trade courses, tertiary preparation level, and community and academic area-specific certificates and bachelors' degrees, with plans to extend to postgraduate study. Short courses are also available in executive management, clerical office support, information and technology, hospitality, and marine and ports. The majority of the 2020 cohort (1,257, 65 per cent of whom were male) was in Honiara, with the main outreach to Buala, Gizo, and Munda. There were 1,835 students enrolled during the first half of 2020, before the COVID-19 pandemic restricted distance enrolments in four centres (including Auki) and caused SINU to close temporarily.[59]

The SINU teaching functions were well entrenched in the SICHE days. However, as with similar upgrading of educational institutions overseas, creating a research agenda, culture, and staff development to meet the requirements of a university remains a long-term project. SINU offers vocational training courses, as do some church groups, nongovernmental organisations (NGOs), and community-based organisations. There were two other tertiary education developments during the 2000s: the University of Papua New Guinea proposed establishing a distance education campus in Honiara (which fizzled out); and Don Bosco School became the Don Bosco Technical Institute, in partnership with the Australian-Pacific Technical College (an Australian aid initiative), offering construction and automotive apprenticeship training at certificate level.

---

59 Information from Dr Jack Maebuta, Doris Rilifia, Martin Otto, and Estee Lonamei, SINU, March and April 2020.

Plate 7.13 Gold medal graduates and two of the medal sponsors at the graduation ceremony for the Solomon Islands National University, 2018.
Source: Office of the Vice-Chancellor, SINU.

Plate 7.14 The senior executive of the Solomon Islands National University at the graduation ceremony, 2018.
Source: Office of the Vice-Chancellor, SINU.

7. BUILDING SOCIETY AND THE NATION

Women in Honiara

Another aspect of the changes in Honiara has been the expansion of the role of women, in education and employment, and as integral citizens in the modern nation. Women began to take up paid employment in the districts and Honiara during the 1950s and 1960s. They also began to be employed in the public service during the 1960s and 1970s, and in other specialised occupations, such as nursing, teaching, the malaria education project, and in hotels, stores, and banks. There were concerted government and church efforts to involve women in education and decision-making. While there should not be too much positive gloss put on this—given the ingrained sexism of many Solomon Islands men and the very few women who are ever elected to political office or climb high in the public service—there were changes taking place that affected the roles of women.

Plate 7.15 Honiara Women's Club, 1962.
Source: *BSIP AR* (1961–62: 48).

In their introductory chapter to *Being the First*, Ruth Basi Afia-Maetala and Alice Aruhe`eta Pollard credit three factors with changing the future of women in Solomon Islands. The first was the mainstreaming of girls' education from the 1960s. The second was the Girl Guides movement. Guiding, established in the 1950s, became an effective and efficient way of training young girls as future leaders:

Guiding provided an opportunity for girls to do things that might otherwise have been condemned, at those times, as masculine activities. For example, Girl Guides were involved in flag raising ceremonies and camping. Guiding was then used in colonial days to help young girls build self-esteem and confidence in themselves within a male dominated society.[60]

In the 1960s, there were 4,000 Guides and Brownies in Solomon Islands. The movement encouraged girls to be involved in activities outside their homes and schools. They learnt leadership and began to feel comfortable in the public sphere.

The third change suggested is the development of Women's Clubs—an exercise in 'colonial feminism', which became a regular feature of urban and village life in the 1960s. The clubs were introduced by the South Pacific Commission to give advice on cooking, sewing by hand and with machines, and child welfare. They were enlivened by community singing. The first club began in Honiara on 15 May 1961, with club rooms opened in November that year. Judy Godfrey from Volunteer Services Overseas arrived to teach women sewing, cookery, child welfare, and English. The South Pacific Commission conducted the first women's leadership courses in Honiara and Gizo during June 1963.[61]

In 1966, there were 80 Women's Clubs throughout the BSIP. So many new clubs formed that a system of registration was established. The Anglican Church's Mothers' Union and the SDA's Dorcas groups augmented the Women's Clubs, which were aimed at providing outreach by women to the poor and needy, and included Christian leadership training. Most Catholic mission stations throughout the islands had a Women's Club, whose members focused their energies on domestic skills, childcare, and gardening. A government-sponsored Women's Interest Officer was appointed in 1964, particularly to facilitate the Women's Clubs.[62] These women's groups engendered a degree of self-empowerment. All Christian denominations included women in their activities and, although one can be critical that these were domestic leadership roles, in the long term, they altered the place of Solomon Islands women. Organisations such as the Young Women's Christian Association (YWCA), which began in Honiara in 1975, were also influential. The YWCA established a kindergarten

---

60   Afia-Maetala and Pollard 2009: 15.
61   *BSIP NS*, 30 May 1961, 30 June 1961, 30 November 1961, 31 May 1963; Afia-Maetala and Pollard 2009: 16.
62   *BSIP AR* 1966: 51; *BSIP NS*, 31 August 1968; Afia-Maetala and Pollard 2009: 17.

and hostel at Rove in 1978. The hostel, upgraded in the early 1980s, enabled young women to live separately but safely away from their families while working in Honiara. The YWCA also provided film nights and sewing classes. There was a sense within the organisation of women's sharing and ownership of urban space, which continues. The South Pacific Commission was also instrumental in the 1960s in introducing leadership courses for women, and a women's hostel was built using British Government funds, providing accommodation for women attending the teachers' training college.[63]

The government's Women's Interest Office was begun to provide training programs for women, to assist the circulation of information, and to train women to participate in leadership and decision-making. After independence in 1978, this translated into the Women and Development Division within the Ministry of Women, Youth, Sports and Recreation. Much of the funding came from overseas aid organisations, which was aimed at improving participation by rural and urban women in the modern nation. Solomon Islands Women's Week began in 1977 and the Solomon Islands National Council of Women was founded in 1983.[64]

Plate 7.16 Selina Tale (YWCA-SI Kindergarten Supervisor), Christina Maezama (General Secretary, 1980–92), and Vera Sautehi (Extension Officer) outside the YWCA premises at Rove, Honiara, in the early 1980s.
Source: Feary and Lai (2012: 42).

63 Feary and Lai 2012: 31–32, 36, 39; Afia-Maetala and Pollard 2009: 16–17.
64 Pollard 2000: 83–91.

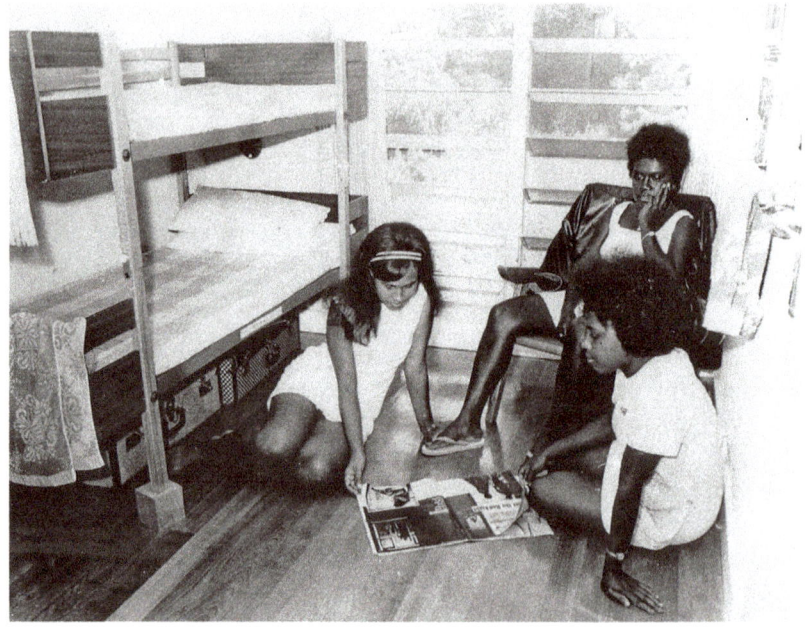

Plate 7.17 A YWCA hostel room, probably in the early 1980s.
Source: Feary and Lai (2012: 49).

Plate 7.18 The YWCA kindergarten in the early 1960s.
Source: Feary and Lai (2012: 49).

There was also a fourth change—a precursor of the mainstreaming of girls' education in the 1960s. In the 1950s, young Solomons women began to go overseas for education. They received scholarships for secondary education and training as primary schoolteachers and nurses in Papua New Guinea, Fiji, New Zealand, and the United Kingdom. These women were provided with world-class training and the certainty that they could succeed when they returned home. Even those who struggled scholastically returned with assurance that they understood something of the outside world.

Census data on women in Honiara are not always uniform enough to use for longitudinal comparisons. A breakdown of the male and female populations of Honiara in 1959 (Table 4.1) indicates there were 827 women: 464 Melanesians, 162 Europeans, 127 Chinese, 48 Polynesians, 11 Fijians, six Gilbertese, and nine others. Indigenous females (including girls) made up 62 per cent of the town's population. Given that they lived in close proximity and most went daily to the market, they must all have known each other, at least by sight.[65] Because the 1970 census included Honiara within Guadalcanal District, it is not possible to establish an ethnic male/female ratio for Honiara, although overall there were 3,954 females and 7,237 males resident in the town.[66] As noted in an earlier chapter, most of the Solomon Islander adults in Honiara from the 1960s to the 1980s were aged from their late teens to 40 years.

The uneven sex ratio in Honiara altered markedly between the 1970s and the end of the century, reflecting the increasing importance of the locally born population in comparison with the male-dominated immigrant population of the early decades. Another characteristic of these years is that, in 1976, more than three in every four people living in Honiara had been born elsewhere. A decade later, the Honiara-born children were more obvious within the population, although by 1999, there had been another wave of migration, with 63 per cent born outside Honiara.[67] Solomon Islands women in Honiara reflected these proportions.

There were exceptional women who rose to the top during these years, although they were few in number. One was Lilly Valahoe Ogatina from Kia, Isabel Island, who reached national prominence in 1965 through her

---

65   BSIP 1961: 51, 57, 60; Tedder 1966: 37.
66   SIG 1999b: 112. Table 4.3 shows the breakdown of the Melanesian male population in Honiara in 1970. See also Table 9.1.
67   SIG 1999b: 22.

election to the Legislative Council, defeating four male candidates to become its first (and only) female member. Her father was George Rubaha, an Anglican catechist, and her mother was Lusuai. One of the first Solomon Islands women to be sent by the government to study overseas, Lilly spent seven years at Queen Victoria School in New Zealand. She returned to begin primary teaching at St Hilda's School, Bungana; then, on 2 January 1966, she married Aubrey Poznanski, a part-Polish, part-Gilbertese member of the Marine Department. Their first child, Aubrey Teaito, was born late in 1966, followed by a daughter, Audrey. Two children joined the family as adoptees.

Plate 7.19 Lilly Valahoe Ogatini Poznanski was a role model for women in the 1960s and 1970s.

Born in 1942 on Isabel Island, she was one of the first women to be educated overseas, at Queen Victoria School for Māori Girls in New Zealand. She became a member of the Legislative Council and represented the Ngosi Ward on the Honiara Town Council. She died in 1989.

Source: Courtesy of Brian Christie, in Clive Moore Collection.

In 1967, Lilly Poznanski stood unsuccessfully for the Honiara seat in the Legislative Council, after which she resumed her teaching career at the Government Primary School in Honiara. In September 1969, she was elected unopposed to the Nggosi Ward of the Honiara Town Council. The next year, she became Assistant Clerk to the Governing Council, while helping part-time in her husband's garage business. In 1978, she became Chief Administrative Officer with the Ministry of Foreign Trade, Industry and Labour—making her the most highly paid indigenous woman in the Solomons. Throughout, she kept close links with her rural kin and was a traditional leader of her Zabana people in their efforts to reconnect with their Logahaza origins—a link that had been ruptured in the late nineteenth century because of slave-raiding. Poznanski was the only woman to achieve high political office during the protectorate years. A role model for all women and very visible in Honiara in the 1960s and 1970s, she died in 1989.[68]

---

68   In 1984, she unsuccessfully contested the West Isabel seat. *BSIP NS*, 30 September 1958, 31 January 1964, 1 April 1965, 15 June 1965, 7 January 1966, 7 May 1967, 30 September 1969, 31 October 1970; Afia-Maetala and Pollard 2009: 22; Moore 2013c: entry for Poznanski; *Melanesian News* [hereinafter *MN*], 9 February 1977.

Few had Poznanski's education and ability, although it would be churlish not to name others: Catherine Adifaka, Angeline Merle Aqorau, Ella Bugotu, Betty Fakarii, Hilda Kari, Margaret Kenilorea, Hilda Kii, Ruth Liloqula, Junelyn Pikacha, Alice Aruhe`eta Pollard, and Phyllis Taloikwai. Even in the 2020s, only a very small number of women have made progress as politicians, businesswomen, and public servants. Nevertheless, Honiara women have been remarkably resilient in their ability to earn an income. They help their families by selling produce on the roadside, ensuring extra cash to feed and clothe their children, and fulfil social obligations. Quietly, they go about maintaining family life, and bridging village and urban life.

Plate 7.20 Women selling barbecued fish at Honiara International Airport—Henderson Field, 2004.
Source: Clive Moore Collection.

Plate 7.21 White River resident Ellen Angofia (centre) selling tie-dyed lap-laps in 1998 at a cultural event.
Source: Clive Moore Collection.

Plate 7.22 A woman selling *bilums* in Honiara, 2010.
Source: Clive Moore Collection.

Children in Honiara

In the 1950s, few Solomon Islander children attended school. Most expatriate children received their schooling overseas, only returning for holidays, and the majority of Solomon Islanders in Honiara were either young single youths and men or those who had left their families in their home village. Slowly, Honiara became a town where families lived. Some children went to kindergarten and school, attended sabbath schools and church services, and joined sporting teams and youth groups such as the SDA's Pathfinder Clubs and the Methodist Boys' Brigade. They also became Scouts, Guides, Cubs, and Brownies, just as they would in any modern Western urban setting. This view needs to be tempered against the number of children in Honiara who moved with their parents from rural areas and often remained illiterate. If they attended school, it was only for a few years of primary education. Even if literate, many remained barely numerate. It is a matter of parental motivation and finances. When there is barely enough money to sustain life, money for education, school uniforms, and youth groups is a luxury some can never afford. This has repercussions all through their adult lives.

Children mixed at school. Photographs from the 1970s to the 1990s indicate the beginnings of multiracial education. Honiara in its early decades was a safer place than it is today. Although they usually socialised in local areas, children could wander to friends' homes to play. Settlements were often made up of people from a single language group and children lived in extended families in the same way as occurred in villages in the districts and, later, provinces.

The children of the elite, like their parents, bridged village and urban societies. They were members of urban families who adopted Western customs like birthday parties and commissioned photographic portraits. Jully Makini was a Honiara child of the 1960s and 1970s. Her description of the carefree days of a Honiara childhood is one of the few published. Her parents had moved the family from Gizo to Honiara, where her father was working in the Customs Department. There were four primary schools during the early 1960s: Chung Wah School, Honiara Government Primary School at 'Namba 3', St John's School at Rove, and Woodford School. Students sat an examination at the end of Year 6 and, if they did well, were awarded scholarships to attend schools in Australia and New Zealand, or local secondary schools. For the majority, education ended at Year 6.

The better-off families bought toys for their children, but like children everywhere, they always played anyway, using everyday objects. They joined youth groups, participated in interschool sports, graduated to more general teams, and attended sabbath schools at the various denominational churches.[69] Makini remembers that most families were new to Honiara:

> Honiara was not busy or crowded, just a few trucks, cars and motorbikes and bicycles. The Government machinery worked well during those years. The town council workers disposed of rubbish from the residences, the houses were repaired and painted by carpenters, and plumbers fixed pipes and unblocked toilets—these were Public Works Department workers. The police carried out their duties faithfully; they were on the beat, always walking two-by-two whether up Lengakiki or Vavaya Ridge or along Mendana Avenue.[70]

Fathers worked and mothers stayed at home and took care of their children. There was intermixing of children from different backgrounds—Melanesian, Polynesian, Gilbertese, Chinese, and European—and they mixed languages while they played:

> Children everywhere have no difficulties making friends with others. Even though the language of communication was Pidgin English [Tok Pisin], through this friendship children from Malaita spoke Roviana. These close friends are still fluent. It is worth noting the early families who resided in this area [opposite the present Central Market]—Osifelos, Tolilius, Takos, Lotis, Pabulus, Buchanans, Dagas, Richardsons, Bosos, Kaukus, Mazinis, Finaus, Hieless, Bisilis, Ririas, Martins and Chottus.[71]

---

69   Makini 2015: 225.
70   ibid., 222–23.
71   ibid., 223.

7. BUILDING SOCIETY AND THE NATION

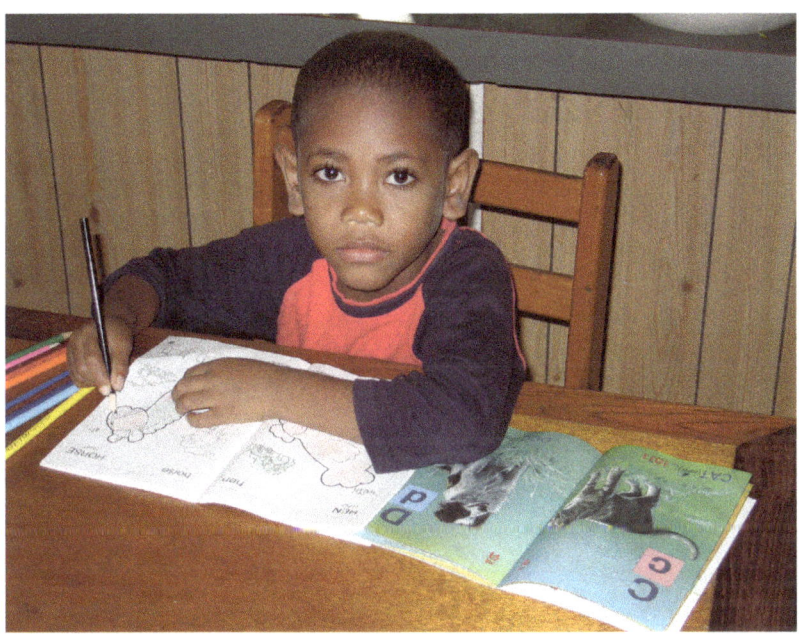

Plate 7.23 Randall Sukumana preparing for his kindergarten class, at Skyline, 2006.
Source: Clive Moore Collection.

Plate 7.24 Woodford School students, 1976.
Source: Transform Aqorau Collection.

Plate 7.25 Girl Guides in Honiara, 2006.
Source: Clive Moore Collection.

One of the hardest areas to assess is the changing role of children and youths in Honiara. In 1976, the 'child'[72] proportion of Honiara's population was 6,037 girls and 8,905 boys, and in 1987, it was 13,120 girls and 17,293 boys. The ethnic division was about 93 per cent Melanesian, with a Malaitan majority. There were 2,724 households in 1976 and 4,317 in 1986.[73] The statistics are clear: the national fertility rate is declining, from an average of 4.8 births per woman in 2000, to 3.36 in 2014, and Honiara's rates are a little below the national average.[74]

There were more children outside the school system than inside. The level of illiteracy has always been frighteningly high. In recent decades, Honiara has always had a high proportion of teenagers, many of them 'dropouts' from school with little chance of finding employment. They have perfected the art of being *masta lius*—wanderers in the urban environment, living largely off their wits and their families. Girls are more likely to assist their mothers with gardening and marketing. Some operate roadside stalls, selling betel nuts and single cigarettes, eking out a living on the poverty line. Youth issues are some of the most significant in Honiara and the most socially combustible elements in urban life. (This theme will be taken up again in Chapter 10.)

---

72 Adulthood was not until 21 years of age.
73 SIG 1988b: 'Report I (Supplement): Summary of Population by Socio-Economic Characteristics, Final Results', pp. 117–21.
74 BSIP 1970: 74, 81.

7. BUILDING SOCIETY AND THE NATION

Plate 7.26 Children at Vura School, 2007.
Source: Clive Moore Collection.

Trade unions and labour activism

Not all education was through formal institutions, and those with employment have had to learn to understand employee–employer relations and workers' rights. Some Solomon Islanders became interested in trade unions and labour activism as a career. Leaders often attended formal training overseas, but for the rank and file, becoming aware of workers' rights was a slow process. This was all part of raising levels of consciousness among future citizens of the nation. Social awareness of individual and collective rights began to challenge the previous overwhelming power of the government and employers. The most significant early Solomon Islander trade unionists were Joses Taungengo Tuhanuku from Bellona Island and Bartholomew (Bart) Ulufa`alu from Langalanga Lagoon, Malaita.

After the war, although the protectorate developed a system of local government, there were no trade unions or political parties. Solomon Islands workers were forbidden to strike by the terms of the indenture contracts under which most of them worked. In 1945, indenture was limited to one-year contracts, and it was abolished two years later. Pressure exerted on the labour market through Maasina Rule was part of the explanation for the demise of the indenture system. However, the change in Papua New Guinea from indenture contracts to agreements occurred at much the same time, and international labour conventions are said to have been the primary reason for these changes. In 1946, steps were taken to legalise trade unions; then, in late 1960 and early 1961, there was an indigenous movement to form a union on Malaita among port and plantation workers, although the first formal trade unions were formed by the BSIP Department of Labour.[75] The British Solomon Islands General Workers Union was registered in 1961 and had considerable success during 1962–63 in negotiating wage increases for government and plantation workers. As part of this, for two weeks in October–November 1962, labourers and classified government workers stopped work over wage disputes and were joined in sympathy by employees of several commercial companies. On 6 November, the government agreed to improve wages and conditions. Those who refused to return to work were repatriated to their home village.

The union had a substantial membership by 1963, when it was split (by the Department of Labour) into the British Solomon Islands Building and General Workers' Union (BSIB&GWU) and the British Solomon Islands Plantation and Farmers' Association (BSIP&FA), both of which were registered in September 1964. Another union, the British Solomon Islands Ports and Copra Workers' Union (BSIP&CWU), was formed in 1963–64, with Joel Kikolo as secretary and Johnson Olisikulu as treasurer. In September 1964, the BSIB&GWU began negotiations for further wage increases, requesting a basic wage of £15 per month (a nearly 100 per cent increase). On 23 March 1965, an agreement was reached for an intermediate wage of £8/15/6 per month (6/9 d. per day), which the union accepted. This was followed a week later by an unofficial strike among government labourers and classified workers. In Honiara, 760 workers, including several hundred private-sector and government workers, went on strike, while 230 government workers continued performing their jobs.

---

75 Bennett 1993: 162; Frazer 1990: 201–2.

The strike spread for a few days to Yandina, Munda, and Gizo. Nineteen men were arrested, charged either with not maintaining essential services or with unlawful assembly. They received prison sentences of between six weeks and three months. The Honiara strike continued until 15 April.

The government was aware that labour issues were becoming important and leading to urban volatility. A conference was held from 29 October to 1 November 1965 between the BSIP&CWU and the BSIB&GWU, although no firm decisions were made because neither union had any subscribed members. Both unions went into temporary suspension. Olisikulu was sent by the BSIP Government to attend the British Trades Unions' Congress in January 1966, then studied in London and Scotland to learn the duties of shop stewards and union clerks. On his return to Honiara, Olisikulu organised the amalgamation of the two unions into one, the British Solomon Islands Workers' Union (BSIWU), which did not last.[76] After the BSIP&CWU, BSIB&GWU, and BSIWU were liquidated, there was no further union development in the second half of the 1960s. The only additions were the teachers' associations that were formed in various districts during the 1960s; the Malaita Teachers' Association was formed in March 1966.

Another strike occurred in April 1965. As Deputy Chief of Police Alan Lindley remembered it, there was labour agitation based at the Kukum Labour Line. Having been told of the activity, and unable to locate Chief of Police David Morgan, Lindley left Rove headquarters and drove to Central Police Station. The area behind the station (where the barracks are today) was almost opposite the old power station, which was staffed mainly by Fijians, who Lindley believed to be part of the discontent. He found several Solomon Islanders sitting outside the wire fence, which, given the gap underneath as it passed over Cruz Creek, made potential access to the power station easy. He stared them down and they moved on, then he returned to the police station, locating Senior Sergeant Gina, after which they both proceeded to the Kukum Labour Line. They confronted a Malaitan dressed in a customary manner and brandishing a club, whom they arrested and took back to Central Police Station, where he was charged with 'conduct likely to cause a breach of the peace'. Next, about 200 Solomon Islanders marched down Mendana Avenue to Central Police Station, demanding the man be released. Lindley, Morgan, District Commissioner Bill Wright, and Ray Viggor, head of the new

---

76 *BSIP NS*, 7 November 1966.

Riot Squad, confronted the crowd as it passed by the Treasury building. The crowd refused to disperse, which led to tear gas shells being fired. There were no arrests because the situation was judged to be too volatile. About three days later, the Riot Squad turned back another crowd that had crossed the bridge over the Mataniko River at Chinatown and was stopped near the new library. These incidents were Honiara's first large-scale civil unrest.[77] Another strike occurred on 6 August 1965 when 65 government employees stopped work at Tulagi to protest their pay and work conditions.

The next union formed was the British Solomon Islands General Workers' Union, begun by Peter Salaka in July 1971, which achieved little and had its registration cancelled at the beginning of 1974.[78] Three other unions were created in 1974–75, none of which had full-time officers: the Solomon Islands Public Servants' Association, the Government Non-Established Workers' Union, and the Guadalcanal Plains General Workers' Union. The first long-term trade union initiated by Solomon Islanders was the Solomon Islands General Workers' Union (SIGWU), later known as the Solomon Islands National Union of Workers (SINUW), which was registered on 15 July 1975.[79] Employers largely ignored the unions. Another problem was that public servants were forbidden from taking an active role in any political party or association, which silenced many of the best-educated voices.

Bart Ulufa`alu, born in 1939, attended Catholic primary schools and Aruligo Secondary School. He studied at the University of Papua New Guinea between 1970 and 1974, where he received a BA in Economics and served as president of the Students' Representative Council. He returned to the Solomons and set up the Rafea and Kwakuna Co-operative Development Society. In 1975, he founded the SIGWU and served as its general secretary for a year. Viewed by the government as a radical, he was blocked from joining the public service and instead chose parliamentary and business paths, establishing the Nationalists Party to contest the 1976 national election for the Legislative Assembly. He was elected and formed the Coalition Opposition Group, which was later renamed the Nationalists Democratic Party. After independence in July 1978, Ulufa`alu became leader of the opposition in the new National

---

77 Bellam 1970: 87.
78 *BSIP AR* 1974: 23; *BSIP NS*, 15 August 1971; Tuhanuku 1983: 120.
79 *BSIP NS*, 15 June 1965; Tuhanuku 1983: 120.

Parliament, and finance minister in the 1981–84 Mamaloni Government. He lost his seat in 1984, spent some time in business ventures, and returned to parliament in 1988, resigning in 1990 to work as a business adviser for the government and in private enterprise. He was re-elected in 1993 and served as prime minister from June 1997 until deposed in a coup in June 2000. Ulufa`alu died in 2007.[80]

Plate 7.27 Bartholomew Ulufa`alu—trade union leader and, later, politician and prime minister—in the 1980s.
Source: Clive Moore Collection.

Plate 7.28 Joses Taungengo Tuhanuku—trade union leader and, later, politician, cabinet minister, and leader of the opposition—in 1981.
Source: Anna Craven Collection, in Clive Moore Collection.

Joses Tuhanuku, born in 1952, attended Su`u primary and secondary schools and KGVI, before studying at the Papua New Guinea University of Technology in Lae and The Australian National University. At various times, he worked as a secondary schoolteacher and as a lecturer at the SICHE. In 1975, he assisted Ulufa`alu in founding the SIGWU and the following year replaced Ulufa`alu as general secretary. A scholarship enabled him to train with the Danish International Development Agency from February 1977 until June 1978. In 1988, Tuhanuku was one of

---

80 SS, 29 May 2007; 'Notes on Contributors' in Larmour 1979: 257; Moore 2004a: 3–19, 61–62, 93–136; STT, 26 July 1978; SND, 9 July 1976; Ulufa`alu 1977, 1983.

the founders of the Solomon Islands Labour Party and was elected to parliament the next year. He served in parliament during 1989–97 and 2002–06, held several ministries, and was also for a period leader of the opposition. He remained a constant force in denouncing corruption.[81]

Tuhanuku described the first strike involving SIGWU as arising from a dispute with the British Solomon Islands Ports Authority. A log of claims for stevedores and an application for recognition of the union was served on the Ports Authority on 15 July 1975. The authority stonewalled the union and, after inactivity, a strike was called on 14 August. The Ports Authority then evicted the striking workers, whom the union rehoused at Central Market for some days, which brought the issue to the attention of the Honiara public and raised unionist and other worker support. Union representatives met with Chief Minister Mamaloni, who ordered the Ports Authority to re-employ the men. The union called off the strike and the wages claim was put to a tribunal. Workers whose contracts had expired were repatriated to their home island. One upshot of this was the creation of a new organisation: the Solomon Islands Federation of Employers, which Tuhanuku says was not legally registered under the *Trade Union Act*.[82]

Further negotiations failed. A general strike was called after the Christmas break and, in the meantime, Mamaloni became embroiled in the Letcher Mint affair.[83] He resigned and cabinet was dissolved, although after a new election, Mamaloni returned to power with a new cabinet chosen from the former opposition members. This manoeuvre did little for the credibility of Mamaloni or his government. On 9 December, the government agent for Central District (the old district commissioner position) refused the union's application to hold a public assembly and procession on 11 December, the intention of which was to present a petition to the chief minister. The issues were the log of claims and a request to delay internal self-government until after the mid-1976 general election. Permission was granted for a public meeting outside Central Market, at which the crowd deputised six men to present the petition to Mamaloni.[84] When the delegation left for the chief minister's office, a crowd of several thousand followed. The meeting went ahead, but when the police were

---

81 See 'Member Biographies: Hon. Joses Taungenga Tuhanuku', available from: www.parliament.gov.sb/memberfiles/memberbiogs/HonTuhanuku.pdf.
82 Tuhanuku 1983: 120–21.
83 The unauthorised manufacture of coins to commemorate self-government.
84 Ulufa'alu, Tuhanuku, Paul Belande, James Maefa'alu, Frank Tafea, and Charles Lesimaoma.

unable to make arrests among the crowd, they chose instead to arrest the six delegates. Each was found guilty in the Magistrate's Court and given a £40 fine with the option of a three-month prison sentence. Four paid their fines, while Ulufa`alu and James Maefa`alu (president of the Government Non-Established Workers' Union) chose prison.

While Ulufa`alu was in prison, one of the union officials decided to organise a demonstration, on 2 January 1976, against self-government without a new national election. The march started at Central Market, then moved towards the governor's office to present a petition. When the marchers reached Central Police Station, the police attempted to halt them and, failing, fired tear gas over their heads. The small demonstration became a riot, shop windows, cars, and offices were damaged, and the gas drifted on to the watching crowd. Nine demonstrators were arrested and were sent to prison for four to nine months. Two days after the riot, Ulufa`alu and Maefa`alu were released. In the ensuing negotiations, most employers, including the government, recognised the union.[85] When Ulufa`alu entered the Legislative Assembly as the Member for East Honiara in the mid-1976 general election, he was replaced as president and general secretary of the SIGWU with Joses Tuhanuku. Ulufa`alu remained an adviser.

Another setback came in October 1977 when the registrar of trade unions suspended the SIGWU for mismanagement. This was resolved in December, although many companies used the situation to withdraw their recognition, refusing to negotiate any log of claims. The office was closed and membership dropped from around 600 to three hundred. Ulufa`alu worked to rebuild the SIGWU, as did Tuhanuku on his return from Denmark, although the union had lost momentum and the nation was preoccupied with the lead-up to independence in July 1978. Membership had risen to 6,000 by the end of that year. Tuhanuku's strategy had been to concentrate on building membership among rural workers on Guadalcanal Plains, which slowed union growth among Honiara's wage-earners. On 27 April 1980, the union's name was altered to the Solomon Islands National Union of Workers (SINUW) to signify its national outlook. Nine strikes occurred that year over gaining recognition from employers and, by the end of 1980, membership was around 10,000, or half the total number of Solomon Islanders in paid employment.[86]

85 Tuhanuku 1983: 123–26.
86 ibid., 127–28.

There were other strike-like movements outside the formal trade unions. In 1991, the nation's doctors who were members of the Solomon Islands Medical Association began a work-to-rule dispute, refusing afterhours work because of longstanding disagreements with the government. To compensate, they opened a medical clinic in Honiara's Chinatown. Better terms and conditions were eventually negotiated during 1993 by Sir Dr Nathan Kere, the new Permanent Secretary of the Ministry of Health and Medical Services.

The public service in the 1950s and 1960s

Many expatriate public servants arrived in the 1950s as part of the transfer of the WPHC from Suva to Honiara. Even so, the expatriate population of around 150 was very small. Those hired in Britain were a little shell-shocked when they reached isolated Honiara, as were others hired from Australia and New Zealand. Living in Honiara in the 1950s was like Pacific time travel back to the 1930s. New Zealand journalist Judy Tudor joined the staff of the *Pacific Islands Monthly* in 1942, becoming assistant editor in 1947. Her articles from the 1950s are memorable, and she was not kind to Honiara or its public servants. Tudor described Honiara as 'the end of the line'. She said the best Pacific public servants were in Suva, Port Moresby, and Rabaul. Those in Honiara were the leftovers:

> A large number of those who come within the latter category are female. Anyone who can pick out words on a typewriter with two fingers can get a job in Honiara as a typist and receive anything up to £15 per week for the effort.
>
> Amongst some of these people—but of course, by no means all, responsibility is thought to end with the receipt of a pay envelope and they are more concerned with acquiring a reputation for drinking their whiskey straight than for hard work.
>
> Although the proportion of tee-total residents is small in any Pacific Island, Honiara is the only place where I have seen a civil servant the worse for liquor in the middle of the working day; and the only place where I have seen female civil servants regularly drink to excess in a public bar. Maybe there is not a bigger proportion of dipsomaniacs in Honiara than elsewhere—maybe it is because they are less fussy about the business that there seems to be more. The behaviour of some of these people could not be

tolerated elsewhere where deportation is still an effective weapon in the hands of the Administration, and probably it will not be tolerated much longer in Honiara.[87]

Although drinking continued to be a major pastime, the standard of the public servants improved. Even though there were still plenty of Quonset huts around and lots of Marston matting being used for ingenious purposes, by the end of the 1960s, Honiara was no longer a town built solely from leftover American war materials. The public service was well established and many of its members tried hard to train Solomon Islanders to achieve independence from Britain. Nevertheless, localisation was slow, and Solomon Islander public servants were outside the union movement. Introducing policies to replace expatriate government employees with suitably qualified Solomon Islanders was first debated by the Legislative Council in February 1963. In that year, 52 Solomon Islanders received promotion to higher grades in the public service.

The size of the public service grew with the needs of the expanded BSIP government departments. Between 1953 and 1976, the addition of the WPHC staff inflated the size of Honiara's public service.[88] By 1971, there were 1,725 public servants, 71.6 per cent of whom were Solomon Islanders, and most were based in Honiara. The public service decreased in size during the first half of the 1970s (as the WPHC wound down) with a slight increase in the proportion of Solomon Islanders (74.6 per cent of 1,569 positions in 1974). There was still a core of high-level public servants who were part of Her Majesty's Overseas Civil Service: 310 in 1971, 315 in 1972, 324 in 1973, 279 in 1974, and 273 in 1975. Localisation was under way through increasing general education training in the BSIP via the new institutions and in-service job training, supervision and management training within departments, or through the regional training development unit.[89] Honiara became the base of the decolonisation process by preparing the new workers who would lead the nation when independence came in 1978. There were some who complained that localisation was too slow; Solomon Mamaloni was one of them.

---

87 Tudor 1953b: 75, 77.
88 *BSIP NS*, 15 February 1963, 31 July 1963. The WPHC was abolished in 1976.
89 *BSIP AR* 1974: 140–41.

Another feature of the public service is earlier retirement than is usual in the twenty-first century. Sir Lloyd Maepeza Gina noted that because the BSIP Government had been active in the western Solomons as early as the 1900s, and the missions had introduced literacy soon after, most of Honiara's offices between the 1950s and 1970s were staffed by people from Western District. Early on, the retirement age was 45, but anyone who began in the public service after 1958 could retire at 50 years of age.

The reason behind this, the British colonial officials said, was to help the economy of the rural districts. Therefore, while you were still young and strong, you could go back home and plant your coconuts, and so on, and still be helpful in the rural communities. Some of those who returned home at that time started coconut plantations or ran trading stores. They worked very hard. Others, however, did not do very much at all.[90]

Since then, the normal public service retirement age has increased to 55 years.

***

Just as elsewhere in the Pacific, work, workers' rights, church, education, sport, and changing roles for women are all part of Honiara's invisible infrastructure. The 'soul' of Honiara is not dependant on town planning and rigorous application of regulations. Solomon Islanders are very adaptable when it comes to living in mixed-ethnicity communities and in urban surroundings. They maintain polite etiquette and respect for their extended families and neighbours. Children are everywhere, which is to be expected in a society with such a high birth rate. Where once they gardened together on public lands, the poor and the rich are now more likely only to mingle at church and on the sports field. New arrivals fresh from villages are always sheltered physically and emotionally by the urban members of their families. Village obligations play out in Honiara and there is a sense of equality even while maintaining respect for those who have become the elite. The next chapter examines the operation of the social hierarchy and national politics.

---

90   Gina 2003: 48–49.

8
Stepping-stones to national consciousness

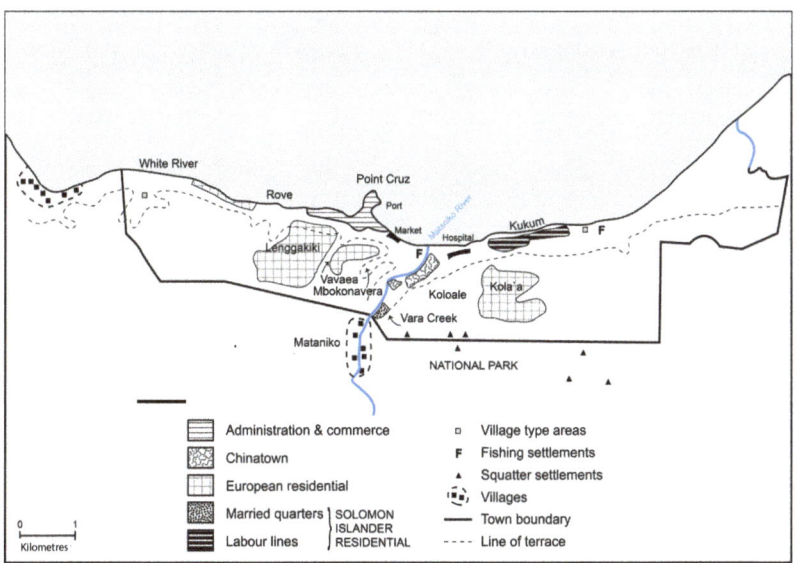

Map 8.1 Honiara in the 1960s, showing the segregated communities.
Source: Based on Bellam (1970). Cartography by Vincent Verheyen.

Honiara has been home to resident commissioners, high commissioners, and governors, then to chief ministers, prime ministers, and governors-general. This chapter begins with the social scene of the colonial European elite, arguing that between the late 1950s and the end of the 1970s, four separate but interlocking 'worlds' developed in Honiara (Figure 0.1). The first two were the worlds of the British administration and the

Chinese business community. Next came Solomon Islanders, the smaller Gilbertese, and Fijian communities, and a scattering of other Pacific Islanders. The Solomon Islanders and other Pacific peoples effectively created a city that was socially theirs and no longer foreign, yet until the mid-1970s, Solomon Islanders had no political or economic power. Alongside these, there was a growing fourth world: a Malaitan community that increasingly grew strong enough to be considered separately from the rest of the Solomon Islander world, while still being part of it. This chapter describes the development of Solomon Islands urban society and its politicisation. One could argue that the pivotal change occurred on 7 July 1978, Independence Day, but it was a longer process as Solomon Islanders took over as leading public servants, politicians, and businesspeople. They began to dominate urban life and to run their own country.[1]

Early Honiara was a socially segregated British colonial town. Economic power rested with Europeans and Chinese, although the Chinese were excluded from the main elite social events. Alan Lindley kept a list of the 194 invitees to the high commissioner's Queen's Birthday ball at Government House in June 1954. Single males predominated. There were 59 couples, seven single women, and two married women with no husbands present. Every name on the list was of European origin. No Chinese or Solomon Islanders were invited, not even the Solomon Islanders who served on the High Commissioner's Advisory Council, nor any of the leading indigenous clergy. The only Solomon Islanders present were servants. The Chinese had their own hierarchy, which operated separately, largely unknown to the Europeans. Solomon Islanders remained at the bottom of the colonial hierarchy, with the rural masses regarded as 'natives'. As outlined in the Introduction, the Maasina Rule movement, which had ended by 1952, gave the British a fright, showing that Solomon Islanders were capable of demanding change. Although Malaita gained a district council and the first government school, this did not mean Malaitan leaders could expect to be invited to soirees at Government House. Another indigenous political grouping, the Moro Movement, based on social, economic, and political improvement, using cooperatives and *kastom* to create a new social order, was active on Guadalcanal. Less threatening than Maasina Rule, Pelise Moro and his movement's followers on Guadalcanal were nevertheless unnerving for the British.

---

1   The phrase that inspired the chapter title comes from Jourdan 1995b.

8. STEPPING-STONES TO NATIONAL CONSCIOUSNESS

Plate 8.1 The High Commissioner's Humber Super Snipe carrying the Duke and Duchess of Kent in 1969, undergoing a traditional challenge from warriors.
Source: Brian Taylor Collection.

An invitation to Government House was considered a social prize. There were also cocktail and dinner party circuits operating both officially and casually among groups of residents. Spearline Wilson, a pre-war Tulagi official and senior protectorate officer in Honiara in 1945–46, was always invited to official events. In 1946, he reported to his wife, who was in Sydney:

> Was at a cocktail dinner on Sunday night, the day the H.C. [High Commissioner] arrived, and at an official dinner on board the 'AMETHYST' yesterday evening. A cocktail party and dinner this evening at the United States Headquarters. Invitation also sent along as a souvenir.[2]

The European elite carried on oblivious to their surroundings. For instance, on the official Queen's Birthday holiday, senior government officers and some civilians would always sign the visitors' book in the guardroom of Government House. The resident commissioner or high commissioner checked the list and there was kudos due for those first to

---

2   UQ FML, Wilson Papers, A.H. Wilson to J.A. Wilson, 16 April 1946.

sign in. Lindley recounted that at cocktail parties in the 1950s men wore black dress trousers, black cummerbunds, and long-sleeved white shirts, but no coats or ties, which was known as 'Red Sea Rig' and was typical of British tropical societies. The women wore long dresses and some even wore knee-length 'mosquito boots', made from soft leather, with a lace inside at the top to pull tight for protection against insect bites.[3] A decade later, the style eccentricities seem to have disappeared, replaced with more modern apparel. Jack Close, part of the commercial elite in Honiara from 1962 to 1967, remembered Honiara as more formal than his previous base at Luganville on Santo Island in the New Hebrides. The Guadalcanal Club was the main centre for entertainment. Expatriate afterwork life seems to have been a whirl of social events:

> Drinks were often taken, by invitation, on the way home from work about 5pm, either at people's houses, the Mendana Hotel or the exclusive Guadalcanal Club on Mendana Avenue. The Cocktail Parties were more formalised and commenced about 7pm, after which came the Dinner Parties, 8.30 or 9pm, which could be casual or formal, one function turning seamlessly into the next.
>
> ... Dinner engagements dress varied from black tie for Government House and official occasions, when ladies wore long gowns and gloves, to shirts and slacks for the casual meals at friends' houses or restaurants. The formal engagements were with government officials and depended on personalities as to how the evenings went. Not one to take refuge in drink, it nevertheless helped sometimes in getting through the evening, and I was taking on board more social alcohol than I wanted to, also smoking more cigarettes than I should. All invitations to dinner had to be reciprocated, so for every night out there was a name to be added to the growing list for our next dinner party.[4]

There was a clear hierarchy among the expatriates. Ron Lawson, whose father was a leading businessman in the late 1940s and 1950s, said 'commercial people were regarded as quite common':

> The senior Administrators were full of their own importance. They had cocktail parties, dinners etc. amongst themselves, wives played bridge and had morning teas. The Administrators generally excluded any natives or commercial people from these

---

3   Information from Alan Lindley, Adelaide, 30 June 2011. See also Tudor 1953a: 121.
4   Close 2011: 199–200, 207.

activities. The only participation the natives enjoyed was as cooks and waiters. Regardless of age, they were always addressed as 'boy'. I played tennis and was told on one occasion by a senior wife that she could not invite me to dinner as my social status was not quite up to it.[5]

Lawson's view is backed up by an incident involving New Zealanders Murray and Linley Chapman, who arrived in Honiara in 1965 on their way to Murray's doctoral research area on the Weather Coast of Guadalcanal. Linley was invited to an afternoon tea that was attended mainly by the wives of administrative officers. It was a stylish affair, and she went well-dressed and wearing Italian sandals, but bare-legged. All the other women were in stockings and high heels—perhaps the reason she was not invited again.[6] Honiara was an isolated colonial outpost that attempted to maintain strict standards, but every now and again there was a hint of something more. For instance, Ken Hay's wife, Susan, is remembered in Honiara's late-colonial history for her party trick: performing the Dance of the Seven Veils. I presume she was not on the afternoon tea invitation list.

Honiara's airport was part of another social pattern. Back in the 1950s, there was only one flight per fortnight. At airport farewells for the flights, which left at 6 am, it was not unusual to find a champagne party in progress. And there were always small sexual scandals among the expatriate community. Alan Lindley remembered an acting district commissioner's wife who ran off with a builder, and an agricultural officer's wife who sailed off with a 'yachtie'. At one stage in the 1950s, the Guadalcanal Club was scandalised by the 'keys in the middle club' when some expatriate married couples randomly swapped house keys for a bit of sexual spice (which led to one officer being sent back to England in disgrace).[7]

Honiara's worlds

The distance between the four or five worlds was maintained through income levels, types and location of housing, customary behaviour, and European racial beliefs. The most upwardly mobile group was the Chinese, who increased their economic power in the 1960s and 1970s. Solomon Islanders remained a separate group. Fijians and Gilbertese

---

5   Lawson n.d. [c. 2000s]: 16.
6   Email from Murray Chapman, 3 May 2016.
7   Lindley 2014: 18.

were also 'natives', but generally regarded as higher status than Solomon Islanders, largely because of their level of education and employment. Students from other Pacific Islands attending the educational institutions also added to the ethnic mix. The European world declined in size and importance from the 1970s, although it picked up again in the 2000s and 2010s, peopled mainly by Australians and New Zealanders while the Regional Assistance Mission to Solomon Islands operated. The Solomon Islander world is now the major political and social force, yet it still lacks economic power, although undeniably there are some very wealthy Solomon Islanders in business and politics. The maturation of a very 'Solomons' way of running the political system has its foundations in the 1960s and 1970s. The Chinese (*waku*) world has now expanded into an Asian world with several internal divisions: old *waku*; and new *waku* from mainland China, South-East Asians (mainly from Malaysia and the Philippines), Koreans, and Japanese. Malaitans hold such a strong place in Honiara that they have become a separate world, although with its own subdivisions.

As illustrated by Map 8.1, Honiara in the 1960s and 1970s was a partially segregated town, but compared with flashpoints in the British Empire, such as the Mau Mau era in British Kenya between 1952 and 1960, urban Solomon Islands was remarkable peaceful. There were no locks on many houses, there were no security guards, and often there was no or only limited electricity, so there were no alarm systems, other than dogs. Expatriates seldom kept firearms. Even so, no matter how senior they became, Solomon Islanders and other Pacific Islanders never felt entirely welcome within the expatriate community. Alcohol consumption was restricted until 1965. Some clubs and hotels were more blatantly racist than others, with 'Natives forbidden' signs, and once alcohol was freely available, 'natives' were restricted to public or '*boi*' bars. The Hotel Woodford was taken over by Ken Hay in 1949, assisted by Mrs E.K. Manning.[8] With a name change to the Mendana Hotel in the late 1950s, Hay continued to own it until the early 1970s. The hotel banned Solomon Islander patrons, except at a rough *boi* bar separated by a fence. Joses Tuhanuku said there was a sign outside the main part of the hotel that said: 'No Dogs, No Natives.' The portly Hay was famed for sitting near the front door, vetting entry while chatting with his patrons.[9]

---

8   *PIM*, February 1951, 68.
9   Tuhanuku 1983: 117; Russell 2003: 116–17. It is now the Kitano Mendana Hotel.

In its early years, the Guadalcanal Cub was another white bastion that banned 'natives' and in later years kept its membership rates at expatriate and elite salary levels, effectively stopping most Solomon Islanders from enjoying the facilities.[10] There was an occasion in the second half of the 1960s when several hundred Solomon Islanders marched on the Guadalcanal Club to protest. The expatriate men present placed themselves defensively outside and the women sheltered in the centre of the dance floor. All entrances were guarded until police assistance arrived.[11] The writing was on the wall and segregation ended soon afterward. The club reformed and encouraged integration. By the 1960s, clubs were unable to discriminate based on race, although some managed to accomplish the same thing by maintaining high membership fees. The Point Cruz Yacht Club was always more friendly than others and the Bugotu, Devesi, and Talasasa Aqorau families were early members. There were two tiers of membership: full members had to own a boat, no matter how small; and others could become associate members. In later years, the golf club, begun in 1957, became less of an expatriate haven and also welcomed a wide range of members.

In their autobiographies, senior public servants (and later national leaders) such as Sir Peter Kenilorea and Sir Lloyd Maepeza Gina make quite clear that Solomon Islanders were not welcomed as equivalents to British public servants, even when they held more senior positions. Writing of his early days, Sir Lloyd said: 'The white masters believed they stood higher than we did and, because of the long-established cross-cultural norms, we knew we could not get close to them in most situations.'[12]

There is a peculiar example of this from the early 1950s, remembered by Alan Lindley. When Lindley first arrived in Honiara, Bill Burley was the only European 'prisoner'. He had been employed at the Mendana Hotel, where he defrauded Ken Hay of a large amount of cash. Burley was tried and sentenced, but not sent to the prison. Instead, he was given a special room beside the guard house at the Rove police barracks, had his food sent in from the hotel, and each evening walked free. He was allowed to borrow a police Mark I Land Rover and set off to have evening drinks with Inspector John Buckingham, the officer in charge of Central District and Honiara Police Station. This situation lasted until mid-1952, when

---

10 Moore 2013c: entries for Mendana Hotel, and Guadalcanal Club.
11 Lindley 2014: 13.
12 Gina 2003: 165.

Buckingham was transferred to Malaita and Lindley took over at Honiara Police Station, ending special privileges.[13] Clearly, there were different standards for black and for white prisoners.

In the introduction to his autobiography, Sir Peter, who crossed swords with several leading British officials, remembered

> the ignominious and ugly head of fallacious white supremacy and the arrogance of colonialism manifested themselves unabashed. The adage 'white is right, if you are brown stick around, but if you are black get back', was the presumed order of the day.[14]

He went on to say:

> In the late colonial years in the Solomon Islands, your worth was judged either by the colour of your skin, the job you held, your upbringing, and the number of letters after your name. There was a Cambridge/Oxford clique amongst the British officers who had made their careers out of 'governing natives', that we locals could never enter. Many of these officers had served previously in other areas of the British empire, particularly in Africa, and they brought with them preconceived ideas about what was 'good' for Solomon Islanders. It was never easy and straightforward for Solomon Islanders to live in their world … I was a black native of Solomon Islands while they were white, British and superior.[15]

Perhaps it was also that being part of the indigenous urban scene was so overwhelming and kin connections so comfortable, along with accompanying social responsibilities, there was little time or need to be part of the afterwork expatriate-dominated social scene. District Commissioner James Tedder wrote in 1966 that most social groups were island-exclusive and, except at the new multiracial Honiara Club, most activities were segregated by choice and design:

> The feeling of 'community' is largely one centred on religion and/or island of origin. This takes the form of associations or clubs formed to maintain island solidarity, to support local councils, and to promote sporting activities and dancing. The organisations formed by religious denominations cut across island identities and promoted sports and social activities.[16]

---

13 Letter from Alan Lindley, Adelaide, 11 March 2016.
14 Kenilorea 2008: xxxii.
15 ibid., 160–61.
16 Tedder 1966: 39.

The BSIP hierarchy

Just as there had been in the early days of the protectorate at Tulagi, there was a clear administrative hierarchy with the resident commissioners (and, after 1953, the high commissioners and, in the 1970s, the governors) at the top, flanked by the Anglican and Catholic bishops. The early resident commissioners lived in a makeshift but comfortable government residency (called Government House after 1953). In 1944, Resident Commissioner Colonel Owen C. Noel (1943–48) was the first to occupy the thatched-roof residency. It had originally been an officers' hospital and then was used to house New Zealand Army nurses. Noel was followed by J.D.A. Germond (acting resident commissioner, 1948–50), and Henry Graham Gregory-Smith (resident commissioner, 1950–52). From 1953, the BSIP was governed directly through the high commissioners and a small executive council. Like all his successors, when Sir Robert Stanley, the new Honiara-based high commissioner, arrived for his first visit in September 1952, he was dressed in white, decked out in his medals, and sporting a feathered white helmet. The next occupants of Government House were Sir John Gutch (1955–61), Sir David Trench (1961–64), and Sir Robert Foster (1964–69).

The official version of the lives of the resident and high commissioners presents a sanitised view that does not always stand up to close scrutiny. Lieutenant Colonel Trench, acting Government Secretary, was acting resident commissioner for periods of 1945 and 1946,[17] much to the dismay of Spearline Wilson, the long-serving head of the Lands and Mining Department and also acting government secretary for a while. Indeed, in December 1945, Wilson had to swear in Trench as acting resident commissioner.[18] Admittedly, Wilson was crotchety and unwell, and not impressed that he had to share a mess with 24 others, including the acting resident commissioner, but in 1946, he expected standards that the protectorate could not provide:

> Things are going from bad to bloody awful down here. The place is just what I imagine Callan Park [an Australian psychiatric hospital] must be like. Trench, who is acting R.C., is, as I have mentioned before, a nitwit. His bosom companion is Judd, who is in the

---

17 SINA BSIP 1/III F58/58II, RC to acting DO D.C.C. Trench, Malaita, 15 October 1945; HC to ARC Alexander Waddell, 14 December 1945, ARC to HC, 27 December 1945.
18 SINA BSIP 1/III F58/58II, HC to RS, 31 December 1945.

Government trade store. Those two and a couple more of the same caliber stay up half the night hanging over the bar, and are good for nothing until late afternoon next day. Nothing but Christian names are used. You can hear Judd's raucous voice at all hours of the day or night calling out, What do you think of that, David, or How is that, David? And Trench's reply, 'pretty good, Arthur', or something like that. I have words with the Res. Com. at least twice a day. I simply will not be party to all the stupid nonsense being indulged in, and don't hesitate to tell Trench exactly what I think about the situation generally, and himself in particular.[19]

We can guess that when Wilson retired at the end of the year, Trench and Judd probably toasted his departure. A few days later, Trench was on his way to Suva as First Assistant Secretary in the WPHC. In October, he was back in the BSIP as Secretary for Development and Native Affairs, to help quell Maasina Rule.[20]

Planning to replace old Government House was under way in 1967, with a new building designed by New Zealand architects. New Government House came into use in mid-1969 and the old building was demolished. The first occupant of this opulent airconditioned home and office was Sir Michael Gass (1969–73), followed by the two pre-independence governors, Sir Donald Luddington (1973–76) and Sir Colin Allan (1976–78). The public section of the house worked well, although the private quarters were cramped. The high commissioners and governors used a black Humber Super Snipe and, later, a black Jaguar to travel on Honiara's few kilometres of sealed roads. Government House had a guard house and, in the early 1950s, when His Excellency departed in the grand car, the police on duty 'turned out' and presented arms to a resounding bugle call.[21] Whenever the resident or high commissioner went on tour around the protectorate in RCS *Coral Queen*, the heads of government departments were expected to be at the wharf, dressed in suits, to farewell him. Some were less popular than others. When Sir Robert Stanley ended his term in 1955, after a polite farewell at the wharf with an 18-gun salute, the relieved senior staff adjourned to the Guadalcanal Club to celebrate his departure as his ship steamed past.[22]

---

19 UQ FML, Wilson Papers, A.H. Wilson to J.A. Wilson, 15 March 1946.
20 SINA BSIP 1/III F58/58II, HC to Secretary of State, 14 January 1947; Secretary to Government BSIP to senior staff, 18 October 1947; HC to Secretary of State, 6 November 1947.
21 Lindley 2013: 3.
22 *BSIP NS*, 21 January 1967, 15 May 1969; Information from Alan Lindley, Adelaide, 30 June 2011.

Plate 8.2 New Government House in 1969. It has since been incorporated into the Heritage Park Hotel.
Source: Brian Taylor Collection.

Ceremonial occasions, such as the Queen's Birthday and Remembrance Day, were always marked with pomp and ceremony. It was a time when dress uniforms, swords, spurs, and plumed helmets received an airing, and all the protocols of the British Empire were observed. The ceremonies did not change over several decades. White pith helmets were still in use at the independence ceremony in 1978 (I remember flying out after the ceremony, sitting next to a British official clutching his helmet, which he told me had been borrowed from the Hong Kong Government). Royal visitors always caused a complete frenzy of admiration. The first was Prince Philip, the Duke of Edinburgh, who visited the protectorate in March 1959. Thirty leading Solomon Islander men and their wives lined up at the Point Cruz wharf, all with small, scripted speeches in case they were asked a question by the prince. The royal party toured the hospital, teacher training college, Joy Biscuit factory, and a plantation, then watched customary dances at Lawson Tama. In the early evening, there was a reception at Government House for around 300 guests, 24 of whom were Solomon Islanders. Later, an exclusive dinner was held onboard the royal yacht HMY *Britannia*.[23]

---

23   SINA BSIP 9/II/FC 23/1; Fox 1958: 57–58. I am indebted to Christopher Chevalier for these references.

Plate 8.3 The Honiara War Cenotaph was constructed in 1959.
Source: BM, Patrick Barrett Collection.

The *Britannia* was the standard vessel used to carry the royals to outposts of the Commonwealth. The Duke and Duchess of Kent visited in 1969, the Duke of Edinburgh returned in March 1971, and the Queen, the Duke of Edinburgh, Princess Anne, Captain Mark Phillips, and Lord Louis Mountbatten visited in 1974. The Duke and Duchess of Gloucester represented the monarch at the Independence Day ceremony in 1978. The Queen and the Duke of Edinburgh visited, again on *Britannia*, in October 1982. The *Britannia* had long been decommissioned when the Duke and Duchess of Cambridge visited in 2012, and Prince Charles passed through in 2019. On each occasion, a combination of loyalty to empire and the Commonwealth, reverence for the monarchy, and sycophancy occurred.

The colonial public service

Most of the colonial public servants worked from 8 am to noon, and from 2 pm to 4.30 pm, Monday to Friday. Those with weekend duties worked from 8 am to noon on Saturdays. From the beginning of 1953, the BSIP Government was merged with the WPHC Secretariat. The position of resident commissioner ceased. The next change was from high commissioner to governor. The official explanation for the change in title was to emphasise the separate nature of the protectorate. The title 'High

Commissioner for the Western Pacific' was archaic and subject to confusion with the diplomatic head of mission in Commonwealth countries. It also concealed the position's almost sole remaining responsibility: for Solomon Islands. At the end of 1971, the Crown Colony of Gilbert and Ellice Islands ceased to come under the WPHC, instead reporting directly to London, and in 1973, the WPHC ceased to act for the British side of the Anglo-French Condominium in the New Hebrides. The BSIP was the only large remaining WPHC territory. The WPHC had outlived its usefulness and was abolished in January 1976.[24] By the time independence was granted in 1978, the BSIP was Britain's last surviving protectorate.

The pre-war and early post-war BSIP courts were the Court of the High Commissioner for the Western Pacific and the Native Courts. Under the separation of powers, the judicial commissioners and judges worked alongside the administrative positions—separate but equal. Several administrative officers also held commissions as deputy commissioners. The High Commissioner's Court was held before a judicial commissioner; it had the full original jurisdiction of a Supreme Court, except that, when held before a deputy commissioner, it had no jurisdiction in matrimonial, Admiralty or lunacy cases, nor in criminal cases for which the offence was punishable with death or imprisonment for seven years or more.[25]

A new Western Pacific (Courts) Order-in-Council, gazetted on 15 August 1961, came into operation on 9 April 1962, restructuring the High Commissioner's Court (constituted under the original 1893 Pacific Order-in-Council, which established the protectorate) as the High Court of the Western Pacific. The High Court also served the Crown Colony of Gilbert and Ellice Islands and the New Hebrides Condominium. This court was a 'Superior Court of Record', possessing all the jurisdiction vested in the High Court in England. It also provided for the appointment of the chief justice, judges, and other officers of the High Court, for the jurisdiction of the court, and for the appellate jurisdiction of the Fiji Court of Appeal in respect to appeals from the High Court. Initially, the court consisted of a chief justice based in Honiara, and two puisne judges—one stationed in Tarawa in the Crown Colony of Gilbert and Ellice Islands and one in

---

24 Sir Donald Collin Cumyn Luddington (1920–2009) served in the Hong Kong civil service before he became District Commissioner, New Territories, and then Secretary for Home Affairs for Hong Kong. He was appointed as the final High Commissioner of the Western Pacific on 10 October 1973, when the position was being transformed into Governor of BSIP. He was knighted in 1976. 'Obituary', *Yorkshire Post*, 29 January 2009.
25 *BSIP AR* 1955–56: 41.

Port Vila in the New Hebrides Condominium. By 1974, the judiciary consisted of the chief justice, who was ordinarily resident in the BSIP, and a puisne judge in the New Hebrides.[26] The last Chief Justice of the Western Pacific, Sir Jocelyn Bodilly, retired in 1975. The first chief justice only for Solomon Islands, D.R. (Renn) Davis OBE, was appointed in April 1976. There were no juries, only two assessors to assist, which made the judicial commissioners and judges extremely powerful.[27]

Separated from them were various government officers, from the chief secretary to the chief of police and senior public servants, such as the heads of departments and the district commissioners. The only district commissioner based in Honiara was for Central District. Most post-war public servants came from the United Kingdom or other British colonies and were new to the BSIP and the WPHC.[28] An earlier chapter described the post-war appointments as technocrats. They usually arrived in the protectorate after service in other parts of the British Commonwealth or within the British Isles. Large numbers of colonial civil servants began to arrive in the Solomons from Africa from the mid-1950s. By the mid-1960s, more than a dozen former colonies and protectorates had become independent as decolonisation took place around the world. Career colonial officers had to be accommodated in the shrinking number of colonial territories. They were often racist and contemptuous of the casual colonial style in the Pacific.

Many of the senior police were former British 'coppers' from London and the Midlands cities who had served in Palestine or Africa. Some of the other senior administrative staff—for instance, District Commissioner James Tedder—came from Australia, but by and large, they were British and had done the colonial circuit, slowly climbing the public service ladder via British Africa or the West Indies. Some moved on reasonably quickly, while others stayed for 10 or 20 years, learning to love the relaxed tropical lifestyle and working with Solomon Islanders. Just as there were public servants full of the swagger of empire, there were always others who were intellectually stimulated by the challenge of moving colonial dependencies along the path to independence. They all had to deal with the labyrinth of the British Colonial Service and their 'bible' was

---

26   The Crown Colony of Gilbert and Ellice Islands gained self-rule in 1971 and separated into two territories in 1975, both of which were granted independence, as Tuvalu (in 1978) and Kiribati (in 1979).
27   *BSIP AR* 1961–62: 54–55; *SND*, 15 April 1976. There are still no juries in Solomon Islands courts.
28   UQ FML, Wilson Papers, A.H. Wilson to J.A. Wilson, 13 December 1946.

the *Colonial Regulations*.[29] The most feared thing they could receive was a 'Red Minute' from His Excellency over something that had caused him displeasure. Such minutes were filed in the individual's confidential personal file for future reference.[30]

It is fair to say that many colonial public servants held jobs beyond the level at which they could expect to have been employed if they had stayed at home. M.P.E. Bellam calculated that the average annual income of European families in Honiara in 1966 was $5,500—many times that of equivalent Solomon Islanders. Even the most senior Solomon Islander public servants only earned $1,000 a year, and their wives seldom worked.[31] The expatriates' base salary was complemented by a tax-free 'inducement allowance', and fringe benefits such as subsidised accommodation, a large tax-free contribution to their children's education at overseas boarding schools, and two free return trips each year for the children. Three months' holiday every two years was usual, and many were on short-term contracts with gratuities set at one-quarter of gross salaries. Most wives managed to find part-time employment to supplement their husbands' salaries. Families employed at least one house servant (sometimes several) and lived in comfortable homes. They drove late-model British Morris and Austin cars, and generally did financially well out of the experience, although there was a downside with the risk of malaria, isolation, and separation from their children when they were at schools in Australia, New Zealand, or England.[32]

Solomon Islander public servants tried to assess the newcomers. Sir Lloyd Maepeza Gina remembered how Solomon Islanders sized up each new administrative arrival:

> In those days, when we Solomon Islands people looked at ourselves sheltered under the Great umbrella of the British colonial administration, we felt that those colonials looked upon us as servants, as black people. As they did in Africa, so too they did in the Solomons. We knew that all along, because of the gossip around the public service we could quickly identify the new comers. When they arrived we said, 'Oh, probably this man has come all the way from Africa or India.' We could feel the kind of

---

29 British Colonial Office 1945.
30 Lindley 2013: 13.
31 Bellam 1970: 82.
32 This is based on Bellam's description (1970: 79), and on my own knowledge of similar employment situations in Port Moresby in the 1970s and 1980s.

attitudes they held. They had probably been the same way in the places they had come from. We were sometimes displeased and would say, 'Oh, be very careful, this man is probably a little bit rough, you know.'[33]

Official precedence was different from status. The senior clergy came high on the list, the Anglican and Catholic bishops sharing their ecclesiastical power with the leaders of the Methodist, South Sea Evangelical and Seventh-day Adventist churches. The managers of the Commonwealth Bank of Australia, the Australia and New Zealand Banking Group (ANZ), and the Hongkong and Shanghai Banking Corporation (HSBC) were also notable as they were independent and knew the financial secrets of individuals living in the protectorate.

The expatriate social scene in the 1950s and 1960s involved cocktail parties, private dinners, trips to the Guadalcanal Club, the golf club, and the one Chinese restaurant. In the 1950s, the social scene expanded to include expeditions to the Point Cruz cinema, with the addition in 1968 of the Point Cruz Yacht Club with its pleasant waterfront bar. There were also outings at weekends to nearby beaches or waterfalls. These were mainly adult-only events as there were very few expatriate children living permanently in Honiara.[34]

Plate 8.4 A government officer's house up on the ridges, 1972.
Source: Brian Taylor Collection.

---

33 Gina 2003: 55.
34 Information from Alan Lindley, Adelaide, 30 June 2011.

8. STEPPING-STONES TO NATIONAL CONSCIOUSNESS

Plate 8.5 The same house as in Plate 8.4, showing its ridge-top position and the view out to sea.
Source: Brian Taylor Collection.

Honiara became a meeting place for Solomon Islanders involved in administration, beginning in November 1949 with the first conference for 150 headmen and their deputies from all over the protectorate.[35] Solomon Islanders did not begin to participate directly in the highest levels of decision-making until 1950–51, when the first four Solomon Islanders were nominated to the Advisory Council.[36] Many of the indigenous leaders did not live in Honiara, coming only for meetings. These early appointments were followed by membership of the Legislative Council (1961–69), Governing Council (1970–74), and Legislative Assembly (1974–78). In most ways, they were outsiders, and were not invited to European social functions, although they did create a bridge between other Solomon Islanders and the colonial elite. John Smith, who arrived as financial secretary in 1970, commented on the strongly expatriate public service and business hierarchy:

---

35 *PIM*, November 1949, 10.
36 These founding fathers of the modern nation were Reverend Kaspar Kakaise (an Anglican priest from Malaita), Silas Sitai from Santa Ana (Clerk to the Eastern District), and Milton Talasasa (district headman from Roviana Lagoon, New Georgia). Jacob (later Sir Jacob) Vouza from Guadalcanal joined them in 1951.

> It was also strange to find that every one of my senior staff, including secretaries, was an expatriate. At first the only Solomon Islanders I met in the working day were the handful of elected members of the Governing Council, messengers and drivers. The most senior local civil servants were doctors, trained at the excellent Fiji medical school, and teachers in the government secondary school and teacher training college.[37]
>
> At something like one in seven of the total [Honiara] population, expatriates were very noticeable. They were not obviously arrogant or patronising and many enjoyed excellent relations with Solomon Islanders but they didn't behave like strangers or guests in somebody else's country. It was their workplace and home and they considered it was the business of government to look after their interests.[38]

Segregated housing and social activities were the order of the day, except when attending church, and even there, expatriates took the front pews. The early expatriate population lived along the coast between Rove and the Mataniko River. The prime location for homes was on the beachfront between Point Cruz and Rove, even though the land had a propensity to flood on high tides and during cyclones. Lengakiki, Kola`a, and Vavaea ridges, and Skyline, with their pleasant views, became the next expatriate and new Solomon Islander elite areas. The houses on the ridges were cooled by breezes from inland and from the sea. Residents there were also less likely to be bothered by mosquitoes. Cars were a necessary addition to these households, as the roads were steep and the sun hot. The Chinese congregated in Chinatown on the banks of the Mataniko and in the valley behind, usually living above their commercial premises. Other Chinese lived next to or above their shops at Point Cruz and at the new Ranadi industrial estate. Solomon Islanders visited these houses only as day-servants or lived with their families in a *boi haus* underneath or at the back of the main houses. The servants in the homes of Honiara expatriates were usually male. Middle-grade housing for Solomon Islander public servants developed at Mbokonavera on the slopes behind the beachside market, around the Rove police barracks, and as far west as White River, in the Mataniko Valley, and on the lower slopes of Kola`a Ridge. They employed *haus meris* (female house servants and child carers), who were usually younger relatives from their home village.

---

37   Smith 2011: 22.
38   ibid., 23.

8. STEPPING-STONES TO NATIONAL CONSCIOUSNESS

Urban culture and building nationalism

The social scene reflected what Christine Jourdan called 'stepping-stones to national consciousness'.[39] The making of modern Solomon Islands and Honiara occurred slowly and involved many different aspects of life. Over decades, the 'world' divisions (Figure 0.1) altered. The European world largely ended in the late 1970s when the public service and political decision-making were localised. The Chinese world remained, although it staggered in the 1970s when about one-quarter of the families left, and then developed in the 1980s and 1990s into old and new *waku*. Honiara became predominantly a Solomon Islander world, with an increasingly wealthy elite who had various levels of linkage back to rural villages.

Among the weaknesses of the late-colonial transition years were the lack of training in business and difficulties accessing finance to begin even small businesses. Solomon Islanders supplemented their wages by growing garden produce for sale or, if they went fishing, by selling their catch to the Fish Marketing Co-operative. The urban economy in which they found themselves enmeshed was totally controlled by foreigners. There were colonial government–supported movements to set up cooperatives, but largely the government viewed business as something for foreigners. The barriers to indigenous entrepreneurship were enormous.

Bellam's 1968 research located only three indigenous businesses in Honiara: one Gilbertese cooperative store at White River, one small Solomon Islander-owned trade store at Kukum, and one firewood supply business. Very few in the 1950s and 1960s had sufficient modern education to be able to cope with large-scale business ventures, and *wantok* pressures destroyed many early entrepreneurs. Little was done to make credit available (except for housing) and there was no training in commercial methods. A decade later, as independence loomed, another survey showed that of 72 shops in Honiara, only five were run by Solomon Islanders: one Solomon Islander–owned trade store in Chinatown, one in each of Mbokonavera and Vura, a furniture workshop at Kukum, and a panel-beating workshop within the Honiara City Council facilities. There were also small building companies such as that run by John Maetea Kaliuae and his brothers. All indigenous businesses had problems raising capital and their main downfall was offering credit facilities that *wantoks*

---

39 Jourdan 1995b.

often did not repay.[40] There were other indigenous businesses involving building or providing services. Most of their start-up funds came from the Agricultural and Industry Loans Board or from Chinese friends, and all lacked business management skills. One Chinese shopkeeper commented that he thought most Solomon Islanders failed in business because they

> lacked capital to start a business with. They prefer to keep their money in boxes in their houses or in bottles and tins buried in the ground, where there is no interest added like in the banks. They do not see that hidden money loses value as time goes on. They cannot get a loan from the bank, for the bank would not see how its money would be recovered.[41]

Although he was exaggerating, the description is correct in that it was extremely hard to get a bank loan. The government concentrated its early assistance on education, health, and housing, not on indigenous business development.[42] Consequently, the Chinese dominated the lower end of the retail market, while larger overseas companies controlled international commercial connections. At independence in 1978, there were still only a handful of Solomon Islander university graduates and few indigenous entrepreneurs.

At one level, a new urban consciousness and a sense of a common destiny leading to nationalism also began to develop once Honiara had its own town council and, from 1964, when a Honiara Member of the Legislative Council was first elected in a secret ballot based on universal adult suffrage and a common roll. Since then, all members for Honiara seats have had to battle with the multiple loyalties of their electorates, where voters make decisions partly based on kin and *wantok* allegiances, but also the competing interests of church, sport, work, and suburban location. Sport and church cut across *wantok* boundaries and create a sense of unity. In the 1960s, there were 14 soccer teams playing in competitions that were usually sponsored by government departments, commercial firms, and churches. Multiracial cricket was played, and rugby union was becoming more popular.[43] Almost all Solomon Islanders attended church at least once a week, for several hours on the sabbath (Saturday or Sunday, depending on the denomination), and often attended other church-related functions on other evenings.

---

40 Bellam 1970: 83; Manedika 1979: 167–68.
41 Manedika 1979: 168.
42 *BSIP AR* 1949–50: 26–27.
43 Tedder 1966: 40.

Alongside working for wages and urban life, Solomon Islanders have maintained customary rituals and performances. The SIBC helped foster this through its recordings of customary music. From the 1950s, celebrations, such as for the Queen's Birthday or visits by foreign dignitaries, involved displays of traditional culture. This was often the first time Solomon Islanders had seen one another's dances, creating a cross-cultural flow that has continued. Honiara also developed some social occasions that mimicked those in neighbouring Australia and other countries, but with a local touch, once more proudly preserving culture. Melbourne Cup Day always had its fans, and the first competition for Miss Custom Queen was held in March 1974. The next year, a Charity Queen contest raised money for the Solomons team to compete in the South Pacific Games. The Catholic Church got in on the act with a Carnival Queen quest, which in 1975 raised A$40,000 for their new cathedral.[44]

Plates 8.6–8.9 Cultural dancers in the 1950s.
Source: BM, Patrick Barrett Collection.

---

44   *BSIP NS*, 15 March 1974; *SND*, 7 March 1975, 12 March 1975.

Plate 8.10 Pelise Moro, leader of the Moro Movement, and some of his followers in Honiara in 1971.

The movement was at its height in the late 1950s and 1960s, when it incorporated half of Guadalcanal's population. Moro had a council made up of advisers and clerks and maintained a 'Custom House' or 'House of Antiquities'. The movement collected taxes and attempted to be self-governing, which was similar to the style of Maasina Rule. Moro was born in the 1920s and died in 2007.

Source: Les Tickle Collection.

Religious customs developed in Honiara. SSEC marching groups performed in Honiara using formation styles that could date back to the late nineteenth century in Queensland Christian missions, but also came out of the Maasina Rule years. I first saw these white-clothed women perform precision marches one night in Vura in the 1980s, at a function arranged by the then local MP, John Maetea Kaliuae.

Occasionally, large customary events occurred. On Christmas Day 1965, a Solomon Islands feast and dancing festival were attended by 3,000 residents, with 2,000 at the feast. Dancers from Sulufou in Lau Lagoon, Malaita, performed, and 500 pigs, 40 bags of rice, and a ton of vegetables were consumed. A few days later, 70 Mbirao people from east-central Guadalcanal walked the 110 kilometres from their highland villages leading pigs for sale at Central Market. They presented a display of dancing and enjoyed a feast laid out on the verandah of the Department of Geological Surveys headquarters.[45]

---

45   *BSIP NS*, 7 January 1966, 21 January 1966.

Plate 8.11 King George VI School students ready to dance, 1968.
The youth in the front is Lawrence Fo'anaota, who later became director of the Solomon Islands National Museum.
Source: Les Tickle Collection.

Honiara developed a vibrant urban culture replete with elements from all over the protectorate, mixed with British, Chinese, and Gilbertese cultures. The first Sea Festival was held in Honiara in 1968 and continued for a few years in the early 1970s. The spectacular centrepiece of the first festival was a race between war canoes from Makira, Santa Ana, Santa Catalina, and Roviana—all decorated in traditional styles. Other events included races for smaller canoes, dinghy racing, and seamanship trials, with competitions for copra-loading, and ship inspections. The next year, the festival was not as successful: the war canoes did not arrive, and drunken Europeans spoilt many of the competitions. There was no festival in 1970, although it resumed in 1971 and 1972. Another was held in February 1974, timed to coincide with the visit of Queen Elizabeth II.[46]

Plate 8.12 A Makira canoe crew at Point Cruz in 1969 during the Sea Festival.
Source: Les Tickle Collection.

Plate 8.13 Makira canoes at Point Cruz in 1969 during the Sea Festival.
Source: Les Tickle Collection.

---

46 ibid., 15 April 1968, 31 May 1969, 31 January 1970, 4 February 1974, 1 March 1974.

Bamboo and string bands began in the 1950s and have never lost their place in the hearts of Solomon Islanders. As in any town or city, musical bands developed and, by local standards, are famous, their leaders achieving rock-star status. Some of the bands began in Christian schools such as Betikama in the 1970s, combining music with witnessing for the Lord. Robert Soaika from Lake Tegano, Rennell Island, was an excellent guitarist in the SDA band the Uplifters, in which Ellison Sade, Honiara-born but from Lau Lagoon, Malaita, and Manasseh Sogavare, from Choiseul Island, got their musical start.

The Gilbert brothers, sons of Gilbert Talo from Fishing Village, were all famous singers in several bands over the decades. Their father always encouraged them by buying musical instruments and amplifiers, or by going guarantor at shops while they paid them off. In the early days, they had to work for the gear by brushing his garden land at Koio Valley; then, as they became financially independent, they purchased their own equipment. They had several rock bands. First, one of them joined a band called the Fleet Swingers, which they eventually took over. Ellison Sade joined them as lyricist and was later a guitarist and keyboard player of renown. Although these bands played international songs they had heard on the radio, they also composed their own material. Getting the foreign lyrics correct, when all they had was the radio version, was always difficult. Sade, who has almost perfect memory for lyrics, also made errors. For some time, they continued to sing The Hollies' 'He Ain't Heavy, He's My Brother' as 'He is in heaven, he's my brother', much to Sade's later amusement.

There were early talent shows in Honiara, which were usually held at Point Cruz cinema. One of the favourite early bands was The Red Sparkle, with H.M. Long on guitar and lead vocals, Hudson Kalita Gilbert on electric guitar and vocals, Inito`o Gilbert on electric rhythm guitar and backup vocals, and younger brother Reddley Loea Gilbert on drums. Hudson Kalita Gilbert was the most famous; he later converted his rock'n'roll band into a gospel band called The Gospel Bells. There were also one-man bands, like that of Jim Herd or Barry Morgan, who played the harmonica and a guitar. Another famous electric guitarist is better known for other things. Back in the early 1970s, Manasseh Sogavare (now four-time prime minister) formed The Tornados, a dance club band, in which he was lead singer and guitarist. They faced tough competition from the Gilberts, the Fa`arodo brothers, and the Ata family, when they won first prize in the Battle of Giants competition held at the Community Centre.[47]

---

47 Information from Ellison Sade, Honiara, 26 November 2017.

Solomon Islands was visited by its first international singing star in 1970—Slim Dusty, a famous Australian country and western singer, who performed in Honiara, Yandina, and Auki. He returned to raise money for cyclone relief in 1986, and again in 1998. Reggae became popular in the 1970s, and the band Pijin Rock moved electric music to a more indigenous level. In the 1980s and 1990s, Unisound was the most famous band, and was later better known for its Unisound recording studios. America's Big Mountain Reggae band performed in Honiara in 1996, as did Lucky Dube from Papua New Guinea in 1997.

Solomon Islanders are rightly proud of their physical cultural heritage. High-quality inlaid pearl-shell wooden carvings, intricately patterned straw bags, shell-wealth, and 'Buka-ware' baskets and trays woven from plant fibre have been sold in Honiara for many decades.[48] More recently, fine stone carvings were added, from Ranongga Island in Western Province. Produced for the tourist trade, the beautiful wooden and stone carvings with traditional motifs help keep old skills and customs alive. A revival in artefact-making from Kwaio Malaita also fed into this market. Large wooden whole-post carvings festoon hotels and public buildings, creating a unique cultural environment. While some of these items are brought to the city from outlying islands, many are now produced in Honiara. Since it was built in 1969, the National Museum has been expanded and has become the centrepiece of this cultural renaissance, through its displays, artefact shop, and at various times the construction of cultural village buildings, plus a performance hall. In recent years, the National Art Gallery has been added on the other side of Mendana Avenue, along with a stage for cultural events, and an artefact sale area. The National Museum is a social scene for artists and musicians who meet casually in its shady central areas. The Artists Association began in Honiara in 1991.

Alcohol consumption

Another factor added to the new urban mix was legal access to alcohol. Selling alcohol to 'natives' was prohibited, although this was impossible to police. Illicit alcohol was always available on Tulagi before World War II; then, during the war, members of the Solomon Islands Defence Force and Labour Corps could obtain free or cheap alcohol through the American armed forces.

---

48   Chick and Chick 1978; Kupiainen 2000.

After the war, one long-term contentious issue was the regulation that denied Solomon Islanders the right to drink alcohol. In 1957, High Commissioner Gutch appointed a select committee to investigate making alcohol more freely available. The committee's deliberations began in January 1958, finding that since the war the drinking of alcohol had become widespread. Beer, wine, spirits, medical alcohol, methylated spirits, and home brew were readily available in Honiara and other towns.[49] The committee, which included Alphonse Daga[50] and Jacob Vuza, recommended that Solomon Islander, Fijian, and Indo-Fijian men over 20 years of age be allowed to drink beer on licensed premises. They said the same groups, if over 30 years of age, should be able to drink wine and spirits on licensed premises, and be allowed to purchase take-away beer and spirits in limited amounts.[51] The ordinance was altered in May 1959. Solomon Islanders, Fijians (including the AMOs), Gilbert Islanders, Ellice Islanders, and New Hebrideans were allowed to drink beer, but only with an official permit (called a chit) issued by the local district commissioner and the officer in charge of the police for the district. They could drink on licensed premises and each month could purchase up to 12 bottles of beer for home consumption. This rule lasted for one year, after which every adult could drink beer, but only those with a chit available through the high commissioner could drink spirits.[52] Women were discouraged from consuming alcohol and were not allowed on licensed premises. They could apply for a permit to drink spirits, which was only granted if their husbands already had one.

The permit system was not a success. There were too many permits for publicans to supervise them adequately, and permits were borrowed by *wantoks*. After 1 February 1962, beer was sold freely in public bars to indigenous people over 21 years, although restrictions on wine and spirits were maintained. Full and restricted licences were introduced for hotels and clubs, sale hours were reduced, and the Liquor Licensing Boards were established in each district. After extensive discussion in the Legislative

---

49 Also see Gina 2003: 170–71.
50 Alphonse Daga was born in 1924 in the western Solomons and educated at Kokeqolo School. During the war, he was a sergeant in the Solomon Islands Labour Corps, then joined the Public Works Department in Gizo and later Honiara. By 1957–58, he was a leading public servant. See also Moore 2013c: entries for Daga, and Vouza.
51 *BSIP NS*, 31 March 1958.
52 Letter from Alan Lindley, Adelaide, 9 March 2016; Moore 2013c: entry on Liquor Policy.

Council during 1964, a Liquor (Amendment) Bill was passed in the December session, which removed all race-based restrictions on alcohol consumption. It came into force on 1 January 1965.[53]

This did not sit well with some Europeans, particularly Ken Hay at the Mendana Hotel. In 1966, Hay told the *Pacific Islands Monthly*:

> You run a hotel as a business, not to please people who might have ideas. I keep out the Solomon Islanders because I don't want to lower my standards. They accuse me of discrimination, but that's rubbish. Solomon Islanders can't stay at my hotel because they are not all at the stage where they are fit to stay there. Certainly, some are, but if I let some in but keep most of them out, then that would be discrimination.[54]

Interestingly, Hay allowed Papua New Guineans and Fijians to stay in his hotel, and various sources say his attitudes were based on a desire to keep high standards, not on racism.[55] Despite this protestation, his general attitudes were colonial and racist.

Constitutional and political change

As Jaap Timmer suggests, 'The ways in which people in Melanesia incorporate the state have a profound impact on how they imagine power relations.'[56] Solomon Islanders have always been flexible in creating new political systems. A good example is the ideology of Maasina Rule, which was grounded in pan-Malaitan *kastom*, interpreted as anticolonial, yet also incorporated aspects of British and American political ideology.[57] Nevertheless, when it came to developing a final post-independence form of government, there was to be no national council of chiefs, such as the Malvatumauri adopted in Vanuatu.[58] Pre-colonial leadership patterns have survived in modified forms, mainly at local levels, although aspects of national political leadership relate to older forms of leadership.

---

53   *BSIP NS*, January 1959, March 1958, February 1959, September 1961, February 1962, 16 December 1964.
54   *PIM*, 1966, quoted by Douglas 2004: 42, no month given.
55   Russell 2003: 116–17; Email from Ann Stevenson, 28 July 2019.
56   Timmer 2019: 132.
57   Akin 2013.
58   Although the Malvatumauri was strengthened by the 2006 *National Council of Chiefs Act*, it is often sidelined in dispute-resolution processes. Demian and Rousseau 2019: 320–21.

Australia's ambitions to take over from the British and add the BSIP to its New Guinea Territories never eventuated;[59] then a series of constitutional and political developments altered the balance of power in the Solomons, transferring decision-making from foreigners to Solomon Islanders. Similar to Christianity and modern business, the state and its apparatus form another 'foreign flower' incorporated into their world view. Between 1921 and 1960, the resident commissioners and high commissioners chaired the Advisory Council to consult on important matters. Provision was made in 1950 to include Solomon Islanders and, from 1951 to 1960, 12 men served on the council in Honiara, representing each district. They were either presidents of the district councils or Anglican clergy. Exactly what influence they had on government processes is difficult to estimate.[60]

The political changes in Solomon Islands need to be viewed in their international and particularly their British Commonwealth contexts. Britain had to deal with agitation for independence in many of its colonies. In 1960, the United Nations passed the Declaration on the Granting of Independence to Colonial Countries and Peoples. The United Nations defined what was considered the subjugation, domination, and exploitation of colonised peoples, and proclaimed the universal rights of all peoples to self-determination. Britain had no choice but to introduce a series of constitutional changes to prepare Solomon Islanders to participate directly in governing their country. The truth was that Britain was also relieved to divest itself of far-flung colonial territories such as the BSIP. In 1960, the Advisory Council was replaced with the nominated Executive Council and the Legislative Council. A range of Solomon Islanders served on the Executive Council—all drawn from the Legislative Council, which had official and unofficial members, who were initially chosen by the resident commissioner and later the high commissioner.[61] Six Solomon Islander members were appointed in 1961, representing the districts. A new order-in-council came into effect on 1 February 1965, providing for the election of eight of the 10 unofficial members of the Legislative Council, with the remaining two nominated by the high commissioner. The first general election was held in all eight constituencies on 7 April 1965. The member

---

59 Waters 2016.
60 They were Salana Ga`a, Reverend Kaspar Kakaise, Stephen Kodovaru, S. Murisigaia, Willie Paia, Eriel Sisili, Silas Sitai, Joash S. Sunaone, Milton Talasasa, Reverend A.C. Tinoni, Reverend Dudley Tute, and Jacob Vouza.
61 They were Reverend Leonard Alufurai, Jack Campbell, Baddeley Devesi, David Kausimae, Mariano Kelesi, Willie Paia, Michael Rapasia, David Ramsay, and Gordon Siama.

for the Honiara constituency was elected by direct ballot, while the other seven were chosen by electoral colleges, the members of which were elected by the members of the local councils.[62]

Plate 8.14 Members of the Legislative Council in 1961.
Source: Alan Lindley Collection, in Clive Moore Collection.

The first direct election occurred in May 1967. Sixty-two candidates contested the election, with 17,689 votes received from 35,101 registered voters—a turnout of 50.3 per cent. Fourteen members were elected, 12 of them indigenous.[63] The early Legislative Council meetings were held at the teachers' college, and later in the High Court chamber. In 1970, the Legislative Council was replaced with the Governing Council. A new constitution became law on 10 April 1970, providing for the Governing Council consisting of the high commissioner, up to nine official members, and 17 elected members, who, for the first time, outnumbered the official members. In the 1970 elections, 55.4 per cent of the registered voters

---

62   There was one Electoral College for the Eastern District, one for the Western District, three for the Malaita District, and two for the Central District, excluding Honiara. The 1965 general election saw three former members returned and the addition of the first (and only) female member of the Legislative Council, Lilly Valahoe Ogatina (later Poznanski). *BSIP AR* 1965: 3; Moore 2013c: entries for Elections, Legislative Council, and Poznanski.
63   The elected members were Willie Betu, Jack Campbell, Baddeley Devesi, John P. Hoka, David Kausimae, Mariano Kelesi, John W. Kere, Edmund Kiva, Leone Laku, Clement Ofai, William D. Ramsay, Gordon Siama, Peter Taloni, and Peter K. Thompson. *BSIP NS*, 22 June 1967, 7 July 1967.

went to the polls, with the average turnout varying between 74.8 per cent in the Isabel electorate and 37.7 per cent in the Central Malaita electorate. There were multiple candidates (usually between two and five) in all constituencies except South Guadalcanal. Campaigning was vigorous in most electorates, particularly in Honiara and Vella Lavella/Kolombangara electoral districts. The style of campaigning was low key, and there were no political parties involved.[64]

The public service members of the Governing Council were withdrawn in 1971.[65] After the 1970 general election, held between 26 May and 30 June, the new Governing Council was officially proclaimed on 15 July. Representation was extended to areas of smaller population, such as Rennell and Bellona, and Ontong Java (as Malaita Outer Islands). As before, in the Eastern Outer Islands constituency, the election was through an electoral college, but otherwise was held through a common roll of registered voters over 21 years of age. The estimated potential electorate was 68,222 (excluding the Eastern Outer Islands), with 49,053 people registered as voters.

In 1971, a political forum was held in Honiara during which leading Solomon Islanders spoke in favour of adopting the Westminster system. They called on Governing Council members to form one political party. This did not occur, although two members of the Governing Council founded political parties soon after. Peter Salaka attempted to begin the Labour Democratic Party and Joe Bryan (an expatriate) tried to form the Peoples' Protection Party. The latter began on Rere plantation in east Guadalcanal among local leaders from the area between Mbokokimbo River and the Kakau district and was intended to combat government forestry policy. The local member of the Legislative Council was Baddeley (later Sir Baddeley) Devesi, who was advised by Joe Bryan. The Peoples' Protection Party was the first environmental protection group. Although a regional party, it was responsible for changes passed in the 1969 Forests and Timber Ordinance. Benedict Kinika, Dr Gideon (later Sir Gideon) Zoloveke, and Ashley Wickham began the United Solomon Islands Party

---

64   The first political party was the Democratic Party, announced in June 1965, with Mariano Kelesi from Lau Lagoon, Malaita, as president and businessman Eric V. Lawson as secretary. It was short-lived. The next, the Solomons United National Party, in 1968, was formed by Bill Ramsay, David Kausimae from `Are`are, Malaita District, and Frank Wickham from Western District, but existed in name only until 1972. *BSIP AR* 1970: 5–6.
65   *BSIP NS*, 15 April 1970, 9 January 1976, 11.

on 27 July 1973; it lapsed later that year and was revived again in 1974.[66] The Independent Group, a consolidation of independent members, was formed by Willie Betu, who was born at Kia on Isabel Island but lived at Roviana Lagoon, New Georgia.

All 23 elected members of the Governing Council met formally in Honiara on 20 November 1970. They agreed to join one party led by Kinika, with Zoleveke as deputy, and Wickham as secretary.[67] Betu, chairman of the Social Services Committee, was appointed head of a steering committee to draw up the policies of the new party including all elected members. The five Governing Council chairmen were on the steering committee.[68] The request for the meeting came from Kinika, the chairman of the United Solomon Islands Party (USIPA). In a strange move, the USIPA agreed to disband and form a new party in March 1974, still using the old name.[69] This was opposed by Solomon Mamaloni, who organised another new party, then withdrew his initial plan, and in January 1974, formed the Peoples' Progressive Party. The 1960s and 1970s in Honiara were a hotbed of intrigue, alliances, deals, and optimistic visions.

Bart Ulufa'alu became a member of the Legislative Assembly in 1976, after which he formed the Coalition Opposition Group, which later became the Nationalists Party and then the National Democratic Party, in 1977.[70] David (later Sir David) Kausimae and Faneta Sirra began the Rural Alliance Party in 1977, which in 1980 merged with the People's Progressive Party, led by Mamaloni, to form the People's Alliance Party. There was also a Melanesian Action Party, which seems to have existed only on paper and, despite its name, was never active. Also in 1977, Peter Kenilorea formed the Solomon Islands United Party—a long-lasting political grouping.[71]

---

66 *KR*, August 1973.
67 The election of one member, Samuel Kuku, was declared invalid, hence 23, not 24 members.
68 Willie Betu, Phillip Solodia Funifaka, Solomon Mamaloni, David Kausimae, and Dr Gideon Zoleveke.
69 *BSIP NS*, 14 December 1973.
70 *SND*, 14 May 1976, 26 August 1977.
71 *BSIP NS*, 15 June 1965; Paia 1975: 83; Kenilorea 2008: 209, 265; Ulufa'alu 1983; Betu 1983; Kausimae 1983; *STT*, 12 October 1977.

The next general election was held in 1973, with 118 candidates vying for 24 seats based on universal adult suffrage, with the voting age set at 21 years. There were 65,534 registered voters—the increase showing the higher interest in the electoral process and more skilful campaigning by candidates. The last general election before independence was held in June 1976. The number of seats increased to 38, with 177 candidates. There were 78,646 registered voters, with a turnout of 44,438 voters.

The format of the Governing Council was not a success. In 1974, it was replaced with a Legislative Assembly, which enabled the creation of a Westminster ministerial system. There were 24 members, with Mamaloni as chief minister. Six portfolios were established: Agriculture and Rural Economy; Education and Cultural Affairs; Home Affairs; Health and Welfare; Trade, Industry and Labour; and Works and Public Utilities. The chief minister kept control of Home Affairs (until a sixth minister was appointed in November), retaining responsibility for immigration and for policy and coordination of the relationship with the South Pacific Commission.[72] In 1975, an order-in-council changed the country's name from the British Solomon Islands to Solomon Islands (with no use of 'the' as a definite article before the name).[73] Mamaloni was replaced as chief minister in 1976 with Kenilorea, who guided the Solomons through to independence and became the country's first prime minister. Between 1974 and 1978, Mamaloni and Kenilorea received the highest annual salaries of any Solomon Islanders: $12,000 each. The National Parliament began to meet after independence, which came on 7 July 1978.

The new political processes added spatial complexity to Honiara, particularly through the direct elections and political parties. Solomon Islanders developed political voices, and Honiara became a hotbed of political activity and intrigue—a quality it has maintained. Individual membership of political parties was not constant as parties lacked any strong ideological basis, except for those with connections to trade unions. Politicians used the parties as vehicles for personal betterment and changed camps easily. Compared with the modern extravagant style, early campaigning was lacklustre.

---

72 *BSIP AR* 1974: 137–38; *BSIP NS*, 6 September 1974.
73 *The British Solomon Islands (Name of Territory) Order 1975*, subsection 2 (1).

Plate 8.15 Chief Minister Peter Kenilorea addressing the motion to adopt the National Constitution, April 1978.
Source: Clive Moore Collection.

Plate 8.16 Prince Richard, Duke of Gloucester, Queen Elizabeth II's representative at the independence ceremony in Honiara, with Prime Minister Peter Kenilorea looking on, 7 July 1978.
Source: Clive Moore Collection.

Parliamentarians did not have an office unless they were a minister. They met constituents in their rooms at the parliamentary hostel in Hibiscus Avenue, at their homes if they happened to be Honiara-based, or wherever they were living with their *wantoks*. In the 1970s, telephones were mainly confined to government offices and were not common in Solomon Islander homes. Constituents found it best to make a personal visit to their Member of Parliament early in the morning, or in the evening at home, or at the hostel.

Sir Peter Kenilorea remembered the politics of the 1970s:

> Lobbying was greatest in the hotels, because while we were accommodated at the Government's expense, there was no subsistence allowance payable to members to attend meetings of Parliament, apart from their appointment grants and monthly salaries … Lobbying tactics included free meals and drinks at the Mendana and Honiara Hotels, the Lantern Inn in Chinatown, and the Honiara Club, the main eating places in town at that time. Expensive parties were also thrown in private homes. Members were easily lured into trading their votes for meals and alcohol. How simple that all seems now compared with the larger-scale corruption that blights the current Parliament.[74]

As still occurs, a great deal of business was conducted while walking along Mendana Avenue or shopping at Central Market, in Chinatown, or in the variety of stores around Point Cruz. The Mendana Hotel, the Point Cruz Yacht Club, and Blum's Hibiscus Hometel café became favourite political gathering places. Church buildings were also integral to the political process, as almost all Solomon Islanders attended church one or more times a week. This was the urban environment in which the parliamentary leaders emerged as part the new elite. Some of the most familiar faces around Honiara in the 1970s were the new generation of politicians who guided the nation from the late colonial days into the early years as an independent state.

***

By the 1970s, Honiara had become a Melanesian city—a city of villages. Education was crucial to developing the dominant Solomon Islander urban world, and Honiara housed the best educational institutions.

---

74 Kenilorea 2008: 207–8, also see p. 205.

Travel and the widening of horizons were another stepping-stone as Solomon Islanders ventured overseas in the 1950s and 1960s, returning with certificates, diplomas, and degrees, but also wiser about international affairs. Localisation progressed in churches, the public service, and the professions. Radio and newspapers enabled quick and wide transmission of information. Sporting facilities encouraged the mixing of and friendly competition between people from different islands. Trade unions developed worker consciousness. There were also self-doubt and blatant colonial racism to overcome. While loyalties to home islands and regions remained strong, slowly, a national consciousness developed. The incorporation of customary behaviours—such as lifestyles, dancing, and singing—into urban culture also helped create the nation. Alcohol became easily available in the 1960s, altering the behaviour of some residents. Whereas Tulagi was clearly a British town, Honiara had become a Pacific city, visited by the British monarch, but adapted to the needs of its inhabitants. The next two chapters cover Honiara after independence. Chapter 9 deals with larger institutional issues and Chapter 10 with the hybrid society that developed in the village-city.

9

Since independence

Plate 9.1 Busy Mendana Avenue in 2014.
Once lined with shade trees, Honiara's main street has become a hot and dusty area dominated by bitumen, concrete, and traffic jams.
Source: Christopher Chevalier Collection.

Modern Honiara

So far, *Honiara: Village-City of Solomon Islands* has concentrated on the years up to 1978—the period of the establishment of institutions that make up the modern nation. The final two chapters are broad essays on the past 40 years. At the time of independence, Honiara was centred on Point Cruz, with most of the business district, government offices, and other public buildings nearby. Low-density housing extended east and west along the coast. The second commercial centre was in Chinatown on the east bank of the Mataniko River, which was an area where rural visitors felt comfortable among the trade stores that were little different from those in the provinces. Further east there were several educational institutions built in the 1960s to serve the nation and surrounding Pacific territories. Ranadi was on the way to becoming the third business centre, based on light industry and warehouses. Henderson Airfield, 11 kilometres east of Point Cruz, was the international gateway, based on an old wartime airstrip. Housing was beginning to fill out the urban area and, as continues, leaf-thatch villages mixed with more permanent houses in the settlements. Leaf-thatch houses were also scattered around the more established houses in the suburbs, subsidiary to the main buildings.

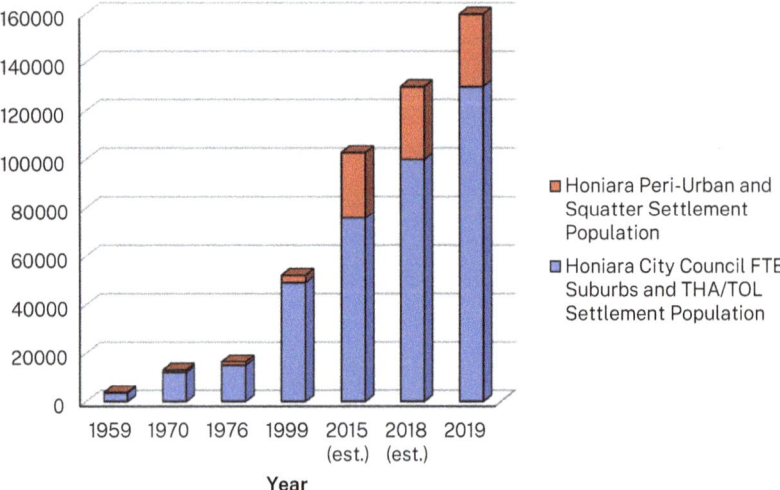

Figure 9.1 The population of Greater Honiara: The Honiara City Council area and the adjacent peri-urban population of Guadalcanal Province, 1959–2019.

Notes: The depiction in this graph should be regarded as approximate. Peri-urban areas of Honiara outside the city boundaries do not show up in statistics until 1999. Over time, squatter areas — many originally outside the town/city boundary — became THA/TOL areas once Honiara's boundary was expanded to incorporate 5,000 hectares of Queen Elizabeth National Park in 1973.

Sources: Based on BSIP (1961); SIG (2014a: 13; 2020g). Graph created by Jessica Carmichael.

Table 9.1 Honiara demographic overview, 1959–2009.

	1959	1970	1976	1986	1999	2009
Population	3,534	11,191	14,942	30,413	48,513	64,609
Males	2,664	7,237	8,905	17,293	27,050	34,089
Females	827	3,954	6,037	13,120	21,462	30,520
Households	445	1,644	2,734	4,317	6,921	8,981
Average household size (persons)	n.a.	n.a.	5.5	7.0	7.1	7.0

n.a. Not available
Note: Some of the figures are deceptive, particularly for 1959 and 1970 for household sizes, as significant numbers lived in barracks.
Sources: BSIP (1961, 1970); SIG (1988a, 1988b, 1999b, 2009).

Figure 9.1 and Table 9.1 provide an outline of population increases between 1959 and 2019 within the Honiara City Council boundaries and in Greater Honiara. The number of urban residents of Solomon Islands (overwhelmingly living in Honiara) increased by approximately 4.7 per cent every year—a doubling every two decades. Some Honiara settlements grew at twice this rate.[1] In 1976, Honiara's population was 14,942, which is comparable with that of a small Australian country town. More than 80 per cent of Honiara's population were Melanesian, and 7 to 8 per cent were Polynesian or Gilbertese. The percentage of Europeans in the town's population fell from 6.1 per cent in 1976 to 4.6 per cent in 1979. Chinese made up only 1.8 per cent in 1979. Malaitans were the main group: approximately 50 per cent of Honiara's residents aged 15 and over. The next largest group, about 12 per cent, was from Western Province. In 1970, there were still two men to every woman; by 1976, this had altered to two women to every three men, indicating the speed of the changes during the 1970s. In 1976, 83 per cent of the Solomon Islanders in Honiara had lived there for less than four years. A decade later, the population was 17,293 males and 13,120 females—a doubling in size and an improvement in the male/female ratio. Urban planners estimated that, based on the rate of increase in the 1970s, the population was likely to be 40,000 by 1996, which was lower than the official figure of 49,107 recorded in the 1999 census, and did not include people living in Greater Honiara beyond the city boundary.[2]

---

1   Keen et al. 2017: 19.
2   Oram 1980: 135–36.

HONIARA

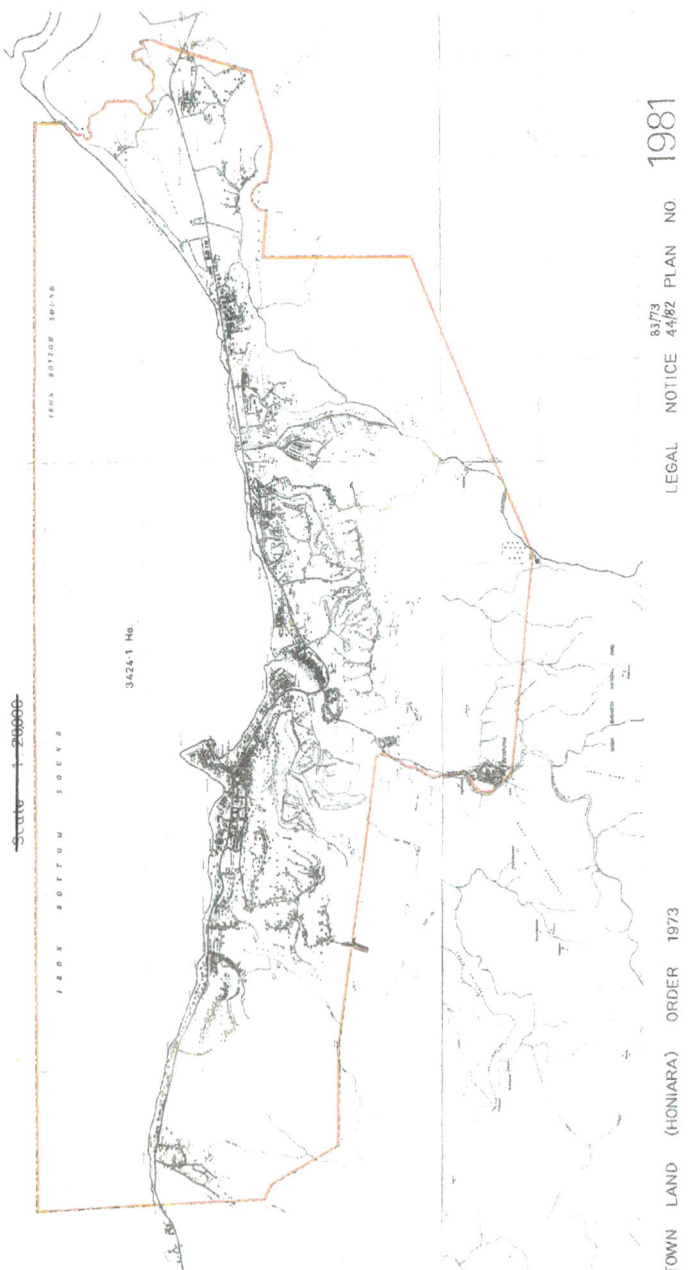

Map 9.1 Honiara town and boundary, 1981.
Although the map shows the section of Queen Elizabeth National Park gifted to the Honiara Town Council, it seems not to include THA/TOL or squatter areas.
Source: Solomon Islands Department of Lands and Survey.

Very few attempts have been made to estimate the full extent of Greater Honiara and its peri-urban fringe. For instance, Map 9.1 indicates that in 1981 about one-third of Honiara City Council land had been developed. However, it seems not to include THA/TOL or squatter areas. Map 10.1 is more accurate, although still limited largely to the area of the Honiara City Council. Recent mapping is much better. Map 10.4 shows the THA/TOL and squatter housing settlements in 2019, and Map 10.5 attempts to show projected growth between 2006 and 2025, and the expected overflow on to Tandai and Malango land.

Point Cruz is emblematic of changing Honiara. Over the past four decades, the promontory has been expanded into a major wharf and storage facility. It bears little resemblance to the original small island joined to the mainland by a reef and a low swampy causeway. To the east, alongside the main wharf and container terminal, is a network of wharves handling interisland shipping. The Point Cruz Yacht Club and the government patrol boat base are on the western side. Increasingly, Honiara has the infrastructure of a modern city, yet the basic geography—Point Cruz, the Mataniko River, the narrow coastal strip, the low ridges, and the many valleys in between—will always shape development. The hills and ridges make it a difficult city for which to provide services. Along with this, human changes and continuities bind Honiara into the modern nation. The number of occupants of settlements equals, or possibly exceeds, that in the suburbs, and housing standards vary enormously.

The population increased at least four or fivefold between 1976 and 2009. In the 2009 census, the male/female ratio had become close to equal. The number of households more than tripled between 1976 and 2009, and the average household size increased. The National Statistics Office's population estimate for the Honiara City Council area in 2009 was 67,000, which it projected would reach 100,000 in 2025.[3] How wrong they were. The official estimate from the 2019 national census is 130,000 within the boundaries of Honiara City Council and another 30,000 in what includes Greater Honiara: a combined total of 160,000 people.

---

3   SIG 2019c: 'Projected Population by Province, 2010–25'.

Plate 9.2 The Honiara waterfront to the east of Point Cruz in 2017, showing international ships at the old main wharf on the right and the smaller interisland shipping wharves to the left.
The fuel storage area is behind and the National Parliament is on the hill.
Source: Clive Moore Collection.

Plate 9.3 Honiara's modern interisland shipping wharves, 2014.
Source: Clive Moore Collection.

Honiara has become the seat of government, the headquarters of Guadalcanal Province, the home of the nation's best schools, and the headquarters of most Christian denominations. It is also home to the head offices of commercial companies and NGOs. It is the 'arrival city' for Solomon Islands, a place where many aspire to live, even with the financial and social difficulties that accompany urban life. However, Honiara City Council has always been weak (compared with many overseas city councils of similar size) and is not really in charge of urban development plans, being subservient to the whims of the national government on most matters. The government has done little to create the necessary infrastructure for anything beyond the more formally planned areas. The results of this lack of forethought are clear in the size of the barely controlled settlements.

The most populous wards in 1970 were Panatina, Mataniko, Vavaea, and Kola`a. Mataniko and Vavaea were central to early settlement (Map 5.2). Kola`a, Vura, and Panatina in the east are geographically the largest wards, stretching furthest inland from the coast. In 1973, Kola`a and Vura absorbed the major part of the national park, and Panatina was also extended. By 1976, Kola`a and Vura in the east, and Nggosi in the west, were all growing fast. In 1986, the most populous wards were Panatina, Vura, Vavaea, and Kola`a Ridge, indicating the population shift to the east. Twenty years later, the largest wards were Nggosi, Kola`a Ridge, Vura, and Panatina. The overall settlement pattern remains the same as earlier: the rich live on the hills and the poor live in the valleys. The population of Point Cruz, the administrative and commercial hub, has remained small. Panatina, once only an education and industrial enclave, has now developed into a major housing area, extending along the coast as far east as (but not quite including) the Burns Creek settlement, and stretching inland. Vura Ward includes Vura suburb, Kobito, and Gilbert Camp, plus numerous other settlements. In 2009, 365 Honiara dwellings were listed as being constructed from makeshift or improvised materials, and 1,586 (of 8,981) had traditional thatched roofs—an indication that squatter settlements and urban villages continued to use local building materials.

Plate 9.4 A prosperous Lengakiki Ridge house, 2014.
Source: Clive Moore Collection.

Plate 9.5 A typical Honiara house combining local and Western materials, 2014.
Source: Christopher Chevalier Collection.

Table 9.2 Population of wards within Honiara, 1970–2009.

Ward	1970	1976	1986	2009
Nggosi	1,130	1,638	3,900	10,068
Mbumbaru	442	440	1,350	3,625
Rove-Lenggakiki[a]	776	1,023	1,554	2,646
Cruz	632	334	545	232
Vavaea	1,402	2,219	4,699	6,954
Vuhokesa	432	576	634	1,191
Mataniko[b]	1,413	1,246	2,317	4,347
Kola`a[c]	1,307	2,447	4,279	10,151
Kukum	862	1,023	1,654	1,835
Naha	544	365	577	356
Vura	586	2,183	4,830	9,096
Panatina	1,624	1,499	4,884	14,108
Total	11,150	14,993	31,223	64,609

[a] Also spelt Langgakiki or Lengakiki.
[b] Also spelt Matanikau.
[c] Also spelt Kolaa or Kola.
Sources: SIG (2011b: 13); Floyd (1976: 7a).

Other social indicators are worth noting here: marriages, religious denominations, and schools. The marriage pattern during the mid-1980s was similar to that in the rest of the country, wherein men married later in life than women by several years—an indication that men were expected to be able to provide a living and accommodation for their wives and potential families before they entered into marriage. The proportions of religious denominations did not entirely mirror the national statistics (Table 7.1). Adherents of the Anglican Church of Melanesia (9,330) were the largest Christian group: 30.6 per cent of Honiara's population, which was lower than their 33.9 per cent nationwide. The SSEC had 7,742 adherents, or 25.4 per cent of Honiara's population, which was much higher than their national level of 17.6 per cent. The same applied to the SDAs: 4,851 adherents, or 15.9 per cent, when the national figure was only 10 per cent. The United Church had 2,551 adherents, or 8.4 per cent. And even though the Catholics had been an important presence on Guadalcanal since the 1890s, they only made up 3,863, or 12.7 per cent, of Honiara's Christians, compared with a national proportion of 19.2 per cent.[4]

---

4   SIG 1988b: 12, 14, 15.

The modern education system begins with early childhood education and six years of primary schooling. The percentage of boys and girls attending primary school is approximately equal. The secondary system divides into junior secondary school (Years 7 to 9) and senior secondary school (Years 10 to 12). The rapid creation of community high schools since the 1990s, which include primary and lower secondary levels, has now swelled the number of secondary school students. As would be expected in a capital city, Honiara has the best-educated population in the nation. Whereas some of the provinces had larger numbers of students at primary school, none matched Honiara for secondary school attendance. The best Honiara upper-level schools are King George VI, the SDA's Betikama, the Catholic St Joseph's Tenaru, the Anglican St Nicholas College, and Woodford International School.

Solving disputes

In a Pacific city the size of Honiara, civil disturbances can easily get out of control, and rivalry between Solomon Islands' diverse peoples is quite usual. The issue has its origins in cultural isolation, the comparative size of the ethnic groups, the power of ancestors and spirituality, and translates to antagonisms in modern society. Before the protectorate administration began in 1896, there was interisland trade and marriage, accompanied by fighting, headhunting, and enslavement. Even closely related kin groups could hold animosities. Canoes were constantly on the move around the coasts of each island and between islands, and groups walked across and around islands, visiting kin, trading, and harvesting seasonal crops. Internecine fighting was ubiquitous. On plantations overseas and in the protectorate, there was also animosity between groups of labourers from different places, although the origins of Pijin, *wantokism*, and pan-island nationalism also date back to these same workplaces.

Sporting games can regularly cause overexcitement in an almost tribal or at least an island-centred manner. Elements of ethnic competition and rivalry are often present at sporting events at Lawson Tama and Town Ground. Lawson Tama is close to Chinatown, with the possibility of looting if any situation gets out of control. The area around Town Ground is also vulnerable as it includes shops, residential accommodation, and government offices. At such times, the police are always very careful in handling crowds. While many events have no relationship to alcoholic excess, once bans were lifted (between 1959 and 1965), alcohol became an extra element, exacerbated more recently by supplies of *kwaso* (home brew).

Solomon Islands is a nation of 900 islands, several of them large and populous, and all divided between descent and language groups. Solomon Mamaloni was correct when he said the nation owed its name to the Spanish and its modern boundaries to the British, who divided the BSIP into four regions for administrative purposes, whereas by his count there were 25 'island nations' inside the Solomon Islands nation. Mamaloni is often quoted as saying: 'Solomon Islands or "the Solomon Islands Community" has never been a Nation and will never be a nation and will never become one.'[5]

His words, written 30 years ago, still have a ring of truth about them. All of this influenced the political events that occurred in Honiara and the way in which the government attempted to ameliorate tense situations. Several cultural mechanisms, and their abuses, paved the way to the Tensions of 1998–2003. Some of the disputes that fed into the Tension years—Maasina Rule and the Moro Movement, for instance—occurred in the days of the British protectorate when an element of anti-government rhetoric was intertwined with the desire to re-establish customary legal systems. As outlined in the previous chapter, trade unions began in the 1960s, flexing their industrial muscle and making demands, which created a voice for working people and an understanding of the power of group action. On the government side, the colonial-era police soon realised that new control methods were needed, which led to the modernisation of the RSIPF during the 1950s. In the late 1960s, a police field force and riot squad were created. While not riots (although that was what Mamaloni called them) and not the first strike (Maasina Rule was the first labour strike), trade union demonstrations in the 1960s and 1970s were the first times the post-war BSIP Government had to deal with crowds of citizens in Honiara refusing to obey police orders. The ability (or lack) of the police to handle riots and civil discontent was part of the mix. In 1993, when Prime Minister Mamaloni authorised the purchase of high-powered weapons for the police (for use in relation to the Bougainville rebellion), this provided modern guns not previously available in Solomon Islands.

---

5   Mamaloni 1992: 10.

One peculiarity leading up to and during the Tension years was the way traditional compensation practices were corrupted. Paying cultural compensation is a standard procedure in Solomon Islands society, and has survived strongly on some islands, particularly Malaita. The origins of the compensation concept relate to payments with traditional valuables—livestock (usually pigs) and food—not modern currency. There are many reasons to demand compensation. After independence, the disputes became more political and a pattern emerged of offering cash payments as compensation. This escalated and, by the time of the Tensions, the practice was accepted as a normal process by the national government.

Compensation is a fundamental contradiction or tension between socially positive and socially destructive behaviours. Exchanges of traditional items maintain equilibrium in society after some slight—perhaps swearing at humans or ancestors, or at a pig destined for sacrifice, or because of insult, injury, or death. In Solomon Islands, a great deal of emphasis is placed on the language of respect within networks, based on age, gender, place, and kin. Any violation of these codes of conduct—for example, swearing and using profanities—can rapidly escalate into conflict, violence, and calls for retribution. In Solomon Islands, 'swears' (as they are referred to in Pijin) have to be heard to be believed. I am most familiar with Malaitan 'swears'. They are vituperative and often involve human anatomy and 'taboo' bodily fluids such as blood and faeces. They are aimed at ancestors or even the mother or grandmother of the victim of the 'swear'. I have never heard any European profane with anything like the intensity of an angry Solomon Islander in full flight. It is a refined cultural form intended to get a reaction and, fuelled by alcohol, it can reach eloquent heights. Compensation is usually demanded for a 'swear'.

The Solomon Islands 'nation' was a British creation; the southern and northern boundaries are arbitrary, created to placate wider German and French colonial interests. Inter-district rivalry is not new. In June 1978, just before independence, a poem was published in the *Solomon Star* that denigrated the people of Western Province. Even now, it is seldom republished (to my knowledge, only once and never within Solomon Islands), such is the antagonism it caused.[6] Called *Ode to the West Wind*, it was scathingly derogatory of what the writer viewed as the high-handed ways of the people of the western Solomons.[7] The author was sent to

---

6   Fraenkel 2004: 116.
7   *SND*, 9 June 1978.

prison and the national government paid SI$9,000 in compensation to Western Province—a sizeable amount more than 40 years ago. This was the beginning of national government payments of cash compensation for events that denigrated ethnic groups within the nation. Western Province—the province closest to Papua New Guinea, at the border with Bougainville—boycotted the 1978 independence ceremonies, not so much because of the poem, but because it wanted maximum autonomy and the National Constitution did not guarantee devolution of powers to the regions. It was eventually coaxed in by Prime Minister Kenilorea in 1979 with a series of ad hoc responses relating to the transfer of Choiseul land held by the national government, and negotiations over the future citizenship status of Gilbertese immigrants.[8] Although relations were patched together, it is a longstanding grievance and, when the Tensions began, once more, a Western breakaway movement emerged. Although phrased in terms of regional autonomy, there was an ethnic element based on the blackness of the Western people's skin—a genetic characteristic that links them to Bougainville—and their belief that Western Province is the economic engine of the nation.[9]

Another incident occurred during 1984–85, when people from the Kwaio language/culture area on Malaita boycotted the national elections because of lack of compensation for a devastating government-organised massacre in 1927, following the killing of their district officer, his deputy, and 13 police on a tax-collecting mission.[10] The 'Kwaio Fadanga'[11] had to be placated: Prime Minister Kenilorea made two trips to talk to the Kwaio, who demanded an almost meaningless SI$300 billion in compensation—best regarded as an ambit claim marking their extreme discontent. Kwaio anger had been simmering for decades. They presented the National Parliament with lists of the dead and items destroyed and raised the issue of compensation with the British High Commission, which refused to engage with an event so long ago. Kenilorea's government paid no compensation. In his autobiography, Kenilorea shows discomfort about dealing with the Kwaio, even though his family is from a neighbouring area on Malaita and he knew Kwaio customs well. As anthropologist

---

8   Premdas et al. 1984.
9   Scales 2007.
10 Moore 2017a: 404–12, 2019: 227–43; Keesing and Corris 1980.
11 *Fadanga* means meeting or discussion. It developed into a political pressure group, operating mainly in the Kwaio language area on Malaita, and in Honiara in a small way. Akin 1999; Kenilorea 2008: 267–71.

David Akin suggests, imbedded in the Kwaio demands was a desire that their customary law ('*kastom* law') should also be recognised, not just British-derived law. They were also opposed to Christian beliefs that banned payments of compensation. There is evidence of this dialogue over law and *kastom* going back at least to the 1930s, and probably as far back as the plantations in Queensland and Fiji in the nineteenth century. A similar element permeates later demands for compensation in Honiara. At its core is non-recognition of the modern state's legal system and a retreat to much older ways of seeking justice.

Kenilorea was responsible for beginning government-sponsored cash payments (to Western Province); Mamaloni took them to new heights. The next serious disturbance was in November 1989 when 5,000 mainly Malaitan youths rioted in Honiara. This riot was triggered by a 'swear' against Malaitans when insulting remarks were written on a shop door at Central Market, supposedly by a Polynesian man from Rennell and Bellona Province. Malaitan youths, fuelled by disenchantment with their lack of access to paid work, quite predictably reacted with anger and violence. Over four days, they used the incident as an excuse to loot stores in Chinatown and along Mendana Avenue.[12] Prime Minister Mamaloni took personal charge of the situation. He prided himself on being able to read the character of the various provinces and knew that antagonisms between Malaitans and Ren/Bels (as those from Rennell and Bellona are known) were longstanding. All Solomon Islanders are aware of this, and often use the 'cats and dogs' simile to describe interaction between the two groups. Although Rennell and Bellona people are few compared with Malaitans, this has never stopped violent interaction. Mamaloni ordered a swift response from the police, who used tear gas to disperse the mob. Access to Chinatown was blocked and the Tandai Highway was closed. White River settlement, with its substantial Malaitan and Ren/Bel populations, was cut off from the city. A few hours after the riot, Mamaloni went on SIBC radio to make a national address in Solomons Pijin. He pleaded for calm in the young nation and asked that the issue be settled through compensation payments. By 3 am, Police Minister Victor Ngele had negotiated a truce and a compensation payment of SI$200,000 from the national government to the Malaita Province Government.

---

12   *SS*, 17 November 1989, 10.

A similar incident occurred in 1996. A man of Polynesian heritage from Reef Islands had supposedly cursed Malaitans at a Honiara night club. The next day, Malaitans assembled at Central Market and demonstrations began. There was a confrontation at the market when several Reef Islanders drew up in a truck and faced a mob of perhaps 1,000 Malaitans. They showed no fear, and the Malaitans showed restraint and respect for Reef fighting prowess.[13] Three days of tension followed. Chinese shops were looted, petrol bombs were readied, and threats were made to burn down Honiara. Shops and schools closed. The government capitulated, using its Community Development Fund to compensate both sides. The 1989 incident was quoted as a precedent for the level of compensation necessary during the Tensions, and Malaitan leaders also referred to *kastom* law as justification. Once again, it marginalised a weak central government and strengthened customary rights.

Unlike Western law, *kastom* law can vary from area to area, even on one island, and enormously between islands. Nor are *kastom* beliefs necessarily external to government processes, as public servants are sympathetic and often unhappy with the weakness of the state they serve. As David Akin concluded:

> The political message that Malaitans delivered in Honiara's streets was not only one of dissatisfaction with the government, but also one of defiance of government control over their island and their affairs.[14]

The 1989 and 1996 riots revealed the underlying, simmering social and economic issues that would emerge fully blown in 1998. While Mamaloni solved the immediate problem in 1989, he was not forthcoming with longer-term solutions. In fact, he closed some schemes in Honiara to assist unemployed youths, seemingly to discourage a further flow of migrants from the provinces, particularly Malaita. He followed this strategy to deal with similar smaller riots and disturbances. Each time, the government provided cash compensation. In 1996, the disturbance was once more between Malaitans and Polynesian groups, the rhetoric directed at all Polynesians, including those from the eastern outer islands of Sikaiana (part of Malaita Province), Ontong Java Atoll, and Tikopia, plus Reef Islanders, who have a mixed Polynesian and Melanesian

---

13   From an eyewitness account.
14   Akin 1999: 61.

heritage. The 1990s riots all involved Malaitans and probably delayed reform of the National Constitution towards adopting a federal rather than a centralised government system. Although Malaitans make up one-third of the Solomons population, their province contains only one-sixth of the land area. This has led to large-scale migration to other provinces and substantial intermarriage outside their own province. The emphasis on central government and the provincial system enabled Malaitans to access services and employment in other provinces, while on Malaita itself there was very little 'modern' development. Malaitans need access to the other provinces to balance out their excess population and to access cash work. It was not clear how the smaller provinces (particularly Rennell and Bellona, and Temotu) could access enough funds under a system of state governments.

Not all prime ministers approved of cash compensation. Prime Minister Ulufa'alu did not, or at least he delayed too long, which was his undoing during the Tensions and led to him being forcibly deposed. In 2000, during Ulufa'alu's term as leader, in response to Guale provocation, disaffected Malaitan young men gained access to guns in the police armouries, which began years of thuggery and extortion by members of the Malaita Eagle Force.

Cost of living in Honiara, 1998–2003

Another aspect of all this was that Honiara was then (and still is) an expensive place to live. Part of what was happening in the 1990s was increasing pressure on its residents, and a sense of hopelessness as conditions deteriorated. No one had faith that the national government was working to improve the situation. The Honiara Retail Price Index—the best gauge of living costs—constantly increased between 1989 and 1999, by an average of 10.7 per cent a year, which was not matched by increases in jobs and incomes. The highest increase was 15.2 per cent in 1991. Food prices increased markedly, as did the cost of alcohol and tobacco, clothing, footwear, housing, and utilities. A 1995 Honiara household income survey showed that many Solomon Islands families in Honiara received an average of only SI$619 (then about A$90) a month in income, and wages were only a small part of that figure. Much of their earnings came from selling their own garden produce, or from onselling other produce, such as betel nuts, from the provinces. The high level of inflation created desperate living conditions during these years, which were compounded during the Tensions. Many families survived on a diet of home-grown tapioca and green vegetables, and as little store-bought food as possible.[15]

The government remained by far the biggest employer in Honiara, with a weak private sector trailing behind. In 1986, there were 29,178 males and 10,032 females employed in Honiara. In 1999, 39,761 males were employed, along with 17,711 females, showing female employment growing faster than for males. Jobs for women were mainly in wholesale and trading services, which were lower in pay and status. In the late 1990s, the beginning of the Gold Ridge mine in the central mountains of Guadalcanal (Maps 0.2 and 9.2) directly stimulated Honiara, which benefited through the development of infrastructure. The mine began operations in 1998, and the next year produced 130,000 ounces of gold, earning approximately US$36.4 million. The inhabitants of the mine site were resettled on the coastal plain 20 kilometres east of Honiara.[16] In 2020, that all seemed like a dream, with the mine closed and the tailings dam in a dangerous condition. The mining company offloaded the mine (and its responsibility for pollution from the tailings dam) to the local landowners for SI$100.

The 1970s–1990s lead-up to the Tension years

Social tensions that were beginning to build in the 1970s and 1980s finally exploded in 1998–99.[17] By the mid-1980s, the Guale were increasingly frustrated by the lack of economic benefits flowing to their province from the agricultural developments on Guadalcanal Plains, and the presence of an ever-expanding Honiara. As already mentioned, on the plains, the landowners owned only 2 per cent of the Commonwealth Development Corporation's SIPL company, although they also received rent for each hectare. The national government held 30 per cent of SIPL, and the company held the rest. There was no involvement from the provincial

---

15   Otter 2002: 65, 'Honiara Income Distribution Survey, 1995'.
16   SIG 2001: 25; Tolia and Petterson 2005.
17   Moore 2004a; Fraenkel 2004; Keesing 1995.

government. By the time of the Tensions, the oil palm estate covered 6,000 hectares, with another 1,000 hectares still under negotiation, and was contributing around 20 per cent to the nation's gross domestic product. When the Gold Ridge mine arranged land leases at a higher level of return, resentment swelled among the traditional owners of the SIPL land. In early 1999, the Ulufa`alu Government announced that as part of its privatisation plans, it wanted to reduce its holdings in SIPL from 30 to 10 per cent, selling the difference to CDC. Although the Guadalcanal Provincial Government objected, wanting the shares to be transferred to it, the financial needs of the national government were too great. A deal was done to sell 10 per cent of the national government's SIPL holdings to Solomon Islanders, in a scheme managed by the Investment Corporation of Solomon Islands. This never occurred and the landowners were left with an unsatisfactory 2 per cent.[18]

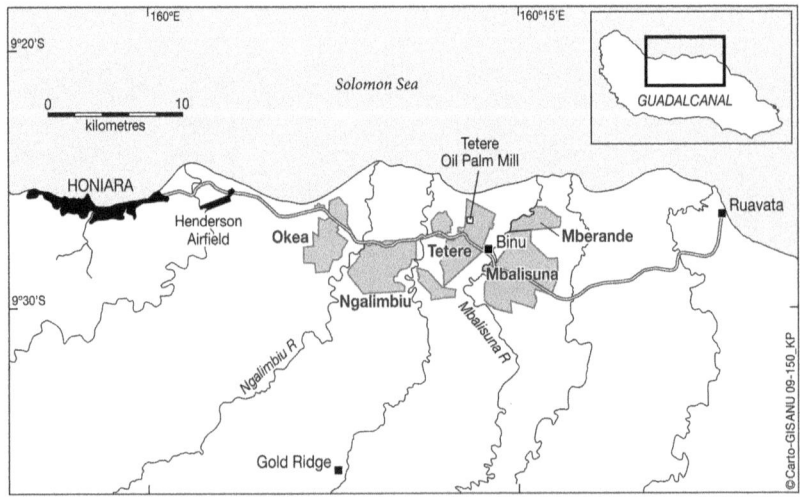

Map 9.2 Honiara (in black) and oil palm plantations (in grey) on Guadalcanal Plains, 2009.
Source: Jon Fraenkel Collection.

There were also difficult and violent elements among the Malaitan settlers on Guadalcanal Plains and in Honiara, who insisted on operating within Malaitan *kastom* realms, which were alien to Guale ways. The Guale felt that Malaitan customary ways were being substituted for their own and that they were losing control of their land. The situation was not unique in

---

18   Moore 2004a: 73–75.

the Pacific Islands. For instance, the same has happened in Port Moresby, where migrants from the Highlands have overridden the local Motu–Koitapu peoples, who have lost control of large areas of their traditional (but now urban) land. Port Moresby's barren hills were transformed into market gardens for industrious Highlanders. The Motu–Koitapu have not been able to compete in commerce with the Highlanders, who dominate transport and many of the small business ventures in the city. It has also happened in Lae, Papua New Guinea's second-largest urban area, where Highlanders and north coast peoples have had easy access to the city via the highways.[19]

While the storm gathered, the number of squatter settlements around Honiara increased. They occupied government-owned and Guale customary land under several arrangements. As explained in Chapter 5, the Guale had 'sold off' (or at least allowed settlement on) some of their lands around Honiara in a complex web of deals that combined cash with customary arrangements. Often, the arrangements were made between men, without involving Guale women, in a matrilineal society in which women were the custodians of the land. Many of the residents on THA/TOL land had been squatters in the 1970s and 1980s; their land had been incorporated into 'formal' arrangements within the boundaries of Honiara City Council. Squatters had also been living on Guadalcanal Plains to the east of Honiara since the 1960s, in ever-increasing numbers, often through customary arrangements with Guale landholders and through intermarriage. Map 6.2 shows the division of land on the Guadalcanal Plains in the 1970s. By the 1990s, there were thousands of settlers on the plains, mainly the families of SIPL employees, and in urban areas they had extended their occupancy far beyond the original customary or THA/TOL boundaries granted for their use. Although their personal rights were tenuous, Malaitan men who married Guale women had some rights through their wives and children. On Guadalcanal, at marriage, women move to their husband's place of residence. Once they are young adults or their father dies, male children usually return to their mother's land and establish themselves there through their relationships with maternal uncles.[20] Many of the newcomers (the migrants from elsewhere) paid no rent, securing their occupancy rights through friendship and kinship. For instance, one group at Abuabili had sweet potato gardens, the crops from

---

19   Stuart 1970; Oram 1976; Strathern 1975; Willis 1974: 145–53.
20   Allen 2012a: 302.

which they sold at Honiara's Central Market, giving a percentage of their profits to the local big-men in the Guale *mamata* (matrilineal landowning group). *Chupu* exchanges (explained in Chapter 5) were paid, but these only provided usufructuary rights for the lifetime of the individual to whom they were granted. Over several decades, the settlements became permanent, although in Guale customary law the settlers did not have permanent ownership rights. Nevertheless, they were inclined to interpret their presence in terms of land rights in the societies from which they originated. Once more, *kastom* was interacting with modern forms of settlement and causing contradictions.[21] The situation was made more complex by the interisland migration of families from the isolated and impoverished Weather Coast to the plains, and to Honiara. Their movements began in the 1950s and intensified from the 1970s.

The Tension years, 1998–2003[22]

The greed of the national elite, most of whom lived in Honiara, was faintly recognisable in the immediate post-independence years (1978–86), and grew exponentially during the years of the logging boom (1987–98). Despite attempts since 2003 to pass anticorruption legislation, since RAMSI departed in mid-2017, corruption has cautiously increased, dampened but not thwarted by government attempts to monitor the practice and increasing numbers of civil society monitoring groups.

Honiara always had a high rate of inward migration. High proportions of the inhabitants supplemented their economic activities with 'village work'—an indication of the importance of the subsistence and cash-crop gardens on the fringes of Honiara.[23] The lifestyles of residents in the settlements, particularly in squatter areas, were basic and lacked certainty. Poverty increased, as did unemployment. The ingredients for civil unrest were all present, mixed with issues surrounding federalism and constitutional reform, which have been argued over continuously since before independence in 1978.

---

21 ibid., 92; Lasaqa 1968; Fraenkel et al. 2010: 67; Allen 2012a.
22 An earlier version of this section was published in Moore 2018.
23 SIG 1988b: 23, 27; Atai 2017. A 2017 report suggests that 79 per cent of Honiara residents are involved in some form of agriculture. SIG 2019d: xiv, 15, Table 4.1.

There is a substantial literature describing the 1998–2003 Tensions and the RAMSI era that followed.[24] There was continuous civil disturbance and militancy that, although it did not affect the whole nation, strongly affected Guadalcanal, Malaita, and Western Province. In the last, it was because of evacuations to there from Honiara, Malaitans already living in the province, and its proximity to Bougainville. Although the circumstances were different, the Bougainville rebellion against the PNG Government was too close to be ignored. During the civil war on Bougainville (1988–98), both the PNG Defence Force and the Bougainville Revolutionary Army made incursions across the border into Western and Choiseul provinces. Around 9,000 Bougainvilleans fled to Solomon Islands, most to Guadalcanal, living there for several years, which meant Guale militants had some direct contact with Bougainville militants.[25]

A long-term underlying reason for the Tensions was lack of economic development on heavily populated Malaita, which caused migration in search of work. Many of the migrants settled in and around Honiara, causing the population to overflow on to surrounding Guadalcanal land.[26] A related reason was Guale discontent with the lack of development on their island beyond the urban and peri-urban areas. There were troubles with unwelcome settlers around the oil palm plantations on the plains, and royalties from the oil palm plantations and the Gold Ridge mine. As well, the Guale lamented what they saw as a lack of respect for their culture. Key issues involved the rights both of free access for all citizens and of traditional custodians of the land. It is also fair to say that governance and political processes had deteriorated, and the rich were gathering wealth at the expense of the poorer majority of people, all of whom were increasingly frustrated as the great promises that had seemed to come with independence receded.

After growing disquiet over several decades, by 1998–99, some of the people of Guadalcanal finally lost patience. One indicative issue going back to 1988 were the multiple murders by Kwaio Malaitans at Mt Austen above Honiara. Anthropologist Roger Keesing's analysis shows the collision between 'two modes of life and two systems of meaning;

---

24 Allen 2007, 2013; Braithwaite et al. 2010; Liloqula and Pollard 2007; Naitoro 2000; Kabutaulaka 2002b. For the literature on Solomon Islands during the RAMSI years, see Moore 2017b.
25 Kabutaulaka 2001: 16; Moore 2004a: 13–14, 53, 97–98; Fraenkel 2004: 127–28.
26 Moore 2007b.

and two moral and legal systems that barely communicate with one another'.[27] To many Guadalcanal people, this seemed to epitomise Malaitans living on their land riding roughshod over their customs. Encouraged by leaders who should have tried alternative approaches within the legal system, in the late 1990s, elements of the Guadalcanal people decided to take the law into their own hands. They purposefully and violently expelled fellow Solomon Islanders—predominantly Malaitan families living around the oil palm plantations on Guadalcanal Plains. Others from all provinces left Honiara once the situation became too dangerous;[28] between 25,000 and 35,000 people fled.

Plate 9.6 Prime Minister Ezekiel Alebua (1986–89), later Premier of Guadalcanal Province (1998–2003), during the Tensions.
He was wounded during an attempted assassination in 2001 and was later imprisoned for corruption.
Source: Christopher Chevalier Collection.

The first militia formed was the Guadalcanal Revolutionary Army, which was later renamed the Isatabu Freedom Movement (IFM). Ezekiel Alebua, then Guadalcanal Premier (and former prime minister, 1986–89), and Sethuel Kelly (a former cabinet minister in the National Parliament) provoked discontent in a manner that was unseemly for national leaders. The behaviour of Alebua and other leading Guadalcanal political figures was probably treasonous, although they were never charged.[29] The turmoil and the mass expulsion were a major catastrophe for the citizens of Honiara and Guadalcanal. Thousands of refugees were dispossessed of their jobs, land, and homes, which led to the counter-formation of the Malaita Eagle Force (MEF), which comprised mainly Malaitans who were current or past residents of Honiara and Guadalcanal Plains. In cahoots with Malaitan sections of the police, the MEF took control of Honiara. The IFM and MEF clashed over the next several years. Raids

---

27   Keesing 1995.
28   Allen 2012b: 164.
29   There will never be agreement on this point. Moore 2004a: 105, 2018: 167, fn. 8. See also Fraenkel 2004: 47–48.

and atrocities became the norm, homes and schools were burned, and no-go zones with roadblocks were declared. The quasi-militant groups fought more through skirmishes than through battles. It was a disastrous situation that brought no credit to either side. Both groups performed traditional magic said to impart martial invincibility—a Solomons touch to modern military confrontation.[30]

Despite national and international attempts to mediate, the government found itself increasingly unable to control the situation. Then, in a June 2000 coup, Malaitans in the police force removed Prime Minister Ulufa`alu, forcing his resignation. The next two governments, led by prime ministers Sogavare and Kemakeza, failed to regain control. All three prime ministers pleaded for international intervention, which eventually came in July 2003 in the form of the Australian-controlled, Pacific Islands Forum–sponsored Regional Assistance Mission to Solomon Islands (RAMSI), which restored law and order and set about strengthening sagging central government processes.

Plate 9.7 Bartholomew Ulufa`alu, Prime Minister of Solomon Islands (1997–2000), addresses the UN General Assembly in New York on 30 September 1999.

He was deposed during a coup on 5 June 2000 and resigned on 14 June. He became leader of the opposition and finance minister in the Sogavare Government in 2006. He died in 2007 after a long battle with diabetes.

Source: UN Photo/Eskinder Debebe, UNO Image 384479, available from: un.org/en/conferences/small-islands/newyork1999.

---

30   Allen 2013: Figure 2.3, pp. 41, 127. Malaitan informants have told me similar stories.

Until then life in Honiara was difficult and dangerous. The police were compromised and largely under MEF control.[31] Terrible things happened. Beheadings and torture occurred: a headless Guale corpse was left in Central Market and, in retaliation, the head of an MEF member was presented to the Multinational Police Assistance Group. There were also assassinations: seven Melanesian religious Brothers were executed on the Weather Coast by Harold Keke and his Guale group; IFM leader Selwyn Saki was killed, his throat cut, and his body mutilated; Father Augustine Geve, the Minister for Youth, Sport and Women, was killed, as was former Police Commissioner Sir Frederick Soaki. Two masked men killed two Guadalcanal militants while they were in a locked ward in hospital in Honiara.[32] People left Honiara to avoid the worst of the confrontations. Solomon Islanders remember the feeling of helplessness during the Tension years. In 2017, reflecting on the Tensions, Sir Allan Kemakeza said:

> We were basically a lawless state with armed criminal militia creating a feeling of fear throughout all layers of the community and impacting all our day to day lives. The impact on the economy was crippling.[33]

Fraudulent 'fast money' and 'pyramid' schemes circulated. One in 2002 was the Princess Diana Family Charity Fund, which was calculated to dupe an already poor and desperate urban population. Another, the Royal Association of Nations and Kingdoms, tempted the Kemakeza Government with an offer of a US$2.6 billion grant.[34] Compensation claims, exploitation, and intimidation became endemic, frightening, and constant. The list below is a sample. In 1998, Premier Alebua announced that his province wanted SI$50 payments for every non-Guale in Honiara and a further payment of SI$100,000 for each of the 24 Guale killed by Malaitans 'for no reason' since independence. In 1999, the national government paid Guadalcanal Province SI$2.5 million as compensation for 'hosting' the capital city and consequent social disruption, but this did not stop attempts to remove Malaitans from Guadalcanal. Often government ministers felt so intimidated they handed over cash to try to ameliorate thuggery. The total amount is difficult to calculate. For instance, in 2000, SI$100,000 went to individuals involved in special police operations,

---

31 Short 2015.
32 Moore 2004b: 4, 131, 141, 152, 190; Carter 2006; Macdonald-Milne 2020: 204–9.
33 Kemakeza 2017.
34 Kabutaulaka 2004: 395.

many with fictitious names, and Prime Minister Ulufa'alu offered both Guadalcanal and Malaita provinces SI$5 million in compensation for incidents in which chiefs had been sworn at or shown disrespect. The money paid to Guadalcanal Province was not accounted for by Premier Alebua, and the money for Malaita Province was seized by the MEF and never reached the province's bank account. The MEF demanded a further SI$50 million. The Honiara Casino was robbed of SI$100,000 in cash. In 2001, the 'special constables' absorbed SI$11 million. Businesses were harassed for money and goods were 'requisitioned', vehicle theft and housebreaking were daily events, and government property was looted. Four-wheel-drive vehicles, particularly new ones owned by members of the diplomatic corps, were keenly sought after for 'road testing' on Malaita. In the 12 months from August 2000, the government gave out SI$140 million in duty remissions, many of them to ex-MEF commanders who had gone into business. Jimmy 'Rasta' Lusibaea received 100 per cent remissions on SI$280,000 of alcohol imported for his bottle shop, and another SI$60,000 in cash compensation for an incident in Fishing Village. More than 300 vehicles entered the country without import tax being paid, plus millions of dollars of duty were forgone on imported tobacco and alcohol. In the lead-up to the 2001 national election, the government paid out more than SI$15 million to ex-militants, police, and politicians, using Taiwanese aid money intended to compensate displaced people.[35]

The total amount rorted was huge and could never be justified in a bankrupt nation. Nevertheless, what happened was often done as a compromise to keep the government functioning at even a minimal level. We need to put ourselves in the shoes of the government ministers and think about what we would do if militants entered our offices and threatened us and our families. Prime ministers Ulufa'alu, Sogavare, and Kemakeza, and their ministerial colleagues can all be criticised, but they were in an unwinnable and unenviable situation. External intervention should probably have come earlier, in about 2000, by which time the downward spiral was clear.[36] The government of Prime Minister John Howard in Australia was guided by Foreign Minister Alexander Downer, who dithered. Howard, Downer, and their advisors had no idea how to deal with the dire situation, and it showed. Previously, Australia had

---

35 Fraenkel 2004: 124, 145; Moore 2004a: 160–63, 168.
36 Moore 2004a: 106, 114, 133, 135, 139–40, 168.

been reluctant to interfere directly in the affairs of its Pacific neighbours. The move to restore law and order and shore up government processes in Solomon Islands began a new chapter in Australian foreign policy. The final answer was RAMSI, which was sent in to regain control.

The Pacific Islands Forum and RAMSI, 2003–17[37]

Most of RAMSI's personnel were based in Honiara. The foreign army and police force members lived in barracks on the edge of town. Although the economy of Honiara was still directly affected by inflation in house prices, RAMSI public servants were entitled to accommodation commensurate with what they could expect elsewhere, and extra NGO staff were based in Honiara. Restaurants flourished and hotels were usually full, with many permanent occupants (some staff spent years living in hotels). Honiara also gained many more high-end four-wheel-drive vehicles, adding to the already worsening traffic.[38] RAMSI tried to quarantine its effect on the overall economy and, although much of its spending was 'boomerang' aid that ended up in the pockets of overseas employees and companies, there was a considerable boost to Honiara's economy. On the plus side, Honiara developed coffee shops like Lime Lounge, Bamboo Bar, and Breakwater Café, where, for the first time, residents could partake of a quality cappuccino or espresso coffee (at international prices).

The Tensions were a low-level conflict, and unique in the Pacific, with Bougainville's rebellion as the closest equivalent, although the circumstances were different. There, the fight was against the national government, which used its army and mercenaries against the rebels. The Solomons' dispute was largely on Guadalcanal between people from two provinces, Guadalcanal and Malaita, and had its basis in long-term development issues.[39] Government processes deteriorated to such an extent that academics debated whether the nation was a 'failing' or 'failed' state. It was not in Australia's interests to have uncertainty on its doorstep, particularly when there was also political volatility in Papua New Guinea, Vanuatu, and Fiji. Australian leaders and the strategic community began

---

37 An earlier draft of this section was published as Moore 2018.
38 Moore 2007a.
39 Moore 2007b.

talking about an 'arc of instability'.[40] To deal with the Tensions crisis, in 2003, the Pacific Islands Forum invoked the 2000 Biketawa Declaration, which outlined guiding principles for good governance and courses of action for responding to crises in the region.

The Pacific Islands Forum's intervention in Solomon Islands was an unprecedented response, and it was also the first time Australia and New Zealand had led a substantial intervention mission beyond their borders that was not under UN auspices. It was an important learning experience for all Pacific Island states, as well as for Australia and New Zealand. There was no blueprint and there were some dead ends and major errors along the way, both from RAMSI and from the Solomon Islands Government. Unlike the situations in East Timor and Kosovo, RAMSI did not take over executive authority. Legally, the sovereignty of the independent Solomon Islands nation continued. There was never any suggestion of a transfer of sovereignty, which would have been against the terms of the Biketawa Declaration.[41] The RAMSI agreement was supposed to be renewed annually by the National Parliament, although this did not always happen. It could have been cancelled had the Solomon Islands Government chosen to do so. This made the situation very different from East Timor and Bougainville.

Large-scale Australian and New Zealand involvement in Solomon Islands' affairs was new. Within the Pacific, Australia had previously concentrated on its former colonial territory of Papua New Guinea, showing minimal interest in the former British protectorate across the border. Australia's annual aid package to Solomon Islands between 1991 and 1998 averaged A$13.3 million—equal to that given to Samoa. Then, suddenly, Australian aid to Solomon Islands increased to A$18.7 million in 1999–2000, and A$20.4 million in 2000–01. It kept increasing and, once RAMSI was established, was always more than A$200 million a year. Similarly, New Zealand—commensurate to its smaller size—increased its aid package, to NZ$13 million in 2003 and spending NZ$347 million between 2003 and 2013.[42] By the time RAMSI was disbanded, Australia had spent A$2.8 billion and New Zealand around half a billion dollars. Suddenly, Australians, New Zealanders, and staff from every Pacific

---

40 Fraenkel 2005; Dobell 2012.
41 Interestingly, when Prime Minister Sogavare spoke at the Lowy Institute in Sydney, in conversation with James Batley in mid-August 2017, he claimed that his early opposition to RAMSI was due to there being a plan to suspend sovereignty. There is no evidence this was ever contemplated.
42 Moore 2004a: 120–21; New Zealand Government 2003; Fraenkel et al. 2014: 85.

Islands Forum nation were very visible. This foreign intervention in law enforcement and bureaucratic agencies altered Honiara. The decade and half of the RAMSI presence created a more ethnically and racially diverse community, and an alternative power base to the central government. RAMSI has been factored into Figure 0.1 in the Introduction, depicting the changing Honiara 'worlds'. Solomon Islanders were exposed to outsiders with good intentions, who were there to make RAMSI and other aid packages work. Most were based in Honiara, although RAMSI and aid project workers travelled widely. The Solomon Islands Government also received many analytical reports on all aspects of government, the economy, and society, which have helped shape and guide subsequent administrative processes.

Most international peacekeeping exercises occur in the wake of civil wars or conflicts between nations. RAMSI was an intervention in a nation with no army (other than the small Royal Solomon Islands Police Field Force) and very few guns. However, Prime Minister Mamaloni's purchase of guns for the police in the early 1990s meant that after raiding the police and prison armouries, the MEF was far better equipped with high-powered weapons than the IFM.

The Solomon Islands conflict was primarily between two civilian militias and between the militias and the police, with overlap between them, particularly between the police and the MEF. Another important difference was that, when measured against many similar events internationally, both the death and the injury rates were low. Nevertheless, the social disruption in a small nation and a small capital city, replete with village-like neighbourhoods, was immense. While there was suffering because health, education, and other government services were either unavailable or declined, if one stands back and examines the Tension-related deaths, many around Honiara, they probably number around 200 (the Truth and Reconciliation Commission's estimate). A larger number died nationwide from lack of access to health services—perhaps another 1,000. If we compare this with other nations that have hosted large peacekeeping missions (East Timor, Iraq, Bosnia, and Sierra Leone) or have faced large internal disputes and genocide (Rwanda, Burundi, and Iraq), the figure is low. Overall, there was a degree of restraint. A lot of posturing occurred, but violent confrontation was relatively rare.

For instance, compare the figures above with the estimated 5,000 deaths in Bougainville (1988–98)[43] and a reported 60,000 to 100,000 deaths in Timor (1975–98).[44]

While the nation mourned the Solomon Islanders and RAMSI staff who died, the low fatality rate shows something about dispute-resolution mechanisms in Solomon Islands. The Tension years were moderated by dispute-resolution approaches that reached back into pre-colonial social mechanisms, mixed with Christian tolerance, and other changes since colonial intervention began in the 1890s. While some individuals and groups abused compensation mechanisms outrageously, *kastom* also played its part in maintaining equilibrium.

A background understanding of what occurred during the 1990s and early 2000s went into RAMSI planning and created its initial success. There was no armed resistance to RAMSI and most of the population (including many of the militants) welcomed the intervention. Although in the beginning there was a substantial military component (the Combined Task Force), the law and order face of the mission was largely led by the Participating Police Force (PPF), which remained an important section of RAMSI, helping to rebuild the RSIPF. No amnesties were offered (which had been a feature of pre-RAMSI peace negotiations), except for the return of firearms. All of this had implications for the command-and-control structure, and the role of the RAMSI Special Coordinators, all of whom were Australian, with the implications of an Australian agenda. Australia ran the operation and paid the majority of RAMSI's bills. This was the largest peacekeeping expense Australia has incurred, and it brought Solomon Islands into Australia's orbit in a way it never had been before. This change in the relationship continues.

---

43 Regan 2013: 123.
44 Rimmer 2013. It needs to be acknowledged that the population of East Timor in 1975 was approximately 630,000, whereas Bougainville had approximately 200,000 people in 1990. This would mean the fatalities in the Indonesian invasion and occupation of East Timor were about four to five times greater than Bougainville's during the conflict with Papua New Guinea.

Plate 9.8 RAMSI soldiers and RSIPF officers talking to a school group, 2000s.
Source: RAMSI Archives.

Plate 9.9 RAMSI soldiers outside the Magistrate's Court in Honiara, 2006.
Source: Clive Moore Collection.

The arrival of the RAMSI forces restored peace to Honiara and neighbouring parts of Guadalcanal. Solomon Islands differs from Papua New Guinea and Fiji in that it never had military forces, only police. The Guadalcanal and Malaitan militants introduced weapons, then RAMSI military forces arrived with armed forces and police. Between 1998 and 2004, Solomon Islands shifted very quickly from a society in which there were very few guns to a militarised community. Initially, there were about 2,000 RAMSI armed services personnel, police, development advisers, and public servants—the majority from Australia, with lesser representation from the other participant nations. By late 2003, 3,700 weapons had been surrendered. Although a few high-powered weapons escaped the net and are still buried around Honiara and on Malaita, the surrender of weapons and ammunition was largely a success, leaving Solomon Islands relatively gun-free. More than half of the troops were withdrawn by the end of 2003, and others left in February and March 2004, leaving behind about 200 police, a few dozen armed forces personnel, and senior public servants in 'line' positions. Although the initial RAMSI activities were accomplished without loss of life, two RAMSI personnel died in action: an Australian police officer was deliberately killed by a sniper in Honiara in December 2004, and another died through misadventure the following March. Four others died while serving in RAMSI.

After strengthening the court facilities and legal system, RAMSI methodically pursued the main corrupt and criminal figures. Many of the key militants faced trial. By November 2003, more than 80 police had been charged, including very senior officers. Members of the MEF supreme council, some IFM leaders, and some politicians, including two former prime ministers, Ezekiel Alebua and Sir Alan Kemakeza, served prison sentences for a variety of crimes. The military presence was more obvious in the first few years, when armed personnel patrolled Honiara's main streets, toting high-powered guns, and helicopters supervised from the sky. In the 2010s, they were more often confined to barracks and less obvious. After the gun amnesty, the second and third phases of RAMSI involved institutional and economic rehabilitation. RAMSI was wound down from 2013 and made a full exit in mid-2017, with aid assistance reverting to the Australian and New Zealand high commissions and other donors, particularly the Republic of China (Taiwan), Japan, and the European Union. Since 2020, the People's Republic of China has replaced Taiwan as a major donor.

RAMSI was always much more than a policing operation and, although on occasions RAMSI opposed government policies, it was never a government. A large amount of development assistance went to rebuilding the machinery of government. This was the 'Three Pillars' approach: restructuring the police, institutional strengthening and accountability, and economic reform. RAMSI and the Solomon Islands Government learnt to be flexible with the agenda, perhaps more so than they usually admitted. Much of the public image was of the Special Coordinators and the smiling PPF. Their activities were far more photogenic than public servants quietly working away behind computers in the Treasury and the courts. Yet there remain unanswered questions. RAMSI largely chose its own agenda, but was it the right one to reorient and rehabilitate the nation? Did RAMSI take sufficient steps to leave behind a functioning reliable bureaucracy to run the nation? Should the RAMSI staff have been kept only in advisory positions and not placed in 'line' positions where they were integrated into the public service? Was the re-localisation process effective? Did any of the RAMSI-era governments really support the 'Three Pillars' approach? The Solomon Islands Government supposedly gave priority to reconciliation and facilitated the Truth and Reconciliation Commission between 2009 and 2012. RAMSI did not, seeing this as beyond its mandate. The commission's report was eventually presented to the National Parliament in September 2014, at the end of Prime Minister Gordon Darcy Lilo's term, although few of its recommendations have been enacted.[45]

There has been no equivalent intervention in any other Pacific nation against which to judge RAMSI's success or failure. Although there was constant outreach to the provinces, much of the work was centred on Honiara, emanating from RAMSI bases at what were previously Lelei Resort in west Honiara, Guadalcanal Beach Resort at Kukum Beach, and in the government ministries. Between 2003 and 2006, RAMSI was overconfident about its success. In the initial phase, guns and ammunition were speedily removed. Solomon Islanders collectively breathed a sigh of relief. RAMSI then worked on its long-term agenda. Unexpectedly, 2006 was RAMSI's worst year. The organisation (through the PPF) must bear a great deal of the responsibility for mishandling the riots in Honiara after the election of Snyder Rini as prime minister. They were not the first

---

45   Prime Minister Lilo tabled the report at the very end of his term (on 5 September 2014). The document does not seem to have been made available through the parliament, although it was published unofficially. There has been minimal debate on the report in the National Parliament or elsewhere. SIG 2014b.

riots in Honiara, but they came when the RSIPF was weak and the PPF was in control. The PPF, largely consisting of Australian Federal Police and seconded state police, who were used to dealing with Australian-style civil unrest, had no idea of the capabilities of a fast-moving Honiara mob. They misjudged the situation and could not rely on the new RSIPF constables, who were not trained to deal with such an emergency. The result was a riot that began at the National Parliament, damaged areas at Point Cruz and around Central Market, and caused immense damage in Chinatown and the Pacific Casino Hotel.[46] Perhaps more interesting than the buildings torched were those that were not: QQQ and Honiara Hotel escaped damage. The Quan and Chan families are old *waku*: married into Solomon Islander families, they used indigenous cultural mechanisms to survive. The PPF and RAMSI learned a salutary lesson: policing techniques that work well in Australia and New Zealand do not necessarily work well in Honiara with a depleted police force. A stronger and more focused RAMSI emerged, and there were also signs that RAMSI's sponsors began to consider a timeframe for withdrawal, or at least a transition to bilateral and multilateral aid programs.[47]

Plate 9.10 The entrance of the Pacific Casino Hotel burning during the April 2006 riot.
Source: Garry Scott Collection.

---

46 Moore 2008a.
47 Allen 2011; Allen and Dinnen 2015, 2016; O'Callaghan 2013.

Plate 9.11 Burnt-out buildings in Chinatown after the April 2006 riot.
Source: Clive Moore Collection.

Plate 9.12 The Quan family's QQQ store in Chinatown, 2006, which was not harmed during the riots.
Source: Clive Moore Collection.

Overall, RAMSI commanded broad respect in the community, although, even with its large budget, there were limitations on what could be accomplished. At various times, particularly in 2005 and 2010, the Solomon Islands Government considered placing limits on RAMSI. Equally, there was rethinking of New Zealand and Australian aid preferences towards bilateral programs. Could it be that RAMSI altered direction after the low ebb of 2006–07 and, after about 2010, was out of kilter with the aims of Solomon Islands governments? Prime Minister Danny Philip's government (2010–11) promoted a five-year exit program, causing friction with Australia, which advocated an open-ended commitment. Did RAMSI stay too long? And why did relations between the government and RAMSI seemingly improve in the final years? Or was it just that the verbal sparring was less obvious? In 2003, Sogavare was a trenchant critic of the original RAMSI concept and, as prime minister (2006–07), he crossed swords with Australia when his government expelled Australian High Commissioner Patrick Cole over alleged interference in a commission of inquiry relating to the April 2006 riots, and over Australia's opposition to Sogavare's appointment of Attorney-General Julian Moti.[48] Eventually, the High Court of Australia found against the Australian Government for its flagrant manipulations of the law over Moti. Yet, at the RAMSI farewell, Moti's and Cole's names never passed Sogavare's lips.[49]

RAMSI's strengths were its ability to constantly reinvent itself in changing circumstances, while declaring that there was a steadfast long-term plan, and its excellent public relations team headed by ace journalist Mary-Louise O'Callaghan, who always managed to present a glowing picture. The RAMSI coordinators were also very skilled diplomats. Despite the 'Three Pillars' rhetoric, there was not one set of goals enunciated in 2003 and followed through. RAMSI learnt along the way and was largely able to run its own agenda with a degree of flexibility.

While the outside intervention has been judged a success, it could never have succeeded without the strength of Solomon Islands society and its own ways of handling cultural complexity. The Tension years brought local institutions to the fore as guiding mechanisms when the state apparatus faltered. The importance of the churches, women, and community government has always been there, but has increased. There were a resilience and manner of behaviour that came from living in diverse

---

48 Colvin 2006; Dorney 2006.
49 Moore 2008b, 2008c; Merrell 2017; Nelson 2007.

communities, as well as the core strength of the cultures. As Reverend Philemon Riti said in his presentation at the June 2017 RAMSI exit symposium, Solomon Islands came 'already equipped with a culture'. This strength prevailed and was the real glue that made the RAMSI years a success, even down to the politicians' ability to compromise. The success did not come from imposed or refurbished government institutions. The place of religion in the nation has always been strong. One theme in the speeches to parliament in RAMSI's last week in June 2017 and in many other presentations and speeches heard at the time was the power of Christianity in providing basic guiding principles for the nation. The churches continue to be essential in the peace-building process.

Although there is a core cultural strength, no one would say all Solomons traditions are suitable for the modern world. Among those not compatible with the future of government and the modern economy and society are gender structures that give emphasis to males and do not fully utilise the joint strength of males and females in creating the modern nation. RAMSI and other aid agencies quietly worked towards the normalisation and valuing of the role of women in all aspects of government and society. The empowerment of women continues to be an important aspect of nation-building. Whereas once women made up 3 per cent of the officers in the RSIPF, by 2016, the figure was a more respectable 20 per cent, and 24 per cent in 2019. The policy since 2017 has been to recruit equal numbers of male and female police each year. While there is much room for improvement, there is now a better recognition that gender equity is necessary to create a modern nation.[50]

Using social mechanisms to remodel society was beyond RAMSI's brief and is best achieved by Solomon Islanders. One issue is to what extent the 2008–12 Truth and Reconciliation Commission's findings have been implemented. Reconciliation remains crucial to the process through which Solomon Islanders come to terms with what happened. In the final days of RAMSI, Prime Minister Sogavare made clear that he felt that RAMSI had acquitted its mandate well and that his government remained committed to implementing the Truth and Reconciliation Commission's findings, with a reparation framework in place. Lessons have been learned and, despite a few political storms over the Coral Sea, there has been goodwill on all sides. As several participants in the final RAMSI symposium noted, errors were made at crucial junctures. This was to be expected with such

---

50   Tavola et al. 2016; SIG 2019b; Brigg 2018; George and Soakai 2020.

a unique, unprecedented Pacific intervention involving many diverse personnel working in difficult situations over many years. Through RAMSI, regional relationships have been strengthened and Pacific countries have been brought closer together through a common cause.

Plate 9.13 The RAMSI Memorial in Honiara, opened in June 2017.
Source: Clive Moore Collection.

***

HONIARA

At its most basic level, RAMSI was about people and goodwill. It was important to Solomon Islanders that RAMSI was a Pacific-wide operation. Bringing other Pacific Islanders into Solomon Islands was part of its success. There was a cultural energy created that reverberated among Solomon Islanders, who appreciated that other Pacific Islanders had come to help them restore normality and progress. This component gave Solomon Islanders confidence in their own ability to move their nation forward.

Many of the underlying causes of the Tensions have not yet been satisfactorily resolved. Perhaps they never will be. Aspects of gender, leadership, corruption, land, logging, decentralisation of development, and urbanisation remain difficult issues. In particular, the increasing size of the national capital's population is a unique challenge. Decisions must be made about Honiara's future, and soon.

Plate 9.14 The Solomon Islands National Parliament building, built in 1994, was a gift from the US Government.
It sits high on Vavaea Ridge overlooking Point Cruz. This photograph is from 2007.
Source: Clive Moore Collection.

The people of Guadalcanal have every right to expect more substantial recompense for the economic and urban developments that have occurred in their province since World War II. They would benefit from any move towards federalism and more regional-level government, enabling strengthening of provincial authority. There are still vast anomalies in development on the island, particularly between the north coast and the remote and impoverished southern Weather Coast. There is also the question of what are acceptable styles of leadership and development. Not everyone believes that logging, mining, and large-scale commercial agricultural production are the answer. A large proportion of people still live in rural areas. They operate under local land tenure systems and support the value of maintaining 'traditional' cultures and *kastom*. There are philosophical issues at stake relating to what type of nation Solomon Islanders want their grandchildren to inherit.[51]

Plate 9.15 Prime Minister Sir Allan Kemakeza (2001–06).

Source: Clive Moore Collection.

Plate 9.16 Prime Minister Rick Hounipwela (2017–19).

Source: Press Secretariat, Office of Prime Minister and Cabinet, Solomon Islands Government.

Plate 9.17 Prime Minister Manasseh Sogavare (2000–01, 2006–07, 2014–17, 2019–).

Source: Press Secretariat, Office of Prime Minister and Cabinet, Solomon Islands Government.

---

51   Aqorau 2011.

10

The village-city

Cities with much longer histories than Honiara's have experienced similarly severe problems as they grew and their functions changed. What the early administrators of Honiara did badly was not planning sufficiently for the large city that now exists. In 1945, residents laughed at the brave town plan and its mild vision for creating a liveable city, but who in 1945 could have envisaged a Greater Honiara in 2020 of 160,000 people?

Planning for the future

In 2015, the Ministry of Lands, Housing and Survey issued a document, *Shaping Honiara's Future*,[1] based on a 2014 study of the Honiara Local Planning Area, which identified various planning issues:

- Uncontrolled land use due to the lack of planning requirements, leading to inefficient use of land.
- Increased pressure on the existing available land for private development, removing opportunities for key infrastructure such as open space, community facilities, and public parks.
- Lack of recognition of the natural environmental affecting some areas of the city, putting properties and people's lives at risk.
- Lack of understanding of the infrastructure requirements of developments and the location of existing infrastructure, resulting in developments blocking access to key infrastructure.

---

1 SIG 2015.

- Lack of requirements for building design, landscaping, and car parking within developments.
- Lack of land to accommodate key public infrastructure to service the growing population.

The emphasis and priorities have been changing as the world has become very conscious of climate change and the environment. Honiara is a coastal city and not much attention has been paid to keeping, let along expanding, recreation areas, nor to the potential for natural disasters. There has been no attempt to control the erosion that occurs in the many creeks and rivers, nor the pollution of these water sources. A good example of what can go wrong is the flooding that occurred in 2014 after a cyclone dumped copious amounts of rain on the city.[2] Honiara's drainage system cannot cope with emergencies like this. Twenty-two people died in the flooding along the Mataniko River. Whole houses floated out to sea. The damage was estimated to have cost SI$108 million—equivalent to 9.2 per cent of gross domestic product—with around 52,000 people affected. The old Mataniko bridge between Chinatown and the coastal road was washed away, and Honiara International Airport–Henderson Field was extensively damaged. Some 675 houses were destroyed, along with food gardens, and farms.[3]

Future natural disasters may cause even worse damage, exacerbated by population growth. A 2017 Asian Development Bank paper rather coyly stated that 'Honiara is relatively far from reaching green city status'.[4] While this is true, and the city planners and politicians should be ashamed of the extent to which they have allowed parks, the seashore, and other areas of government land to be plundered for commercial developments, it will now be difficult to 'green' the city without clearing the settlements, which is unlikely to happen. And as the policy to change land tenure in the settlements from THA/TOL to FTE proceeds, 'greening' will become even more difficult.

---

2   SIG 2014e.
3   ibid., 14.
4   ADB 2017: 15.

10. THE VILLAGE-CITY

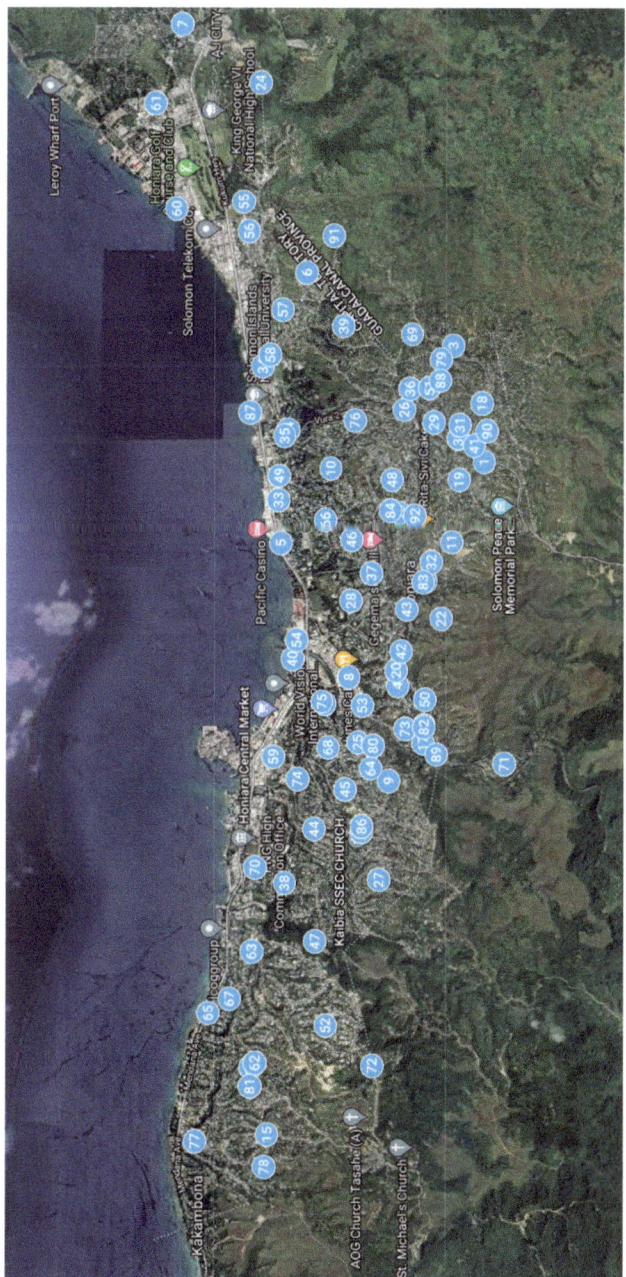

Map 10.1 Settlements (THA/TOL and squatter) within or on the Honiara City Council boundaries, 2019.

Source: Regina Souter, International WaterCentre at Griffith University (modified from World Bank and Honiara City Council: Community Access and Urban Services Enhancement Project).

HONIARA

Code for Map 10.1: Settlements (THA/TOL and squatter) within or on the Honiara City Council boundaries, 2019, on the accompanying map.

1 Adaliua	32 Kombivatu	63 Rove
2 Aefako	33 Kukum	64 Skyline
3 Aefako 2	34 Kukum Campus	65 Tandai
4 Antioch	35 Kukum Community	66 Tanuli Ridge
5 Bahai	36 Lau Valley	67 Tavioa Ridge
6 Baranaba	37 Lawson Tama	68 Tehamurina
7 Burns Creek	38 Lengakiki	69 Tolo
8 Chinatown	39 Lio Creek	70 Town Ground
9 Choviri	40 Mamanawata	71 Tuvaruhu
10 East Kola Ridge	41 Mamulele	72 Upper Tasahe
11 Ferakusia	42 Matafali	73 Vara Creek
12 Feraladoa	43 Matariu	74 Vavaea Ridge
13 Fijian Quarter	44 Mbokona	75 Vuhokesa
14 Fishing Village	45 Mbokonavera	76 Vura
15 Forest Valley	46 Mbua Valley	77 White River
16 Fulisango	47 Mbumburu	78 Wind Valley
17 Gegema	48 Naha	79 Windy Valley
18 Gilbert Camp	49 Naha Community	80 Koa Hill (below US Memorial)
19 Green Valley	50 Namoliki	81 Banana Valley
20 Gwaimaoa	51 New Valley	82 Cana Hill
21 Independence Valley	52 Ngossi	83 Feraladoa (beside Pakoe Lodge)
22 Jericho	53 Number 3	84 Green Valley (SIWA)
23 Kaibia	54 Ontong Java/ Lord Howe	85 Kaibia (East)
24 King George	55 Panatina Campus	86 Kaibia Heights
25 Koa Hill	56 Panatina Ridge	87 Kukum Fishing Village
26 Kofiloko	57 Panatina Valley	88 Kwaio Valley
27 Kokomulevuha	58 Panatina Village	89 Marble Street
28 Kola`ale	59 Point Cruz	90 Master Liu
29 Kombito 1	60 Ranadi	91 Ohiola
30 Kombito 2	61 Ranadi Industrial	92 Zion
31 Kombito 3	62 Rifle Range	

Source: Souter and Orams (2019).

In *Shaping Honiara's Future*'s six 'visions', the planners' stated aims were to make Honiara a liveable cultural and economic hub for the nation, with an efficient transport system and resilience to natural events and environmental risks. Congestion within the city centre is recognised as a major issue, which requires improvements to the road and transport systems. The plan is to eventually decentralise Honiara by developing multiple nodes and centres, and to create centrally located precincts showcasing the best of Honiara—including heritage, art, culture, and the natural landscape. Planners suggest the best solution is to diversify development away from Point Cruz to satellite areas. Utilising the river systems, the hills, and the sea would make it a pleasant city, both for locals and for international tourists. However, the rivers and creeks are polluted, and the coast has been locked up under commercial developments.

Two key plans may alter the situation. One is a new highway bypass inland from Honiara, skirting through what is now Tandai, and presumably also Malango and Lengo, land (Map 9.3). There are also plans to develop a second city at Mamara, still within the Tandai area, west of Honiara—a new, planned city to relieve the pressure on existing urban areas.[5] The sketches for the future Point Cruz area show apartments built above a commercial precinct, rather than the present low-rise street scene. As well, moving the fuel depot facilities from the centre of Honiara is once more up for discussion, along with the redevelopment of downtown Point Cruz. While the plan is laudable, an important issue remains unanswered: the cost of achieving these changes in a nation that has vast structural weaknesses in its economic base.

The planners seem to have modelled future urban development on First World cities, not Pacific reality. There is insufficient understanding of how Honiara has evolved since 1945 and of the limits of a cash-strapped developing nation. Town planners create nice words and pictures, but if there is no political will or cash to finance new developments, their concepts fail. The government cannot afford to restructure urban development on Guadalcanal without substantial inputs of foreign aid or becoming beholden to foreign developers, such as with the Mamara plan. The COVID-19 shutdown of much of the national economy has further reduced the government's ability to make structural changes to the urban environment, at least for some years. The next important goal will be creating sufficient infrastructure for and running the Pacific Games in 2023, with not much leeway left for anything else.

---

5   SIG 2018; *SIBC*, 24 February 2021, 26 April 2021.

HONIARA

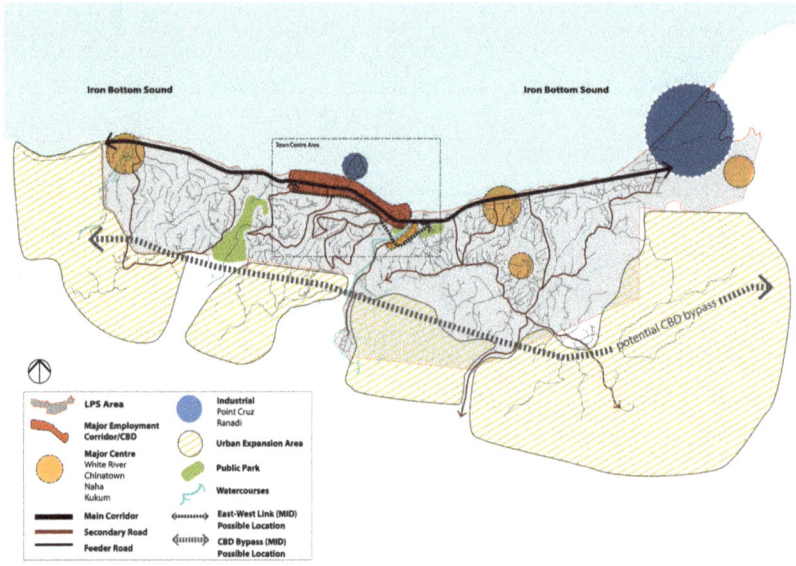

Map 10.2 A 2015 Honiara citywide structural plan showing the proposed bypass road.
Source: SIG (2015).

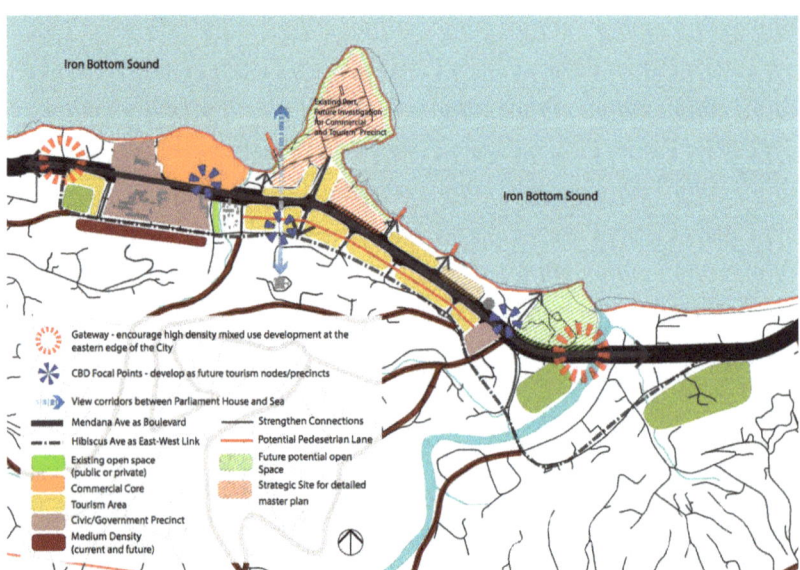

Map 10.3 A 2015 Honiara city centre structural plan.
Source: SIG (2015).

Hybridity

The Tensions and the RAMSI years brought to the fore various cultural forms that have always been part of the national make-up: *wantokism*, *kastom*, linguistic diversity, and dispute-resolution mechanisms. With little government-sponsored social security beyond basic health care, and limited primary education, much of which failed to function during the Tensions and early RAMSI years, life in Honiara is always difficult. New arrivals are sustained by established social networks, which enable them eventually to integrate into urban life, although there is also a strong element of circulation with a constant flow from and to the provinces. In Honiara's expanding urban settlements, and elsewhere in Melanesia, many of the features of people's rural origins survive, including significant ongoing circulation. Life in the settlements seldom enables a transition into the more affluent suburbs. The small size of the formal economy and the lack of employment mean it is a constant battle to survive. The measurable economy remains weak and the saving grace for the nation is self-sufficiency at the village level, which represents 80 per cent of the population.

Many of the issues of the Tensions and the decade after are writ large in Honiara. The size of Greater Honiara means that understanding its history and social dynamics will be crucial to all future development in Solomon Islands. Although there is now relative quiet after six years of turmoil, and 14 years of outside intervention, like a dormant volcano, Honiara has the capacity to erupt again. After RAMSI departed at the end of June 2017, in August, the Solomon Islands Government signed an agreement with Australia assuring direct military assistance if there was any recurrence of civil unrest. Let us hope the rebuilt RSIPF can cope without further outside help.

In 2016, the country's gross domestic product was around A$1.4 billion: 38 per cent came from agriculture, and 26 per cent was generated from the export of natural resources. Although there have been attempts to reopen the Gold Ridge mine, this has not occurred, and other mining ventures are still at an investigation phase, except for Bintan Mining's small-scale bauxite mining on Rennell Island, which has returned negligible revenue to the government since it began in 2014. The other major mining venture is Axiom's nickel mining project on San Jorge Island in Isabel Province. Axiom planned to begin exports in late 2019, but had its export and investment licences withdrawn in November that year by the Solomon Islands Government.[6] In 2017, the country's exports were dominated by large commodity-based industries: A$390 million from round logs; A$14 million from sawn timber; A$35 million from fish (whole, processed, and canned); A$30 million from palm oil; A$18 million from coconut products (copra, mature nuts, coconut oils, and meals); and A$10 million from cocoa beans.[7] Timber is Solomon Islands' largest export, and corruption enables companies to circumvent many of the logging regulations. Log exports are underreported, and reforestation seldom occurs. Asian companies are stripping out trees at an alarmingly unsustainable rate. As well, logging revenue will decline in the long term; it must, as overlogging has been occurring for at least 30 years.

The closure in the late 1990s of the Guadalcanal Plains oil palm estates provided a chance to rethink the area's economic and social structure. Since the Tensions, the plantations outside Honiara slowly have been regenerated by Guadalcanal Plains Palm Oil Limited (GPPOL), which controls 6,500 hectares and is now the leading agricultural company in Solomon Islands. The company is an offshoot of New Britain Palm Oil Limited, which was originally part of British agricultural company Harrisons and Crosfield, and then part of Malaysian state-owned company Kulim (Malaysia) Berhad. The parent company is Sime Darby Plantation, a huge agribusiness that is the world's largest producer of sustainable palm oil. From 2004, agreement was made with the Tasimboko landowners to restart the oil palm estates, with better arrangements to limit the spread of settlement and include an outgrower component. GPPOL began operations in 2005 and the mill restarted in mid-2006.[8]

This poses significant economic challenges. Until 2020 and the COVID-19 pandemic, Honiara was a sprawling, booming, vibrant Pacific city. There was a constant sense of hybridity, a joining of several cultural forms—none of them triumphant—that formed the beauty of the place. This chapter argues that the authorities must come to terms with squatters, settlements, villages, and cultural hybridity. They must face the issues still outstanding from the Tensions and RAMSI years, incorporating solutions into planning, or face future urban and national turmoil. Long-established FTE areas such as Kola'a Ridge, Panatina, and Vura can perhaps be

---

6   Wasuka 2019; 'Axiom failed to meet the ministry's conditions', *SIBC*, 6 December 2019; Sei 2019b.
7   PHAMA 2013.
8   Fraenkel et al. 2010; Allen 2012a.

regarded as suburbs, yet, so, too, can White River's urban village and the Malaitan Fishing Village at Kukum, both of which have moved from their squatter origins to THA/TOL and now FTE status. White River is a multiethnic community that includes modern Western housing and semitraditional buildings. Fishing Village is a Malaitan stronghold that looks rather like an artificial island village washed up from Lau Lagoon on the Kukum shore. Its narrow spaces and closely positioned houses owe as much to the origins of the people—on crowded artificial islands—as to Honiara, and clearly city council building regulations are being ignored. To an outsider, Fishing Village appears chaotic, but the housing clusters are in extended family groupings, which enable social support.

Plate 10.1 Hybridity: A rest house at the Honiara Trade Show in 2008—symbolic of the old and the new.
Source: Clive Moore Collection.

The THA/TOL districts and squatter areas (Maps 10.1 and 10.4) are best described as settlements, although residents call them villages, in recognition of traditional domiciliary characteristics and the hybrid spaces created. Squatter areas can be large—for example, at Burns Creek— or quite small, wedged into more established areas. The settlements operate like villages with functioning local communities, plus a few basic municipal services. Extended families gather for rites of passage such as births, marriages, and funerals, and maintain aspects of village authority. The FTE suburbs lack this characteristic; residents there do not feel closely bound to their neighbours. Settlements are urban villages, the strengths of which lie in customary relationships. Market stalls are built at road junctions, providing easy access to meet common household needs, while enabling village-style socialisation.

Plate 10.2 Hybridity: Neighbouring houses at Fishing Village are often built close together.

While perhaps not within city council regulations, the practice is used by extended families and provides shade and cover in bad weather. This photograph is from 2013.

Source: Clive Moore Collection.

Honiara's hybrid nature relates to the operation of *wantokism*, extended kinship relationships, and *kastom*. In *The Chiefs' Country*, Malaitan Michael Kwa'ioloa and anthropologist Ben Burt provide a window into settlement life in east Honiara. Kwa'ioloa lives in Kobito, surrounded by family and other Kwara'ae relatives and *wantoks*. He and other Malaitan leaders there operate with many of the trappings of Malaitan big-men:

> In Honiara, although we are not at home, we understand that our tradition stays wherever we stay. If we are without our tradition, everything will be all over the place. People of different languages are involved, because our area of south-east Honiara is one community including Kombito, Kofiloko, Lau Valley, and up to Gilbert Camp. Other areas have other groups. We call this a community, because everyone knows each other. We coordinate the chiefs and if there are any problems we deal with them.[9]

Kwa'ioloa describes having formed a Malaitan house of chiefs in Honiara, although other accounts suggest this customary authority is limited to areas close to his Kobito home. Nevertheless, many customary elements have survived the transition to the urban world. Some disputes are dealt with inside the communities, and 'red shell wealth' changes hands in compensation.

In the FTE areas, there is an emerging group of richer urbanites who prefer to minimise their obligations to poorer relatives, or at least make access difficult.[10] Yet, in the end, they never totally ignore their kin as the responsibility is too ingrained. Even in areas such as Gilbert Camp and Kobito, some people engage with the market economy and heed the government's promotion of individualistic behaviours, rather than following provincial or Honiara versions of *kastom*. At most, they operate a modernist version of *kastom* based on their socioeconomic context. Ethnicity flows into national politics. Malaitans make up the major ethnic component living between Vura and Gilbert Camp, and it is rare for anyone other than a Malaitan to win the large East Honiara parliamentary seat.[11] From a national political perspective, the Malaitan dominance in east Honiara combines modern politics with indigenous practices.

---

9   Kwa'ioloa and Burt 2012: 168.
10 Gooberman-Hill 1999.
11 Over 12 elections, four of seven members were Malaitans and another two were part-Malaitan. Since 2018, when the Electoral Commission allowed cross-border registration for voting, it is now much harder to anticipate the results in the three Honiara seats, as electors can choose to vote away from their primary place of residence. Batley et al. 2019.

Although traditional leadership remains important, the Christian denominations and their leadership are just as crucial in Honiara. These spread through all of Honiara's settlements and the more developed suburban FTE communities, providing stable social networks and leadership. While those with cars, or bus fares, may choose to travel to the central churches and halls, there are many local-area churches operated by the long-established denominations, as well as the newer Pentecostal groups. Most of these are within walking distance of the homes of their congregations. Activities are not confined to the sabbath, and many residents in the settlements are involved in evening meetings.

Social activities, obligations, and aspirations are similar, whether one lives in established suburbs like Lengakiki or Kola`a Ridge, in a THA/TOL settlement like Kobito, or a squatter settlement like Burns Creek. When money is available, people upgrade their homes or get water and electricity connected. Extended families flow through houses, children play, everyone is fed and housed. Weddings occur, linking families in a manner no different from life in villages in the provinces. These events vary, some including exchanges of traditional wealth, while others follow the style of European weddings, with bridesmaids and groomsmen in matching outfits.

Another, less noticeable change in Honiara is that girls and young women are now much freer in urban surroundings. Even if cloaked as participation in church or sporting activities, women can mix, use the transport system to visit relatives and friends, and develop their own varieties of popular culture. Young women attend concerts (religious and secular), explore new clothing and hair fashions, and use electronic music devices and mobile phones. They mirror many of the behavioural patterns of their Western counterparts. While not as free as Honiara males, and bound by limited finances, modern women can enjoy the pleasures of hotels and clubs, but with more risk than in Western society. Nevertheless, there is far more parental control over girls and young women than over their brothers, and a large percentage of them are confined to home environments and church activities.

10. THE VILLAGE-CITY

Plate 10.3 Hendry Billy Toa Te'e's house at Kobito 2, which was built over a few years in the 2010s as money became available.
Source: Clive Moore Collection.

Plate 10.4 Emelda Davis (left), an Australian South Sea Islander, visiting the family of Hendry Billy Toa Te'e at Kobito, 2014.
Source: Clive Moore Collection.

Alongside this, domestic violence is increasing, fuelled by the male-dominated traditional culture, established use of physical violence for discipline, lack of education, poverty, *kwaso* (home brew), and conservative Christianity.[12] In 2016, the National Parliament passed the *Family Protection Act*, which criminalised domestic violence, although implementation and training have been slow and poorly resourced. Women do not want to shame their extended families by revealing the violent secrets within their marriage; and the payment of bride-wealth, which must be returned if a marriage breaks down, discourages divorce.[13]

Land and corruption

The availability of land is a major and contentious issue. The 2010 unimproved capital value of all land within the Honiara City Council boundary was SI$2.46 billion, of which approximately SI$2.1 billion was then fixed-term estates. A decade later, the figures have increased considerably, and would be even higher if we included land on the peri-urban fringe. High-quality housing seems to cover every available ridge, and people claim there is a shortage of land both for housing and for commercial use. Deals have been done by rich Asians and Solomon Islanders to transfer land from government control to private use. The government owns around 3,200 houses in Honiara and the provinces, although a significant number are illegally occupied or beyond economic repair. The government also operates a public service rental scheme, which in 2009 was worth SI$53 million, and was estimated to be between 24 and 40 per cent of the rental market. Rents are far too low to be economic and, in 2009, the government was owed SI$24 million by public lease tenants. Public servants who own their homes are entitled to rental allowances, which in 2008 cost the government SI$11.37 million.[14] With this level of incompetence in the administration of public land and housing, and the lucrative perks and commercial possibilities governing land acquisition, the poor in the settlements and squatter areas have little chance of gaining access to suitable long-term ownership of land. Even paying annual land licence fees is often beyond them.

---

12   Ming et al. 2016; Waka Mere 2019. Solomon Islands has high rates of family and sexual violence: 64 per cent of women aged 19 to 49 surveyed at the National Referral Hospital between 1994 and 2011 reported physical and sexual abuse from a partner.
13   Marks 2019.
14   Williams 2011: 2; Evans 2012.

The rezoning and allocation of land in Honiara are a fraught business. There are too many examples of obvious corruption over the years to believe that the process is fair and uninfluenced by bribery. As lawyer Transform Aqorau argued in a 2013 essay:

> [L]and allocation, in particular allocation of urban land ... clearly reflects corruption as evident by the standard of commercial buildings built by the more recent Chinese arrivals. It is argued that these lands could only have been allocated through corrupt means as there has never been any government tender by the Commissioner of Lands in the last ten years. The replacement of what were once residential homes at Kukum Labour Line by commercial buildings owned and operated by these new Chinese arrivals could only have been done by corrupt means. There were no tenders issued for these areas, and the fact that Solomon Islanders who lived there could have been given an opportunity to own those plots of lands where their houses were located arguably points to corruption. It is argued that government machinery that disenfranchises its own citizens by making them homeless to give way to a new wave of Chinese is evidence of serious inherent weaknesses in the government systems particularly in the Lands Department, Physical Planning Division, and Honiara Municipal Authority.[15]

Corruption, says Aqorau, 'has left a terrible legacy ... that has permeated all levels of Solomon Islands society'.[16]

Corruption is obvious in Honiara at all levels. In the early 1990s, Prime Minister Mamaloni sold government land in Mendana Avenue to a Chinese friend. During the same years, the then Premier of Guadalcanal Province sold land at the other end of Mendana Avenue for SI$50,000, without consulting his executive. In his forthcoming biography of Mamaloni, Christopher Chevalier summed up the corruption nicely: 'Gradually, valuable plots of land in the middle of Honiara and along the Kukum Highway were sold off to developers—mainly Asian businessmen who bought the land corruptly.'[17]

More recently, rich Solomon Islanders and Asian business interests have been busy buying up land around the airport to the east and Kakabona to the west—sometimes with dubious legality. Prices for land blocks

---

15   Aqorau 2013.
16   Wairiu 2007.
17   Chevalier 2017: 252.

are largely dependent on location and size and vary from SI$100,000 to SI$500,000. These costs have pushed many middle-class Solomon Islanders to buy land further east, where prices are not as high and land parcels are smaller. The area around Lungga River and Alligator Creek is particularly sought-after by people working around Ranadi and the airport. Landowners are building small rental houses and 'single men's quarters' to cater for this demand.

There are numerous examples of past commissioners of lands exercising their powers in a manner beyond the terms of the *Land and Titles Act*. In 2013, Honiara City Mayor Andrew Mua complained that the then commissioner had sold pieces of land that formed part of Honiara's garbage dump to Asian investors and other individuals. There have been media reports of other land set aside for public use or future utilities being sold by various commissioners, including land next to the Mataniko River bridge that had been designated for expanding crucial transport infrastructure, which was sold to an Asian businessman. Reports suggest corruption is widespread throughout the Ministry of Lands, Housing and Survey, with many staff gaining personal control of FTE land. The decisions of the Honiara Town Planning Board, which oversaw overall urban planning, were frequently overridden.[18] The situation was so corrupt that the legislation was amended in 2015 to introduce a Land Board, stripping the commissioner's position of its discretionary powers. These land deals have enriched a few and thrown poor people off land on which they have lived for decades.

There is an Institute of Public Administration Management Learning in Honiara and SINU runs short administrative training courses, which help lift public servants to higher standards. Regardless of these endeavours, a substantial black market has developed for government services. Making a little extra money at the expense of both the public and the government has become commonplace. Getting a water meter connected quickly (rather than waiting for six to 12 months) can be accomplished with a SI$1,000 bribe, while gaining swift progress through the system for a minor land matter costs SI$500 as a 'salary supplement'. Gaining a copy of a birth certificate can be hurried through the system or the issuing of a passport can be speeded up—both through small bribes, which are euphemistically called 'lunch money'. There appear to be different levels

---

18   Foukona and Allen 2017: 94–98.

of corruption for different races: Solomon Islanders get the cheapest deals but resent the avaricious public servants; Europeans pay considerably more; and Asians are usually willing to splash a lot of cash around to get instant attention. And, despite Prime Minister Lilo's assurance on *Radio New Zealand* in August 2013 that it was not true that politicians can be lured to change sides in Parliament,[19] 10 years ago the rumour was that this could be achieved with a bribe of SI$50,000; now it routinely costs more like SI$500,000. Luring top politicians to change sides is said to cost up to SI$1 million.[20] All of this money circulates in the 'grey economy' in Honiara and the provinces. Aqorau stated the future consequences:

> Donors … should be concerned that their tax money is helping to sustain a situation that will fuel a revolution: a revolt that would be instigated by young Solomon Islanders who are well informed through social networks to what is happening within the deepest corners of the Government.[21]

Since 2003, Solomon Islanders have returned to settle in Honiara in large numbers, with an annual urban population growth rate of 4.7 per cent. Daniel Evans suggested the growth rate of Honiara's urban settlements was 26 per cent over the three years following the arrival of RAMSI. Many of these settlers were returning to try to regenerate their lives after becoming refugees to the provinces in 1998–99. The squatter settlement at Burns Creek grew enormously during these years. Much of the peri-urban expansion was beyond the city council's control as it occurred in Guadalcanal Province on the fringes of the city, on customary or reclassified land. The strain on the urban and peri-urban settlements caused by the Tensions has been immense. It took years to restore water supplies that were damaged or had been allowed to deteriorate. During the Tension years, many households in settlements made do with public water supplies, walking long distances to access water for drinking and washing, using wells, springs, and limited council supplies.[22] Even when reticulated water is available, many cannot afford to connect the service to their homes, nor to pay the water usage charges.

---

19 Husband 2013.
20 There was a remarkable front-page article in the *IS* on 3 November 2017, which claimed that Jeremiah Manele, the leader of the opposition, was offered SI$1 million to become deputy prime minister in a Sogavare-led government.
21 Aqorau 2013.
22 Evans 2012: 8; Storey 2003; Chand and Yala 2008; Information from Hendry Billy Toa Te`e, Kobito, 17 October 2013.

Urban characteristics

The provision of urban services in Honiara and its environs is more extensive than in other parts of the country, although still minimal compared with some other capital cities in the Pacific. In 2009, only 75 per cent of the city had access to piped water, while only two-thirds had lighting linked to the electricity grid. Sewerage coverage is also limited: only 54 per cent of households had a flush toilet, and another 9 per cent had shared flush toilets. The raw sewage outfalls to the sea and the Mataniko River. For areas not connected to the sewerage system, a septic tank emptying service is available, but the coverage and quality of this service are limited. For others, shared pit toilets remain the only possibility.[23]

What is the future for this village-city? Honiara's population increased from 3,000 in the late 1950s to 160,000 in 2020—an astounding growth rate. In the 1970s, with a population of around 15,000, it seemed that everyone knew everyone else. In modern Honiara, this is no longer possible, although one has only to spend time at the docks to see the constant human traffic circulating between the provinces and Honiara, with the urban middle class and elites still closely involved in this movement, looking after relatives from their villages of origin. People seldom arrive without contacts; every provincial village has members living in Honiara. The hybrid strength of Honiara society depends on individual and community-level resources, with little support from, or links with, municipal authorities or the state.

Modern Honiara, through both British planning and Solomon Islands ingenuity, comprises five types of land occupancy. First, as a remnant from earlier years, a small area of customary land has been preserved, although it is no longer controlled by the Tandai landowners to whom it was granted. By and large, customary landownership was expunged from urban Honiara, but not from the surrounding areas of sea and land. Map 9.1 shows the Honiara City Council boundary on land and sea, in almost equal proportions. In August 2017, a court case provided a win for the Tandai landowners, with 1,500 hectares of the ocean now registered in the name of Vincent Kurilau, on behalf of the Tandai.[24]

---

23 UN-Habitat 2012: 14.
24 Information from Michael Ben Walahoula, Honiara, October 2017.

The remainder of Honiara belongs to the state, with the non-customary land either reserved for government and council purposes or released under various forms of long-term lease or licence arrangement. The second type of land is national government and council land in the form of reserves held for public purposes, such as playing fields and areas for recreational use, road reserves, and areas earmarked for future development. Until the end of 2014, government land could be obtained through the Commissioner of Lands either as FTE or as THA/TOL. The newly created Land Board now holds this responsibility, and FTE is available for a renewable tenure of 75 years, whereas some of the earlier FTE land was provided for shorter periods.[25] Reports from the early 2010s suggested there were 5,049 FTEs in Honiara, covering 12.7 square kilometres.[26] The fourth land type is THA/TOL, which is described in Chapter 5. For a fee, THA/TOL land can now be converted into FTEs under 75-year leases—a logical extension of what have become permanent suburban settlements. A remaining problem is the high cost of the conversion for those on subsistence incomes.

The fifth category covers 20,000 to 25,000 people in more than 3,000 households in Honiara (about one-quarter of the population) who live as squatters on land occupied without formal land title or licence, mainly Tandai land on the peri-urban fringe, in unused crevices, or on government or council reserves in FTE and THA/TOL areas. Permanent structures are often built in squatter areas, and customary arrangements have been made with Guale landholders to safeguard their occupancy.[27] FTE, THA/TOL, and squatter lands are sometimes side by side.

When asked whether there are suburbs, Honiara residents look surprised and say there are none in the way urban tenure is understood in places like Australia. To accommodate relatives, even the middle class and elites sometimes build houses from local materials alongside their substantial homes, and squatters may occupy unused land nearby. One feature of the city council over the past decade is a modernisation of rules and building codes, although no one seems to take much notice in THA/TOL and FTE areas. With no street mail delivery system, it is difficult to communicate with the bulk of residents and, even if it were possible, there are issues

---

25   'New resolution reached by Lands & Housing Board on lands', *SIBC*, 20 June 2015.
26   Evans 2012.
27   Larden and Sullivan 2008: 316–17; SIG 2013; Maebuta and Maebuta 2009; Evans 2010; Jourdan 2010: 269.

with literacy. The 2014 Honiara Planning Scheme uses formal language that does not acknowledge the reality of thousands of illegal residences, nor suggest how to incorporate them into the city.

Living in Honiara

In the absence of full reports from the 2019 national census, a contemporary picture can be gained from one RAMSI project, the People's Survey, which began with a pilot survey in 2006 and was completed every year until 2013, interviewing 3,000 to 4,000 individuals each year all over the nation.[28] The final People's Survey is used here to create a picture of modern Honiara. In 2013, there were 613 interviewees from Honiara in a total of 3,405 nationally.[29] Those surveyed saw RAMSI's biggest achievements as bringing peace to the country and restoring law and order, although just over 50 per cent of the Honiara residents surveyed had no idea who paid for RAMSI.[30] Residents wanted economic development and a curb on corruption. About 65 per cent said they would be willing to report misuse of power or public monies, but similar numbers said they had never known an official to behave improperly, which indicates faulty collective memory in relation to petty corruption.[31]

Almost 97 per cent of the Honiara interviewees identified Honiara as their permanent home. In FTE areas, there was an equal balance of couples from the same and different provinces, whereas those living in Honiara settlements were more likely to have partners from the same province. Still, the interprovincial marriage rates were three times higher in Honiara than on the rest of Guadalcanal, or on Malaita. Urban Solomon Islanders are beginning to shed their regionalism, becoming citizens of the nation, not just of provinces.[32] As suggested in the Introduction, in terms of Malaitan dominance in Honiara and in the nation, it may mean that in the long term, mixed-province marriages will create a more united national community and Malaitan influence will lessen. This may take another 30 to 50 years to produce obvious changes.

---

28   RAMSI 2006, 2007, 2008, 2010, 2011, 2012, 2013.
29   RAMSI 2013: 101.
30   ibid., 102, 104.
31   ibid., 111, 118, 119–21.
32   ibid., 20–21.

Plate 10.5 'No weapons (sharp or pointed)': The Pipeline Disco, Hibiscus Hotel, Honiara, 1994.
Source: Clive Moore Collection.

Plate 10.6 Youths dressed up for a dance competition entitled 'Battlegrounds', 2016.
Source: Vincent Verheyen Collection.

In the 1940s and 1950s, there were few children or youths in the city. In the early twenty-first century, Honiara's child population is comparable with the level in the provinces. Household size has generally decreased in the provinces since the 1980s. In Honiara, the 2009 national census showed that household sizes remained high, at around seven people per dwelling—an indication of family size and the number of people arriving to look for work and staying with *wantoks*.[33] There are many reports of houses with 10 to 15 occupants, including children, all subsisting on a single basic income. One of the ticking time-bombs in Honiara is the future of the youth population. The 1999 census showed a substantial number of 15 to 29 year olds in Honiara—exceeded only by Malaita Province, with Guadalcanal and Western provinces not far behind.[34] This age group was likely to be unemployed. Urban youths can often only find low-status work as labourers on family or community projects, and less often with businesses.[35] Young men felt alienated from decision-making and the People's Surveys showed them to be concerned about alcohol use and abuse, violence, aggression, and stealing. Young women were equally disadvantaged and were even more 'invisible' in most decision-making processes. They were concerned about alcohol, marijuana, and teenage pregnancy. All youths wanted better skills training, greater access to opportunities for income generation, and increased sporting facilities. There have been many schemes to develop policies to improve the situation for youths in Honiara, back to the Masta Liu Project of the mid-1970s, but until there is some improvement in employment opportunities, the level of disenchantment will continue to increase.[36]

Water and electricity services are not secure and the cost prohibits many people from connecting to the main supply grids. In the 2013 People's Survey, 16.7 per cent of Honiara people surveyed described the water supply as insufficient and unreliable. The electricity supply in the Solomons is expensive, partly because it is produced by diesel fuel. Slowly, there have been moves away from diesel generation. Australian aid has assisted the development of the Tina River hydro project, which will connect to the Lungga power station and the Honiara grid by the early 2020s. A few years back, there was an investigation into ways to harness nearby Savo

---

33   UNICEF 2012: 5, 8.
34   Hassall & Associates and AusAID 2004: 11.
35   Evans 2016, 2018; Ride 2019.
36   Evans 2019.

Island's volcanic thermal power as the basis for electricity generation.[37] 'Cash Power' (pay-as-you-go meters) is used to power domestic lighting and electrical appliances, and small solar systems are gaining popularity, but refrigeration is still rare in many settlement houses. Cooking is done on stoves powered by bottled gas, kerosene, wood, and coconut shell, with stone-pit cooking still in use, particularly to prepare food for the sabbath and for feasts. In the FTE suburbs, 83.8 per cent of households had a main grid electricity supply, while this figure was only 37.8 per cent in the settlements. Almost 12 per cent of residents in the suburbs and 33.9 per cent in the settlements had access to small solar electricity systems (capable of providing basic lighting and recharging mobile phones), which are fast becoming a cheaper alternative to the main grid supply. Almost 9 per cent of people living in the suburbs and 29.3 per cent in the settlements had no electricity at all.[38]

Honiara's residents, like many in other parts of the developing world, have skipped the installation of telephone landlines and moved straight to mobile phones. In 2009, only 23 per cent of those surveyed had a mobile phone.[39] That year, the new *Telecommunications Act* broke the one-carrier monopoly held by Our Telekom (formerly Solomons Telecom) and introduced Bemobile, a PNG company backed by Hong Kong equity fund GEMS and the international telecommunications firm Trilogy. Mobile phone charges fell sharply, leading to a surge in the number of subscribers—to an extent that mobile phones have become ubiquitous. In 2013, more than 80 per cent of Honiara's adult residents had access to a mobile phone—up from the 2011 and 2012 levels. The proportion is now much higher.[40] The mobile network has been extended to far-flung rural areas (even isolated Tikopia Island and Ontong Java Atoll), which encourages nationwide communications. Overseas calls remain expensive, providing no encouragement to business. Internet speeds are faster than they were a few years ago, although download costs remain prohibitive. Conditions improved when a fibre-optic cable from Sydney reached Honiara in late 2019. Digital access figures continue to increase all through the nation—one consequence of which will be that future social disturbances are likely to be orchestrated through mobile phones and Facebook.

---

37   SIG 2011a; Geodynamics Limited 2014.
38   RAMSI 2013: 52, 55, 58.
39   ibid., 60; O'Callaghan 2013: 45.
40   There were 479,800 mobile phone connections operating in January 2020 (71 per cent of the population) and 147,000 internet users (22 per cent of the population). Kemp 2020.

Radio listening, both AM and FM, is widespread, mainly to keep up with news services, followed by music, and community notices. Radio remains the preferred media for information, along with newspapers. Access to television—from overseas satellite services, along with short local programming—is limited and not usually available in the settlements.[41] Mobile phones are used mainly for voice and text messages, with limited use of the internet because of the cost.

Education

The education system begins with early childhood education and six years of primary schooling. The secondary system divides into junior secondary school (Years 7 to 9) and senior secondary school (Years 10 to 12). The rapid creation of community high schools since the 1990s, which include primary and lower secondary levels, has now swelled the number of secondary school students. Schools are often under-resourced, with limits on teacher training, overcrowded classrooms, and not enough teaching materials. Education is not compulsory, and schooling has basic fees per child.

The People's Surveys provided information on education. During the 1990s, Honiara primary school enrolment statistics increased, then decreased, showing the effect of inflation in the economy and growing poverty: 5,493 enrolments in 1990, 11,775 in 1995, and 6,455 in 1997.[42] In the 2010s, the ratios between students and certified teachers in Honiara primary and secondary schools were higher than in any of the provinces.[43] In 2020, there were 15 Honiara Education Authority primary schools (Years 1–6) and 12 secondary schools (Years 7–12) spread throughout the city, in various combinations.[44] There are also early childhood education centres, and training in technical vocational education.

---

41 RAMSI 2013: 65, 69.
42 Otter 2002: 91.
43 UNICEF 2012: 26. Only in Rennell/Bellona is the student/certified teacher ratio higher and only in primary schools.
44 Honiara City Council Schools, available from: honiaracitycouncil.com/index.php/education-and-recreation-2/hcc-schools-parents-2/hcc-secondary-schools/; and honiaracitycouncil.com/index.php/education-and-recreation-2/hcc-schools-parents-2/hcc-primary-schools/.

Year 13, a pre-university foundation program, is offered only by a few schools.[45] The best schools are private, such as Woodford International School and the Anglican Church of Melanesia's St Nicholas College, which take students from preschool to matriculation. Woodford began in the mid-1950s as a small school on Mendana Avenue in Point Cruz, catering mainly for expatriate children. By the early 1970s, it had outgrown its downtown space and its redevelopment was included in the Solomon Islands National Development Plan. The school moved to its new site at Kukum in 1979. A decade later, its name was changed to Honiara International School, and then to Woodford International School. St Nicholas College began more than 30 years ago and has included secondary level for 20 years.

Some 30 to 40 per cent of children attended primary schools in their local communities, although about half travelled for more than an hour to reach their primary school of choice. Most of those surveyed thought the quality of teaching at primary and secondary schools had improved over the previous five years.[46] Ninety-three per cent of the occupants of the FTE areas had more than five years of formal education, although only 84.5 per cent in the settlements had achieved this level. In the FTE suburbs, 22.7 per cent had no secondary education, 24.4 per cent had one to three years, and 52.8 per cent had more than four years. In the settlements, 36.7 per cent had no secondary education, 23.3 per cent had one to three years, and 39.9 per cent had four or more years. A minority of those surveyed had attended tertiary courses: 22.2 per cent in the suburbs and 18 per cent in the settlements had done so, for one to three years—presumably, mostly through SICHE and USP courses.

The background to tertiary education was outlined in Chapter 7. Since the 1980s, there has been consolidation and considerable expansion. SINU has begun to adopt a mixed-mode delivery system (face-to-face combined with distance education), aiming to establish provincial centres and nationwide outreach. Informal adult education (from basic literacy to community development courses) is available, run by women's groups, churches, and NGOs. Some education is available for 'push-outs' who have failed to gain a place in school. The Ministry of Education and

---

45 Galokale 2013: 9–10.
46 RAMSI 2013: 23, 24, 25, 27–30, 32–34.

Human Resources Development receives substantial donor funding and its Honiara-based Curriculum Development Centre has been instrumental in national curriculum reform.

While Honiara is the best Western-educated community in the country, a surprising degree of adult illiteracy continues, and many young adults in Honiara have been left outside the school system. A significant proportion of Honiara residents in the settlements (8.1 per cent) had received no formal education—a higher proportion than in the FTE districts (3.5 per cent). In Kobito, for instance, some illiterate adult men and women manage to hold down steady jobs. One man I know is a baggage-handler at the airport; one aged in his 20s has become a hairdresser, resplendent in dyed and braided blond hair; and another, aged in his 40s, sells barbecued chickens and betel nuts by the roadside. There is also a generation of students who in normal circumstances could have expected to continue through the system but who received no schooling during the Tension years. They have been left stunted educationally by being unable to complete school. While the government has recognised the necessity of achieving national literacy and expanded the provision of education, the reality is a lack of finances and expertise. The result has been the expansion of a disadvantaged underclass with no chance of finding employment, surviving through the *wantok* system and the *liu* process. It is this group that is volatile and opportunistic in any political disturbance, such as the Tension years and the 2006 Chinatown riot. Governments have much to fear from anyone who harnesses their discontent.

Plate 10.7 The next generation: Vura Primary School students, 2007.
Source: Clive Moore Collection.

Health

Based on access to health and educational services, Honiara is usually seen as a good place to live. Health services there are better than in the provinces, although some who participated in the 2013 People's Survey indicated that it could take more than an hour to travel from their homes to health facilities. There are several clinics around Honiara and, despite some shortcomings, the National Referral Hospital is the best and largest medical facility in the country. Most of those surveyed thought access to health services had improved over the previous five years, although less than half were happy with the service they received.

Life expectancy is slightly higher in Honiara than in the provinces. Analysis of the 1999 and 2009 census results shows some general health advantages of living in Honiara. Although overall prenatal and postnatal death rates remain high by Pacific standards, Honiara's infant mortality rate is the lowest in the nation. The incidence of malaria has declined over recent decades, which is perhaps responsible for fewer households using chemically treated bed-nets to ward off mosquitoes.[47] Dengue fever has made a resurgence, probably due to increasing urbanisation providing more breeding sites for the main vector, the *Aedes aegypti* mosquito. Pregnant women and children under five are most at risk. Improvements in child health are attributed to immunisation, exclusive breastfeeding, and better child nutrition. Waterborne diseases are still a problem. In 2009, out of a total of 7,379 households in Honiara, 4,415 had access to clean drinking water inside dwellings, 1,368 only had access outside their dwellings, 1,072 used outside shared water supplies, and 353 households reported no piped water was available.[48]

Hanson's disease (leprosy) is still active in Honiara, with 30 new cases reported in 2017.[49] HIV prevalence among the general population appears to be low. The Solomons introduced HIV monitoring procedures and community education earlier than any other Pacific nation. The first case was officially recorded in 1994, and there have only been 25 reported cases, six of them currently in Honiara. Most transmission is via heterosexual activity. As HIV testing is client-initiated and there are limited laboratory testing facilities, along with poorly trained health workers, it is likely that sexual diseases in Honiara are not being detected accurately and are significantly under-reported. Rates for other sexual diseases, particularly syphilis, are high and indicate underlying behavioural risks. Reported condom use is low. The major vector area for sexual diseases is Western Province (this relates to workers in the logging industry), not Honiara, although this probably means cases in Honiara are under-reported.[50]

Alcohol and marijuana consumption are high and, since the 1990s, *kwaso* (homemade potent alcoholic spirit) has increased in availability. Alcohol in particular fuels domestic violence. Honiara residents suggested the Solomon Islands Government should give priority to improving health and education services. In the People's Surveys, they also mentioned police and agricultural advice services as important. Respondents signalled that they received virtually no information relating to agricultural practices—an important omission for people who partly depend on the sale of their agricultural produce.

---

47   Otter 2002: 17, 18, 20, 34; Kere 2017.
48   UN-Habitat 2012: 34, 45.
49   'Health broadcast', *SIBC*, 24 January 2018.
50   SIG 2016b: 11–12; Marks et al. 2015; *SIBC*, 18 December 2018.

10. THE VILLAGE-CITY

Plate 10.8 Small health clinics run by the Honiara City Council are spread through the suburbs. This one is in White River, 2008.
Source: Clive Moore Collection.

Earning a living

Just under half of those surveyed in 2013 thought their financial situation was much the same as two years earlier. About one-quarter thought their economic circumstances were worse. Only 33.7 per cent of the Honiara residents interviewed were involved in paid work, 31 per cent depended on money from members of their family, and 61.7 per cent made money from selling commodities. Marginally more males than females were in paid work. This result is amplified by Maebuta and Maebuta's 2009 study of livelihoods in Honiara squatter settlements, which found that the main sources of household income are selling betel-nuts and cigarettes to supplement full time and casual jobs. The average income from informal activities is two times more than the average fortnightly income from casual and full-time employment and 1.5 times more than the national minimum wage.[51]

Small local markets thrive, with thousands of betel nut and tobacco stalls, and others selling fresh green vegetables and sweet potatoes, plus fish of dubious quality (bought frozen, then thawed). The main sales at roadside markets and Central Market came from betel nuts and cigarettes, garden crops, canteen goods, fish, and other foods, ice, drinks, and livestock. Many households operate small kiosks attached to their houses, functioning as mini-trade stores.[52] Just under half those surveyed had never paid direct taxation and more than half had no bank account, living totally in the cash economy. They have no comprehension of or access to loan facilities, and do not even fully understand the necessity to pay urban annual land fees. Some families relied on remittances from relatives working away from home, mainly in New Zealand and Australia.[53] The COVID-19 pandemic scare showed just how fragile the domestic economy is.[54]

---

51   Maebuta and Maebuta 2009.
52   These local markets are regulated by Honiara City Council officers, who were once known as the Honiara City Constabulary, a branch of the RSIPF. My thanks to Eric Grimm for his clarification of this service, 13 May 2020.
53   RAMSI 2013: 75, 76, 77, 78–79, 85–92.
54   Australian Government 2020.

10. THE VILLAGE-CITY

Plate 10.9 The Sunday Fishing Village market on Kukum Highway, 2011.
Source: Clive Moore Collection.

Plate 10.10 Central Market on the waterside, 2017.
Source: Clive Moore Collection.

Plate 10.11 Thousands of people visit Honiara's Central Market every day.
This photograph is from 2004.
Source: Clive Moore Collection.

Plate 10.12 A market stall at Honiara International Airport—Henderson Field, 2004.
Source: Clive Moore Collection.

Central Market and the Malaita Fishing Village Sunday market provide the bulk of fresh produce for Honiara. Women vendors dominate these two markets. The unregulated White River market spreads along both sides of the road west out of Honiara, made up of closely packed rows of small huts. It is male-dominated and sells mainly betel nuts. Council-owned Kukum market now sells little fresh produce. The vendors concentrate on betel nuts and illegal home brew, in a space dominated by men, to an extent that women feel unsafe there. Smaller markets operate at Naha and Borderline. There was also a small market at Rove and another near King George VI School—both of which are now closed.[55] In the late 2010s, vendors at Central Market on average made SI$104 per market visit—60 per cent more than the 2019 daily minimum wage.[56] The economic benefits of market selling are huge. Central Market is well run and now has at least 1,000 vendors on weekends. About two-thirds of them grow their own produce, with the other third onselling produce grown by others. The vegetables and fruits come mainly from north and central Guadalcanal, the Ngela Group and Savo, the Russells, Malaita, and Isabel. The fish on sale come mainly from Noro, and direct from trawlers operating in Western Province, with some also from the Ngela Group, the Russells, Isabel, and Malaita. Overall market earnings per annum are around SI$30 million, which flow back into Honiara and provincial economies. After household costs and business needs, about 34 per cent of the remaining market income is spent on school fees, church tithes, building materials, and supporting kin.[57] About 90 per cent of the market venders are women, and their experiences of Honiara differ from those of men. A recent urban development report says:

> For some, the city offers opportunities for leadership and skills development generally not found in the village. They value the greater role they can have in earning income for the family—often becoming the main bread winner. More women work in the informal sector than men … These opportunities allow them access to the finances necessary to provide for their families' needs.
>
> While women can earn money, they can be harassed by males in their community to 'share' their earnings. The lack of access to saving facilities or banks increases their vulnerability to these

---

55 UN Women 2009; Keen and Ride 2018.
56 Georgeou et al. 2019: 113.
57 Keen et al. 2017: 109–11.

demands, as most have to keep their savings in cash. This is a significant issue impacting on empowerment, education for children, food security and poverty; unaddressed it can lead to violence against women. Some women leaders believe that access to trustworthy and easily accessible savings facilities can reduce this problem.[58]

The market economy is entirely based on cash and still contains elements of local provincial marketing, expanded to Honiara. The vendor skills necessary are little different from those in village markets, which allows visitors from the provinces and rural areas on Guadalcanal to participate in the urban economy. Central Market, in particular, has been the social, economic, and often political hub of Honiara for more than 60 years.

Transport

Most Honiara residents surveyed felt that cheap transport was sufficiently available. They used it for access to work, visiting their families and friends, and to attend sport and church activities.[59] Over decades, minibuses have provided an excellent service all over Honiara, while recently bigger buses have been added to the fleet. Over the past decade, traffic has become a dominant issue in Honiara, with substantial traffic jams. Partly, this is because Honiara has been swamped by cheap Japanese second-hand cars. There are hundreds of taxis, which are also used as family cars. The congested roads have reduced the financial viability of taxis, which once charged by the kilometre but now charge by the hour. In the period 2017–21, Japanese funding enabled a massive upgrade of Kukum Highway from the airport, including building a second bridge across the Mataniko River, and the creation of large roundabouts at the city council building intersection and at Kukum. The project will be completed before the 2023 Pacific Games. The city desperately needs a highway bypass, although construction will be financially and logistically difficult (Map 10.2).

---

58   ibid., 84.
59   RAMSI 2013: 39–40.

Plate 10.13 Chinatown from lower Skyline Ridge, 2011.
Source: Clive Moore Collection.

Plate 10.14 Mendana Avenue, 2008.
Source: Clive Moore Collection.

Plate 10.15 View of the Point Cruz area from Parliament, 2008.
Source: Clive Moore Collection.

Law and Order

One of RAMSI's Three Pillars was the strengthening of policing and the justice system. Most of the Honiara residents surveyed in 2013 had no contact with the police over the previous year. Where contact was made, it was to deal with theft, violence, or community disputes. The general feeling was that the level of police assistance was not satisfactory, because the police did not help or were too slow to arrive, although one-third of respondents thought police assistance had improved over the previous five years.[60] Those in Honiara's FTE suburbs were twice as likely as those in settlements to say they felt unsafe in the downtown area (23 per cent compared with 11 per cent). Young men and women were more likely than older respondents to say they felt unsafe in Honiara. Drunks abound in the settlements, particularly at weekends. They cause a nuisance, wandering the streets, and are responsible for violent incidents. One slowly increasing community problem is the production

---

60 ibid., 43–45.

of *kwaso* in primitive stills. Although the police constantly target *kwaso* production, it still flourishes. *Kwaso* and marijuana, but not 'hard' drugs, are available in all settlements, squatter areas, and markets. The drinking of *kava* (a beverage made from *Piper methysticum*) is a new and spreading phenomenon, with *kava* bars operating. The survey found community disputes were common, although the majority of those interviewed were satisfied with the ways available to them to solve these disputes. Local and traditional justice systems were thought to be superior mechanisms to calling the police. Although domestic and community violence did not emerge as particular themes, a 2019 Oxfam survey suggests 'women's behaviour is strongly policed and their transgression often resulted in severe punishment'. Men are far less likely to be held accountable for their actions.[61]

Life in middle-class Honiara is not yet lived behind razor wire, although those with the most to lose do protect themselves with guards, dogs, and high fences. 'Rascal' (criminal) gangs do not operate to the same extent as in Port Moresby or Lae. There are criminal groups involved in opportunistic break-ins and other crimes, and youth gangs exist.[62] One of the oldest groups is Borderline Original Gangsters (BOG), which is made up mainly of young Kwara`ae and Kwaio Malaitans. Other gangs are similar and usually have a shared ethnic origin.

There is considerable indigenous resentment over the extent of Asian political and economic influence, which always smoulders but seldom breaks into flames.[63] The old *waku* have moved into large-scale commerce and the professions. They are also culturally skilled at operating in Solomon Islands and are never as confrontational or as uncaring as the new *waku*. Control of three of Honiara's main hotels is in old *waku* hands. The main resentment is against the smaller new *waku* traders who make little attempt to accommodate themselves to Solomons ways. The shopkeepers sitting on their high chairs in the trade stores, keeping their untrusting eyes on their cash, staff, and customers, cause resentment, as do new *waku* ventures into business areas usually reserved for Solomon Islanders. Recently, the new *waku* began moving into the bus industry (which is reserved for locals).[64] The image of parallel but overlapping

---

61 Homan et al. 2019: 5.
62 Dinnen 1994, 2001; Jourdan 2008; Allen 2007: 125–26.
63 Moore 2008a.
64 In December 2017, Honiara City Council banned foreign-owned buses. Kafo 2017.

'worlds', introduced in earlier chapters, remains valid. As the centrality of Chinatown diminishes, there is a joke circulating in Honiara: the decline is not important as the whole of Honiara has become a Chinatown.

The events of 1998–2003, the large 2006 riot, and smaller riots in 2014 and 2019 make clear that there remains a potential for violence to arise again in Honiara. Many of the same ingredients that created the Tensions remain: dissatisfaction with lack of development in Guadalcanal and Malaita provinces; continued Malaitan migration, particularly to Honiara; a burgeoning population of disaffected youths with no prospects of paid employment; a growing Honiara constantly encroaching on Guale land; blatant political corruption that has flourished despite RAMSI; and the possibility of future misguided rogue leadership. The national government is aware of these problems, but is obviously incapable of dealing with them, and the Honiara City Council has no capacity to do so. After flash floods in May 2014, when small riots occurred over the maldistribution of relief funds, a Chinese store was burnt down. Once more, the Chinese community braced for a larger riot that, mercifully, did not come.[65] The recently rearmed RSIPF performed well in handling riots after the 24 April 2019 election of Prime Minister Sogavare, which gives reason for future optimism.[66]

Parliament and local council representatives

Most people interviewed had little contact with parliamentarians or town councillors. Politicians fill a different role than in developed nations. Because national politicians have large Constituency Development Funds (CDFs) (now SI$350,000 per member)[67] and access to shipping grants and other direct funding, they are called on to provide community services such as coffins for burials in Honiara or coffins and costs for transporting bodies back to the provinces. They also provide water tanks for households in their electorates. There are three national electorates

---

65   Australia Network News 2014; *SIBC*, 17 May 2014, 23 May 2014; *SS*, 19 May 2014; Wood 2014.
66   *SIBC*, 24 April 2019. There are still more than 40 Australian Federal Police in supporting roles.
67   Aqorau 2019. Until 2019, the Taiwanese funded 20 per cent of the Constituency Development Fund system, which was down 50 per cent from their contribution 10 years ago.

based in Honiara.⁶⁸ Given the high turnover in parliament each election, members need to prove their local usefulness. There is a great deal of criticism over the existence of the Constituency Development Funds, which have grown exponentially and are seldom acquitted properly. They show the hybridity of the political and social system. Parliamentarians dispense their CDFs rather like chiefs and big-men giving handouts to families in their villages.

Creating an urban culture

Honiara is a hybrid Pacific urban space, while also a Pacific 'arrival city' and a developing-world city.⁶⁹ The relatively small size of Honiara and Solomon Islands, plus the resilience of aspects of village culture, argue against applying models from other developing-world cities.

In Honiara's expanding urban settlements, and elsewhere in the Pacific, many of the features of the people's rural origins survive. Pathways from settlements into the more affluent suburbs and middle-class life seldom exist, owing to the smallness of the formal economy and constraints on the informal economy. In some ways, these Pacific cities are not vehicles of development comparable with 'arrival cities' beyond the Pacific. They operate more as extensions of rural life, and circulation is a dominant feature. In the 1960s, M.E.P. Bellam noted that two-thirds of his Honiara informants associated mainly with kin, half of them lived with kin, and one-quarter worked with kin.⁷⁰ This remains true half a century later, particularly within the THA/TOL and squatter areas. One argument put forward here is that a Malaitan 'world' has developed in Honiara. While there are middle-class and elite Malaitan families, the majority still lives in THA/TOL settlements and squatter areas where leaf-thatch houses mingle with more substantial houses.

In his study of Honiara in the 1990s, Cato Berg suggested Honiara's elite was not representative of the rest of Solomon Islands. Berg concluded that Honiara's elite was based on Solomon Islands families who became prominent during the late nineteenth and early twentieth centuries,

---

68 RAMSI 2013: 98, 127–29. In November 2017, Prime Minister Sogavare calculated the total amount given directly to the 50 parliamentarians was more than SI$500 million annually. *SS*, 9 November 2017.
69 Saunders 2010.
70 Bellam 1968: 10.

usually through connections to Christian missions or the serendipity of living near trading stations or BSIP district headquarters. He argued that the 'British protectorate may have left behind an implicit hierarchy which now manifests itself in the composition of the urban elite'.[71] Honiara's indigenous elite of the 1990s was descended from the second generation of the colonial elite. Their families were the ones who first migrated to Honiara after the war, although how much of this elite formation was British-inspired and how much was indigenous-motivated or created anew in Honiara is not clear. Solomon Islanders masterfully managed to modernise their indigenous cultures, and little of the British influence remains.

As described in Chapter 5, *masta liu*, a term in use since the 1970s, depicts another cultural phenomenon: temporary and permanent urban residents, usually youths and men, who depend on their *wantoks* and wander opportunistically in urban space. It is a lifestyle adopted out of necessity in a harsh urban setting with few jobs. Other more recent related terms are *hospaep* (from 'hosepipe'), which means to suck up resources from the wider group of primary affiliation, and the graphic *nila* (to insert a needle to drain blood). Many *masta liu* become adept at *nila* and *hospaep* techniques, draining the financial body of dollars under the pretext of *wantokism*. They can also turn to crime to support themselves, usually through theft.[72] Another word has also recently entered the vocabulary: *beliga* (meaning thieves, who often have a violent edge).[73] *Masta liu* are just conniving gentlemen by comparison. *Beliga* have more in common with Papua New Guinea's *raskols* and are hardcore criminals. The introduction of the term *beliga* is an indication that urban tensions are increasing.

Language, kinship networks, circulation, and integration are all woven into urban strategies for survival and success. Linguistic complexity is part of everyday life in Honiara. There are 65 to 70 languages still used in Solomons Islands, with another 50 or so dialect variations.[74] Each is probably spoken in Honiara. Solomons Pijin is the lingua franca linking

---

71   Berg 2000: 193.
72   Frazer 1985; Chapman and Prothero 1985: 10; Berg 2000: 37–59; Jourdan 1995a; Keesing 1994.
73   *Beliga* literally means 'theft' in the To'ambaita language from north Malaita. The rise of street crime in Honiara in the 2010s led to the general adoption of the term as a label for a range of antisocial youth behaviour—predominantly pickpocketing and street theft, as well as violent harassment and muggings. The bus stop at Central Market is now often called 'Beliga Point'.
74   Lewis et al. 2013; Jourdan 2014: 77.

all groups, and most residents also use or at least understand standard English. Most Honiara residents speak more than one vernacular language and understand phrases in others. Often, they say they can 'hear' other languages, even when they cannot speak them. This linguistic world is part of the complexity of Honiara. Vernacular languages are intermingled with Pijin, the verbal context varying, depending on the language groups and individuals involved. For some, Pijin has become their mother tongue. Conversations among *wantoks* may remain in a particular vernacular language or begin with pleasantries in the language, then retreat to Pijin. The educated elite will often begin with pleasantries in Pijin, before turning to English peppered with Pijin words and phrases. Humour, casual style, and good manners permeate most conversations. Solomon Islanders choose their words carefully, indicating familial relationships, and showing respect, even changing linguistic kin categories to fit difficult situations.[75] Outsiders can often be blissfully unaware of the interpersonal relationships being played out around them, spinning on the slang meanings of a single word or an oblique cultural reference.

Invisible boundaries, such as *tambu* ('taboo'), which in some Solomons cultures regulates gender relationships in spatial and behavioural ways, need to be added to this mix. My favourite examples relate to the three walkways installed by well-meaning planners trying to make the busy coast road safer to cross. The two walkways under Mendana Avenue have remained closed for years, largely because the more traditional Malaitan men would never allow women to pass over their heads; it would be a *tambu* pollutant that traditionally requires a compensation payment. Recently, I was told of Kwaio Malaita men in a taxi, confronted by the third walkway, an overpass between the hospital and Chinatown. They asked the driver to stop, and they got out and walked around the overpass, thus avoiding any chance of pollution.[76] The Central Market's underground walkway has now reopened, although with guards to stop misuse. Languages also contain subtle cultural codes that help individuals negotiate relationships; swearing or cursing via reference to offensive sexual scenarios is common. Breaches of *tambu* codes and curses are usually compensated in cash and

---

75   Berg (2000: 115) gives an example of two Rennellese brothers who met at a hotel and conducted their conversation as if they were uncle and nephew to escape the implications of the disrespect of two brothers meeting in that situation.
76   This was related to me by David Akin, July 2018.

customary wealth items, forming another thread in the social fabric. Compensation can also be misused, with claims engineered and relying more on gullibility and fear than actuality.[77]

Anthropologist Christine Jourdan reminds us that living in town is a new phenomenon for Solomon Islanders with no model to follow and no path of evolution:

> [T]hey are continuously creating a culture in which they are immersed. They are both agents and recipients in this process, as marginal participants in a worldwide capitalist consumerism and as cultural creators. In this case one can confidently argue that this urban culture in the making is being created by urbanites as they live it, although the creative possibilities of urban life-styles are constrained by town structures, the type of socioeconomic activities of urbanites, and the type of social relationships they establish in urban settings.[78]

As well as operating within a customary framework, Honiara is a modern city in which Western popular culture thrives, mixed with Pacific variations. Church-based singing is part of a modern vibrant music and youth culture. Christianity, the Bahá`í Faith, and now Islam are essential parts of the social glue that makes it all work.

Music and popular culture are important aspects of nation-building and national consciousness. Traditional panpipe music, local bamboo bands, country and western, gospel, love ballads, and black music like Pijin rock, reggae, and rap, are all available on CDs and are played on local radio stations, enabling learning and the mixing of languages in enjoyable circumstances. Musicians from Papua New Guinea and Australia visit Honiara. Rock concerts by visiting and local reggae and rap artists are standard entertainment. Some bands base themselves at hotel venues, such as the outdoor bar at the Iron Bottom Sound Hotel. CHM, the big PNG recording studio, has signed up Solomons' groups. Honiara musicians, such as Sharzy, often play in Brisbane. Singers such as Sharzy, Papa Yanni, Lulu, Sisiva, Litol Rastas, 2-4-1 Band, and Native Stoneage have replaced the earlier musical scene. The use of Solomons Pijin and local languages is commonplace in song lyrics. Bands are male-dominated, and women

---

77   Much of this paragraph is based on my observations since the 1970s. See also Berg 2000: 176–79.
78   Jourdan 1995b: 142.

are seldom lead singers—an indication of ingrained cultural attitudes. YouTube allows Solomons' music to reach around the world, and digital networks in the Solomons have improved rapidly, enabling anyone to watch and listen on their mobile phones.

Modern Honiara is in part a replica of international urban societies. Fashion consciousness in clothes and hairstyles, modern body language, and the most evolved use of Solomons Pijin—all emanate from Honiara. There is now a small gay and lesbian scene, although sexuality and gender variations are not easily welcomed in Honiara. A few LGBTQ refugees have ended up in Australia, granted residence on compassionate grounds because of their lack of acceptance in Honiara.

Festivals are always welcome diversions. The annual Trade Show (an agriculture and industry fair) is an opportunity for tens of thousands of residents to wander the exhibits. National ceremonies are choreographed occurrences executed with great skill. The 11th Pacific Arts Festival, held in Honiara between 1 and 14 July 2012, was a unique opportunity for Solomon Islanders to highlight and celebrate their cultural diversity. The theme was 'Culture in Harmony with Nature'. The festival provided a chance for Solomon Islanders to show pride in their nation and its many cultures, and to invite the peoples of the Pacific to join them in celebration. It was a time for unification, an opportunity to build infrastructure, and to create long-term cultural, economic, and spiritual benefits for artists and communities. The festival cemented Honiara's place in Pacific tourism and was also a peaceful event that involved all residents of the capital. The crowds walked to and from the Panatina venue every day and evening, reclaiming the streets. The festival restored the confidence of the people of Honiara. After dismal years, they were on the international stage and created a memorable, peaceful event showcasing their city and nation, and the entire Pacific. It was emblematic of a newly self-assured Honiara. The 2023 Pacific Games will generate a similar pride in Honiara and the nation.

Plate 10.16 A women's marching group in Vura, Honiara, 1995.
Source: Clive Moore Collection.

Plate 10.17 Cultures are preserved through cultural groups performing at public events. Here, Malaitan panpipe dancers perform at the Art Gallery in 1995.
Source: Clive Moore Collection.

Plates 10.18–10.20 A Malaitan bride-price ceremony for Clive Maesae and Salome Stella in August 2011.

It began at Fishing Village (trucks have replaced canoes) (Plate 10.18) and moved to the bride's family home at Rove, where a wall of 50 Malaitan shell valuables (Plate 10.19) was presented to the bride's family by the groom's family, along with SI$24,000 in cash and 40 rolls of cloth. The feast was held back at Fishing Village, where taros and yams were being prepared (Plate 10.20).

Source: Clive Moore Collection.

HONIARA

2020: Iumi Tugeda against COVID-19

COVID-19 eventually reached Solomon Islands after a valiant effort to keep the virus out. In early 2021, as this book was being finalised, there had been no deaths, no community transmission, and the national coordination effort had been well planned. Solomon Islanders are not new to disease epidemics, although their isolation over several thousand years protected them from diseases common in Europe and Asia. Then, during the nineteenth century, whaling ships introduced outside diseases, as did labourers returning from work on overseas plantations, missionaries and their converts, and traders. There was no immunity in Solomon Islands to diseases such as the common cold, and some gastrointestinal and influenza-type infections, mumps, measles, and chickenpox, which caused large-scale depopulation.[79] Solomon Islands escaped the eighteenth and nineteenth-century smallpox epidemics that ravaged Aboriginal Australians and affected New Guineans. The first known major epidemics were of measles in 1875, introduced by labourers returning from Queensland, the influenza epidemic (Spanish flu) of 1919–20, and various poliomyelitis outbreaks, particularly those in the 1950s. Government reports also note other large influenza and infectious disease epidemics. Tens of thousands died in their villages during colonial-era disease outbreaks; on some islands, perhaps half the population died.

When the COVID-19 virus began to sweep around the world early in 2020, grave fears were held for the effect it would have on Solomon Islands. From 1 February, restrictions were placed on entry to the country from overseas.[80] The National Referral Hospital and the provincial hospital system operate under strain at the best of times. Government policy was focused on stopping the virus entering the country, which provided sufficient time to build up domestic defences. In March, commercial international travel ceased entirely in an attempt to stop entry of the virus, and both the governor-general and the prime minister addressed the nation. Prime Minister Sogavare made many radio broadcasts to the nation on COVID-19 planning, and government agencies issued competent planning advice, all of which engendered confidence. The *Emergency Powers Act* was invoked to institute the Emergency Powers (COVID-19) Regulations 2020 to deal with any public emergency.

---

79   Moore 2017a: 54, 86, 307, 401–2, 417, 430–3; Scott 2007: 84–87.
80   SIG 2020a; Pagepitu 2020.

Honiara was declared an emergency zone and all nightclubs, *kava* and other bars, and casinos, were closed; *kava* and alcohol bars reopened in mid-May. Initially, many residents chose to return to their home provinces and villages, and Members of Parliament were allowed to use their discretionary funds to return constituents to their home villages, although this flow soon stopped as interisland movement was closed. Initially, churches were encouraged to stay open, although during Easter (10–12 April), many members chose to worship at home. Schools were closed and, just as in the rest of the world, a sense of fear spread through Honiara's population. This slowly lifted as it became clear that the nation had no recorded cases of COVID-19. With no flights to Australia until July, the government relied on the People's Republic of China to provide the capacity for local testing. The first COVID-19 testing supplies arrived in Honiara on 22 April, allowing local testing from mid-May, even though doubts were raised in some quarters about the quality of the Chinese testing equipment. There were also questions about a Chinese vessel said to have broken quarantine and entered the country illegally.[81]

In late March, the public service was scaled down and staff in non-essential services were authorised to take emergency paid leave of absence. The economy went into negative growth (with gross domestic product predicted to be –5 per cent), and the Solomon Islands Provident Fund was allowed to assist its members beyond the usual facilities. In May, the government announced the sale of a COVID-19 Domestic Development Bond of SI$120 million to help fund a SI$309 million stimulus package for the economy.[82]

Solomon Islands had poor facilities for palliative care, which required immediate upgrading.[83] By mid-April 2020, quarantine facilities were established in Honiara, utilising 442 rooms at Guadalcanal Beach Resort, Telekom Recreational Area, the VIMO apartments on the outskirts of the airport, and at King George VI School. Provincial sites were also established. In late April, limited numbers of schools were allowed to reopen, but not on Guadalcanal, at Noro, Munda, Choiseul Bay, or in the Shortland Islands. All early childhood centres and primary schools up to Year 6 remained closed, as did rural training centres.

---

81 *IS*, 1 May 2020; *SIBC*, 14 May 2020; Osifelo 2020a; Kaukui 2020; Saeni 2020.
82 SIG 2020b, 2020c, 2020d, 2020e, 2020i; Fanasia 2020.
83 Spratt and Spencer 2018.

Attempts were made to close the border between Bougainville and the Shortlands, instituting the Coastwatchers 20/20 Program for local communities to report boat traffic to police—a throwback to the Coastwatchers of World War II.[84] Betel nut and other local market stalls were closed, although these quickly sprang up again in new locations. Planning also began for satellite markets to take the pressure off Central Market, where social distancing was virtually impossible. This strategy, already in Honiara City Council planning documents, was brought forward by COVID-19 preparations.[85]

By mid-May, with no cases reported in the nation, Prime Minister Sogavare allowed businesses and schools to reopen. Short lockdowns were practised in Honiara. One result of the May 2020 trial lockdown was eerie photographs of Honiara without vehicles and people. However, cracks had begun to appear in the united front when, in late April and early May, the Premier of Malaita Province was involved in a slanging match with the national government over provincial and national powers relating to COVID-19 and China.[86] And, just as in the Tension years, pyramid financial schemes emerged. One Link Pacifica, which collected more than SI$300,000, was condemned by the central bank and the prime minister; charges were laid against the directors.[87]

The situation in Solomon Islands remained remarkably stable for several months. Occasional planeloads of citizens and diplomats returned, from the Philippines, Australia, New Zealand, Fiji, and China and were placed in quarantine in Honiara, although from late July this was at their own expense. Solomon Islands recorded its first cases of COVID-19 on 3 October: two students who had returned from the Philippines, both of whom were asymptomatic and in quarantine. Four more were diagnosed at the end of the month: professional soccer players returning from the United Kingdom. By mid-November, there were 16 cases. Prime Minister Sogavare showed his fury with those who had been dishonest in their pre-departure information, warning of possible prosecutions for endangering the nation.[88]

---

84   *SIBC*, 19 April 2020; SIG 2020e; *SS*, 16 April 2020.
85   *SS*, 29 April 2020.
86   Osifelo 2020b; *SIBC*, 15 May 2020.
87   Buchanan 2020.
88   Maka`a and Piringi 2020; *SIBC*, 10 October 2020; Kusu 2020; Iroga 2020.

The quarantine facilities for overseas arrivals have worked well. On 15 November, 105 'repatriates' were released from the quarantine facilities into the general community, with 85 remaining. *The Island Sun*'s description made it sound like a class graduating from a short course.[89] In early December, there were 170 individuals in quarantine or isolation wards. Even with more 'rescue' flights arriving, the situation was under control. By the end of 2020, there had been 17 positive cases: 10 had recovered, seven remained in isolation, and three were still testing positive.[90] By early 2021, the situation was stable with no positive cases. In March, vaccines from Australia and China began to arrive, with the aim of vaccinating all adults during 2021.[91] One of the main fears is that, as COVID-19 spreads out of control in Papua New Guinea, Solomon Islands' northern border is a likely future entry point.

The future

UN-Habitat data suggest that, in 2016, there were close to 4,000 informal settlement households within Honiara's municipal boundary. Keen and Kiddle estimated that this included about 28,000 people, or approximately 20 per cent of Honiara's official population (excluding the peri-urban population). The 2019 estimate, illustrated in Map 10.1, suggested there were 92 THA/TOL and squatter settlements within or on the Honiara City Council boundaries. This figure does not include the peri-urban population, nor its continuing expansion inland into areas that are customary Tandai or Malango land, other registered land in Guadalcanal Province, or land designated as part of Queen Elizabeth National Park. The new squatter and THA/TOL areas, which are largely on Honiara's inland fringes, will become ever more substantial. The government now recognises that many of these informal settlements are permanent and is seeking ways to legitimise their tenure and to provide urban services.[92] The forward estimate in Maps 10.4 and 10.5 is sobering, with future expansion mostly in the city's east.

---

89 Podokolo 2020a.
90 Podokolo 2020b; SIG 2020f; *SIBC*, 21 December 2020.
91 *SIBC*, 16 March 2021.
92 Keen and Kiddle 2016; see also SIG 2016a.

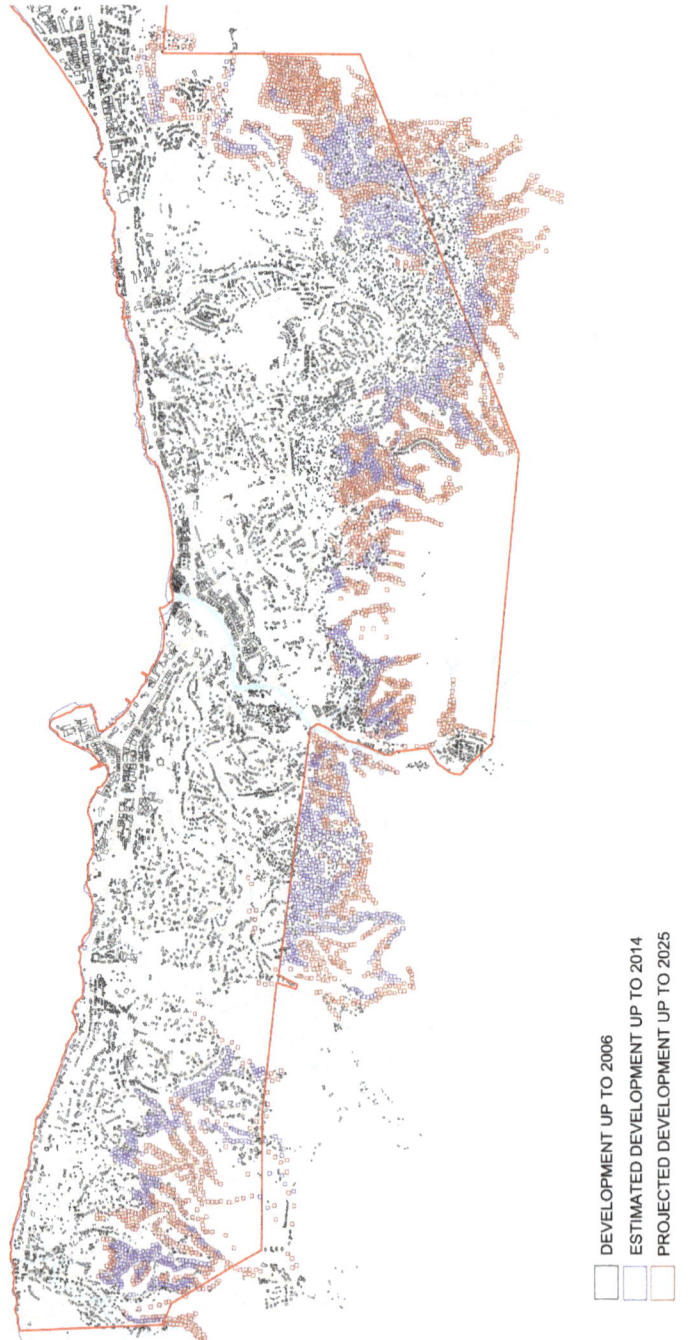

Map 10.4 Honiara's current and projected urban growth, 2006–25.
Source: Ministry of Lands, Housing and Survey.

If Honiara doubles in size—which is predicted in the next few decades—it will begin to operate like Port Moresby and Suva, which have more in common with other developing-world cities. It may absorb all the adjacent Tandai and Malango wards of the Guadalcanal Provincial Government. In 2018, an Asian Development Bank study produced a future development strategy for Greater Honiara and Tandai and Malango land—an area of 133 square kilometres (Map 10.5). The first phase suggested was upgrading the present facilities in time for the 2023 Asian Games. The second phase covers the period 2023–27, with an emphasis on upgrading the city centre to encourage investments in business, particularly tourism, to improve connectivity between areas, to increase resilience to natural hazards and climate change, and to enlarge and upgrade urban centres and services. The third phase, 2028–35, focuses on strengthening economic potential, tourism, and housing expansion to the city's south.[93]

Plate 10.21 Point Cruz Yacht Club, 2008.
Source: Clive Moore Collection.

---

93   SIG 2018.

Plate 10.22 Sabot racing in front of the Point Cruz Yacht Club, looking out to the patrol boat wharf, 2007.
Source: Clive Moore Collection.

Plate 10.23 The front entrance of King Solomon Hotel, 2006.
Source: Clive Moore Collection.

10. THE VILLAGE-CITY

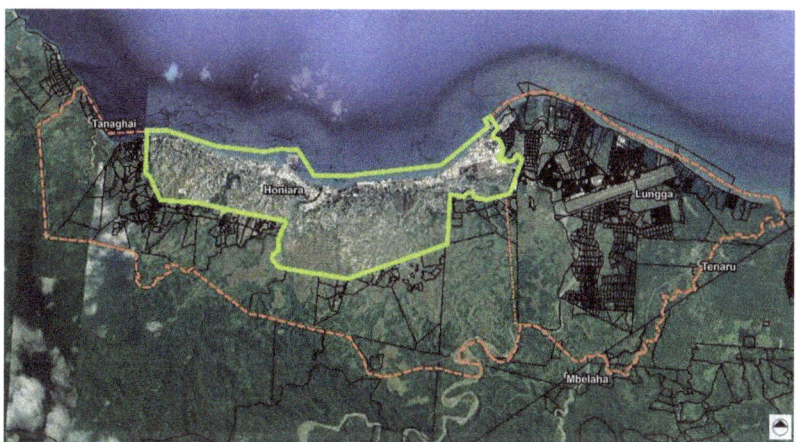

Map 10.5 Greater Honiara, including the area of the Honiara City Council (in green) and Tandai and Malango wards (in red) of Guadalcanal Provincial Government.
Source: SIG (2018: 3).

If we are to believe the planning reports, eventually the village-city concept will disappear, which I find unlikely. The city council and the national government have limited funds to spend on urban development. Urban services have always favoured the FTE and not the settlement areas. Honiara's houses may be creaking at the seams, but they continue to shelter and maintain their occupants. Families still manage to look after their own, despite the financial challenges. Beggars are rare in Honiara, unlike Port Moresby, where for decades they have been a common sight in downtown Boroko. Honiara's many settlements are home to the most vulnerable and marginal residents. Town planning must allow for their presence and enable them to live with dignity. Government, at all levels, must fulfil its obligations to its citizens. If this course is not followed, the unresolved issues that caused the Tension years—with full reconciliation and economic progress not achieved—may well bring a recurrence of urban turmoil.

A 2019 UN survey commissioned to examine Solomon Islanders' perceptions of peacebuilding after RAMSI found that about half the Malaitans and Guale surveyed were dissatisfied with the way the government had handled issues arising from the Tensions. The two most important changes identified as lacking were increased access to economic opportunities and the need to grant greater power to provincial authorities. Improving employment, health, and education and reducing corruption had the highest ratings. Interestingly, achieving reconciliation relating to Tensions issues did not rate highly.[94]

***

For 45 years, I have visited and lived in Honiara. I like the place and feel comfortable there. I visit friends and adopted family members, and look forward to each trip. The city has its detractors—mainly outsiders who find it an ugly, hot, and dusty sprawl over barren hills, lacking in charm. They are missing something. Honiara is a Solomon Islands canvas of startling complexity, both geographically and through its people. The hills, ridges, and valleys create small communities, each separate from the other, rather like villages. It is boisterous but also refined, respectful of differences, and on occasions almost demure. Its people are proud and nationalistic, relaxed, and full of smiles. The same cultural strengths that helped Solomon Islands survive the Tensions and RAMSI years will carry on. Although I worry about the poverty and the insecure land tenure, there is a sense of self-contained confidence and calm. Even so, those at the bottom of urban society have every reason to be concerned about their future.

Although there are now one or two urban-born generations, even the richest members of the elite are not far away in time from the village origins of their parents and grandparents. A pre-Christian spiritual world still operates, alongside and including the most fervent Christians, and is respected by all. There is an acknowledgement that Solomon Islands' spirituality is anchored in land owned under customary tenure, and that these land rights must be preserved. Yet, half of Honiara's people live on land to which they have no legal rights. The big losers could be the Tandai on whose land Honiara sits, although with a little legal ingenuity, the government could rezone the customary land surrounding Honiara, allowing the owners to benefit from their proximity to the huge urban centre, and thus receive ample compensation.

---

94 Sloan et al. 2019.

There are few signs that national, provincial, and urban authorities have learnt lessons from the 1998–2017 Tensions and RAMSI years, or that they are willing to tackle looming issues. Two more large changes came in 2020. First, the Solomon Islands Government dropped its long-term diplomatic allegiance with Taiwan, transferring recognition to the People's Republic of China. Although it is a foreign policy issue, this has caused some social unrest, and the Malaitan Provincial Government has been at loggerheads with the national government. Because of the size of Honiara's Malaitan population, this has a flow-on effect. The second change is of course COVID-19. The Solomons has done remarkably well in containing the pandemic.

Let us hope it does not take another period of civil upheaval to force the hands of leaders on any of these issues. The hybridity that I have stressed is part of the answer for future success. If the government realises this, Honiara can succeed as a bourgeoning major Pacific urban settlement—and a village-city. Urban planning must be an indigenous process and it is up to the citizens of the nation to create a Honiara that fits their needs.

Plate 10.24 Governor-General Sir David Vunagi GCMG KStJ and Lady Mary Vunagi, 2020.
Source: Government House Collection.

Plate 10.25 Isabel Province dancers on Independence Day, 2005, at Lawson Tama.

They are playing large panpipes and a bamboo percussion instrument that is struck with thongs (rubber slippers).

Source: Clive Moore Collection.

Plate 10.26 Independence Day celebrations at Lawson Tama, Honiara, 2008.

Source: Clive Moore Collection.

Bibliography

Newspaper articles are listed only if the names of the authors are known. Anonymous articles are referenced in individual footnotes. Some websites are only referenced in footnotes.

Afia-Maetala, Ruth Basi and Alice Aruhe`eta Pollard. 2009. Turning the Tide: Celebrating Women's History in the Solomon Islands, 1948–2009. In *Being the First: Storis Blong Oloketa Mere Lo Solomon Aelan*, edited by Alice Aruhe`eta Pollard and Marilyn J. Waring, 9–33. Honiara and Auckland: RAMSI and Institute of Public Policy and Pacific Media Centre, AUT University.

Akin, David. 1999. Compensation and the Melanesian State: Why the Kwaio Keep Claiming. *Contemporary Pacific* 11(1): 35–67.

Akin, David. 2005. *Kastom* as Hegemony? A Response to Babadzan. *Anthropological Theory* 5(1): 97–105. doi.org/10.1177/1463499605050871.

Akin, David. 2013. *Colonialism, Maasina Rule, and the Origins of Malaitan Kastom*. Honolulu: University of Hawai`i Press. doi.org/10.21313/hawaii/9780824838140.001.0001.

Allan, Colin Hamilton. 1989. *Solomons Safari, 1953–58 (Part I)*. Christchurch, NZ: Nag's Head Press.

Allan, Colin Hamilton. 1990. *Solomons Safari, 1953–58 (Part II)*. Christchurch, NZ: Nag's Head Press.

Allen, Matthew G. 2007. Greed and grievance in the conflict in Solomon Islands, 1998–2003. PhD thesis, The Australian National University, Canberra. Available from: openresearch-repository.anu.edu.au/handle/1885/150055.

Allen, Matthew G. 2011. *Long-term engagement: The future of the Regional Assistance Mission to Solomon Islands*. Strategic Insights No. 51. Canberra: Australian Strategic Policy Institute.

Allen, Matthew G. 2012a. Informal Formalisation in a Hybrid Property Space: The Case of Smallholder Oil Palm Production in Solomon Islands. *Asia Pacific Viewpoint* 53(3): 300–13. doi.org/10.1111/j.1467-8373.2012.01489.x.

Allen, Matthew G. 2012b. Land, Identity and Conflict on Guadalcanal, Solomon Islands. *Australian Geographer* 43(2): 163–80. doi.org/10.1080/00049182.2012.682294.

Allen, Matthew G. 2013. *Greed and Grievance: Ex-Militants' Perspectives on the Conflict in Solomon Islands, 1998–2003*. Honolulu: University of Hawai`i Press. doi.org/10.21313/hawaii/9780824838546.001.0001.

Allen, Matthew G. and Sinclair Dinnen. 2015. Solomon Islands in Transition? *Journal of Pacific History* 50(4): 381–97. doi.org/10.1080/00223344.2015.1101194.

Allen, Matthew and Sinclair Dinnen. 2016. Beyond Life Support? Reflections on Solomon Islands after the Regional Assistance Mission. *Asia and Pacific Policy Studies* 3(1): 3–12. doi.org/10.1002/app5.120.

Amherst, W.A.T.A. and Basil H. Thomson (trans and eds). 1901. *The Discovery of the Solomon Islands by Alvaro de Mendana 1568, Translated from the Original Spanish Manuscripts; Edited, with Introduction and Notes.* London: Hakluyt Society. [Facsimile republished by Kraus Reprint, Nendein, Liechtenstein, 1967.]

Aplin, Douglas. 1980. *Rabaul, 1942*. Melbourne: 2/22 Battalion AIF Lark Force Association. [Reprinted Broadbeach Waters, Qld, 1994.]

Aqorau, Transform. 2011. *The Reflections of a Solomon Islander: Development and Governance of a Small Island State*. Shanghai: Self-Published.

Ariki, Ann Lindvall. 2020. *Solomon Grassroots*. Stockholm: BoD–Books on Demand.

Aruafu, Carlos. 2016. We got it! Country to host 2023 Pacific Games. *Solomon Star*, 12 May.

Asian Development Bank (ADB). 1977. *A Report on Housing in Honiara*. Manila: Asian Development Bank.

Asian Development Bank (ADB). 2016. *The Emergence of Pacific Urban Villages: Urbanization Trends in the Pacific Islands*. Manila: Asian Development Bank. Available from: uploads.habitat3.org/hb3/The-Emergence-of-Pacific-Urban-Villages-Urbanization-Trends-in-the-Pacific-Islands.pdf.

Asian Development Bank (ADB). 2017. *Pacific Economic Monitor*. December. Manila: Asian Development Bank. Available from: www.adb.org/publications/pacific-economic-monitor-december-2017.

Atai, John. 2017. Big fear over bill. *Solomon Star*, 17 October.

Australia Network News. 2014. Police out in force to prevent fresh riots in Solomons capital. *ABC News*, 18 May. Available from: www.abc.net.au/news/2014-05-17/an-solomon-riots/5460094.

Australian Government. 2020. Solomon Islands COVID-19 Development Response Plan. October. *Partnership for Recovery: Australia's COVID-19 Development Response*. Canberra: Australian Government. Available from: www.dfat.gov.au/sites/default/files/covid-response-plan-solomon-islands.pdf.

Babadzan, Alain. 2004. Kastom as Culture? *Anthropological Theory* 4(3): 325–28. doi.org/10.1177/1463499604045567.

Ballard, Robert D. 1993. *The Lost Ships of Guadalcanal*. Sydney: Allen & Unwin.

Bartlett, Jay. 2017. Statement by Hatanga Limited Re: Eviction in Solomon Islands and Related Violence. *Pacific Islands Report*, 5 May 2017. Honolulu: East-West Center.

Bathgate, Murray A. 1973. *A Study of Economic Change and Development in the Indigenous Sector, West Guadalcanal, British Solomon Islands Protectorate*. Wellington: Department of Geography, Victoria University.

Bathgate, Murray A. 1977. The Honiara market in the Solomon Islands: A study of the supply of food from the rural area and the marketing behaviour of the vendors. Presented to Food, Shelter and Transport in the Third World Seminar. The Australian National University, Canberra, 29 July.

Bathgate, Murray A. 1978a. Marketing Distribution Systems in the Solomon Islands: The Supply of Food to Honiara. In *Food, Shelter and Transport in Southeast Asia and the Pacific*, edited by P.J. Rimmer and D.W. Drakakis-Smith, 63–100. Department of Human Geography Publication HG/12. Canberra: School of Pacific Studies, The Australian National University.

Bathgate, Murray A. 1978b. *The structure of rural supply to the Honiara Market in the Solomon Islands*. Development Studies Centre Occasional Paper No. 11. Canberra: The Australian National University.

Bathgate, Murray A. 1985. Movement Processes from Precontact to Contemporary Times: The Ndi-Nggai, West Guadalcanal, Solomon Islands. In *Circulation in Population Movement*, edited by Murray Chapman and R. Mansell Prothero, 83–118. London: Routledge & Kegan Paul.

Batley, James, Colin Wiltshire, Joanne Ridolfi, and Athena Rogers. 2019. *The voter as commodity: The phenomenon of cross-border voter registration in Solomon Islands*. In Brief No. 21. Canberra: Department of Pacific Affairs, The Australian National University.

Bau, Rickson Jordan. 2019a. NOAA has more to offer. *SIBC*, 4 September.

Bau, Rickson Jordan. 2019b. New nurses to join the workforce. *SIBC*, 12 September.

Beckett, Jeremy. 1986. Ian Hogbin. *American Ethnology* 13(4): 799–801. doi.org/10.1525/ae.1986.13.4.02a00120.

Beckett, Jeremy and Geoffrey Gray. 2007. Hogbin, Herbert Ian Priestley (1904–1989). In *Australian Dictionary of Biography*, vol. 17, 539. Melbourne: Melbourne University Press. Available from: adb.anu.edu.au/biography/hogbin-herbert-ian-priestley-12644.

Bedford, Richard D. 1967. Resettlement: Solution to economic and social problems in the Gilbert and Ellice Islands colony. MA thesis, University of Auckland. Available from: www.researchgate.net/publication/288041601_Resettlement_Solution_to_Economic_and_Social_Problems_in_the_Gilbert_and_Ellice_Islands_Colony.

Bellam, M.E.P. 1964. The Melanesian in town: A preliminary study of the urbanisation of adult male Melanesians in Honiara, British Solomon Islands Protectorate. MA thesis, Victoria University of Wellington.

Bellam, M.E.P. 1968. Urbanization and regional development in the British Solomon Islands Protectorate. Report to the Western Pacific High Commission, Honiara. General Correspondence Files, 300–499 series, relating to the WPHC and BSIP: 1967–1971 (1962–1972). WPHC 29/11, 312/2/3. Great Britain. High Commission for the Western Pacific Islands.

Bellam, M.E.P. 1970. The Colonial City: Honiara, a Pacific Islands Case Study. *Pacific Viewpoint* 11(1): 6–96. doi.org/10.1111/apv.111004.

Bellshaw, Cyril. 1957. *The Great Village: The Economic and Social Welfare of Hanuabada, an Urban Community in Papua*. London: Routledge & Kegan Paul.

Bennett, Judith A. 1981. Oscar Svensen: A Solomons Trader among 'The Few'. *Journal of Pacific History* 16(4): 170–89. doi.org/10.1080/00223348108572426.

Bennett, Judith A. 1987. *Wealth of the Solomons: A History of a Pacific Archipelago, 1800–1978*. Honolulu: University of Hawai`i Press.

Bennett, Judith A. 1993. 'We Do Not Come Here to Be Beaten': Resistance and the Plantation System in the Solomon Islands to World War II. In *Plantation Workers: Resistance and Accommodation*, edited by Brij V. Lal, Doug Munro, and Edward D. Beechert, 129–86. Honolulu: University of Hawai`i Press.

Bennett, Judith A. 2000. *Pacific Forest: A History of Resource Control and Contest in Solomon Islands, c. 1800–1997*. Leiden and Cambridge, UK: Brill and White Horse Press. doi.org/10.1163/9789004475854.

Bennett, William. 1988. Behind Japanese Lines in the Western Solomons. With an Introduction by Geoffrey M. White and David W. Gegeo. In *The Big Death: Solomon Islanders Remember World War II*, edited by Geoffrey M. White, David W. Gegeo, David Akin, and Karen Watson-Gegeo, 133–48. Honiara and Suva: Solomon Islands College of Higher Education and University of the South Pacific.

Berg, Cato. 2000. Managing difference: Kinship, exchange and urban boundaries in Honiara, Solomon Islands. MA thesis, University of Bergen, Norway.

Betu, Willy. 1983. The Origins of the Independent Group. In *Solomon Islands Politics*, edited by Peter Larmour with Sue Tarua, 107–13. Suva: Institute of Pacific Studies, University of the South Pacific.

Bobai, Tebano. 1979. Gilbertese Settlement. In *Land in Solomon Islands*, edited by Peter Larmour, 131–41. Suva and Honiara: Institute of Pacific Studies, University of the South Pacific, and Ministry of Agriculture and Lands, Solomon Islands Government.

Bolton, Lissant. 1999. Radio and the Redefinition of Kastom in Vanuatu. *The Contemporary Pacific* 11(2): 335–60.

Bowman, Robert G. 1946. Army Farms and Agricultural Development in the Southwest Pacific. *Geographical Review* 36(3): 420–66. doi.org/10.2307/210826.

Braithwaite, John, Sinclair Dinnen, Matthew Allen, Valerie Braithwaite, and Hilary Charlesworth. 2010. *Pillars and Shadows: Statebuilding as Peacebuilding in Solomon Islands*. Canberra: ANU E Press. doi.org/10.22459/PS.11.2010.

Brigg, Morgan. 2018. Beyond the Thrall of the State: Governance as a Relational-Affective Effect in Solomon Islands. *Cooperation and Conflict* 53(2): 154–72.

British Colonial Office. 1945. *Colonial Regulations: Regulations for His Majesty's Colonial Service, Part 1, Public Officers, Part 2, Public Business*. London: Colonial Office.

Buchanan, Assumpta. 2020. Bail refused for One Link director. *Solomon Star*, 15 May.

Burt, Ben. 1983. The Remnant Church: A Christian Sect of the Solomon Islands. *Oceania* 53(4): 334–46. doi.org/10.1002/j.1834-4461.1983.tb01997.x.

Butcher, Mike. 2012. '... *when the long trick's over': Donald Kennedy in the Pacific*. Bendigo, Vic.: Holland House Publishing.

Carter, Richard A. 2006. *In Search of the Lost: The Death and Life of Seven Peacemakers of the Melanesian Brotherhood*. Norwich, UK: Canterbury Press.

Chand, Satish and Charles Yala. 2008. Informal Land Systems with Urban Settlements in Honiara and Port Moresby. In AusAID, *Making Land Work, Volume 2: Case Studies on Customary Land and Development*, 85–106. Canberra: AusAID.

Chapman, Murray and R. Mansell Prothero. 1985. Circulation between 'Home' and Other Places: Some Propositions. In *Circulation in Population Movement: Substance and Concepts from the Melanesian Case*, edited by Murray Chapman and R. Mansell Prothero, 1–12. London: Routledge & Kegan Paul.

Chick, John and Sue Chick, eds. 1978. *Grass Roots Art of the Solomon Islands*. Sydney: Pacific Publications.

Clemens, Martin. 2004. *Alone on Guadalcanal: A Coastwatcher's Story*. Annapolis, MD: Naval Institute Press.

Clifford, William, Louise Morauta, and Barry Stuart. 1984. *Law and Order in Papua New Guinea. Volume 1: Report and Recommendations. Volume 2: Appendices*. Port Moresby: Institute of National Affairs and Institute of Applied Social and Economic Research.

Cline, Dennis and Bob Michel. 2002. *Skeeter Beaters: Memories of the South Pacific, 1941–1945*. Elk River, MN: Deforest Press.

Close, Jack. 2011. *South Pacific Adventure*. Hull, UK: Riverhead.

Cochrane, Glynn. 1970. The Administration of Waigina Resettlement Scheme. *Human Organization* 29(2): 123–32. doi.org/10.17730/humo.29.2.q07m95236n7q28h4.

Colvin, Mark. 2006. Australian High Commissioner sent home. *PM*, [ABC Radio], 12 September. Available from: www.abc.net.au/pm/content/2006/s1739354.htm.

Connell, John and John P. Lea. 1994. *Pacific 2010: Urbanisation in Polynesia.* Canberra: National Centre for Development Studies, Research School of Pacific and Asian Studies, The Australian National University.

Davenport, William. 1970. Two Social Movements in the British Solomons that Failed and their Political Consequences. In *The Politics of Melanesia*, edited by Marion W. Ward, Susan C. Tarua, and May Dudley, 162–72. Canberra and Port Moresby: Research School of Pacific Studies, The Australian National University, and University of Papua New Guinea.

Davenport, William H. and Gülbün Çoker. 1967. The Moro Movement of Guadalcanal, British Solomon Islands Protectorate. *Journal of the Polynesian Society* 76(2): 123–75.

Demian, Melissa and Benedicta Rousseau. 2019. Owning the Law in Melanesia. In *The Melanesian World*, edited by Eric Hirsch and Will Rollason, 315–29. London: Routledge. doi.org/10.4324/9781315529691-18.

Dinnen, Sinclair. 1994. *Praise the Lord and Pass the Ammunition: Criminal Group Surrender in Papua New Guinea.* Boroko, PNG: Papua New Guinea National Research Institute. doi.org/10.1002/j.1834-4461.1995.tb02539.x.

Dinnen, Sinclair. 2001. *Law and Order in a Weak State: Crime and Politics in Papua New Guinea.* Honolulu: University of Hawai'i Press.

Dinnen, Sinclair and Allison Ley, eds. 2000. *Reflections on Violence in Melanesia.* Sydney and Canberra: Hawkin Press and Asia Pacific Press.

Dobell, Graeme. 2012. From 'Arc of Instability' to 'Arc of Responsibility'. *Security Challenges* 8(4): 33–45.

Donner, William W. 2002. Rice and Tea, Fish and Taro: Sikaiana Migration to Honiara. *Pacific Studies* 25(1–2): 23–44.

Dorney, Sean. 2006. Expulsion of high commissioner in Solomon Islands unacceptable, says John Howard. *The World Today*, [ABC Radio], 13 September. Available from: www.abc.net.au/worldtoday/content/2006/s1739879.htm.

Dorney, Sean. 2012. Interview with Dorothy Wickham, bringing local television to Solomon Islands. *Radio Australia*, 15 February.

Douglas, Ngaire. 2004. Towards a History of Tourism in Solomon Islands. *Journal of Pacific Studies* 26(1–3): 29–49.

Downs, Ian. 1980. *The Australian Trusteeship: Papua New Guinea, 1945–75.* Canberra: Australian Government Publishing Service.

Emberson-Bain, `Atu. 1994. *Labour and Gold in Fiji*. Cambridge, UK: Cambridge University Press.

Ernst, Manfred. 2006. Solomon Islands. In *Globalization and the Re-Shaping of Christianity in the Pacific Islands*, edited by Manfred Ernst, 159–204. Suva: Pacific Theological College.

Evans, Daniel. 2016. *Hard work: Youth employment programming in Honiara, Solomon Islands*. State, Society and Governance in Melanesia Discussion Paper No. 7. Canberra: The Australian National University.

Evans, Daniel. 2019. 'Things Still Fall Apart': A Political Economy Analysis of State–Youth Engagement in Honiara, Solomon Islands. In *Pacific Youth: Local and Global Futures*, edited by Helen Lee, 79–109. Canberra: ANU Press. doi.org/10.22459/PY.2019.04.

Fanasia, Andrew. 2020. PM launches economic stimulus package. *Solomon Star*, 5 May.

Feary, Sue and Jocelyn Lai. 2012. *Stori Blo YWCA: A History of the Young Women's Christian Association in Solomon Islands*. Honiara: YWCA.

Feinberg, Richard. 1996. Outer Islanders and Urban Resettlement in the Solomon Islands: The Case of Anutans on Guadalcanal. *Journal de la Société des Océanistes* 103(2): 207–17. doi.org/10.3406/jso.1996.1990.

Feinberg, Richard. 2002. Anutans in Honiara: A Polynesian People's Struggle to Maintain Community in the Solomon Islands. *Pacific Studies* 25(1–2): 45–70.

Feldt, Eric C. 1946. *The Coast Watchers*. New York: Ballantine Books.

Feuer, A.B., ed. 1992. *Coast Watching in the Solomon Islands: The Bougainville Reports, December 1941 – July 1943*. Westport, CT: Praeger, Greenwood Publishing Group. [Reprinted as *Coast Watching in WWII: Operations against the Japanese on the Solomon Islands, 1941–43*. Mechanicsburg, PA: Stackpole Books, 2006.]

Floyd, C.H. 1974. *Physical Planning in the British Solomon Islands Protectorate*. Suva: United Nations Development Advisory Team for the South Pacific.

Floyd, C.H. 1975. *Physical Planning Comments on Four Development Proposals in Honiara, Solomon Islands*. Suva: United Nations Development Advisory Team for the South Pacific.

Floyd, C.H. 1976. *Housing in Honiara: A Contribution from the Physical Planning Aspect*. Suva: United Nations Development Advisory Team for the South Pacific.

Floyd, C.H. 1978. *Industrial and Housing Areas in Honiara*. Suva: United Nations Development Advisory Team for the South Pacific.

Foukona, Joseph D. and Matthew G. Allen. 2017. Urban Land in Solomon Islands: Powers of Exclusion and Counter-Exclusion. In *Kastom, Property and Ideology: Land Transformations in Melanesia*, edited by Siobhan McDonnell, Matthew G. Allen, and Colin Filer, 85–110. Canberra: ANU Press. doi.org/10.22459/KPI.03.2017.03.

Fox, Charles E. 1958. *Lord of the Southern Isles: Being the Story of the Anglican Mission in Melanesia, 1849–1949*. London: Mowbray.

Fraenkel, Jon. 2004. *The Manipulation of Custom: From Uprising to Intervention in the Solomon Islands*. Wellington: Victoria University Press.

Fraenkel, Jon. 2005. South-West Pacific: Arc of Instability or Matrix of Discontent? In *New Zealand in a Globalising World*, edited by Ralph Pettman, 119–37. Wellington: Victoria University Press.

Fraenkel, Jon, Matthew Allen, and Harry Brock. 2010. The Resumption of Palm-Oil Production on Guadalcanal's Northern Plains. *Pacific Economic Bulletin* 25(1): 64–75.

Fraenkel, Jon, Joni Madraiwiwi, and Henry Okole. 2014. *The RAMSI Decade: A Review of the Regional Assistance Mission to Solomon Islands, 2003–2013*. Honiara and Suva: Solomon Islands Government and Pacific Islands Forum. Available from: www.eastwestcenter.org/sites/default/files/filemanager/pidp/pdf/Independent%20RAMSI%20Review%20Report%20Final.pdf.

Frank, Richard B. 1990. *Guadalcanal*. New York: Random House.

Frazer, Ian. 1973. *To`ambaita Report: A Study of Socio-Economic Change in North-West Malaita*. Wellington: Department of Geography, Victoria University.

Frazer, Ian. 1985. Walkabout and Urban Movement: A Melanesian Case Study. In *Mobility and Identity in the Island Pacific*, edited by Murray Chapman and Philip S. Morrison. *Pacific Viewpoint* [Special Issue] 26(7): 185–205. doi.org/10.1111/apv.261010.

Frazer, Ian. 1990. Maasina Rule and Solomon Islands Labour History. In *Labour in the South Pacific*, edited by Clive Moore, Jacqueline Leckie, and Doug Munro, 191–203. Townsville, Qld: Department of History and Politics and Melanesian Studies Centre, James Cook University of North Queensland.

Galokale, Kerryn Sogha. 2013. The potential of professional learning communities for teacher learning in the community high schools in the Solomon Islands. MEd thesis, Massey University (Manawatu), Palmerston North, NZ. Available from: mro.massey.ac.nz/bitstream/handle/10179/4810/02_whole.pdf?sequence=1&isAllowed=y.

Gegeo, David Welchman. 1991. World War II in the Solomons: Its Impact on Society, Politics, and World View. In *Remembering the Pacific War*, edited by Geoffrey M. White, 27–35. Occasional Paper. Honolulu: University of Hawai`i at Manoa.

Gegeo, David Welchman. 2015. Tasimauri Sojourns and Journeys: Interview with Murray Chapman. In *Oceanian Journeys and Sojourns: Home Thoughts from Abroad*, edited by Judith A. Bennett, 37–64. Dunedin, NZ: University of Otago Press.

Geodynamics Limited. 2014. *Savo Island Geothermal Power Project Prospectus*. Brisbane: Geodynamics Limited.

George, Nicole and Pauline Soakai. 2020. 'Our struggle, our cry, our sweat': Challenging the Gendered Logics of Participation and Conflict Transition in Solomon Islands. *International Feminist Journal of Politics* 22(4): 572–93. doi.org/10.1080/14616742.2020.1798798.

Georgeou, Nichole, Charles Hawksley, James Monks, and Melinda Ki`i. 2019. Food Security and Asset Creation in Solomon Islands: Gender and the Political Economy of Agricultural Production for Honiara Central Market. *Portal Journal of Multidisciplinary International Studies* 16(1–2): 101–18. doi.org/10.5130/pjmis.v16i1-2.6542.

Gibson, Lorena. 2019. Class, Labour and Consumption in Urban Melanesia. In *The Melanesian World*, edited by Eric Hirsch and Will Rollason, 164–79. London: Routledge. doi.org/10.4324/9781315529691-9.

Gina, Lloyd Maepeza. 2003. *Journeys in a Small Canoe: The Life and Times of a Solomon Islander*, edited by Judith A. Bennett and Khyla J. Russell. Suva and Canberra: Institute of Pacific Studies, University of the South Pacific, and Pandanus Books.

Goddard, Michael. 2019. Searching for Melanesian Urbanity. In *The Melanesian World*, edited by Eric Hirsch and Will Rollason, 223–36. London: Routledge. doi.org/10.4324/9781315529691-12.

Golden, Graeme A. 1993. *The Early European Settlers of the Solomon Islands*. Melbourne: Self-published.

Gooberman-Hill, Rachael J.S. 1999. Constraints of 'feeling free': Becoming middle class in Honiara (Solomon Islands). PhD thesis, University of Edinburgh. Available from: era.ed.ac.uk/handle/1842/22253.

Gutch, John. 1987. *Colonial Servant*. Padstow, UK: T.J. Press.

Hadlow, Martin. 2004. The Mosquito Network: American Military Radio in the Solomon Islands during World War II. *Journal of Radio Studies* 11(1): 73–86. doi.org/10.1207/s15506843jrs1101_7.

Hadlow, Martin. 2015. Radio broadcasting: 63 years on and counting! *SIBC*, 25 September. Available from: www.sibconline.com.sb/sibssibc-63rd-anniversary/.

Hadlow, Martin. 2016. Wireless and empire ambition: Wireless telegraphy/telephony and radio broadcasting in the British Solomon Islands Protectorate, South-West Pacific (1914–1947)—Political, social and developmental perspectives. PhD thesis, University of Queensland, Brisbane. Available from: espace.library.uq.edu.au/view/UQ:411422.

Hægland, Pål. 2010. 'I want my music to be my own': A contemporary music scene in Honiara, Solomon Islands. MA thesis, University of Bergen, Norway.

Hansell, J.R.F. and J.R.D Wall. 1974. *The British Solomon Islands Protectorate, Volume 2: Guadalcanal and the Florida Islands*. Surbiton, UK: Land Resources Division, Ministry of Overseas Development.

Harwood, Frances. 1971. The Christian Fellowship Church: A revitalization movement in Melanesia. PhD thesis, University of Chicago.

Hassall & Associates and Australian Agency for International Development (AusAID). 2004. *Youth in Solomon Islands: A Participatory Study of Issues, Needs and Priorities—Final report*. Canberra: AusAID. Available from: www.trove.nla.gov.au/work/25660401.

Heath, Ian. 1975. *Physical Planning Comments on Four Development Proposals in Honiara, Solomon Islands*. Suva: United Nations Development Advisory Team for the South Pacific.

Heath, Ian. 1978. *Report on Land Research Project in Solomon Islands*. Suva: United Nations Development Advisory Team.

Heath, Ian. 1981. Solomon Islands: Land Policy and Independence. *Kabar Seberang: Sulating Maphilindo* 8–9: 62–77.

H.E.C. Robinson. c. 1940. *Map of the Solomon Islands*. Sydney: H.E.C. Robinson Pty Ltd.

Hilder, Brett. 1955. Hugo Colchester-Wemyss. *Pacific Islands Monthly*, February: 78.

Hilder, Brett. 1957. Romulus Dethridge. *Pacific Islands Monthly*, June: 81.

Hobbis, Geoffrey. 2017a. The MicroSDs of Solomon Islands: An Offline Remittance Economy of Digital Multi-Media. *Digital Culture & Society* 3(2): 21–40. doi.org/10.14361/dcs-2017-0203.

Hobbis, Geoffrey. 2017b. The Shifting Moralities of Mobile Phones in Lau Communicative Ecologies (Solomon Islands). *Oceania* 87(2): 173–87. doi.org/10.1002/ocea.5160.

Hobbis, Geoffrey. 2017c. A technographic anthropology of mobile phone adoption in the Lau Lagoon, Malaita, Solomon Islands. PhD thesis, École des hautes études en sciences sociales, Paris, and Concordia University, Montreal. Available from: spectrum.library.concordia.ca/982334/1/Hobbis_PhD_S2017.pdf.

Hogbin, Ian. 1964. *A Guadalcanal Society: The Kaoka Speakers*. New York: Holt, Rinehart & Winston.

Holloway, John P. 1973. Rove: The New Headquarters. *Solomon Islands Police Force Newsletter*, December: 5–6.

Homan, Sarah, Tomoko Honda, Loksee Leung, Emma Fulu, and Jane Fisher. 2019. *Transforming Harmful Gender Norms in Solomon Islands: A Study of the Oxfam Safe Families Program*. Melbourne: The Equality Institute, Monash University, and Oxfam Australia. Available from: www.oxfam.org.au/wp-content/uploads/2019/10/Transforming-Gender-Norms-Report-FINAL.pdf.

Hookey, J.F. 1969. The Establishment of a Plantation Economy in the British Solomon Islands Protectorate. In *The History of Melanesia, 2nd Waigani Seminar*, edited by K.S. Inglis, 229–38. Canberra and Port Moresby: Research School of Pacific Studies, The Australian National University, and University of Papua New Guinea.

Hornfischer, James D. 2011. *Neptune's Inferno: The U.S. Navy at Guadalcanal*. New York: Random House.

Horton, Dick C. 1965. *The Happy Isles: A Diary of the Solomons*. London: Heinemann.

Horton, Dick C. 1970. *Fire Over the Islands: Coast Watchers of the Solomons*. Sydney: A.H. & A.W. Reed.

Husband, Annell. 2013. Solomon Islands after RAMSI. *Insight*, [Radio New Zealand], 25 August. Available from: www.radionz.co.nz/national/programmes/insight/audio/2566779/insight-for-25-august-2013-solomon-islands-after-ramsi.

Hviding, Edvard. 2005. Christian Fellowship Church. In *Encyclopedia of Religion and Nature*, edited by Bron Taylor, 306–7. London: Continuum Books.

Innes, John. 2017. *Guide to the Guadalcanal Battlefields*. Brisbane: Self-published.

Iroga, Robert. 2020. PM fury at footballers, some students for dishonesty as COVID-19 cases rise. *Solomon Business Magazine Online*, 9 November 2020. Available from: sbm.sb/2020/11/09/pm-fury-at-footballers-some-students-for-dishonesty-as-covid-19-cases-rise/.

Ishimori, Daichi. 2007. Disentangling Fundamentalism and Nativistic Movements: An Analysis of the Christian Fellowship Church in the Solomon Islands. *People and Culture in Oceania* 23: 33–52.

Jersey, Stanley C. 2008. *Hell's Islands: The Untold Story of Guadalcanal*. College Station, TX: Texas A&M University Press.

Jones, Paul. 2012. *The State of Pacific Towns and Cities: Urbanization in ADB's Pacific Developing Member Countries*. Pacific Studies Series. Mandaluyong City, Philippines: Asian Development Bank.

Jourdan, Christine. 1985. Sapos iumi mitim iumi: Urbanization and creolization in the Solomon Islands. PhD thesis, The Australian National University, Canberra. Available from: openresearch-repository.anu.edu.au/handle/1885/10894.

Jourdan, Christine. 1995a. Masta Liu. In *Youth Cultures: A Cross Cultural Perspective*, edited by Vered Amit-Talai and Helena Wulff, 75–98. London: Routledge.

Jourdan, Christine. 1995b. Stepping-Stones to National Consciousness: The Solomon Islands Case. In *Nation Making: Emergent Identities in Postcolonial Melanesia*, edited by Robert J. Foster, 127–49. Ann Arbor: University of Michigan Press.

Jourdan, Christine. 2008. Youth and Mental Health in Solomon Islands: A Situational Analysis—Tingting Helti, Tingting Siki! Suva: Foundation of the Peoples of the South Pacific International. Available from: fspiblog.files.wordpress.com/2011/08/solomon-islands-youth-and-mental-health-analysis-situation-analysis-march-08.pdf.

Jourdan, Christine. 2010. The Cultural Localization of Rice in the Solomon Islands. *Ethnology* 49(4): 263–82.

Jourdan, Christine. 2014. 'Multilinguisme et identités urbaines a Honiara (Îsles Salomon) [Multilingualism and Urban Identities in Honiara (Solomon Islands)]. In *Villes invisibles: Anthropologie urbaine du Pacifique* [*Invisible Cities: Urban Anthropology of the Pacific*], edited by Dorothée Dussy and Éric Wittersheim, 75–98. Paris: L'Harmattan.

Kabutaulaka, Tarcisius Tara. 1998. *Pacific Islands stakeholder participation in development: Solomon Islands*. Pacific Islands Discussion Paper No. 6. Washington, DC: The World Bank. Available from: documents.worldbank.org/en/publication/documents-reports/documentdetail/921981468777288988/pacific-islands-stakeholder-participation-in-development-solomon-islands.

Kabutaulaka, Tarcisius Tara. 2001. *Beyond ethnicity: The political economy of the Guadalcanal crisis in Solomon Islands*. State, Society and Governance in Melanesian Program Working Paper No. 01/1. Canberra: The Australian National University. Available from: dpa.bellschool.anu.edu.au/experts-publications/publications/1557/beyond-ethnicity-political-economy-guadalcanal-crisis-solomon\.

Kabutaulaka, Tarcisius Tara. 2002a. *Footprints in the Tasimauri Sea: A Biography of Dominiko Alebua*. Suva: Institute of Pacific Studies, University of the South Pacific.

Kabutaulaka, Tarcisius Tara. 2002b. *A weak state and the Solomon Islands peace process*. East-West Center Working Papers, Pacific Islands Development Series, No. 14. Honolulu: East-West Center and Center for Pacific Islands Studies, University of Hawai`i at Manoa.

Kabutaulaka, Tarcisius Tara. 2004. Political Reviews, Melanesia: Solomon Islands. *The Contemporary Pacific* 16(2): 393–401. doi.org/10.1353/cp.2004.0050.

Kabutaulaka, Tarcisius Tara. 2019. Land Groups, Land Registration, and Economic Development Projects on Guadalcanal, Solomon Islands. *Pacific Studies* 42(3): 107–38.

Kafo, Teddy. 2017. HCC to ban foreign owned buses. *Solomon Star*, 12 December.

Kaukui, Ian. 2020. COVID-19 tests can be done here as of next week, Secretary to the Prime Minister Dr Jimmy Rogers says. *Solomon Star*, 29 April.

Kausimae, David. 1983. The Origins of the People's Alliance Party. In *Solomon Islands Politics*, edited by Peter Larmour with Sue Tarua, 114–16. Suva: Institute of Pacific Studies, University of the South Pacific.

Keen, Meg, Julien Barbara, Jessica Carpenter, Daniel Evans, and Joseph Foukona. 2017. *Urban development in Honiara: Harnessing opportunities, embracing change*. State, Society and Governance in Melanesia Research Paper. Canberra: Department of Pacific Affairs, The Australian National University. Available from: dpa.bellschool.anu.edu.au/experts-publications/publications/5567/urban-development-honiara-harnessing-opportunities-embracing.

Keen, Meg and Luke Kiddle. 2016. *Priced out of the market: Informal settlements in Honiara, Solomon Islands*. SSGM In Brief 2016/28. Canberra: State, Society and Governance in Melanesia Program, The Australian National University. Available from: openresearch-repository.anu.edu.au/bitstream/1885/142754/1/ib-2016-28-keenkiddle.pdf.

Keen, Meg and Anouk Ride. 2018. *Markets matter: ANU–UN Women project on Honiara's informal markets in Solomon Islands*. SSGM In Brief 2018/9. Canberra: State, Society and Governance in Melanesia Program, The Australian National University. Available from: dpa.bellschool.anu.edu.au/experts-publications/publications/6066/ib-201809-markets-matter-anu-un-women-project-honiaras.

Keesing, Roger M. 1978a. Politico-Religious Movements and Anticolonialism on Malaita: Maasina Rule in Historical Perspective. Part I. *Oceania* 48(4): 241–61. doi.org/10.1002/j.1834-4461.1978.tb01350.x.

Keesing, Roger M. 1978b. Politico-Religious Movements and Anticolonialism on Malaita: Maasina Rule in Historical Perspective. Part II. *Oceania* 49(1): 46–73. doi.org/10.1002/j.1834-4461.1978.tb01374.x.

Keesing, Roger M. 1982. Kastom and Anticolonialism on Malaita: 'Culture' as Political Symbol. *Mankind* 13(4): 357–73. doi.org/10.1111/j.1835-9310.1982.tb01000.x.

Keesing, Roger M. 1993. Kastom Re-Examined. *Anthropological Forum* 6(4): 587–96. doi.org/10.1080/00664677.1993.9967434.

Keesing, Roger M. 1994. Foraging in the Urban Jungle: Notes from the Kwaio Underground. *Journal de la Société des Océanistes* 99: 167–75. doi.org/10.3406/jso.1994.1934.

Keesing, Roger M. 1995. Murder on Mount Austen: Kwaio Framing of an Act of Violence. In *Beyond Textuality: Asceticism and Violence in Anthropological Interpretation*, edited by Gilles Bibeau and Ellen E. Corin, 209–29. Berlin: Mouton de Gruyter.

Keesing, Roger M. and Peter Corris. 1980. *Lightning Meets the West Wind: The Malaita Massacre*. Melbourne: Oxford University Press.

Keesing, Roger M. and Robert Tonkinson, eds. 1982. Reinventing Traditional Culture: The Politics of Kastom in Island Melanesia. *Mankind* [Special Issue] 13(4).

Kemp, Simon. 2020. Digital 2020: Solomon Islands. *DataReportal*, 18 February. Available from: datareportal.com/reports/digital-2020-solomon-islands.

Kendrick, A.R. 1968. Large Scale Agriculture on the Guadalcanal Plains. *World Crops* 20(6): 48–50.

Kengava, Clement. 1979. Choiseul Immigrants in Honiara. In *Land in Solomon Islands*, edited by Peter Larmour, 155–66. Suva and Honiara: Institute of Pacific Studies, University of the South Pacific, and Solomon Islands Ministry of Agriculture and Lands, Solomon Islands Government.

Kenilorea, Peter. 2008. *Tell It As It Is: Autobiography of Rt Hon. Sir Peter Kenilorea, KBE, PC, Solomon Islands' First Prime Minister*, edited by Clive Moore. Taipei: Centre for Asia-Pacific Area Studies, Academia Sinica.

Kituai, August Imbrum Kumaniara. 1982. An Example of Pacific Micro-Nationalism: The Banaban Case. *Bikmaus: A Journal of Papua New Guinea Affairs, Ideas and the Arts* 3(4): 3–48.

Knudson, Kenneth E. 1965. *Titiana: A Gilbertese community in the Solomon Islands*. Department of Anthropology Project for the Comparative Study of Cultural Change and Stability in Displaced Communities in the Pacific No. 1. Eugene, OR: Department of Anthropology, University of Oregon.

Knudson, Kenneth E. 1977. Sydney Island, Titiana, and Kamamleai: Southern Gilbertese in the Phoenix and Solomon Islands. In *Exiles and Migrants in Oceania*, edited by Michael D. Lieber, 195–241. Honolulu: University of Hawai`i Press.

Koli, Jared. 2017. Settlers fight back. *The Island Sun*, [Honiara], 4 May.

Kupiainen, Jari. 2000. *Tradition, Trade and Woodcarving in Solomon Islands*. Issue 45 of Transactions of the Finnish Anthropological Society. Aarhus, Denmark: The Intervention Press.

Kusu, Frederick. 2020. Four Covid-19 patients come from UK. *Solomon Star*, 27 October.

Kwa`ioloa, Michael and Ben Burt. 2012. *The Chiefs' Country: Leadership and Politics in Honiara, Solomon Islands*. Brisbane: University of Queensland Press.

Kwai, Anna Annie. 2017. *Solomon Islanders in World War II: An Indigenous Perspective*. State, Society and Governance in Melanesia Series. Canberra: ANU Press. doi.org/10.22459/SIWWII.12.2017.

Laracy, Hugh M. 1974. Unwelcome Guests: The Solomons' Chinese. *New Guinea* 8(4): 27–37.

Laracy, Hugh M. 1976. *Marists and Melanesians: A History of the Catholic Missions in the Solomon Islands*. Canberra: Australian National University Press.

Laracy, Hugh M. 1983. *Pacific Protest: The Maasina Rule Movement, Solomon Islands, 1944–1952*. Suva: Institute of Pacific Studies, University of the South Pacific.

Laracy, Hugh and Geoffrey White, eds. 1988. Taem Blong Faet: World War II in Melanesia. *'O'O: A Journal of Solomon Islands Studies*. Honiara: University of the South Pacific Honiara Centre.

Larden, Douglas and Marjorie Sullivan. 2008. Strengthening Land Administration in Solomon Islands. In Australian Agency for International Development, *Making Land Work. Volume 2: Case Studies*, 307–25. Canberra: AusAID. Available from: www.dfat.gov.au/sites/default/files/MLW_VolumeTwo_Case Study_15.pdf.

Larmour, Peter, ed. 1979. *Land in Solomon Islands*. Suva and Honiara: Institute of Pacific Studies, University of the South Pacific, and Ministry of Agriculture and Lands, Solomon Islands Government.

Larmour, Peter, ed. 2005. *Foreign Flowers: Institutional Transfer and Good Governance in the Pacific Islands*. Honolulu: University of Hawai`i Press. doi.org/10.1515/9780824874568/

Lasaqa, Isireli Q. 1968. Melanesians' choice: A geographical study of Tasimboko participation in the cash economy, Guadalcanal, British Solomon Islands. PhD thesis, The Australian National University, Canberra. Available from: openresearch-repository.anu.edu.au/handle/1885/128299.

Lawrence, David R. 2014. *The Naturalist and His 'Beautiful Islands': Charles Morris Woodford in the Western Pacific*. Canberra: ANU Press. doi.org/10.22459/NBI.10.2014.

Laxton, P.B. 1951. Nikumaroro. *Journal of the Polynesian Society* 60(2–3): 134–60.

Leckie, Jacqueline (with contributors). 2018. *A University for the South Pacific: 50 Years of USP*. Suva: University of the South Pacific.

Lee, Betty. 2019. *Right Man, Right Place, Worst Time: Commander Eric Feldt— His Life and His Coastwatchers*. Brisbane: Boolarong Press.

Lewis, Martin. 2017. *In the Shadow of Empire: My Life in the Colonies*. UK: Self-published. Available from: www.britishempire.co.uk/article/intheshadowof empire.htm.

Lewis, M. Paul, Gary F. Simons, and Charles D. Fennig, eds. 2013. *Ethnologue: Languages of the World*. 17th edn. Dallas, TX: SIL International. Available from: www.ethnologue.com.

Liloqula, Ruth and Alice Aruhe'eta Pollard. 2000. *Understanding conflict in Solomon Islands: A practical means to peacemaking*. State, Society and Governance in Melanesia Discussion Paper No. 7. Canberra: The Australian National University. Available from: openresearch-repository.anu.edu.au/bitstream/1885/142361/1/SSGM%20-2000%20number%207%20-%20 Understanding%20conflict%20in%20Solomon%20Islands.pdf.

Lord, Walter. 1977. *Lonely Vigil: Coastwatchers of the Solomons*. New York: Viking Press.

Macdonald-Milne, Brian. 2020. *Seeking Peace in the Pacific: The Story of Conflict and Christianity in the Central Solomon Islands*. Leicester, UK: Christians Aware and the Melanesian Mission.

McDougall, Debra. 2009. Becoming Sinless: Converting to Islam in the Christian Solomon Islands. *American Anthropologist* 111(4): 480–91. doi.org/10.1111/ j.1548-1433.2009.01157.x.

McIntyre, W. David. 2014. *Winding Up the British Empire in the Pacific Islands*. Oxford, UK: Oxford University Press.

MacQuarrie, Hector. 1946. *Vouza and the Solomon Islands*. Sydney: Angus & Robertson.

Maebuta, Helen Esther and Jack Maebuta. 2009. Generating Livelihoods: A Study of Urban Squatter Settlements in Solomon Islands. *Pacific Economic Bulletin* 24(3): 118–31.

Maetoloa, Meshach. 1985. The Remnant Church: Two Studies. In *New Religious Movements in Melanesia*, edited by Carl Loeliger and Garry Trompf, 120–48. Suva and Port Moresby: University of the South Pacific and University of Papua New Guinea.

Maggio, Rololfo. 2014. 'Honiara is hard': The domestic moral economy of the Kwara'ae people of Gilbert Camp, Solomon Islands. PhD thesis, University of Manchester. Available from: www.research.manchester.ac.uk/portal/files/84022513/FULL_TEXT.PDF.

Maka'a, Gina and Charley Piringi. 2020. Solomon Islands lost its COVID-19 free status. *SIBC*, 4 October.

Makini, Jully. 2015. The Duress of Movement: Reflections on the Time of the Ethnic Tension, Solomon Islands. In *Oceanian Journeys and Sojourns: Home Thoughts Abroad*, edited by Judith A. Bennett, 220–44. Dunedin, NZ: University of Otago Press.

Mamaloni, Solomon. 1992. The Road to Independence. In *Independence, Dependence, Interdependence: The First 10 Years of Solomon Islands Independence*, edited by Ron Crocombe and Ezau Tuza, 7–18. Suva: Institute of Pacific Studies, University of the South Pacific.

Mamu, Moffat. 2021. Bomb blast kills top aviation engineer and youth leader. *Solomon Star*, 11 May.

Manedika, Daniel. 1979. Solomon Islands Businessmen. In *Land in Solomon Islands*, edited by Peter Larmour, 167–75. Suva and Honiara: Institute of Pacific Studies, University of the South Pacific, and Ministry of Agriculture and Lands, Solomon Islands Government.

Marks, Kathy. 2019. Cry in the dark. *The Australian*, [*Weekend Magazine*], 14–15 December: 24–28.

Marks, M., H. Kako, R. Butcher, B. Lauri, E. Puiahi, R. Pitakaka, O. Sokana, G. Kilua, A. Roth, A.W. Solomon, and D.C. Mabey. 2015. Prevalence of Sexually Transmitted Infections in Female Clinic Attendees in Honiara, Solomon Islands. *BMJ Open* 5(4): e007276. doi.org/10.1136/bmjopen-2014-007276.

Mason, Joseph Lawrence. 2004. War and peace, environment and society: Guadalcanal, Solomon Islands and the Second World War. PhD thesis, University of Iowa, Iowa City.

Merillat, Herbert L. 2010. *The Island: A History of the First Marine Division on Guadalcanal*. Yardley, PA: Westholm.

Merrell, Susan. 2017. *Redeeming Moti*. Australia: Pacific Perspectives.

Michener, James. 1951. *Return to Paradise*. Harmondsworth, UK: Penguin.

Ming, Mikaela A., Molly G. Stewart, Rose E. Tiller, Rebecca G. Rice, Louise E. Crowley, and Nicola J. Williams. 2016. Domestic Violence in Solomon Islands. *Journal of Family Medicine and Primary Care* 5(1): 16–19. doi.org/10.4103/2249-4863.184617.

Monson, Rebecca. 2015. From *Taovia* to Trustee: Urbanisation, Land Disputes and Social Differentiation in Kakabona. *Journal of Pacific History* 50(4): 437–49. doi.org/10.1080/00223344.2015.1106642.

Montford, C.L. 1994. *The Long Dark Island*. Wellington: The Desk Top Press.

Montgomery, Charles. 2004. *The Last Heathen: Encounters with Ghosts and Ancestors in Melanesia*. Vancouver: Douglas & McIntyre.

Moore, Clive. 1981. Kanaka Maratta: A history of Melanesian Mackay. PhD thesis, James Cook University, Townsville, Qld. Available from: researchonline.jcu.edu.au/24019/.

Moore, Clive. 1985. *Kanaka: A History of Melanesian Mackay*. Port Moresby: Institute of Papua New Guinea Studies and University of Papua New Guinea Press. Available from: espace.library.uq.edu.au/view/UQ:678886.

Moore, Clive. 2004a. *Happy Isles in Crisis: The Historical Causes for a Failing State in Solomon Islands, 1998–2004*. Canberra: Asia Pacific Press. Available from: espace.library.uq.edu.au/view/UQ:40809.

Moore, Clive. 2004b. Rakwane. In *Pacific Places, Pacific Histories: Essays in Honour of Robert C. Kiste*, edited by Brij V. Lal, 135–52. Honolulu: University of Hawai`i Press.

Moore, Clive. 2007a. External Intervention: The Solomon Islands beyond RAMSI. In *Development and Security in the South West Pacific*, edited by Anne Browne, 169–96. New York: International Peace Academy.

Moore, Clive. 2007b. The Misappropriation of Malaitan Labour: Historical Origins of the Recent Solomon Islands Crisis. *Journal of Pacific History* 42(2): 211–32. doi.org/10.1080/00223340701461668.

Moore, Clive. 2008a. No More Walkabout Long Chinatown: Asian Involvement in the Solomon Islands Economic and Political Processes. In *Politics and State Building in Solomon Islands*, edited by Sinclair Dinnen and Stewart Firth, 64–95. Canberra: Asia Pacific Press. doi.org/10.22459/PSBS.05.2008.03.

Moore, Clive. 2008b. Pacific View: The Meaning of Governance and Politics in the Solomon Islands. *Australian Journal of International Affairs* 62(3): 386–407. doi.org/10.1080/10357710802286833.

Moore, Clive. 2008c. Uncharted Pacific Waters: The Solomon Islands Constitution and the Government of Prime Minister Manasseh Sogavare, 2006–2007. *History Compass* 6(2): 488–509. doi.org/10.1111/j.1478-0542.2008.00511.x.

Moore, Clive. 2013a. Peter Abu'ofa and the Founding of the South Sea Evangelical Mission in the Solomon Islands, 1894–1904. *Journal of Pacific History* 48(1): 23–42. doi.org/10.1080/00223344.2012.756162.

Moore, Clive. 2013b. Indigenous Participation in Constitutional Development: Case Study of the Solomon Islands Constitutional Review Committees of the 1960s and 1970s. *Journal of Pacific History* 48(2): 162–76. doi.org/10.1080/00223344.2013.77678.

Moore, Clive. 2013c. *Solomon Islands Historical Encyclopaedia 1893–1978*. [Online.] Available from: www.solomonencyclopaedia.net/.

Moore, Clive. 2014. *Looking beyond RAMSI: Solomon Islanders' Perspectives on their Future*. Honiara: Regional Assistance Mission to Solomon Islands.

Moore, Clive. 2017a. *Making Mala: Malaita in Solomon Islands, 1870s–1930s*. Canberra: ANU Press. doi.org/10.22459/MM.04.2017.

Moore, Clive. 2017b. *Select Bibliography on Solomon Islands, 2003–2017*. [Online.] Canberra: Department of Pacific Affairs, The Australian National University. Available from: ssgm.bellschool.anu.edu.au/news-events/stories/5644/select-bibliography-solomon-islands-2003-2017.

Moore, Clive. 2018. The End of Regional Assistance Mission to Solomon Islands (2003–17). *Journal of Pacific History* 53(2): 164–79. doi.org/10.1080/00223344.2018.1472521.

Moore, Clive. 2019. *Tulagi: Pacific Outpost of British Empire*. Canberra: ANU Press. doi.org/10.22459/T.2019.

Mullins, Steve. 2019. *Octopus Crowd: Maritime History and the Business of Australian Pearling in its Schooner Age*. Tuscaloosa, AL: University of Alabama Press.

Naitoro, John Houainamo. 2000. Solomon Islands conflict: Demands for historical rectification and restorative justice. Paper Presented at the Pacific Updates on Solomon Islands, Fiji and Vanuatu, National Centre for Development Studies, Asia Pacific School of Economics and Management, The Australian National University, Canberra, 6 June. Available from: restorativejustice.org/rj-library/solomon-islands-conflict-demands-for-historical-rectification-and-restorative-justice/1737/#sthash.LRAMr6F2.dpbs.

Nanau, Gordon Leua. 2011. The Wantok System as a Socio-Economic and Political Network in Melanesia. *OMNES: The Journal of Multicultural History* 2(1): 31–55. doi.org/10.15685/omnes.2011.06.2.1.31.

Nanau, Gordon Leua. 2014. Land Ownership, Livelihoods and Sustainable Development in Guadalcanal, Solomon Islands. In *La Mélanésie Actualités et etudes: Foncier et développement durable* [*Melanesia News and Studies: Land and Sustainable Development*], edited by Frederic Angleviel and Marcelin Abong, 173–89. Paris: L'Harmattan. Available from: www.researchgate.net/publication/272780026_Land_Ownership_Livelihoods_and_Sustainable_Development_in_Guadalcanal_Solomon_Islands.

Nelson, Hank. 2007. *The Moti affair in Papua New Guinea*. State, Society and Governance in Melanesia Working Paper No. 2007/1. Canberra: The Australian National University. Available from: ssgm.bellschool.anu.edu.au/sites/default/files/publications/attachments/2015-12/07_01wp_Nelson_0.pdf.

New Zealand Government. 2003. *New Zealand's Aid in the Solomon Islands: Fact Sheet*, 25 July. Wellington: New Zealand Agency for International Development. Available from: reliefweb.int/report/solomon-islands/new-zealands-aid-solomon-islands-fact-sheet.

O'Brien, Claire. 1995. *A Greater than Solomon Here: A Story of Catholic Church in Solomon Islands, 1567–1967*. Honiara: Catholic Church Solomon Islands.

O'Callaghan, Mary Louise, ed. 2013. *Rebuilding a Nation: Ten Years of the Solomon Islands–RAMSI Partnership*. Canberra: CanPrint.

O'Connor, Gülbün Çoker. 1973. The Moro Movement of Guadalcanal. PhD thesis, University of Pennsylvania, Philadelphia.

Oliver, Douglas. 1991. *Black Islanders: A Personal Perspective of Bougainville, 1937–1991*. Honolulu: University of Hawai`i Press.

Oram, Nigel. 1976. *Colonial Town to Melanesian City: Port Moresby 1884–1974*. Canberra: Australian National University Press. Available from: pacificinstitute.anu.edu.au/sites/default/files/resources-links/ANU_Press_Colonial_Town_to_Melanesian_City.pdf.

Oram, Nigel. 1980. Land, Housing and Administration in Honiara: Towards a Concerted Policy. `O`O: Journal of Solomon Islands Studies* 1(1–2): 133–63.

Osifelo, Eddie. 2020a. Medical equipment for Covid-19 arrives in the country. *The Island Sun*, [Honiara], 23 April.

Osifelo, Eddie. 2020b. Face to face. *The Island Sun*, [Honiara], 11 May.

Osifelo, Fred. 2018. We are responsible for Honiara's roads: MID. *SIBC*, 19 February.

Osifelo, Frederick. 1985. *Kanaka Boy: An Autobiography*. Suva: Institute of Pacific Studies and Solomon Islands Extension Centre, University of the South Pacific.

Osmond, Frederick Gary. 2006. Nimble savages: Myth, race, social memory and Australian aquatic sport. PhD thesis, University of Queensland, Brisbane. Available from: espace.library.uq.edu.au/view/UQ:328892.

Otter, Mark, ed. 2002. *Solomon Islands: Human Development Report 2002—Building a Nation*. Brisbane: Mark Otter for the Government of Solomon Islands.

Pacific Horticultural and Agricultural Market Access Program (PHAMA). 2013. *Technical Report 43: Feasibility Study on Developing Exports of Selected Products from Solomon Islands to Australia (SOLS13)*, 25 January. Prepared for AusAID, Canberra. Available from: phamaplus.com.au/wp-content/uploads/2016/05/TR-43-SOLS13-Marketing-Study-v1.0-FINAL.pdf.

Pagepitu, Alfred. 2020. SI in 'high risk' areas, prevention efforts continue. *The Island Sun*, [Honiara], 3 February.

Paia, Warren A. 1975. Aspects of Constitutional Development in the Solomon Islands. *Journal of Pacific History* 10(2): 81–89. doi.org/10.1080/00223347508572268.

Parakoro, H. 1971. Do you know? *Solomon Islands Police Force Newsletter*, August: 9.

Pitakaka, Voyce. 1979. Gilbertese in Titiana. In *Land in Solomon Islands*, edited by Peter Larmour, 142–46. Suva and Honiara: Institute of Pacific Studies, University of the South Pacific, and Ministry of Agriculture and Lands, Solomon Islands Government.

Pitakaka, Voyce and Tebano Bobai. 1979. Nei Matangare Dancers. In *Land in Solomon Islands*, edited by Peter Larmour, 147–49. Suva and Honiara: Institute of Pacific Studies, University of the South Pacific, and Ministry of Agriculture and Lands, Solomon Islands Government.

Podokolo, Mavis Nishimura. 2020a. Quarantine graduation. *The Island Sun*, [Honiara], 16 November.

Podokolo, Mavis Nishimura. 2020b. 10 recovered, 3 remain positive. *The Island Sun*, [Honiara], 28 December.

Pollard, Alice Aruhe'eta. 2000. *Givers of Wisdom, Labourers without Gain: Essays on Women in Solomon Islands*. Suva: Institute of Pacific Studies, University of the South Pacific.

Premdas, Ralph R., Jeffrey S. Steeves, and Peter Larmour. 1984. The Western Breakaway Movement in the Solomon Islands. *Pacific Studies* 7(2): 34–67.

Price, Charles with Elizabeth Baker. 1976. Origins of Pacific Islanders in Queensland, 1863–1904: A Research Note. *Journal of Pacific History* 11(2): 106–21. doi.org/10.1080/00223347608572294.

Putz, Catherine. 2018. An Indigenous Perspective on World War II's Solomon Islands Campaign. *The Diplomat*, 7 February. Available from: thediplomat.com/2018/02/an-indigenous-perspective-on-world-war-iis-solomon-islands-campaign/.

Randall, Will. 2002. *Solomon Time: Adventures in the South Pacific*. London: Abacus.

Raucaz, L.M. 1928. *In the Savage South Solomons: The Story of a Mission*. Dublin: The Society for the Propagation of the Faith.

Regan, Anthony J. 2013. Bougainville: Conflict Deferred. In *Diminishing Conflicts in Asia and the Pacific: Why Some Subside and Others Don't*, edited by Edward Aspinall, Robin Jeffrey, and Anthony Regan, 119–33. Abingdon, UK: Routledge.

Regan, Anthony J. and Helga Griffin, eds. 2005. *Bougainville Before the Conflict*. Canberra: Pandanus Books.

Regional Assistance Mission to Solomon Islands (RAMSI). 2006. *People's Survey: Pilot 2006—Solomon Islands*. Canberra: ANU Enterprise. Available from: www.ramsi.org/wp-content/uploads/2014/07/Peoples-Survey-2006-Pilot-Complete-report-d6cc0b53-723e-4a14-800a-2c3f23d5cc61-0.pdf.

Regional Assistance Mission to Solomon Islands (RAMSI). 2007. *People's Survey 2007*. Canberra: ANU Enterprise. Available from: www.ramsi.org/wp-content/uploads/2014/07/Peoples-Survey-2007-Complete-report-302d1ba8-2602-492e-a81f-a79435f0808f-0.pdf.

Regional Assistance Mission to Solomon Islands (RAMSI). 2008. *People's Survey 2008*. Canberra: ANU Enterprise. Available from: www.ramsi.org/wp-content/uploads/2014/07/Peoples-Survey-2008-Complete-Report-145bc48c-adad-4b0b-8e3f-8b0c196a72e4-0.pdf.

Regional Assistance Mission to Solomon Islands (RAMSI). 2010. *People's Survey 2009*. Canberra: ANU Enterprise. Available from: www.ramsi.org/wp-content/uploads/2014/07/Peoples-Survey-2009-Complete-Report-de573d10-1d01-4db6-b615-5361ee1d2c3d-0.pdf.

Regional Assistance Mission to Solomon Islands (RAMSI). 2011. *Solomon Islands Government RAMSI People's Survey 2010*. Canberra: ANU Enterprise. Available from: www.ramsi.org/wp-content/uploads/2017/07/People-Survey-2010-Complete-report-90d3652b-dacf-4dc7-a4d0-1d40075a9848-0.pdf.

Regional Assistance Mission to Solomon Islands (RAMSI). 2012. *The People's Survey 2011*. Canberra: ANU Enterprise. Available from: www.ramsi.org/wp-content/uploads/2017/07/Peoples-Survey-2011-FULL-REPORT-WEB-c7ead65c-d16d-4c2a-8c24-9bc8ef741bd8-0.pdf.

Regional Assistance Mission to Solomon Islands (RAMSI). 2013. *SIG RAMSI People's Survey Report*. Canberra: ANU Edge and University of the South Pacific. Available from: www.ramsi.org/wp-content/uploads/2014/07/FINAL-Peoples-Survey-2013-1-final-111900c1-79e2-4f41-9801-7f29f6cd2a66-0.pdf.

Ride, Anouk. 2019. *Youth-inclusive development: Challenges and potential in Solomon Islands*. Department of Pacific Affairs In Brief No. 2019/1. Canberra: The Australian National University. Available from: dpa.bellschool.anu.edu.au/sites/default/files/publications/attachments/2019-01/ib2019_1_ride.pdf.

Rimmer, Susan Harris. 2013. Timor-Leste: International Intervention, Gender and the Dangers of Negative Peace. In *Diminishing Conflicts in Asia and the Pacific: Why Some Subside and Others Don't*, edited by Edward Aspinall, Robin Jeffrey, and Anthony Regan, 19–36. Abingdon, UK: Routledge.

Roe, David. 1993. Prehistory without pots: Prehistoric settlement and economy on north-west Guadalcanal, Solomon Islands. PhD thesis, The Australian National University, Canberra. Available from: openresearch-repository.anu.edu.au/handle/1885/8040.

Runa, Lynnissha. 2017. Power cuts hit hard on national broadcaster. *Solomon Star*, 24 December.

Russell, Tom. 2003. *I Have the Honour to Be: A Memoir of a Career Covering Fifty-Two Years of Service for British Overseas Territories*. Spennymoor, UK: The Memoir Club.

Ruthven, David. 1979a. Capitalist and Traditional Leaders. In *Land in Solomon Islands*, edited by Peter Larmour, 58–73. Suva and Honiara: Institute of Pacific Studies, University of the South Pacific, and Ministry of Agriculture and Lands, Solomon Islands Government.

Ruthven, David. 1979b. Land Legislation from the Protectorate to Independence. In *Land in Solomon Islands*, edited by Peter Larmour, 239–48. Suva and Honiara: Institute of Pacific Studies, University of the South Pacific, and Ministry of Agriculture and Lands, Solomon Islands Government.

Saeni, Wilson. 2020. Suidani: Don't accept coronavirus kits from China. *Solomon Star*, 4 April.

Salani, Charlie. 2019. Wale calls on govt to fix Honiara water issue. *SIBC*, 9 July.

Sas, Nick. 2019. China on the mind with Scott Morrison in Solomon Islands, but there is more to discuss. *ABC News*, 1 June. Available from: abc.net.au/news/2019-06-01/china-on-the-table-in-scott-morrisons-trip-to-solomon-islands/11162326.

Sasako, Alfred. 2016. Taiwan offers to build new National Referral Hospital without gynaecology. *The Island Sun*, [Honiara], 18 May.

Saunders, Doug. 2010. *Arrival City: The Final Migration and Our Next World*. Sydney: Allen & Unwin.

Saunders, Keithie. 2013. *Of Wars and Worship: The Extraordinary Story of Gertrude and Alvin Blum*. Oxford, UK: George Ronald Publisher.

Scales, Ian. 2007. The Coup Nobody Noticed: The Solomon Islands Western State Movement in 2000. *Journal of Pacific History* 42 (2): 187–209. doi.org/10.1080/00223340701461643.

Scott, Michael W. 2007. *The Severed Snake: Matrilineages, Making Place, and a Melanesian Christianity in Southeast Solomon Islands*. Durham, NC: Carolina Academic Press.

Sei, Lowen. 2017. New National Referral Hospital re-location 'progressing well'. *SIBC*, 2 May.

Sei, Lowen. 2018. Police destroy dangerous projectile near White River market. *SIBC*, 19 February.

Sei, Lowen. 2019a. Country not benefitting from Rennell mining: Govt. *SIBC*, 7 March.

Sei, Lowen. 2019b. New filtration plant for Kongulai soon. *SIBC*, 18 March.

Short, Frank. 2015. *Policing a Clash of Cultures*. Bangkok: Self-published.

Siegel, Jeff. 1985. Origins of Pacific Islanders in Fiji. *Journal of Pacific History* 20(1): 42–54. doi.org/10.1080/00223348508572504.

Sloan, Tom, Sinclair Dinnen, Nicole Sweaney, and Chris Chevalier. 2019. *Perceptions of peacebuilding in Solomon Islands post-RAMSI*. Department of Pacific Affairs In Brief No. 2019/6. Canberra: The Australian National University.

Smith, John. 2011. *An Island in the Autumn*. Morayshire, UK: Librario.

Smith, Michael S. 2000. *Bloody Ridge: The Battle that Saved Guadalcanal*. Novato, CA: Presidio.

Smyth, Rosaleen. 1984. A Note on the 'Saucepan Special': The People's Radio of Central Africa. *Historical Journal of Film, Radio and Television* 4(2): 195–201. doi.org/10.1080/01439688400260191.

Souter, Regina and Pablo Orams. 2019. *Water, sanitation, and hygiene in the informal settlements of Honiara, Solomon Islands*. Water Global Practice Working Paper, August. Washington, DC: International Bank for Reconstruction and Development, World Bank Group. Available from: documents.worldbank.org/curated/en/514751574138362122/pdf/Water-and-Sanitation-Services-for-Informal-Settlements-in-Honiara-Solomon-Islands.pdf.

Spratt, Joanna and Gabriel Spencer. 2018. *Palliative care in Solomon Islands*. Development Policy Centre Discussion Paper No. 74, 12 December. Canberra: Development Policy Centre, The Australian National University. Available from: papers.ssrn.com/sol3/papers.cfm?abstract_id=3299814. doi.org/10.2139/ssrn.3299814.

Stone, Peter. 1995. *Hostages to Freedom: The Fall of Rabaul*. Yarram, Vic.: Oceans Enterprises.

Storey, Donovan. 2003. The Peri-Urban Pacific: From Exclusive to Inclusive Cities. *Asia Pacific Viewpoint* 44(3): 259–79. doi.org/10.1111/j.1467-8373.2003.00214.x.

Strathern, Marilyn. 1975. *No money on our skins: Hagen migrants in Port Moresby, New Guinea*. Research Bulletin No. 61. Port Moresby and Canberra: New Guinea Research Unit and The Australian National University.

Stuart, Ian. 1970. *Port Moresby: Yesterday and Today*. Sydney: Pacific Publications.

Svensen, O. 1943. Rubber in the Solomons: How plants were introduced. [Letter to the editor], *Pacific Islands Monthly*, 29 April.

Tahal, James Prasad and Stephen Oxenham. 1981. Solomon Islands: Remnants of Empire. In *Pacific Indians: Profiles in 20 Pacific Countries*, edited by Ron Crocombe, 55–61. Suva: Institute of Pacific Studies, University of the South Pacific.

Tatua, Nanette. 2014. Empowering Women in Business and Politics. In *Looking beyond RAMSI: Solomon Islanders' Perspectives on their Future*, edited by Clive Moore, 41–47. Honiara: Regional Assistance Mission to Solomon Islands.

Tavola, Helen, Afu Billy, and Josephine Kama. 2016. *Advancing Australia's Work on Leadership and Decision-Making: 'The Next Level'—Scoping Study on Women in Leadership and Decision-Making*. Canberra: Department of Foreign Affairs and Trade. Available from: www.dfat.gov.au/sites/default/files/solomon-islands-scoping-study-womens-leadership-decision-making.pdf.

Teaiwa, Katerina. 2000. Banaba Island: Paying the Price for Other People's Development. *Indigenous Affairs* 1: 38–45.

Teaiwa, Katerina. 2015. *Consuming Ocean Island: Stories of People and Phosphate from Banaba*. Bloomington, IN: Indiana University Press.

Tedder, John L.O. 1966. Honiara (Capital of the British Solomon Islands Protectorate). *South Pacific Bulletin* 16(1): 36–41.

Tedder, John L.O. 1973. Solomon Islands Information and Broadcasting Services: The Broadcasting Section. *South Pacific Bulletin* 23(4): 27–32.

Tedder, John L.O. 2008. *Solomon Islands Years: A District Administrator in the Islands, 1952–1974*. Stuarts Point, NSW: Tuatu Studies.

Theroux, Paul. 1992. *The Happy Isles in Oceania: Paddling the Pacific*. New York: Putnam.

Tickle, Les. 1970. Search for Culture. *Colour Review: The Art Teacher's Journal* (Spring): 4–13.

Timmer, Jaap. 2015. Being-in-the-Covenant: Reflections on the Crisis of Historicism in North Malaita, Solomon Islands. In *Phenomenology in Anthropology: A Sense of Perspective*, edited by Kalpana Ram and Christopher Houston, 175–94. Bloomington, IN: Indiana University Press.

Timmer, Jaap. 2019. Regional Overview: From Diversity to Multiple Singularities. In *The Melanesian World*, edited by Eric Hirsch and Will Rollason, 126–39. London: Routledge. doi.org/10.4324/9781315529691-7.

Tippett, Alan R. 1967. *Solomon Islands Christianity: A Study of Growth and Obstruction*. London: Lutterworth Press.

Tolia, Donn H. and M.G. Petterson. 2005. The Gold Ridge Mine, Guadalcanal, Solomon Islands' First Gold Mine: A Case Study in Stakeholder Consultation. *Geological Society, London, Special Publications* 250(1): 149–59. doi.org/10.1144/GSL.SP.2005.250.01.15.

Tozaka, Milner and James Nage. 1981. Administering Squatter Settlements in Honiara. In *Land, People and Government: Public Lands Policy in the South Pacific*, edited by Peter Larmour, Ron Crocombe, and Anna Taungega, 114–18. Suva: Institute of Pacific Studies, University of the South Pacific.

Treadaway, Julian. 2007. *Dancing, Dying, Crawling, Crying: Stories of Continuity and Change in the Polynesian Community of Tikopia*. Suva: IPS Publications, University of the South Pacific.

Trench, D.C.C. 1956a. Marchant on Malaita. *Corona* 8(5): 106–8.

Trench, D.C.C. 1956b. Marchant on Malaita. *Corona* 8(6): 230–33.

Trench, D.C.C. 1956c. Marchant on Malaita. *Corona* 8(7): 58–61.

Tryon, Darrell T. and Brian D. Hackman. 1983. *Solomon Islands Languages: An Internal Classification*. Pacific Linguistics Series C, No. 72. Canberra: Department of Linguistics, Research School of Pacific Studies, The Australian National University. Available from: openresearch-repository.anu.edu.au/handle/1885/145227.

Tudor, Judy. 1953a. The Taralala in the Solomons. *Pacific Islands Monthly*, April: 119, 121.

Tudor, Judy. 1953b. Report on Honiara: Dwelling place of bods. *Pacific Islands Monthly*, June: 68–77.

Tuhanuku, Joses. 1983. Trade Unions and Politics. In *Solomon Islands Politics*, edited by Peter Larmour and Sue Tarua, 117–32. Suva: Institute of Pacific Studies, University of the South Pacific.

Tuza, Esau Taqasabo. 1975. The emergence of the Christian Fellowship Church: A historical view of Silas Eto, founder of the Christian Fellowship Church. MA thesis, University of Papua New Guinea, Port Moresby.

Ulufa`alu, Bart. 1977. The Effects of Colonialism and Christianity on Customary Land Tenure in the Solomons. In *The Melanesian Environment: Papers at and Arising from the 9th Waigani Seminar, Port Moresby, 2–8 May 1975*, edited by John H. Winslow, 537–43. Singapore: Angus & Robertson.

Ulufa`alu, Bart. 1983. The Development of Political Parties. In *Solomon Islands Politics*, edited by Peter Larmour with Sue Tarua, 101–6. Suva: Institute of Pacific Studies, University of the South Pacific.

United Nations Children's Fund (UNICEF). 2012. *Children in Solomon Islands, 2011: An Atlas of Social Indicators*. Suva: UNICEF Pacific.

United Nations Human Settlements Programme (UN-Habitat). 2012. *Solomon Islands: National Urban Profile*. Nairobi: UN-Habitat.

University of the South Pacific Solomon Islands Centre. 1983. *University of the South Pacific Solomon Islands Centre Information Booklet*. Honiara: University of the South Pacific Solomon Islands Centre.

UN Women. 2009. *Solomon Islands Markets Profiles*. Honiara: UN Women Asia and the Pacific. Available from: asiapacific.unwomen.org/en/digital-library/publications/2009/8/solomon-islands-markets-profiles.

Wairiu, Morgan. 2007. History of the Forestry Industry in Solomon Islands: The Case of Guadalcanal. *Journal of Pacific History* 42(2): 233–46. doi.org/10.1080/00223340701461684.

Waka Mere. 2019. *The Impact of Domestic and Sexual Violence on the Workplace in Solomon Islands: Survey Report*. March. Honiara: International Finance Corporation. Available from: www.ifc.org/wps/wcm/connect/36087fa5-b699-453d-a558-f7a79e08906e/Survey+report+Solomon+Islands+impact+of+violence+on+workplace.pdf?MOD=AJPERES.

Wasuka, Evan. 2019. Logging company 'reinvented' itself as bauxite miner in Solomon Islands, says researcher. *Pacific Beat*, [ABC Radio Australia], 14 March. Available from: www.abc.net.au/radio-australia/programs/pacificbeat/logging-company-reinvented-itself-as-miner/10899386.

Waters, Christopher. 2016. The Last of Australian Imperial Dreams for the Southwest Pacific: Paul Hasluck, the Department of Territories and a Greater Melanesia in 1960. *Journal of Pacific History* 51(2): 169–85. doi.org/10.1080/00223344.2016.1195595.

Webb, Michael. 2005. Melanesia. In *Continuum Encyclopedia of Popular Music of the World. Volume V: Asia and Oceania*, edited by John Shepherd, David Horn, and Dave Laing, 289–92. London: Continuum.

White, Geoffrey M. 1988. Introduction: Scouting and Fighting in Santa Isabel. In *The Big Death: Solomon Islanders Remember World War II*, edited by Geoffrey M. White, David Gegeo, David Akin, and Karen Watson-Gegeo, 149–53. Honiara: Solomon Islands College of Higher Education and University of the South Pacific.

White, Geoffrey M., David Gegeo, David Akin, and Karen Watson-Gegeo, eds. 1988a. *The Big Death: Solomon Islanders Remember World War II*. Honiara: Solomon Islands College of Higher Education and University of the South Pacific.

White, Geoffrey M., David Gegeo, David Akin, and Karen Watson-Gegeo. 1988b. Preface. In *The Big Death: Solomon Islanders Remember World War II*, edited by Geoffrey M. White, David Gegeo, David Akin, and Karen Watson-Gegeo, 127–32. Honiara: Solomon Islands College of Higher Education and University of the South Pacific.

Wickham, Dorothy and Ofani Eremae. 2020. Australian and British bomb disposal workers killed in blast in Solomon Islands. *The Guardian*, 21 September. Available from: www.theguardian.com/world/2020/sep/21/solomon-island-bomb-blast-australian-and-briton-killed.

Williams, Shaun. 2011. *Public land governance in Solomon Islands*. Justice for the Poor Briefing Note 6(1). Washington, DC: The World Bank.

Willis, Ian. 1974. *Lae, Village and City*. Melbourne: Melbourne University Press.

Wood, Terence. 2014. From floods to flames in Honiara. *Devpolicy Blog*, 21 May. Canberra: Development Policy Centre, The Australian National University. Available from: devpolicy.org/in-brief/from-floods-to-flames-in-honiara-20140521/.

Zoleveke, Gideon. 1980. *Zoleveke: A Man from Choiseul*. Edited by John Chick. Suva: Institute of Pacific Studies, University of the South Pacific.

Newspapers and magazines

Bahá`í World News Service
British Solomon Island News Sheet (Honiara)
Focus (Canberra)
The Island Sun (Honiara)
Kakamora Reporter (Honiara)
Pacific Islands Monthly (Sydney)
Pacific Islands Report (Honolulu)
Solomon Islands Police Force Newsletter (Honiara)
Solomon News Drum (Honiara)
Solomon Star (Honiara)
Solomons Toktok (Honiara)
Solomon Women (Honiara)

HONIARA

Unpublished manuscripts in the possession of the author

Aqorau, Transform. 2013. Solomon Islands post-RAMSI: Falling down in bits and pieces.

Aqorau, Transform. 2019. Taiwan or China? Solomon Islands growing foreign policy dilemma!

Chevalier, Christopher. 2017. Understanding Solomon(s): A biography of Solomon Mamaloni. Canberra.

Evans, Daniel. 2010. The urban land environment—Honiara. Background paper prepared for Sources of Growth Discussion Paper. World Bank, Honiara.

Evans, Daniel. 2012. Unpublished internal World Bank document. Honiara.

Evans, Daniel. 2018. The trouble with young men: An engagement with moral panics, tropes and historical representations of male youth in Honiara, Solomon Islands. Paper presented at the Pacific History Association Conference, Cambridge, UK, December.

Kemakeza, Allan. 2017. Speech to the RAMSI Farewell Symposium. Honiara, 28 June.

Kere, Nathan. 2017. Cyclic malaria in Solomon Islands. East Medical Centre Limited, Honiara.

Lawson, Ronald A. n.d. [c. 2000s]. A story of the Solomon Islands.

Lindley, Alan. 2011a. Notes on Honiara.

Lindley, Alan. 2011b. Notes on Keesing and Corris (1980), February.

Lindley, Alan. 2013. Manuscript.

Lindley, Alan. 2014. Manuscript, April–September.

Lindley, Alan. 2015. Manuscript, May–September.

Macgregor, J.D. 2000. Musings on the Solomons.

Maeliau, Michael. 1976. The remnant church: A separatist church. Long essay written at Christian Leaders Training College, Banz, Papua New Guinea.

Maeliau, Michael. 2003. Trouble in paradise, Aroma Ministries.

Maggio, Rololfo. 2016. Big confusion: The land question in Honiara and the history of land policy in Solomon Islands.

Manakako, Philip and Emmanuelle Mangalle. 2018. In the name of Nahona`ara (Honiara). List of Guadalcanal names for sites in Honiara prepared for the Guadalcanal Province Land Summit, Honiara, 28–29 March.

Palmer, Norman and Caulton Medobu. 2003. Transcript of an interview with Bishop Norman Palmer by Reverend Caulton Medobu, 25 June.

Tandai House of Chiefs and Tandai Landowners Association. n.d. [2010s]. Justification of ownership.

Other sources

British Museum (London)

Alexander Wilson Collection

John Tod Collection, containing Bob Wright Collection

Patrick Barrett Collection

British Solomon Islands Protectorate (Honiara)

1896–1974. *British Solomon Islands Annual and Biannual reports*.

1949. Superintendent of Police and Prisons Hugo Colchester-Wemyss, *Report on the Police and Prisons Department in the British Solomon Islands Protectorate*, 30 August 1949.

1954. *National Park Regulation*.

1957. Colin Hamilton Allan, *Report of the Special Lands Commission, Customary Land Tenure in the British Solomon Islands Protectorate*. Honiara: Western Pacific High Commission.

1957–66. *Gazette*.

1959. *Land and Titles Ordinance No. 13*.

1960. *The Guadalcanal Campaign*. Honiara: British Solomon Islands Information Services.

1961. Norma McArthur, *Report of the Population Census of 1959*. Honiara: British Solomon Islands Protectorate.

1960–69. *Legislative Council Debates*.

1962. *Report on the Honiara Town Development Plan*, 1 March. Honiara: Town Planning Board.

1970. *Report on the Census of the Population of the British Solomon Islands Protectorate, 1970*.

1975. *The British Solomon Islands (Name of Territory) Order, 1975*. Available from: www.legislation.gov.uk/uksi/1975/808/made.

Solomon Islands Government

1988a. Solomon Islands 1986 Population Census Report 1: Population by Sex, Age and Ward, Final Results. *Solomon Islands National Statistics Office Statistical Bulletin No. 03*. Honiara: Solomon Islands National Statistics Office.

1988b. Solomon Islands 1986 Population Census Report. *Solomon Islands National Statistics Office Statistical Bulletin No. 12*. Honiara: Solomon Islands National Statistics Office.

1997. *The Provincial Government Act 1997*, (No. 7 of 1997). National Parliament. Available from: www.parliament.gov.sb/files/legislation/Acts/1997/The%20 Provincial%20Government%20Act%201997.pdf.

1999a. *The Honiara City Act 1999*, (No. 2 of 1999). National Parliament. Available from: www.parliament.gov.sb/files/legislation/Acts/1999/THE%20 HONIARA%20CITY%20ACT%201999.pdf.

1999b. *Solomon Islands Population and Housing Census*. Honiara: Solomon Islands National Statistics Office.

2001. *Guadalcanal Province Development Profile, August 2001*. Honiara: Rural Development Division, Ministry of Provincial Government and Rural Development.

2009. *Solomon Islands National Census*. Honiara: Solomon Islands National Statistics Office.

2011a. *Business Advantage Solomon Islands, 2010–11*. Honiara: Foreign Investment Division, Department of Commerce, Industry, Labour and Immigration.

2011b. Solomon Islands Population and Housing Census 2009, Basic Tables and Census Description. *Solomon Islands National Statistics Office Statistical Bulletin No. 06*. Honiara: Solomon Islands National Statistics Office.

2012a. Genesis E. Kofana, Report on the claim by landowners that west of Honiara starting from Rove to the Western Town Boundary has not been properly acquired. In Honiara City Council Constitutional Congress Team, *Report of the Honiara–Guadalcanal Maritime and Land Boundaries Consultation Meetings, 2011*. Honiara: Honiara City Council.

2012b. Tapualiki Samasoni and Joseph Hula, *Report on the Honiara–Guadalcanal Maritime and Land Boundaries*. Honiara: Honiara City Council.

2013. *Concept Note: Solomon Islands Urban Management Programme of Support (SUMPS) No. 10*. Honiara: Ministry of Lands, Housing and Survey.

2014a. *Draft Honiara Local Planning Scheme, 2015*. Honiara: Ministry of Lands, Housing and Survey.

2014b. *Final Report: Solomon Islands Truth and Reconciliation Commission—Confronting the Truth for a Better Solomon Islands*. 5 vols. Tabled in Solomon Islands National Parliament, *Hansard*, 5 September 2014. Available from: catalogue.nla.gov.au/Record/6613097.

2014c. *Land and Titles (Amendment) Act 2014*, (No. 11 of 2014). National Parliament. Available from: www.parliament.gov.sb/files/legislation/9th%20Parliament/Acts/2014/Lands%20and%20Titles%20(Amendment)%20Act%202014.pdf.

2014d. *Report on the Need to Upgrade and Relocate the National Referral Hospital, Honiara, Solomon Islands*. Honiara: Ministry of Health and Medical Services.

2014e. *Solomon Islands: Rapid Assessment of the Macro and Sectoral Impacts of Flash Floods in the Solomon Islands, April 2014*. Honiara: Ministry of Development Planning and Aid Coordination and Ministry of Finance and Treasury. Available from: www.gfdrr.org/sites/default/files/publication/pda-2014-solomonislands.pdf.

2015. *Shaping Honiara's Future: Honiara Local Planning Scheme 2015, Gazetted 13 October*. Honiara: Ministry of Lands, Housing and Survey and Honiara City Council.

2016a. Luke Kiddle, *Honiara City-Wide Informal Settlement Analysis*. Report Prepared for the Solomon Islands Government and Honiara City Council. Supported by UN-Habitat as part of the Participatory Slum Upgrading Programme. Honiara: Solomon Islands Government and Honiara City Council.

2016b. *Solomon Islands: Global AIDS Response Progress Report 2016*. Honiara: Ministry of Health and Medical Services STI/HIV Division.

2018. *Greater Honiara Urban Development Strategy and Action Plan, Volume 1.* Honiara and Manila: Ministry of Lands, Housing and Survey and Asian Development Bank. Available from: adb.org/sites/default/files/project-documents/49460/49460-001-dpta-en.pdf.

2019a. Barana Nature Park launched. Press release, 23 July. Ministry of Environment, Climate Change, Disaster Management and Meteorology, Honiara. Available from: mecdm.gov.sb/-mecdmgov/faq-s/158-barana-nature-park-launched.html.

2019b. Commissioner of RSIPF: Launch of the RSIPF Gender Strategy 2019–2021. Speech. Royal Solomon Islands Police Force, Honiara. Available from: www.rsipf.gov.sb/sites/default/files/Launch%20of%20Gender%20Strategy%20-CRSIPF%20TP%27s.pdf.

2019c. *National Statistics Office, Population Statistics.* [Online.] Available from: statistics.gov.sb/statistics/social-statistics/population.

2019d. *Report on National Agricultural Survey, 2017.* Honiara: Solomon Islands National Statistics Office, Ministry of Finance and Treasury and Ministry of Agriculture and Livestock, in collaboration with the Food and Agriculture Organization of the United Nations and the World Bank.

2020a. Government advice for travellers. Press release, 1 February. Press Secretariat, Office of Prime Minister and Cabinet, Honiara.

2020b. Hon. Prime Minister Statement to the Nation on state of public emergency. 27 March, Honiara. Available from: solomons.gov.sb/wp-content/uploads/2020/03/PMs-STATEMENT-TO-THE-NATION-27-3-20.pdf.

2020c. *Ministry of Public Service Circular Memorandum No. 03/2020*, 31 March.

2020d. COVID-19: PM Sogavare announces $120 COVID-19 domestic development bond. Media release, 24 April. Press Secretariat, Office of Prime Minister and Cabinet, Honiara.

2020e. COVID-19: PM Sogavare announces schools reopening. Media release, 24 April. Press Secretariat, Office of Prime Minister and Cabinet, Honiara.

2020f. *National Situational Report 18: SIG Response to COVID-19.* NSR18_12/20, 2 December. Honiara: National Disaster Council, National Disaster Management Office.

2020g. *Provisional Count: 2019 National Population and Housing Census.* Census Release 1/2020, 16 November. Honiara: Census Office, National Statistics Office, Ministry of Finance and Treasury. Available from: www.solomonchamber.com.sb/media/1997/provisional_count-2019_census_result.pdf.

2020h. *Solomon Islands General Map*. Honiara: National Geographical Information Centre.

2020i. *Solomon Islands Government Economic Stimulus Package to Address the Impacts of the COVID-19 Pandemic*. Honiara: Ministry of Finance and Treasury and Office of Prime Minister and Cabinet.

Other archives and libraries

Anglican Church of Melanesia

The Anglican Church of Melanesia (ACOM) Solomon Islands Collection is housed in the Solomon Islands National Archives.

Pacific Manuscripts Bureau (The Australian National University, Canberra)

Barrow, G. Lennox. 1942–47. *An Account of Life in the British Solomon Islands Protectorate Where the Author was a District Officer, 1942–1947*. PMB 517.

Levers Pacific Plantations Pty Ltd. 1902–22. Lever Solomons Ltd. PMB 1121.

Oram, Nigel. 1962–93. Papers on Town Planning in Bougainville and Honiara, and Provincial Government in Papua New Guinea. PMB 1371.

Woodford, C.M. 1888–89. Diary, 16 August 1888 to 3 January 1889. PMB 1290, Woodford Papers, Reel 5, Bundle 29, PMB 151.

National Archives of the Solomon Islands (Honiara)

BSIP and Solomon Islands Government Archives, and the Anglican Church of Melanesia (ACOM) Collection, Honiara.

Marchant, William S. 1942–43. Diary for 2 January 1942 to 6 May 1943. Transcribed by J. French, Aide-de-Camp to the High Commissioner, 29 December 1962, BSIP 5/IV/1.

United States National Archives and Records Administration (College Park, MD)

University of Queensland

Wilson, Alexander H. and Jessie. 1930s–1950s. Papers and photographs of Alexander and Jessie Wilson, including material from their daughter Andrea Gordon Bannatyne. Fryer Library, University of Queensland, Brisbane.

Western Pacific High Commission (University of Auckland)

1958. *Housing Committee Report*. Honiara: Western Pacific High Commission.

Index

Page numbers in bold refer to maps, tables and plates.

A page number followed by an 'n' indicates a reference appearing in a footnote on that page.

Afia-Maetala, Ruth B., 333
Akin, David, 23, 189, 239, 404, 405
Alebua, Dominiko, 29
Alebua, Ezekiel, **412**
    premier, Guadalcanal Province, 414–15
    prime minister, 412, 421
Alexander, G.C., 56, 57
Allan, Sir Colin, 148, 149, 364
Allen, Matthew, 38
Alligator Creek (Ilu River), 30, 48, 78, 80, 85, 133, 446
Andersen, Val J., 309
Andresen, Albert M. (Andy), 70
Aqorau, Francis Talasasa, 312, 361
Aqorau, Transform, 445
Assemblies of God Church, 307
Asian business community, 169
    see also Chinese
Atkin, George, 289
Aubin, Bishop Jean M., 301
Australian Government
    aid to Pacific nations, 417
    Army Bomb Disposal Section, 134
    Australian-Pacific Technical College, 331
    High Commissioner to Solomon Islands, deported (2006), 425
    High Court decision on Moti case (2011), 425
    RAMSI, role in, 360, 413
    security assistance agreement (2017), 437
    Solomon Islanders, deported (1906–08), 47
    Solomon Islands, territorial interest in, 253
    White Australia Policy, 47
aviation
    airlines, 137, 255, 286, 287
    Honiara Airfield (Kukum), 125, **284**
    Honiara International Airport–Henderson Field, 5, 6, 48, 102, 111, 284, 286, 287, 392, 432
    see also World War II—Japan—airfields; World War II—US—airfields

Baddeley, Bishop Walter, 116, 145
Bahá'í Faith, 299, 301, 307, 309, 472
Bain, Robert, 45
banking
    Australia and New Zealand Banking Group (ANZ), 262, 312, 370

Commonwealth Bank of
    Australia, **138**, 142, 262
Hongkong and Shanghai Banking
    Corporation (HSBC), 262,
    370
postal orders, 142
Barley, Jack C., 56
Barrow, Lennox, 116
Bathgate, Murray, 176, 180, 181, 241
Bavadra, Timothy, 175
Bellam, M.P.E., 256, 373, 469
Bellona Island, 345, 404, 406
Belshaw, Cyril, 11
Bennett, Bill, 70, 72, 291, 294
Bennett, Captain P., 286
Bennett, Judith, 23, 102, 105
Berg, Cato, 469
Betu, Willie, 386
Blum, Alvin J. and Gertrude, 258,
    259, 307
    A.J. and G. Blum and Company,
    259
Bodilly, Sir Jocelyn, 368
Boseto, Bishop Sir Lesley, 305, 306
Boso, Billy, 312, 342
Boye, Samuel S. and Ruby O., 70
Bradley, Edward, 272
bridges, 10, **81**, **86**, 105, **137**, 139,
    144, 149, **167**, 203, 254, 255,
    348, 432, 446, 464
Briggs, G.G., 128
British colonial society
    alcoholics, 352–53
    colonial mentality, 359–62
    hierarchy, 297, 356–59, 363–66
    housing, **370–71**, 372
    racism, 144n73, 259, 360–62,
        369–70, 382, 390
    'Red Sea Rig', 358
    salaries, 168, 273, 369
    segregation, 134, 160, 175, 259,
        355
    see also clubs, societies and
        associations

British Government
    Colonial Development and
        Welfare Fund, 119, 250, 292
    Colonial Office, 42, 43
    Colonial Regulations, 369
    Foreign Liquidation Commission,
        131
    Ministry of Food, 120, 140
    royal family, visits, **357**, 365–66,
        388
    Secretary of State for the
        Colonies, 57, 108
British Solomon Islands Protectorate
    (BSIP)
    Advisory Council, 118, 356, 371,
        383
    Agricultural and Industry Loans
        Board, 374
    Agriculture Department, 142, 178
        Copra Board, 140
        Dodo Creek Agricultural
            Station, 4
        experimental farms, 142, 178,
            237, 249
        Forests and Timber
            Ordinance, 1969, 385
    *British Solomon Islands (Name of
        Territory) Order, 1975*, 387
    British Solomon Islands Trade
        Scheme, 119, 140
    BSIP Trading Corporation
        Ltd, 140, **141**, 143, 144
    Censorship Board, 150
    census results, 15, 159, 168, 174,
        184, 186, 187, 193
    see also Solomon Islands
        Government
    constitutions, 25, 382–84, **388**,
        403, 406
    Customs Department, 431
    Districts
        see Central; Eastern;
            Guadalcanal; Isabel;
            Malaita; Western

INDEX

Education Department, 314
elections, 338, 349, 350, 351, 383, 384, 385, 387
Executive Council, 363, 383
Geological Surveys Department, 376
Governing Council, 173, 292, 293, 338, 371, 372, 384–87
Government House, 30, 132, **146**, 153, 255, 356–58, 363–64, 365, **365**
Government Information Service, 288
Government Residency, **122**, 146, 363
governors, 4, 148, **326**, 351, 355, 363, 364, 366
high commissioners, 253, 364, 366–67
Housing Authority, 208, 211–17, 220, **229**
Independence, 4, 16, 243, 356, 365, 366, 367, **388**
  'Ode to the West Wind', 402
  Western Province breakaway movement, 403
Labour Department
  indenture, abolished (1947), 182, 346
  labour shortages, 139
  Trade Union Act, 350
  see also trade unions
Lands and Survey Department
  land acquisition, 126, 173, 444
  Land and Titles Ordinances, 214
  land regulations, 42, 43
  Phillips Lands Commission (1920s), 47, 50, 51, 56, 57, 128
Legislative Assembly, 214, 235, 290, 348, 386, 387
Legislative Council, 173, 185, 210, 250, 317, 321, 338–84, **384**, 385

Local Government Ordinance, 1963, 200
Marine Department, 144, 325, 338
Medical Department, 176, 264, 267, 268, 326
  Central Hospital ('Namba 9'), 5, 20, 123, 263–65, **263**, **265**, 267–69, 328
  leprosaria, 265, 266, 267–68
  nurse and dresser training, 268, 327, 328
  ophthalmology, 268
military governors, 95, 108, 116, 162
National Park Regulation, 1954, 129
Native Courts, 367
parliamentary hostel, 389
Police and Prisons Department, 181, 182
  see also police
Ports Act 1956, 281
Ports Authority, 112, 140, 185, 245, 281, 283, 350
proclaimed, 3
public service
  appointments to, 368
  chief secretaries, 151
  Colonial Regulations, 369
  district commissioners (government agents), 16, 29, 130, 179, 219, 230, 243, 290, 291, 347, 350, 359, 378, 381
  district officers, 29, 39, 55–56, 70, 76, 95, 107, 116, 148, 178, 243, 291, 403
  housing, 160, **370–71**, 215, 217, 372
  localisation, 20, 210, 217, 306, 325, 353, 390
  'Red Minutes', 369

527

resident commissioners, 28, 55, 56, 75, 95, 107, 117, 132, 144, 253, 254, 325, 355, 357, 363, 366, 383
retirement age, 115, 354
Secretariat, 20, 131, 132, 144, 145, 146, 148, 149, 210, 254, 309, 366
work hours, 366
Public Works Department, 144, 185, 200, 210, 211, 311, 342
resident commissioners, 75, 107, 108, 109, 116, 165, 363
Town Councils Ordinances, 200
see also Western Pacific High Commission
Brown, H., 278
Bryan, Joe, 385
Buckingham, John, 272, 361
Bulocokocoko, Sakiusa, 159
Burley, Bill, 261
Burns, Philp & Company, 47, 136
Burt, Ben, 441

Calvert, Ron F., 290, 291
Camp Guadal, *see* World War II—US
Campbell, Fred, 76
Carney, Captain J.V., 106n69
Carpenters, *see* W.R. Carpenter & Company
Carter, Reverend George, 305
Catholic Church
    Daughters of Mary Immaculate, 303
    Dominican Sisters, 303
    Dominicans (Order of Preachers), 302
    Holy Cross Cathedral, 247, 301, 303, **304**
    Marist Mission, 58, 76, 268, 299, 300, 302, 306
    Mendaña expedition friars (1568), 32
    Missionnaires du Sacré-Coeur-Issoudun, 300
    Prefectures, 300
    priests, first indigenous, 306
    printing press, 301
    Rua Sura, 300
    schools, 302, 320
    Society of the Divine Word, 300
    Vicariate Apostolic of Melanesia, 299
    Visale, 75, 301
Cenotaph, 111, 131, 132, **366**
Central District, 67, 77, 116, 130, 151, 186, **202**, 272, 350, 361, 368
Central Islands Province, 12
Chamber of Commerce, 151, 244, 259
Chan Chee, 166
Chan, Laurie, 169
Chan, Sir Tommy, 169
Chan, William, 262
Chand, Ganesh, 331
Chapman, Murray and Linley, 359
Chevalier, Christopher, 445
children, 20, 139, 150, 173, 190, 191, 297, 337, 339, 341–45, **345**
    birth rates, 354, 452
    elite families, 341–42
    health, 219, 458
    households, 189, 457
    literacy levels, 274, 344, 450, 455, 456
    multiracial education, 341, 455
    overseas education for expatriates, 341, 369
    see also educational institutions—school entries; Solomon Islanders—youth organisations
Chinese
    artisans, 166
    Bookshop, The (department store), 169
    British Solomon Islands Chinese Association, 166

INDEX

Chinatown, 5, 18, 120, 134, 138, 139, 151, 157, 158, 160, 161, 162–70, **163–64**, **167**, 201, 392, **465**, 467
Christianity, 166
Chung Wah School, 165–66, 314, 341
demography, 166, 168, 255, 393
employed at Camp Guadal, 162
Joy Biscuit factory, 168, 365
Kwan How Yuan Pty Ltd, 168
market gardens, 178
parliamentarians, 169
plantations, 168
QQQ store, 169, 423, **424**
trade ships, 162
Tulagi, 162
waku, 21, 165, 169, 360, 373, 423, 467
wholesale trading, 168
Choiseul Province, 16, 46
Christian Fellowship Church, 277, 299
Christian Life Centre, 307
Church of Melanesia (Anglican)
All Saints' Pro-Cathedral, 301
Community of the Cross, 306
Community of the Sisters of the Church, 306
Diocese of Melanesia, 267, 268, 289, 301, 311
Maravovo School, 76, 254
Melanesian Brotherhood (Ira Retatasiu, or Tasiu), 4, 306, 414
Norfolk Island College, 300
Provincial Press, 289
schools, 125, 321, 400, 456
Siota, 67, 301
Southern Cross, 311
St Barnabas' Cathedral, 147, 239, 247, 301, **303**
Taraoniara, 301

Churches, *see* individual Church entries
Clemens, Martin, **68**, 69, 71, 75, 79, 85, 95, 107
Close, Jack, 258
clubs, societies and associations, 150, 151, 153, 166, 259, 309, 311, 312, 333, **334**, 341
Guadalcanal Club, 152, 312, 359, 361
Honiara Club (Solomon Islands Club), 151, **154**, 166, 321, 362, 389
Honiara Golf Club, 106, 136, 152, 204, 312, 313, 361, 370
Point Cruz Yacht Club, 140, 152, 153, 312, 361, 370, 389, 395, **481–82**
Women's Clubs, 312, **333**, 334
Colchester-Wemyss, Hugo, 272
Cole, Patrick, 425
Coleman-Porter, C.A., 315
Connell, John, 11
Coronation Gardens, 131
Corrigan, J.A., 70
Crichlow, Dr Nathaniel, 109
Crone, Ben, 266
Cross, Dr Tony, 268
Crowley, Captain Laurie, 286
cultural artefacts, production and sale
artefact shops, 162, 191, 259, 282, 380
building decoration, 318, 321
cultural events
11th Pacific Arts Festival (2012), 473
bride-price ceremonies, **475**
Burns Night, 153
charity events, 375
cinemas, 105, **110**, 140, 149, 150, **155**, 205, 208, 255, 259, 370, 379
customary dances, 16, 173, **375**, 376, **377**, **378**, **474**, **475**, **486**

529

customary wealth, 9, 190, **475**
hotel entertainment, 9, 174
Melbourne Cup Day, 375
National Agricultural and Produce Show, 262
ceremonies, 366, 378, 473, **486**
    Queen's Birthday, **124**, 153, 274, **275**, 278, 356, 357, 365, 375
    Sea Festival, 377, **378**
    South Sea Evangelical Church marching groups, 376
    St Andrew's Society, 153
    see also music

Daga, Alphonse, 342, 381
Dakei, Solomon, 158, 266, 292
Davis, D.R. (Renn), 368
Dethridge, Romulus, 147, 180
Devesi, Sir Baddeley, 313, 361, 385
D.J. Gubbay & Company (New Hebrides) Pty Ltd, 142, 258
d'Oliveyra, Joseph T., 48–50, 128
Dovi, Ratu Tom, 174
Downer, Alexander, 415
Dumphy, William, 48

Eastern District, 12, 13, 70, 142, 162, 267, 272, 279
economy
    cattle, 73, 142, 237, 250, 251
    cocoa, 438
    cooperatives, 182, 225, 356, 373
    copra, 12, 19, 43–60, 119–20, 172, 249, 253, 354, 438
    fishing, 12, 14, 40, 161, 191, 205, 219, 225, 283, 312, 373
    gardening, 130, 178, 189, 190, 191, 205, 215, 219, 334, 344
    Honiara Retail Price Index, 406
    indigenous businesses, 373, 374
    logging, 410, 428, 429, 438, 458
    mining, 123, 248, 407, 411, 437–38
    oil palms, 217, 250, 251, 252, 408, **408**, 411, 412, 438
    rice, 217, 237, 250–51
    see also Asian business community; British Solomon Islands Protectorate—British Solomon Islands Trade Scheme; Chinese; markets
Edson, Colonel Merritt A. (Red Mike), 89
education system
    Cambridge School Certificate (O Levels), 316, 317
educational institutions
    Agricultural College, 225
    Agricultural Staff Training Institute, 315
    Auki Boat-Building School, 315
    Betikama Adventist School, 237, 242, 304, 320, 379, 400
    Bishop Epalle School, 321
    British Solomon Islands Teachers' and Vocational Training College, 135, 309, 315, 317, 321–23
    British Solomon Islands Teachers' Training College, 323–24, **323**, 335, 365, 372
    Burns Creek School, 236
    Chung Wah School, 165–66, 314, 341
    Don Bosco Technical Institute, 331
    Florence Young School, 321
    Honiara Education Authority schools, 454
    Honiara Government Primary School, 315, 338
    Honiara High School, 321
    Honiara Technical Institute, 324–25
    Hospital Training School, 315

King George VI School, 9, 152, **154**, 255, 262, 309, 312, 313, 316–21, **318–20**, **377**, 400, 477
Nurses' and Dressers' Training Schools, 315–16, 326–27, **328**
Solomon Islands College of Higher Education, 330–31
Solomon Islands National University, 138, 313, 324, 331, **332**, 327
St John's School, 341
St Joseph's School, Tenaru, 400
St Nicholas' College, 400
Survey and Draughting Institute, 324
TS (Training Ship) *Ranadi* Marine Training School, 205, 315, 325, **326**
University of Papua New Guinea Open College, proposal, 331
University of the South Pacific Campus, 328–29, **330**
Villa Maria Training College, Visale, 301
Vura School, **345**, **457**
Woodford International School, 400, 455
Woodford School, 5, 314, **343**
YWCA Kindergarten, 334, **336**
Edwards, Rodger, 278
electorates, 374, 385, 468
electricity, 147, 211, 217, 219, 223, 262, 278, 360, 442, 448, 452–53
Elliot, Edith Elizabeth, 326
Epalle, Bishop Jean-Baptiste, 300
Evans, Daniel, 447

Fairymead Sugar Company Ltd, 120, 303
Fatnowna family, 4
Fiji, 4, 6, 11, 43, 123, 158, 253, 254, 337
Fiji Medical School, 144, 326, 372

labour trade, 22, 36, 37, 185, 403
see also Western Pacific High Commission
Fijians in Solomon Islands
Fijian guerrilla company (World War II), 95
Fijian Quarter, 19, 139, 147, 161, 174–75
Fijians, 21, 139, 160
Indo-Fijians, 21, 139, 160, 173
Firth, Bob, 140
flooding, 432
Forrest, A.E.C., 46
Forster, Michael, 70
Foster, Sir Robert, 363
Foukona, Joseph, 38
Fox, Reverend Charles, 310
Frank, Richard, 110
Frazer, Ian, 185, 243
Freshwater, Bert, 76
Fung Shiu Kat, 165

Galbraith, Dr J.E.K. (Dick), 268
Galo, Dr Glynn, 331
Gass, Sir Michael, 151, 364
gay and lesbian scene, 473
Germond, J.D.A., 165, 363
Geve, Father Augustine, 414
Ghormley, Vice-Admiral Robert, 103
Gilbert, Hudson Kalita, Inito'o, and Reddley Loea, 379
Gilbert and Ellice Islands, Crown Colony of, 171, 293, 315, 316, 324, 367
Gilbertese migrants, 19, 20, 160, 170, 171–74, **171**, 192, 227, 278, 337, 338, 342, 356, 359, 373, 377, 393
citizenship, 20, 403
Ellice Islanders, 171
fixed-term estate (FTE), 172, 214–15
perpetual estate (PE), 173
Gina, Reverend Belshazaar (Bill), 306, 310

Gina, Senior Sergeant, 347
Gina, Sir Lloyd Maepeza, 354, 361, 369
Gloucester, Duke and Duchess of, 366, **388**
Golden, Graeme, 48, 49
Goldie College, Banga, New Georgia Island, 172
Goldie, Reverend John, 145
Goraiga, Joseph, 15
Gregory-Smith, Henry Graham, 363
Guadalcanal District, **61**
    Aola government station, 12, 55, 71
    Aola plantation, 46, 48
    Commonwealth Development Corporation, 217, 250, 407
    Foxwood Timber Ltd, 217, 252
    Gold Ridge mining, 71, 74, 76, 123
    Guadalcanal Council, 14, 15, 235
    Ilu experimental farm, 142, 178, 180, 181, 235, 249, 251, 270
    Maasina Rule, 13
    Makaruka village, 14, 15, 16
    Mamara (Tau`utu) plantation, 39, 47, 48–52, **57**, 125, **126**, 128, **129**
    Marau-Hauba Council, 14–15
    Vulolo administrative subdistrict, 59
    Wards, **184**
Guadalcanal Island, 28
    agriculture, subsistence, 12, 32, 35, 36, 37
    Avuavu, 15, 76, 300
    Balo, 15
    Bonegie River, 84, 94, 103
    Cape Esperance, 78, 82, 83, 91, 94
    Chiri, 181
    Cruz (Tanakua) Creek, 34
    demography, 15, 28, 35–37, 59, 78, 95, 111, 252, 392
    descent groups, 37–38
    Domma, 50, 329
    Duidui, 15
    geography, 3, 8, 28, 34
    gold, Spanish search for, 32–33
    human occupation of, 29
    Hylavo River, 71
    Ilu River, *see* Alligator Creek
    irrigation, 35, 36
    Isatabu, use of name, 14, 15, 16, 29, 412
    Kakau Bay, 15, 56, 76, 128, 385
    Koli Point, 36, 89, 91, 135
    Komuvada, 172
    labour trade, effect on population, 37
    Lambi Bay, 75, 182
    land, concepts of ownership, 37–38
    languages, **27**, 29
    Lavoro (Lavuro), 71
    Lengo language/culture area, 29, 34, 37, 42, 45, 52, 59, 435
    Lungga River, 35, 36, 52, 85, **88**, 90, **104**, 106, 121, 136, **137**, 204, 237, 249, 262, 446
    Malango language/culture area, 29, 34, 42, 45, 59, 60, 224, 395, 435, 479, 481, **483**
    Marau Sound, 14, 15, 29, 35, 46, 75, 76
    Mbalisuna River, 250, 254
    Mbokokimbo River, 385
    Metapono River, 91
    Mt Austen, 92, 94, 102, 111, 130, 131, 197, 230, 231, 411
    Mt Popomanaseu, 8
    Nahona`ara, 30, 124, 225
    name, origin of, 28
    Ndi language/culture area, 29
    Ngalimbiu River, 251, 254
    Nggae language/culture area, 176, 178, 179
    Nginia language/culture area, 29

plantations, 36–61
Poha River, 36, 49, 91, 92, 179, 261
raiding parties to, 36
Rere, 15, 56, 76
Ruaniu, 53
Taivu Point, 85, 89
Takemboru, 181, 182
Tamatangga, 181
Tanakake, 39, 56, 128, 325
Tandai language/culture area, 29, 30, **51**, **52**, **57**, **58**, 123–31, **126–27**, **129**, 161, 191, 195, 197, 217, 218, 220, 222, 223, 224, 230, 261, 395, 448–49, 479, 481, **483**, 484
  Barana Nature and Heritage Reserve, 130
  chapu customary exchanges, 60, 230–40
  court cases (2017), 48, **127**, 128, 195, 448
  highway bypass plans, 435, **436**
  Honiara, incorporation into, 124–28, 240
  Horahi, **30**, 50, **53–54**, 58, **80**, 82, 84, 126, 127, 128, 301
  Kakabona, 36, 50, 85, **88**, 90, 91, 92, 161, 178, 179, 181, 182, 197, 301
  Komulevuha canoe reserve, 126, 448
  land alienation for plantations, 38–60
  Malagili, 55, 56, 57, 58, 126, 128
  Mataniko right-of-way, 126–27, 448
  Queen Elizabeth National Park, 129–30, 197
  squatters, 218, 433–34, 449–50
  see also Honiara City Council—Greater Honiara concept; Mendaña expedition (1568)
Tangare, 76
Tasimboko, 29, 45, 71, 89, 181, 191, 438
Tassafaronga Point, 83, 84, 90, 91
Tavanipupu Island, 46
Tenaru River, 36, 39, 85, 254
Vatamunu, 127
Vatuboia, 50
Vatudaki, 50
Veramboli, 181
Visale, 182, 300, 301
Vura River, 36, 179, 181
Weather Coast (*Tasimauri*), 14–16, 28, 29, 59, 75, 359, 410, 414, 429
Guadalcanal Plains, 45, 59, 105, 118, 143, 185, 238, 243, 248, 249–53, **249**, 348, 351, 407, 408, **408**, 409, 411, 412, 438
  Brewers Solomon' Associate Ltd, 251
  Commonwealth Development Corporation, 217, 250, 407
  Foxwood Timber Ltd, 217, 252
  labour force, 185, 217, 243, 252, 351, 412
  oil palms, 250, 252
  rice, 250, 251
Guadalcanal Province, **2**, 7, 18, **184**, 245, 397, 414, 415, 447
  Gold Ridge mining, 248, 407, 408, 411, 437
  Wards, 16, 19, 191, 481
  see also Tension Years—Isatabu Freedom Movement
Gutch, Sir John, 149, 200, 254, 327, 363, 381
Hackman, Brian, 29
Hall, Hugh, 316
Hart, Clarry, 76

Hay, Kenneth and Susan, 70, 76, 131, 143, 144, 147, 181, 250–51, 259, 359, 360, 361, 382
    Guadalcanal Plains Ltd, 143, 250
    K.H. Dalrymple Hay Pty Ltd, 131
    Mendana Enterprises Ltd, 144
health issues
    alcohol, 10, 206, 308, 360, 380, 380–82, 389, 390, 400–1, 402, 406, 444, 415, 452, 458, 467
    kava, 477
    kwaso, see above alcohol
    malaria, 73, 81,131,265, 266, 268, 311
    marijuana, 10, 452, 458
    poliomyelitis, 476
    tobacco, 133, 182, 185, **186**, 255, **298**, 406, 415, 460
    tuberculosis, **265**
    venereal diseases, 95
    viral diseases, 36, 475
        COVID-19, 243, 331, 435, 476–79
    see also British Solomon Islands Protectorate —Medical Department—Central Hospital; Solomon Islands Government—National Referral Hospital
Hell's Point ordnance dump, 132, 133–36
Henderson, Maj. Lofton R., 106
Hill, Ralph, 56
historiography, 21–23
Ho Man, 178
Hoai, Baranaba, 128
Hogbin, Ian, 28–29
Holland, John, 272
Holloway, John, 278
Honiara City Council (1999–), 7
    boundary, 11, 60, 124, 131, 195, 197, 200, 222, 223, 224, 232, 240, 393, 395, 409, 444, 479
    Chachapa Kondomamba, 50
    demography, 16, **180**, **187**, **220**, **256**, 393, **393**, 448, 392, **393**, **394**, 395, **399**, **448**
    Education Authority schools, 454
    future planning, 210, 431–36
    Greater Honiara concept, 9, 11, 16, 30, 45, 48, 60, 121, 222, 240, 243, 297, **392**, 393, 395, 431, 437, 481, **483**
    health clinics, **459**
    Honiara City Act 1999, 18
    inland highway bypass plan, **436**
    Local Planning Scheme, 195
    Matavale, 125
    minibuses, 5, 6, 464
    pollution, 9, 268, 432
    sewerage system, 211, 448
    town planning, 6, 297, 354, 483, **436**, **480**
    Town Planning Board, 446
    traffic jams, 6, **391**
    transport, 5–6, **241**
    Wards, 18, 338, **399**
Honiara geography, 5, **30**, 32, 121–24, 200
Honiara hotels
    Blums, 258–59, **260**
    Coral Sea Casino, 125
    Heritage Park, 30
    Hibiscus, 259, **451**
    Honiara, 153, 258, 389, 423
    Iron Bottom Sound (IBS), 125, 169, 472
    King Solomon, 178, 259, **482**
    Kwong Chow, 258
    Mendana, 143, **154**, 258, 259, 358, 360, 361, 382, 389
    Pacific Casino, 169, **423**
    Solomon Kitano Mendana, 143
    Woodford, 143
Honiara housing, 139
    Fijian Quarter, 19, 139, 147, 161, 174–75

government officers, 146, 160, **370–71**
'schickers alley', 146–47, **146**
Housing Authority, 208, 211, 213, 215, 216, 217, 229
Labour Line, 132, 140, 161, 180, 205, 208, **209**, 218, 219, 227, 277, 347, 445
ridges, 5, 122–23, 133, 160–61, **170**, 200, 244, 261–62, 342, **370–71**
Solomon Islanders, 122, 160–61, 201, 205–45
Honiara settlements, 220, 222, **433–34**
Abira`ado`e, 234
Adaliua, 234
Aekafo, 220
Borderline, 234
Burns Creek, 6, 224, 227, 234, 237–38, 244, 304, 313, 397, 439, 442
Fera`ladoa, 234
Fulisango, 231, 234
Gilbert Camp, 10, 130, 224, 227, 232, 234–35, 237, 238, 240, 397, 441
Green Valley, 224, 234
Kaibia, 217, 234
Koa Hill, 127, 197, 224, 234, 235
Kobito, 10, 130, 219, 224, 227, 231–33, **231–32**, 233, 234, **236**, 238, 310, 397, 441, 442, **443**, 439, 456
Kongulai, 240
Lau Valley, 234, 441
Lord Howe (Komulevuha canoe reserve), 126
Malaita Fishing Village, 6, 9, 181, 199, 201, 208, 220, 225–27, **226**, 379, 439, **440**, **461**, 462, **475**
Mamulele (Namulele), 234
New Mala, 234

`Ofi`olo, 234
squatters, 195, 197, 199, 206, 217–27, **221**, 230–38, 240, 313, 395, 397, 410, **433–34**, 438–39, 442, 444, 447, 449, 459, 467, 469
official attitudes to, 199, 201, 221, 223, 224, 226, 230, 232, 238, 244, 253, 409, 438
Sun Valley, 234
THA/TOL land, 217–19, 221, 222–24, 226, 227, 230, 233–34, 238, 240, 242, **392**, 395, 432, **433–34**, 439, 449, 469, 479
Tolo, 234
White River, 9, 49, 122, 128–29, **129**, 151, 201, 208, 227–30, **228–29**, 340, 404, 439, **459**, 463
Honiara streets, roads and highways
Commonwealth Street, 112
Hibiscus Avenue, **202**, 204, 258, 389
Kukum Highway, 6, 10, 102, 204, 261, 301, 304, 445, **461**, 464
Mendana Avenue, 5, 6, 131, 132, 140, **141**, 146, 149, 151, **155**, 169, **241**, 261, 321, 347, 380, **391**, **396**, **465**, **471**
Mud Alley, **145**, 146, 147, 261
Skyline Road, 235, 261, 235
Tandai Highway, 261, 404
Honiara suburbs and estates
Kola`a Ridge, 215, 218, 219, 160, **221**, 244, 277, 284, 397
Kombuvatu, 215
Kukum, 6, 9, 161, 125, 140, 151, 161, 180, 197, 205, 208, **209**, 213, 218, 219, **226**, 255, 277, **280**, **284**, 311, 312, 322, 347, 445, **461**, 463

Kuromulevuhu, 215
Lengakiki Ridge, 5, 32, **122**, 136, 148, **155**, 160, 204, 215, 261, 309, 342, 372, **398**
Lungga, 6, 446
Mbokona, 9, 215, 217
Mbokonavera, 32, 161, 205, 213, 215, **209**, **273**, 373
Mbua Valley, 213, 216
Mbumburu Ridge, 32, 197, 205
Naha, 102, 463, 388
Nggosi, 5, 144, 387
Panatina, 5, 130, 168, 197, 204, 215, 217, 317, 397, 438, 473
Point Cruz, 30, **41**, **122**, 125, 203, 205, **241**, 370, 372, 389, 395, 397, 435, **466**
   cinema, 150, **155**, 370
   government offices, 119, 151, 161, 203, 392
   shops, 140, 166, 191
   wharves, 116, 122, 161, 261, 279, **280**, 282, **282**, 283, **396**
   Woodford School, 455
   yacht club, 152, 312, 361, 370, 395
Ranadi, 5, 106, 191, 197, 204, 205, 237, 244, **284**, 325, 372, 392, 446
Rove, 5, **112**, 126, 203, 293, 294, 335, 463
   see also police—Royal Solomon Islands Police Force; police—Solomon Islands Police Force
Seventh-day Adventist Valley, 215, 217
Skyline, 5, 11, 235, 261, 262, 301, 372
Symes Valley, 215
Tasahe Ridge, 136
Tehamurina, 213
Tuvaruhu, 213
Vara Creek, 132, 210, 213
Vavaea Ridge, 6, 32, 84, 205, 292, 372, 397
Vura, 4, 130, 179, 181, 197, 211, **212**, 213, **345**, **357**, 376, 397, 441, 474, **474**
White River, 9, 122, 199, **199**, 208, **226**, 227–230, **228–29**, 404, 439, 440, **459**, **461**, 463
Honiara Town Council (1957–98)
   abattoir, 204, 237, 268
   boundary, 127, 128, 132, **196**, 197, **198**, **199**, 230, 233, **247**, 392, **298**, **355**, **394**, **433**, **448**
   demography, 139, 140, 149, 159–60, **180**, 182, **188**, 192–93, 200, 255, **256**, 344, 393, **399**
   elections, 203
   Guadalcanal Bus Service, 262
   high-rise buildings, **257**
   minibuses, **241**, 262, 464
   Municipal Authority, created (1980), 195, 203
   Queen Elizabeth National Park, 128, 129–30, 190, 479
   Rove Botanic Gardens, 203
   Town Planning Board, 201, 203, 210
   Town Planning Ordinance, 200
   Wards, **184**, 203, 397, **399**
Honiara water supply, 18, 122, 147, 223, 261–62
Honiara 'worlds' concept, 20–21, 23–26
Hoskins, R.J. (Dick), 294
Hounipwela, Rick, prime minister, **429**
Howard, John, Australian prime minister, 415
Hughes, Peter, 253

Ichiki, Colonel Kiyoano, 84
Inoue, Admiral Shigeyoshi, 74
Iromea, John Seti, 237
Isa, Henry, 312
Isabel District, 267
Isabel Province, 16, 46, 267, 277, 331, **486**
Islam, 308
Itea, Ishmael, 4

Japan
    aid projects, 10
    Henderson International Airport upgrade, 5n6
    Kukum Highway upgrade, 10, 464
    see also World War II
Jehovah's Witnesses Church, 301, 305, 308
Jersey, Stanley, 110
Johnson, Frederick (Pop), 108
Johnstone, J.A. (Johno), 143, 144
Josselyn, Henry, 70, 79
Jourdan, Christine, 25, 472

Kabutaulaka, Tarcisius Tara, 29, 38, 189
Kabwere, John, 278
Kaliuae, John Maetia and Caroline, 4, 373, 376
Kaliuae, John Ru`ugwata and Ella, **212**
Kanaf, Walter, 132
Karibanang, Te, 172
Karuru, Enele, 266
Kausimae, Sir David, 386
Kawaguchi, Major General Kiyotake, 89, 90
Keenan, John, 70
Keesing, Roger, 411
Keke, Harold, 414
Kelly, Sethuel, 412
Kelly, Thomas Garvin, 39, 45, 46
Kemakeza, Sir Allan, 414, 421, **429**
    prime minister, 413, 415

Kennedy, Donald, G., 70
Kenilorea, Sir Peter, 22, 239, 361, 389
    chief minister, 294, 386, 387, **388**
    prime minister, 294, 403
Kere, Dr Sir Nathan, 266, 352
Kikolo, Joel, 346
Kinika, Benedict, 385, 386
Kiriau, W.B. (Ben), 277, 278
Knibbs, Stanley, 50, 51, 56
Kukum 'labour line', 140, 180, 205, 208, 218, 219, 277, 347, 445
Kukum Single Officers' Quarter, 161, 180
Kuper, Albert, 311
Kuper, Heinrich and Kafagamurironga, 144
Kuper, Geoffrey, 144
Kurilau, Vincent, 448
Kwa`ioloa, Michael, 231, 232, 233, 441
Kwai, Annie, 94
Kwan How Yuan, 162
Kwan Toor, 163
Kwan, James, 262
Kwok Hing Chung, 150

Lai Yuen Wo, 166
law and order
    beliga, 470
    corruption, 9, 21, 350, 410, 428, 444–47, 450, 484
    domestic violence, 206, 444, 458, 467
    riots, 5, 18, 277, 348, 351, 401, 404, 405, 406, 422, 423, 425, 468
    safety concerns, 463–64, 466
    youth gangs, 467
    see also health issues—alcohol; health issues—marijuana; police; Tension Years—riots
Lawson, Eric V., 309
Lawson, Ron, 358
Lea, John, 11

Legacy, 28
Levers Pacific Plantations Pty Ltd, 39, 42, 43, 50, 55, 56, 57, 75, 105, 119, 120, 126, 128, 137, 143, 217, 250
    Aola plantation, 46–47
    compensation for Honiara land, 125
    harassment of Tandai landholders, 39, 55
    Ilu plantation, **44**, 48, 105, 249, 250
    Kukum plantation, 39, 45, 47, 197
    Lungga plantation, **44**, 45, 47, **57**, 75
    Pacific Islands Company, 42, 47
    Russell Islands Plantation Estate Ltd, 48, 237
    Tenaru plantation, **44**, 45, 47, 48
    Tenavatu (Ilu) plantation, 47–48, 52, 57, 78, 312
    Yandina plantation, 143
Lewis, Captain M., 286
Lindley, Alan and Doreen, 137, **145**, 146, 272, 273, 274, 277, 295, 347, 358, 359, 361, 362
Lotze, Jack, 140
Luddington, Sir Donald, **326**, 364
Lusibaea, Jimmy 'Rasta', 415

MacArthur, General Douglas, 66, 103
McDougall, Debra, 308
Macfarlan, Lieutenant Don, 71, 76
Macgregor, Dr J.D., 147, 265, 266
Mackenzie, Lieutenant Commander Hugh, 72, 79
Maefa`alu, James, 351
Maesae, Clive and Salome Stella, 475
Maesae, Harry, 225
Maesatana, John, 233
Maggio, Rodolfo, 234
Makini, Jully, 341, 342
Malaita District
    Atoifi Hospital, 267, 268, 287
    Auki, 12, 67, 142, 163, 259, 267, 272, 273, 277, 279, 286, 293, 380
    Auki Boatbuilding School, 315
    Auki Experimental Primary School, 315, 316
    Hospital of the Epiphany, Fauaabu, 327
    Kilu`ufi Hospital, 225, 267
    King George VI School, 316
    Maasina Rule, 13–14, 139
    Malaita Council, 14
Malaita Island
    `Are`are language/cultural area, 13–14, 15, 159, 234
    Baegu language/cultural area, 132, 232, 237
    Fataleka language/cultural area, 4, 227, 232, 234, 238
    Kwaio language/cultural area, 25, 235, 380, 403, 404, 411, 471
    Kwara`ae language/cultural area, 192, 232, 441
    Lau language/cultural area, 208, 225, 226, 234, 379, 441
    Maasina Rule, 13, 15, 23, 99, 139, 175, 186, 239, 271, 273, 316, 346, 356, 364, 376, 382, 401
    Maramasike Passage, 46
    Marau Sound colony, Guadalcanal, 14–15
    pan-Malaitan characteristics, 192
    To`ambaita language/cultural area, 185
Malaita Province, 12, 16, 19, 267, 278
    Kwaio boycott of national elections (1984–85), 403
Mamaloni, Solomon, 99, 312
    chief minister, 294, 350, 386, 387, 401
    prime minister, 401, 404, 405, 418, 445
Mamata, Loea, 225

Marchant, William, 75, 107, 108, 109
markets, 9–10, 436
  Central Market, 176, 177–82, **179**, **183–84**, 203, 225, 241, **339**, 350, 404–5, 414, 423, **461–62**, 463–64
  Malaita Fishing Village, 9, 463, **461**
Mason, Paul, 69, 78
media and communication, 288–96
  digital, 288, 453, 473
  fibreoptic cable, undersea, 288
  mobile phones, 288, 293, 253, 454
  newspapers, 105, 175, 288, 289, 290, 296, 402
  Solomon Islands Broadcasting Corporation (SIBC), 290–96, **295**
  television, 16, 296, 454
Melbourne Solomon Islands Pty Ltd, 49
Mendaña expedition (1568), 5, 31–36, **31**
Merillat, Herbert, 92
Michener, James, 132, 133
Mikawa, Vice-Admiral Gunichi, 78
Milner, G.F., 291
Mitchell, Sir Philip, 107, 108, 109, 116
Mitsui & Company, 142, 258
Miyazaki, Captain Shigetoshi, 73
Monrad, Alex, 46
Montford, Reverend Con L., 148, 150, 206
Montgomery, Charles, 8
Monzen, Captain Kanae, 75, 84
Moore, Father D.J., 58
Moore, Frank, 270
Morgan, David, 277, 347, 379
Moro Movement, 13, 14–16, 29, 175, 277, 356, 401
Moro, Pelise, 14–16, 356, **376**

Moti, Julian, 425
Muruyama, Lieutenant General Masao, 90
music, 99, 152–53, 157, 158–59, **158**, 291, 472, 375, 379, 380, 391, 472, **486**
  see also World War II—US—music

nahona'ara, origin of Honiara's name, 30, 125
Nanau, Gordon, 37, 38
Naqu, Rone, 158
Neilsen, Lars, 46
Nerdrum brothers, 46
New Caledonia, 6, 22, 37, 67, 116, 137
New Zealand
  New Zealand Leper Trust Board, 268
  RAMSI, role in, 417
  timber, 105
Nga Kwak Kwan, 262
Ngela Group
  Siota, 67, 301
  Tulagi enclave, 3, 12, 17, 46, 56, 65, 67, 71, 75, 78, 82, 118, 338
Ngele, Victor, 404
Nimitz, Admiral Chester W., 67, 77, 103
Noel, Owen Cyril, 109, 116, 363
Norris, C.G. 55, 56

O'ai, Baranaba, 234
Okamura, Lieutenant Commander Norinaga, 75
Olisikulu, Johnson, 346
Ontong Java (Luangiua or Lord Howe) Atoll, 12, 45, 220, 385, 453
Osifelo, Sir Fred, 132, 162, 292, 342
Otuana, Dominic, 312

Pacific Islands Forum, 416–28
Pacific Islands Monthly, 116, 118, 352, 382
Paige, Lieutenant Mitchell, 102
Papua New Guinea, 11, 18
    Bougainville, 66, 69, 70, 71, 72, 78, 94, 104, 105, 137, 401, 403, 411, 416, 419
    Buka, 66, 72, 83, 105, 286, 380
    Kavieng, 69, 71
    Milne Bay, 65, 66
    New Britain, 65, 66, 96, 137
    New Britain Palm Oil Ltd, 438
    New Ireland, 69
    Papua New Guinea University of Technology, 349
    Port Moresby, 6, 11, 18, 66, 72, 73, 77, 127, 191, 213, 287, 352, 409, 467, 483
    Rabaul, 65, 66, 69, 71, 72, 75, 78, 83, 94, 104, 105, 137, 191, 304, 352
    University of Papua New Guinea, 331, 348
Paravicini, Eugen, 36
Pentecostal churches, 307, 308, 442
People's Republic of China, 313, 421, 477, 485
Philip, Danny, prime minister, 435
police
    Armed Constabulary, 96, **124**, 144, 270, 273, 361
    prisons, 139, 144, 178, 180, 271, 272, 273, 351, 418
    Royal Solomon Islands Police Force (1978–), 467
        armouries raided, 418
        rebuilt during RAMSI years, 422, 466
        recruitment policy, 426
    Solomon Islands Police Force (1954–78), 270–78
        barracks, 361, 372

        Central Police Station, 111, 131, 274, **276**, 277, 347, 351
        Criminal Investigation Division, 274
        Explosive Ordnance Disposal Unit, 136
        Field Force and Riot Unit, 277, 401, 418
        police band, 278
        Queen's Birthday parades and celebrations, **124**, 153, 274, **275**
        radio communication, 277
        Rove Headquarters, 126, **271**, 272, 274, **275**, 278
        uniforms, 274–75
political parties, 385–86
Pollard, Alice Aruhe'eta, 333, 339
Polynesian Outliers, 184, 310, 379, 385
Pope, William, 50
Poznanski, Aubrey and Lily Valahoe Ogatina, 337–38, **338**
Public Library, 152, 255, 294, 384
Pullen, Reg, 266

Quan Hong, Augustine, 132, 150, 162
Que, Jason, 158
Queensland, 4, 66, 72, 73, 108, 137, 281, 287, 295, 311, 472
    labour trade, 22, 36, 37, 47, 192, 303, 310, 376, 404
Quonset huts, reuse of, 116, 119, 123, 131, 133, **138**, 140, **141**, 143, 146, 150, 151, 152, **155**, 255, 263, **263**, **276**, **282**, 301, 353

Rabut, Alex J., 46–47, 49, 51
Ramosaea, Jack and Leonga, 227, **228**
Ramosaea, Rau, 227
Randall, Will, 8
Raqachaphau, 125
R.C. Symes Pty Ltd, 129, 131, 279

Read, W.J. (Jack), 69, 78
Red Beach, 48, 75, 78, 172
Regional Assistance Mission to Solomon Islands (RAMSI), 10, 416–27, **240**, **427**, 450, 466
Remnant Church, 308
Rendova Island, 70, 104
Rennell and Bellona Province, 385, 404
Rennell Island, 70, 77, 83, 220, 404, 406, 437
Republic of China (Taiwan), 269, **270**, 313, 421
Rhoades, Frederick Ashton (Snowy), 70, 71
Richardson, Dick, 272, 342
Riti, Reverend Philemon, 426
Robson, R.W., 116
Rotoava, Jobi, 306
Rove (Vutudaki, or Le Sage) Creek, 32, 34, 124, 125, 261
Rowley, Frederick, 76
Russell Islands, 36, 119, 137, 237
    Yandina, 137, 142, 143, 237, 277, 278, 279, 284, 286, 380

Sade, Ellison, 225, 242, 379
Saki, Selwyn, 414
Salaka, Peter, 348
Samoa, labour trade, 22, 37
Sampson, Lieutenant W.S., 79
Sandars, Eustace, 108
Santa Cruz District, 12, 16, 46, 70, 72, 132, 278, 279, 405
Sato, Yukio, 169
Saunders, Sir Bruce and Lady Keithie, 258, 259
Savo Island, 8, 14, 28, 29, 36, 78, 82, 83, 91, 121, 176, 452
Schroeder, Lief, 71
Semple, James, 272, 273
Seton, Carden, 70
Seventh-day Adventist Church, 9
    Atoifi hospital, Malaita, 267

Western Pacific Union Mission, 304
see also educational institutions—Betikama Adventist School; Burns Creek School
shipping
    Burns, Philp & Co, 47, 136, 140, 281
    container terminal, 283, 395
    Kukum wharves, 95, 105, 144, 279, **280**
    local shipping wharves, 4, 112, 116, 161, **282**, **283**, 395, **396**
    Point Cruz wharves, **280**, **396**, 466
    Point Cruz, expansion of, 280, 281, 283
    Solomon Islands Ports Authority, 140
    Tulagi wharves and shipyard, 116, 162, 279
    see also British Solomon Islands Protectorate—Ports Authority
ships
    Bina, 181
    Compass Rose II, 4, **183**
    HMAS *Australia*, 77
    HMAS *Canberra*, 77, 79
    HMAS *Hobart*, 77
    HMS *Amethyst*, 357
    HMY *Britannia*, 365, 366
    IJN *Oite*, 84
    Kurimaru, 144
    Malaita, 136
    Morinda, 136
    Muliama, 136
    Pacific Eden, 5
    RCS *Coral Queen*, 364
    RCS *Melanesian*, 281
    Southern Cross, 311
    SS *Orcades*, 282
    TSMV *Oriental Queen*, 282
    Turkmenia, 4
    USS *Astoria*, 79

541

USS *Chicago*, 78
USS *Enterprise*, 78, 91
USS *Hornet*, 91
USS *Long Island*, 79
USS *Quincy*, 79
USS *Saratoga*, 78
USS *Vincennes*, 79
USS *Wasp*, 78
Shortland Islands, 12, 66, 72, 90, 104, 135, 172, 477
Sirra, Faneta, 386
Sitai, Silas, 292
Sitori, Edwin, 158, 159
Smith, John, 371
Soaika, Robert, 379
Soaki, Sir Fredrick, 278, 414
Sogavare, Manasseh
   leader of the opposition, 425
   member of The Tornados, 379
   prime minister, 379, 413, 415, 425, 426, **429**, 468, 476, 478
Solomon Islanders, 8
   ancestral beliefs, 13, 14, 98, 191, 234, 299, 308
   craft markets, **340**
   cultural characteristics, 9, 20, 26, 161, 189, 192, 439–40
   cultural events, 16, **375**, **377**, **378**, **474**, **475**, **486**
   dispute resolution, 419, 437
   demography, 11, 13, 343
   elite, 6, 20, 211, 239, 244, 317, 341, 354, 372, 373, 389, 410, 448, 449, 469, 470, 471, 484
   hybridity, concept, 6, 9, 20, 159, 161, 238, 240–41, 299, 390, 437–44, **439–40**, 448, 469, 485
   kastom, 159, 189, 242, 299, 308, 356, 382, 404–5, 408, 410, 419, 429, 437, 441
   laen (genealogy), 38–39
   land, concepts of, 13, 14
   languages, 26, **27**, 28, 29, 31

   masta lius, 242–43, 344
   mixed-race, 70, 72, 144, 182, 272
   political movements, 13–16
   Solomons Pijin English, 26, 38, 99, 132, 158, 165, 166, 242, 292, 293, 294, 400, 402, 404, 470–71, 473
      classes for foreigners, 325, 329
   tambu (taboo), 471
   wages, 96, 99, 182, 185, 190, 206, 208, 218, 346, 350, 373, 375, 406
   wantok system, 18, 113, 185, 189–91, 192, 218, 241–43, 256, 299, 373–74, 381, 389, 400, 437, 441, 452, 456, 470, 471, 472
   youth concerns, 466–67, **451**
   youth organisations, 341
   see also children; Christianity; Word War II
Solomon Islands Government
   census results, 307, 337, 393, 450, 457
      male/female ratios, 187, 337, 393, 395
   chief justices, 128, 367, 368
   Community Development Fund, 405
   Constituency Development Fund, 469
   Emergency Powers Act, 476
   Family Protection Act, 444
   gross domestic product, 408, 432, 437, 477
   Honiara City Act 1999, 18
   Independence (1978), 278, 366, 378, 486
   Land and Titles (Amendment) Act 2014, 195, 446
   ministries
      Education and Human Resources Development, 445–46

Health and Medical Services, 352
  Lands, Housing and Survey, 195, 243, 431
    Land Board, 195, 449
  Women, Youth, Sports and Recreation, 335
National Art Gallery, 380
National Constitution, **388**, 403, 406
National Fisheries Development Company, 175
National Museum, 5, 20, **31**, 131, 255, **257**, 380
National Parliament, 6, 18, 32, **248**, 387, **396**, 412, 417, 422, 423, **428**, 444
National Referral Hospital ('Namba 9'), 5, 270
  operating theatres, 263, 269
  patient numbers, 264, 269
  provincial hospitals, links, 267, 268
  rural health centres, links, 267
  upgraded by Republic of China (Taiwan), 269
  see also British Solomon Islands Protectorate—Medical Department—Central Hospital; health
Provincial Government Act 1997, 18
Solomon Islands Ports Authority, 112, 140, 185, 281, 283, 350
Telecommunications Act 2009, 453
see also British Solomon Islands Protectorate; economy; health issues—viral diseases—COVID-19; media and communication—Solomon Islands Broadcasting Corporation
South Pacific Commission, 311, 322, 334

South Pacific Fishing Company, 142
South Sea Evangelical Church, 239, 287, 300, 303, 304, 370, 399
  marching groups, 376
South Sea Evangelical Mission, 303, 306
Spain, *see* Mendaña expedition
sport
  cricket, 152, 205, 309, 310, 311, 312, 313, 316, 374
  cups and shields awarded, 312
  King George VI School ovals, 309
  Ko'o football team, **314**
  Kobito oval, 310
  Kukum field, 311
  Lawson Tama, 239, 309, 313, 328, 365, 400, **486**
  National Sports Council, 238
  national stadium plans, 238, 313
  Pacific Games (2023), 435, 464, 473
  soccer, 205, 311, 312, 316, 374, 478
  South Pacific Games, 311, 375
  sports complex planning, 313
  swimming, 103, 152, 310, 312
  Town Ground, 9, 310, 313
  see also clubs, societies and associations
Stanley, Sir Robert C.S., 253, 254, 321, 363, 364
Stateside, 123, 144, 270
Stevens, Harry, 45
Stevenson, Jock, 153, 255
Stibbard, Reverend Leslie, 76
Sukumana, Randall, **343**
Svensen, Carl Oscar, 39, 46–51, 55, 128, 129
Svensen, Theodore, 46

Tabua, Sefanaia, 266
Tahal, James Prasad, 175
Takahashi, Lieutenant Tatsunosuke, 84

Talasasa, Francis Aqorau, *see* Aqorau
Talo, Gilbert, 225, 379
Tanaka, Rear-Admiral Raizo, 85
Tarakabu, Reverend Takarebu, 172
Tarakabu, Reverend Tim, 172
Tedder, James, 16, 29
Temotu Province, 16–17, 244, 252, 296
Tension Years (1998–2003), 7–8, 18
 assassinations, 278, 414
 Bougainville Revolutionary Army incursions, 411
 Bougainvilleans living on Guadalcanal, 411
 breakdown of services, 406–7
 cost of living, 406–7
 economic pressures, 406–10
 evacuations, 411
 extortion, 406, 414–15
 'fast money' and 'pyramid' schemes, 414
 Guadalcanal discontent, 248, 252–53, 411
 Guadalcanal Revolutionary Army, 412
 Isatabu Freedom Movement, 16, 412, 414, 418, 421
 Malaita Eagle Force, 230, 406, 412, 414, 415, 418, 421
 mediation attempts, 413
 mortality, 418
 Multinational Police Assistance Group, 414
 refugees, 412, 447
 riots (2006), 5, 18, 163, 169, 422–23, **423**, **424**, 425, 456, 468
 squatter settlements on Guadalcanal land, 409
 Truth and Reconciliation Commission, 240, 418, 426
 Western breakaway movement, 403
 see also Regional Assistance Mission to Solomon Islands
Theodore, E.G. (Ted), 123
Theroux, Paul, 7
Timmer, Jaap, 26, 299, 382
Tina River hydro project, 452
Toa Te`e, Billy and Roselyn Aona, **236**
Toa Te`e, Hendry, house, **443**
Togonu, Walter, 132
trade unions, 346–48, 350, 351
 Solomon Islands Medical Association, 352
 strikes, 346–47, 348, 350, 351, 352, 401
 see also Tuhanuku, Joses Taungengo; Ulufa`alu, Bartholomew
Trench, Sir David C.C., 109, 162, 363, 364
Tryon, Darrell, 29
Tuadubi, Tayla village, 35
Tudor, Judy, 143, 352
Tuhanuku, Joses Taungengo, 345, **349**
 parliamentarian, 349
 trade union leader, 345, 349–51
Tulagi enclave, *see* Central District
Turner, Rear-Admiral Kelly, 77, 79
Tuza, Reverend Esau, 306
Ulawa Island, 12
Ulufa`alu, Bartholomew (Bart), 345, 348, **349**
 parliamentarian, 348–49
 prime minister, 349, **413**
 trade union leader, 348
Un Tak Fook, 168
United Church in Papua New Guinea and the Solomon Islands, **54**, 84, 172, 173, 239, 268, 287, **304**, 305, 320, 399
United States of America (US), **428**, 259
 see also World War II

INDEX

urbanisation, 3, 10–12, 447
  indigenous movements, 13–16
  Maasina Rule, impact of, 13
  urban settlements, 16–19, 220, 433–34
  village-city concept, 19–21
Usi, Peter, 237

Valusa, David, 15
Vandegrift, Major General Alexander A., 77, 79
Vanuatu, 6, 11, 24, 158, 288, 315, 382, 416
Verali, Bennie, 145
Viggor, Ray, 277, 347
Vunagi, Sir David, **485**
Vunagi, Lady Mary, **485**
Vuza, Sir Jacob, 69, 111, **112**, 144, 38

Waddell, Alexander (Nick), 70
Waena, Sir Nathaniel, 331
Waigagu, Robert, 312
Walahoula, Michael Ben, 45
Wale, Matthew, 262
Waneba, Station Sergeant, 274
Wang, James, 165
Ward, B.S., 278
W.D. & H.O. Wills Company, tobacco factory, 185, **186**
Western District, 12, 70, 104
  Gizo, 12, 16, 142, 148, 172, 286
  Munda, 276, 286, 287
  New Georgia Islands, 36–37, 70, 94, 143, 267, 279, 300
  Rendova Island, 70, 104
  Roviana Lagoon, 300, 310, 342, 377, 386
  Shortland Islands, 12, 66, 72, 104, 172
  Vella Lavella Island, 284, 287, 385
Western Pacific High Commission, 3, 4, 254n17
  chief justices, 128, 367–68,
  deputy commissioners, 367

Fiji Court of Appeal, 367
high commissioners, 151, 149, 200, 253, 254, 321, 327, 263, 364
High Court of the Western Pacific, 6, 20, 125, 128, **248**, 255, 367, 376
  chief justices, 128, 368
  pusine judges, 368
Secretariat, 20, 148, 254, 255, 366
special commissioners, 109
transfer to Honiara, 4, 148, 253, 254, 352
Western Pacific (Courts) Order in Council, 1961, 367
Western Province, 143, 287, 385, 402–3, 411
  economy, 403
  Gizo, 16, 174, 268, 296, 331, 334, 341
  Kolombangara Island, 158, 385
  Munda, 283, 287, 331, 347, 477
  Noro, 12, 16, 283, 477
  Shortland Islands, 477, 478
Wheatley, Hugh, 70
Wickham, Adrian, 312
Wickham, Alick, 310, 312
Wickham, Ashley, 295, 385, 386
Wickham, Harry, 70
Wickham, Martin, 312
Widdy, Charles, 79
Wilikai, John, 312
Williams, John, 39, 45, 46
Wilmot, A., 76
Wilson, Alexander (Spearline), 109, 144, 145, 177, 357, 363, 364
women, 293, 333–40, 367, 381, 442
  Christian Orders, 425
  demography, **187**, 337, 393
  domestic violence, 206, 444, 458, 467
  education, 317, 320, **332**, 455
  employment, 333, 407, 456, 472, **339**

empowerment, 426, 452
Girl Guides Movement, 333–34
haus meris (domestic servants), 372
health, 458
hostels, 327, 335, **336**
leadership, 335, 337–39
markets, produce and craft, **339, 340**, 463–64
marriage, 399, 409
Ministry of Women, Youth, Sports and Recreation, 335
Mothers' Union (Anglican), 334
nursing, 326, **328**, 330, 333
public service, 339
religion, 425
role in modern nation, 324, 333, 426
safety concerns, 463–64, 466
scholarships, 337
Seventh-day Adventist Church's Dorcas groups, 334
Solomon Islands National Council of Women, 335
Solomon Islands Women's Week, 335
South Sea Evangelical Church marching groups, **474**
teaching, 333, 335
Women's Clubs, **333**, 334
Women's Interest Officer, 334
Young Women's Christian Association, 334–35, **335**
Woodford, Charles, 28, 45, 46, 47
Woodhouse, Thomas, 39, 45, 46
Woods, Christine, 366
Woothia, 45
World War II
  battles, 65, 73, 75, 77, 78, 82, 83, **83**, 85, 86, 89, 91, 94, **66**, 102
  British Solomon Islands Protectorate policy, 67–68, 162
  Coastwatchers and Scouts, 67–72
  compensation, lack of, 102, 119, 120, 140

Iron Bottom Sound, 82, **83**
Japan, **64**
  Aichi 'Val' dive-bombers, 83
  airfields, 66, **74**, 102, 106
  Bougainville, 66, 71, 104
  Buka, 66, 72, 83, 105
  Bushido, concept, 84
  Chuuk Island, 63, 65, 66
  evacuation from Guadalcanal, 82
  expansion into Pacific, 63, **64**, 65
  Ichiki's Detachment, 84, 85
  Korean labourers, 75, 79
  military units, 73, 75, 78, 84, 89, 90, 91
  Mitsubishi G4M 'Betty' bombers, 71
  Rabaul, 65, 66, 69, 71, 72, 75, 78, 83, 92, 94, 104, 105
  railway, 74
  seaplanes, 72, 73
  Shortland Islands, 72, 89, 90, 104, 135
  South-east Asia, supply lines, 73
  troop numbers, 91, 110
  Zero fighters, 69, 71, 72, 78, 83
memorials, 110, **112–13**
mortality, 110–11
New Zealand
  New Zealand Army nurses' hostel, 363
  RNZAF No. 6 Flying Boat Squadron, 118
Slot, The, 78
Solomon Islanders
  artefact trade, 162
  casual labourers, 95
  mortality, 98, 111
  motivations, 96
  relationship with Allied and Japanese forces, 95–99, **100–3**

Scouts, *see above*
  Coastwatchers and Scouts
Solomon Islands Defence
  Force, 67, 68, **68**, 95, 96,
  162, 175, 270, 380
Solomon Islands Labour
  Corps, 13, 76, 92, **93**, 95,
  97, **98**, 99, **100**, 102, 109,
  139, 143, 162, 175, 380
South Pacific Scouts, in the
  Fijian guerrilla company,
  95
Tulagi enclave, 46, 65, 75, 77, 78,
  82, 116
Tulagi, 46, 55, 67, 69, 71, 72, 73,
  78, 85, 86, 89, 95, 103, 107,
  109
United States of America (US)
  African American
    Construction Battalion,
    13, 98, 175
  airfields
    Carney, 106, **108**
    Fighter I, 86, 106, 133,
      107
    Fighter II, 106, 125, 133,
      136, **107**, 248
    Henderson, 65, 67, 72,
      74, 79, 82, 85, 86, 89,
      90, 94, 105, 106, **107**,
      131, 133, **137**
    Koli, 106, **108**
  Boeing B-17 Flying Fortress
    bombers, 104
  Camp Guadal, 19, 30, **41**, 61,
    67, **93**, **97–98**, **100–1**,
    103–9, **110**, **115**, **122**, 162
  chapel, 106n68, 301, **302**
  chemical weapons, 134, 135
  cinema, 105, **110**
  F4F Grumman 'Wildcat'
    fighters, 79
  gardens, 105

Gavutu-Tanambogo base, 67,
  75, 78
Goettge Patrol, 84
Hell's Point ordnance dump,
  132–36
herbicides, use of, 102
hospital ('Namba 9'), 5, **263**
Kakabona, **88**
Kukum docks, 105, 133, **280**
logging, 105
Lungga River, **88**, **93**, **104**,
  137
M3A1 General Stuart light
  'Honey' tanks, 85
Marine Corps air arm, 110
Marston matting, 102, 106,
  117, **131**, **333**
Mataniko River, 5, 9, **80**, **81**,
  86
military units, 77, 79, 84, 86,
  90, 92, 106, 271
music, 99
P-400 fighters, 79
PT boats, 82
PX stores, 117
Quonset huts, 116, 119, 123,
  218, **263**
  see also Quonset huts,
    reuse of
radio station, 105, 290
railways, **97**, 105
seaplanes, 82
supply lines, 73
telephones, **97**, 105, 148
troop numbers, 110
W.R. Carpenter & Company, 119,
  120, 140, 165, 174
Wright, Bill, 347

Yates, Ronald, 272
Yee Fai, George, 151
Yo, Colin, 283

Zoleveke, Dr Sir Gideon, 293, 386

www.ingramcontent.com/pod-product-compliance
Lightning Source LLC
Chambersburg PA
CBHW040319300426
44111CB00023B/2949